THE OXFORD AUTHORS

General Editor: Frank Kermode

JONATHAN SWIFT (1667–1745) left Dublin for England in 1689, where he was secretary to Sir William Temple and taught Temple's ward Esther Johnson ('Stella'), who remained his close friend until her death in 1728. A great Anglo-Irish publicist, Swift first came to public and political attention in England with *Contests and Dissensions* (1701) and *A Tale of a Tub* (1704). He supported Harley's Tory administration in *The Conduct of the Allies* (1711), and in 1713 became Dean of St Patrick's, Dublin. When the Government fell with the death of Queen Anne the following year he retired there, emerging as a popular Irish patriot with publications such as *The Drapier's Letters* (1724) and *A Modest Proposal* (1729). His best-known work today, *Gulliver's Travels*, was published in London in 1726. He is buried in St Patrick's Cathedral, beneath the epitaph he composed himself. A master of prose style, he is also a considerable poet, excelling in ironical anti-'poetic' imagination.

ANGUS ROSS, Reader in English at the University of Sussex, writes on eighteenth-century and other literature in English and has edited texts and anthologies including *Robinson Crusoe*, *Gulliver's Travels*, and Richardson's *Clarissa*.

DAVID WOOLLEY commenced collecting first and early editions of Swift in Australia in 1946. During a residence of twenty years in London, he has studied the texts of Swift's verse and prose, including the extensive correspondence, from the originals in England, Ireland, and the United States.

THE OXFORD AUTHORS

JONATHAN SWIFT

EDITED BY
ANGUS ROSS
AND
DAVID WOOLLEY

Oxford   New York

OXFORD UNIVERSITY PRESS

Oxford University Press, Walton Street, Oxford OX2 6DP

Oxford New York Toronto
Delhi Bombay Calcutta Madras Karachi
Petaling Jaya Singapore Hong Kong Tokyo
Nairobi Dar es Salaam Cape Town
Melbourne Auckland

and associated companies in
Berlin Ibadan

Oxford is a trade mark of Oxford University Press

First published 1984 in hardback and simultaneously in a paperback edition
Paperback reprinted 1989 (with corrections), 1991, 1992

British Library Cataloguing in Publication Data

Swift, Jonathan
Jonathan Swift.—(The Oxford authors)
1. English literature
I. Title II. Ross, Angus, 19—
III. Woolley, David
828'.509 PR3722

ISBN 0–19–281337–4 Pbk

Library of Congress Cataloging in Publication Data

Swift, Jonathan, 1667–1745.
Jonathan Swift.
(The Oxford authors)
Bibliography: p.
Includes index.
I. Ross, Angus. II. Woolley, David. III. Title.
IV. Series.
PR37.22.R68 1984 828'.509 83–17225
ISBN 0–19–281337–4 (pbk.)

Printed in Great Britain by
Biddles Ltd.
Guildford & King's Lynn

To
Diana Okkalides and Frances Woolley

CONTENTS

Italic titles of Swift's works in this volume indicate poems

INTRODUCTION

OUR selection is made from Swift's 150 or so separate prose works, some 280 poems, and over 750 known letters. With only two exceptions, all the works are given complete. To allow representation with some solidity of an active writing career of half a century spanning the period from the last decade of the seventeenth century to the fourth of the eighteenth, *Gulliver's Travels* is omitted as being easily available elsewhere.

The big collections of Swift's works, with some basis it is true in his own publishing practice, have perpetuated a series of editorial judgements which over the years interfered with the critical appreciation of his *œuvre*. The difficulty stems from the custom of classifying his writings, placing them in groups according to ostensible subject-matter or apparent genre. The arrangement of the present selection is chronological and is meant, by fruitful juxtaposition, to offer a new and clearer awareness of the unity as well as the complexity of Swift's vision, indicating the powerful bonds between disparate pieces. The poems are not segregated, though they may easily be read as a group by reference to the Contents (see p. vii). Basic information about the circumstances, politics, and ideas that prompted individual pieces is given in the Notes. A Biographical Index of the contemporaries he mentions is also provided for handy reference in reading literature so precisely aimed in the first instance at a highly self-conscious, perceptive, and homogeneous audience. The Glossary lists words whose meaning may now be obscure and translates or paraphrases foreign or difficult phrases. The Chronology sets out the principal events in Swift's public life (in lieu of a biographical sketch), and lists some of his own publications as well as the dates of the appearance of contemporary books which contribute to an understanding of his works. The scope of this series precluded the provision for each work selected of a rationale of the text printed in this volume.

Jonathan Swift's life, character, and writing are distinguished not merely by the normal tensions and contrasts of human experience, but by the powerful clash of violently opposed forces. Further, in his case at least, it has always been not only difficult, but finally impossible, to read the author out of the works and treat the texts as free-standing objects, uncomplicated by authorial intention, biographical complexities, or historical relationships. F. R. Leavis in his essay on 'The Irony of Swift' (*The Common Pursuit*, 1952) very properly seeks to clear his discussion from focusing unawares on 'the kind of man that Swift was' and to stop 'well on this side of pathology'. Yet the same critic invokes Swift's 'insane egotism' that 'reinforced the savagery' which he finds in parts of the writing.

At the opposite extreme, some readers have been impelled to place Swift's writing in a wholly biographical or psychological context. His powerful if perplexing character has fascinated later generations, just as it strongly attracted, or made bitter enemies of, those who met him in life. In common with other men of his time, and several members of his own circle such as Addison, Steele, or Pope, who lived in the first age of English culture from which letters and personal papers survive in relative plenty, Swift left extensive documentation of his private life. The information appears to delineate an inner life peculiarly susceptible to theoretical analysis using the psychologies of this century. Rashly moving backwards and forwards between such records and Swift's works, or parts of them, readers of such a taste have emphasized the disturbing texture of Swift's writing, and sought explanations for this undoubted literary quality in corresponding disorders of his personality. He is not of course alone in having his art judged by appeals to anal fixation and technical notions on the far side of pathology.

It is, however, the qualities of Swift's writing itself and the power of his vision of the human lot that in the last resort justify to any extent, if at all, such theorizing. Clear and open as the appeal of the writing is, there are areas of deep unfamiliarity for the modern reader, not only in political doctrines, allusions, and content related to the life and concerns of a past time, but more seriously involving rhetorical and critical principles, a context of past literature accessible and living to Swift's contemporary readers. Much of this has been opened up to us by the extensive commentary on his works. There is a constant struggle, though, between immediate, personal response to Swift's text and a historical modification of this response. The following paragraphs seek to outline some of the context without, it is hoped, inhibiting too much the reader's own inventiveness and pleasure.

The circumstances of Swift's birth and earliest years neatly illustrate the critical problems. He was the posthumous child of his father, and a perhaps even more traumatic experience followed. He tells this story himself in the paragraphs he wrote in his early sixties or later under the title 'Family of Swift' and which has been given the in part misleading modern title *Fragment of Autobiography to 1714* (*Prose*, v. 187–95):

. . . when he was a year old, an event happened to him that seems very unusual; for his nurse who was a woman of Whitehaven [in Cumberland], being under an absolute necessity of seeing one of her relations, who was then extremely sick, and from whom she expected a legacy; and being at the same time extremely fond of the infant, she stole him on shipboard unknown to his mother and uncle, and carried him with her to Whitehaven, where he continued for almost three years. For when the matter was discovered, his mother sent orders by all means not to hazard a second voyage, till he could be better able to bear it. The nurse was so careful of him that before he returned he had learned to spell, and by the time that he was three years old he could read any chapter in the Bible.

All this must have had an effect on Swift's character, feelings, and ideas; but what effect? Biographers are in duty bound to flesh out the psycho-drama, but the reader of Swift's works is not condemned to the long chain of inference. On the other hand, two immediate consequences flowed from Swift's parentage. His birth in Dublin and his family heritage fated him to be one of the English of Ireland. As an Anglo-Irish writer he received an irrevocable cultural stamp, a set of preoccupations, a social and historical role; certain more speculative characteristics, linguistic, tactical, and imaginative, may also ensue. A discussion of the Irish dimension of his writing, however, forms a later section of this Introduction. The second important consequence of his origins was the family connection that led, after a rather old-fashioned course of study at Trinity College, Dublin, to Swift's employment as his secretary by Sir William Temple (see p. 717) at Moor Park for the best part of the decade from 1689 to 1699. This is worth some elaboration, since the effect of the experience on his writing and thinking can hardly be overemphasized, and the effect is more than a historical 'influence', it is felt in the whole tone and ambience of his prose.

It is not too much to say that practically every political, moral, and literary doctrine that Swift held may be traced to the formative presence of Temple. At first sight this would seem to confirm a historicist reading of Swift's work, but what actually in Swift's hands became of those doctrines, and even of the literary professionalism, the principles of unity of sentence and construction of paragraph that his service taught him, is another matter, and the measure of his art as a writer. The transcription of Temple's own works and the correction of them under the author's instructions, perhaps by dictation, formed part of the literary training Swift received in Temple's circle. Swift's legacy on his employer's death was the right to publish the retired diplomat's remaining writings. Three volumes, more than half of Temple's *Works*, consist of carefully selected (and adjusted) letters, public and personal, in the writing of which Temple formed his mature prose style, the famous eloquence of his *Essays* and the neatness of his *Memoirs*. Not on oath, Swift in the 'Preface' to the first two volumes (1700) declares that, 'It is generally believed, that this author has advanced our English tongue to as great a perfection as it can well bear.' Throughout the succeeding century, Temple was admired as a reformer of English prose. On Thursday, 9 April 1778, according to Boswell, Dr Johnson drew attention to a quality of style which Swift specially valued, claiming that 'Sir William Temple was the first writer who gave cadence to English prose. Before his time they were careless of arrangement, and did not mind whether a sentence ended with an important word or an insignificant word, or with what part of speech it was concluded.' From close editorial work on these *Letters*, Swift acquired his respect for the letter as a literary form and its importance in history-writing, as well as his own mastery of its narrative and imaginative possibilities.

Temple's essays were published in three volumes of *Miscellanea* (1680, 1690, 1701), the third edited by Swift. The comparative discussion of cultures, based on wide reading of the available accounts, however inaccurate, of China, Peru, the Islamic world, as well as of the ancient world of the Mediterranean basin, and the modern world of northern Europe, is the chief claim Temple has to originality. Swift, a lifelong reader of books of travels, made only indirect but pervasive use of such comparisons of culture. He also seems to have ingrained in him two rooted notions of Temple's. These are the profound belief that human nature everywhere and in all ages is the same, and that the true end of the study of history is moral philosophy. Temple's essays are scattered with the seeds of ideas which Swift develops in his own works, and traits of style he made his own, in all bettering his instruction. A short passage from Temple's essay, 'Of Popular Discontents', will illustrate this relationship. Temple's characteristic parallelisms would have been tightened by Swift, but the ironical opening is Swiftian:

When anybody is angry, somebody must be in fault; and those of seasons which cannot be remedied, of accidents that could not be prevented, of miscarriages that could not be foreseen, are often laid upon the government, and, whether right or wrong, have the same effect of raising or increasing the common and popular discontents.

Temple argues in the same essay that an excellent constitution of government may be established, 'but none can provide that all magistrates or officers necessary to conduct or support it shall be wise and good . . .'. This was one of the reasons for the decay of any human structures which haunted Swift when he contemplated the English constitution or the Anglican Church. Swift constantly followed

Temple's practice of working from 'heads' or hints, of thinking in terms of pieces of prose shaped by the personality projected by the writer, of publishing collections of such pieces in miscellany volumes. He followed Temple's lead in publishing documents of recent history where appropriate in an argument. This also met a growing demand by the contemporary reading public; it is of course a common practice now and may be seen in *The Conduct of the Allies* and the *Drapier's Letters*, and Swift constantly had this market in view.

From his years of working under Temple Swift drew his preoccupation with history itself. Temple sketched *An Introduction to the History of England*, published in 1694 (from a manuscript written out by Swift) as a 'small endeavour' intended 'to invite and encourage some worthy spirit and true lover of our country' to produce the good general history of England, the want of which Temple considered a disgrace to English learning. Temple's superficial piece expresses his scorn at 'the dirt and rubbish of such barbarous times' and dismisses Alfred the Great in a single sentence. The transcendental vision of history as a record of God's intervention in human affairs, a Puritan belief which Swift ridicules in *A Tale of a Tub*, has in Temple's work given way to generalizations, laws, and maxims, illustrated by historical events. Swift followed Temple in three pieces (*Prose*, v. 1–78): the first, *An Abstract of English History*, may represent the 'heads' for his own history of England, or reading notes on Temple's work; the second and third form the so-called *Fragment of English History*, a substantial block of narrative covering the reigns of William II, Henry I, Stephen, and Henry II in part. Swift's aim was to produce a smooth chronicle of events with character analysis, not detailing sources though he worked reasonably hard on what chronicles or compilations he read. From this apprentice work comes the sure touch and digested information underlying the historical asides that strike the reader as playing an important part in his great satires such as *A Tale of a Tub*. In his early historical writing, he cautiously embarks on a theory of mixed governments and the balance of power, the kind of generalization which, with brief historical illustrations, often gives firmness to his political pamphlets. Many of his short theoretical passages develop out of one of his most fundamental political tenets, 'power, by the common maxim, always accompanying property'. This argument in his *History* links Swift, through Temple, with an important group of seventeenth-century English political and historical theorists known as 'classical republicans'.

One other aspect of history-writing is worth noting, which Swift clearly adopted from his years at Moor Park. He justifies the publication of Temple's letters (*Prose*, i. 258) by saying that they give 'a true account of story'; they do not fulfil this function well if they only consist of 'long dry subjects of business' (ibid. 266). The true account sought by Temple (and Swift) is imaginative, giving the feel of events, 'actions while they are alive and breathing', imbued with psychological and rhetorical life, ordering differences of style in the letters according to the recipients. We may well think that Temple himself only imperfectly realized these ambitions, but Swift embodied them in the *Journal to Stella* (see pp. 230–6 and 272–9). Another straightforward use of this instinct for direct historical writing is the letter, *Swift to Alexander Pope* 10 January 1721 (see pp. 411–17), and his *Epitaph* may be judged as a condensed piece of lapidary history.

Swift's relationship with Temple was more ambiguous, or ambivalent, than has so far been suggested. It has been dramatized as a clash between a second-rate patron and a brilliant dependant. There is clearly much in this, and Swift's later references to his employer are not uniformly laudatory; they also sometimes take the form of eulogy the sincerity of which has been questioned. More interesting are the rich variations Swift creates from the historical theme, extending to ironic subversion of the very genre of historical writing itself, which had entered so deeply into his artistic consciousness. *The Battle of the Books*, his earliest mature work, exploits the satirical possibilities of guying 'contemporary history' as recorded in newspapers or perhaps practised by Temple. *The Contests and Dissensions in Athens and Rome* takes the contemporary custom of studying ancient history and creates from this conventional interest a mosaic that tests the reader's ingenuity. History as a living human concern, its pitfalls, excesses, blindnesses, is a profound concern in *A Tale of a Tub*, with its 'modern' rhetoric, and joking citations of Herodotus and other ancient historians. This concern is continued in the similar complexity of *Gulliver's Travels*. Gulliver's performance as historian, in his discussions with the king of Brobdingnag, for example, is one of the witty and sombre areas of the satire.

History, in fact, is a very good example of a fundamental organizing principle of Swift's entire literary achievement. This is the way in which traits of expression and style, threads or networks of ideas and preoccupations, run through and through his works, in prose and verse, many (if not most) stemming from his years at Moor Park. Such features may have a 'straight' or straightforward expression, and a 'double' or playful, satirical, devious, sometimes anarchic, embodiment. The latter marks Swift's deeply ironic and satirical cast of mind, a temper profoundly resistant to convention, at the same time as his didactic, preaching side was allied with a vulnerable idealism and passionate honesty.

The strands of his lifelong concerns surface at different times, in different kinds of works. His conviction that good conversation and polite behaviour are supreme manifestations of the civilized defences of human life, for example, was at least fortified in Temple's circle. It can become active in many different places and forms, 'straight' in *On the Death of Mrs. Johnson*, outraged in *A Short Character of Thomas Earl of Wharton* or his letter to John Evans, Bishop of Meath, 22 May 1719, savagely mocking in *A Complete Collection of Genteel and Ingenious Conversation*. He held a doctrine, reminiscent of Temple, of the hesitant, fragile, and perhaps doomed improvement in language; he adds to this a characteristic sense of the vivifying but dangerous bond between language and social behaviour, which underlies the humour of ['The continual Corruption of our English Tongue'] in *The Tatler*, No. 230, 28 September 1710, his attack on Steele in *The Importance of the Guardian Considered* (1713), and the wit of *The Grand Question Debated*, an occasional poem of 1729. Temple's notion of history did not neglect economic considerations. Swift makes use of a straightforward if partisan exposition of such matters in many of his political pieces, such as *The Conduct of the Allies* (1711), and finds a basis in his theory of political economy for the imagery of a powerful set of verses, *The Run upon the Bankers* (1720). Economics, too, is the backbone of the writing that dominated the last twenty-five years of his life, the pamphlets on Ireland, a country in whose culture history, and the writing of history, have played a major and shaping role.

This is a convenient place to turn to Swift's Irish context, the second formative heritage of his birth in Dublin. An appreciation of the complicated relationship in Swift's day between the metropolis and the Anglo-Irish periphery helps our understanding of the powerful complexity of Swift's writing, which is at once a great contribution to the written culture in English, and also a dominant component of the Anglo-Irish tradition of literature and political rhetoric. One of the violent tensions characteristic of Swift's life and art lies here, and mirrors the deep divisions in Irish society at that time. Swift's Ireland had been created by three cataclysmic events and a related fundamental change in Irish politics and government. The early seventeenth-century political struggle in England, which led to the outbreak of civil war, the execution of the king in 1649, and the overthrow of the monarchy, precipitated a formidable rebellion of the native Irish leaders against the English Government. This erupted in October 1641. A bloody reconquest of

Ireland was effected by Cromwell, who after a campaign in all ways parallel with the ferocity of the Thirty Years War in Germany imposed an Act of Settlement in 1652 dispossessing in varying degrees the Catholic rebels, both native Irish and Old English, and placing all land titles in doubt. The new settlers were largely Cromwellian veterans cashing in their rewards for military service. The second upheaval followed Charles II's restoration in 1660. A new Act of Settlement in 1661, which aimed at paying in Irish land some of Charles II's debts to his supporters, was passed by the Protestant Irish Parliament. This threw land titles into new confusion that provided ample pickings for English carpet-bagging lawyers, among whom was Swift's father. Amid much injustice, the Cromwellians were powerful enough to keep their lands but Catholics were expelled to less favourable locations, mostly in the west. The Anglican Church of Ireland was restored as the established Church, supported by tithes levied on all land, though that Church was the religious embodiment of a minority of the Protestant minority.

The third convulsion in Ireland took place between Swift's eighteenth and twenty-third years. When in 1688 the Roman Catholic monarch James II withdrew in the face of the invasion of William, Prince of Orange (who became William III), civil war broke out in Ireland. In March 1689 James, with French assistance, joined his army in Ireland. He summoned a Catholic Parliament (the Patriot Parliament), which did not really represent the Celtic Irish leaders. The Catholic Old English majority in this body set about demolishing Charles II's settlement, expropriating the large numbers of Protestant landowners who had fled on James's approach, and yet again threw land tenure into chaos. In the exodus, the young Swift himself fled to England. On 1 July 1690 William decisively defeated his uncle and father-in-law James at the Battle of the Boyne. The Jacobite field army was effectively destroyed at Aughrim on 12 July 1691. The ruin of the Catholic landowners was completed by partial abrogation of the Treaty of Limerick negotiated in 1691, but not ratified by the new Protestant Irish Parliament until 1697, and then in a mutilated form.

The fundamental political organization of Ireland was divisive and unjust. There were three groups of inhabitants. The Catholic majority are estimated at a million and a half, the Protestant minority at half a million. The Protestants, however, were divided between the homogeneous and resolute *bloc* of about 350,000 Ulster Presbyterians, chiefly small farmers but also including flourishing entrepreneurs and tradesmen, and 150,000 Anglican Anglo-Irish. The political nation was formed of the latter (together with English appointees). The complete

English establishment of government was replicated in Ireland by this small group, a king (the Lord-Lieutenant), Lord Treasurer, Lord Chancellor, judges, archbishops, bishops, two Houses of Parliament. Many officers were absentees. The tenure of land was the key to power and the process of extruding the Irish Catholic leaders had gone on steadily. From owning in 1641 more than half the land in the country, by 1703 Catholics owned only between one-tenth and one-fifth, and that mostly marginal. Swift's co-religionists deemed themselves reconquerors of the country; twice within living memory menaced by dispossession, they were savagely determined not to incur this danger again. They disenfranchised the Presbyterians by the Irish Test Act of 1703, and sought by a series of Penal Laws (accepted but not initiated in London) to condemn the Catholic majority to a state of ignorant and landless dependence. The Anglo-Irish domination was, however, validated by the armed force of the metropolitan power, a rankling, irreducible guarantee of the political subservience of the Dublin Government and Parliament. The English executive's orders were carried out by the Lord-Lieutenant and a group of largely English office-holders, the English interest, who were responsible for bargaining with local politicians.

His birth and nurture gave Swift a divided culture, and had other profound consequences in all his writing, apart from the obvious course of his later life as Dean of St Patrick's and the Irish themes in his political and personal writing. At the risk of over-simplification, it may be suggested that Swift has conflicting 'English' and 'Irish' sides. In this he may be no more than the best-known example of that Anglo-Irish ambivalence or ambiguity of outlook which J. C. Beckett (see p. 697) suggests led to the detachment and aggression of insecurity and which Andrew Carpenter (see p. 697) calls 'double vision'. This was, the latter argues, a reaction to life in Ireland as it became after the Battle of the Boyne, 'a more enigmatic and ambiguous affair than life in England'. Swift's English side scorned Ireland, 'the land of slaves and fens'. He wrote to the second Earl of Oxford in an often-quoted letter from Dublin dated 14 June 1737 of Lord Treasurer Oxford's 'want of power to keep me in what I ought to call my own country; though I happened to be dropped here, and was a year old before I left it, and to my sorrow did not die before I came back to it again'. His Irish side is more Irish than his Anglo-Irish contemporaries, defiant in the *Drapier's Letters*, responding with oblique fellow-feeling and passionate humanity to the misery of the oppressed Catholics in *A Modest Proposal*.

As a young man from the periphery, Swift sought fame and reward in the metropolis. Here we may consider the way his works gather into clusters, a feature of the distribution of his poetry *and* prose, which is obscured by printing the poems by themselves, and collecting the prose pieces into groups by apparent topic. The *History of England* cluster of 1697, as 'English' as can be imagined, we have already noted. There is a more problematic cluster of pieces related to *A Tale of a Tub*, which is deeply rooted in his ambivalent relationship with Temple and his English circle. *A Tale of a Tub* and its companions, like *The Mechanical Operation of the Spirit*, are outrageously devious in their rhetoric and their demands on the reader, sabotaging the easy urbanity that Temple strives to project. Swift's writing seems in places to reflect the ironic and subversive inspection which the wit from the periphery gives to metropolitan pretensions. The *Bickerstaff Papers* (1708–9), the *Tatler* contributions such as the sets of verses, *A Description of the Morning* (1709) and *A Description of a City Shower* (1710), various verse 'imitations' of Horace like [*Part of*] *The Seventh Epistle of the First Book* (1713), all form part of another 'English' cluster aimed at showing the polite world of London that the author was a native of the Town.

Swift's straightforward discussion of language clearly attached itself to this 'English' side of his writing. His encomium of Temple as the supreme improver of the English language has already been referred to; in *A Proposal for Correcting, Improving and Ascertaining the English Tongue* (1712), he appears as a prescriptivist, trying vainly to halt the decay of the English language, a nationalist conservative. He thought this service important enough to embody it in a letter to Lord Treasurer Oxford and, almost uniquely among his works, sign it with his name. A satirical obverse of this argument is to be found in his essay in *The Tatler*, No. 230 (28 September 1710), where, characteristically more English than the English, he mocks the betrayal of linguistic and social propriety by those who should in the metropolis be the transmitters of such values, the men of quality and fashion. A similar satirical attack is found in *A Complete Collection of Genteel and Ingenious Conversation*, which, though published posthumously, may date in embryo at least from these London years. There is another side, however, to Swift's attitude to language, which links him not to Temple or Dr Johnson, but to James Joyce. In some of his practice, far from being a prescriptivist, Swift shows an awareness and adept use of the widest variation of registers, polite and non-polite, spoken, written, technical, old and new. He has a very large lexicon, and his works are cited from time to time in the *Oxford English Dictionary* as giving examples of early printed usages of words and senses of words. This width of linguistic sympathy, and daring, are two of the sources of his power as a writer. *A Tale of a Tub* is a linguistic *tour de force*; the *Humble Petition of Frances Harris* in verse is another example of his exploitation of an ear for turns of phrase, tones of voice, and all the social nuances of language. The enjoyment of the *Journal to Stella* comes from his informality of language: as he rightly says, 'my letters are too good to be lost'. It is speculative, but not too far-fetched, to say that this is an 'Irish' feeling for English, ironical, aware of the social complexities of discourse, enjoying the anarchy and discontinuity in conversation and communication. The 'foreign' languages in *Gulliver's Travels* give a sense of the threat of half-understanding or misunderstanding a strange tongue, the feeling that might be experienced in living in a country split by two languages, English and Irish. The language games that Swift played with Sheridan and other friends, in which English words form Latin words, and vice versa, his deep interest in punning, riddles, old sayings, and puzzles, are aspects of the profound feeling that Swift has for all forms of English, at all levels, and which he can command in his writings at will for diverse purposes.

One of Temple's stylistic traits, and perhaps one of his fundamental habits of thought, lay in the framing of well-expressed general statements. To this gesture the custom of writing from 'heads' may be related. Swift starts where Temple left off; his writing is far tighter, his tone infinitely sharper, but the same attraction to maxims is the basis of many of his best and most effective passages such as the opening of *The Contests and Dissensions* or the first paragraph of *The Examiner*, No. 39 (26 April 1711). *Verses on the Death of Dr. Swift* (1731) issues from a similar pithy beginning, in this case rendered from the writing of La Rochefoucauld, whose *Réflexions ou Sentences et Maximes Morales* (1665) Swift greatly admired. His own *Thoughts on Various Subjects* and other epigrams show how consistently he practised this art (see [*Apothegms*], p. 181). He also worked against this characteristic power, however, in *A Tale of a Tub*; there, the generalizations and maxims of the 'modern' writer are mocked or evolved into ambiguous and fantastic forms: for example, '. . . For, if we take an examination of what is generally understood by *happiness*, as it has respect, either to the understanding or the senses, we shall find all its properties and adjuncts will herd under this short definition: that, *it is the perpetual possession of being well deceived*. . .' Maxims and political generalizations, as in the opening five paragraphs of *The Conduct of the Allies*, give his political writing a solidity remarkable in comparison with contemporary pieces, even though his argument may take an extreme position in the guise of offering central and agreed thoughts. Swift's imagination, on the other hand, resists the generalizations, seizes on the multifarious details, the doubts, the chaos. His experience in Ireland after 1714 increases the force of this loss of confidence in political formulae. The passion remains, and the hatred of tyranny, the scorn of dishonesty, the contempt for oppression. 'Fair Liberty was all his cry', but how could the immediate reaction of feeling be generalized in thought? Where could he find a resting place for framing maxims? It is true that Swift continues to strike out remarkable sentences like: 'Am I a free man in England, and do I become a slave in six hours by crossing the channel?' (*Some observations upon a Paper, called the Report of the Committee*, see p. 671, III.) The 'maxims of the schools', the general formulae of political philosophy, are more or less absent, or present only to be satirized.

In his *Essay upon the Advancement of Trade in Ireland* (1673), Temple begins his discussion with the maxim that 'the true and natural ground of trade and riches is, number of people in proportion to the compass of ground they inhabit . . .'. He continues, 'the want of trade in Ireland proceeds from the want of people . . .'. Swift's experience of politics and court intrigue in London from 1710 to 1714 and in the exacerbated difficulties of the Irish political scene after 1714 did not alter his political and constitutional opinions, but they strengthened the imaginative difficulties he had, in his finest and most powerful writing, in assenting to the magisterial, crisp general statements of theoretical political argument. *A Modest Proposal* (1729) takes the form of an 'argument' starting from an unstated Templeian maxim of political economy. This maxim is in fact set out in a short undated piece, obviously written at this time, but not printed until 1765 under the title *Maxims Controlled* [i.e. refuted, invalidated] *in Ireland* (*Prose*, xii. 131–7). The piece opens with the statement: 'There are certain maxims of state, founded upon long observation and experience, drawn from the constant practice of the wisest nations, and from the very principles of government, nor ever controlled by any writer upon politics.' The penultimate of those listed is, 'that people are the riches of a nation'. Swift's contention is that Ireland is not a normal kingdom or commonwealth, with 'the same natural rights common to the rest of mankind'. But the power and complexity of *A Modest Proposal* undercuts this relatively simple irony. It is the very truth of the maxims as they are embodied in the human situation that is sabotaged. The satirist himself is as threatened and vulnerable as his unconcerned targets, the political nation of Ireland, the guilty English reader, or the hypocritical readership in general. 'But, as to myself,' he bitterly says, correctly identifying himself as in his time a promoter of schemes of thought and action, 'having been wearied out for many years with offering vain, idle visionary thoughts; and at length utterly despairing of success, I fortunately fell upon this proposal . . .' Swift indeed never wrote a treatise in his life, only books with the appearance of treatises; his imagination came to resist extended arguments, and his wisdom is offered in broken generalizations. Even language itself, though an enjoyable game, is an uncertain tool, disabling the hand that holds it.

Swift was a political animal; his political tracts and poems, therefore, form a very substantial part of his achievement, and his preoccupation with politics and politicians ran all through his life. But just as, for him, history provided moral reflections for modern readers, so political actions, conflicts, and crises were located in a context of historical and moral argument. Swift's political tracts were stylish contributions to actual controversy, and gain weight from his reach of imagination and reference. The relationship in such political writing, however, between immediate circumstances, events, persons, and intentions on the one hand, and on the other political doctrines, moral principles, or lasting literary worth and enjoyment, is often strained. At the simplest level, Swift's very effective response to the current of affairs and the sometimes rebarbative subject-matter drawn from insistent contemporary political topics can defeat modern readers who are not specialists in the history of the time. This difficulty masks passages as good as anything he ever wrote. Although such political concerns and references feature in many of his pieces, his strictly political writing is chiefly distributed in three groups. Some early pieces were written as he was trying to make his way in London. Secondly, from October 1710 to summer 1714 he lived in London, active as a writer in support of Harley's administration and its Tory majority in the Commons; during this time he wrote more than thirty weekly essays in the pro-Government *Examiner*, twenty or so other known prose pieces and pamphlets, and about thirteen verse broadsides; he may have written other fugitive pieces and was one of those through whom Harley, in a very modern way, managed his administration's publicity and public image. The effectiveness of this propaganda, and Swift's participation in it, decreased as the quarrel between Harley and St John grew more bitter, until the final fatal breach in late 1713. Lastly, from 1720, Swift published sixty or so prose pieces directly concerned with Irish political affairs, including several essays in the *Intelligencer*, a journal briefly conducted by Swift and Thomas Sheridan in 1728, as well as writing more than that number of sets of political verses on the same topic, many of them printed separately as broadsides.

His political beliefs and doctrines did not materially alter throughout his writing career, but his allegiances changed from time to time. As we see (p. 612), his early *Contests and Dissensions in Athens and Rome* was not a very practical political piece, but used politics for a virtuoso essay. He wrote directly in support of Harley's ministry, but in assessing this commitment we should keep in mind an earlier sentence of his: 'To enter into a *party* as into an order of *friars*, with so resigned an obedience to superiors, is very unsuitable both with the civil and religious liberties, we so zealously assert' (*The Sentiments of a Church-of-England Man* (1708); *Prose*, ii. 24). Swift's ideal State was a strictly hierarchical one, in which power followed the possession of land. The Church by law established was part of the political balance. He deeply believed that those who would not conform to the Church should be disenfranchised. Thus, his *stated* doctrines of liberty and representation were very heavily qualified and conservative. He naturally considered as betrayal, not only the changes forced by the rise of the 'moneyed men' who financed the cost of the war against Louis XIV, but also any departures from his model which flowed from pragmatic political action, the give and take of the fierce political struggles in the last years of William III and the reign of Queen Anne. This did no harm to the power of his political writing. He could and did in this way convince himself that justice lay on one side of the political argument in England. His support for an argument, or a politician, or a policy often has about it, therefore, an air of powerful alarm, as if the very order of things is on the edge of collapse.

One of the great themes of his political writing up to 1714 is his support for a peaceful end to the great European war against Louis XIV and his French expansionism. Swift's involvement in the debate surrounding this European conflict was of long standing. Sir William Temple's diplomacy was from the 1670s aimed at creating and strengthening an effective coalition against the *grand monarque*. Swift was engaged, therefore, in writing the ex-ambassador's self-justificatory history of the beginning of the struggle. He played a major part in bringing about the success of Harley's deeply felt anti-war policy of concluding the vast conflict with a negotiated peace, if necessary at the expense of violating agreement with England's allies. *The Conduct of the Allies* remains Swift's most effective pamphlet in terms of actual political results. One of the most powerful feelings awakened in the reader by Swift's political rhetoric is a hatred of war:

It will, no doubt, be a mighty comfort to our grandchildren when they see a few rags hang up in Westminster Hall, which cost an hundred millions whereof they are paying the arrears, and boasting, as beggars do, that their grandfathers were rich and great.

His contemporary success was gained by a sure instinct in reaching the audience he sought; his modern achievement lies in making his political writing transcend not only the details on which it is built, but the explicit doctrines which he held and argued for in form.

The latter point is more fully illustrated in the Irish tracts. The deep, irreconcilable pressures on Swift as an Anglo-Irish writer have already been outlined, and this sketch is amplified in the notes to the Irish pamphlets included in this selection. Practically, as a publicist, Swift in the *Drapier's Letters* led the Anglo-Irish resistance to English administrative government of Ireland, which forced the abandonment of Wood's patent to provide new copper coins for Ireland. He was also, however, compelled to witness the success of Walpole and the English executive, working through Boulter, Archbishop of Armagh, in following this tactical defeat by a more ruthless control of the Dublin establishment, by the more insistent appointment of Englishmen to place and office, and in other ways ignoring the Anglo-Irish argument for some independence of political action. His long-term victory lay in articulating in memorable and usable form the spirit of the Irish political nation. Further, his voice made that political nation gradually aware, amid the oppression of the eighteenth-century constitution, that in some way it was responsible for 'the whole people of Ireland'. Swift is no nationalist, but as 'the Hibernian patriot' his stylish and powerful rhetoric addresses the modern reader directly, sweeping away the complex enmities of the Irish situation in his own day. It was Swift's ringing phrases that were invoked by the establishment rationalists at the end of the eighteenth century, as in Grattan's speech to the Irish Commons on 16 April 1782, when he proposed the unanimously adopted declaration of Irish legislative independence and said: 'Spirit of Swift, spirit of Molyneux, your genius has prevailed. Ireland is now a nation; in that new character I hail her and bowing to her august presence, I say *esto perpetua*.' But that particular arrangement was not to 'be perpetual'. It has passed away, leaving Swift's final achievement as one of conscience, imagination, and the art of writing.

Parallel with Swift's political concerns runs another of his profound preoccupations, the demands of his religious belief and office. From the reign of Henry VIII, Swift argued, though not itself free from the overweening tendency of all political constituents and powers, the Church of England worked for the establishment of the balance between King, Lords, and Commons, and added its own force on the side of order, civilization, and peace. Charles II's restoration put an end to the anti-monarchical and anti-Church usurpation of the

Cromwellians, and it was in this theory of the Restoration that Swift was educated.

The overtly political place of the Church of Ireland in Charles II's and the Williamite settlements of Ireland is obvious. Membership of that minority body became the shibboleth of the ownership of land, from which flowed power. The dignitaries of the Irish Church, mostly appointees from England, were officers of the Anglo-Irish Government, the bishops sat in the House of Lords, and the Archbishops of Dublin and Armagh were frequently Lords Justices in the absence of the Lord-Lieutenant. It is true that Archbishop King represented an Anglo-Irish resistance movement in the Church, a tendency in which Swift himself played a notable part. The situation of his Church, and the stress of his own place in it, galled Swift's ideas of the Church in Christian tradition, his ideal of the Church as an independent force. The political rub for the Church and churchmen lay not so much in the secularizing reformation of Henry VIII, who 'robbed' it (*Sermon upon the Martyrdom of Charles I*, in *Prose*, ix. 220) and to whom, Swift says, 'Nero . . . was a saint in comparison' (*Prose*, v. 249). A resigned acceptance in the face of the human misfortunes recounted by history could to some extent cope with such oppression. The serious politico-religious crisis came in the Glorious Revolution of 1688. In this upheaval, the *de jure* king, James II, to whom (though a Catholic) all ecclesiastics had taken solemn oaths as head of the Church by divine arrangement, was excluded by parliamentary legislation, and replaced in the same fashion by William III. Thus the monarch was created by Parliament, and the Church, though a divinely instructed body, had even its religious supremacy guaranteed by the Lords and Commons. Swift held steadfastly to the belief that dissenters, those who did not accept the supremacy of the State Church, should by the Test Acts be excluded from public office. Again, however, this ecclesiastical position was guaranteed by the will of the Lords and Commons; what they had granted they could take away, and there were constant movements in the Commons to repeal the Test.

The institutionalized, regulatory side of Christianity, the Church, is only part of the religious life. So far as the other part, personal religious belief, is concerned, Swift scrupulously kept himself out of religious controversy. One of the sharpest thrusts of *A Tale of a Tub*, however, is the implicit argument against building on any sense of personal religious illumination, or acting on any belief in inspiration. But there is a very long tradition in Christianity of ecstatic religion, trance, possession, mysticism, and all the social concomitants of such revelations, namely shamanism, cults, quietism, protest. Swift's rejection of the extremes of personal belief led him in *A Tale of a Tub* into exploring the deep connections linking religious ecstasy with sexual excitement and other psychosomatic states. Critics at the time protested that the satire was in danger of attacking traditionally revered religious qualities, if it did not in fact do so. This is one of the instances in Swift's work where a compelling awareness of social and ecclesiastical imperatives intersects an equally strong realization of the power, for good and evil, in the individual spirit. His expressed moral and ethical doctrine, in, for example, his sermon *The Testimony of Conscience*, is practical, low-key, and repressive. The questions he raises by his imagination in the feeling projected through his wit and social conscience are much less contained and containable. The yoking together in the satire of *A Tale of a Tub* of Alexander the Great, Monsieur Descartes, and the Anabaptist Jack of Leyden (p. 143), all examples of men whose transcendental inner compulsions are psychologically complex and not always admirable, is an extremely vivid instance of the uncomfortable texture of his writing. Just as his crisp political generalizations are given force by the unresolved conflicts hovering over them, so the apparent staidness of his straightforward expression of moral doctrine is made grimmer by its context, in his works as a whole, of spectres and forces awakened by his wit.

So much may be said of the political and religious complexity of Swift's position, not to 'explain' his writing, but to suggest the centres of potential disturbance in it, from which may be felt the heat and activity of his own imaginative doubt, perplexity, striving for certainty. All readers have sensed the suppressed power in Swift's writing, the feeling of force barely confined, or in some passages not quite contained.

To great mastery of writing in verse and prose Swift joined a passionate wish for order, a clear and steady awareness not only of how far human beings fell short of their potential, but also of that 'treasury of vileness and baseness' which his friend Dr Arbuthnot 'always believed to be in the heart of man'. Swift's personal, political, and religious circumstances were complex and galling, and he responded fully to their painful complexity, but also strove for clear ideas and true judgements. The power of his feelings and the keenness of his thought do not produce some simple, single doctrine or confident resolution of doubts. In varied writing that still has the ability to move his readers, he continues to elicit equally varied, sometimes contradictory, responses.

Acknowledgements

Students of Swift will at once detect where the work of other scholars has been laid under contribution in this volume. The debt, too large to be indicated throughout the text, is fully acknowledged here. The editors wish to give particular thanks for help to: John Bell, Paul-Gabriel Boucé, Colin Brooks, Andrew Carpenter, Frank Ellis, Frank Kermode, Hermann Real, James Shiel, Norman Vance, Heinz Vienken; and to the staff of the British Library; Cambridge University Library; Bodleian Library; English Faculty Library, Oxford; Forster Collection, Victoria and Albert Museum; Trinity College Library, Cambridge; University of Sussex Library. The editors are grateful for financial and other assistance from the University of Sussex.

CHRONOLOGY

1667   30 November, Jonathan Swift born in Hoey's Court, Dublin.

1672   Addison and Steele born.

1673   Swift sent to Kilkenny College; Test Act in England.

1674   Milton dies.

1677   Bunyan, *Pilgrim's Progress*.

1678   Popish Plot; St John (Bolingbroke) born; Andrew Marvell dies.

1681   Dryden, *Absalom and Achitophel*.

1682   Swift enters Trinity College, Dublin.

1685   Charles II dies, accession of Roman Catholic James II; Monmouth's rebellion and execution.

1686   Swift graduates BA in Dublin.

1688   Birth of Pope; death of Bunyan; William of Orange invades England by invitation; James II flees to France.

1688–9 James II appeals to his Roman Catholic subjects in Ireland and civil war breaks out; Trinity College suspends its session; Swift flees to England; James II establishes himself in Ireland.

1689   Under family patronage Swift employed by Sir William Temple at Moor Park in Surrey; becomes tutor to 8-year-old Esther Johnson (Stella).

1690   1 July, William III defeats James II at the Battle of the Boyne; James flees to France; Swift returns to Ireland to seek preferment.

1691   Swift returns to Moor Park as Temple's secretary; 12 July, Jacobite army defeated at Aughrim; 3 October, the Treaty of Limerick ends the fighting.

1692   *Ode to the Athenian Society*, Swift's first publication; he graduates MA at Hart Hall, Oxford.

1694   Swift leaves Moor Park and is ordained priest in Dublin; he is given the Church of Ireland prebend of Kilroot in a presbyterian area near Belfast.

1695   Press Licensing Act lapses; first of the Penal Laws imposing restrictions on Irish Catholics.

1696   Swift returns to Temple's service at Moor Park; during the next three years writes *The Battle of the Books* in support of Temple in the Ancients and Moderns controversy; completes most of *A Tale of a Tub*.

1699   Death of Temple (*When I come to be old*); Swift returns to Dublin as chaplain to the Earl of Berkeley; William Molyneux, *The Case of Ireland's being bound by Acts of Parliament in England, Stated* (1698).

1700   Swift presented to vicarage of Laracor near Dublin and prebend
        in St Patrick's Cathedral; Swift ed. *Temple's Letters*, i and ii; death of
        Dryden.

1701   Swift returns to England and publishes *Contests and Dissensions . . . in
        Athens and Rome*; *The Humble Petition of Frances Harris*; returns to
        Ireland; Swift ed. *Temple's Miscellanea*, iii; James II dies.

1702   Swift graduates DD at Trinity College, Dublin; Esther Johnson and
        Rebecca Dingley come to live in Dublin; death of Pepys; William III
        dies, accession of Queen Anne; allies declare war on France (War of
        the Spanish Succession).

1704   Swift publishes anonymous volume containing *A Tale of a Tub* and
        associated pieces; Defoe's periodical *The Review* (to 1713); Locke dies;
        Test Act in Ireland; Battle of Blenheim.

1707   Swift appointed a Church of Ireland commissioner to solicit from
        Queen Anne the remission of the 'first fruits'; becomes known in
        London to Addison and other writers as well as to men in power; allied
        army defeated in Spain at Almanza; Union of Scots and English
        Parliaments.

1708–9 *Bickerstaff Papers*; Steele, *The Tatler* (to 1711), to which Swift contri-
        butes; Swift ed. *Temple's Memoirs*, iii; Samuel Johnson born; May,
        peace negotiations at Geertruidenberg break down; August, bloody
        Battle of Malplaquet; Barrier Treaty signed with Dutch to keep them
        in the Alliance; first real Copyright Act; Swift returns to Ireland.

1710   August, fall of Lord Treasurer Godolphin; Harley to power as
        Chancellor of the Exchequer; secret peace negotiations with France
        begin informally; 7 September, Swift arrives in London and starts the
        Journal to Stella; October, the Tories win a landslide victory in the
        general election; Swift agrees to support Harley and the new ministry;
        he turns on the Whig ex-ministers in *A Short Character of Thomas Earl
        of Wharton* and *The Virtues of Sid Hamet's Rod* against Godolphin;
        November, Swift begins his series of thirty-three weekly papers in *The
        Examiner* as the administration's chief party writer.

1711   The politicians direct Swift to conclude his *Examiner* series; *The
        Conduct of the Allies* published in November; Swift's anti-Whig squib
        The Windsor Prophecy angers the Queen; he becomes closely involved
        with Hester Vanhomrigh (Vanessa); Steele–Addison *Spectator* (to
        1712), to which Swift contributes; Harley made Earl of Oxford and
        Lord Treasurer; December, Marlborough dismissed; crisis over peace
        negotiations; *Miscellanies in Prose and Verse*.

1712   Swift, *Some Remarks on the Barrier Treaty*, attacks the Dutch; split
        opens between Oxford and Secretary St John; Ministers cannot agree
        on form and contents of Swift's justificatory piece for forthcoming
        session of Parliament; Swift, *A Proposal for Correcting the English
        Tongue*; Pope, *Rape of the Lock*; Stamp Act seeks to censor the periodical
        press by taxation; Rousseau born; St John made Viscount Bolingbroke.

1713   Swift tries to cool Hester Vanhomrigh's passion by writing *Cadenus and Vanessa*; Oxford can obtain for Swift only the Deanery of St Patrick's, not in the Queen's gift; he is installed in Dublin; Swift attacks Steele's Whig journalism in *The Importance of the Guardian Considered*; Addison, *Cato* (tragedy); Anthony Collins, *Discourse of Free-thinking* (answered by Swift); Scriblerus Club (Swift, Pope, Arbuthnot, Oxford, Parnell, etc.) develops out of the Brothers' Club, to satirize pedantry and dullness; Treaties of Peace and Commerce with France are signed at Utrecht; the Commons refuses to ratify Bolingbroke's Treaty of Commerce.

1714   The Ministry disintegrates; Swift's attack on Steele, *The Public Spirit of the Whigs*, attracts price of £300 on the head of the author; Swift retires to Letcombe Regis in Berkshire; *The Author upon Himself*; Oxford dismissed, Bolingbroke not made Lord Treasurer; 1 August, Queen Anne dies, accession of George I; dismissal of Bolingbroke; Swift leaves for Dublin, 16 August, and takes up residence in his deanery; his letters are opened in the post.

1715   March, Bolingbroke flees to France and takes service with the Pretender; Bolingbroke, Ormond, and Oxford impeached; Jacobite Rebellion in Scotland; Louis XIV dies.

1717   Oxford's impeachment discontinued on a technicality and he is released.

1719   Defoe, *Robinson Crusoe*; Addison dies; British Declaratory Act establishes British House of Lords as final Court of Appeal for Irish suits and asserts right of British Parliament to legislate for Ireland.

1720   Swift, *A Proposal for the Universal Use of Irish Manufacture*, the printer prosecuted; South Sea Bubble; Jacobite conspiracy in England to exploit crisis; patent issued to William Wood for the manufacture of copper coins for Ireland.

1721   A manuscript of part of *Gulliver's Travels* is seen by friends and Swift is writing domestic and occasional verse; Smollett born; Prior dies; Walpole, Chancellor of the Exchequer and Prime Minister.

1722   Defoe, *Journal of the Plague Year* and *Moll Flanders*; Atterbury committed to the Tower; Habeas Corpus suspended; Wood's patent published, provoking Irish administrative protest.

1723   Hester Vanhomrigh (Vanessa) dies; Atterbury found guilty of 'high crimes and misdemeanours' by Act of Parliament; Swift's friend Carteret jockeyed out of power by Walpole and Townshend.

1724   *Drapier's Letters* attack English Government for Wood's patent, Swift a national hero in Ireland; Carteret arrives in Dublin as Lord-Lieutenant and counters the *Letter to the Whole People of Ireland* by offering £300 for the discovery of the 'anonymous' Drapier, the reward going unclaimed.

1725   Carteret calls the Irish Parliament to announce Wood's surrender of his patent.

1726   Swift arrives in London with the manuscript of *Gulliver's Travels* and stays four months, chiefly with Pope at Twickenham; he meets Walpole to discuss Irish problems and finds him unsympathetic and unresponsive; 28 October, *Gulliver's Travels* published in London after Swift's departure for Dublin; Bolingbroke *et al.*, *Craftsman* (to 1748), the chief Opposition periodical.

1727   April to September, Swift again in England; he returns to the final sickness and death of Esther Johnson (Stella); *Pope–Swift Miscellanies*, i and ii; George I dies, accession of George II; Sir Isaac Newton dies.

1728–9 *Miscellanies* [iii]; Swift spends eight months with Achesons near Armagh, source of the 'Market Hill' poems; Swift collaborates with Sheridan in writing the periodical, the *Intelligencer*; Gay, *Beggar's Opera*; Pope, *Dunciad*, i–iii.

1729   *A Modest Proposal.*

1731   *Verses on the Death of Dr. Swift*; Pope, *Epistle to Burlington*; Defoe dies.

1732   *Miscellanies* [iv].

1733   *On Poetry. A Rhapsody*; Pope, *Essay on Man* and *First Satire of II Horace, Imitated*; Voltaire, *English Letters*.

1734   General election, Walpole wins.

1735   Bolingbroke retires to France; George Faulkner publishes the 4-vol. Dublin edition of Swift's *Works*; Swift makes his will; Pope, *Epistle to Dr. Arbuthnot*.

1736   *The Legion Club*; Swift unsuccessfully attempts to publish the *History of the Four Last Years of the Queen*.

1737   Pope, *Imitations of Horace* and *Letters*; Queen Caroline dies.

1738   Johnson, *London*; *Polite Conversation*.

1740   Swift makes his last will; Richardson, *Pamela*, i; Boswell born.

1741   Pope ed. *Memoirs of Scriblerus*; *Letters to and from Dr. Swift.*

1742   17 August, Swift is declared 'of unsound mind and memory' and his affairs are handed over to trustees; Pope, (*New*) *Dunciad*, iv; Fielding, *Joseph Andrews*; Walpole resigns.

1744   Death of Pope.

1745   *Directions to Servants*; Jacobite Rebellion; Walpole dies; 19 October, Swift dies in his Deanery of St Patrick's, Dublin; buried in his cathedral church; the Epitaph he composed is carved and placed according to his directions.

NOTE ON THE TEXT

THE text of the present selection from Swift's *œuvre* is based on a wide-ranging review of all the textual sources of the seventy-two items chosen. Where more than one witness is available to help determine and establish the earliest state of a text and its subsequent revision, a fresh collation was undertaken of each, which took cognizance of substantive variation and of such significant minutiae as spelling, capitalization, and even typographical presentation, as might conceivably betray an authorial origin.

Thus manuscripts, first and subsequent editions, English or Irish reprints, and the authorized collections of 1711, 1727, and 1735 have been scrutinized, as well as the texts of some posthumous editions. To take the extreme case of *A Tale of a Tub*, upwards of twenty-three editions printed before 1756 were collated or examined, and for the *Verses on the Death of Dr. Swift* eleven editions printed before 1746 and three annotated copies containing the completed text of poem and notes.

Although in the result the broad outline of familiar works remains unchanged, it will be found that many long-standing errors have been retrieved and, more important, that the present text answers for the first time faithfully to the whole range of nuances imparted by the author to individual works, in somewhat haphazard fashion, over perhaps twenty-five years.

In the area of revision it can be seen that Swift's changes, once a work had appeared in print, occur almost exclusively in local repairs of a word or two for the sake of euphony or exactness of meaning, and very occasionally in straight omissions, usually on the grounds of mere prudence. Rewriting of even so little as a paragraph is so out of character as to be virtually non-existent, and this fact alone underlines the absurdity of the recent contention that the nine sorry paragraphs in Motte's 1726 text of *Gulliver's Travels*, later replaced with authentic material in Faulkner's 1735 text, were directly from Swift's pen.

As to genuine variants, however, it is a legitimate question whether, as between original readings and revisions, an editor is ever at liberty to assert his own preference for a discarded variant and thus effectively to overrule the author himself. After an extended and intensive survey of the smallest changes throughout Swift's prose and verse, one may recall these memorable words: 'when a man's thoughts are clear, the properest words will generally offer themselves first, and his own judgement will direct him in what order to place them, so as they may be best understood'. Equally relevant is Swift's deep concern for euphony, expressed in *A Proposal for Correcting the English Tongue*. Applying these canons one may see, time and again, that afterthoughts in the form of casual revision, often years after the original act of composition, have been imposed upon a text which in its first form was expressed to perfection in its clarity, its shape, its sound and rhythm, some or all of which qualities are violated by the random change. Too often it is evident that the author himself has lost the overall impulse of the original expression. Consequently an editor, seeking to serve the best interests of both writer and reader, is driven to favour a general rule to retain the early readings among variants, unless some overriding consideration is present which makes acceptance of the revision mandatory.

This rule, which is applied in the present selection, constitutes a departure from the orthodoxy by which in recent years Swift's writings in prose and verse have for the most part exhibited the late variants. The textual foundations of each work have been reassessed for this edition, and each work therefore has been treated individually on the merits and defects of its surviving texts.

The decision to modernize affects spelling, punctuation, and the older conventions of capitals and non-emphatic italics. Nevertheless, it has not been so rigorously applied as to reduce a lively original to the sustained monotony of today's newspaper or novel. The expansive display of the title-page and its epigraph have been converted into a dropped heading. Not infrequently old spellings have been reprieved for the same reason that some obsolete words demanded to survive, namely that to modernize in these cases is to discard a deliberate option taken by the author for the sake of sound or rhythm or sense.

Paradoxically, a more creative view has been taken of the duty to respect the author's intentions, often presumed, in punctuation. The holographs exhibit an inconsistent practice; transcripts vary from scribe to scribe; compositors and printers' readers contributed a measure of error and individual bias; Swift's own instinctive habits reflect conventions long since abandoned.

In this situation, affecting both verse and prose, it was judged best to start anew. Having identified first those manuscripts and early editions closest to author's copy for the printer and most likely to reflect even intermittently his directions, and then consulted reprints for possible changes, a new punctuation has been devised which both respects those authorial directions and conveys them to the reader in the simpler modern practice, allowing free rein to the tempo of the writing.

A related consideration is Swift's joy in the use of emphatic typography, which transmits his unfailing sense of concurrent multiple meanings (of which puns are only one manifestation), and his keen ear for rhetorical pace and climax. His deliberate use of italics and of full capitals for whole words and passages has been carefully preserved, and gives further testimony to the energy of his writing.

Exceptional editorial treatment has been given to the text of certain works. For example, the present text of Swift's greatest poem, *Verses on the Death of Dr. Swift*, is a new recension which draws upon the superior variants in the parallel passages of Pope's London folio of 1739. *On Poetry* has been expanded by restoring within half-brackets the fifty-four lines omitted in 1733, though the standard line numbers are retained in a much-quoted work. In the very early *Battle of the Books*, where conceivably the improving hand of the compositor was responsible for a level of italics verging on slapstick, the incidence has been tactfully reduced to those few instances clearly characteristic of Swift.

The degree sign (°) indicates a note at the end of the book. More general notes and headnotes are not cued. All material between square brackets [ ] is editorial.

A Full and True Account of the BATTEL Fought last FRIDAY, Between the *Antient* and the *Modern* BOOKS in St. JAMES's LIBRARY.

THE BOOKSELLER° TO THE READER.

THE following Discourse, as it is unquestionably of the same author, so it seems to have been written about the same time with the former; I mean the year 1697, when the famous dispute was on foot about ancient and modern learning. The controversy took its rise from an essay of Sir William Temple's upon that subject, which was answered by W. Wotton, B.D., with an Appendix by Dr. Bentley, endeavouring to destroy the credit of Æsop and Phalaris for authors, whom Sir William Temple had, in the essay before-mentioned, highly commended. In that appendix the doctor falls hard upon a new edition of Phalaris put out by the Honourable Charles Boyle, now Earl of Orrery, to which Mr. Boyle replied at large, with great learning and wit; and the doctor voluminously rejoined. In this dispute, the town highly resented to see a person of Sir William Temple's character and merits roughly used by the two reverend gentlemen aforesaid, and without any manner of provocation. At length, there appearing no end of the quarrel, our author tells us that the BOOKS in St. James's Library,° looking upon themselves as parties principally concerned, took up the controversy and came to a decisive battle. But the manuscript by the injury of fortune or weather being in several places imperfect, we cannot learn to which side the victory fell.

I must warn the reader to beware of applying to persons what is here meant only of books, in the most literal sense. So, when Virgil is mentioned, we are not to understand the person of a famous poet called by that name, but only certain sheets of paper, bound up in leather, containing in print the works of the said poet; and so of the rest.

THE PREFACE OF THE AUTHOR.

SATIRE is a sort of glass, wherein beholders do generally discover everybody's face but their own; which is the chief reason for that kind of reception it meets in the world, and that so very few are offended with it. But if it should happen otherwise, the danger is not great; and I have learned from long experience never to apprehend mischief from those understandings I have been able to provoke; for anger and fury, though they add strength to the sinews of the body, yet are found to relax those of the mind, and to render all its efforts feeble and impotent.

There is a brain that will endure but one scumming; let the owner gather it with discretion, and manage his little stock with husbandry; but of all things, let him beware of bringing it under the lash of his betters, because that will make it all bubble up into impertinence, and he will find no new supply. Wit, without knowledge, being a sort of cream, which gathers in a night to the top, and by a skilful hand may be soon whipped into froth; but once scummed away, what appears underneath will be fit for nothing but to be thrown to the hogs.

A FULL AND TRUE ACCOUNT OF THE BATTLE FOUGHT LAST FRIDAY, &c.

WHOEVER examines with due circumspection into the **Annual Records of Time*, will find it remarked that War is the child of Pride, and Pride the daughter of Riches. The former of which assertions may be soon granted, but one cannot so easily subscribe to the latter; for Pride is nearly related to Beggary and Want, either by father or mother, and sometimes by both: and to speak naturally, it very seldom happens among men to fall out when all have enough, invasions usually travelling from north to south, that is to say, from poverty upon plenty. The most ancient and natural grounds of quarrels are lust and avarice; which, though we may allow to be brethren, or collateral branches of pride, are certainly the issues of want. For, to speak in the phrase of writers upon politics, we may observe in the Republic of Dogs° (which, in its original, seems to be an institution of the Many) that the whole state is ever in the profoundest peace after a full meal; and that civil broils arise among them when it happens for one great bone to be seized on by some leading dog, who either divides it among the few and then it falls to an oligarchy, or keeps it to himself and then it runs up to a tyranny. The same reasoning also holds place among them in those dissensions we behold upon a turgescency in any of their females. For the right of possession lying in common (it being impossible to establish a property in so delicate a case) jealousies and suspicions do so abound that the whole commonwealth of that street is reduced to a manifest state of war, of every citizen against every citizen, till some one of more courage, conduct, or fortune than the rest, seizes and enjoys the prize; upon which naturally arises plenty of

* 'Riches produceth pride; pride is war's ground, &c.' *Vide* Ephem. de Mary Clarke; opt. edit.°

heart-burning, and envy, and snarling against the happy dog. Again, if we look upon any of these republics engaged in a foreign war either of invasion or defence, we shall find the same reasoning will serve as to the grounds and occasions of each, and that poverty or want in some degree or other (whether real or in opinion, which makes no alteration in the case) has a great share, as well as pride, on the part of the aggressor.

Now, whoever will please to take this scheme, and either reduce or adapt it to an intellectual state or commonwealth of learning, will soon discover the first ground of disagreement between the two great parties at this time in arms, and may form just conclusions upon the merits of either cause. But the issue or events of this war are not so easy to conjecture at; for the present quarrel is so inflamed by the warm heads of either faction, and the pretensions *somewhere or other* so exorbitant, as not to admit the least overtures of accommodation. This quarrel first began (as I have heard it affirmed by an old dweller in the neighbourhood) about a small spot of ground, lying and being upon one of the two tops of the hill Parnassus; the highest and largest of which had, it seems, been time out of mind in quiet possession of certain tenants called the Ancients, and the other was held by the Moderns. But these, disliking their present station, sent certain ambassadors to the Ancients, complaining of a great nuisance; how the height of that part of Parnassus quite spoiled the prospect of theirs, especially towards the *East*;° and therefore, to avoid a war, offered them the choice of this alternative— either that the Ancients would please to remove themselves and their effects down to the lower summity, which the Moderns would graciously surrender to them, and advance in their place; or else that the said Ancients will give leave to the Moderns to come with shovels and mattocks, and level the said hill as low as they shall think it convenient. To which the Ancients made answer, how little they expected such a message as this from a colony whom they had admitted, out of their own free grace, to so near a neighbourhood. That, as to their own seat, they were aborigines of it, and therefore to talk with them of a removal or surrender, was a language they did not understand. That if the height of the hill on their side shortened the prospect of the Moderns, it was a disadvantage they could not help; but desired them to consider whether that injury (if it be any) were not largely recompensed by the shade and shelter it afforded them. That as to levelling or digging down, it was either folly or ignorance to propose it, if they did, or did not know, how that side of the hill was an entire rock, which would break their tools and hearts without any damage to itself. That they would therefore advise the Moderns rather to raise their own side of the hill than dream of pulling down that of the Ancients; to the former of which they would not only give licence, but also largely contribute. All this was rejected by the Moderns with much indignation, who still insisted upon one of the two expedients. And so this difference broke out into a long and obstinate war, maintained on the one part by resolution and by the courage of certain leaders and allies; but on the other by the greatness of their number, upon all defeats affording continual recruits. In this quarrel whole rivulets of ink have been exhausted, and the virulence of both parties enormously augmented. Now, it must here be understood that ink is the great missive weapon in all battles of the learned, which, conveyed through a sort of engine called a quill, infinite numbers of these are darted at the enemy by the valiant on each side, with equal skill and violence, as if it were an engagement of porcupines. This malignant liquor was compounded by the engineer who invented it, of two ingredients, which are gall and copperas; by its bitterness and venom to suit in some degree, as well as to foment, the genius of the combatants. And as the Grecians, after an engagement, when they could not agree about the victory, were wont to set up trophies on both sides, the beaten party being content to be at the same expense to keep itself in countenance (a laudable and ancient custom, happily revived of late in the art of war); so the learned, after a sharp and bloody dispute, do on both sides hang out their trophies too, whichever comes by the worst. These trophies have largely inscribed on them the merits of the cause, a full impartial account of such a battle, and how the victory fell clearly to the party that set them up. They are known to the world under several names, as *disputes*, *arguments*, *rejoinders*, *brief considerations*, *answers*, *replies*, *remarks*, *reflections*, *objections*, *confutations*. For a very few days they are fixed up in all public places either by themselves or their *representatives, for passengers to gaze at;° from whence the chiefest and largest are removed to certain magazines they call libraries, there to remain in a quarter purposely assigned them, and from thenceforth begin to be called *Books of Controversy*.

In these books is wonderfully instilled and preserved the spirit of each warrior, while he is alive; and after his death his soul transmigrates there to inform them. This at least is the more common opinion; but I believe it is with libraries as with other cemeteries, where some philosophers affirm that a certain spirit, which they call *brutum hominis*,° hovers over the monument till the body is corrupted and turns to dust or to worms, but then vanishes or dissolves. So, we may say, a restless spirit haunts over every book till dust or worms have seized upon it, which to some may

* Their title-pages.

happen in a few days, but to others, later; and therefore books of controversy, being of all others haunted by the most disorderly spirits, have always been confined in a separate lodge from the rest; and, for fear of mutual violence against each other, it was thought prudent by our ancestors to bind them to the peace with strong iron chains.° Of which invention the original occasion was this. When the works of Scotus° first came out, they were carried to a certain library and had lodgings appointed them; but this author was no sooner settled than he went to visit his master Aristotle; and there both concerted together to seize Plato by main force and turn him out from his ancient station among the divines, where he had peaceably dwelt near eight hundred years. The attempt succeeded, and the two usurpers have reigned ever since in his stead: but to maintain quiet for the future, it was decreed that all *polemics* of the larger size should be held fast with a chain.

By this expedient the public peace of libraries might certainly have been preserved, if a new species of controversial books had not arose of late years, instinct with a most malignant spirit, from the war above-mentioned between the learned, about the higher summity of Parnassus.

When these books were first admitted into the public libraries, I remember to have said upon occasion to several persons concerned, how I was sure they would create broils wherever they came, unless a world of care were taken; and therefore I advised that the champions of each side should be coupled together or otherwise mixed, that, like the blending of contrary poisons, their malignity might be employed among themselves. And it seems I was neither an ill prophet nor an ill counsellor; for it was nothing else but the neglect of this caution which gave occasion to the terrible fight that happened on Friday last, between the ancient and modern books in the King's Library. Now, because the talk of this battle is so fresh in everybody's mouth, and the expectation of the town so great to be informed in the particulars; I, being possessed of all qualifications requisite in an historian, and retained by neither party, have resolved to comply with the urgent *importunity of my friends* by writing down a full impartial account thereof.

The guardian of the regal library, a person of great valour but chiefly renowned for his *humanity,° had been a fierce champion for the Moderns; and, in an engagement upon Parnassus, had vowed, with his own hands, to knock down two of the Ancient chiefs° who guarded a small pass on the superior rock; but endeavouring to climb up was cruelly

* The Honourable Mr. Boyle, in the preface to his edition of Phalaris, says he was refused a manuscript by the library-keeper, '*pro solita humanitate suâ*'.

obstructed by his own unhappy weight and tendency towards his centre, a quality to which those of the Modern party are extreme subject; for, being light-headed, they have in speculation a wonderful agility, and conceive nothing too high for them to mount; but in reducing to practice, discover a mighty pressure about their posteriors and their heels. Having thus failed in his design, the disappointed champion bore a cruel rancour to the Ancients, which he resolved to gratify by showing all marks of his favour to the books of their adversaries, and lodging them in the fairest apartments; when at the same time, whatever book had the boldness to own itself for an advocate of the Ancients, was buried alive in some obscure corner, and threatened upon the least displeasure to be turned out of doors. Besides, it so happened that about this time there was a strange confusion of place among all the books in the library,° for which several reasons were assigned. Some imputed it to a great heap of learned dust, which a perverse wind blew off from a shelf of Moderns into the keeper's eyes. Others affirmed he had a humour to pick the worms out of the schoolmen, and swallow them fresh and fasting; whereof some fell upon his spleen, and some climbed up into his head, to the great perturbation of both. And lastly, others maintained that by walking much in the dark about the library, he had quite lost the situation of it out of his head; and therefore, in replacing his books, he was apt to mistake and clap Des Cartes next to Aristotle; poor Plato had got between Hobbes and the *Seven Wise Masters*,° and Virgil was hemmed in with Dryden on one side, and Withers° on the other.

Meanwhile, those books that were advocates for the Moderns chose out one from among them to make a progress through the whole library, examine the number and strength of their party, and concert their affairs. This messenger performed all things very industriously, and brought back with him a list of their forces, in all fifty thousand, consisting chiefly of light-horse, heavy-armed foot, and mercenaries;° whereof the foot were in general but sorrily armed, and worse clad; their horses large, but extremely out of case and heart; however, some few, by trading among the Ancients, had furnished themselves tolerably enough.

While things were in this ferment, discord grew extremely high; hot words passed on both sides, and ill blood was plentifully bred. Here a solitary Ancient, squeezed up among a whole shelf of Moderns, offered fairly to dispute the case, and to prove by manifest reasons, that the priority was due to them, from long possession, and in regard of their prudence, antiquity, and, above all, their great merits towards the Moderns. But these denied the premises, and seemed very much to wonder how the Ancients could pretend to insist upon their antiquity, when it was so plain (if they went to that) that the Moderns were much the more *ancient of the two.° As for any obligations they owed to the Ancients, they renounced them all. ' 'Tis true,' said they, 'we are informed some few of our party have been so mean to borrow their subsistence from you; but the rest, infinitely the greater number (and especially we French and English), were so far from stooping to so base an example that there never passed, till this very hour, six words between us. For our horses are of our own breeding, our arms of our own forging, and our clothes of our own cutting out and sewing.' Plato was by chance upon the next shelf, and observing those that spoke to be in the ragged plight mentioned a while ago; their jades lean and foundered, their weapons of rotten wood, their armour rusty, and nothing but rags underneath; he laughed loud, and in his pleasant way swore, by G— he believed them.

Now, the Moderns had not proceeded in their late negotiation with secrecy enough to escape the notice of the enemy. For those advocates who had begun the quarrel by setting first on foot the dispute of precedency, talked so loud of coming to a battle, that Temple happened to overhear them, and gave immediate intelligence to the Ancients, who thereupon drew up their scattered troops together, resolving to act upon the defensive; upon which several of the Moderns fled over to their party, and among the rest Temple himself. This Temple, having been educated and long conversed among the Ancients, was, of all the Moderns, their greatest favourite, and became their greatest champion.

Things were at this crisis, when a material accident fell out. For, upon the highest corner of a large window, there dwelt a certain spider, swollen up to the first magnitude by the destruction of infinite numbers of flies, whose spoils lay scattered before the gates of his palace, like human bones before the cave of some giant. The avenues to his castle were guarded with turnpikes and palisadoes, all after the modern way of fortification. After you had passed several courts, you came to the centre, wherein you might behold the constable himself in his own lodgings, which had windows fronting to each avenue, and ports to sally out upon all occasions of prey or defence. In this mansion he had for some time dwelt in peace and plenty, without danger to his person by swallows from above, or to his palace by brooms from below; when it was the pleasure of fortune to conduct thither a wandering bee, to whose curiosity a broken pane in the glass had discovered itself, and in he went; where, expatiating a while, he at last happened to alight upon one of the outward walls of the spider's citadel, which, yielding to the unequal weight, sunk down to the very foundation. Thrice he endeavoured to force his passage, and thrice

* According to the modern paradox.

the centre shook. The spider within, feeling the terrible convulsion, supposed at first that nature was approaching to her final dissolution; or else that Beelzebub, with all his legions, was come to revenge the death of many thousands of his subjects, whom this enemy had slain and devoured. However, he at length valiantly resolved to issue forth, and meet his fate. Meanwhile the bee had acquitted himself of his toils, and, posted securely at some distance, was employed in cleansing his wings and disengaging them from the ragged remnants of the cobweb. By this time the spider was adventured out, when, beholding the chasms and ruins and dilapidations of his fortress, he was very near at his wit's end; he stormed and swore like a madman, and swelled till he was ready to burst. At length, casting his eye upon the bee, and wisely gathering causes from events (for they knew each other by sight), 'A plague split you,' said he, 'for a giddy son of a whore. Is it you, with a vengeance, that have made this litter here? Could you not look before you, and be d—d? Do you think I have nothing else to do (in the devil's name) but to mend and repair after your arse?'—'Good words, friend,' said the bee (having now pruned himself and being disposed to droll) 'I'll give you my hand and word to come near your kennel no more; I was never in such a confounded pickle since I was born.'—'Sirrah,' replied the spider, 'if it were not for breaking an old custom in our family never to stir abroad against an enemy, I should come and teach you better manners.'—'I pray have patience', said the bee, 'or you will spend your substance, and for aught I see, you may stand in need of it all towards the repair of your house.'—'Rogue, rogue,' replied the spider, 'yet, methinks you should have more respect to a person whom all the world allows to be so much your betters.'—'By my troth,' said the bee, 'the comparison will amount to a very good jest, and you will do me a favour to let me know the reasons that all the world is pleased to use in so hopeful a dispute.' At this the spider, having swelled himself into the size and posture of a disputant, began his argument in the true spirit of controversy with a resolution to be heartily scurrilous and angry, to urge *on* his own reasons without the least regard to the answers or objections of his opposite, and fully predetermined in his mind against all conviction.

'Not to disparage myself', said he, 'by the comparison with such a rascal, what art thou but a vagabond without house or home, without stock or inheritance? Born to no possession of your own, but a pair of wings and a drone-pipe. Your livelihood is an universal plunder upon nature; a free-booter over fields and gardens; and for the sake of stealing, will rob a nettle as readily as a violet. Whereas I am a domestic animal, furnished with a native stock within myself. This large castle (to show my improvements in the mathematics°) is all built with my own hands, and the materials extracted altogether out of my own person.'

'I am glad', answered the bee, 'to hear you grant at least that I am come honestly by my wings and my voice; for then, it seems, I am obliged to Heaven alone for my flights and my music; and Providence would never have bestowed me two such gifts, without designing them for the noblest ends. I visit indeed all the flowers and blossoms of the field and the garden; but whatever I collect from thence enriches myself without the least injury to their beauty, their smell, or their taste. Now, for you and your skill in architecture and other mathematics, I have little to say. In that building of yours there might, for aught I know, have been labour and method enough; but, by woeful experience for us both, 'tis too plain the materials are naught, and I hope you will henceforth take warning, and consider duration and matter as well as method and art. You boast, indeed, of being obliged to no other creature but of drawing and spinning out all from yourself; that is to say, if we may judge of the liquor in the vessel by what issues out, you possess a good plentiful store of dirt and poison in your breast; and though I would by no means lessen or disparage your genuine stock of either, yet I doubt you are somewhat obliged, for an increase of both, to a little foreign assistance. Your inherent portion of dirt does not fail of acquisitions by sweepings exhaled from below; and one insect furnishes you with a share of poison to destroy another. So that, in short, the question comes all to this—Whether is the nobler being of the two, that which, by a lazy contemplation of four inches round, by an overweening pride, which feeding and engendering on itself, turns all into excrement and venom, produc[es] nothing at last but flybane and a cobweb; or that which, by an universal range, with long search, much study, true judgment, and distinction of things, brings home honey and wax.'

This dispute was managed with such eagerness, clamour, and warmth, that the two parties of books in arms below stood silent a while, waiting in suspense what would be the issue, which was not long undetermined. For the bee, grown impatient at so much loss of time, fled straight away to a bed of roses without looking for a reply, and left the spider like an orator, *collected* in himself, and just prepared to burst out.

It happened upon this emergency, that Æsop broke silence first. He had been of late most barbarously treated by a strange effect of the regent's *humanity*,° who had tore off his title-page, sorely defaced one half of his leaves, and chained him fast among a shelf of Moderns. Where, soon discovering how high the quarrel was like to proceed, he tried all his arts, and turned himself to a thousand forms. At length, in the borrowed shape of an ass,° the regent mistook him for a Modern, by which means he had time and opportunity to escape to the Ancients, just when the spider and the bee were entering into their contest, to which he gave his attention with a world of pleasure; and when it was ended, swore in the loudest key that in all his life he had never known two cases so parallel and adapt to each other, as that in the window, and this upon the shelves. 'The disputants', said he, 'have admirably managed the dispute between them, have taken in the full strength of all that is to be said on both sides, and exhausted the substance of every argument *pro* and *con*. It is but to adjust the reasonings of both to the present quarrel, then to compare and apply the labours and fruits of each, as the bee has learnedly deduced them, and we shall find the conclusions fall plain and close upon the Moderns and us. For pray, gentlemen, was ever anything so modern as the spider in his air, his turns, and his paradoxes? He argues in the behalf of you his brethren, and himself, with many boastings of his native stock and great genius; that he spins and spits wholly from himself, and scorns to own any obligation or assistance from without. Then he displays to you his great skill in architecture and improvement in the mathematics. To all this the bee, as an advocate retained by us the Ancients, thinks fit to answer—that if one may judge of the great genius or inventions of the Moderns by what they have produced, you will hardly have countenance to bear you out in boasting of either. Erect your schemes with as much method and skill as you please; yet if the materials be nothing but dirt, spun out of your own entrails (the guts of modern brains), the edifice will conclude at last in a cobweb, the duration of which, like that of other spiders' webs, may be imputed to their being forgotten, or neglected, or hid in a corner. For anything else of genuine that the Moderns may pretend to, I cannot recollect, unless it be a large vein of wrangling and satire,° much of a nature and substance with the spider's poison; which, however they pretend to spit wholly out of themselves, is improved by the same arts, by feeding upon the insects and vermin of the age. As for us, the Ancients, we are content, with the bee, to pretend to nothing of our own beyond our wings and our voice, that is to say, our flights and our language. For the rest, whatever we have got has been by infinite labour, and search, and ranging through every corner of nature; the difference is that instead of dirt and poison, we have rather chose to fill our hives with honey and wax, thus furnishing mankind with the two noblest of things, which are sweetness and light.'°

'Tis wonderful to conceive the tumult arisen among the books, upon the close of this long descant of Æsop; both parties took the hint, and heightened their animosities so on a sudden that they resolved it should come to a battle. Immediately the two main bodies withdrew under their several ensigns to the further parts of the library, and there entered into cabals and consults° upon the present emergency. The Moderns were in very warm debates upon the choice of their leaders; and nothing less than the fear impending from their enemies could have kept them from mutinies upon this occasion. The difference was greatest among the horse, where every private trooper pretended to the chief command, from Tasso and Milton to Dryden and Withers. The light-horse were commanded by Cowley and Despréaux.° There came the bowmen under their valiant leaders, Des Cartes, Gassendi, and Hobbes,° whose strength was such that they could shoot their arrows beyond the atmosphere, never to fall down again, but turn like that of Evander° into meteors; or, like the cannon-ball, into stars. Paracelsus brought a squadron of stink-pot-flingers from the snowy mountains of Rhœtia. There came a vast body of dragoons, of different nations, under the leading of Harvey, their great aga:° part armed with scythes, the weapons of death, part with lances and long knives, all steeped in poison; part shot bullets of a most malignant nature, and used white powder which infallibly killed without report. There came several bodies of heavy-armed foot, all mercenaries, under the ensigns of Guicciardine, Davila, Polydore Virgil, Buchanan, Mariana, Cambden,° and others. The engineers were commanded by Regiomontanus and Wilkins.° The rest were a confused multitude, led by Scotus, Aquinas, and Bellarmine;° of mighty bulk and stature, but without either arms, courage, or discipline. In the last place came infinite swarms of *calones*, a disorderly rout led by L'Estrange;° rogues and ragamuffins that follow the camp for nothing but the plunder, all without coats to cover them.

The army of the Ancients was much fewer in number. Homer led the horse, and Pindar the light-horse; Euclid was chief engineer; Plato and Aristotle commanded the bowmen, Herodotus and Livy the foot, Hippocrates the dragoons. The allies, led by Vossius° and Temple, brought up the rear.

All things violently tending to a decisive battle, Fame, who much frequented, and had a large apartment formerly assigned her in the regal library, fled up straight to Jupiter to whom she delivered a faithful account of all that had passed between the two parties below (for, among the gods, she always tells truth). Jove, in great concern, convokes a council in the Milky-Way. The senate assembled, he declares the occasion of convening them: a bloody battle just impendent between two mighty armies of Ancient and Modern creatures called books, wherein

* These are pamphlets, which are not bound or covered.

the celestial interest was but too deeply concerned. Momus, the patron of the Moderns, made an excellent speech in their favour, which was answered by Pallas,° the protectress of the Ancients. The assembly was divided in their affections, when Jupiter commanded the book of fate to be laid before him. Immediately were brought by Mercury three large volumes in folio containing memoirs of all things, past, present, and to come. The clasps were of silver double gilt, the covers of celestial turkey leather, and the paper such as here on earth might pass almost for vellum. Jupiter, having silently read the decree, would communicate the import to none, but presently shut up the book.

Without the doors of this assembly, there attended a vast number of light, nimble gods, menial servants to Jupiter: these are his ministering instruments in all affairs below. They travel in a caravan, more or less together, and are fastened to each other like a link of galley-slaves, by a light chain which passes from them to Jupiter's great toe; and yet, in receiving or delivering a message they may never approach above the lowest step of his throne, where he and they whisper to each other through a long hollow trunk. These deities are called by mortal men *accidents* or *events*; but the gods call them second causes.° Jupiter having delivered his message to a certain number of these divinities, they flew immediately down to the pinnacle of the regal library, and consulting a few minutes, entered unseen and disposed the parties according to their orders.

Meanwhile, Momus fearing the worst, and calling to mind an ancient prophecy which bore no very good face to his children the Moderns, bent his flight to the region of a malignant deity called Criticism. She dwelt on the top of a snowy mountain in Nova Zembla; there Momus found her extended in her den, upon the spoils of numberless volumes half devoured. At her right hand sat Ignorance, her father and husband, blind with age; at her left, Pride her mother, dressing her up in the scraps of paper herself had torn. There was Opinion her sister, light of foot, hoodwinked, and headstrong, yet giddy and perpetually turning. About her played her children, Noise and Impudence, Dulness and Vanity, Positiveness, Pedantry, and Ill-Manners. The goddess herself had claws like a cat; her head, and ears, and voice, resembled those of an ass; her teeth fallen out before, her eyes turned inward as if she looked only upon herself; her diet was the overflowing of her own gall; her spleen was so large as to stand prominent like a dug of the first rate, nor wanted excrescencies in form of teats, at which a crew of ugly monsters were greedily sucking; and what is wonderful to conceive, the bulk of spleen increased faster than the sucking could diminish it. 'Goddess,' said

Momus, 'can you sit idly here while our devout worshippers the Moderns are this minute entering into a cruel battle, and perhaps now lying under the swords of their enemies? Who then hereafter will ever sacrifice or build altars to our divinities? Haste, therefore, to the British Isle, and if possible prevent their destruction, while I make factions among the gods and gain them over to our party.'

Momus, having thus delivered himself, stayed not for an answer, but left the goddess to her own resentments. Up she rose in a rage and, as it is the form upon such occasions, began a soliloquy. ' 'Tis I' (said she) 'who give wisdom to infants and idiots; by me, children grow wiser than their parents; by me, beaux become politicians, and schoolboys judges of philosophy;° by me, sophisters debate and conclude upon the depths of knowledge; and coffeehouse wits, instinct by me, can correct an author's style and display his minutest errors without understanding a syllable of his matter or his language. By me, striplings spend their judgment as they do their estate, before it comes into their hands. 'Tis I who have deposed wit and knowledge from their empire over poetry, and advanced myself in their stead. And shall a few upstart Ancients dare to oppose me?—But come, my aged parents, and you my children dear, and thou my beauteous sister; let us ascend my chariot and haste to assist our devout Moderns, who are now sacrificing to us a hecatomb, as I perceive by that grateful smell which from thence reaches my nostrils.'

The goddess and her train having mounted the chariot, which was drawn by tame geese, flew over infinite regions shedding her influence in due places, till at length she arrived at her beloved island of Britain; but in hovering over its metropolis, what blessings did she not let fall upon her seminaries of Gresham and Covent Garden!° And now she reached the fatal plain of St. James's Library, at what time the two armies were upon the point to engage; where, entering with all her caravan unseen, and landing upon a case of shelves, now desert but once inhabited by a colony of virtuosos, she stayed a while to observe the posture of both armies.

But here the tender cares of a mother began to fill her thoughts and move in her breast. For, at the head of a troop of Modern bowmen, she cast her eyes upon her son Wotton, to whom the fates had assigned a very short thread; Wotton, a young hero, whom an unknown father of mortal race begot by stolen embraces with this goddess. He was the darling of his mother above all her children, and she resolved to go and comfort him. But first according to the good old custom of deities she cast about to change her shape, for fear the divinity of her countenance might dazzle his mortal sight and overcharge the rest of his senses. She therefore gathered up her person into an octavo compass: her body grew white and arid, and split in pieces with dryness; the thick turned into pasteboard, and the thin into paper, upon which her parents and children artfully strewed a black juice, or decoction of gall and soot, in form of letters; her head, and voice, and spleen, kept their primitive form, and that which before was a cover of skin did still continue so. In which guise she marched on towards the Moderns, undistinguishable in shape and dress from the divine Bentley, Wotton's dearest friend. 'Brave Wotton,' said the goddess, 'why do our troops stand idle here, to spend their present vigour and opportunity of the day? Away, let us haste to the generals and advise to give the onset immediately.' Having spoke thus, she took the ugliest of her monsters, full glutted from her spleen, and flung it invisibly into his mouth, which flying straight up into his head squeezed out his eyeballs, gave him a distorted look, and half overturned his brain. Then she privately ordered two of her beloved children, Dulness and Ill-Manners, closely to attend his person in all encounters. Having thus accoutred him she vanished in a mist, and the hero perceived it was the goddess his mother.

The destined hour of fate being now arrived, the fight began; whereof, before I dare adventure to make a particular description, I must, after the example of other authors, petition for a hundred tongues, and mouths, and hands, and pens, which would all be too little to perform so immense a work. Say, goddess, that presidest over History, who it was that first advanced in the field of battle! Paracelsus, at the head of his dragoons, observing Galen° in the adverse wing, darted his javelin with a mighty force, which the brave Ancient received upon his shield, the point breaking in the second fold. *   *   *   *   *

*   *   *   *   *   *   * *Hic pauca*
*   *   *   *   *   *   * *desunt.°*
*   *   *   *   *   *   *

They bore the wounded aga on their shields to his chariot   *
*   *   *   *   *   *   *   *

Desunt *   *   *   *   *   *   *
nonnulla. *   *   *   *   *   *   *
*   *   *   *   *   *   *   *

Then Aristotle, observing Bacon° advance with a furious mien, drew his bow to the head and let fly his arrow, which missed the valiant Modern and went hizzing over his head. But Des Cartes it hit; the steel point quickly found a defect in his head-piece; it pierced the leather and the pasteboard and went in at his right eye. The torture of the pain whirled the valiant bowman round till death, like a star of superior influence, drew him into his own vortex.°

*   *   *   *   *   *   *   *

Ingens hiatus   *   *   *   *   *   *
hic in MS.   *   *   *   *   *   *

*   *   *   *   *   *   *   *

*   *   *   * when Homer appeared at the head of
the cavalry, mounted on a furious horse with difficulty managed by the
rider himself, but which no other mortal durst approach; he rode among
the enemy's ranks, and bore down all before him. Say, goddess, whom he
slew first and whom he slew last! First, Gondibert° advanced against him,
clad in heavy armour and mounted on a staid, sober gelding, not so
famed for his speed as his docility in kneeling whenever his rider would
mount or alight. He had made a vow to Pallas, that he would never leave
the field till he had spoiled *Homer of his armour; madman, who had
never once seen the wearer nor understood his strength! Him Homer
overthrew, horse and man, to the ground, there to be trampled and
choked in the dirt. Then with a long spear he slew †Denham, a stout
Modern° who from his father's side derived his lineage from Apollo, but
his mother was of mortal race. He fell, and bit the earth. The celestial
part Apollo took and made it a star, but the terrestrial lay wallowing upon
the ground. Then Homer slew Wesley° with a kick of his horse's heel; he
took Perrault by mighty force out of his saddle, then hurled him at
Fontenelle,° with the same blow dashing out both their brains.

On the left wing of the horse, Virgil appeared in shining armour,
completely fitted to his body. He was mounted on a dapple grey steed, the
slowness of whose pace was an effect of the highest mettle and vigour. He
cast his eye on the adverse wing, with a desire to find an object worthy of
his valour, when, behold, upon a sorrel gelding of a monstrous size
appeared a foe issuing from among the thickest of the enemy's
squadrons; but his speed was less than his noise, for his horse, old and
lean, spent the dregs of his strength in a high trot, which though it made
slow advances yet caused a loud clashing of his armour, terrible to hear.
The two cavaliers had now approached within the throw of a lance, when
the stranger desired a parley, and, lifting up the vizard of his helmet, a
face hardly appeared from within, which after a pause was known for that
of the renowned Dryden. The brave Ancient suddenly started, as one
possessed with surprise and disappointment together; for the helmet was
nine times too large for the head, which appeared situate far in the hinder
part, even like the lady in a lobster,° or like a mouse under a canopy of

---

* *Vid.* Homer.

 † Sir John Denham's poems are very unequal, extremely good and very indifferent; so that his detractors said he was not the real author of *Cooper's Hill*.

state, or like a shrivelled beau from within the penthouse of a modern periwig; and the voice was suited to the visage, sounding weak and remote. Dryden, in a long harangue,° soothed up the good Ancient, called him 'father' and by a large deduction of genealogies made it plainly appear that they were nearly related. Then he humbly proposed an exchange of armour, as a lasting mark of hospitality between them. Virgil consented (for the goddess Diffidence came unseen and cast a mist before his eyes), though his was of gold* and cost a hundred beeves, the other's but of rusty iron. However, this glittering armour became the Modern yet worse than his own. Then they agreed to exchange horses; but when it came to the trial, Dryden was afraid and utterly unable to mount.   *   *   *   *   *   *   *
*   *   *   *   *   *
*   *   *   *   *   *   *Alter hiatus*
*   *   *   *   *   *   *in MS.*
*   *   *   *   *   *   *

Lucan° appeared upon a fiery horse of admirable shape, but headstrong, bearing the rider where he list over the field; he made a mighty slaughter among the enemy's horse, which destruction to stop, Blackmore,° a famous Modern (but one of the mercenaries) strenuously opposed himself and darted a javelin with a strong hand, which falling short of its mark, struck deep in the earth. Then Lucan threw a lance, but Æsculapius came unseen and turned off the point. 'Brave Modern,' said Lucan, 'I perceive some god protects you, for never did my arm so deceive me before. But what mortal can contend with a god? Therefore let us fight no longer, but present gifts to each other.' Lucan then bestowed the Modern a pair of spurs, and Blackmore gave Lucan a bridle.   *   *   *   *   *   *   *
*   *   *   *   *   *   *
Pauca de-   *   *   *   *   *   *
sunt.   *   *   *   *   *   *
*   *   *   *   *   *   *   *

Creech;° but the goddess Dulness took a cloud, formed into the shape of Horace, armed and mounted, and placed it in a flying posture before him. Glad was the cavalier to begin a combat with a flying foe, and pursued the image, threatening loud, till at last it lead him to the peaceful bower of his father Ogleby,° by whom he was disarmed and assigned to his repose.

Then Pindar slew —, and —, Oldham, and — and Afra the Amazon,° light of foot. Never advancing in a direct line but wheeling with

* *Vid.* Homer

incredible agility and force, he made a terrible slaughter among the enemy's light horse. Him when Cowley° observed, his generous heart burnt within him and he advanced against the fierce Ancient, imitating his address, and pace, and career, as well as the vigour of his horse and his own skill would allow. When the two cavaliers had approached within the length of three javelins, first Cowley threw a lance, which missed Pindar, and passing into the enemy's ranks, fell ineffectual to the ground. Then Pindar darted a javelin so large and weighty that scarce a dozen cavaliers,° as cavaliers are in our degenerate days, could raise it from the ground; yet he threw it with ease, and it went by an unerring hand singing through the air; nor could the Modern have avoided present death, if he had not luckily opposed the shield that had been given him by Venus. And now both heroes drew their swords, but the Modern was so aghast and disordered that he knew not where he was; his shield dropped from his hands; thrice he fled, and thrice he could not escape. At last he turned, and lifting up his hand in the posture of a suppliant, 'Godlike Pindar,' said he, 'spare my life, and possess my horse with these arms, besides the ransom which my friends will give when they hear I am alive and your prisoner.' 'Dog!' said Pindar, 'let your ransom stay with your friends; but your carcass shall be left for the fowls of the air and the beasts of the field.' With that he raised his sword, and with a mighty stroke cleft the wretched Modern in twain, the sword pursuing the blow; and one half lay panting on the ground, to be trod in pieces by the horses' feet; the other half was borne by the frighted steed through the field. This *Venus took, washed it seven times in ambrosia, then struck it thrice with a sprig of amaranth; upon which the leather grew round and soft, and the leaves turned into feathers, and being gilded before, continued gilded still; so it became a dove, and she harnessed it to her chariot.

* * * * * * * *
* * * * * * *Hiatus valdè de-*
* * * * * * *flendus in MS.*
* * * * * * * *

Day being far spent, and the numerous forces of the Moderns half inclining to a retreat, there issued forth from a squadron of their heavy-armed foot, a captain whose name was Bentley, in *The Episode* person the most deformed of all the Moderns; tall, but *of Bentley* without shape or comeliness; large, but without strength or *and Wotton.* proportion. His armour was patched up of a thousand incoherent pieces,° and the sound of it as he marched was loud and dry, like that made by the fall of a sheet of lead which an Etesian wind° blows suddenly

* I do not approve the author's judgment in this, for I think Cowley's Pindarics are much preferable to his *Mistress*.

down from the roof of some steeple. His helmet was of old rusty iron, but the vizard was brass, which tainted by his breath corrupted into copperas, nor wanted gall from the same fountain; so that whenever provoked by anger or labour, an atramentous quality of most malignant nature was seen to distil from his lips. In his *right hand he grasped a flail; and (that he might never be unprovided of an *offensive* weapon) a vessel full of ordure in his left. Thus completely armed he advanced with a slow and heavy pace where the Modern chiefs were holding a consult upon the sum of things; who, as he came onwards, laughed to behold his crooked leg and hump shoulder, which his boot and armour vainly endeavouring to hide, were forced to comply with and expose. The generals made use of him for his talent of railing which, kept within government, proved frequently of great service to their cause, but at other times did more mischief than good; for at the least touch of offence, and often without any at all, he would like a wounded elephant convert it against his leaders. Such at this juncture was the disposition of Bentley: grieved to see the enemy prevail, and dissatisfied with everybody's conduct but his own. He humbly gave the Modern generals to understand that he conceived, with great submission, they were all a pack of *rogues*, and *fools*, and *sons of whores*, and *d—mned cowards*, and *confounded loggerheads*, and *illiterate whelps*, and *nonsensical scoundrels*; that if himself had been constituted general, those presumptuous dogs the Ancients would long before this have been beaten out of the field. †'You', said he, 'sit here idle; but when I or any other valiant Modern kill an enemy, you are sure to seize the spoil. But I will not march one foot against the foe till you all swear to me that whomever I take or kill, his arms I shall quietly possess.' Bentley having spoke thus, Scaliger,° bestowing him a sour look, 'Miscreant prater!' said he, 'eloquent only in thine own eyes, thou railest without wit, or truth, or discretion. The malignity of thy temper perverteth nature; thy learning makes thee more barbarous, thy study of humanity° more inhuman; thy converse amongst poets more grovelling, miry, and dull. All arts of civilizing others render thee rude and untractable; courts have taught thee ill manners, and polite conversation has finished thee a pedant. Besides, a greater coward burdeneth not the army. But never despond; I pass my word, whatever spoil thou takest shall certainly be thy own, though I hope that vile carcass will first become a prey to kites and worms.'

Bentley durst not reply, but half choked with spleen and rage

* The person here spoken of is famous for letting fly at everybody without distinction, and using mean and foul scurrilities.

† *Vid.* Homer de Thersite.

withdrew, in full resolution of performing some great achievement. With him, for his aid and companion, he took his beloved Wotton; resolving by policy or surprise to attempt some neglected quarter of the Ancients' army. They began their march over carcasses of their slaughtered friends; then to the right of their own forces; then wheeled northward, till they came to Aldrovandus's tomb° which they passed on the side of the declining sun. And now they arrived, with fear, towards the enemy's out-guards, looking about if haply they might spy the quarters of the wounded, or some straggling sleepers, unarmed and remote from the rest. As when two mongrel curs, whom native greediness and domestic want provoke and join in partnership, though fearful, nightly to invade the folds of some rich grazier, they with tails depressed, and lolling tongues, creep soft and slow; meanwhile, the conscious moon, now in her zenith, on their guilty heads darts perpendicular rays; nor dare they bark, though much provoked at her refulgent visage, whether seen in puddle by reflection, or in sphere direct; but one surveys the region round, while t'other scouts the plain, if haply to discover, at distance from the flock, some carcass half devoured, the refuse of gorged wolves or ominous ravens. So marched this lovely, loving pair of friends, nor with less fear and circumspection when, at distance, they might perceive two shining suits of armour hanging upon an oak, and the owners not far off in a profound sleep. The two friends drew lots, and the pursuing of this adventure fell to Bentley; on he went, and in his van Confusion and Amaze, while Horror and Affright brought up the rear. As he came near, behold two heroes of the Ancients' army, Phalaris and Æsop, lay fast asleep. Bentley would fain have dispatched them both, and stealing close, aimed his flail at Phalaris's breast. But then the goddess Affright interposing caught the Modern in her icy arms, and dragged him from the danger she foresaw; for both the dormant heroes happened to turn at the same instant, though soundly sleeping and busy in a dream. *For Phalaris was just that minute dreaming how a most vile poetaster had lampooned him, and how he had got him roaring in his bull.° And Æsop dreamed that as he and the Ancient chiefs were lying on the ground, a wild ass broke loose, ran about, trampling and kicking and dunging in their faces. Bentley, leaving the two heroes asleep, seized on both their armours and withdrew in quest of his darling Wotton.

He in the meantime had wandered long in search of some enterprize, till at length he arrived at a small rivulet that issued from a fountain hard by, called in the language of mortal men, Helicon. Here he stopped, and

* This is according to Homer, who tells the dreams of those who were killed in their sleep.

parched with thirst resolved to allay it in this limpid stream. Thrice with profane hands he essayed to raise the water to his lips, and thrice it slipped all through his fingers. Then he stooped prone on his breast, but ere his mouth had kissed the liquid crystal, Apollo came and in the channel held his shield betwixt the Modern and the fountain, so that he drew up nothing but mud. For, although no fountain on earth can compare with the clearness of Helicon, yet there lies at bottom a thick sediment of slime and mud; for so Apollo begged of Jupiter, as a punishment to those who durst attempt to taste it with unhallowed lips, and for a lesson to all not to *draw too deep* or *far from the spring*.

At the fountain-head Wotton discerned two heroes. The one he could not distinguish but the other was soon known for Temple, general of the allies to the Ancients. His back was turned, and he was employed in drinking large draughts in his helmet from the fountain, where he had withdrawn himself to rest from the toils of the war. Wotton, observing him, with quaking knees and trembling hands spoke thus to himself:* 'O that I could kill this destroyer of our army, what renown should I purchase among the chiefs! But to issue out against him, man for man, shield against shield, and lance against lance, what Modern of us dare? For he fights like a god, and Pallas or Apollo are ever at his elbow. But, O mother! if what Fame reports be true, that I am the son of so great a goddess, grant me to hit Temple with this lance that the stroke may send him to hell, and that I may return in safety and triumph, laden with his spoils.' The first part of his prayer, the gods granted at the intercession of his mother and of Momus; but the rest, by a perverse wind sent from Fate, was scattered in the air. Then Wotton grasped his lance, and brandishing it thrice over his head, darted it with all his might, the goddess, his mother, at the same time adding strength to his arm. Away the lance went hizzing, and reached even to the belt of the averted Ancient, upon which, lightly grazing, it fell to the ground. Temple neither felt the weapon touch him, nor heard it fall; and Wotton might have escaped to his army, with the honour of having remitted his lance against so great a leader, unrevenged; but Apollo, enraged that a javelin flung by the assistance of so foul a goddess should pollute his fountain, put on the shape of ————,° and softly came to young Boyle, who then accompanied Temple. He pointed first to the lance, then to the distant Modern that flung it, and commanded the young hero to take immediate revenge. Boyle, clad in a suit of armour which had been *given him by all the gods*, immediately advanced against the trembling foe, who now fled before him. As a young lion in the Libyan plains, or Araby desert, sent by

* *Vid.* Homer.

his aged sire to hunt for prey, or health, or exercise, he scours along wishing to meet some tiger from the mountains or a furious boar; if chance a wild ass, with brayings importune, affronts his ear, the generous beast, though loathing to distain his claws with blood so vile, yet much provoked at the offensive noise which Echo, foolish nymph, like her ill-judging sex, repeats much louder and with more delight than Philomela's song, he vindicates the honour of the forest, and hunts the noisy long-eared animal. So Wotton fled, so Boyle pursued. But Wotton, heavy-armed and slow of foot, began to slack his course, when his lover Bentley appeared, returning laden with the spoils of the two sleeping Ancients. Boyle observed him well, and soon discovering the helmet and shield of Phalaris his friend, both which he had lately with his own hands new polished and gilded,° rage sparkled in his eyes, and leaving his pursuit after Wotton, he furiously rushed on against this new approacher. Fain would he be revenged on both, but both now fled different ways. And, as a woman *in a little house, that gets a painful livelihood by spinning,†if chance her geese be scattered o'er the common, she courses round the plain from side to side, compelling here and there the stragglers to the flock; they cackle loud, and flutter o'er the champaign,—so Boyle pursued, so fled this pair of friends. Finding at length their flight was vain, they bravely joined, and drew themselves in phalanx. First, Bentley threw a spear with all his force, hoping to pierce the enemy's breast; but Pallas came unseen, and in the air took off the point and clapped on one of lead, which, after a dead bang against the enemy's shield, fell blunted to the ground. Then Boyle, observing well his time, took a lance of wondrous length and sharpness; and as this pair of friends compacted stood close side to side, he wheeled him to the right, and with unusual force darted the weapon. Bentley saw his fate approach, and flanking down his arms close to his ribs, hoping to save his body, in went the point passing through arm and side, nor stopped or spent its force till it had also pierced the valiant Wotton, who, going to sustain his dying friend, shared his fate. As when a skilful cook has trussed a brace of woodcocks, he with iron skewer pierces the tender sides of both, their legs and wings close pinioned to the ribs; so was this pair of friends transfixed, till down they fell, joined in their lives, joined in their deaths; so closely joined that Charon will mistake them both for one and waft them over Styx for half his fare. Farewell, beloved loving pair!

* *Vid.* Homer.

† This is also after the manner of Homer; the woman's getting a painful livelihood by spinning, has nothing to do with the similitude, nor would be excusable without such an authority.

Few equals have you left behind. And happy and immortal shall you be, if all my wit and eloquence can make you.

    And, now   *   *   *   *   *   *
*   *   *   *   *   *   *
*   *   *   *   *   *   *
*   *   *

Desunt cætera.

When I come to be old
1699

Not to marry a young woman.

Not to keep young company unless they really desire it.

Not to be peevish, or morose, or suspicious.

Not to scorn present ways, or wits, or fashions, or men, or war, &c.

Not to be fond of children, or let them come near me hardly.

Not to tell the same story over and over to the same people.

Not to be covetous.

Not to neglect decency, or cleanliness, for fear of falling into nastiness.

Not to be over severe with young people, but give allowances for their youthful follies and weaknesses.

Not to be influenced by, or give ear to knavish tattling servants, or others.

Not to be too free of advice, nor trouble any but those that desire it.

To conjure some good friends to inform me which of these resolutions I break, or neglect, and wherein; and reform accordingly.

Not to talk much, nor of myself.

Not to boast of my former beauty, or strength, or favour with ladies, &c.

Not to hearken to flatteries, nor conceive I can be beloved by a young woman. Et eos qui hereditatem captant, odisse ac vitare.°

Not to be positive or opiniatre.

Not to set up for observing all these rules, for fear I should observe none.

A DISCOURSE OF THE *Contests* and *Dissensions* BETWEEN THE NOBLES and the COMMONS IN *ATHENS* and *ROME*, WITH THE Consequences they had upon both those STATES.

——Si tibi vera videtur
Dede 'manus; & si falsa est accingere contra.°

Lucret.

CHAP. I.

'Tis agreed, that in all government there is an absolute unlimited power, which naturally and originally seems to be placed in the whole body, wherever the executive part of it lies. This holds in the body natural; for wherever we place the beginning of motion, whether from the head, or the heart, or the animal spirits in general, the body moves and acts by a consent of all its parts. This unlimited power, placed fundamentally in the body of a People, is what the best legislators of all ages have endeavoured, in their several schemes or institutions of government, to deposit in such hands as would preserve the people from rapine and oppression within, as well as violence from without. Most of them seem to agree in this, that it was a trust too great to be committed to any one man or assembly, and therefore they left the right still in the whole body; but the administration or executive part, in the hands of one, the few, or the many, into which three powers all independent bodies of men seem naturally to divide; for by all I have read of those innumerable and petty commonwealths in Italy, Greece, and Sicily, as well as the great ones of Carthage and Rome, it seems to me, that a free People met together, whether by compact, or family government, as soon as they fall into any acts of civil society, do of themselves divide into three powers. The first is that of some one eminent spirit,° who, having signalized his valour and fortune in defence of his country, or by the practice of popular arts at home, becomes to have great influence on the people, to grow their leader in warlike expeditions, and to preside, after a sort, in their civil assemblies; and this is grounded upon the principles of nature and common reason, which, in all difficulties and dangers, where prudence or courage is required, do rather incite us to fly for counsel or assistance to a single person, than a multitude. The second natural division of power is of such men who have acquired large possessions, and consequently dependences, or descend from ancestors who have left them great inheritances, together with an hereditary authority. These easily uniting in thoughts and opinions, and acting in concert, begin to enter upon measures for securing their properties, which are best upheld by preparing against invasions from abroad, and maintaining peace at home; this commences a great council, or Senate of Nobles, for the weighty affairs of the nation. The last division is of the mass or body of the people, whose part of power is great and undisputable, whenever they can unite either collectively, or by deputation, to exert it. Now the three forms of government so generally known in the schools, differ only by the civil administration being placed in the hands of one, or sometimes two (as in Sparta) who were called Kings; or in a senate, who were called the Nobles; or in the people collective or representative, who may be called the Commons. Each of these had frequently the executive power in Greece, and sometimes in Rome; but the power in the last resort was always meant by legislators to be held in balance among all three. And it will be an eternal rule in politics among every free people, that there is a balance of power to be carefully held by every state within itself, as well as among several states with each other.

The true meaning of a balance of power, either without or within a state, is best conceived by considering what the nature of a balance is. It supposes three things. First, the part which is held, together with the hand that holds it; and then the two scales, with whatever is weighed therein. Now consider several states in a neighbourhood; in order to preserve peace between these states, it is necessary they should be formed into a balance, whereof one or more are to be directors, who are to divide the rest into equal scales, and, upon occasions, remove from one into the other, or else fall with their own weight into the lightest; so, in a state within itself, the balance must be held by a third hand, who is to deal the remaining power with the utmost exactness into each scale. Now it is not necessary, that the power should be equally divided between these three; for the balance may be held by the weakest, who, by his address and conduct, removing from either scale and adding of his own, may keep the scales duly poised. Such was that of the two kings of Sparta, the consular power in Rome, that of the kings of Media before the reign of Cyrus, as represented by Xenophon; and that of the several limited states in the Gothic institutions.

When the balance is broke, whether by the negligence, folly, or weakness of the hand that held it, or by mighty weights fallen into either scale, the power will never continue long in equal division between the two remaining parties, but (till the balance is fixed anew) will run entirely into one. This gives the truest account of what is understood in the most ancient and approved Greek authors, by the word Tyranny,° which is not meant for the seizing of the uncontrolled or absolute power into the hands of a single person (as many superficial men have grossly mistaken) but for the breaking of the balance by whatever hand, and leaving the power wholly in one scale. For tyranny and usurpation in a state are by no means confined to any number, as might easily appear from examples enough; and, because the point is material, I shall cite a few to prove it.

The Romans* having sent to Athens and the Greek cities of Italy, for the copies of the best laws, chose ten legislators to put them into form, and during the exercise of their office, suspended the consular power, leaving the administration of affairs in their hands. These very men, though chosen for such a work, as the digesting a body of laws for the government of a free state, did immediately usurp arbitrary power, ran into all the forms of it, had their guards and spies after the practice of the tyrants of those ages, affected kingly state, destroyed the Nobles, and oppressed the People; one of them proceeding so far as to endeavour to force a lady of great virtue: the very crime,° which gave occasion to the expulsion of the regal power but sixty years before, as this attempt did to that of the Decemviri.

The Ephori in Sparta were at first only certain persons deputed by the kings to judge in civil matters, while *they* were employed in the wars. These men, at several times, usurped the absolute authority, and were as cruel tyrants as any in their age.

Soon after the unfortunate expedition into Sicily,† the Athenians chose four hundred men for administration of affairs, who became a body of tyrants, and were called in the language of those ages, an Oligarchy, or Tyranny of the Few; under which hateful denomination they were soon after deposed in great rage by the People.

When Athens was subdued by Lysander,‡ he appointed thirty men for the administration of that city, who immediately fell into the rankest tyranny; but this was not all; for conceiving their power not founded on a basis large enough, they admitted three thousand into a share of the government; and thus fortified, became the cruellest tyranny upon record. They murdered in cold blood great numbers of the best men, without any provocation, from the mere lust of cruelty, like Nero or Caligula. This was such a number of tyrants together, as amounted to near a third part of the whole city; for Xenophon tells us,§ that the city contained about ten thousand houses; and allowing one man to every

---

* Dionys. Hal. lib. 10.   † Thucyd. lib. 8.
‡ Xenoph. de Rebus Graec. l. 2.   § Memorab. lib. 3.

house, who could have any share in the government (the rest consisting of women, children, and servants), and making other obvious abatements, these tyrants, if they had been careful to adhere together, might have been a majority even of the people collective.

In the time of the second Punic war,* the balance of power in Carthage was got on the side of the people, and this to a degree, that some authors reckon the government to have been then among them a *dominatio plebis*, or Tyranny of the Commons; which it seems they were at all times apt to fall into, and was at last among the causes that ruined their state: and the frequent murders of their generals, which Diodorus† tells us was grown to an established custom among them, may be another instance that tyranny is not confined to numbers.

I shall mention but one example more among a great number that might be produced; it is related by the author last cited.‡ The orators of the people at Argos (whether you will style them, in modern phrase, *Great Speakers in the House*; or only, in general, representatives of the people collective) stirred up the commons against the nobles, of whom 1600 were murdered at once; and at last, the orators themselves, because they left off their accusations, or, to speak intelligibly, because they *withdrew their impeachments*; having, it seems, raised a spirit they were not able to lay. And this circumstance, as cases have lately stood, may perhaps be worth noting.

From what hath been already advanced several conclusions may be drawn.

First, That a mixed government, partaking of the known forms received in the schools, is by no means of Gothic invention, but hath place in nature and reason, seems very well to agree with the sentiments of most legislators, and to have been followed in most states, whether they have appeared under the name of monarchies, aristocracies, or democracies. For, not to mention the several republics of this composition in Gaul and Germany, described by Cæsar and Tacitus, Polybius tells us, the best government is that which consists of three forms, *Regno, Optimatium, et Populi Imperio*;§° which may be fairly translated, the King, Lords, and Commons. Such was that of Sparta, in its primitive institution by Lycurgus; who, observing the corruptions and depravations to which every of these was subject, compounded his scheme out of all; so that it was made up of *Reges, Seniores, et Populus*.° Such also was the state of Rome under its consuls; and the author tells us, that the Romans fell upon this model purely by chance (which I take to have been nature and common reason), but the Spartans by thought and design. And such at

* Polyb. Frag. lib. 6.   † Lib. 20.   ‡ Lib. 15.   § Frag. lib. 6.

Carthage was the *summa reipublicæ*,* or power in the last resort; for they had their kings, called *Suffetes*, and a Senate, which had the power of nobles, and the people had a share established too.

Secondly, it will follow, that those reasoners who employ so much of their zeal, their wit, and their leisure for upholding the balance of power in Christendom, at the same time that by their practices they are endeavouring to destroy it at home, are not such mighty patriots, or so much in the true interest of their country, as they would affect to be thought, but seem to be employed like a man who pulls down with his right hand what he has been building with his left.

Thirdly, this makes appear the error of those who think it an uncontrollable maxim, that power is always safer lodged in many hands than in one. For, if these many hands be made up only from one of the three divisions before-mentioned, it is plain from those examples already produced, and easy to be paralleled in other ages and countries, that they are as capable of enslaving the nation, and of acting all manner of tyranny and oppression, as it is possible for a single person to be, although we should suppose their number not only to be of four or five hundred, but above three thousand.

Again, it is manifest, from what hath been said, that in order to preserve the balance in a mixed state, the limits of power deposited with each party° ought to be ascertained, and generally known. The defect of this is the cause that introduces those strugglings in a state about Prerogative and Liberty; about Encroachments of the Few upon the Rights of the Many, and of the Many upon the Privileges of the Few, which ever did and ever will conclude in a Tyranny; first, either of the Few or the Many, but at last, infallibly of a single person. For whichever of the three divisions in a state is upon the scramble for more power than its own (as one or other of them generally is), unless due care be taken by the other two, upon every new question that arises they will be sure to decide in favour of themselves, talk much of Inherent Right; they will nourish up a dormant power, and reserve privileges° *in petto*, to exert upon occasions, to serve expedients, and to urge upon necessities; they will make large demands, and scanty concessions, ever coming off considerable gainers. Thus at length the balance is broke, and Tyranny let in, from which door of the three it matters not.

To pretend to a declarative right upon any occasion whatsoever, is little less than to make use of the whole power; that is, to declare an opinion to be law, which hath always been contested, or perhaps never started before such an incident brought it on the stage. Not to consent to

* Id. ib.

the enacting of such a law, which has no view besides the general good, unless another law° shall at the same time pass with no other view but that of advancing the power of one party alone; what is this but to claim a positive voice as well as a negative? To pretend that great changes and alienations of property° have created new and great dependences, and consequently new additions of power, as some reasoners have done, is a most dangerous tenet. If dominion must follow property, let it follow in the same pace; for changes in property through the bulk of a nation make slow marches, and its due power always attends it. To conclude that whatever attempt is begun by an assembly ought to be pursued° to the end, without regard to the greatest incidents that may happen to alter the case; to count it mean, and below the *dignity of a House*, to quit a prosecution; to resolve upon a conclusion before it is possible to be apprised of the premisses; to act thus, I say, is to affect not only absolute power, but infallibility too. Yet such unaccountable proceedings as these have popular assemblies engaged in, for want of fixing the due limits of power and privilege.

Great changes may indeed be made in government, yet the form continue and the balance be held. But large intervals of time must pass between every such innovation, enough to melt down and make it of a piece with the constitution. Such, we are told, were the proceedings of Solon when he modelled anew the Athenian Commonwealth. And what convulsions in our own as well as other states have been bred by a neglect of this rule, is fresh and notorious enough. It is too soon, in all conscience, to repeat this error again.

Having shown that there is a natural balance of power in all free states, and how it hath been divided, sometimes by the people themselves, as in Rome, at others by the institutions of the legislators, as in the several states of Greece and Sicily; the next thing is to examine what methods have been taken to break or overthrow this balance, which every one of the three parties hath continually endeavoured, as opportunities have served; as might appear from the stories of most ages and countries. For, absolute power in a particular state is of the same nature with universal monarchy in several states adjoining to each other. So endless and exorbitant are the desires of men, whether considered in their persons or their states, that they will grasp at all, and can form no scheme of perfect happiness with less. Ever since men have been united into governments, the hopes and endeavours after universal monarchy have been bandied among them, from the reign of Ninus to this of the Most Christian King;° in which pursuits commonwealths have had their share, as well as monarchs. So the Athenians, the Spartans, the Thebans, and the

Achaians, did several times aim at the universal monarchy of Greece; so the commonwealths of Carthage and Rome affected the universal monarchy of the then known world. In like manner hath absolute power been pursued by the several parties of each particular state; wherein single persons have met with most success, though the endeavours of the Few and the Many have been frequent enough; yet, being neither so uniform in their designs, nor so direct in their views, they neither could manage nor maintain the power they had got; but were ever deceived by the popularity and ambition of some single person. So that it will be always a wrong step in policy for the Nobles and Commons to carry their endeavours after power so far as to overthrow the balance. And it would be enough to damp their warmth in such pursuits, if they could once reflect that in such a course they will be sure to run upon the very rock that they meant to avoid; which, I suppose, they would have us think is the tyranny of a single person.

Many examples might be produced of the endeavours of each of these three rivals after absolute power; but I shall suit my discourse to the time I am writing in, and relate only such dissensions in Greece and Rome, between the Nobles and Commons, with the consequences of them, wherein the latter were the aggressors.

I shall begin with Greece, where my observations shall be confined to Athens, though several instances might be brought from other states thereof.

CHAP. II.

Of the Dissensions in ATHENS, *between the* FEW *and the* MANY.

Theseus is the first who is recorded, with any appearance of truth, to have brought the Grecians from a barbarous manner of life among scattered villages, into cities; and to have established the popular state in Athens, assigning to himself the guardianship of the laws, and chief command in war. He was forced after some time to leave the Athenians to their own measures, upon account of their seditious temper, which ever continued with them till the final dissolution of their government by the Romans. It seems the country about Attica was the most barren of any in Greece; through which means it happened that the natives were never expelled by the fury of invaders (who thought it not worth a conquest), but continued always aborigines, and therefore retained, through all revolutions, a tincture of that turbulent spirit wherewith their government began. This institution of Theseus appears to have been rather a sort of mixed monarchy than a popular state, and for aught we know, might continue so during that series of kings till the death of Codrus. From this last prince, Solon was said to be descended; who, finding the people engaged in two violent factions of the Poor and the Rich, and in great confusions thereupon; refusing the monarchy which was offered him, chose rather to cast the government after another model, wherein he made due provision for settling the balance of power, choosing a senate of four hundred and disposing the magistracies and offices according to men's estates; leaving to the multitude their votes in electing, and the power of judging certain processes by appeal. This council of 400 was chosen, 100 out of each tribe, and seems to have been a body representative of the people; though the people collective reserved a share of power to themselves. It is a point of history perplexed enough; but thus much is certain, that the balance of power was provided for; else Pisistratus, called by authors the Tyrant of Athens, could never have governed so peaceably as he did, without changing any of Solon's laws.* These several powers, together with that of the Archon or chief magistrate, made up the form of government in Athens, at what time it began to appear upon the scene of action and story.

The first great man bred up under this institution was Miltiades, who lived about ninety years after Solon, and is reckoned to have been the first great captain not only of Athens, but of all Greece. From the time of Miltiades to that of Phocion, who is looked upon as the last famous general of Athens, are about 130 years; after which they were subdued and insulted by Alexander's captains, and continued under several revolutions a small truckling state of no name or reputation, till they fell with the rest of Greece under the power of the Romans.

During this period from Miltiades to Phocion, I shall trace the conduct of the Athenians with relation to their dissensions between the People and some of their Generals; who at that time, by their power and credit in the army, in a warlike commonwealth, and often supported by each other, were with the magistrates and other civil officers a sort of counterpoise to the power of the people, who since the death of Solon had already made great encroachments. What these dissension were, how founded, and what the consequences of them, I shall very briefly and impartially relate.

I must here premise, that the Nobles in Athens were not at this time a corporate assembly, that I can gather; therefore the resentments of the Commons were usually turned against particular persons, and by way of articles of impeachment. Whereas the Commons in Rome and some

* Herodot. lib. 1.

other states, as will appear in a proper place, though they followed this method upon occasion, yet generally pursued the enlargement of their power by more set quarrels of one entire assembly against another. However, the custom of particular impeachments being not limited to former ages, any more than that of general struggles and dissensions between fixed assemblies of Nobles and Commons; and the ruin of Greece having been owing to the former, as that of Rome was to the latter; I shall treat on both expressly; that those states who are concerned in either (if at least there be any such now in the world) may, by observing the means and issues of former dissensions, learn whether the causes are alike in theirs; and if they find them to be so, may consider whether they ought not justly to apprehend the same effects.

To speak of every particular person impeached by the Commons of Athens, within the compass designed, would introduce the history of almost every great man they had among them. I shall therefore take notice only of six who, living in that period of time when Athens was at the height of its glory° (as indeed it could not be otherwise while such hands were at the helm), though *impeached for high crimes and misdemeanours* such as bribery, arbitrary proceedings, misapplying or embezzling public funds, ill conduct at sea, and the like, were honoured and lamented by their country as the preservers of it, and have had the veneration of all ages since justly paid to their memories.

Miltiades was one of the Athenian generals against the Persian power, and the famous victory at Marathon was chiefly owing to his valour and conduct. Being sent some time after to reduce the Island Paros, he mistook a great fire at a distance for the Persian fleet, and being no ways a match for them, set sail to Athens. At his arrival he was *impeached* by the Commons for treachery, though not able to appear by reason of his wounds, fined 30,000 crowns, and died in prison. Though the consequences of this proceeding upon the affairs of Athens were no more than the untimely loss of so great and good a man, yet I could not forbear relating it.

Their next great man was Aristides. Besides the mighty service he had done his country in the wars, he was a person of the strictest justice, and best acquainted with the laws as well as forms of their government, so that he was in a manner the Chancellor of Athens. This man, upon a slight and false accusation of favouring arbitrary power, was banished by ostracism; which, rendered into modern English, would signify, that they voted *he should be removed from their presence and councils for ever.*° But they had soon the wit to recall him, and to that action owed the preservation of their state by his future services. For it must be still confessed in behalf of the Athenian People, that they never conceived themselves perfectly infallible, nor arrived to the heights of modern assemblies to make obstinacy confirm what sudden heat and temerity began. They thought it not below the dignity of an assembly to endeavour at correcting an ill step; at least to repent, though it often fell out too late.

Themistocles was at first a Commoner himself. It was he who raised the Athenians to their greatness at sea, which he thought to be the true and constant interest of that Commonwealth; and the famous naval victory over the Persians at Salamis was owing to his conduct. It seems the people observed somewhat of haughtiness in his temper and behaviour, and therefore banished him for five years; but finding some slight matter of accusation against him, they sent to seize his person, and he hardly escaped to the Persian court; from whence, if the love of his country had not surmounted its base ingratitude to him, he had many invitations to return at the head of the Persian fleet, and take a terrible revenge; but he rather chose a voluntary death.

The people of Athens impeached Pericles for misapplying the public revenues to his own private use. He had been a person of great deservings from the Republic, was an admirable speaker, and very popular. His accounts were confused, and he wanted time to adjust them; therefore, merely to divert that difficulty and the consequences of it, he was forced to engage his country in the Peloponnesian war, the longest that ever was known in Greece, and which ended in the utter ruin of Athens.

The same people having resolved to subdue Sicily, sent a mighty fleet under the command of Nicias, Lamachus, and Alcibiades: the two former, persons of age and experience; the last, a young man of noble birth, excellent education, and a plentiful fortune. A little before the fleet set sail, it seems one night the stone-images of Mercury, placed in several parts of the city, were all pared in the face. This action the Athenians interpreted for a design of destroying the popular state; and Alcibiades, having been formerly noted for the like frolics and excursions, was immediately accused of this. He, whether conscious of his innocence, or assured of the secrecy, offered to come to his trial before he went to his command; this the Athenians refused; but as soon as he was got to Sicily, they sent for him back, designing to take the advantage and prosecute him in the absence of his friends, and of the army, where he was very powerful. It seems he understood the resentments of a popular assembly too well to trust them; and therefore instead of returning, escaped to Sparta, where his desire of revenge prevailing over his love to his country, he became its greatest enemy. Meanwhile the Athenians, before Sicily, by the death of one commander, and the superstition, weakness, and perfect ill conduct of the other, were utterly destroyed, the whole fleet taken, [and] a miserable slaughter made of the army, whereof hardly one ever returned. Some time after this Alcibiades was recalled upon his own conditions by the necessities of the People, and made chief commander at sea and land; but his lieutenant engaging against his positive orders, and being beaten by Lysander, Alcibiades was again disgraced and banished. However, the Athenians having lost all strength and heart since their misfortune at Sicily, and now deprived of the only person that was able to recover their losses, repent of their rashness, and endeavour in vain for his restoration; the Persian lieutenant to whose protection he fled, making him a sacrifice to the resentments of Lysander, the general of the Lacedemonians, who now reduces all the dominions of the Athenians, takes the city, razes their walls, ruins their works, and changes the form of their government; which, though again restored for some time by Thrasybulus (as their walls were rebuilt by Conon) yet here we must date the fall of the Athenian greatness; the dominion and chief power in Greece from that period to the time of Alexander the Great, which was about fifty years, being divided between the Spartans and Thebans. Though Philip, Alexander's father (the Most Christian king of that age) had indeed some time before begun to break in upon the republics of Greece by conquest or bribery, particularly *dealing large money among some popular orators*, by which he brought many of them (as the term of art was then) to *Philippize*.°

In the time of Alexander and his captains, the Athenians were offered an opportunity of recovering their liberty and being restored to their former state; but the wise turn they thought to give the matter was by an impeachment and sacrifice of the author to hinder the success. For, after the destruction of Thebes by Alexander, this prince designing the conquest of Athens, was prevented by Phocion the Athenian general, then ambassador from that state; who by his great wisdom and skill at negotiation diverted Alexander from his design, and restored the Athenians to his favour. The very same success he had with Antipater after Alexander's death, at which time the government was new regulated by Solon's laws. But Polyperchon, in hatred to Phocion, having by order of the young king (whose governor he was) restored those whom Phocion had banished, the plot succeeded; Phocion was accused by popular orators, and put to death.

Thus was the most powerful commonwealth of all Greece, after great degeneracies from the institution of Solon, utterly destroyed by that rash, jealous, and inconstant humour of the People, which was never satisfied to see a general either victorious or unfortunate; such ill judges, as well as rewarders, have Popular Assemblies been, of those who best deserved from them.

Now, the circumstance which makes these examples of more importance, is, that this very power of the People in Athens, claimed so confidently for an inherent right, and insisted on as the undoubted privilege of an Athenian born, was the rankest encroachment imaginable, and the grossest degeneracy from the form that Solon left them. In short, their government was grown into a *dominatio plebis*, or Tyranny of the People, who by degrees had broke and overthrown the balance which that legislator had very well fixed and provided for. This appears not only from what hath been already said of that lawgiver, but more manifestly from a passage in Diodorus;* who tells us that Antipater, one of Alexander's captains, 'abrogated the popular government (in Athens) and restored the power of suffrages and magistracy to such only as were worth two thousand drachmas; by which means (says he) that Republic came to be again administered by the laws of Solon.' By this quotation 'tis manifest that this great author looked upon Solon's institution, and a popular government, to be two different things. And as for this restoration by Antipater, it had neither consequence nor continuance worth observing.

I might easily produce many more examples, but these are sufficient: and it may be worth the reader's time to reflect a little upon the merits of the cause, as well as of the men, who had been thus dealt with by their country. I shall direct him no further than by repeating, that Aristides was the most renowned by the people themselves for his exact *justice and knowledge in the law*. That Themistocles was a most fortunate admiral, and had got *a mighty victory over the great King of Persia's fleet*; that Pericles was *an able minister of state, an excellent orator, and a man of letters*; and, lastly, that Phocion, besides the success of his arms, was also renowned for his *negotiations abroad, having in an embassy brought the greatest monarch of the world at that time, to the terms of an honourable peace, by which his country was preserved*.

I shall conclude my remarks upon Athens with the character given us of that People by Polybius.† 'About this time (says he) the Athenians were governed by two men, quite sunk in their affairs; had little or no commerce with the rest of Greece, and were become great reverencers of crowned heads.'

For, from the time of Alexander's captains till Greece was subdued by the Romans (to the latter part of which this description of Polybius falls

* Lib. 18. † Lib. 5.

in) Athens never produced one famous man either for counsels or arms, or hardly for learning. And, indeed, it was a dark insipid period through all Greece: for except the Achaian league under Aratus and Philopœmen,* and the endeavours of Agis and Cleomenes to restore the state of Sparta, so frequently harassed with tyrannies occasioned by the popular practices of the Ephori, there was very little worth recording. All which consequences may perhaps be justly imputed to this degeneracy of Athens.

CHAP. III.

Of the Dissensions between the PATRICIANS *and* PLEBEIANS *in* ROME, *with the Consequences they had upon that State.*

Having in the foregoing Chapter confined myself to the proceedings of the Commons only, by the method of *impeachments* against particular persons, with the fatal effects they had upon the state of Athens, I shall now treat of the dissensions at Rome, between the People and the collective body of the Patricians or Nobles. It is a large subject, but I shall draw it into as narrow a compass as I can.

As Greece, from the most ancient accounts we have of it, was divided into several kingdoms, so was most part of Italy† into several petty commonwealths. And as those kings in Greece are said to have been deposed by their People upon the score of their arbitrary proceedings; so, on the contrary, the commonwealths of Italy were all swallowed up, and concluded in the tyranny of the Roman emperors. However, the differences between those Grecian monarchies and Italian Republics were not very great: for, by the accounts Homer gives us of those Grecian princes who came to the siege of Troy, as well as by several passages in the Odysseys, it is manifest that the power of these princes in their several states was much of a size with that of the kings in Sparta, the Archon at Athens, the Suffetes at Carthage, and the Consuls in Rome. So that a limited and divided power seems to have been the most ancient and inherent principle of both those People, in matters of government. And such did that of Rome continue from the time of Romulus, though with some interruptions, to Julius Cæsar, when it ended in the tyranny of a single person. During which period (not many years longer than from the Norman conquest to our age) the Commons were growing by degrees into power and property, gaining ground upon the Patricians, as it were, inch by inch, till at last they quite overturned the balance, leaving

* Polyb.   † Dionys. Halicar.

all doors open to the practices of popular and ambitious men, who destroyed the wisest republic, and enslaved the noblest people that ever entered upon the stage of the world. By what steps and degrees this was brought to pass, shall be the subject of my present enquiry.

While Rome was governed by kings, the monarchy was altogether elective. Romulus himself, when he had built the city, was declared king by the universal consent of the People, and by augury, which was then understood for Divine appointment. Among other divisions he made of the People, one was into Patricians and Plebeians: the former were like the Barons of England some time after the conquest; and the latter are also described to be almost exactly what our Commons were then. For they were dependents upon the Patricians, whom they chose for their patrons and protectors, to answer for their appearance, and defend them in any process; they also supplied their patrons with money in exchange for their protection. This custom of patronage, it seems, was very ancient and long practised among the Greeks.

Out of these Patricians Romulus chose an hundred to be a Senate, or Grand Council, for advice and assistance to him in the administration. The Senate, therefore, originally consisted all of nobles, and were of themselves a standing council, the People being only convoked upon such occasions as by this institution of Romulus fell into their cognizance. These were, to constitute magistrates, to give their votes for making laws, and to advise upon entering on a war. But the two former of these popular privileges were to be confirmed by authority of the Senate; and the last was only permitted at the King's pleasure.° This was the utmost extent of power pretended to by the Commons in the time of Romulus; all the rest being divided between the King and the Senate, the whole agreeing very nearly with the constitution of England for some centuries after the conquest.

After a year's interregnum from the death of Romulus, the Senate of their own authority chose a successor, and a stranger, merely upon the fame of his virtue, without asking the consent of the Commons; which custom they likewise observed in the two following kings. But in the election of Tarquinius Priscus, the fifth king, we first hear mentioned that it was done, *populi impetratâ veniâ;*° which indeed was but very reasonable for a free people to expect; though I cannot remember, in my little reading, by what incidents they were brought to advance so great a step. However it were, this prince, in gratitude to the People by whose consent he was chosen, elected a hundred Senators out of the Commons, whose number with former additions was now amounted to three hundred.

The People having once discovered their own strength, did soon take occasion to exert it, and that by very great degrees. For at this king's death (who was murdered by the sons of a former), being at a loss for a successor, Servius Tullius, a stranger, and of mean extraction, was chosen protector of the kingdom by the People, without the consent of the Senate; at which the Nobles being displeased, he wholly applied himself to gratify the Commons, and was by them declared and confirmed no longer protector, but King.°

This prince first introduced the custom of giving freedom to servants, so as to become citizens of equal privileges with the rest, which very much contributed to increase the power of the People.

Thus in a very few years the Commons proceeded so far as to wrest even the power of choosing a king, entirely out of the hands of the Nobles; which was so great a leap and caused such a convulsion and struggle in the state, that the constitution could not bear it; but civil dissensions arose, which immediately were followed by the tyranny of a single person, as this was by the utter subversion of the regal government, and by a settlement upon a new foundation. For the Nobles, spited at this indignity done them by the Commons, firmly united in a body, deposed this prince by plain force, and chose Tarquin the Proud, who, running into all the forms and methods of tyranny, after a cruel reign, was expelled by an universal concurrence of Nobles and People, whom the miseries of his reign had reconciled.

When the Consular government began, the balance of power between the Nobles and Plebeians was fixed anew. The two first Consuls were nominated by the Nobles, and confirmed by the Commons; and a law was enacted, that no person should bear any magistracy in Rome, *injussu populi*; that is, without consent of the Commons.

In such turbulent times as these, many of the poorer citizens had contracted numerous debts, either to the richer sort among themselves, or to senators and other nobles: and the case of debtors in Rome for the first four centuries* was, after the set time for payment, no choice but either to pay or be the creditor's slave. In this juncture, the Commons leave the city in mutiny and discontent, and will not return but upon condition to be acquitted of all their debts; and moreover, that certain magistrates be chosen yearly, whose business it shall be to defend the Commons from injuries. These are called Tribunes of the People,° their persons are held sacred and inviolable, and the People bind themselves by oath never to abrogate the office. By these Tribunes, in process of time, the People were grossly imposed on to serve the turns and

* Ab urbe condita [from the founding of the city].

occasions of revengeful or ambitious men, and to commit such exorbitances as could not end but in the dissolution of the government.

These Tribunes, a year or two after their institution, kindled great dissensions between the Nobles and the Commons on the account of Coriolanus, a nobleman, whom the latter had *impeached*, and the consequences of whose impeachment (if I had not confined myself to Grecian examples for that part of my subject) had like to have been so fatal to their state. And from this time the Tribunes begun a custom of accusing to the People whatever Noble they pleased, several of whom were banished or put to death in every age.

At this time the Romans were very much engaged in wars with their neighbouring states; but upon the least intervals of peace, the quarrels between the Nobles and the Plebeians would revive; and one of the most frequent subjects of their differences was the *conquered lands*,° which the Commons would fain have divided among the public; but the Senate could not be brought to give their consent. For several of the wisest among the Nobles began to apprehend the growing power of the People; and therefore, knowing what an accession thereof would accrue to them by such an addition of property, used all means to prevent it: for this the Appian family was most noted, and thereupon most hated by the Commons. One of them having made a speech against this division of lands, was impeached by the People of high treason, and a day appointed for his trial; but he disdaining to make his defence, chose rather the usual Roman remedy of killing himself, after whose death the Commons prevailed, and the lands were divided among them.

This point was no sooner gained, but new dissensions began; for the Plebeians would fain have a law enacted to lay all men's rights and privileges upon the same level; and to enlarge the power of every magistrate within his own jurisdiction, as much as that of the Consuls. The Tribunes also obtained to have their number doubled, which before was five; and the author tells us that their insolence and power increased with their number, and the seditions were also doubled with it.*

By the beginning of the fourth century from the building of Rome, the Tribunes proceeded so far in the name of the Commons, as to accuse and fine the Consuls themselves,° who represented the kingly power. And the Senate observing, how in all contentions they were forced to yield to the Tribunes and People, thought it their wisest course to give way also to time. Therefore a decree was made to send ambassadors to Athens and the other Grecian commonwealths planted in that part of Italy called Græcia Major, to make a collection of the best laws; out of

* Dionys. Halicar.

which, and some of their own, a new complete body of law was formed, afterwards known by the name of the Laws of the Twelve Tables.

To digest these laws into order, ten men were chosen, and the administration of all affairs left in their hands; what use they made of it hath been already shown. It was certainly a great revolution, produced entirely by the many unjust encroachments of the People; and might have wholly changed the fate of Rome, if the folly and vice of those, who were chiefly concerned, could have suffered it to take root.

A few years after, the Commons made further advances on the power of the Nobles; demanding among the rest that the Consulship, which hitherto had only been disposed to the former, should now lie in common to the pretensions of any Roman whatsoever. This, though it failed at present, yet afterwards obtained, and was a mighty step to the ruin of the commonwealth.

What I have hitherto said of Rome hath been chiefly collected out of that exact and diligent writer Dionysius Halicarnasseus; whose history (through the injury of time) reaches no farther than to the beginning of the fourth century after the building of Rome. The rest I shall supply from other authors, though I do not think it necessary to deduce this matter any further so very particularly as I have hitherto done.

To point at what time the balance of power was most equally held between the Lords and Commons in Rome would perhaps admit a controversy. Polybius tells us,* that in the second Punic war the Carthaginians were declining because the balance was got too much on the side of the People, whereas the Romans were in their greatest vigour by the power remaining in the Senate; yet this was between two and three hundred years after the period Dionysius ends with; in which time the Commons had made several further acquisitions. This however must be granted, that (till about the middle of the fourth century) when the Senate appeared resolute at any time upon exerting their authority, and adhered closely together, they did often carry their point. Besides, it is observed by the best authors,† that in all the quarrels and tumults at Rome from the expulsion of the kings, though the People frequently proceeded to rude contumelious language, and sometimes so far as to pull and hale one another about the forum; yet no blood was ever drawn in any popular commotions, till the time of the Gracchi. However, I am of opinion that the balance had begun many years before to lean to the popular side. But this default was corrected, partly by the principle just mentioned, of never drawing blood in a tumult; partly by the warlike genius of the People, which in those ages was almost perpetually

* Fragm. lib. 6   † Dionys. Hal., Plutarch, &c.

employed; and partly by their great commanders, who by the credit they had in their armies fell into the scales as a further counterpoise to the growing power of the People. Besides, Polybius, who lived in the time of Scipio Africanus the younger, had the same apprehensions of the continual encroachments made by the Commons; and being a person of as great abilities and as much sagacity as any of his age; from observing the corruptions, which, he says, had already entered into the Roman constitution, did very nearly foretell what would be the issue of them. His words are very remarkable, and with little addition may be rendered to this purpose.* 'That those abuses and corruptions which in time destroy a government,° are sown along with the very seeds of it, and both grow up together; and that as rust eats away iron, and worms devour wood, and both are a sort of plagues born and bred along with the substance they destroy; so with every form and scheme of government that man can invent, some vice or corruption creeps in with the very institution, which grows up along with and at last destroys it.' The same author,† in another place, ventures so far as to guess at the particular fate which would attend the Roman government. He says, its ruin would arise from popular tumults, which would introduce a *dominatio plebis*, or Tyranny of the People; wherein it is certain he had reason, and therefore might have adventured to pursue his conjectures so far as to the consequences of a popular tyranny, which, as perpetual experience teaches, never fails to be followed by the arbitrary government of a single person.

About the middle of the fourth century from the building of Rome, it was declared lawful for nobles and plebeians to intermarry; which custom, among many other states, has proved the most effectual means to ruin the former, and raise the latter.

And now the greatest employments in the state were, one after another by laws forcibly enacted by the Commons, made free to the People: the Consulship itself, the office of Censor, that of the Quæstors or Commissioners of the Treasury, the office of Prætor or Chief Justice, the priesthood, and even that of Dictator. The Senate, after long opposition, yielding merely for present quiet to the continual urging clamours of the Commons, and of the Tribunes their advocates. A law was likewise enacted, that the *plebiscita*, or *A Vote of the House of Commons*, should be of universal obligation; nay, in time the method of enacting laws was wholly inverted: for whereas the Senate used of old to confirm the *plebiscita*, the People did at last, as they pleased, confirm or disannul the *senatusconsulta*.‡

Appius Claudius brought in a custom of admitting to the Senate the

* Lib. 5.   † Fragm. lib. 6.   ‡ Dionys. Hal. lib. 2.

sons of freedmen, or of such who had once been slaves; by which, and succeeding alterations of the like nature, that great council degenerated into a most corrupt and factious body of men, divided against itself, and its authority became despised.

The century and half following, to the end of the third Punic war by the entire destruction of Carthage, was a very busy period at Rome: the intervals between every war being so short, that the Tribunes and People had hardly leisure or breath to engage in domestic dissensions; however, the little time they could spare was generally employed the same way. So, Terentius Leo, a Tribune, is recorded to have basely prostituted the privileges of a Roman citizen, in perfect spite to the Nobles. So, the great African Scipio and his brother, after all their mighty services, were impeached by an ungrateful Commons.

However, the warlike genius of the people and continual employment they had for it, served to divert this humour from running into a head, till the age of the Gracchi.°

These persons, entering the scene in the time of a full peace, fell violently upon advancing the power of the People, by reducing into practice all those encroachments which they had been so many years gaining. There were at that time certain *conquered lands* to be divided, beside a *great private estate left by a king*.° These the Tribunes, by procurement of the elder Gracchus, declared by their legislative authority were not to be disposed of by the Nobles, but by the Commons only. The younger brother pursued the same design; and besides, obtained a law that all Italians should vote at elections as well as the citizens of Rome: in short, the whole endeavours of them both perpetually turned upon retrenching the Nobles' authority in all things, but especially in the matter of judicature. And though they both lost their lives in those pursuits, yet they traced out such ways as were afterwards followed by Marius, Sylla, Pompey, and Cæsar, to the ruin of the Roman freedom and greatness.

For in the time of Marius, Saturninus, a Tribune, procured a law that the Senate should be bound by oath to agree to whatever the People would enact. And Marius himself while he was in that office of Tribune is recorded to have with great industry used all endeavours for depressing the Nobles, and raising the People; particularly for cramping the former in their *power of judicature*, which was their most *ancient and inherent right*.

Sylla, by the same measures, became absolute tyrant of Rome; he added three hundred Commons to the Senate, which perplexed the power of the whole order and rendered it ineffectual; then flinging off the mask, he abolished the office of Tribune, as being only a scaffold to tyranny, whereof he had no further use.

As to Pompey and Cæsar, Plutarch tells us that their union for pulling down the Nobles (by their credit with the People) was the cause of the civil war, which ended in the tyranny of the latter; both of them in their consulships having used all endeavours and occasions for sinking the authority of the Patricians, and giving way to all encroachments of the People, wherein they expected best to find their own accounts.

From this deduction of popular encroachments in Rome, the reader will easily judge, how much the balance was fallen upon that side. Indeed, by this time the very foundation was removed, and it was a moral impossibility that the Republic could subsist any longer. For the Commons having usurped the offices of the state, and trampled on the Senate, there was no government left but a *dominatio plebis*. Let us, therefore, examine how they proceeded in this conjuncture.

I think it is an universal truth, that the People are much more dexterous at pulling down and setting up, than at preserving what is fixed; and they are not fonder of seizing more than their own than they are of delivering it up again to the worst bidder, with their own into the bargain. For, although in their corrupt notions of divine worship, they are apt to multiply their gods; yet their earthly devotion is seldom paid to above one idol at a time, of their own creation; whose oar they pull with less murmuring, and much more skill, than when they share the lading, or even hold the helm.

The several provinces of the Roman empire were now governed by the great men of their state, those upon the frontiers with powerful armies, either for conquest or defence. These governors, upon any designs of revenge or ambition, were sure to meet with a divided power at home, and therefore bent all their thoughts and applications to close in with the People, who were now by many degrees the stronger party. Two of the greater spirits that Rome ever produced, happened to live at the same time and to be engaged in the same pursuit; and this at a juncture the most dangerous for such a contest. These were Pompey and Cæsar, two stars of such a magnitude that their conjunction was as likely to be fatal as their opposition.

The Tribunes and People, having now subdued all competitors, began the last game of a prevalent populace, which is that of choosing themselves a master; while the Nobles foresaw, and used all endeavours left them to prevent it. The People at first made Pompey their admiral, with full power over all the Mediterranean; soon after Captain-General of all the Roman forces, and governor of Asia. Pompey, on the other side, restored the office of Tribune which Sylla had put down; and in his Consulship procured a law for *examining into the miscarriages of men in office or command for twenty years past*. Many other examples of Pompey's popularity are left us on record, who was a perfect favourite of the People, and designed to be more; but his pretensions grew stale for want of a timely opportunity to introduce them upon the stage. For Cæsar, with his legions in Gaul, was a perpetual check upon his designs; and in the arts of pleasing the People, did soon after get many lengths beyond him. He tells us* himself that the Senate by a bold effort, having made some severe decrees against his proceedings, and against the Tribunes; these all left the city, and went over to his party, and consequently along with them the affections and interests of the People; which is further manifest from the accounts he gives us of the citizens in several towns mutinying against their commanders, and delivering both to his devotion. Besides, Cæsar's public and avowed pretensions for beginning the civil war were to restore the Tribunes and the People, oppressed (as he pretended) by the Nobles.

This forced Pompey, against his inclinations, upon the necessity of changing sides, for fear of being forsaken by both; and of closing in with the Senate and chief magistrates, by whom he was chosen general against Cæsar.

Thus at length the Senate (at least the primitive part of them, the Nobles) under Pompey, and the Commons under Cæsar, came to a final decision of the long quarrels between them. For, I think, the ambition of private men did by no means begin or occasion this war; though civil dissensions never fail of introducing and spiriting the ambition of private men; who thus become indeed the great instruments for deciding of such quarrels, and at last are sure to seize on the prize. But no man who sees a flock of vultures hovering over two armies ready to engage, can justly charge the blood drawn in the battle to them, though the carcasses fall to their share. For while the balance of power is equally held, the ambition of private men, whether orators or great commanders, gives neither danger nor fear, nor can possibly enslave their country; but, that once broken, the divided parties are forced to unite each to its head, under whose conduct or fortune one side is at first victorious, and at last both are slaves. And to put it past dispute, that this entire subversion of the Roman liberty and constitution, was altogether owing to those measures which had broke the balance between the Patricians and Plebeians, whereof the ambition of particular men was but an effect and consequence; we need only consider that when the uncorrupted part of

* De bello civili [*Civil War*], l. 1.

the Senate had, by the death of Cæsar, made one great effort to restore their former state and liberty, the success did not answer their hopes; but that whole assembly was so sunk in its authority that those patriots were forced to fly, and give way to the madness of the People; who, by their own dispositions, stirred up with the harangues of their orators, were now wholly bent upon a single and despotic slavery. Else, how could such a profligate as Antony, or a boy of eighteen like Octavius, ever dare to dream of giving the law to such an empire and People? Wherein the latter succeeded, and entailed the vilest tyranny that Heaven, in its anger, ever inflicted on a corrupt and poisoned People. And this with so little appearance at Cæsar's death, that when Cicero wrote to Brutus how he had prevailed by his credit with Octavius to promise him (Brutus) pardon and security for his person; that great Roman received the notice with the utmost indignity, and returned Cicero an answer (yet upon record) full of the highest resentment and contempt for such an offer, and from such a hand.

Here ended all show or shadow of liberty in Rome. Here was the repository of all the wise contentions and struggles for power, between the Nobles and Commons, lapped up safely in the bosom of a Nero and a Caligula, a Tiberius and a Domitian.

Let us now see, from this deduction of particular impeachments, and general dissensions in Greece and Rome, what conclusions may naturally be formed for instruction of any other state, that may haply upon many points labour under the like circumstances.

CHAP. IV.

Upon the subject of *impeachments* we may observe that the custom of accusing the Nobles to the People, either by themselves or their orators (now styled *An Impeachment in the Name of the Commons*) has been very ancient both in Greece and Rome, as well as Carthage; and therefore may seem to be the inherent right of a free People; nay, perhaps it is really so. But then it is to be considered, first, that this custom was peculiar to republics, or such states where the administration lay principally in the hands of the Commons, and ever raged more or less, according to their encroachments upon absolute power; having been always looked upon by the wisest men and best authors of those times, as an effect of licentiousness, and not of liberty; a distinction, which no multitude, either represented or collective, hath been at any time very nice in observing. However, perhaps this custom in a popular state, of impeaching particular men, may seem to be nothing else but the People's choosing upon occasion to exercise their own jurisdiction in person; as if a king of England should sit as chief justice in his court of King's Bench; which they say in former times he sometimes did. But in Sparta, which was called a kingly government, though the People were perfectly free, yet because the administration was in the two kings and the Ephori (with the assistance of the Senate) we read of no impeachments by the People. Nor was the process against great men, either upon account of ambition or ill conduct, though it reached sometimes to kings themselves, ever formed that way as I can recollect, but only passed through those hands where the administration lay. So likewise, during the regal government in Rome, though it were instituted a mixed monarchy, and the People made great advances in power, yet I do not remember to have read of one impeachment from the Commons against a patrician, till the consular state began, and the People had made great encroachments upon the administration.

Another thing to be considered is, that allowing this right of impeachment to be as inherent as they please, yet if the Commons have been perpetually mistaken in the merits of the causes and the persons as well as in the consequences of such impeachments upon the peace of the state, we cannot conclude less than that the Commons in Greece and Rome (whatever they may be in other states) were by no means qualified, either as prosecutors or judges in such matters; and therefore, that it would have been prudent to reserve these privileges dormant, never to be produced but upon very great and urging occasions, where the state is in apparent danger, the universal body of the people in clamours against the administration, and no other remedy in view. But for a few popular orators or tribunes, upon the score of *personal piques*; or *to employ the pride they conceive in seeing themselves at the head of a party*; or *as a method for advancement*; or *moved by certain powerful arguments that could make* Demosthenes *philippize*:° for such men, I say, when the state would of itself gladly be quiet, and hath besides, affairs of the last importance° upon the anvil, to *impeach* Miltiades, *after a great naval victory, for not pursuing the Persian fleet*; to impeach Aristides, *the person most versed among them in the knowledge and practice of their laws, for a blind suspicion of his acting in an arbitrary way (that is, as they expounded it, not in concert with the People)*; to impeach Pericles, *after all his services, for a few inconsiderable accounts*; or *to impeach* Phocion, *who had been guilty of no other crime but negotiating a treaty for the peace and security of his country*: what could the continuance of such proceedings end in, but the utter discouragement of all virtuous actions and persons, and consequently in the ruin of a state? Therefore the historians of those ages seldom fail to set this matter in all its lights, leaving us the highest and most honourable ideas of those persons who suffered by the persecution of the People, together with the fatal consequences they had, and how the prosecutors seldom failed to repent, when it was too late.

These impeachments perpetually falling upon many of the best men both in Greece and Rome, are a cloud of witnesses° and examples enough to discourage men of virtue and abilities from engaging in the service of the public; and help on t'other side to introduce the ambitious, the covetous, the superficial and the ill-designing; who are as apt to be bold, and forward, and meddling, as the former are to be cautious, and modest, and reserved. This was so well known in Greece that an eagerness after employments in the state was looked upon by wise men as the worst title a man could set up; and made Plato say,° 'That if all men were as good as they ought, the quarrel in a commonwealth would be, not as it is now, who *should* be ministers of state, but who should *not* be so.' And Socrates is introduced by Xenophon,* severely chiding a friend of his for not entering into the public service, when he was every way qualified for it. Such a backwardness there was at that time among good men to engage with an usurping People, and a set of *pragmatical ambitious orators*. And Diodorus tells us,† that when the petalism was erected at Syracuse° in imitation of the ostracism at Athens, it was so notoriously levelled against all who had either birth or merit to recommend them, that whoever possessed either withdrew for fear, and would have no concern in public affairs. So that the people themselves were forced to abrogate it, for fear of bringing all things into confusion.

There is one thing more to be observed, wherein all the popular impeachments in Greece and Rome seem to have agreed; and that was, a notion they had of being concerned in point of honour to condemn whatever person they impeached; however frivolous the articles were upon which they began, or however weak the surmises whereon they were to proceed in their proofs. For, to conceive that the body of the People could be mistaken, was an indignity not to be imagined, till the consequences had convinced them when it was past remedy. And I look upon this as a fate to which all popular accusations are subject; though I should think that the saying, *Vox populi vox Dei*, ought to be understood of the universal bent and current of a People, not the bare majority of a few representatives; which is often procured by little arts, and great industry and application; wherein those who engage in the pursuits of malice and revenge, are much more sedulous than such as would prevent them.

* Lib. 3. Memorab.   † Lib. 11.

From what has been deduced of the dissensions in Rome between the two bodies of Patricians and Plebeians, several reflections may be made.

First, that when the balance of power is duly fixed in a state, nothing is more dangerous and unwise than to give way to the first steps of popular encroachments, which is usually done either in hopes of procuring ease and quiet from some vexatious clamour, or else *made merchandise, and merely bought and sold.* This is breaking into a constitution to serve a present expedient, or supply a present exigency: the remedy of an empiric to stifle the present pain, but with certain prospect of sudden and terrible returns. When a child grows easy and content by being humoured, and when a lover becomes satisfied by small compliances, without further pursuits; then expect to find popular assemblies content with small concessions. If there could one single example be brought from the whole compass of history, of any one popular assembly, who after beginning to contend for power ever sat down quietly with a certain share; or if one instance could be produced of a popular assembly that ever knew, or proposed, or declared what share of power was their due; then might there be some hopes that it were a matter to be adjusted by reasonings, by conferences, or debates. But since all that is manifestly otherwise, I see no other course to be taken in a settled state, than a steady constant resolution in those to whom the rest of the balance is entrusted, never to give way so far to popular clamours as to make the least breach in the constitution, through which a million of abuses and encroachments will certainly in time force their way.

Again, from this deduction it will not be difficult to gather and assign certain marks of popular encroachments; by observing which, those who hold the balance in a state may judge of the degrees, and by early remedies and application put a stop to the fatal consequences that would otherwise ensue. What those marks are hath been at large deduced, and need not be here repeated.

Another consequence is this, that (with all respect for popular assemblies be it spoke) it is hard to recollect one folly, infirmity or vice, to which a single man is subjected, and from which a body of Commons, either collective or represented, can be wholly exempt. For, besides that they are composed of men with all their infirmities about them, they have also the ill fortune to be generally led and influenced by the very worst among themselves; I mean popular orators, tribunes, or, as they are now styled, *great speakers, leading men,* and the like. From whence it comes to pass that in their results we have sometimes found the same spirit of cruelty and revenge, of malice and pride, the same blindness and obstinacy and unsteadiness, the same ungovernable rage and anger, the same injustice, sophistry, and fraud, that ever lodged in the breast of any individual.

Again, in all free states, the evil to be avoided is tyranny, that is to say, the *summa imperii*, or unlimited power solely in the hands of the One, the Few, or the Many. Now, we have shown that although most revolutions of government in Greece and Rome began with the Tyranny of the People, yet they generally concluded in that of a single person. So that a usurping populace is its own dupe, a mere underworker, and a purchaser in trust for some single tyrant whose state and power they advance to their own ruin, with as blind an instinct as those worms that die with weaving magnificent habits for beings of a superior nature to their own.

CHAP. V.

Some reflections upon the late public proceedings among us, and that variety of factions in which we are still so intricately engaged, gave occasion to this discourse. I am not conscious that I have forced one example, or put it into any other light than it appeared to me long before I had thoughts of producing it.

I cannot conclude without adding some particular remarks upon the present posture of affairs and dispositions in this kingdom.

The fate of empire is grown a common-place: that all forms of government having been instituted by men, must be mortal like their authors, and have their periods of duration limited, as well as those of private persons; this is a truth of vulgar knowledge and observation. But there are few who turn their thoughts to examine how those diseases in a state are bred, that hasten its end; which would, however, be a very useful inquiry. For, though we cannot prolong the period of a commonwealth beyond the decree of Heaven, or the date of its nature, any more than human life beyond the strength of the seminal virtue, yet we may manage a sickly constitution, and preserve a strong one; we may watch and prevent accidents; we may turn off a great blow from without, and purge away an ill humour that is lurking within: and by these, and other such methods, render a state long-lived, though not immortal. Yet some physicians have thought that if it were practicable to keep the several humours of the body in an exact equal balance of each with its opposite, it might be immortal, and so perhaps would a political body, if the balance of power could be always held exactly even. But, I doubt, this is as almost impossible in practice as the other.

It hath an appearance of fatality, and that the period of a state approaches, when a concurrence of many circumstances, both within and without, unite towards its ruin; while the whole body of the People are either stupidly negligent, or else giving in with all their might to those very practices that are working their destruction. To see whole bodies of men breaking a constitution by the very same errors that so many have been broke before; to observe opposite parties who can agree in nothing else, yet firmly united in such measures as must certainly ruin their country; in short, to be encompassed with the greatest dangers from without, to be torn by many virulent factions within; then to be secure and senseless under all this, and to make it the very least of our concern; these, and some others that might be named, appear to me to be the most likely symptoms in a state of a sickness unto death.°

> *Quod procul à nobis flectat fortuna gubernans.*
> *Et ratio potius, quam res persuadeat ipsa.*°
>
> LUCR.

There are some conjunctures, wherein the death or dissolution of government is more lamentable in its consequences, than it would be in others. And I think a state can never arrive to its period in a more deplorable crisis than at a time when some *prince in the neighbourhood,*° of vast power and ambition, lies hovering like a vulture to devour, or at least, dismember its dying carcase; by which means it becomes only a province or acquisition to some mighty monarchy, without hopes of a resurrection.

I know very well there is a set of sanguine tempers, who deride and ridicule in the number of fopperies all such apprehensions as these. They have it ready in their mouths, that the people of England are of a genius and temper never to admit slavery among them; and they are furnished with a great many commonplaces upon that subject. But it seems to me, that such discoursers do reason upon short views and a very moderate compass of thought. For I think it a great error to count upon the genius of a nation as a standing argument in all ages, since there is hardly a spot of ground in Europe where the inhabitants have not frequently and entirely changed their temper and genius. Neither can I see any reason, why the genius of a nation should be more fixed in the point of government than in their morals, their learning, their religion, their common humour and conversation, their diet and their complexion; which do all notoriously vary almost in every age, and may every one of them have great effects upon men's notions of government.

Since the Norman conquest the balance of power in England has often varied, and sometimes been wholly overturned. The part which the

Commons had in it, *that most disputed point in its original, progress, and extent*, was by their own confessions but a very inconsiderable share. Generally speaking, they have been gaining ever since, although with frequent interruptions and slow progress. The abolishing of villeinage, together with the custom introduced (or permitted) among the Nobles of selling their lands in the reign of Henry the Seventh, was a mighty addition to the power of the Commons: yet I think a much greater happened in the time of his successor, at the dissolution of the abbeys; for this turned the clergy wholly out of the scale, who had so long filled it, and placed the Commons in their stead, who in a few years became possessed of vast quantities of those and other lands, by grant or purchase. About the middle of Queen Elizabeth's reign, I take the power between the Nobles and the Commons to have been in more equal balance than it was ever before or since. But then, or soon after, arose a faction in England, which under the name of Puritan began to grow popular, by moulding up their new schemes of religion with republican principles in government; who, gaining upon the prerogative as well as the Nobles, under several denominations, for the space of about sixty years, did at last overthrow the constitution and, according to the usual course of such revolutions, did introduce a Tyranny, first of the People, and then of a single person.°

In a short time after, the old government was revived. But the progress of affairs for almost thirty years, under the reigns of two weak princes,° is a subject of a different nature; when the balance was in danger to be overturned by the hands that held it, which was at last very seasonably prevented by the late Revolution. However, as it is the talent of human nature to run from one extreme to another, so in a very few years we have made mighty leaps from prerogative heights into the depth of popularity,° and, I doubt, to the very last degree that our constitution will bear. It were to be wished, that the most august assembly of the Commons would please to form a Pandect of their own power and privileges, to be confirmed by the entire legislative authority, and that in as solemn a manner (if they please) as the *Magna Charta*. But to fix one foot of their compass wherever they think fit, and extend the other to such terrible lengths, without describing any circumference at all, is to leave us and themselves in a very uncertain state, and in a sort of *rotation*, that the author of the *Oceana* never dreamed on.° I believe the most hardy tribune will not venture to affirm at present that any just fears of encroachment are given us from the regal power, or the Few: and is it then impossible to err on the other side? How far must we proceed, or where shall we stop? The raging of the sea, and the madness of the people,° are put together in Holy Writ; and it is God alone who can say to either, *Hitherto shalt thou pass, and no farther.*°

The balance of power in a limited state is of such absolute necessity that Cromwell himself, before he had perfectly confirmed his tyranny, having some occasions for the appearance of a parliament, was forced to create and erect an entire new House of Lords (such as it was) for a counterpoise to the Commons. And indeed, considering the vileness of the clay, I have sometimes wondered that no tribune of that age durst ever venture to ask the potter, What dost thou make?° But it was then about the last act of a popular usurpation; and Fate, or Cromwell, had already prepared them for that of a single person.

I have been often amazed at the rude, passionate, and mistaken results, which have at certain times fallen from great assemblies, both ancient and modern, and of other countries as well as our own. This gave me the opinion I mentioned a while ago, that public conventions are liable to all the infirmities, follies, and vices of private men. To which, if there be any exception, it must be of such assemblies who act by *universal concert, upon public principles, and for public ends*; such as proceed upon debates without *unbecoming warmths*, or *influence from particular leaders and inflamers*; such whose members, instead of *canvassing to procure majorities for their private opinions, are ready to comply with general sober results, though contrary to their own sentiments.* Whatever assemblies act by these, and other methods of the like nature, must be allowed to be exempt from several imperfections to which particular men are subjected. But I think the source of most mistakes and miscarriages in matters debated by public assemblies, ariseth from the influence of private persons upon great numbers, styled, in common phrase, *leading men and parties.* And therefore, when we sometimes meet a few words put together, which is called the Vote or Resolution of an Assembly, and which we cannot possibly reconcile to prudence, or public good, it is most charitable to conjecture that such a Vote has been conceived, and born, and bred in a private brain; afterwards raised and supported by an obsequious party; and then with usual methods confirmed by an artificial majority. For, let us suppose five hundred men, mixed in point of sense and honesty as usually assemblies are; and let us suppose these men proposing, debating, resolving, voting, according to the mere natural motions of their own little or much reason and understanding; I do allow, that abundance of indigested and abortive, many pernicious and foolish overtures would arise and float a few minutes; but then they would die and disappear. Because this must be said in behalf of human kind, that common sense and plain reason, while men are disengaged from acquired opinions, will ever have some general influence upon their minds; whereas the species of folly and vice are infinite, and so different in every individual, that they could never procure a majority if other corruptions did not enter to pervert men's understandings, and misguide their wills.

To describe how parties are bred in an assembly would be a work too difficult at present, and perhaps not altogether safe. *Periculosæ plenum opus aleæ.*° Whether those who are leaders, usually arrive at that station more by a sort of instinct or secret composition of their nature, or influence of the stars, than by the possession of any great abilities, may be a point of much dispute. But when the leader is once fixed, there will never fail to be followers. And man is so apt to imitate, so much of the nature of sheep (*imitatores, servum pecus*)°, that whoever is so bold to give the first *great leap over the heads of those about him* (though he be the worst of the flock), shall be quickly followed by the rest. Besides, when parties are once formed, the stragglers look so ridiculous and become so insignificant, that they have no other way but to run into the herd, which at least will hide and protect them; and where to be much considered requires only to be very violent.

But there is one circumstance with relation to parties, which I take to be of all others most pernicious in a state; and I would be glad any partisan would help me to a tolerable reason, that because Clodius and Curio happen to agree with me in a few singular notions, I must therefore blindly follow them in all: or, to state it at best, that because Bibulus the party-man is persuaded that Clodius and Curio do really propose the good of their country as their chief end, therefore Bibulus shall be wholly guided and governed by them in the means and measures towards it. Is it enough for Bibulus and the rest of the herd to say, without further examining, 'I am of the side with Clodius', or 'I vote with Curio'? Are these proper methods to form and make up what they think fit to call the *united wisdom of the nation?* Is it not possible that upon some occasions Clodius may be bold and insolent, borne away by his passion, malicious and revengeful? that Curio may be corrupt, and expose to sale his tongue or his pen? I conceive it far below the dignity both of human nature and human reason, to be engaged in any party, the most plausible soever, upon such servile conditions.

This influence of One upon Many, which seems to be as great in a People represented, as it was of old in the Commons collective, together with the consequences it has had upon the legislature, hath given me frequent occasion to reflect upon what Diodorus tells us° of one Charondas, a lawgiver to the Sybarites an ancient people of Italy, who was so averse from all innovation, especially when it was to proceed from particular persons (and, I suppose, that he might put it out of the power of men fond of their own notions to disturb the constitution at their pleasures, by advancing private schemes), as to provide a statute that whoever proposed any alteration to be made, should step out and do it with a rope about his neck: if the matter proposed were generally approved, then it should pass into a law; if it went in the negative, the proposer to be immediately hanged. Great ministers may talk of what projects they please; but I am deceived if a more effectual one could ever be found for *taking off* (as the present phrase is) those hot, unquiet spirits, who disturb assemblies, and obstruct public affairs, by gratifying their pride, their malice, their ambition, their vanity, or their avarice.

Those who in a late reign began the distinction between the personal and political capacity, seem to have had reason if they judged of princes by themselves; for, I think there is hardly to be found through all nature a greater difference between two things, than there is between a representing commoner in the function of his public calling, and the same person when he acts in the common offices of life. Here he allows himself to be upon a level with the rest of mortals; here he follows his own reason, and his own way, and rather affects a singularity in his actions and thoughts, than servilely to copy either from the wisest of his neighbours. In short, here his folly and his wisdom, his reason and his passions, are all of his own growth, not the echo or infusion of other men. But when he is got near the walls of his assembly, he assumes and affects an entire set of very different airs; he conceives himself a being of a superior nature to those *without*, and acting in a sphere where the vulgar methods for the conduct of human life can be of no use. He is listed in a party where he neither knows the temper, nor designs, nor perhaps the person of his leader, but whose opinions he follows and maintains with a zeal and faith as violent, as a young scholar does those of a philosopher whose sect he is taught to profess. He hath neither thoughts, nor actions, nor talk, that he can call his own, but all conveyed to him by his leader, as wind is through an organ. The nourishment he receives has been not only chewed but digested, before it comes into his mouth. Thus instructed, he followeth his party right or wrong, through all its sentiments, and acquires a courage and stiffness of opinion not at all congenial with him.

This encourages me to hope that during the present lucid interval,° the members retired to their homes may suspend a while their *acquired complexions*, and taught by the calmness of the scene and the season, reassume the native sedateness of their temper. If this should be so, it would be wise in them, as individual and private mortals, to look back a little upon the storms they have raised, as well as those they have escaped:

to reflect, that they have been authors of a new and wonderful thing in England, which is, for a House of Commons to lose the universal favour of the numbers they represent:° to observe how those whom they thought fit to persecute for righteousness' sake have been openly caressed by the people; and to remember how themselves sat in fear of their persons from popular rage. Now, if they would know the secret of all this unprecedented proceeding in their *masters*, they must not impute it to their freedom in debate, or declaring their opinions; but to that unparliamentary abuse of setting individuals upon their shoulders, who were hated by God and man. For it seems the mass of the people, in such conjunctures as this, have opened their eyes, and will not endure to be governed by *Clodius* and *Curio*, at the head of their *myrmidons*, though these be ever so numerous, and composed of their own representatives.

This aversion of the people against the late proceedings of the Commons is an accident, that if it last a while, might be improved to good uses for setting the balance of power a little more upon an equality than their late measures seem to promise or admit. This accident may be imputed to two causes: the first is an universal fear and apprehension of the greatness and power of France, whereof the people in general seem to be very much and justly possessed, and therefore cannot but resent to see it, in so critical a juncture, wholly laid aside by their ministers, the Commons. The other cause is a great love and sense of gratitude in the people towards their present King, grounded upon a long opinion and experience of his merit, as well as concessions to all their reasonable desires; so that it is for some time they have begun to say, and to fetch instances where he has in many things been hardly used. How long these humours may last (for passions are momentary, and especially those of a multitude) or what consequences they may produce, a little time will discover. But whenever it comes to pass that a popular assembly, free from such obstructions, and already possessed of more power than an equal balance will allow, shall continue to think they have not enough, but by cramping the hand that holds the balance, and by impeachments or dissensions with the nobles endeavour still for more; I cannot possibly see, in the common course of things, how the same causes can produce different effects and consequences among us, from what they did in Greece and Rome.

[There is one thing I must needs add, though I reckon it will appear to many as a very unreasonable paradox. When the Act passed some years ago against bribing of elections, I remember to have said upon occasion to some persons of both Houses, that we should be very much deceived in the consequences of that Act: and upon some discourse of the

conveniences of it, and the contrary (which will admit reasoning
enough), they seemed to be of the same opinion. It has appeared since
that our conjectures were right: for I think the late Parliament° was the
first-fruits of that Act; the proceedings whereof, as well as of the present,
have been such as to make many persons wish that things were upon the
old foot in that matter. Whether it be that so great a reformation was too
many degrees beyond so corrupt an Age as this; or that according to the
present turn and disposition of men in our nation, it were a less abuse to
bribe elections, than leave them to the discretion of the choosers, this at
least was Cato's opinion, when things in Rome were at a crisis much
resembling ours; who is recorded to have gone about with great industry,
dealing money among the people to favour Pompey (as I remember)
upon a certain election in opposition to Cæsar. And he excused himself
in it upon the necessities of the occasion, and the corruptions of the
people; an action that might well have excused Cicero's censure of him,
that he reasoned and acted *tanquam in Republica Platonis, non in fæce
Romuli.*° However it be, 'tis certain that the talents which qualify a man
for the service of his country in Parliament, are very different from those
which give him a dexterity at making his court to the people, and do not
often meet in the same subject. Then for the moral part, the difference is
inconsiderable; and whoever practices upon the weakness and vanity of
the people is guilty of an immoral action as much as if he did it upon their
avarice. Besides, the two trees may be judged by their fruits. The former
produces a set of popular men, fond of their own merits and abilities,
their opinions, and their eloquence; whereas the bribing of elections
seems to be at worst but an ill means of keeping things upon the old foot,
by leaving the defence of our properties chiefly in the hands of those who
will be the greatest sufferers, whenever they are endangered. It is easy to
observe in the late and present Parliament, that several boroughs and
some counties have been represented by persons who little thought to
have ever had such hopes before: and how far this may proceed, when
such a way is laid open for the exercise and encouragement of popular
arts, one may best judge from the consequences that the same causes
produced both in Athens and Rome. For, let speculative men reason, or
rather refine as they please; it ever will be true among us, that as long as
men engage in the public service upon private ends, and whilst all
pretences to a sincere Roman love of our country, are looked upon as an
affectation, a foppery, or a disguise (which has been a good while our
case, and is likely to continue so), it will be safer to trust our property and
constitution in the hands of such who have paid for their elections, than
of those who have obtained them by servile flatteries of the people.]°

To Their EXCELLENCIES the
Lords Justices of Ireland.

The Humble Petition of Frances Harris,
Who must Starve, and Die a Maid if it miscarries.

Humbly sheweth, that I went to warm myself in Lady Betty's
    chamber, because I was cold;°
And I had in a purse seven pound, four shillings, and sixpence
    (besides farthings) in money and gold;
So because I had been buying things for my lady last night,
I was resolved to tell my money, to see if it was right.
Now you must know, because my trunk has a very bad lock,
Therefore all the money I have, which God knows is a very small
    stock,
I keep in a pocket, tied about my middle, next my smock.
So when I went to put up my purse, as God would have it, my smock
    was unript,
And instead of putting it into my pocket, down it slipt;
Then the bell rung, and I went down stairs to put my lady to
    bed;   10
And, God knows, I thought my money was as safe as my
    maidenhead.
So, when I came up again, I found my pocket feel very light;
But when I search'd, and miss'd my purse, Lord! I thought I should
    have sunk outright.
'Lord! madam,' says Mary, 'how d'ye do?'—'Indeed,' says I, 'never
    worse:
But pray, Mary, can you tell what I have done with my purse?'
'Lord help me!' says Mary, 'I never stirr'd out of this place!'
'Nay,' said I, 'I had it in Lady Betty's chamber, that's a plain case.'
So Mary got me to bed, and cover'd me up warm:
However, she stole away my garters, that I might do myself no harm.
So I tumbled and toss'd all night, as you may very well think,   20
But hardly ever set my eyes together, or slept a wink.
So I was a-dream'd, methought, that we went and search'd the folks
    round,
And in a corner of Mrs. Dukes' box, tied in a rag, the money was
    found.°
So next morning we told Whittle, and he fell a swearing:°

Then my dame Wadgar came, and she, you know, is thick of
    hearing.°
'Dame,' said I, as loud as I could bawl, 'do you know what a loss I
    have had?'
'Nay,' says she, 'my Lord Colway's folks are all very sad:°
For my Lord Dromedary comes a Tuesday without fail.'°
'Pugh!' said I, 'but that's not the business that I ail.'
Says Cary, says he, 'I have been a servant this five and twenty years
    come spring,°   30
And in all the places I lived I never heard of such a thing.'
'Yes,' says the steward 'I remember when I was at my Lady
    Shrewsbury's,°
Such a thing as this happen'd, just about the time of *gooseberries*.'
So I went to the party suspected, and I found her full of grief.
(Now, you must know, of all things in the world I hate a thief.)
However, I was resolved to bring the discourse slily about:
'Mrs. Dukes,' said I, 'here's an ugly accident has happened out:
'Tis not that I value the money three skips of a louse:°
But the thing I stand upon is the credit of the house.
'Tis true, seven pound, four shillings, and sixpence makes a great
    hole in my wages: 40
Besides, as they say, service is no inheritance in these ages.°
Now, Mrs. Dukes, you know, and everybody understands,
That though 'tis hard to judge, yet money can't go without hands.'°
'The devil take me!' said she (blessing herself), 'if ever I saw't!'
So she roar'd like a bedlam, as tho' I had call'd her all to naught.
So, you know, what could I say to her any more?
I e'en left her, and came away as wise as I was before.
Well; but then they would have had me gone to the Cunning Man:
'No,' said I, ' 'tis the same thing, the Chaplain will be here anon.'°
So the Chaplain came in. Now the servants say he is my sweetheart,   50
Because he's always in my chamber, and I always take his part.
So, as the devil would have it, before I was aware, out I blunder'd,
'Parson,' said I, 'can you cast a *nativity*, when a body's plunder'd?'
(Now you must know, he hates to be called *Parson*, like the *devil*.)
'Truly,' says he, 'Mrs. Nab, it might become you to be more civil;°
If your money be gone, as a learned *Divine* says, d'ye see,
You are no *text* for my handling; so take that from me.
I was never taken for a *Conjurer* before, I'd have you to know.'
'Lord!' said I, 'don't be angry, I'm sure I never thought you so;
You know I honour the cloth; I design to be a Parson's wife;   60

I never took one in *your coat* for a Conjurer in all my life.'
With that he twisted his girdle at me like a rope, as who should say,
'Now you may go hang yourself for me!' and so went away.
Well; I thought I should have swoon'd. 'Lord!' said I, 'what shall I
    do?
I have lost my *money*, and shall lose my *true-love* too!'
Then my lord call'd me: 'Harry,' said my lord, 'don't cry;
I'll give something towards thy loss.' 'And', says my lady, 'so will I.'
'Oh! but', said I, 'what if after all the Chaplain won't *come to?*'
For that, he said (an't please your Excellencies), I must petition you.

  The premisses tenderly consider'd, I desire your Excellencies'
    protection,   70
And that I may have a share in next Sunday's collection;
And, over and above, that I may have your Excellencies' letter,
With an order for the Chaplain aforesaid; or instead of him, a better:
And then your poor petitioner, both night and day,
Or the Chaplain (for 'tis his *trade*) as in duty bound, shall ever *pray*.°

A MEDITATION

UPON A

Broom-Stick

ACCORDING TO THE STYLE AND MANNER OF THE HONOURABLE ROBERT BOYLE'S MEDITATIONS.

THIS single stick, which you now behold ingloriously lying in that neglected corner, I once knew in a flourishing state in a forest; it was full of sap, full of leaves, and full of boughs; but now, in vain does the busy art of man pretend to vie with nature, by tying that withered bundle of twigs to its sapless trunk; 'tis now at best but the reverse of what it was, a tree turned upside down, the branches on the earth, and the root in the air; 'tis now handled by every dirty wench, condemned to do her drudgery, and, by a capricious kind of fate, destined to make other things clean, and be nasty itself: at length, worn to the stumps in the service of the maids, 'tis either thrown out of doors, or condemned to its last use, of kindling a fire. When I beheld this I sighed, and said within myself, **Surely mortal man is a Broomstick!** Nature sent him into the world strong and lusty, in a thriving condition, wearing his own hair on his head, the proper branches of this reasoning vegetable, till the axe of intemperance has lopped off his green boughs, and left him a withered trunk: he then flies to art, and puts on a periwig, valuing himself upon an unnatural bundle of hairs, all covered with powder, that never grew on his head; but now should this our broomstick pretend to enter the scene, proud of those birchen spoils it never bore, and all covered with dust, though the sweepings of the finest lady's chamber, we should be apt to ridicule and despise its vanity. Partial judges that we are of our own excellencies, and other men's defaults!

But a broomstick, perhaps you will say, is an emblem of a tree standing on its head; and pray what is man, but a topsyturvy creature, his animal faculties perpetually mounted on his rational, his head where his heels should be, grovelling on the earth! And yet with all his faults, he sets up to be an universal reformer and corrector of abuses, a remover of grievances, rakes into every slut's corner of Nature, bringing hidden corruptions to the light, and raises a mighty dust where there was none before; sharing deeply all the while in the very same pollutions he pretends to sweep away. His last days are spent in slavery to women, and generally the least deserving, till, worn out to the stumps, like his brother besom, he is either kicked out of doors, or made use of to kindle flames for others to warm themselves by.

A
TALE
OF A
TUB.

Written for the Universal Improvement of Mankind

Diu multumque desideratum°

Basima eacabasa eanaa irraurista, diarba da caeotaba
fobor camelanthi.   *Iren. Lib.* 1. *C.* 18.°

——————— *Juvatque novos decerpere flores,*
Insignemque meo capiti petere inde coronam,
Unde prius nulli velarunt tempora Musæ.°   Lucret.

Treatises written by the same Author, most of them mentioned in the following
  Discourses; which will be speedily published.

  A Character of the present set of Wits *in this Island.*
  A panegyrical Essay upon the Number THREE.
  A Dissertation upon the principal Productions of Grub Street.
  Lectures upon a Dissection of Human Nature.
  A Panegyric upon the World.
  An analytical Discourse upon Zeal, histori-theo-physi-logically *considered.*
  A general History of Ears.
  A modest Defence of the Proceedings of the Rabble *in all ages.*
  A Description of the Kingdom of Absurdities.
  A Voyage into England, *by a Person of Quality in* Terra Australis incognita,°
translated from the Original.
  A critical Essay upon the Art of Canting, *philosophically, physically, and musically*
considered.

AN APOLOGY

For the [Tale of a Tub.]

IF *good and ill nature equally operated upon Mankind, I might have saved*
myself the trouble of this Apology; for it is manifest by the reception the following
discourse hath met with, that those who approve it are a great majority among
the men of taste; yet there have been two or three treatises written expressly
against it° besides many others that have flirted at it occasionally, without one
syllable having been ever published in its defence, or even quotation to its

*advantage that I can remember, except by the polite author of a late discourse°
between a Deist and a Socinian.*

*Therefore, since the book seems calculated to live at least as long as our
language and our taste admit no great alterations, I am content to convey some
Apology along with it.*

*The greatest part of that book was finished above thirteen years since, 1696,
which is eight years before it was published. The author was then young, his
invention at the height, and his reading fresh in his head. By the assistance of
some thinking, and much conversation, he had endeavour'd to strip himself of as
many real prejudices as he could; I say real ones because, under the notion of
prejudices, he knew to what dangerous heights some men have proceeded. Thus
prepared, he thought the numerous and gross corruptions in Religion and
Learning might furnish matter for a satire that would be useful and diverting.
He resolved to proceed in a manner that should be altogether new, the world
having been already too long nauseated with endless repetitions upon every
subject. The abuses in Religion he proposed to set forth in the Allegory of the
Coats and the three Brothers, which was to make up the body of the discourse.
Those in Learning he chose to introduce by way of digressions. He was then a
young gentleman much in the world, and wrote to the taste of those who were like
himself; therefore in order to allure them, he gave a liberty to his pen, which
might not suit with maturer years or graver characters, and which he could have
easily corrected with a very few blots, had he been master of his papers for a year
or two before their publication.*

*Not that he would have governed his judgment by the ill-placed cavils of the
sour, the envious, the stupid, and the tasteless, which he mentions with disdain.
He acknowledges there are several youthful sallies which, from the grave and the
wise, may deserve a rebuke. But he desires to be answerable no farther than he is
guilty, and that his faults may not be multiplied by the ignorant, the unnatural,
and uncharitable applications of those who have neither candour to suppose good
meanings, nor palate to distinguish true ones. After which he will forfeit his life if
any one opinion can be fairly deduced from that book which is contrary to
Religion or Morality.*

*Why should any clergyman of our church be angry to see the follies of
fanaticism and superstition exposed, though in the most ridiculous manner; since
that is perhaps the most probable way to cure them, or at least to hinder them
from farther spreading? Besides, though it was not intended for their perusal, it
rallies nothing but what they preach against. It contains nothing to provoke
them, by the least scurrility upon their persons or their functions. It celebrates the
Church of England as the most perfect of all others in discipline and doctrine; it
advances no opinion they reject, nor condemns any they receive. If the clergy's
resentments lay upon their hands, in my humble opinion they might have found*

more proper objects to employ them on: nondum tibi defuit hostis;° *I mean those heavy, illiterate scribblers, prostitute in their reputations, vicious in their lives, and ruined in their fortunes, who, to the shame of good sense as well as piety, are greedily read merely upon the strength of bold, false, impious assertions, mixed with unmannerly reflections upon the priesthood, and openly intended against all Religion; in short, full of such principles as are kindly received because they are levelled to remove those terrors that Religion tells men will be the consequence of immoral lives. Nothing like which is to be met with in this discourse, though some of them are pleased so freely to censure it. And I wish there were no other instance of what I have too frequently observed, that many of that reverend body are not always very nice in distinguishing between their enemies and their friends.*

 Had the author's intentions met with a more candid interpretation from some whom out of respect he forbears to name, he might have been encouraged to an examination of books written by some of those authors above described, whose errors, ignorance, dulness and villainy, he thinks he could have detected and exposed in such a manner that the persons who are most conceived to be affected by them, would soon lay them aside and be ashamed. But he has now given over those thoughts; since the weightiest *men in the* weightiest *stations° are pleased to think it a more dangerous point to laugh at those corruptions in Religion, which they themselves must disapprove, than to endeavour pulling up those very foundations wherein all Christians have agreed.*

 He thinks it no fair proceeding that any person should offer determinately to fix a name upon the author of this discourse, who hath all along concealed himself from most of his nearest friends. Yet several have gone a farther step, and Letter of *pronounced another book° to have been the work of the same hand* Enthusiasm. *with this, which the author directly affirms to be a thorough mistake, he having as yet never so much as read that discourse; a plain instance how little truth there often is in general surmises, or in conjectures drawn from a similitude of style or way of thinking.*

 Had the author written a book to expose the abuses in Law, or in Physic, he believes the learned professors in either faculty would have been so far from resenting it as to have given him thanks for his pains, especially if he had made an honourable reservation for the true practice of either science. But Religion, they tell us, ought not to be ridiculed, and they tell us truth. Yet surely the corruptions in it may; for we are taught by the tritest maxim in the world° that Religion being the best of things, its corruptions are likely to be the worst.

 There is one thing which the judicious reader cannot but have observed, that some of those passages in this discourse which appear most liable to objection, are what they call parodies, where the author personates the style and manner of other writers whom he has a mind to expose. I shall produce one instance, it is in the [93]*d page. Dryden, L'Estrange,° and some others I shall not name, are here levelled at, who having spent their lives in faction and apostacies and all manner of vice, pretended to be sufferers for Loyalty and Religion. So Dryden tells us in one of his prefaces° of his merits and suffering, and thanks God that he possesses his soul in patience. In other places he talks at the same rate, and L'Estrange often uses the like style; and I believe the reader may find more persons to give that passage an application. But this is enough to direct those who may have overlooked the author's intention.*

There are three or four other passages which prejudiced or ignorant readers have drawn by great force to hint at ill meanings, as if they glanced at some tenets in religion. In answer to all which, the author solemnly protests he is entirely innocent; and never had it once in his thoughts that anything he said would in the least be capable of such interpretations, which he will engage to deduce full as fairly from the most innocent book in the world. And it will be obvious to every reader that this was not any part of his scheme or design, the abuses he notes being such as all Church of England men agree in; nor was it proper for his subject to meddle with other points than such as have been perpetually controverted since the Reformation.

To instance only in that passage about the three wooden machines mentioned in the Introduction: in the original manuscript there was a description of a fourth, which those who had the papers in their power blotted out, as having something in it of satire that I suppose they thought was too particular; and therefore they were forced to change it to the number Three, from whence some have endeavoured to squeeze out a dangerous meaning° that was never thought on. And indeed the conceit was half spoiled by changing the numbers, that of Four being much more cabalistic, and therefore better exposing the pretended virtue of Numbers, a superstition there intended to be ridiculed.

Another thing to be observed is, that there generally runs an irony through the thread of the whole book, which the men of taste will observe and distinguish, and which will render some objections that have been made, very weak and insignificant.

This Apology being chiefly intended for the satisfaction of future readers, it may be thought unnecessary to take any notice of such treatises as have been written against this ensuing discourse, which are already sunk into waste paper and oblivion after the usual fate of common answerers to books which are allowed to have any merit. They are indeed like annuals, that grow about a young tree and seem to vie with it for a summer, but fall and die with the leaves in autumn and are never heard of any more. When Dr. Eachard writ his book about the Contempt of the Clergy,° numbers of these answerers immediately started up, whose memory if he had not kept alive by his replies it would now be utterly unknown that he were ever answered at all. There is indeed an exception, when any great genius thinks it worth his while to expose a foolish piece; so we still read Marvell's Answer to Parker with pleasure, though the book it answers be sunk long ago: so the Earl of Orrery's Remarks° will be read with delight when the Dissertation he exposes will neither be sought nor found: but these are no enterprizes for common hands, nor to be hoped for above once or twice in an age. Men would be more cautious of losing their time in such an undertaking, if they did but consider that to answer a book effectually requires more pains and skill, more wit, learning, and judgment than were employed in the writing it. And the author assures those gentlemen who have given themselves that trouble with him, that his discourse is the product of the study, the observation, and the invention of several years; that he often blotted out much more than he left, and if his papers had not been a long time out of his possession, they must have still undergone more severe corrections: and do they think such a building is to be battered with dirt-pellets, however envenomed the mouths may be that discharge them? He hath seen the productions but of two answerers, one of which at first appeared as from an unknown hand,° but since avowed by a person who upon some occasions hath discovered no ill vein of humour. 'Tis a pity any occasions should put him under a necessity of being so hasty in his productions, which otherwise might often be entertaining. But there were other reasons obvious enough for his miscarriage in this; he writ against the conviction of his talent, and entered upon one of the wrongest attempts in nature, to turn into ridicule by a week's labour a work which had cost so much time and met with so much success in ridiculing others: the manner how he has handled his subject I have now forgot, having just looked it over when it first came out, as others did, merely for the sake of the title.

The other answer is from a person of a graver character,° and is made up of half invective and half annotation, in the latter of which he hath generally succeeded well enough. And the project at that time was not amiss, to draw in readers to his pamphlet, several having appeared desirous that there might be some explication of the more difficult passages. Neither can he be altogether blamed for offering at the invective part, because it is agreed on all hands that the author had given him sufficient provocation. The great objection is against his manner of treating it, very unsuitable to one of his function. It was determined by a fair majority that this answerer had in a way not to be pardoned drawn his pen against a certain great man° then alive and universally reverenced for every good quality that could possibly enter into the composition of the most accomplished person; it was observed how he was pleased, and affected to have that noble writer called his adversary; and it was a point of satire well directed, for I have been told Sir W[illiam] T[emple] was sufficiently mortified at the term. All the men of wit and politeness were immediately up in arms through indignation, which prevailed over their contempt, by the consequences they apprehended from such an example, and it grew Porsenna's case, idem trecenti juravimus.° *In short, things were ripe for a general insurrection till my Lord Orrery had a little laid the spirit and settled the ferment. But his lordship being principally engaged with another antagonist,° it was thought necessary in order to quiet the minds of men, that this opposer should receive a reprimand, which partly occasioned that discourse of the Battle of the Books; and the author was further at the pains to insert one or two remarks on him in the body of the book.*

This answerer has been pleased to find fault with about a dozen passages, which the author will not be at the trouble of defending further than by assuring the reader that for the greater part the reflecter is entirely mistaken, and forces interpretations which never once entered into the writer's head, nor will he is sure into that of any reader of taste and candour; he allows two or three at most, there produced, to have been delivered unwarily: for which he desires to plead the excuse offered already, of his youth, and frankness of speech, and his papers being out of his power at the time they were published.

But this answerer insists, and says what he chiefly dislikes is the design: *what that was I have already told, and I believe there is not a person in England, who can understand that book, that ever imagined it to have been anything else but to expose the abuses and corruptions in Learning and Religion.*

But it would be good to know what design *this reflecter was serving when he concludes his pamphlet with a caution to readers to beware of thinking the author's wit was entirely his own: surely this must have had some allay of personal animosity at least mixed with the* design *of serving the public, by so useful a discovery; and it indeed touches the author in a tender point, who insists upon it that through the whole book he has not borrowed one single hint from any writer in the world; and he thought, of all criticisms, that would never have been one. He conceived it was never disputed to be an original, whatever faults it might have. However, this answerer produces three instances to prove* this author's wit is not his own in many places. *The first is, that the names of Peter, Martin and Jack, are borrowed from a Letter of the late Duke of Buckingham.° Whatever wit is contained in those three names the author is content to give it up, and desires his readers will subtract as much as they placed upon that account; at the same time protesting solemnly that he never once heard of that letter except in this passage of the answerer: so that the names were not borrowed, as he affirms, though they should happen to be the same, which however is odd enough, and what he hardly believes, that of Jack being not quite so obvious as the other two. The second instance to show the author's wit is not his own, is Peter's banter (as he calls it in his Alsatia phrase)° upon Transubstantiation, which is taken from the same Duke's conference with an Irish priest, where a cork is turned into a horse. This the author confesses to have seen about ten years after his book was writ, and a year or two after it was published. Nay, the answerer overthrows this himself, for he allows the Tale was written in 1697, and I think that pamphlet was not printed in many years after. It was necessary that corruption should have some allegory as well as the rest, and the author invented the properest he could, without inquiring what other people had writ; and the commonest reader will find there is not the least resemblance between the two stories. The third instance is in these words: 'I have been assured, that the Battle in St. James's Library is,* mutatis mutandis, taken out of a French book entitled* Combat des Livres,° if I misremember not.' In which passage there are two clauses observable, 'I have been assured' and, 'if I misremember not'. I desire first to know whether, if that conjecture proves an utter falsehood, those two clauses will be a sufficient excuse for this worthy critic? The matter is a trifle; but would he venture to pronounce at this rate upon one of greater moment? I know nothing more contemptible in a writer than the character of a plagiary, which he here fixes at a venture; and this not for a passage but a whole discourse taken out from another book, only* mutatis mutandis. The author is as much in the dark about this as the answerer, and will imitate him by an affirmation at random; that if there be a word of truth in this reflection, he is a paltry, imitating pedant and the answerer is a person of wit, manners and truth. He takes his boldness from never having seen any such treatise in his life nor heard of it before; and he is sure it is impossible for two writers of different times and countries to agree in their thoughts after such a manner that two continued discourses shall be the same, only* mutatis mutandis. Neither will he insist upon the mistake of the title, but let the answerer and his friend° produce any book they please, he defies them to show one single particular where the judicious reader will affirm he has been obliged for the smallest hint; giving only allowance for the accidental encountering of a single thought, which he knows may sometimes happen, though he has never yet found it in that discourse, nor has heard it objected by anybody else.*

So that if ever any design was unfortunately executed, it must be that of this answerer who, when he would have it observed that the author's wit is not his own, is able to produce but three instances, two of them mere trifles, and all three manifestly false. If this be the way these gentlemen deal with the world in those criticisms where we have not leisure to defeat them, their readers had need be cautious how they rely upon their credit; and whether this proceeding can be reconciled to humanity or truth, let those who think it worth their while determine.

It is agreed this answerer would have succeeded much better if he had stuck wholly to his business as a commentator upon the Tale of a Tub, *wherein it cannot be denied that he hath been of some service to the public, and has given very fair conjectures towards clearing up some difficult passages; but it is the frequent error of those men (otherwise very commendable for their labours) to make excursions beyond their talent and their office, by pretending to point out the beauties and the faults; which is no part of their trade, which they always fail in, which the world never expected from them, nor gave them any thanks for endeavouring at. The part of Minellius or Farnaby° would have fallen in with his genius, and might have been serviceable to many readers who cannot enter into the abstruser parts of that discourse; but* optat ephippia bos piger:° *the dull, unwieldy, ill-shaped ox, would needs put on the furniture of a horse, not considering he was born to labour, to plough the ground for the sake of superior beings, and that he has neither the shape, mettle nor speed of that nobler animal he would affect to personate.*

It is another pattern of this answerer's fair dealing to give us hints that the author is dead,° and yet to lay the suspicion upon somebody, I know not who, in the country; to which can only be returned that he is absolutely mistaken in all his conjectures; and surely conjectures are at best too light a pretence to allow a man to assign a name in public. He condemns a book and consequently the author, of whom he is utterly ignorant, yet at the same time fixes, in print, what he thinks a disadvantageous character upon those who never deserved it. A man who receives a buffet in the dark may be allowed to be vexed, but it is an odd kind of revenge to go to cuffs in broad day with the first he meets with, and lay the last night's injury at his door. And thus much for this discreet, candid, pious, and ingenious *answerer.*

How the author came to be without his papers is a story not proper to be told and of very little use, being a private fact of which the reader would believe as little or as much as he thought good. He had, however, a blotted copy by him which he intended to have writ over with many alterations, and this the publishers° were well aware of, having put it into the bookseller's preface,° that they apprehended a surreptitious copy, which was to be altered, &c. *This though not regarded by readers, was a real truth, only the surreptitious copy was rather that which was printed; and they made all haste they could, which indeed was needless, the author not being at all prepared; but he has been told the bookseller was in much pain, having given a good sum of money for the copy.*

In the author's original copy there were not so many chasms as appear in the book, and why some of them were left, he knows not; had the publication been trusted to him, he would have made several corrections of passages against which nothing hath been ever objected. He would likewise have altered a few of those that seem with any reason to be excepted against; but to deal freely, the greatest number he should have left untouched as never suspecting it possible any wrong interpretations could be made of them.

The author observes at the end of the book there is a discourse called A Fragment, *which he more wondered to see in print than all the rest. Having been a most imperfect sketch, with the addition of a few loose hints, which he once* lent a gentleman who had designed a discourse of somewhat the same subject, he never thought of it afterwards; and it was a sufficient surprise to see it pieced up together, wholly out of the method and scheme he had intended, for it was the ground work of a much larger discourse, and he was sorry to observe the materials so foolishly employed.

There is one further objection made by those who have answered this book, as well as by some others, that Peter is frequently made to repeat oaths and curses. Every reader observes it was necessary to know that Peter did swear and curse. The oaths are not printed out, but only supposed; and the idea of an oath is not immoral like the idea of a profane or immodest speech. A man may laugh at the Popish folly of cursing people to hell, and imagine them swearing, without any crime; but lewd words or dangerous opinions though printed by halves, fill the reader's mind with ill ideas; and of these the author cannot be accused. For the judicious reader will find that the severest strokes of satire in his book are levelled against the modern custom of employing wit upon those topics, of which there is a remarkable instance in the [132]d page as well as in several others, though perhaps once or twice expressed in too free a manner, excusable only for the reasons already alleged. Some overtures have been made by a third hand to the bookseller, for the author's altering those passages which he thought might require it; but it seems the bookseller will not hear of any such thing, being apprehensive it might spoil the sale of the book.

The author cannot conclude this Apology without making this one reflection; that, as wit is the noblest and most useful gift of human nature, so humour is the most agreeable; and where these two enter far into the composition of any work they will render it always acceptable to the world. Now, the great part of those who have no share or taste of either, but by their pride, pedantry, and ill manners, lay themselves bare to the lashes of both, think the blow is weak because they are insensible; and where wit hath any mixture of raillery, 'tis but calling it banter and the work is done. This polite word of theirs was first borrowed from the bullies in White-Friars,° then fell among the footmen, and at last retired to the pedants, by whom it is applied as properly to the production of wit as if I should apply it to Sir Isaac Newton's mathematics. But, if this bantering as they call it be so despisable a thing, whence comes it to pass they have such a perpetual itch towards it themselves? To instance only in the answerer already mentioned, it is grievous to see him in some of his writings at every turn going out of his way to be waggish, to tell us of a cow that pricked up her tail and in his answer to this discourse he says, it is all a farce and a ladle; with other passages equally shining. One may say of these impedimenta literarum,° that wit owes them a shame, and they cannot take wiser counsel than to keep out of harm's way, or at least, not to come till they are sure they are called.

To conclude: with those allowances above required this book should be read;

after which the author conceives few things will remain which may not be excused in a young writer. He wrote only to the men of wit and taste, and he thinks he is not mistaken in his accounts when he says they have been all of his side, enough to give him the vanity of telling his name, wherein the world, with all its wise conjectures, is yet very much in the dark; which circumstance is no disagreeable amusement either to the public or himself.

The author is informed, that the bookseller has prevailed on several gentlemen to write some explanatory notes,° for the goodness of which he is not to answer, having never seen any of them, nor intends it, till they appear in print, when it is not unlikely he may have the pleasure to find twenty meanings which never entered into his imagination.

June 3, 1709.

POSTSCRIPT.

*S*INCE *the writing of this, which was about a year ago, a prostitute bookseller hath published a foolish paper° under the name of* Notes on the Tale of a Tub, *with some account of the author, and with an insolence which I suppose is punishable by law, hath presumed to assign certain names. It will be enough for the author to assure the world that the writer of that paper is utterly wrong in all his conjectures upon that affair. The author further asserts that the whole work is entirely of one hand, which every reader of judgment will easily discover. The gentleman who gave the copy° to the bookseller being a friend of the author, and using no other liberties besides that of expunging certain passages where now the chasms appear under the name of* desiderata. *But if any person will prove his claim to three lines in the whole book, let him step forth and tell his name and titles; upon which the bookseller shall have orders to prefix them to the next edition, and the claimant shall from henceforward be acknowledged the undisputed author.*

TO THE RIGHT HONOURABLE
JOHN LORD SOMERS.

MY LORD,

THO' the author has written a large Dedication, yet that being addressed to a prince whom I am never likely to have the honour of being known to (a person besides, as far as I can observe, not at all regarded, or thought on by any of our present writers) and I being wholly free from that slavery which booksellers usually lie under to the caprices of authors, I think it a wise piece of presumption to inscribe these papers to your Lordship and to implore your Lordship's protection of them. God and your Lordship know their faults and their merits; for as to my own particular, I am altogether a stranger to the matter, and though everybody else should be equally ignorant, I do not fear the sale of the book at all the worse, upon that score. Your Lordship's name on the front in capital letters will at any time get off one edition, neither would I desire any other help to grow an alderman than a patent for the sole privilege of dedicating to your Lordship.

I should now, in right of a dedicator, give your Lordship a list of your own virtues and at the same time be very unwilling to offend your modesty; but chiefly I should celebrate your liberality towards men of great parts and small fortunes, and give you broad hints that I mean myself. And I was just going on in the usual method, to peruse a hundred or two of dedications, and transcribe an abstract to be applied to your Lordship; but I was diverted by a certain accident. For, upon the covers of these papers, I casually observed written in large letters the two following words, *DETUR DIGNISSIMO*; which, for aught I knew, might contain some important meaning. But it unluckily fell out that none of the authors I employ understood Latin (though I have them often in pay to translate out of that language); I was therefore compelled to have recourse to the curate of our parish, who Englished it thus, *Let it be given to the worthiest*: and his comment was, that the author meant his work should be dedicated to the sublimest genius of the age for wit, learning, judgment, eloquence, and wisdom. I called at a poet's chamber (who works for my shop) in an alley hard by, showed him the translation and desired his opinion who it was that the author could mean. He told me after some consideration, that vanity was a thing he abhorred, but by the description, he thought himself to be the person aimed at; and at the same time he very kindly offered his own assistance *gratis* towards penning a Dedication to himself. I desired him, however, to give a second guess. Why, then, said he, it must be I, or my Lord Somers. From thence I went to several other wits of my acquaintance, with no small hazard and weariness to my person, from a prodigious number of dark, winding stairs; but found them all in the same story, both of your Lordship and themselves. Now, your Lordship is to understand that this proceeding was not of my own invention; for I have somewhere heard it is a maxim that those to whom everybody allows the second place, have an undoubted title to the first.°

This infallibly convinced me that your Lordship was the person

intended by the author. But being very unacquainted in the style and
form of dedications, I employed those wits aforesaid to furnish me with
hints and materials towards a panegyric upon your Lordship's virtues.

In two days they brought me ten sheets of paper, filled up on every
side. They swore to me that they had ransacked whatever could be found
in the characters of *Socrates*, *Aristides*, *Epaminondas*, *Cato*, *Tully*, *Atticus*,
and other hard names which I cannot now recollect. However, I have
reason to believe they imposed upon my ignorance, because when I came
to read over their collections, there was not a syllable there but what I and
everybody else knew as well as themselves. Therefore I grievously suspect a cheat, and that these authors of mine stole and transcribed every
word from the universal report of mankind. So that I look upon myself as
fifty shillings out of pocket to no manner of purpose.

If by altering the title I could make the same materials serve for
another Dedication (as my betters have done) it would help to make up
my loss; but I have made several persons dip here and there in those
papers, and before they read three lines they have all assured me plainly
that they cannot possibly be applied to any person besides your Lordship.

I expected, indeed, to have heard of your Lordship's bravery at the
head of an army; of your undaunted courage in mounting a breach, or
scaling a wall; or to have had your pedigree traced in a lineal descent from
the House of Austria; or of your wonderful talent at dress and dancing; or
your profound knowledge in algebra, metaphysics, and the oriental
tongues. But to ply the world with an old beaten story of your wit, and
eloquence, and learning, and wisdom, and justice, and politeness, and
candour, and evenness of temper in all scenes of life; of that great
discernment in discovering, and readiness in favouring deserving men;
with forty other common topics; I confess I have neither conscience nor
countenance to do it. Because there is no virtue, either of a public or
private life, which some circumstances of your own have not often
produced upon the stage of the world; and those few which, for want of
occasions to exert them, might otherwise have passed unseen, or unobserved by your *friends*, your *enemies* have at length brought to light.°

'Tis true, I should be very loth the bright example of your Lordship's
virtues should be lost to after-ages, both for their sake and your own; but
chiefly because they will be so very necessary to adorn the history of a *late
reign*.° And that is another reason why I would forbear to make a recital
of them here, because I have been told by wise men that as Dedications
have run for some years past, a good historian will not be apt to have
recourse thither in search of characters.

There is one point, wherein I think we dedicators would do well to change our measures; I mean, instead of running on so far upon the praise of our patrons' *liberality*, to spend a word or two in admiring their *patience*. I can put no greater compliment on your Lordship's than by giving you so ample an occasion to exercise it at present; though perhaps I shall not be apt to reckon much merit to your Lordship upon that score, who having been formerly used to tedious harangues,° and sometimes to as little purpose, will be the readier to pardon this, especially when it is offered by one who is with all respect and veneration,

MY LORD,

Your Lordship's most obedient,
and most faithful servant,

THE BOOKSELLER.

THE BOOKSELLER TO THE READER.

I T *is now six years since these papers came first to my hands, which seems to have been about a twelvemonth after they were writ; for the author tells us in his preface° to the first treatise, that he has calculated it for the year* 1697, *and in several passages of that Discourse, as well as the second, it appears they were written about that time.*

As to the author, I can give no manner of satisfaction. However, I am credibly informed that this publication is without his knowledge, for he concludes the copy is lost, having lent it to a person since dead, and being never in possession of it after. So that whether the work received his last hand, or whether he intended to fill up the defective places, is like to remain a secret.

If I should go about to tell the reader by what accident I became master of these papers, it would in this unbelieving age pass for little more than the cant or jargon of the trade. I therefore gladly spare both him and myself so unnecessary a trouble. There yet remains a difficult question, why I published them no sooner. I forbore upon two accounts. First, because I thought I had better work upon my hands; and secondly, because I was not without some hope of hearing from the author, and receiving his directions. But I have been lately alarmed with intelligence of a surreptitious copy which a certain great wit had new polished and refined, or as our present writers express themselves, fitted to the humour of the age, as they have already done with great felicity to Don Quixote, Boccalini,° la Bruyere, *and other authors. However, I thought it fairer dealing to offer the whole work in its naturals. If any gentleman will please to furnish me with a key in order to explain the more difficult parts, I shall very gratefully acknowledge the favour, and print it by itself.*

THE EPISTLE DEDICATORY,

TO HIS ROYAL HIGHNESS

PRINCE POSTERITY.*

SIR,

I HERE present Your Highness with the fruits of a very few leisure hours, stolen from the short intervals of a world of business and of an employment quite alien from such amusements as this; the poor production of that refuse of time, which has lain heavy upon my hands during a long prorogation of parliament, a great dearth of foreign news, and a tedious fit of rainy weather; for which and other reasons, it cannot choose extremely to deserve such a patronage as that of Your Highness, whose numberless virtues, in so few years, make the world look upon you as the future example to all princes; for although Your Highness is hardly got clear of infancy, yet has the universal learned world already resolved upon appealing to your future dictates with the lowest and most resigned submission; fate having decreed you sole arbiter of the productions of human wit, in this polite and most accomplished age. Methinks, the number of appellants were enough to shock and startle any judge, of a genius less unlimited than yours: but in order to prevent such glorious trials, the *person*° (it seems) to whose care the education of Your Highness is committed, has resolved (as I am told) to keep you in almost an universal ignorance of our studies, which it is your inherent birthright to inspect.

It is amazing to me that this *person* should have assurance, in the face of the sun, to go about persuading Your Highness that our age is almost wholly illiterate, and has hardly produced one writer upon any subject. I know very well that when Your Highness shall come to riper years, and have gone through the learning of antiquity, you will be too curious to neglect inquiring into the authors of the very age before you: and to think that this *insolent*, in the account he is preparing for your view, designs to reduce them to a number so insignificant as I am ashamed to mention, it moves my zeal and my spleen for the honour and interest of our vast

---

* The Citation out of Irenæus in the title-page, which seems to be all *gibberish*, is a form of initiation used anciently by the Marcosian Heretics.° W. WOTTON.

It is the usual style of decried writers to appeal to Posterity, who is here represented as a prince in his nonage, and Time as his governor; and the author begins in a way very frequent with him, by personating other writers who sometimes offer such reasons and excuses for publishing their works, as they ought chiefly to conceal and be ashamed of.

flourishing body, as well as of myself, for whom, I know by long experience, he has professed and still continues a peculiar malice.

'Tis not unlikely that when Your Highness will one day peruse what I am now writing, you may be ready to expostulate with your governor upon the credit of what I here affirm, and command him to shew you some of our productions. To which he will answer (for I am well informed of his designs) by asking Your Highness, where they are? and what is become of them? and pretend it a demonstration that there never were any, because they are not then to be found. Not to be found! Who has mislaid them? Are they sunk in the abyss of things? 'Tis certain that in their own nature they were *light* enough to swim upon the surface for all eternity. Therefore the fault is in him who tied weights so heavy to their heels as to depress them to the centre. Is their very essence destroyed? Who has annihilated them? Were they drowned by *purges*, or martyred by *pipes*? Who administered them to the posteriors of —— ? But that it may no longer be a doubt with Your Highness who is to be the author of this universal ruin, I beseech you to observe that large and terrible *scythe* which your governor affects to bear continually about him. Be pleased to remark the length and strength, the sharpness and hardness, of his *nails* and *teeth*: consider his baneful, abominable *breath*, enemy to life and matter, infectious and corrupting. And then reflect whether it be possible for any mortal ink and paper of this generation to make a suitable resistance. O! that Your Highness would one day resolve to disarm this usurping *maitre de palais**° of his furious engines, and bring your empire *hors du page.*†

It were endless to recount the several methods of tyranny and destruction which your governor is pleased to practise upon this occasion. His inveterate malice is such to the writings of our age that of several thousands produced yearly from this renowned city, before the next revolution of the sun there is not one to be heard of. Unhappy infants, many of them barbarously destroyed before they have so much as learnt their *mother tongue* to beg for pity. Some he stifles in their cradles; others he frights into convulsions, whereof they suddenly die; some he flays alive; others he tears limb from limb. Great numbers are offered to Moloch,° and the rest, tainted by his breath, die of a languishing consumption.

But the concern I have most at heart, is for our corporation of *poets*, from whom I am preparing a petition to Your Highness, to be subscribed with the names of one hundred thirty six of the first rate, but whose immortal productions are never likely to reach your eyes, though each of

* Comptroller.   † Out of guardianship.

them is now an humble and an earnest appellant for the laurel,° and has large comely volumes ready to show for a support to his pretensions. The *never-dying* works of these illustrious persons, your governor, sir, has devoted to unavoidable death, and Your Highness is to be made believe that our age has never arrived at the honour to produce one single poet.

We confess *Immortality* to be a great and powerful goddess, but in vain we offer up to her our devotions and our sacrifices if Your Highness's governor, who has usurped the *priesthood*, must by an unparalleled ambition and avarice, wholly intercept and devour them.

To affirm that our age is altogether unlearned, and devoid of writers in any kind, seems to be an assertion so bold and so false that I have been some time thinking the contrary may almost be proved by uncontrollable demonstration. 'Tis true indeed, that although their numbers be vast, and their productions numerous in proportion, yet are they hurried so hastily off the scene, that they escape our memory, and delude our sight. When I first thought of this address, I had prepared a copious list of *titles* to present Your Highness as an undisputed argument for what I affirm. The originals were posted fresh upon all gates and corners of streets° but, returning in a very few hours to take a review, they were all torn down, and fresh ones in their places. I inquired after them among readers and booksellers, but I inquired in vain; the *memorial of them was lost among men, their place was no more to be found*;° and I was laughed to scorn for a clown and a pedant, without all taste and refinement, little versed in the course of present affairs, and that knew nothing of what had passed in the best companies of court and town. So that I can only avow in general to Your Highness, that we *do* abound in learning and wit; but to fix upon particulars, is a task too slippery for my slender abilities. If I should venture in a windy day to affirm to Your Highness that there is a large cloud near the *horizon* in the form of a *bear*, another in the *zenith* with the head of an *ass*, a third to the westward with claws like a *dragon*, and Your Highness should in a few minutes think fit to examine the truth, 'tis certain they would all be changed in figure and position: new ones would arise, and all we could agree upon would be that clouds there were, but that I was grossly mistaken in the *zoography* and *topography* of them.°

But your governor perhaps may still insist, and put the question, What is then become of those immense bales of paper which must needs have been employed in such numbers of books? Can these also be wholly annihilate, and so of a sudden as I pretend? What shall I say in return of so invidious an objection? It ill befits the distance between Your Highness and me to send you for ocular conviction to a *jakes*, or an *oven*, to the windows of a *bawdy-house*, or to a sordid *lantern*. Books, like men their authors, have no more than one way of coming into the world, but there are ten thousand to go out of it and return no more.

I profess to Your Highness, in the integrity of my heart, that what I am going to say is literally true this minute I am writing. What revolutions may happen before it shall be ready for your perusal, I can by no means warrant. However, I beg you to accept it as a specimen of our learning, our politeness, and our wit. I do therefore affirm, upon the word of a sincere man, that there is now actually in being a certain poet called John Dryden, whose translation of Virgil° was lately printed in a large folio, well bound, and if diligent search were made, for aught I know is yet to be seen. There is another called Nahum Tate, who is ready to make oath that he has caused many reams of verse to be published, whereof both himself and his bookseller (if lawfully required) can still produce authentic copies, and therefore wonders why the world is pleased to make such a secret of it. There is a third, known by the name of Tom Durfey, a poet of a vast comprehension, an universal genius, and most profound learning. There are also one Mr. Rymer, and one Mr. Dennis, most profound critics. There is a person styled Dr. B[en]tl[e]y, who has written near a thousand pages of immense erudition, *giving a full and true account* of a certain *squabble*, of wonderful importance, between himself and a bookseller. He is a writer of infinite wit and humour; no man rallies with a better grace, and in more sprightly turns. Further, I avow to Your Highness that with these eyes I have beheld the person of William W[o]tt[o]n,° B.D., who has written a good sizeable volume against a *friend of your governor*° (from whom, alas! he must therefore look for little favour) in a most gentlemanly style, adorned with utmost politeness and civility, replete with discoveries equally valuable for their novelty and use, and embellished with *traits* of wit so poignant and so apposite, that he is a worthy yokemate to his forementioned *friend*.

Why should I go upon further particulars which might fill a volume with the just elogies of my cotemporary brethren? I shall bequeath this piece of justice to a larger work, wherein I intend to write a character of the present set of *wits* in our nation. Their persons I shall describe particularly and at length, their genius and understandings in *miniature*.

In the meantime I do here make bold to present Your Highness with a faithful abstract, drawn from the universal body of all arts and sciences, intended wholly for your service and instruction. Nor do I doubt in the least but Your Highness will peruse it as carefully, and make as considerable improvements, as *other* young *princes* have already done by the many volumes of late years written for a help to their studies.

That Your Highness may advance in wisdom and virtue, as well as years, and at last outshine all your royal ancestors, shall be the daily prayer of,

SIR,

Your Highness's

Most devoted, &c.

Decemb. 1697.

THE PREFACE.

THE wits of the present age being so very numerous and penetrating, it seems the grandees of Church and State begin to fall under horrible apprehensions lest these gentlemen, during the intervals of a long peace, should find leisure to pick holes in the weak sides of Religion and Government. To prevent which there has been much thought employed of late upon certain projects for taking off the force and edge of those formidable enquirers from canvassing and reasoning upon such delicate points. They have at length fixed upon one which will require some time as well as cost to perfect. Meanwhile, the danger hourly increasing by new levies of wits, all appointed (as there is reason to fear) with pen, ink, and paper, which may at an hour's warning be drawn out into pamphlets and other offensive weapons ready for immediate execution, it was judged of absolute necessity that some present expedient be thought on, till the main design can be brought to maturity. To this end, at a Grand Committee° some days ago, this important discovery was made by a certain curious and refined observer: that seamen have a custom when they meet a *whale*, to fling him out an empty *tub* by way of amusement, to divert him from laying violent hands upon the ship. This parable was immediately mythologised; the whale was interpreted to be Hobbes's *Leviathan*,° which tosses and plays with all schemes of Religion and Government, whereof a great many are hollow, and dry, and empty, and noisy, and wooden, and given to rotation.° This is the *Leviathan* whence the terrible wits of our age are said to borrow their weapons. The *ship* in danger is easily understood to be its old antitype, the Commonwealth.° But how to analyze the tub was a matter of difficulty; when, after long enquiry and debate, the literal meaning was preserved, and it was decreed that in order to prevent these *Leviathans* from tossing and sporting with the Commonwealth (which of itself is too apt to *fluctuate*) they should be diverted from that game by *a Tale of a Tub*. And my genius being conceived to lie not unhappily that way, I had the honour done me to be engaged in the performance.

This is the sole design in publishing the following treatise, which I hope will serve for an *interim* of some months to employ those unquiet spirits till the perfecting of that great work; into the secret of which it is reasonable the courteous reader should have some little light.

It is intended that a large Academy be erected, capable of containing nine thousand seven hundred forty and three persons, which by modest computation is reckoned to be pretty near the current number of *wits* in this island. These are to be disposed into the several schools of this academy, and there pursue those studies to which their genius most inclines them. The undertaker himself will publish his proposals with all convenient speed, to which I shall refer the curious reader for a more particular account, mentioning at present only a few of the principal schools. There is first a large *Pederastic* School, with French and Italian masters. There is also the *Spelling* School,° *a very spacious building*: the School of *Looking-glasses*: the School of *Swearing*: the School of *Critics*: the School of *Salivation*: the School of *Hobby-horses*: the School of *Poetry*: the School of *Tops*:* the School of *Spleen*: the School of *Gaming*: with many others too tedious to recount. No person to be admitted member into any of these schools without an attestation under two sufficient persons' hands, certifying him to be a *wit*.

But, to return. I am sufficiently instructed in the principal duty of a preface, if my genius were capable of arriving at it. Thrice have I forced my imagination to make the *tour* of my invention, and thrice it has returned empty, the latter having been wholly drained by the following treatise. Not so, my more successful brethren the *moderns*, who will by no means let slip a preface or dedication without some notable distin-guishing stroke to surprise the reader at the entry, and kindle a wonderful expectation of what is to ensue. Such was that of a most ingenious poet who, soliciting his brain for something new, compared himself to the *hangman*, and his patron to the *patient*. This was *insigne, recens, indictum ore alio.*†° When I went through that necessary and noble course of study‡ I had the happiness to observe many such egregious touches, which I shall not injure the authors by transplanting; because I have remarked that nothing is so very tender as a *modern* piece of wit, and

---

* This I think the author should have omitted, it being of the very same nature with the *School of Hobby-horses*, if one may venture to censure one who is so severe a censurer of others, perhaps with too little distinction.

† Horace. Something extraordinary, new and never hit upon before.

‡ Reading Prefaces, &c.

which is apt to suffer so much in the carriage. Some things are extremely witty *today*, or *fasting*, or *in this place*, or *at eight o'clock*, or *over a bottle*, or *spoke by* Mr. What d'y'call'm, or *in a summer's morning*: any of the which, by the smallest transposal or misapplication, is utterly annihilate. Thus, *wit* has its walks and purlieus, out of which it may not stray the breadth of a hair, upon peril of being lost. The *moderns* have artfully fixed this *mercury*,° and reduced it to the circumstances of time, place, and person. Such a jest there is that will not pass out of Covent Garden, and such a one that is nowhere intelligible but at Hyde Park corner. Now, though it sometimes tenderly affects me to consider that all the towardly passages I shall deliver in the following treatise will grow quite out of date and relish with the first shifting of the present scene, yet I must need subscribe to the justice of this proceeding; because I cannot imagine why we should be at expense to furnish wit for succeeding ages, when the former have made no sort of provision for ours; wherein I speak the sentiment of the very newest, and consequently the most orthodox refiners,° as well as my own. However, being extremely solicitous that every accomplished person who has got into the taste of wit calculated for this present month of August 1697, should descend to the very *bottom* of all the *sublime* throughout this treatise, I hold fit to lay down this general maxim. Whatever reader desires to have a thorough comprehension of an author's thoughts cannot take a better method than by putting himself into the circumstances and posture of life that the writer was in upon every important passage as it flowed from his pen. For this will introduce a parity and strict correspondence of ideas between the reader and the author. Now, to assist the diligent reader in so delicate an affair as far as brevity will permit, I have recollected that the shrewdest pieces of this treatise were conceived in bed in a garret; at other times (for a reason best known to myself) I thought fit to sharpen my invention with hunger; and in general the whole work was begun, continued, and ended, under a long course of physic, and a great want of money. Now, I do affirm it will be absolutely impossible for the candid peruser to go along with me in a great many bright passages unless, upon the several difficulties emergent, he will please to capacitate and prepare himself by these directions. And this I lay down as my principal *postulatum*.

Because I have professed to be a most devoted servant of all *modern* forms, I apprehend some curious *wit* may object against me for proceeding thus far in a preface, without declaiming according to the custom against the multitude of writers, whereof the whole multitude of writers most reasonably complains. I am just come from perusing some hundreds of prefaces, wherein the authors do at the very beginning address the gentle reader concerning this enormous grievance. Of these I have preserved a few examples and shall set them down as near as my memory has been able to retain them.

One begins thus:

For a man to set up for a writer, when the press swarms with, &c.

Another:

The tax upon paper° does not lessen the number of scribblers, who daily pester, &c.

Another:

When every little would-be wit takes pen in hand, 'tis in vain to enter the lists, &c.

Another:

To observe what trash the press swarms with, &c.

Another:

Sir, It is merely in obedience to your commands that I venture into the public; for who upon a less consideration would be of a party with such a rabble of scribblers, &c.

Now, I have two words in my own defence against this objection. First, I am far from granting the number of writers a nuisance to our nation, having strenuously maintained the contrary in several parts of the following Discourse. Secondly, I do not well understand the justice of this proceeding, because I observe many of these polite prefaces to be not only from the same hand, but from those who are most voluminous in their several productions. Upon which, I shall tell the reader a short tale.

A mountebank in Leicester-Fields° *had drawn a huge assembly about him. Among the rest, a fat unwieldy fellow, half stifled in the press, would be every fit crying out, Lord! what a filthy crowd is here! Pray, good people, give way a little. Bless me! what a devil has raked this rabble together! Z—ds, what squeezing is this! Honest friend, remove your elbow. At last a weaver that stood next him could hold no longer. A plague confound you* (said he) *for an overgrown sloven; and who* (in the devil's name) *I wonder, helps to make up the crowd half so much as yourself? Don't you consider* (with a pox) *that you take up more room with that carcase than any five here? Is not the place as free for us as for you? Bring your own guts to a reasonable compass* (and be d—n'd) *and then I'll engage we shall have room enough for us all.*

There are certain common privileges of a writer, the benefit whereof I hope there will be no reason to doubt; particularly, that where I am not understood it shall be concluded that something very useful and profound is couched underneath; and again, that whatever word or sentence is printed in a different character shall be judged to contain something extraordinary either of *wit* or *sublime*.

As for the liberty I have thought fit to take of praising myself upon some occasions or none, I am sure it will need no excuse if a multitude of great examples be allowed sufficient authority. For it is here to be noted that *praise* was originally a pension paid by the world; but the *moderns*, finding the trouble and charge too great in collecting it, have lately bought out the *fee-simple*, since which time the right of presentation is wholly in ourselves. For this reason it is that when an author makes his own elogy, he uses a certain form to declare and insist upon his title which is commonly in these or the like words, 'I speak without vanity'; which I think plainly shows it to be a matter of right and justice. Now, I do here once for all declare that in every encounter of this nature through the following treatise, the form aforesaid is implied; which I mention to save the trouble of repeating it on so many occasions.

'Tis a great ease to my conscience that I have written so elaborate and useful a discourse without one grain of satire intermixed; which is the sole point wherein I have taken leave to dissent from the famous originals of our age and country. I have observed some satirists to use the public much at the rate that pedants do a naughty boy ready horsed for discipline: first expostulate the case, then plead the necessity of the rod from great provocations, and conclude every period with a lash. Now if I know anything of mankind, these gentlemen might very well spare their reproof and correction, for there is not through all nature another so callous and insensible a member as the *world's posteriors*, whether you apply to it the *toe* or the *birch*. Besides, most of our late satirists seem to lie under a sort of mistake, that because *nettles* have the prerogative to sting, therefore all *other weeds* must do so too. I make not this comparison out of the least design to detract from these worthy writers; for it is well known among *mythologists* that *weeds* have the pre-eminence over all other vegetables; and therefore the first *monarch* of this island, whose taste and judgment were so acute and refined, did very wisely root out the *roses* from the collar of the *Order*, and plant the *thistles* in their stead,° as the nobler flower of the two. For which reason it is conjectured by profounder antiquaries that the satirical itch, so prevalent in this part of our island, was first brought among us from beyond the Tweed. Here may it long flourish and abound. May it survive and neglect the scorn of the world with as much ease and contempt as the world is insensible to the lashes of it. May their own dulness, or that of their party, be no discouragement for the authors to proceed, but let them remember it is with *wits* as with *razors*, which are never so apt to *cut* those they are employed on as when they have *lost their edge*. Besides, those whose teeth are too rotten to bite, are best of all others, qualified to revenge that defect with their breath.

I am not like other men to envy or undervalue the talents I cannot reach; for which reason I must needs bear a true honour to this large eminent sect of our British writers. And I hope this little panegyric will not be offensive to their ears since it has the advantage of being only designed for themselves. Indeed, nature herself has taken order that fame and honour should be purchased at a better pennyworth by satire than by any other productions of the brain, the world being soonest provoked to *praise* by *lashes*, as men are to *love*. There is a problem in an ancient author, why Dedications and other bundles of flattery run all upon stale musty topics, without the smallest tincture of anything new; not only to the torment and nauseating of the Christian reader, but (if not suddenly prevented) to the universal spreading of that pestilent disease the lethargy, in this island: whereas there is very little satire which has not something in it untouched before. The defects of the former are usually imputed to the want of invention among those who are dealers in that kind, but I think with a great deal of injustice, the solution being easy and natural; for the materials of panegyric, being very few in number, have been long since exhausted. For, as health is but one thing and has been always the same, whereas diseases are by thousands, besides new and daily additions; so, all the virtues that have been ever in mankind are to be counted upon a few fingers; but his follies and vices are innumerable and time adds hourly to the heap. Now the utmost a poor poet can do is to get by heart a list of the cardinal virtues, and deal them with his utmost liberality to his hero or his patron: he may ring the changes as far as it will go, and vary his phrase till he has talked round, but the reader quickly finds it is all *pork** with a little variety of sauce. For there is no inventing terms of art beyond our ideas, and when our ideas are exhausted, terms of art must be so too.

But though the matter for panegyric were as fruitful as the topics of satire, yet would it not be hard to find out a sufficient reason why the latter will be always better received than the first. For, this being bestowed only upon one or a few persons at a time, is sure to raise envy, and consequently ill words from the rest who have no share in the blessing. But satire being levelled at all is never resented for an offence by any, since every individual person makes bold to understand it of others, and very wisely removes his particular part of the burden upon the shoulders of the world, which are broad enough and able to bear it. To this purpose I have sometimes reflected upon the difference between

* Plutarch.°

Athens and England, with respect to the point before us. In the Attic commonwealth* it was the privilege and birthright of every citizen and poet to rail aloud and in public, or to expose upon the stage by name, any person they pleased, though of the greatest figure, whether a C[l]eon, an Hyperbolus,° an Alcibiades, or a Demosthenes. But on the other side, the least reflecting word let fall against the *people* in general was immediately caught up and revenged upon the authors, however considerable for their quality or their merits. Whereas in England, it is just the reverse of all this. Here you may securely display your utmost *rhetoric* against mankind, in the face of the world; tell them, 'That all are gone astray, that there is none that doth good, no not one;° that we live in the very dregs of time; that knavery and atheism are epidemic as the pox; that honesty is fled with Astræa';° with any other commonplaces, *equally* new and eloquent, which are furnished by the *splendida bilis*.†° And when you have done, the whole audience, far from being offended, shall return you thanks as a deliverer of precious and useful truths. Nay, further, it is but to venture your lungs, and you may preach in Covent Garden° against foppery and fornication, and *something else*: against pride, and dissimulation, and bribery, at White-Hall:° you may expose rapine and injustice in the Inns of Court Chapel: and in a city° pulpit be as fierce as you please against avarice, hypocrisy, and extortion. 'Tis but a *ball* bandied to and fro, and every man carries a *racket* about him to strike it from himself among the rest of the company. But on the other side, whoever should mistake the nature of things so far as to drop but a single hint in public, how *such a one* starved half the fleet and half poisoned the rest: how *such a one*, from a true principle of *love* and *honour*, pays no debts but for *wenches* and *play*: how *such a one* has got a clap, and runs out of his estate: how Paris bribed by Juno and Venus,‡ loth to offend either party, slept out the whole cause on the bench: or, how *such an orator* makes long speeches in the senate, with much thought, little sense, and to no purpose; whoever, I say, should venture to be thus particular must expect to be imprisoned for *scandalum magnatum*, to have *challenges* sent him, to be sued for *defamation*, and to be *brought before the bar of the house*.

But I forget that I am expatiating on a subject wherein I have no concern, having neither a talent nor an inclination for satire. On the other side I am so entirely satisfied with the whole present procedure of human

---

* *Vide* Xenophon.°

† Spleen. *Hor.*

‡ Juno and Venus are money and a mistress, very powerful bribes to a judge, if scandal says true. I remember such reflections were cast about that time, but I cannot fix the person intended here.

things that I have been for some years preparing materials towards *A Panegyric upon the World*, to which I intended to add a second part entitled *A Modest Defence of the Proceedings of the Rabble in all Ages*.° Both these I had thoughts to publish by way of appendix to the following treatise; but finding my commonplace book fill much slower than I had reason to expect, I have chosen to defer them to another occasion. Besides, I have been unhappily prevented in that design by a certain domestic misfortune, in the particulars whereof, though it would be very seasonable and much in the *modern* way to inform the *gentle reader*, and would also be of great assistance towards extending this preface into the size now in vogue, which by rule ought to be *large* in proportion as the subsequent volume is *small*; yet I shall now dismiss our impatient reader from any further attendance at the *porch*, and having duly prepared his mind by a preliminary discourse, shall gladly introduce him to the sublime mysteries that ensue.

A TALE OF A TUB, &c.

SECT. I.

The Introduction.

WHOEVER hath an ambition to be heard in a crowd must press, and squeeze, and thrust, and climb, with indefatigable pains, till he has exalted himself to a certain degree of altitude above them. Now, in all assemblies though you wedge them ever so close, we may observe this peculiar property that over their heads there is room enough, but how to reach it is the difficult point, it being as hard to get quit of *number* as of *hell*;

> *—— *Evadere ad auras,*
> *Hoc opus, hic labor est.*°

To this end, the philosopher's way in all ages has been by erecting certain *edifices in the air*.° But whatever practice and reputation these kind of structures have formerly possessed, or may still continue in, not excepting even that of Socrates when he was suspended in a basket° to help contemplation, I think with due submission they seem to labour under two inconveniences. First, that the foundations being laid too

---

* But to return, and view the cheerful skies;
  In this the task and mighty labour lies.

high, they have been often out of *sight*, and ever out of *hearing*. Secondly, that the materials being very transitory have suffered much from inclemencies of air, especially in these north-west regions.

Therefore, towards the just performance of this great work there remain but three methods that I can think on; whereof the wisdom of our ancestors being highly sensible, has, to encourage all aspiring adventurers, thought fit to erect three wooden machines for the use of those orators who desire to talk much without interruption. These are the *pulpit*, the *ladder*°, and the *stage itinerant*. For, as to the *Bar*, though it be compounded of the same matter and designed for the same use, it cannot however be well allowed the honour of a fourth, by reason of its level or inferior situation exposing it to perpetual interruption from collaterals. Neither can the *Bench* itself, though raised to a proper eminency, put in a better claim whatever its advocates insist on. For, if they please to look into the original design of its erection and the circumstances or adjuncts subservient to that design, they will soon acknowledge the present practice exactly correspondent to the primitive institution, and both to answer the etymology of the name, which in the Phœnician tongue is a word of great signification, importing if literally interpreted, *the place of sleep*; but in common acceptation, *a seat well bolstered and cushioned for the repose of old and gouty limbs: senes ut in otia tuta recedant.*° Fortune being indebted to them this part of retaliation that, as formerly they have long *talked* whilst others *slept*, so now they may *sleep* as long, whilst others *talk*.

But if no other argument could occur to exclude the Bench and the Bar from the list of oratorial machines, it were sufficient that the admission of them would overthrow a number which I was resolved to establish whatever argument it might cost me; in imitation of that prudent method observed by many other philosophers and great clerks, whose chief art in division has been to grow fond of some proper mystical number which their imaginations have rendered sacred, to a degree that they force common reason to find room for it in every part of nature; reducing, including, and adjusting every *genus* and *species* within that compass, by coupling some against their wills, and banishing others at any rate. Now, among all the rest the profound number *THREE* is that which hath most employed my sublimest speculations, nor ever without wonderful delight. There is now in the press (and will be published next Term) a panegyrical essay of mine upon this number, wherein I have by most convincing proofs not only reduced the *senses* and the *elements* under its banner, but brought over several deserters from its two great rivals, *SEVEN* and *NINE*.

Now, the first of these oratorial machines, in place as well as dignity, is the *pulpit*. Of pulpits there are in this island several sorts, but I esteem only that made of timber from the *sylva Caledonia*,° which agrees very well with our climate. If it be upon its decay, 'tis the better both for conveyance of sound and for other reasons to be mentioned by and by. The degree of perfection in shape and size, I take to consist in being extremely narrow with little ornament, and, best of all, without a cover (for by ancient rule it ought to be the only uncovered *vessel* in every assembly where it is rightfully used) by which means, from its near resemblance to a pillory, it will ever have a mighty influence on human ears.°

Of *ladders* I need say nothing. 'Tis observed by foreigners themselves, to the honour of our country, that we excel all nations in our practice and understanding of this machine. The ascending orators do not only oblige their audience in the agreeable delivery, but the whole world in their *early* publication of these speeches° which I look upon as the choicest treasury of our British eloquence, and whereof, I am informed, that worthy citizen and bookseller, Mr. John Dunton, hath made a faithful and a painful collection which he shortly designs to publish in twelve volumes in folio, illustrated with copperplates. A work highly useful and curious, and altogether worthy of such a hand.

The last engine of orators is the *stage itinerant*,* erected with much sagacity *sub Jove pluvio, in triviis et quadriviis*.† It is the great seminary of the two former, and its orators are sometimes preferred to the one and sometimes to the other, in proportion to their deservings, there being a strict and perpetual intercourse between all three.

From this accurate deduction it is manifest that for obtaining attention in public, there is of necessity required a *superior position of place*. But although this point be generally granted, yet the cause is little agreed in; and it seems to me that very few philosophers have fallen into a true, natural solution of this phenomenon. The deepest account, and the most fairly digested of any I have yet met with, is this, that air being a heavy body, and therefore (according to the system of Epicurus‡) continually descending, must needs be more so when loaden and pressed down by words, which are also bodies of much weight and gravity, as it is manifest from those deep *impressions* they make and leave upon us; and therefore

---

* Is the *mountebank's stage*, whose orators the author determines either to the *gallows* or a *conventicle*.

† In the open air, and in streets where the greatest resort is.

‡ Lucret. Lib. 2.

must be delivered from a due altitude, or else they will neither carry a good aim nor fall down with a sufficient force.

> Corpoream quoque enim vocem constare fatendum est,
> Et sonitum, quoniam possunt impellere sensus.*
>
> LUCR. Lib. 4.

And I am the readier to favour this conjecture, from a common observation that in the several assemblies of these orators, nature itself has instructed the hearers to stand with their mouths open and erected parallel to the horizon, so as they may be intersected by a perpendicular line from the zenith to the centre of the earth. In which position, if the audience be well compact, every one carries home a share and little or nothing is lost.

I confess there is something yet more refined in the contrivance and structure of our modern theatres. For, first, the pit is sunk below the stage, with due regard to the institution above deduced; that whatever *weighty* matter shall be delivered thence (whether it be *lead* or *gold*) may fall plumb into the jaws of certain *critics* (as I think they are called) which stand ready open to devour them. Then the boxes are built round and raised to a level with the scene, in deference to the ladies, because that large portion of wit laid out in raising pruriences and protuberancies, is observed to run much upon a line and ever in a circle. The whining passions and little starved conceits are gently wafted up by their own extreme levity to the middle region, and there fix and are frozen by the frigid understandings of the inhabitants. Bombast and buffoonery, by nature lofty and light, soar highest of all and would be lost in the roof, if the prudent architect had not with much foresight contrived for them a fourth place called *the twelve-penny gallery*, and there planted a suitable colony who greedily intercept them in their passage.

Now this physico-logical scheme of oratorial receptacles or machines contains a great mystery, being a type, a sign, an emblem, a shadow, a symbol, bearing analogy to the spacious commonwealth of writers, and to those methods by which they must exalt themselves to a certain eminency above the inferior world. By the *pulpit* are adumbrated the writings of our *modern saints*° in Great Britain, as they have spiritualized and refined them from the dross and grossness of *sense* and *human reason*. The matter, as we have said, is of rotten wood, and that upon two considerations; because it is the quality of rotten wood to give *light* in the dark, and secondly, because its cavities are full of worms; which is a type

---

* 'Tis certain then, that *voice* that thus can wound,
   Is all *material*; *body* every *sound*.

with a pair of handles,* having a respect to the two principal qualifications of the orator and the two different fates attending upon his work.

The *ladder* is an adequate symbol of *faction* and of *poetry*, to both of
which so noble a number of authors are indebted for their fame. Of
faction because†   *   *   *   *   *   *

*   *   *   *   *   *   *   *

Hiatus in MS.   *   *   *   *   *   *

*   *   *   *   *   Of *poetry*, because its
orators do *perorare* with a song° and because climbing up by slow degrees,
fate is sure to turn them off before they can reach within many steps of
the top, and because it is a preferment attained by transferring of
propriety, and a confounding of *meum* and *tuum*.

Under the *stage itinerant* are couched those productions designed for
the pleasure and delight of mortal man, such as Sixpenny-worth of Wit,
Westminster Drolleries, Delightful Tales, Compleat Jesters, and the
like, by which the writers of and for *GRUB-STREET*° have in these latter
ages so nobly triumphed over Time; have clipped his wings, pared his
nails, filed his teeth, turned back his hour-glass, blunted his scythe, and
drawn the hobnails out of his shoes. It is under this classis I have
presumed to list my present treatise, being just come from having the
honour conferred upon me to be adopted a member of that illustrious
fraternity.

Now, I am not unaware how the productions of the Grub Street
brotherhood have of late years fallen under many prejudices, nor how it
has been the perpetual employment of two *junior* start-up societies to
ridicule them and their authors as unworthy their established post in the
commonwealth of wit and learning. Their own consciences will easily
inform them whom I mean, nor has the world been so negligent a
looker-on, as not to observe the continual efforts made by the societies of
Gresham° and of *Will*'s‡ to edify a name and reputation upon the ruin of
OURS. And this is yet a more feeling grief to us upon the regards of

---

* The two principal qualifications of a fanatic preacher are his inward light, and his
head full of maggots; and the two different fates of his writings are to be burnt, or
worm-eaten.

† Here is pretended a defect in the manuscript; and this is very frequent with our
author either when he thinks he cannot say anything worth reading, or when he has no
mind to enter on the subject, or when it is a matter of little moment; or perhaps to
amuse his reader (whereof he is frequently very fond) or lastly, with some satirical
intention.

‡ *Will*'s Coffee-House, was formerly the place where the poets usually met, which
though it be yet fresh in memory, yet in some years may be forgot, and want this
explanation.

tenderness as well as of justice, when we reflect on their proceedings not only as unjust, but as ungrateful, undutiful, and unnatural. For how can it be forgot by the world or themselves (to say nothing of our own records, which are full and clear in the point) that they both are seminaries not only of our *planting*, but our *watering* too? I am informed our two *rivals* have lately made an offer to enter into the lists with united forces, and challenge us to a comparison of books both as to *weight* and *number*. In return to which (with licence from our president) I humbly offer two answers. First, we say the proposal is like that which Archimedes made upon a *smaller* affair,* including an impossibility in the practice, for, where can they find scales of *capacity* enough for the first, or an arithmetician of *capacity* enough for the second? Secondly, we are ready to accept the challenge, but with this condition, that a third indifferent person be assigned, to whose impartial judgment it should be left to decide which society each book, treatise, or pamphlet, do most properly belong to. This point, God knows, is very far from being fixed at present, for we are ready to produce a catalogue of some thousands which in all common justice ought to be entitled to our fraternity, but by the revolted and newfangled writers most perfidiously ascribed to the others. Upon all which we think it very unbecoming our prudence that the determination should be remitted to the authors themselves, when our adversaries, by briguing and caballing, have caused so universal a defection from us that the greatest part of our society hath already deserted to them, and our nearest friends begin to stand aloof as if they were half ashamed to own us.

This is the utmost I am authorized to say upon so ungrateful and melancholy a subject, because we are extreme unwilling to inflame a controversy whose continuance may be so fatal to the interests of us all, desiring much rather that things be amicably composed. And we shall so far advance on our side as to be ready to receive the two *prodigals* with open arms, whenever they shall think fit to return from their *husks* and their *harlots*° (which, I think from the present course of their studies,† they most properly may be said to be engaged in) and, like an indulgent parent, continue to them our affection and our blessing.

But the greatest maim given to that general reception which the writings of our society have formerly received (next to the transitory state of all sublunary things) hath been a superficial vein among many readers of the present age, who will by no means be persuaded to inspect beyond the surface and the rind of things. Whereas, *Wisdom* is a *fox* who after

---

* *Viz.* About moving the earth.

† Virtuoso experiments, and modern comedies.

long hunting will at last cost you the pains to dig out. 'Tis a *cheese* which, by how much the richer, has the thicker, the homelier, and the coarser coat, and whereof, to a judicious palate, the *maggots* are the best. 'Tis a *sack-posset*, wherein the deeper you go you will find it the sweeter. *Wisdom* is a *hen* whose *cackling* we must value and consider because it is attended with an *egg*. But then lastly 'tis a *nut*, which unless you choose with judgment may cost you a tooth, and pay you with nothing but a *worm*. In consequence of these momentous truths, the Grubæan Sages have always chosen to convey their precepts and their arts shut up within the vehicles of types and fables; which having been perhaps more careful and curious in adorning than was altogether necessary, it has fared with these vehicles after the usual fate of coaches over-finely painted and gilt, that the transitory gazers have so dazzled their eyes and filled their imaginations with the outward lustre, as neither to regard nor consider the person or the parts of the owner within. A misfortune we undergo with somewhat less reluctancy because it has been common to us with Pythagoras, Æsop, Socrates,° and other of our predecessors.

However, that neither the world nor ourselves may any longer suffer by such misunderstandings, I have been prevailed on, after much importunity from my friends, to travail in a complete and laborious dissertation upon the prime productions of our society, which besides their beautiful externals for the gratification of superficial readers, have darkly and deeply couched under them the most finished and refined systems of all sciences and arts; as I do not doubt to lay open by untwisting or unwinding, and either to draw up by exantlation or display by incision.

This great work was entered upon some years ago by one of our most eminent members. He began with the History of Reynard the Fox*° but neither lived to publish his essay nor to proceed further in so useful an attempt; which is very much to be lamented because the discovery he made and communicated with his friends is now universally received; nor do I think any of the learned will dispute that famous treatise to be a complete body of civil knowledge and the *revelation*, or rather the *apocalypse*, of all State *Arcana*. But the progress I have made is much greater, having already finished my annotations upon several dozens, from some of which I shall impart a few hints to the candid reader, as far as will be necessary to the conclusion at which I aim.

The first piece I have handled is that of Tom Thumb,° whose author

* The Author seems here to be mistaken, for I have seen a Latin edition of *Reynard the Fox*, above a hundred years old, which I take to be the original; for the rest, it has been thought by many people to contain some satyrical design in it.

was a Pythagorean philosopher. This dark treatise contains the whole scheme of the Metempsychosis, deducing the progress of the soul through all her stages.

The next is Dr. Faustus, penned by Artephius, an author *bonæ notæ* and an *adeptus*. He published it in the *nine-hundred-eighty-fourth year of his age; this writer proceeds wholly by *reincrudation*, or in the *via humida*; and the marriage between Faustus and Helen does most conspicuously dilucidate the fermenting of the *male* and *female dragon*.

Whittington and his Cat is the work of that mysterious rabbi Jehuda Hannasi, containing a defence of the Gemara of the Jerusalem Mishna and its just preference to that of Babylon, contrary to the vulgar opinion.

The Hind and Panther. This is the masterpiece of a famous writer now living,† intended for a complete abstract of sixteen thousand schoolmen from Scotus to Bellarmin.

Tommy Potts. Another piece supposed by the same hand, by way of supplement to the former.

The Wise Men of Gotham, *cum appendice*. This is a treatise of immense erudition, being the great original and fountain of those arguments bandied about both in France and England, for a just defence of the modern learning and wit, against the presumption, the pride, and ignorance of the ancients. This unknown author hath so exhausted the subject that a penetrating reader will easily discover whatever hath been written since upon that dispute, to be little more than repetition. An abstract of this treatise hath been lately published by a *worthy member* of our society.‡

These notices may serve to give the learned reader an idea as well as a taste of what the whole work is likely to produce; wherein I have now altogether circumscribed my thoughts and my studies, and if I can bring it to a perfection before I die, shall reckon I have well employed the poor remains of an unfortunate life.§ This, indeed, is more than I can justly expect from a quill worn to the pith in the service of the State, in *pros* and *cons* upon *Popish plots*, and *meal-tubs*,||° and *exclusion bills*, and *passive obedience*, and *addresses of lives and fortunes*, and *prerogative*, and *property*,

* He lived a thousand.

† Viz. In the year 1698.

‡ This is I suppose to be understood of Mr. W[o]tt[o]n's Discourse of Ancient and Modern Learning.

§ Here the author seems to personate L'Estrange, Dryden, and some others, who, having passed their lives in vice, faction, and falsehood, have the impudence to talk of merit and innocence and sufferings.

|| In King Charles the Second's time, there was an account of a Presbyterian plot, found in a meal-tub, which then made much noise.

and *liberty of conscience*, and *Letters to a Friend*: from an understanding and
a conscience threadbare and ragged with perpetual turning; from a head
broken in a hundred places by the malignants of the opposite factions;
and from a body spent with poxes ill cured by trusting to bawds and
surgeons who (as it afterwards appeared) were professed enemies to me
and the government, and revenged their party's quarrel upon my nose
and shins. Fourscore and eleven pamphlets have I writ under three
reigns, and for the service of six and thirty factions. But finding the state
has no further occasion for me and my ink, I retire willingly to draw it out
into speculations more becoming a philospher, having, to my un-
speakable comfort, passed a long life with a conscience void of offence°
[towards God and towards Men].

But to return. I am assured from the reader's candour that the brief
specimen I have given will easily clear all the rest of our society's
productions from an aspersion grown, as it is manifest, out of envy and
ignorance: that they are of little farther use or value to mankind beyond
the common entertainments of their wit and their style. For these I am
sure have never yet been disputed by our keenest adversaries, in both
which, as well as the more profound and mystical part, I have throughout
this treatise closely followed the most applauded originals. And to render
all complete I have, with much thought and application of mind, so
ordered that the chief title prefixed to it (I mean, that under which I
design it shall pass in the common conversations of court and town) is
modelled exactly after the manner peculiar to *our* society.

I confess to have been somewhat liberal in the business of titles,*
having observed the humour of multiplying them to bear great vogue
among certain writers whom I exceedingly reverence. And indeed it
seems not unreasonable, that books, the children of the brain, should
have the honour to be christened with variety of names as well as other
infants of quality. Our famous Dryden has ventured to proceed a point
farther, endeavouring to introduce also a multiplicity of *godfathers*†°
which is an improvement of much more advantage, upon a very obvious
account. 'Tis a pity this admirable invention has not been better
cultivated so as to grow by this time into general imitation, when such an
authority serves it for a precedent. Nor have my endeavours been
wanting to second so useful an example. But it seems there is an unhappy
expense usually annexed to the calling of a godfather which was clearly
out of my head, as it is very reasonable to believe. Where the pinch lay, I

---

* The title-page in the original was so torn, that it was not possible to recover several
titles which the author here speaks of.

† See Virgil translated, &c.

cannot certainly affirm; but having employed a world of thoughts and pains to split my treatise into forty sections, and having entreated forty lords of my acquaintance that they would do me the honour to stand, they all made it a matter of conscience and sent me their excuses.

SECT. II.

Once upon a time, there was a man who had three sons by one wife,* and all at a birth, neither could the midwife tell certainly which was the eldest. Their father died while they were young, and upon his deathbed, calling the lads to him, spoke thus:

'Sons, because I have purchased no estate, nor was born to any, I have long considered of some good legacies to bequeath you; and at last, with much care as well as expense, have provided each of you (here they are) a new coat.† Now, you are to understand that these coats have two virtues contained in them: one is, that with good wearing they will last you fresh and sound as long as you live: the other is that they will grow in the same proportion with your bodies, lengthening and widening of themselves so as to be always fit. Here; let me see them on you before I die. So; very well; pray, children, wear them clean and brush them often. You will find in my will‡ (here it is) full instructions in every particular concerning the wearing and management of your coats, wherein you must be very exact to avoid the penalties I have appointed for every transgression or neglect, upon which your future fortunes will entirely depend. I have also commanded in my will that you should live together in one house like brethren and friends, for then you will be sure to thrive and not otherwise.'

Here the story says this good father died, and the three sons went all together to seek their fortunes.

I shall not trouble you with recounting what adventures they met for the first seven years,° any further than by taking notice that they carefully observed their father's will, and kept their coats in very good order, that

---

* By these three sons, Peter, Martin, and Jack; Popery, the Church of England, and our Protestant dissenters, are designed. W. Wotton.

† By his *coats* which he gave his sons, the Garments of the Israelites.° W. Wotton. An error (with submission) of the learned commentator; for by the coats are meant the Doctrine and Faith of Christianity, by the Wisdom of the divine Founder fitted to all times, places, and circumstances. Lambin.°

‡ The New Testament.

they travelled through several countries, encountered a reasonable quantity of giants, and slew certain dragons.

Being now arrived at the proper age for producing themselves, they came up to town and fell in love with the ladies, but especially three who about that time were in chief reputation, the Duchess d'Argent, Madame de Grands Titres, and the Countess d'Orgueil.* On their first appearance our three adventurers met with a very bad reception, and soon with great sagacity guessing out the reason, they quickly began to improve in the good qualities of the town: they writ, and rallied, and rhymed, and sung, and said, and said nothing; they drank, and fought, and whored, and slept, and swore, and took snuff; they went to new plays on the first night, haunted the *chocolate*-houses, beat the watch, lay on bulks, and got claps; they bilked hackney-coachmen, ran in debt with shopkeepers, and lay with their wives; they killed bailiffs, kicked fiddlers down stairs, eat at Locket's,° loitered at Will's; they talked of the drawing-room and never came there; dined with lords they never saw; whispered a duchess, and spoke never a word; exposed the scrawls of their laundress for billets-doux of quality; came ever just from court and were never seen in it; attended the Levee *sub dio*; got a list of the peers by heart in one company, and with great familiarity retailed them in another. Above all, they constantly attended those Committees of Senators who are silent in the *House*, and loud in the *Coffee-House*, where they nightly adjourn to chew the cud of politics, and are encompassed with a ring of disciples who lie in wait to catch up their droppings. The three brothers had acquired forty other qualifications of the like stamp too tedious to recount, and by consequence were justly reckoned the most accomplished persons in town. But all would not suffice and the ladies aforesaid continued still inflexible. To clear up which difficulty I must, with the reader's good leave and patience, have recourse to some points of weight which the authors of that age have not sufficiently illustrated.

For about this time it happened a sect arose† whose tenets obtained and spread very far, especially in the *grande monde* and among everybody of good fashion. They worshipped a sort of *idol*‡ who, as their doctrine delivered, did daily create men by a kind of manufactory operation. This idol they placed in the highest parts of the house, on an altar erected

* Their mistresses are the Duchess d'Argent, Mademoiselle de Grands Titres, and the Countess d'Orgueil, *i.e. covetousness, ambition,* and *pride*; which were the three great vices that the ancient fathers inveighed against as the first corruptions of Christianity. W. WOTTON.

† This is an occasional satire upon dress and fashion, in order to introduce what follows.

‡ By this *idol* is meant a tailor.

about three foot. He was shewn in the posture of a Persian emperor, sitting on a *superficies* with his legs interwoven under him. This god had a *goose* for his ensign, whence it is that some learned men pretend to deduce his original from Jupiter Capitolinus.° At his left hand beneath the altar, *Hell*° seemed to open and catch at the animals the idol was creating; to prevent which, certain of his priests hourly flung in pieces of the uninformed mass or substance, and sometimes whole limbs already enlivened, which that horrid gulf insatiably swallowed, terrible to behold. The goose was also held a subaltern divinity or *deus minorum gentium*,° before whose shrine was sacrificed that creature°whose hourly food is human gore, and who is in so great renown abroad for being the delight and favourite of the Ægyptian Cercopithecus.* Millions of these animals were cruelly slaughtered every day to appease the hunger of that consuming deity. The chief idol was also worshipped as the inventor of the *yard* and *needle*, whether as the god of seamen or on account of certain other mystical attributes, hath not been sufficiently cleared.

The worshippers of this deity had also a system of their belief which seemed to turn upon the following fundamentals. They held the universe to be a large *suit of clothes*, which *invests* everything: that the earth is invested by the air; the air is invested by the stars; and the stars are invested by the *primum mobile*.° Look on this globe of earth, you will find it to be a very complete and fashionable *dress*. What is that which some call *land*, but a fine coat faced with green? or the sea, but a waistcoat of water-tabby? Proceed to the particular works of the creation, you will find how curious *Journeyman* Nature hath been, to trim up the *vegetable* beaux; observe how sparkish a periwig adorns the head of a *beech*, and what a fine doublet of white satin is worn by the *birch*. To conclude from all, what is man himself but a *micro-coat*,† or rather a complete suit of clothes with all its trimmings? As to his body, there can be no dispute; but examine even the acquirements of his mind, you will find them all contribute in their order towards furnishing out an exact dress. To instance no more: is not religion a *cloak*, honesty a *pair of shoes* worn out in the dirt, self-love a *surtout*, vanity a *shirt*, and conscience a *pair of breeches* which, though a cover for lewdness as well as nastiness, is easily slipped down for the service of both?

These *postulata* being admitted, it will follow in due course of reasoning that those beings which the world calls improperly *suits of clothes* are in

---

* The Ægyptians worshipped a monkey, which animal is very fond of eating lice, styled here, creatures that feed on human gore.

† Alluding to the word *microcosm*, or a little world, as man hath been called by philosophers.

reality the most refined species of animals; or to proceed higher, that they are rational creatures, or men. For is it not manifest that they live, and move, and talk, and perform all other offices of human life? Are not beauty, and wit, and mien, and breeding, their inseparable proprieties? In short, we see nothing but them, hear nothing but them. Is it not they who walk the streets, fill up *parliament—, coffee—, play—, bawdy-houses*? 'Tis true indeed, that these animals which are vulgarly called *suits of clothes*, or *dresses*, do, according to certain compositions, receive different appellations. If one of them be trimmed up with a gold chain, and a red gown, and a white rod, and a great horse, it is called a *Lord Mayor*; if certain ermines and furs be placed in a certain position we style them a *Judge*; and so an apt conjunction of lawn and black satin we entitle a *Bishop*.

Others of these professors, though agreeing in the main system, were yet more refined upon certain branches of it, and held that man was an animal compounded of two *dresses*, the *natural* and the *celestial suit*, which were the body and the soul; that the soul was the outward, and the body the inward clothing; that the latter was *ex traduce*° but the former of daily creation and circumfusion. This last they proved by scripture, because *in them we live, and move, and have our being*;° as likewise by philosophy because they are *all in all*,° *and all in every part*.° Besides, said they, separate these two, and you will find the body to be only a senseless unsavoury carcase. By all which it is manifest that the outward dress must needs be the soul.

To this system of religion were tagged several subaltern doctrines which were entertained with great vogue; as particularly, the faculties of the mind were deduced by the learned among them in this manner: *embroidery* was *sheer wit*; *gold fringe* was *agreeable conversation*; *gold lace* was *repartee*; a huge long *periwig* was *humour*; and a *coat full of powder* was very good *raillery*; all which required abundance of *finesse* and *delicatesse* to manage with advantage, as well as a strict observance after times and fashions.

I have with much pains and reading collected out of ancient authors this short summary of a body of philosophy and divinity, which seems to have been composed by a vein and race° of thinking very different from any other systems either *ancient* or *modern*. And it was not merely to entertain or satisfy the reader's curiosity but rather to give him light into several circumstances of the following story; that knowing the state of dispositions and opinions in an age so remote, he may better comprehend those great events which were the issue of them. I advise therefore the courteous reader to peruse with a world of application, again and again, whatever I have written upon this matter. And so leaving these broken ends, I carefully gather up the chief thread of my story, and proceed.

These opinions therefore were so universal, as well as the practices of them, among the refined part of court and town, that our three brother-adventurers as their circumstances then stood were strangely at a loss.* For, on the one side, the three ladies they addressed themselves to (whom we have named already) were ever at the very top of the fashion, and abhorred all that were below it but the breadth of a hair. On the other side, their father's will was very precise, and it was the main precept in it with the greatest penalties annexed, not to add to, or diminish from their coats one thread without a positive command in the will. Now the coats† their father had left them were, 'tis true, of very good cloth and, besides, so neatly sewn you would swear they were all of a piece, but at the same time very plain, and with little or no ornament. And it happened that before they were a month in town, great *shoulder-knots*‡° came up. Straight, all the world was *shoulder-knots*; no approaching the ladies' *ruelles*° without the *quota* of shoulder-knots. 'That fellow,' cries one, 'has no soul; where is his shoulder-knot?' Our three brethren soon discovered their want by sad experience, meeting in their walks with forty mortifications and indignities. If they went to the playhouse, the door-keeper showed them into the twelve-penny gallery. If they called a boat, says a waterman, 'I am first sculler'.° If they stepped to the Rose° to take a bottle, the drawer would cry, 'Friend, we sell no ale.' If they went to visit a lady, a footman met them at the door with, 'Pray send up your message.' In this unhappy case they went immediately to consult their father's Will, read it over and over, but not a word of the *shoulder-knot*. What should they do? What temper° should they find? Obedience was absolutely necessary, and yet *shoulder-knots* appeared extremely requisite. After much thought one of the brothers who happened to be

---

* The first part of the Tale is the History of Peter; thereby Popery is exposed: everybody knows the Papists have made great additions to Christianity; that indeed is the great exception which the Church of England makes against them; accordingly Peter begins his pranks with *adding a shoulder-knot to his coat*. W. WOTTON.

† His description of the cloth of which the coat was made, has a farther meaning than the words may seem to import, 'The coats their father had left them were of very good cloth, and besides so neatly sewn, you would swear it had been all of a piece; but, at the same time, very plain with little or no ornament.' This is the distinguishing character of the Christian religion: *christiana religio absoluta et simplex* was Ammianus Marcellinus's description of it, who was himself a heathen. W. WOTTON.

‡ By this is understood the first introducing of pageantry, and unnecessary ornaments in the Church, such as were neither for convenience nor edification; as a *shoulder-knot*, in which there is neither symmetry nor use.

more book-learned than the other two, said he had found an expedient. ' 'Tis true,' said he, 'there is nothing here in this Will, *totidem verbis*,* making mention of *shoulder-knots*, but I dare conjecture we may find them *inclusivè*, or *totidem syllabis*.' This distinction was immediately approved by all, and so they fell again to examine the will. But their evil star had so directed the matter that the first syllable was not to be found in the whole writing. Upon which disappointment, he who found the former evasion took heart and said, 'Brothers, there is yet hopes; for though we cannot find them *totidem verbis*, nor *totidem syllabis*, I dare engage we shall make them out *tertio modo*, or *totidem literis*.' This discovery was also highly commended, upon which they fell once more to the scrutiny, and soon picked out *S,H,O,U,L,D,E,R*, when the same planet, enemy to their repose, had wonderfully contrived that a *K* was not to be found. Here was a weighty difficulty! But the distinguishing brother (for whom we shall hereafter find a name) now his hand was in, proved by a very good argument that *K* was a modern, illegitimate letter, unknown to the learned ages nor anywhere to be found in ancient manuscripts. ' 'Tis true,' said he, 'the word Calendæ hath in *Q.V.C.*† been sometimes writ with a *K*, but erroneously, for in the best copies, it is ever spelt with a *C*. And by consequence it was a gross mistake in our language to spell "knot" with a *K*'; but that from henceforward he would take care it should be writ with a *C*. Upon this all further difficulty vanished; *shoulder-knots* were made clearly out to be *jure paterno*,° and our three gentlemen swaggered with as large and as flaunting ones as the best.

But as human happiness is of a very short duration, so in those days were human fashions upon which it entirely depends. Shoulder-knots had their time, and we must now imagine them in their decline; for a certain lord came just from Paris with fifty yards of *gold lace* upon his coat, exactly trimmed after the court fashion of that *month*. In two days all mankind appeared closed up in bars of gold lace:‡ whoever durst peep abroad without his complement of gold lace, was as scandalous as a [eunuch], and as ill received among the women. What should our three knights do in this momentous affair? They had sufficiently strained a point already in the affair of shoulder-knots. Upon recourse to the Will

* When the Papists cannot find anything which they want in Scripture they go to *Oral Tradition*: thus Peter is introduced dissatisfied with the tedious way of looking for all the letters of any word which he has occasion for in the *Will*, when neither the constituent syllables, nor much less the whole word, were there *in terminis*. W. WOTTON.

† [Quibusdam veteribus codicibus.] Some ancient manuscripts.

‡ I cannot tell whether the author means any new innovation by this word, or whether it be only to introduce the new methods of forcing and perverting scripture.

nothing appeared there but *altum silentium*.° That of the shoulder-knots was a loose, flying, circumstantial° point; but this of gold lace seemed too considerable an alteration without better warrant. It did *aliquo modo essentiæ adhærere*,° and therefore required a positive precept. But about this time it fell out that the learned brother aforesaid had read *Aristotelis Dialectica*, and especially that wonderful piece *de Interpretatione*° which has the faculty of teaching its readers to find out a meaning in everything but itself, like commentators on the Revelations who proceed prophets without understanding a syllable of the text. 'Brothers,' said he, 'you are to be informed,* that of wills *duo sunt genera*, nuncupatory† and scriptory; that in the scriptory will here before us, there is no precept or mention about gold lace, *conceditur*: but, *si idem affirmetur de nuncupatorio, negatur*.° For brothers, if you remember, we heard a fellow say when we were boys, that he heard my father's man say, that he heard my father say, that he would advise his sons to get *gold lace* on their coats, as soon as ever they could procure money to buy it.' 'By G—! that is very true,' cries the other. 'I remember it perfectly well,' said the third. And so without more ado they got the largest gold lace in the parish, and walked about as fine as lords.

A while after there came up *all in fashion* a pretty sort of *flame-coloured satin*‡ for linings, and the mercer brought a pattern of it immediately to our three gentlemen. 'An please your worships,' said he,§ 'my Lord C[lifford] and Sir J[ohn] W[alters] had linings out of this very piece last night; it takes wonderfully, and I shall not have a remnant left enough to make my wife a pin-cushion, by tomorrow morning at ten o'clock.' Upon this, they fell again to rummage the Will, because the present case also

* The next subject of our author's wit is the *glosses* and *interpretations of scripture*, very many absurd ones of which are allowed in the most authentic books of the Church of Rome. W. WOTTON.

† By this is meant *tradition*, allowed to have equal authority with the scripture, or rather greater.

‡ This is *purgatory*, whereof he speaks more particularly hereafter, but here, only to show how scripture was perverted to prove it, which was done by giving equal authority with the *canon* to *Apocrypha*, called here a *codicil annexed*.

It is likely the author, in every one of these changes in the brothers' dresses, refers to some particular error in the Church of Rome, though it is not easy, I think, to apply them all: but by this of *flame-coloured satin* is manifestly intended *purgatory*; by *gold lace* may perhaps be understood the lofty ornaments and plate in the churches; the *shoulder-knots* and *silver fringe* are not so obvious, at least to me; but the Indian figures of men, women, and children, plainly relate to the pictures in the Romish churches, of God like an old man, of the Virgin Mary, and our Saviour as a child.

§ This shows the time the author writ, it being about fourteen years since those two persons were reckoned the fine gentlemen of the town.

required a positive precept, the lining being held by orthodox writers to be of the essence of the coat. After long search they could fix upon nothing to the matter in hand except a short advice of their father's in the Will to take care of *fire* and put out their *candles* before they went to sleep.* This, though a good deal for the purpose and helping very far towards self-conviction, yet not seeming wholly of force to establish a command; and being resolved to avoid farther scruple, as well as future occasion for scandal, says he that was the scholar, 'I remember to have read in wills of a codicil annexed,° which is indeed a part of the will, and what it contains hath equal authority with the rest. Now, I have been considering of this same will here before us, and I cannot reckon it to be complete, for want of such a codicil. I will therefore fasten one in its proper place very dexterously. I have had it by me some time; it was written by a dog-keeper° of my grandfather's,† and talks a great deal (as good luck would have it) of this very flame-coloured satin.' The project was immediately approved by the other two; an old parchment scroll was tagged on according to art, in the form of a *codicil annexed*, and the *satin* bought and worn.

Next winter a *player*, hired for the purpose by the corporation of *fringe-makers*, acted his part in a new comedy all covered with silver fringe,‡ and according to the laudable custom, gave rise to that fashion. Upon which the brothers consulting their father's Will, to their great astonishment found these words, '*Item*, I charge and command my said three sons to wear no sort of *silver fringe* upon or about their said coats,' etc., with a penalty in case of disobedience, too long here to insert. However, after some pause, the brother so often mentioned for his erudition, who was well skilled in criticisms, had found in a certain author which he said should be nameless, that the same word which in the will is called *fringe*, does also signify a *broomstick*, and doubtless ought to have the same interpretation in this paragraph. This, another of the brothers disliked because of that epithet *silver*, which could not, he humbly conceived, in propriety of speech be reasonably applied to a *broomstick*; but it was replied upon him that this epithet was understood in a *mythological* and *allegorical* sense. However, he objected again why their father should forbid them to wear a *broomstick* on their coats, a caution that seemed unnatural and impertinent; upon which he was taken up

---

* That is, to take care of hell, and in order to do that, to subdue and extinguish their lusts.

† I believe this refers to that part of the Apocrypha where mention is made of Tobit and his dog.

‡ This is certainly the further introducing the pomps of habit and ornament.

short, as one who spoke irreverently of a *mystery* which doubtless was very useful and significant, but ought not to be over-curiously pried into or nicely reasoned upon. And in short, their father's authority being now considerably sunk, this expedient was allowed to serve as a lawful dispensation for wearing their full proportion of silver fringe.

A while after was revived an old fashion, long antiquated, of *embroidery* with *Indian figures* of men, women, and children.* Here they had no occasion to examine the Will. They remembered but too well how their father had always abhorred this fashion; that he made several paragraphs on purpose importing his utter detestation of it, and bestowing his everlasting curse to his sons, whenever they should wear it. For all this, in a few days they appeared higher in the fashion than anybody else in town. But they solved the matter by saying that these figures were not at all the *same* with those that were formerly worn and were meant in the will. Besides, they did not wear them in that sense as forbidden by their father, but as they were a commendable custom, and of great use to the public. That these rigorous clauses in the will did therefore require some *allowance*, and a favourable intepretation, and ought to be understood *cum grano salis*.

But fashions perpetually altering in that age, the scholastic brother grew weary of searching further evasions and solving everlasting contradictions. Resolved, therefore, at all hazards to comply with the modes of the world, they concerted matters together and agreed unanimously to lock up their father's Will in a *strong box*,† brought out of Greece or Italy (I have forgot which) and trouble themselves no further to examine it, but only refer to its authority whenever they thought fit. In consequence whereof, a while after it grew a general mode to wear an infinite number of *points*, most of them tagged with silver: upon which, the scholar pronounced *ex cathedra*‡ that *points* were absolutely *jure paterno*, as they might very well remember. 'Tis true indeed, the fashion

* The images of saints, the blessed Virgin, and our Saviour as an infant.

Ibid. Images in the Church of Rome give him but too fair a handle. *The brothers remembered*, &c. The allegory here is direct. W. WOTTON.

† The Papists formerly forbade the people the use of scripture in a vulgar tongue; Peter therefore *locks up his father's will in a strong box, brought out of Greece or Italy*. Those countries are named because the New Testament is written in Greek; and the vulgar Latin, which is the authentic edition of the Bible in the Church of Rome, is in the language of old Italy. W. WOTTON.

‡ The popes, in their decretals and bulls, have given their sanction to very many gainful doctrines which are now received in the Church of Rome, that are not mentioned in scripture, and are unknown to the primitive church. Peter accordingly pronounces *ex cathedra*, that *points tagged with silver were absolutely jure paterno*, and so they wore them in great numbers. W. WOTTON.

prescribed somewhat more than were directly named in the Will; however, that they as heirs general of their father had power to make and add certain clauses for public emolument, though not deducible *totidem verbis* from the letter of the Will, or else, *multa absurda sequerentur*. This was understood for *canonical*, and therefore on the following Sunday they came to church all covered with *points*.

The learned brother, so often mentioned, was reckoned the best scholar in all that or the next street to it; insomuch as, having run something behind-hand with the world, he obtained the favour from a *certain lord*,* to receive him into his house and to teach his children. A while after the lord died, and he, by long practice upon his father's Will, found the way of contriving a *deed of conveyance* of that house to himself and his heirs; upon which he took possession, turned the young squires out, and received his brothers in their stead.†

SECT. III.

A Digression concerning Critics.

Though I have been hitherto as cautious as I could, upon all occasions most nicely to follow the rules and methods of writing laid down by the example of our illustrious *moderns*; yet has the unhappy shortness of my memory led me into an error from which I must immediately extricate myself, before I can decently pursue my principal subject. I confess with shame it was an unpardonable omission to proceed so far as I have already done, before I had performed the due discourses expostulatory, supplicatory, or deprecatory, with my *good lords* the *critics*. Towards some atonement for this grievous neglect, I do here make humbly bold to present them with a short account of themselves and their *art*, by looking into the original and pedigree of the word as it is generally understood among us, and very briefly considering the ancient and present state thereof.

By the word *critic*, at this day so frequent in all conversations, there have sometimes been distinguished three very different species of mortal

---

* This was Constantine the Great, from whom the popes pretend a donation of St. Peter's patrimony, which they have never been able to produce.

† The bishops of Rome enjoyed their privileges in Rome at first by the favour of emperors, whom at last they shut out of their own capital city, and then forged a donation from Constantine the Great, the better to justify what they did. In imitation of this, Peter *having run something behind-hand in the world obtained leave of a certain lord*, &c. W. WOTTON.

men, according as I have read in *ancient books and pamphlets*. For first, by this term was understood such persons as invented or drew up rules for themselves and the world, by observing which a careful reader might be able to pronounce upon the productions of the *learned*, from his taste to a true relish of the *sublime* and the *admirable*, and divide every beauty of matter or of style from the corruption that apes it: in their common perusal of books singling out the errors and defects, the nauseous, the fulsome, the dull, and the impertinent, with the caution of a man that walks through Edinburgh streets in a morning,° who is indeed as careful as he can to watch diligently and spy out the filth in his way; not that he is curious to observe the colour and complexion of the ordure, or take its dimensions, much less to be paddling in or tasting it, but only with a design to come out as cleanly as he may. These men seem, though very erroneously, to have understood the appellation of *critic* in a literal sense; that one principal part of his office was to praise and acquit; and that a *critic* who sets up to read only for an occasion of censure and reproof, is a creature as barbarous as a *judge* who should take up a resolution to hang all men that came before him upon a trial.

Again, by the word *critic* have been meant the restorers of ancient learning from the worms, and graves, and dust of manuscripts.

Now the races of those two have been for some ages utterly extinct; and besides, to discourse any further of them would not be at all to my purpose.

The third, and noblest sort, is that of the *TRUE CRITIC*, whose original is the most ancient of all. Every *true critic* is a hero born, descending in a direct line from a celestial stem by Momus and Hybris, who begat Zoilus, who begat Tigellius,° who begat Etcætera the elder; who begat B[e]ntly, and Rym[e]r, and W[o]tton, and Perrault, and Dennis, who begat Etcætera the younger.

And these are the *critics* from whom the commonwealth of learning has in all ages received such immense benefits that the gratitude of their admirers placed their origin in Heaven, among those of Hercules, Theseus, Perseus, and other great deservers of mankind. But heroic virtue itself, hath not been exempt from the obloquy of evil tongues. For it hath been objected that those ancient heroes, famous for their combating so many giants, and dragons, and robbers, were in their own persons a greater nuisance to mankind than any of those monsters they subdued; and therefore to render their obligations more complete, when all *other* vermin were destroyed should, in conscience, have concluded with the same justice upon themselves; as Hercules most generously did,° and hath upon that score procured to himself more temples and votaries than the best of his fellows. For these reasons I suppose it is, why some have conceived it would be very expedient for the public good of learning that every *true critic*, as soon as he had finished his task assigned, should immediately deliver himself up to ratsbane, or hemp, or from some convenient altitude; and that no man's pretensions to so illustrious a character should by any means be received before that operation were performed.

Now, from this heavenly descent of *criticism*, and the close analogy it bears to *heroic virtue*, 'tis easy to assign the proper employment of a *true ancient genuine critic*;° which is to travel through this vast world of writings; to pursue and hunt those monstrous faults bred within them; to drag out the lurking errors, like Cacus from his den; to multiply them like Hydra's heads; and rake them together like Augeas's dung; or else to drive away a sort of *dangerous fowl* who have a perverse inclination to plunder the best branches of the *tree of knowledge*, like those Stymphalian birds that eat up the fruit.

These reasonings will furnish us with an adequate definition of a *true critic*: that he is *a discoverer and collector of writers' faults*, which may be further put beyond dispute by the following demonstration: That whoever will examine the writings in all kinds wherewith this ancient sect has honoured the world, shall immediately find, from the whole thread and tenor of them, that the ideas of the authors have been altogether conversant and taken up with the faults, and blemishes, and oversights, and mistakes of other writers; and let the subject treated on be whatever it will, their imaginations are so entirely possessed and replete with the defects of other pens that the very quintessence of what is bad, does of necessity distil into their own; by which means the whole appears to be nothing else but an *abstract* of the *criticisms* themselves have made.

Having thus briefly considered the original and office of a *critic*, as the word is understood in its most noble and universal acceptation, I proceed to refute the objections of those who argue from the silence and pretermission of authors; by which they pretend to prove that the very art of *criticism* as now exercised, and by me explained, is wholly *modern*; and consequently that the *critics* of Great Britain and France have no title to an original so ancient and illustrious as I have deduced. Now, if I can clearly make out on the contrary, that the most ancient writers have particularly described both the person and the office of a *true critic*, agreeable to the definition laid down by me, their grand objection from the silence of authors will fall to the ground.

I confess to have for a long time borne a part in this general error, from which I should never have acquitted myself but through the assistance of

our noble *moderns* whose most edifying volumes I turn indefatigably over°
night and day, for the improvement of my mind and the good of my
country. These have with unwearied pains made many useful searches
into the weak side of the *ancients*, and given us a comprehensive list of
them.* Besides, they have proved beyond contradiction that the very
finest things delivered of old, have been long since invented and brought
to light by much later pens; and that the noblest discoveries those *ancients*
ever made, of art or of nature, have all been produced by the
transcending genius of the present age. Which clearly shows how little
merit those *ancients* can justly pretend to, and takes off that blind
admiration paid them by men in a corner, who have the unhappiness of
conversing too little with *present things*. Reflecting maturely upon all this,
and taking in the whole compass of human nature, I easily concluded that
these *ancients*, highly sensible of their many imperfections, must needs
have endeavoured from some passages in their works, to obviate, soften,
or divert the censorious reader by *satire*, or *panegyric* upon the *true critics*,
in imitation of their *masters*, the *moderns*. Now, in the *commonplaces* of
both these† I was plentifully instructed by a long course of useful study in
prefaces and *prologues*; and therefore immediately resolved to try what I
could discover of either, by a diligent perusal of the most ancient writers,
and especially those who treated of the earliest times. Here I found to my
great surprise that although they all entered, upon occasion, into
particular descriptions of the *true critic*, according as they were governed
by their fears or their hopes; yet whatever they touched of that kind was
with abundance of caution, adventuring no farther than *mythology* and
hieroglyphic. This, I suppose, gave ground to superficial readers for
urging the silence of authors against the antiquity of the *true critic*, though
the *types* are so apposite, and the applications so necessary and natural,
that it is not easy to conceive how any reader of a *modern eye* and *taste*
could overlook them. I shall venture from a great number to produce a
few, which I am very confident will put this question beyond dispute.

It well deserves considering that these *ancient writers*, in treating
enigmatically upon this subject, have generally fixed upon the very *same*
hieroglyph, varying only the story according to their affections, or their
wit. For first; Pausanias is of opinion° that the perfection of writing
correct was entirely owing to the institution of *critics*; and, that he can
possibly mean no other than the *true critic*, is I think manifest enough
from the following description. He says, *they were a race of men who
delighted to nibble at the superfluities and excrescencies of books; which the*

---

* See Wotton *of Ancient and Modern Learning.*
† Satire and Panegyric upon Critics.

learned at length observing, took warning of their own accord, to lop the luxuriant, the rotten, the dead, the sapless, and the overgrown branches from their works. But now, all this he cunningly shades under the following allegory; *that the Nauplians in Argia learned the art of pruning their vines by observing, that when an* ASS *had browsed upon one of them, it thrived the better and bore fairer fruit.* But Herodotus,*° holding the very same *hieroglyph*, speaks much plainer and almost *in terminis.* He hath been so bold as to tax the *true critics* of ignorance and malice, telling us openly, for I think nothing can be plainer, that *in the western part of Libya, there were* ASSES *with* HORNS. Upon which relation Ctesias† yet refines,° mentioning the very same animal about India, adding, *that whereas all other* ASSES *wanted a gall, these horned ones were so redundant in that part that their flesh was not to be eaten because of its extreme bitterness.*

Now, the reason why those ancient writers treated this subject only by types and figures was, because they durst not make open attacks against a party so potent and terrible as the *critics* of those ages were, whose very voice was so dreadful, that a legion of authors would tremble and drop their pens at the sound; for so Herodotus‡ tells us expressly in another place, how *a vast army of Scythians was put to flight in a panic terror, by the braying of an* ASS. From hence it is conjectured by certain profound *philologers*, that the great awe and reverence paid to a *true critic* by the writers of Britain have been derived to us from those our Scythian ancestors.° In short, this dread was so universal that in process of time those authors who had a mind to publish their sentiments more freely, in describing the *true critics* of their several ages were forced to leave off the use of the former *hieroglyph*, as too nearly approaching the *prototype*, and invented other terms instead thereof that were more cautious and mystical. So Diodorus, speaking to the same purpose, ventures° no farther than to say that in the mountains of Helicon there grows a certain *weed*, which bears a flower of so damned a scent as to poison those who offer to smell it. Lucretius gives exactly the same relation:°

> Est etiam in magnis Heliconis montibus arbos,
> Floris odore hominem retro consueta necare.§
>
> Lib. 6.

But Ctesias,° whom we lately quoted, hath been a great deal bolder; he had been used with much severity by the *true critics* of his own age, and therefore could not forbear to leave behind him at least one deep mark of

---

* Lib. 4.   † Vide excerpta ex eo apud Photium.   ‡ Lib. 4. [129].
      § Near Helicon, and round the learned hill,
         Grow trees, whose blossoms with their odour kill.

his vengeance against the whole tribe. His meaning is so near the surface that I wonder how it possibly came to be overlooked by those who deny the antiquity of the *true critics*. For, pretending to make a description of many strange animals about India, he hath set down these remarkable words: 'Among the rest,' says he, 'there is a *serpent* that wants *teeth*, and consequently cannot bite; but if its *vomit* (to which it is much addicted) happens to fall upon anything, a certain rottenness or corruption ensues. These *serpents* are generally found among the mountains where *jewels* grow, and they frequently emit a *poisonous juice*, whereof whoever drinks, that person's brains fly out of his nostrils.'

There was also among the *ancients* a sort of critic not distinguished in *specie* from the former but in growth or degree, who seem to have been only the *tyros* or *junior* scholars; yet, because of their differing employments, they are frequently mentioned as a sect by themselves. The usual exercise of these younger students was to attend constantly at theatres, and learn to spy out the *worst parts* of the play, whereof they were obliged carefully to take note and render a rational account to their tutors. Fleshed at these smaller sports, like young wolves, they grew up in time to be nimble and strong enough for hunting down large game. For it hath been observed both among ancients and moderns, that a *true critic* hath one quality in common with a *whore* and an *alderman*, never to change his title or his nature; that a *grey critic* has been certainly a *green* one, the perfections and acquirements of his age being only the improved talents of his youth; like *hemp*, which some naturalists inform us is bad for *suffocations* though taken but in the seed. I esteem the invention or at least the refinement of *prologues*, to have been owing to these younger proficients, of whom Terence makes frequent and honourable mention under the name of *malevoli*.°

Now, 'tis certain, the institution of the *true critics* was of absolute necessity to the commonwealth of learning. For all human actions seem to be divided like Themistocles and his company:° one man can *fiddle*, and another can make *a small town a great city*; and he that cannot do either one or the other deserves to be kicked out of the creation. The avoiding of which penalty has doubtless given the first birth to the nation of *critics*, and withal, an occasion for their secret detractors to report that a *true critic* is a sort of mechanic, set up with a stock and tools for his trade at as little expense as a tailor; and that there is much analogy between the utensils and abilities of both: that the tailor's *hell* is the type of a critic's *commonplace book*, and his wit and learning held forth by the *goose*; that it requires at least as many of these to the making up of one scholar, as of the others to the composition of a man;° that the valour of both is equal, and their *weapons* near of a size. Much may be said in answer to those invidious reflections, and I can positively affirm the first to be a falsehood. For on the contrary, nothing is more certain than that it requires greater layings out to be free of the *critic*'s company, than of any other you can name. For, as to be a *true beggar* it will cost the richest candidate every groat he is worth; so, before one can commence a *true critic* it will cost a man all the good qualities of his mind; which, perhaps for a less purchase, would be thought but an indifferent bargain.

Having thus amply proved the antiquity of *criticism* and described the primitive state of it, I shall now examine the present condition of this empire and show how well it agrees with its ancient self. A certain author* whose works have many ages since been entirely lost, does, in his fifth book and eighth chapter, say of *critics*, that 'their writings are the mirrors of learning.' This I understand in a literal sense, and suppose our author must mean that whoever designs to be a perfect writer must inspect into the books of *critics*, and correct his invention there as in a mirror. Now, whoever considers that the *mirrors* of the ancients were made of brass and *sine mercurio*,° may presently apply the two principal qualifications of a *true modern critic*, and consequently must needs conclude that these have always been and must be for ever the same. For *brass* is an emblem of duration, and when it is skilfully burnished will cast *reflections* from its own *superficies*, without any assistance of *mercury* from behind. All the other talents of a *critic* will not require a particular mention, being included or easily deducible to these. However, I shall conclude with three maxims which may serve both as characteristics to distinguish a *true modern critic* from a pretender, and will be also of admirable use to those worthy spirits who engage in so useful and honourable an art.

The first is that *criticism*, contrary to all other faculties of the intellect, is ever held the truest and best when it is the very *first* result of the *critic*'s mind; as fowlers reckon the first aim for the surest, and seldom fail of missing the mark if they stay for a second.

Secondly, the *true critics* are known by their talent of swarming about the noblest writers, to which they are carried merely by instinct, as a rat to the best cheese, or a wasp to the fairest fruit. So when the king is a horseback, he is sure to be the *dirtiest* person of the company, and they that make their court best, are such as *bespatter* him most.

Lastly, a *true critic* in the perusal of a book is like a *dog* at a feast, whose thoughts and stomach are wholly set upon what the guests *fling away*, and consequently is apt to *snarl* most when there are the fewest *bones*.

---

* A quotation after the manner of a great author. Vide Bently's *Dissertation*, &c.

Thus much, I think, is sufficient to serve by way of address to my patrons, the *true modern critics*, and may very well atone for my past silence as well as that which I am like to observe for the future. I hope I have deserved so well of their whole *body* as to meet with generous and tender usage from their *hands*. Supported by which expectation, I go on boldly to pursue those adventures already so happily begun.

SECT. IV.

A Tale of a Tub

I have now, with much pains and study, conducted the reader to a period where he must expect to hear of great revolutions. For no sooner had our *learned brother*, so often mentioned, got a warm house of his own over his head than he began to look big, and to take mightily upon him; insomuch that unless the gentle reader, out of his great candour, will please a little to exalt his idea, I am afraid he will henceforth hardly know the *hero* of the play when he happens to meet him, his part, his dress, and his mien being so much altered.

He told his brothers he would have them to know that he was their elder, and consequently his father's sole heir; nay, a while after he would not allow them to call him *brother*, but *Mr. PETER*; and then he must be styled *Father PETER*; and sometimes, *My Lord PETER*. To support this grandeur, which he soon began to consider could not be maintained without a better *fonde* than what he was born to, after much thought he cast about at last to turn *projector* and *virtuoso*, wherein he so well succeeded that many famous discoveries, projects, and machines, which bear great vogue and practice at present in the world, are owing entirely to Lord Peter's invention. I will deduce the best account I have been able to collect of the chief amongst them, without considering much the order they came out in, because I think authors are not well agreed as to that point.

I hope, when this treatise of mine shall be translated into foreign languages (as I may without vanity affirm that the labour of collecting, the faithfulness in recounting, and the great usefulness of the matter to the public, will amply deserve that justice) that the worthy members of the several *academies* abroad, especially those of France and Italy, will favourably accept these humble offers for the advancement of universal knowledge. I do also advertise the most reverend Fathers the Eastern Missionaries, that I have, purely for their sakes, made use of such words and phrases as will best admit an easy turn into any of the oriental languages, especially the Chinese. And so I proceed with great content of mind, upon reflecting how much emolument this whole globe of the earth is likely to reap by my labours.

The first undertaking of Lord Peter was to purchase a large continent,* lately said to have been discovered in *Terra Australis Incognita.*° This tract of land he bought at a very great pennyworth from the discoverers themselves (though some pretended to doubt whether they had ever been there), and then retailed it into several cantons to certain dealers, who carried over colonies but were all shipwrecked in the voyage. Upon which Lord Peter sold the said continent to other customers *again*, and *again*, and *again*, and *again*, with the same success.

The second project I shall mention was his sovereign remedy for the *worms*,†° especially those in the *spleen*. The patient was to eat nothing after supper for three nights:‡ as soon as he went to bed he was carefully to lie on one side, and when he grew weary, to turn upon the other. He must also duly confine his two eyes to the same object, and by no means break wind at both ends together without manifest occasion. These prescriptions diligently observed, the *worms* would void insensibly by perspiration, ascending through the *brain*.

A third invention was the erecting of a *whispering-office*,§ for the public good and ease of all such as are hypochondriacal, or troubled with the colic; likewise of all eavesdroppers, physicians, midwives, small politicians, friends fallen out, repeating poets,° lovers happy or in despair, bawds, privy-councillors, pages, parasites, and buffoons: in short, of all such as are in danger of bursting with too much *wind*. An *ass*'s head was placed so conveniently that the party affected might easily with his mouth accost either of the animal's ears; which he was to apply close for a certain space, and by a fugitive faculty, peculiar to the ears of that animal, receive immediate benefit either by eructation, or expiration, or evomition.

Another very beneficial project of Lord Peter's was, an *office of*

---

* That is, Purgatory.

† *Penance* and *absolution* are played upon under the notion of a *sovereign remedy for the worms*, especially in the spleen, which by observing Peter's prescription would void sensibly by perspiration, ascending through the brain, &c. W. WOTTON.

‡ Here the author ridicules the penances of the Church of Rome, which may be made as easy to the sinner as he pleases, provided he will pay for them accordingly.

§ By his *whispering-office* for the relief of eavesdroppers, physicians, bawds, and privy-councillors, he ridicules auricular confession; and the priest who takes it, is described by the ass's head. W. WOTTON.

insurance for tobacco-pipes,* martyrs of the modern zeal, volumes of poetry, shadows,————and rivers: that these, nor any of these, shall receive damage by *fire.*° From whence our *friendly societies* may plainly find themselves to be only transcribers from this original, though the one and the other have been of *great* benefit to the undertakers, as well as of *equal* to the public.

Lord Peter was also held the original author of *puppets* and *raree-shows*† the great usefulness whereof being so generally known, I shall not enlarge further upon this particular.

But another discovery for which he was much renowned was his famous universal *pickle.*‡ For, having remarked how your common *pickle,*§ in use among housewives, was of no further benefit than to preserve dead flesh and certain kinds of vegetables, Peter, with great cost as well as art, had contrived a *pickle* proper for houses, gardens, towns, men, women, children, and cattle, wherein he could preserve them as sound as insects in amber. Now, this *pickle* to the taste, the smell, and the sight, appeared exactly the same with what is in common service for beef and butter and herrings (and has been often that way applied with great success); but for its many sovereign virtues, was quite a different thing. For Peter would put in a certain quantity of his *powder pimperlim-pimp,*¶° after which it never failed of success. The operation was performed by *spargefaction* in a proper time of the moon. The patient who was to be *pickled*, if it were a house, would infallibly be preserved from all spiders, rats, and weasels. If the party affected were a dog, he should be exempt from mange, and madness, and hunger. It also infallibly took away all scabs and lice, and scalled heads from children, never hindering the patient from any duty either at bed or board.

But of all Peter's rarities he most valued a certain set of *bulls,*‖ whose

* This I take to be the office of Indulgences, the gross abuses whereof first gave occasion for the Reformation.

† I believe are all the monkeries and ridiculous processions, &c., among the papists.

‡ Holy water, he calls an *universal pickle*, to preserve houses, gardens, towns, men, women, children, and cattle, wherein he could preserve them as sound as insects in amber. W. WOTTON.

§ This is easily understood to be holy water, composed of the same ingredients with many other pickles.

¶ And because holy water differs only in consecration from common water, therefore he tells us that his pickle by the powder of *pimperlim-pimp* receives new virtues, though it differs not in sight nor smell from the common pickle, which preserves beef, and butter, and herrings. W. WOTTON.

‖ The *papal bulls* are ridiculed by name, so that here we are at no loss for the author's meaning. W. WOTTON.

Ibid. Here the author has kept the name, and means the pope's Bulls, or rather his race was by great fortune preserved in a lineal descent from those that guarded the *golden fleece*. Though some who pretended to observe them curiously, doubted the breed had not been kept entirely chaste, because they had degenerated from their ancestors in some qualities, and had acquired others very extraordinary, but a foreign mixture. The bulls of Colchos° are recorded to have *brazen feet*; but whether it happened by ill pasture and running, by an allay from intervention of other parents, from stolen intrigues; whether a weakness in their progenitors had impaired the seminal virtue, or by a decline necessary through a long course of time, the originals of nature being depraved in these latter sinful ages of the world; whatever was the cause, it is certain that Lord Peter's *bulls* were extremely vitiated by the rust of time in the metal of their feet, which was now sunk into common *lead*.° However, the terrible *roaring* peculiar to their lineage, was preserved, as likewise that faculty of breathing out *fire* from their nostrils; which, notwithstanding, many of their detractors took to be a feat of art, and to be nothing so terrible as it appeared, proceeding only from their usual course of diet, which was of *squibs* and *crackers*.* However, they had two peculiar marks which extremely distinguished them from the bulls of Jason, and which I have not met together in the description of any other monster beside that in Horace—

Varias inducere plumas;

and

Atrum desinit in piscem.°

For these had *fishes' tails*, yet upon occasion could *outfly* any bird in the air. Peter put these *bulls* upon several employs. Sometimes he would set them a-*roaring* to fright *naughty boys*† and make them quiet. Sometimes he would send them out upon errands of great importance; where, it is wonderful to recount, and perhaps the cautious reader may think much to believe it, an *appetitus sensibilis*° deriving itself through the whole family from their noble ancestors, guardians of the *golden fleece*, they continued so extremely fond of *gold*, that if Peter sent them abroad though it were only upon a compliment, they would *roar*, and *spit*, and *belch*, and *piss*, and *fart*, and snivel out *fire*, and keep a perpetual coil, till you flung them a bit of *gold*; but then, *pulveris exigui jactu*,° they would grow calm and quiet as lambs. In short, whether by secret connivance or encouragement from fulminations and excommunications of heretical princes, all signed with lead and the seal of the fisherman.

* These are the fulminations of the pope, threatening hell and damnation to those princes who offend him.

† That is, kings who incur his displeasure.

their master, or out of their own liquorish affection to gold, or both; it is certain they were no better than a sort of sturdy, swaggering beggars; and where they could not prevail to get an alms, would make women miscarry and children fall into fits, who to this day usually call sprites and hobgoblins by the name of *bull-beggars*.° They grew at last so very troublesome to the neighbourhood that some gentlemen of the *north-west*° got a parcel of right English *bull-dogs*, and baited them so terribly that they felt it ever after.

I must needs mention one more of Lord Peter's projects, which was very extraordinary and discovered him to be a master of a high reach and profound invention. Whenever it happened that any rogue of Newgate was condemned to be hanged, Peter would offer him a pardon for a certain sum of money, which when the poor caitiff had made all shifts to scrape up and send, his lordship would return a piece of paper in this form.*

'TO all mayors, sheriffs, jailors, constables, bailiffs, hangmen, &c. Whereas we are informed that A. B. remains in the hands of you, or any of you, under the sentence of death. We will and command you upon sight hereof, to let the said prisoner depart to his own habitation, whether he stands condemned for murder, sodomy, rape, sacrilege, incest, treason, blasphemy, &c., for which this shall be your sufficient warrant. And if you fail hereof, G—d d—mn you and yours to all eternity. And so we bid you heartily farewell.

Your most humble
man's man,°
EMPEROR PETER.'

The wretches trusting to this, lost their lives and money too.

I desire of those whom the *learned* among posterity will appoint for commentators upon this elaborate treatise, that they will proceed with great caution upon certain dark points wherein all who are not *verè adepti*° may be in danger to form rash and hasty conclusions, especially in some mysterious paragraphs where certain *arcana* are joined for brevity sake, which in the operation must be divided. And I am certain that future sons of art will return large thanks to my memory, for so grateful, so useful an *innuendo*.

It will be no difficult part to persuade the reader that so many worthy discoveries met with great success in the world, though I may justly

---

* This is a copy of a general pardon, signed *servus servorum*.

Ibid. Absolution *in articulo mortis*, and the tax *cameræ apostolicæ*,° are jested upon in Emperor Peter's letter. W. WOTTON.

assure him that I have related much the smallest number, my design having been only to single out such as will be of most benefit for public imitation, or which best served to give some idea of the reach and wit of the inventor. And therefore it need not be wondered, if by this time, Lord Peter was become exceeding rich. But alas, he had kept his brain so long and so violently upon the rack, that at last it *shook* itself and began to *turn round* for a little ease. In short, what with pride, projects, and knavery, poor Peter was grown distracted, and conceived the strangest imaginations in the world. In the height of his fits (as it is usual with those who run mad out of pride) he would call himself *God Almighty*,* and sometimes *monarch of the universe*. I have seen him (says my author) take three old *high-crowned hats*† and clap them all on his head three storey high, with a huge bunch of *keys* at his girdle,‡ and an *angling-rod* in his hand. In which guise, whoever went to take him by the hand in the way of salutation, Peter with much grace, like a well-educated spaniel, would present them with his *foot*;§ and if they refused his civility then he would raise it as high as their chops, and give them a damned kick on the mouth, which hath ever since been called a *salute*. Whoever walked by without paying him their compliments, having a wonderful strong breath he would blow their hats off into the dirt. Meantime his affairs at home went upside down, and his two brothers had a wretched time; where his first *boutade*¶ was to kick both their *wives* one morning out of doors, and his own too;‖ and in their stead, gave orders to pick up the first three strollers could be met with in the streets. A while after, he nailed up the cellar-door, and would not allow his brothers a drop of *drink* to their victuals.** Dining one day at an alderman's in the city, Peter observed him expatiating after the manner of his brethren, in the praises of his sirloin of beef. 'Beef', said the sage magistrate, 'is the king of meat; beef comprehends in it the quintessence of partridge, and quail, and venison,

* The Pope is not only allowed to be the Vicar of Christ, but by several divines is called God upon Earth, and other blasphemous titles.

† The triple crown.

Ibid. The Pope's universal monarchy, and his triple crown, and fisher's ring. W. WOTTON.

‡ The keys of the Church.

§ Neither does his arrogant way of requiring men to kiss his slipper escape reflection. W. WOTTON.

¶ This word properly signifies a sudden jerk, or lash of a horse, when you do not expect it.

‖ The Celibacy of the Romish clergy is struck at in Peter's beating his own and brothers' wives out of doors. W. WOTTON.

** The Pope's refusing the cup to the laity, persuading them that the blood is contained in the bread, and that the bread is the real and entire body of Christ.

and pheasant, and plum-pudding, and custard.' When Peter came home, he would needs take the fancy of cooking up this doctrine into use and apply the precept, in default of a sirloin, to his brown loaf. 'Bread,' says he, 'dear brothers, is the staff of life; in which bread is contained, *inclusivè*, the quintessence of beef, mutton, veal, venison, partridge, plum-pudding, and custard. And to render all complete, there is intermingled a due quantity of water whose crudities are also corrected by yeast or barm, through which means it becomes a wholesome fermented liquor, diffused through the mass of the bread.' Upon the strength of these conclusions, next day at dinner was the brown loaf served up in all the formality of a city feast. 'Come, brothers,' said Peter, 'fall to, and spare not; here is excellent good mutton;* or hold, now my hand is in, I'll help you.' At which word, in much ceremony, with fork and knife, he carves out two good slices of the loaf and presents each on a plate to his brothers. The elder of the two, not suddenly entering into Lord Peter's conceit, began with very civil language to examine the mystery. 'My lord,' said he, 'I doubt, with great submission, there may be some mistake.' 'What,' says Peter, 'you are pleasant; come then, let us hear this jest your head is so big with.' 'None in the world, my lord, but unless I am very much deceived, your lordship was pleased a while ago to let fall a word about mutton, and I would be glad to see it with all my heart.' 'How,' said Peter, appearing in great surprise, 'I do not comprehend this at all.'—Upon which, the younger interposing to set the business aright, 'My lord,' said he, 'my brother, I suppose, is hungry, and longs for the mutton your lordship hath promised us to dinner.' 'Pray,' said Peter, 'take me along with you: either you are both mad, or disposed to be merrier than I approve of. If *you* there do not like your piece I will carve you another, though I should take that to be the choice bit of the whole shoulder.' 'What then, my lord,' replied the first 'it seems this is a shoulder of mutton all this while?' 'Pray, sir,' says Peter, 'eat your victuals and leave off your impertinence if you please, for I am not disposed to relish it at present.' But the other could not forbear, being over provoked at the affected seriousness of Peter's countenance. 'By G—, my lord,' said he, 'I can only say that to my eyes, and fingers, and teeth, and nose, it seems to be nothing but a crust of bread.' Upon which the second put in his word, 'I never saw a piece of mutton in my life so nearly resembling a slice from a twelve-penny loaf.' 'Look ye, gentlemen,' cries Peter in a rage, 'to convince you what a couple of blind, positive, ignorant, wilful

---

* *Transubstantiation.* Peter turns his bread into mutton, and according to the popish doctrine of concomitants, his wine too, which in his way he calls *palming his damned crusts upon the brothers for mutton.* W. WOTTON.

puppies you are, I will use but this plain argument: By G—, it is true, good, natural mutton as any in Leadenhall market, and G— confound you both eternally if you offer to believe otherwise.' Such a thundering proof as this left no further room for objection. The two unbelievers began to gather and pocket up their mistake as hastily as they could. 'Why, truly,' said the first, 'upon more mature consideration'—'Ay,' says the other, interrupting him, 'now I have thought better on the thing, your lordship seems to have a great deal of reason.' 'Very well,' said Peter, 'here boy, fill me a beer-glass of claret. Here's to you both, with all my heart.' The two brethren, much delighted to see him so readily appeased, returned their most humble thanks and said they would be glad to pledge his lordship. 'That you shall,' said Peter, 'I am not a person to refuse you anything that is reasonable: wine, moderately taken, is a cordial; here is a glass apiece for you; 'tis true natural juice from the grape, none of your damned *vintners*' brewings.' Having spoke thus, he presented to each of them another large dry crust, bidding them drink it off and not be bashful, for it would do them no hurt. The two brothers after having performed the usual office in such delicate conjunctures, of staring a sufficient period at Lord Peter and each other, and finding how matters were like to go, resolved not to enter on a new dispute but let him carry the point as he pleased; for he was now got into one of his mad fits, and to argue or expostulate further would only serve to render him a hundred times more untractable.

I have chosen to relate this worthy matter in all its circumstances, because it gave a principal occasion to that great and famous *rupture** which happened about the same time among these brethren, and was never afterwards made up. But of that, I shall treat at large in another section.

However, it is certain that Lord Peter, even in his lucid intervals, was very lewdly given in his common conversation, extreme wilful and positive, and would at any time rather argue to the death than allow himself once to be in an error. Besides, he had an abominable faculty of telling huge palpable *lies* upon all occasions; and swearing not only to the truth, but cursing the whole company to Hell if they pretended to make the least scruple of believing him. One time he swore he had a *cow*† at home, which gave as much milk at a meal as would fill three thousand churches, and what was yet more extraordinary, would never turn sour.

---

* By this *Rupture* is meant the *Reformation*.

† The ridiculous multiplying of the Virgin Mary's *milk* among the papists, under the allegory of a *cow*, which gave as much milk at a meal as would fill three thousand churches. W. WOTTON.

Another time he was telling of an old *sign-post** that belonged to his *father*, with nails and timber enough on it to build sixteen large men-of-war. Talking one day of Chinese waggons,° which were made so light as to sail over mountains: 'Z—ds,' said Peter, 'where's the wonder of that? By G—, I saw a large house of lime and stone† travel over sea and land (granting that it stopped sometimes to bait) above two thousand German leagues.' And that which was the good of it, he would swear desperately all the while that he never told a lie in his life, and at every word, 'By G—, gentlemen, I tell you nothing but the truth, and the D—l broil them eternally that will not believe me.'

In short, Peter grew so scandalous that all the neighbourhood began in plain words to say, he was no better than a knave. And his two brothers, long weary of his ill usage, resolved at last to leave him; but first they humbly desired a copy of their father's *Will*, which had now lain by neglected time out of mind. Instead of granting this request he called them *damned sons of whores*, *rogues*, *traitors*, and the rest of the vile names he could muster up. However, while he was abroad one day upon his projects, the two youngsters watched their opportunity, made a shift to come at the *Will*‡ and took a *copia vera*, by which they presently saw how grossly they had been abused; their father having left them equal heirs, and strictly commanded that whatever they got should lie in common among them all. Pursuant to which their next enterprise was to break open the cellar-door, and get a little good *drink*§ to spirit and comfort their hearts. In copying the *Will* they had met another precept against whoring, divorce, and separate maintenance; upon which their next work¶ was to discard their concubines and send for their wives. While all this was in agitation there enters a solicitor from Newgate, desiring Lord Peter would please procure a *pardon* for a *thief* that was to be *hanged* tomorrow. But the two brothers told him he was a coxcomb to seek pardons from a fellow who deserved to be hanged much better than his client, and discovered all the method of that imposture, in the same form I delivered it a while ago, advising the solicitor to put his friend upon

---

* By this *sign-post* is meant the *cross* of our Blessed Saviour.

† The chapel of Loretto, which travelled from the Holy Land to Italy. He falls here only upon the ridiculous inventions of popery. The Church of Rome intended by these things to gull silly, superstitious people, and rook them of their money; the world had been too long in slavery, and our ancestors gloriously redeemed us from that yoke. The Church of Rome therefore ought to be exposed, and he deserves well of mankind that does expose it. W. WOTTON.

‡ Translated the scriptures into the vulgar tongues.

§ Administered the cup to the laity at the communion.

¶ Allowed the marriages of priests.

obtaining *a pardon from the king*.* In the midst of all this clutter and revolution, in comes Peter with a file of dragoons at his heels,† and gathering from all hands what was in the wind, he and his gang, after several millions of scurrilities and curses, not very important here to repeat, by main force very fairly kicks them both out of doors,‡ and would never let them come under his roof from that day to this.

SECT. V.

A Digression in the Modern Kind.

We whom the world is pleased to honour with the title of *modern authors* should never have been able to compass our great design of an everlasting remembrance, and never-dying fame, if our endeavours had not been so highly serviceable to the general good of mankind. This, *O Universe*, is the adventurous attempt of me thy secretary;

> —— Quemvis perferre laborem
> Suadet, et inducit noctes vigilare serenas.°

To this end I have some time since, with a world of pains and art, dissected the carcass of *human nature* and read many useful lectures upon the several parts, both *containing* and *contained*, till at last it *smelt* so strong I could preserve it no longer. Upon which, I have been at a great expense to fit up all the bones with exact contexture and in due symmetry, so that I am ready to show a complete anatomy thereof to all curious *gentlemen and others*. But not to digress further in the midst of a digression, as I have known some authors enclose digressions in one another, like a nest of boxes, I do affirm that having carefully cut up *human nature*, I have found a very strange, new, and important discovery,° that the public good of mankind is performed by two ways, *instruction* and *diversion*. And I have further proved in my said several readings (which perhaps the world may one day see, if I can prevail on any friend to steal a copy, or on certain gentlemen of my admirers to be very importunate) that as mankind is now disposed, he receives much greater advantage by being *diverted* than *instructed*; his epidemical

---

* Directed penitents not to trust to pardons and absolutions procured for money, but sent them to implore the mercy of God, from whence alone remission is to be obtained.

† By Peter's dragoons is meant the civil power, which those princes who were bigotted to the Romish superstition employed against the reformers.

‡ The Pope shuts all who dissent from him, out of the Church.

diseases being *fastidiosity*, *amorphy*, and *oscitation*;° whereas, in the present universal empire of wit and learning, there seems but little matter left for *instruction*. However, in compliance with a lesson of great age and authority I have attempted carrying the point in all its heights, and accordingly, throughout this divine treatise, have skilfully kneaded up both together with a layer of *utile* and a layer of *dulce*.

When I consider how exceedingly our illustrious *moderns* have eclipsed the weak glimmering lights of the *ancients* and turned them out of the road of all fashionable commerce, to a degree that our choice town wits,* of most refined accomplishments, are in grave dispute whether there have been ever any *ancients* or no° (in which point we are like to receive wonderful satisfaction from the most useful labours and lucubrations of that worthy *modern*, Dr. B[e]ntly); I say, when I consider all this I cannot but bewail that no famous *modern* hath ever yet attempted an universal system, in a small portable volume, of all things that are to be known, or believed, or imagined, or practised in life. I am, however, forced to acknowledge that such an enterprize was thought on some time ago by a great philosopher of *O. Brazile*.†° The method he proposed was by a certain curious *receipt*, a *nostrum*, which after his untimely death I found among his papers, and do here, out of my great affection to the *modern learned*, present them with it, not doubting it may one day encourage some worthy undertaker.

You take fair correct copies, well bound in calf-skin, and lettered at the back, of all modern bodies of arts and sciences whatsoever, and in what language you please. These you distil in balneo Mariæ, *infusing* quintessence of poppy Q.S.,° *together with three pints of* Lethe, *to be had from the apothecaries. You cleanse away carefully the* sordes *and* caput mortuum,° *letting all that is volatile evaporate. You preserve only the first running, which is again to be distilled seventeen times, till what remains will amount to about two drams. This you keep in a glass vial,* hermetically *sealed, for one and twenty days. Then you begin your Catholic*° *treatise, taking every morning fasting (first shaking the vial) three drops of this* elixir, *snuffing it strongly up your nose. It will dilate itself about the brain (where there is any) in fourteen minutes, and you immediately perceive in your head an infinite number of* abstracts, summaries, compendiums, extracts, collections, medullas, excerpta

---

* The learned person, here meant by our author, hath been endeavouring to annihilate so many ancient writers that, until he is pleased to stop his hand, it will be dangerous to affirm whether there have been ever any ancients in the world.

† This is an imaginary island, of kin to that which is called the *Painters' Wives Island*,° placed in some unknown part of the ocean, merely at the fancy of the map-maker.

quædams, florilegias,° *and the like, all disposed into great order, and reducible upon paper.*

I must needs own it was by the assistance of this *arcanum* that I, though otherwise *impar*, have adventured upon so daring an attempt, never achieved or undertaken before but by a certain author called Homer, in whom, though otherwise a person not without some abilities and, *for an ancient*, of a tolerable genius, I have discovered many gross errors which are not to be forgiven his very ashes, if by chance any of them are left. For whereas we are assured he designed his work for a complete body of all knowledge,* human, divine, political, and mechanic, it is manifest he hath wholly neglected some, and been very imperfect in the rest. For first of all, as eminent a *cabalist°* as his disciples would represent him, his account of the *opus magnum°* is extremely poor and deficient; he seems to have read but very superficially either Sendivogius, Behmen, or *Anthroposophia Theomagica.*†° He is also quite mistaken about the *sphæra pyroplastica,°* a neglect not to be atoned for, and (if the reader will admit so severe a censure) *vix crederem autorem hunc, unquam audivisse ignis vocem.°* His failings are not less prominent in several parts of the *mechanics*. For, having read his writings with the utmost application usual among *modern wits*, I could never yet discover the least direction about the structure of that useful instrument, a *save-all*. For want of which, if the *moderns* had not lent their assistance, we might yet have wandered *in the dark*. But I have still behind a fault far more notorious to tax the author with; I mean, his gross ignorance‡ in the *common laws of this realm*, and in the doctrine as well as discipline of the Church of England. A defect, indeed, for which both he and all the ancients stand most justly censured by my worthy and ingenious friend Mr. W[o]tt[o]n, Bachelor of Divinity, in his incomparable treatise of *Ancient and Modern Learning:* a book never to be sufficiently valued, whether we consider the happy turns and flowings of the author's wit, the great usefulness of his sublime discoveries upon the subject of *flies* and *spittle*, or the laborious eloquence of his style. And I cannot forbear doing that author the justice of my public acknowledgments for the great *helps* and *liftings* I had out of his incomparable piece while I was penning this treatise.

* Homerus omnes res humanas poematis complexus est.—*Xenoph. in conviv.°*

† A treatise written about fifty years ago, by a Welsh gentleman of Cambridge. His name, as I remember, was Vaughan, as appears by the answer to it writ by the learned Dr. Henry More.° It is a piece of the most unintelligible *fustian*, that perhaps was ever published in any language.

‡ Mr. W[o]tt[o]n (to whom our author never gives any quarter) in his comparison of ancient and modern learning, numbers divinity, law, &c., among those parts of knowledge wherein we excel the ancients.

But, besides these omissions in Homer already mentioned, the curious reader will also observe several defects in that author's writings for which he is not altogether so accountable. For whereas every branch of knowledge has received such wonderful acquirements since his age, especially within these last three years° or thereabouts, it is almost impossible he could be so very perfect in modern discoveries as his advocates pretend. We freely acknowledge him to be the inventor of the *compass*, of *gunpowder*, and the *circulation of the blood*: but I challenge any of his admirers to show me in all his writings, a complete account of the *spleen*. Does he not also leave us wholly to seek in the art of *political wagering*?° What can be more defective and unsatisfactory than his long dissertation upon *tea*? And as to his method of *salivation without mercury*, so much celebrated of late, it is to my own knowledge and experience a thing very little to be relied on.

It was to supply such momentous defects that I have been prevailed on, after long solicitation, to take pen in hand; and I dare venture to promise the judicious reader shall find nothing neglected here that can be of use upon any emergency of life. I am confident to have included and exhausted all that human imagination can *rise* or *fall* to. Particularly, I recommend to the perusal of the learned, certain discoveries that are wholly untouched by others, whereof I shall only mention among a great many more, my *New Help* [*for*] *Smatterers*, or the *Art of being Deep-learned and Shallow-read*; *A Curious Invention about Mouse-Traps*; *An Universal Rule of Reason, or every Man his own Carver*; together with a most useful engine for *catching of owls*. All which, the judicious reader will find largely treated on, in the several parts of this discourse.

I hold myself obliged to give as much light as is possible into the beauties and excellencies of what I am writing, because it is become the fashion and humour most applauded among the first authors of this polite and learned age, when they would correct the ill nature of critical, or inform the ignorance of courteous readers. Besides, there have been several famous pieces lately published both in verse and prose, wherein if the writers had not been pleased, out of their great humanity and affection to the public, to give us a nice detail of the *sublime* and the *admirable* they contain, it is a thousand to one whether we should ever have discovered one grain of either. For my own particular, I cannot deny that whatever I have said upon this occasion had been more proper in a preface, and more agreeable to the mode which usually directs it there. But I here think fit to lay hold on that great and honourable privilege, of being the *last writer*. I claim an absolute authority in right, as the *freshest modern*, which gives me a despotic power over all authors before me. In the strength of which title I do utterly disapprove and declare against that pernicious custom of making the preface a bill of fare to the book. For I have always looked upon it as a high point of indiscretion in *monster-mongers* and other *retailers of strange sights*, to hang out a fair large picture over the door, drawn after the life with a most eloquent description underneath. This hath saved me many a threepence, for my curiosity was fully satisfied and I never offered to go in, though often invited by the urging and attending orator with his last *moving* and *standing* piece of rhetoric, 'Sir, upon my word, we are just going to begin.' Such is exactly the fate at this time of Prefaces, Epistles, Advertisements, Introductions, Prolegomenas, Apparatuses, To the Reader's. This expedient was admirable at first. Our great Dryden has long carried it as far as it would go, and with incredible success. He has often said to me in confidence that the world would have never suspected him to be so great a poet, if he had not assured them so frequently in his Prefaces that it was impossible they could either doubt or forget it. Perhaps it may be so. However, I much fear his instructions have edified out of their place, and taught men to grow wiser in certain points where he never intended they should; for it is lamentable to behold with what a lazy scorn many of the yawning readers in our age do nowadays twirl over forty or fifty pages of *preface* and *dedication* (which is the usual *modern* stint) as if it were so much Latin. Though it must be also allowed on the other hand, that a very considerable number is known to proceed *critics* and *wits* by reading nothing else.° Into which two factions, I think, all present readers may justly be divided. Now, for myself, I profess to be of the former sort; and therefore, having the *modern* inclination to expatiate upon the beauty of my own productions and display the bright parts of my discourse, I thought best to do it in the body of the work, where, as it now lies, it makes a very considerable addition to the bulk of the volume, *a circumstance by no means to be neglected by a skilful writer*.

Having thus paid my due deference and acknowledgment to an established custom of our newest authors, by *a long digression unsought for*, and *an universal censure unprovoked*, by forcing into the light, with much pains and and dexterity, my own excellencies and other men's defaults, with great justice to myself and candour to them, I now happily resume my subject, to the infinite satisfaction both of the reader and the author.

SECT. VI.

A Tale of a Tub.

We left Lord Peter in open rupture with his two brethren, both for ever discarded from his house and resigned to the wide world, with little or nothing to trust to; which are circumstances that render them proper subjects for the charity of a writer's pen to work on, scenes of misery ever affording the fairest harvest for great adventures. And in this, the world may perceive the difference between the integrity of a generous author and that of a common friend. The latter is observed to adhere close in prosperity but on the decline of fortune, to drop suddenly off. Whereas the generous author, just on the contrary, finds his hero on the dunghill, from thence by gradual steps raises him to a throne, and then immediately withdraws, expecting not so much as thanks for his pains. In imitation of which example I have placed Lord Peter in a noble house, given him a title to wear, and money to spend. There I shall leave him for some time, returning where common charity directs me, to the assistance of his two brothers at their lowest ebb. However, I shall by no means forget my character of an historian to follow the truth step by step, whatever happens or wherever it may lead me.

The two exiles, so nearly united in fortune and interest, took a lodging together, where, at their first leisure, they began to reflect on the numberless misfortunes and vexations of their life past, and could not tell on the sudden to what failure in their conduct they ought to impute them, when, after some recollection, they called to mind the copy of their father's Will which they had so happily recovered. This was immediately produced, and a firm resolution taken between them to alter whatever was already amiss, and reduce all their future measures to the strictest obedience prescribed therein. The main body of the Will (as the reader cannot easily have forgot) consisted in certain admirable rules about the wearing of their coats, in the perusal whereof the two brothers, at every period, duly comparing the doctrine with the practice, there was never seen a wider difference between two things, horrible downright transgressions of every point. Upon which they both resolved, without further delay, to fall immediately upon reducing the whole, exactly after their father's model.

But here it is good to stop the hasty reader, ever impatient to see the end of an adventure before we writers can duly prepare him for it. I am to record that these two brothers began to be distinguished at this time by certain names. One of them desired to be called *MARTIN*,* and the other took the appellation of *JACK*.† These two had lived in much friendship and agreement under the tyranny of their brother Peter, as it is the talent of fellow-sufferers to do; men in misfortune being like men in the dark, to whom all colours are the same. But when they came forward into the world and began to display themselves to each other and to the light, their complexions appeared extremely different, which the present posture of their affairs gave them sudden opportunity to discover.

But, here the severe reader may justly tax me as a writer of short memory, a deficiency to which a true *modern* cannot but, of necessity, be a little subject. Because, *memory* being an employment of the mind upon things past, is a faculty for which the learned in our illustrious age have no manner of occasion, who deal entirely with *invention*, and strike all things out of themselves, or at least by collision from each other; upon which account, we think it highly reasonable to produce our great forgetfulness as an argument unanswerable for our great wit. I ought in method to have informed the reader, about fifty pages ago, of a fancy Lord Peter took, and infused into his brothers, to wear on their coats whatever trimmings came up in fashion; never pulling off any, as they went out of the mode, but keeping on all together, which amounted in time to a medley the most antic you can possibly conceive, and this to a degree that upon the time of their falling out there was hardly a thread of the original coat to be seen, but an infinite quantity of *lace* and *ribbons*, and *fringe*, and *embroidery*, and *points* (I mean only those *tagged with silver*,‡ for the rest fell off). Now this material circumstance having been forgot in due place, as good fortune hath ordered, comes in very properly here, when the two brothers are just going to reform their vestures into the primitive state, prescribed by their father's Will.

They both unanimously entered upon this great work, looking sometimes on their coats and sometimes on the Will. Martin laid the first hand; at one twitch brought off a large handful of *points*; and with a second pull, stripped away ten dozen yards of *fringe*. But when he had gone thus far he demurred a while. He knew very well there yet remained a great deal more to be done; however, the first heat being over, his violence began to cool, and he resolved to proceed more moderately in the rest of the work; having already narrowly scaped a swingeing rent in pulling off the *points*, which being *tagged with silver* (as we have observed

* Martin Luther.   † John Calvin.
‡ Points tagged with silver are those doctrines that promote the greatness and wealth of the church, which have been therefore woven deepest into the body of popery.

before) the judicious workman had, with much sagacity, double sewn to preserve them from *falling*. Resolving therefore to rid his coat of a great quantity of *gold lace*, he picked up the stitches with much caution, and diligently gleaned out all the loose threads as he went, which proved to be a work of time. Then he fell about the embroidered Indian figures of men, women, and children, against which, as you have heard in its due place, their father's testament was extremely exact and severe: these, with much dexterity and application, were after a while quite eradicated, or utterly defaced. For the rest, where he observed the embroidery to be worked so close as not to be got away without damaging the cloth, or where it served to hide or strengthen any flaw in the body of the coat contracted by the perpetual tampering of workmen upon it, he concluded the wisest course was to let it remain, resolving in no case whatsoever that the substance of the stuff should suffer injury; which he thought the best method for serving the true intent and meaning of his father's Will. And this is the nearest account I have been able to collect of Martin's proceedings upon this great revolution.

But his brother Jack, whose adventures will be so extraordinary as to furnish a great part in the remainder of this discourse, entered upon the matter with other thoughts and a quite different spirit. For the memory of Lord Peter's injuries produced a degree of hatred and spite which had a much greater share of inciting him, than any regards after his father's commands, since these appeared at best only secondary and subservient to the other. However, for this medley of humour he made a shift to find a very plausible name, honouring it with the title of *zeal*; which is perhaps the most significant word° that hath been ever yet produced in any language, as I think I have fully proved in my excellent *analytical* discourse upon that subject, wherein I have deduced a *histori-theo-physi-logical* account of *zeal*, showing how it first proceeded from a *notion* into a *word*, and thence, in a hot summer, ripened into a *tangible substance*. This work, containing three large volumes in folio, I design very shortly to publish by the *modern* way of *subscription*, not doubting but the nobility and gentry of the land will give me all possible encouragement, having already had such a taste of what I am able to perform.

I record, therefore, that brother Jack, brimful of this miraculous compound, reflecting with indignation upon Peter's tyranny, and further provoked by the despondency of Martin, prefaced his resolutions to this purpose. 'What!' said he, 'a rogue that locked up his drink, turned away our wives, cheated us of our fortunes; palmed his damned crusts upon us for mutton; and, at last, kicked us out of doors; must we be in his fashions, with a pox? A rascal, besides, that all the street cries out against.' Having thus kindled and inflamed himself as high as possible, and by consequence in a delicate temper for beginning a reformation, he set about the work immediately, and in three minutes made more dispatch than Martin had done in as many hours. For (courteous reader) you are given to understand, that *zeal* is never so highly obliged as when you set it a-*tearing*; and Jack, who doated on that quality in himself, allowed it at this time its full swinge. Thus it happened that, stripping down a parcel of *gold lace* a little too hastily, he rent the *main body* of his *coat* from top to bottom; and whereas his talent was not of the happiest in *taking up a stitch*, he knew no better way than to darn it again with *packthread* and a *skewer*. But the matter was yet infinitely worse (I record it with tears) when he proceeded to the *embroidery*: for being clumsy by nature, and of temper impatient; withal, beholding millions of stitches that required the nicest hand, and sedatest constitution, to extricate; in a great rage he tore off the whole piece, cloth and all, and flung them into the kennel, and furiously thus continuing his career: 'Ah, good brother Martin,' said he, 'do as I do, for the love of God; strip, tear, pull, rend, flay off all, that we may appear as unlike the rogue Peter as it is possible. I would not for a hundred pounds carry the least mark about me, that might give occasion to the neighbours of suspecting that I was related to such a rascal.' But Martin, who at this time happened to be extremely phlegmatic and sedate, begged his brother, of all love, not to damage his coat by any means; for he never would get such another: desired him to consider that it was not their business to form their actions by any reflection upon Peter's, but by observing the rules prescribed in their father's Will. That he should remember Peter was still their brother, whatever faults or injuries he had committed, and therefore they should, by all means, avoid such a thought as that of taking measures for good and evil, from no other rule than of opposition to him. That it was true, the testament of their good father was very exact in what related to the wearing of their *coats*; yet it was no less penal, and strict, in prescribing agreement and friendship and affection between them. And therefore, if straining a point were at all dispensible, it would certainly be so rather to the advance of unity, than increase of contradiction.

Martin had still proceeded as gravely as he began, and doubtless would have delivered an admirable lecture of morality, which might have exceedingly contributed to my reader's *repose both of body and mind* (the true ultimate end of *ethics*); but Jack was already gone a flight-shot beyond his patience. And as in scholastic disputes nothing serves to rouse the spleen of him that *opposes*, so much as a kind of pedantic affected calmness in the *respondent*; disputants being for the most part like unequal scales, where the *gravity* of one side advances the *lightness* of the other, and causes it to fly up and kick the beam; so it happened here that the *weight* of Martin's argument exalted Jack's *levity*, and made him fly out and spurn against his brother's moderation. In short, Martin's *patience* put Jack in a *rage*; but that which most afflicted him was to observe his brother's coat so well reduced into the state of innocence, while his own was either wholly rent to his shirt, or those places which had scaped his cruel clutches were still in Peter's livery. So that he looked like a drunken *beau*, half rifled by bullies; or like a fresh tenant of Newgate when he has refused the payment of *garnish*; or like a discovered *shoplifter*, left to the mercy of *Exchange-women*;° or like a *bawd* in her old velvet petticoat, resigned into the secular hands of the *mobile*. Like any or like all of these, a medley of *rags*, and *lace*, and *rents*, and *fringes*, unfortunate Jack did now appear: he would have been extremely glad to see his coat in the condition of Martin's, but infinitely gladder to find that of Martin in the same predicament with his. However, since neither of these was likely to come to pass he thought fit to lend the whole business another turn, and to dress up necessity into a virtue. Therefore, after as many of the *fox*'s arguments° as he could muster up for bringing Martin to *reason*, as he called it; or as he meant it, into his own ragged, bobtailed condition; and observing he said all to little purpose; what, alas! was left for the forlorn Jack to do, but after a million of scurrilities against his brother, to run mad with spleen, and spite, and contradiction. To be short, here began a mortal breach between these two. Jack went immediately to *new lodgings*, and in a few days it was for certain reported that he had run out of his wits. In a short time after, he appeared abroad and confirmed the report by falling into the oddest whimseys that ever a sick brain conceived.

And now the little boys in the streets began to salute him with several names. Sometimes they would call him Jack the Bald;* sometimes, Jack with a Lantern;† sometimes, Dutch Jack; ‡° sometimes, French Hugh;§ sometimes, Tom the Beggar;¶ and sometimes, Knocking Jack of the North.‖ And it was under one, or some, or all of these appellations (which I leave the learned reader to determine) that he hath given rise to the most illustrious and epidemic sect of *Æolists*,° who, with honourable

* That is, *Calvin*, from *calvus*, bald.
† All those who pretend to inward light.
‡ Jack of Leyden, who gave rise to the Anabaptists.
§ The Huguenots.
¶ The Gueuses, by which name some Protestants in Flanders were called.
‖ John Knocks, the reformer of Scotland.

commemoration, do still acknowledge the renowned *JACK* for their author and founder. Of whose original, as well as principles, I am now advancing to gratify the world with a very particular account.

— Mellæo contingens cuncta Lepore.°

SECT. VII.

A Digression in Praise of Digressions.

I have sometimes *heard* of an Iliad in a *nutshell*, but it hath been my fortune to have much oftener *seen* a *nutshell* in an Iliad. There is no doubt that human life has received most wonderful advantages from both; but to which of the two the world is chiefly indebted, I shall leave among the curious as a problem worthy of their utmost inquiry. For the invention of the latter, I think the commonwealth of learning is chiefly obliged to the great *modern* improvement of *digressions*: the late refinements in knowledge running parallel to those of diet in our nation, which among men of a judicious taste are dressed up in various compounds, consisting in *soups* and *olios*, *fricassees*, and *ragouts*.

'Tis true there is a sort of morose, detracting, ill-bred people, who pretend utterly to disrelish these polite innovations; and as to the similitude from diet, they allow the parallel but are so bold to pronounce the example itself a corruption and degeneracy of taste. They tell us that the fashion of jumbling fifty things together in a dish was at first introduced in compliance to a depraved and *debauched appetite*, as well as to a *crazy constitution*: and to see a man hunting through an *olio* after the *head* and *brains* of a *goose*, a *widgeon*, or a *woodcock*, is a sign he wants a stomach and digestion for more substantial victuals. Further, they affirm that *digressions* in a book are like *foreign troops* in a *state*, which argue the nation to want a *heart* and *hands* of its own, and often either *subdue* the *natives* or drive them into the most *unfruitful corners*.

But, after all that can be objected by these supercilious censors, 'tis manifest the society of writers would quickly be reduced to a very inconsiderable number, if men were put upon making books with the fatal confinement of delivering nothing beyond what is to the purpose. 'Tis acknowledged that were the case the same among us as with the Greeks and Romans, when learning was in its *cradle*, to be reared and fed and clothed by *invention*, it would be an easy task to fill up volumes upon particular occasions, without further expatiating from the subject than by moderate excursions, helping to advance or clear the main design. But with *knowledge* it has fared as with a numerous army encamped in a fruitful country, which for a few days maintains itself by the product of the soil it is on; till provisions being spent, they are sent to forage many a mile, among friends or enemies it matters not. Meanwhile the neighbouring fields, trampled and beaten down, become barren and dry, affording no sustenance but clouds of dust.

The whole course of things being thus entirely changed between *us* and the *ancients*, and the *moderns* wisely sensible of it, we of this age have discovered a shorter and more prudent method to become *scholars* and *wits*, without the fatigue of *reading* or of *thinking*. The most accomplished way of using books at present is two-fold; either first, to serve them as some men do *lords*, learn their *titles* exactly and then brag of their acquaintance. Or secondly, which is indeed the choicer, the profounder, and politer method, to get a thorough insight into the *index*,° by which the whole book is governed and turned, like *fishes* by the *tail*. For, to enter the palace of learning at the *great gate* requires an expense of time and forms; therefore men of much haste and little ceremony are content to get in by the *back door*. For the arts are all in a *flying* march, and therefore more easily subdued by attacking them in the *rear*. Thus physicians discover the state of the whole body by consulting only what comes from *behind*. Thus men catch knowledge by throwing their *wit* on the *posteriors* of a book, as boys do sparrows with flinging *salt* upon their *tails*. Thus human life is best understood by the wise man's rule, of *regarding the end*.° Thus are the sciences found like Hercules's oxen, by *tracing them backwards*.° Thus are *old sciences* unravelled like *old stockings*, by beginning at the *foot*.

Besides all this, the army of the sciences hath been of late, with a world of martial discipline, drawn into its *close order*, so that a view or a muster may be taken of it with abundance of expedition. For this great blessing we are wholly indebted to *systems* and *abstracts*, in which the *modern* fathers of learning, like prudent usurers, spent their sweat for the ease of us their children. For *labour* is the seed of *idleness*, and it is the peculiar happiness of our noble age to gather the *fruit*.

Now, the method of growing wise, learned, and *sublime*, having become so regular an affair, and so established in all its forms, the number of writers must needs have increased accordingly, and to a pitch that has made it of absolute necessity for them to interfere continually with each other. Besides, it is reckoned that there is not at this present a sufficient quantity of new matter left in nature to furnish and adorn any one particular subject to the extent of a volume.° This I am told by a very skilful *computer*, who hath given a full demonstration of it from rules of *arithmetic*.

This, perhaps, may be objected against by those who maintain the infinity of matter, and therefore will not allow that any *species* of it can be exhausted. For answer to which, let us examine the noblest branch of *modern* wit or invention planted and cultivated by the present age, and which of all others hath borne the most and the fairest fruit. For though some remains of it were left us by the *ancients*, yet have not any of those, as I remember, been translated or compiled into systems for *modern* use. Therefore we may affirm to our own honour, that it has, in some sort, been both invented and brought to perfection by the same hands. What I mean is that highly celebrated talent among the *modern* wits, of deducing similitudes, allusions, and applications, very surprising, agreeable, and apposite, from the *pudenda* of either sex, together with *their proper uses*. And truly, having observed how little invention bears any vogue besides what is derived into these *channels*, I have sometimes had a thought that the happy genius of our age and country was prophetically held forth by that ancient typical description of the Indian pigmies,* *whose stature did not exceed above two foot*; *sed quorum pudenda crassa, et ad talos usque pertingentia.*° Now, I have been very curious to inspect the late productions wherein the beauties of this kind have most prominently appeared. And although this *vein* hath bled so freely, and all endeavours have been used in the power of human breath to dilate, extend, and keep it open; like the Scythians,† *who had a custom, and an instrument, to blow up the privities of their mares, that they might yield the more milk*; yet I am under an apprehension it is near growing dry, and past all recovery, and that either some new *fonde* of wit should if possible be provided, or else that we must even be content with repetition here, as well as upon all other occasions.

This will stand as an uncontestable argument that our *modern* wits are not to reckon upon the infinity of matter for a constant supply. What remains therefore but that our last recourse must be had to large *indexes*, and little *compendiums*? *Quotations* must be plentifully gathered and booked in alphabet; to this end, though authors need be little consulted, yet *critics*, and *commentators*, and *lexicons*, carefully must. But above all, those judicious collectors of *bright parts*, and *flowers*, and *observandas*, are to be nicely dwelt on, by some called the *sieves* and *boulters* of learning, though it is left undetermined whether they dealt in *pearls* or meal, and consequently, whether we are more to value that which *passed through*, or what *stayed behind*.

By these methods, in a few weeks, there starts up many a writer capable of managing the profoundest and most universal subjects. For,

* Ctesiæ fragm. apud Photium.°   † Herodot. L. 4. [2].

what though his *head* be empty provided his *commonplace book* be full, and if you will bate him but the circumstances of *method*, and *style*, and *grammar*, and *invention*; allow him but the common privileges of transcribing from others and digressing from himself as often as he shall see occasion; he will desire no more ingredients towards fitting up a treatise that shall make a very comely figure on a bookseller's shelf; there to be preserved neat and clean for a long eternity, adorned with the heraldry of its title fairly inscribed on a label; never to be thumbed or greased by students nor bound to everlasting chains of darkness in a library:° but, when the fulness of time is come, shall haply undergo the trial of purgatory in order *to ascend the sky*.

Without these allowances, how is it possible we *modern* wits should ever have an opportunity to introduce our collections, listed under so many thousand heads of a different nature; for want of which, the learned world would be deprived of infinite delight as well as instruction, and we ourselves buried beyond redress in an inglorious and un-distinguished oblivion?

From such elements as these, I am alive to behold the day wherein the corporation of authors can outvie all its brethren in the *guild*. A happiness derived to us with a great many others from our Scythian ancestors, among whom the number of *pens* was so infinite that the Grecian* eloquence had no other way of expressing it, than by saying that in the regions far to the *north*, it was hardly possible for a man to travel, the very air was so replete with *feathers*.

The necessity of this digression will easily excuse the length, and I have chosen for it as proper a place as I could readily find. If the judicious reader can assign a fitter, I do here impower him to remove it into any other corner he please. And so I return with great alacrity, to pursue a more important concern.

SECT. VIII.

A Tale of a Tub.

The learned Æolists†° maintain the original cause of all things to be *wind*, from which principle this whole universe was at first produced and into which it must at last be resolved; that the same breath which had kindled and blew *up* the flame of nature, should one day blow it *out*.

Quod procul à nobis flectat fortuna gubernans.°

* Herodot. L. 4. [7 and 31]. † All pretenders to inspiration whatsoever.

This is what the *adepti* understand by their *anima mundi;*° that is to say, the *spirit*, or *breath*, or *wind* of the world; or examine the whole system by the particulars of nature, and you will find it not to be disputed. For whether you please to call the *forma informans*° of man by the name of *spiritus*, *animus*, *afflatus*, or *anima*, what are all these but several appellations for *wind*, which is the ruling *element* in every compound and into which they all resolve upon their corruption? Further, what is life itself, but as it is commonly called, the *breath* of our nostrils?° Whence it is very justly observed by naturalists that *wind* still continues of great emolument in *certain mysteries* not to be named, giving occasion for those happy epithets of *turgidus* and *inflatus*, applied either to the *emittent* or *recipient* organs.

By what I have gathered out of ancient records I find the *compass* of their doctrine took in two and thirty points, wherein it would be tedious to be very particular. However, a few of their most important precepts, deducible from it, are by no means to be omitted, among which the following maxim was of much weight: That since *wind* had the master share as well as operation in every compound, by consequence those beings must be of chief excellence wherein that *primordium* appears most prominently to abound, and therefore *man* is in the highest perfection of all created things, as having, by the great bounty of philosophers, been endued with three distinct *animas*° or *winds*, to which the sage Æolists with much liberality have added a fourth of equal necessity as well as ornament with the other three, by this *quartum principium* taking in the four corners of the world. Which gave occasion to that renowned *cabalist Bumbastus*,* of placing the body of man in due position to the four *cardinal* points.°

In consequence of this, their next principle was that *man* brings with him into the world a peculiar portion or grain of *wind*, which may be called a *quinta essentia*, extracted from the other four. This *quintessence* is of a catholic use upon all emergencies of life, is improveable into all arts and sciences, and may be wonderfully refined as well as enlarged, by certain methods in education. This, when *blown* up to its perfection, ought not to be covetously hoarded up, stifled, or hid under a bushel, but freely communicated to mankind. Upon these reasons and others of equal weight, the wise Æolists affirm the gift of BELCHING to be the noblest act of a rational creature. To cultivate which art and render it more serviceable to mankind, they made use of several methods. At certain seasons of the year, you might behold the priests amongst them,

* This is one of the names of Paracelsus; he was called Christophorus, Theophrastus, Paracelsus, Bumbastus.

in vast numbers, with their *mouths** *gaping wide against a storm*. At other times were to be seen several hundreds linked together in a circular chain, with every man a pair of bellows applied to his neighbour's breech, by which they blew up each other to the shape and size of a *tun*; and for that reason, with great propriety of speech, did usually call their bodies, their *vessels*. When by these and the like performances they were grown sufficiently replete, they would immediately depart, and disembogue for the public good a plentiful share of their acquirements into their disciples' chaps. For we must here observe that all learning was esteemed among them to be compounded from the same principle. Because first, it is generally affirmed, or confessed, that learning *puffeth men up*;° and secondly, they proved it by the following syllogism: *Words are but wind*; *and learning is nothing but words*; ergo, *learning is nothing but wind*. For this reason, the philosophers among them did in their schools deliver to their pupils all their doctrines and opinions by *eructation*, wherein they had acquired a wonderful eloquence, and of incredible variety. But the great characteristic by which their chief sages were best distinguished, was a certain position of countenance, which gave undoubted intelligence to what degree or proportion the spirit agitated the inward mass. For, after certain gripings, the *wind* and vapours issuing forth, having first by their turbulence and convulsions within caused an earthquake in man's little world, distorted the mouth, bloated the cheeks, and gave the eyes a terrible kind of *relievo*. At which junctures all their *belches* were received for sacred, the sourer the better, and swallowed with infinite consolation by their meagre devotees. And to render these yet more complete, because the breath of man's life is in his nostrils, therefore the choicest, most edifying, and most enlivening *belches*, were very wisely conveyed through that vehicle° to give them a tincture as they passed.

Their gods were the four *winds*, whom they worshipped as the spirits that pervade and enliven the universe, and as those from whom alone all *inspiration* can properly be said to proceed. However, the chief of these, to whom they performed the adoration of *latria*,° was the *almighty North*, an ancient deity whom the inhabitants of Megalopolis, in Greece, had likewise in highest reverence: *omnium deorum Boream maxime celebrant.*†° This god, though endued with ubiquity, was yet supposed by the profounder Æolists to possess one peculiar habitation, or (to speak in form) a *cœlum empyræum*, wherein he was more intimately present. This was situated in a certain region well known to the ancient Greeks, by

---

* This is meant of those seditious preachers, who blow up the seeds of rebellion, &c.

† Pausan. L. 8.

them called Σκοτία,° or the *Land of Darkness*. And although many controversies have arisen upon that matter, yet so much is undisputed that from a region of the *like denomination* the most refined Æolists have borrowed their original, from whence, in every age, the zealous among their priesthood have brought over their choicest *inspiration*, fetching it with their own hands from the fountain-head in certain *bladders*, and disploding it among the sectaries in all nations, who did, and do, and ever will, daily gasp and pant after it.

Now, their mysteries and rites were performed in this manner. 'Tis well known among the learned that the virtuosos of former ages had a contrivance for carrying and preserving *winds* in casks or barrels, which was of great assistance upon long sea voyages, and the loss of so useful an art at present is very much to be lamented though, I know not how, with great negligence omitted by Pancirollus.*° It was an invention ascribed to Æolus himself, from whom this sect is denominated, and who, in honour of their founder's memory, have to this day preserved great numbers of those *barrels*, whereof they fix one in each of their temples, first beating out the top; into this *barrel*, upon solemn days, the priest enters, where having before duly prepared himself by the methods already described a secret funnel is also conveyed from his posteriors to the bottom of the barrel, which admits new supplies of inspiration, from a *northern* chink or cranny. Whereupon, you behold him swell immediately to the shape and size of his *vessel*. In this posture he disembogues whole tempests upon his auditory, as the spirit from beneath gives him utterance, which issuing *ex adytis* and *penetralibus*,° is not performed without much pain and gripings. And the wind in breaking forth deals with his face† as it does with that of the sea, first *blackening*, then *wrinkling*, and at last *bursting it into a foam*. It is in this guise the sacred Æolist delivers his oracular *belches* to his panting disciples; of whom some are greedily gaping after the sanctified breath, others are all the while hymning out the praises of the *winds*, and, gently wafted to and fro by their own humming, do thus represent the soft breezes of their deities appeased.

It is from this custom of the priests that some authors maintain these Æolists to have been very ancient in the world; because the delivery of their mysteries, which I have just now mentioned, appears exactly the same with that of other ancient oracles whose inspirations were owing to certain subterraneous *effluviums* of *wind*, delivered with the *same* pain to the priest and much about the *same* influence on the people. It is true

---

* An author who writ *De Artibus perditis* &c., of arts lost, and of arts invented.

† This is an exact description of the changes made in the face by Enthusiastic preachers.

indeed, that these were frequently managed and directed by *female* officers, whose organs were understood to be better disposed for the admission of those oracular *gusts*, as entering and passing up through a receptacle of greater capacity, and causing also a pruriency by the way, such as with due management hath been refined from a carnal into a spiritual ecstasy. And, to strengthen this profound conjecture, it is further insisted that this custom of *female* priests* is kept up still in certain refined colleges of our *modern* Æolists, who are agreed to receive their inspiration, derived through the receptacle aforesaid, like their ancestors the Sybils.

And whereas the mind of man, when he gives the spur and bridle to his thoughts, doth never stop but naturally sallies out into both extremes of high and low, of good and evil, his first flight of fancy commonly transports him to ideas of what is most perfect, finished, and exalted; till, having soared out of his own reach and sight, not well perceiving how near the frontiers of height and depth border upon each other; with the same course and wing he falls down plumb into the lowest bottom of things, like one who travels the *East* into the *West*, or like a straight line drawn by its own length into a circle. Whether a tincture of malice in our natures makes us fond of furnishing every bright idea with its reverse; or whether reason, reflecting upon the sum of things, can like the sun serve only to enlighten one half of the globe, leaving the other half by necessity under shade and darkness; or whether fancy, flying up to the imagination of what is highest and best, becomes overshot, and spent, and weary, and suddenly falls like a dead bird of paradise to the ground; or whether, after all these *metaphysical* conjectures, I have not entirely missed the true reason; the proposition however which hath stood me in so much circumstance is altogether true; that, as the most uncivilized parts of mankind have some way or other climbed up into the conception of a *God* or Supreme Power, so they have seldom forgot to provide their fears with certain ghastly notions, which instead of better have served them pretty tolerably for a *devil*. And this proceeding seems to be natural enough; for it is with men whose imaginations are lifted up very high, after the same rate as with those whose bodies are so; that, as they are delighted with the advantage of a nearer contemplation upwards, so they are equally terrified with the dismal prospect of the precipice below. Thus, in the choice of a *devil*, it hath been the usual method of mankind to single out some being, either in act or in vision, which was in most antipathy to the god they had framed. Thus also the sect of Æolists possessed themselves with a dread and horror and hatred of two malignant natures, betwixt

---

* Quakers, who suffer their women to preach and pray.

whom and the deities they adored, perpetual enmity was established. The first of these was the *chameleon*,* sworn foe to *inspiration*, who in scorn devoured large influences of their god without refunding the smallest blast by *eructation*. The other was a huge terrible monster called Moulinavent, who with four strong arms waged eternal battle with all their divinities, dexterously turning to avoid their blows and repay them with interest.

Thus furnished, and set out with *gods* as well as *devils*, was the renowned sect of Æolists, which makes at this day so illustrious a figure in the world, and whereof that polite nation of Laplanders are, beyond all doubt, a most authentic branch; of whom I therefore cannot without injustice here omit to make honourable mention, since they appear to be so closely allied in point of interest as well as inclinations with their brother Æolists among us, as not only to buy their *winds* by wholesale from the *same* merchants, but also to retail them after the *same* rate and method, and to customers much alike.

Now, whether the system here delivered was wholly compiled by Jack, or as some writers believe, rather copied from the original at Delphos,° with certain additions and emendations suited to times and circumstances; I shall not absolutely determine. This I may affirm, that Jack gave it at least a new turn, and formed it into the same dress and model as it lies deduced by me.

I have long sought after this opportunity of doing justice to a society of men for whom I have a peculiar honour; and whose opinions, as well as practices, have been extremely misrepresented and traduced by the malice or ignorance of their adversaries. For I think it one of the greatest and best of human actions, to remove prejudices and place things in their truest and fairest light; which I therefore boldly undertake without any regards of my own, beside the conscience, the honour, and the thanks.

SECT. IX.

A Digression concerning the Original, the Use, and Improvement of Madness in a Commonwealth.

Nor shall it any ways detract from the just reputation of this famous sect, that its rise and institution are owing to such an author as I have described Jack to be: a person whose intellectuals were overturned, and

---

* I do not well understand what the Author aims at here, any more than by the terrible Monster mentioned in the following lines, called *Moulinavent*, which is the French word for a windmill.

his brain shaken out of its natural position, which we commonly suppose to be a distemper and call by the name of *madness* or *frenzy*. For, if we take a survey of the greatest actions that have been performed in the world under the influence of single men, which are *the establishment of new empires by conquest, the advance and progress of new schemes in philosophy, and the contriving, as well as the propagating, of new religions*; we shall find the authors of them all to have been persons whose natural reason hath admitted great revolutions, from their diet, their education, the prevalency of some certain temper, together with the particular influence of air and climate. Besides, there is something individual in human minds that easily kindles at the accidental approach and collision of certain circumstances, which though of paltry and mean appearance, do often flame out into the greatest emergencies of life. For great turns are not always given by strong hands, but by lucky adaption and at proper seasons; and it is of no import where the fire was kindled if the vapour has once got up into the brain. For the *upper region* of man is furnished like the *middle region* of the air; the materials are formed from causes of the widest difference, yet produce at last the same substance and effect. Mists arise from the earth, steams from dunghills, exhalations from the sea, and smoke from fire; yet all clouds are the same in composition as well as consequences, and the fumes issuing from a jakes will furnish as comely and useful a vapour as incense from an altar. Thus far, I suppose, will easily be granted me; and then it will follow that, as the face of nature never produces rain but when it is overcast and disturbed, so human understanding, seated in the brain, must be troubled and overspread by vapours ascending from the lower faculties to water the invention, and render it fruitful. Now, although these vapours (as it hath been already said) are of as various original as those of the skies, yet the crop they produce differs both in kind and degree, merely according to the soil. I will produce two instances to prove and explain what I am now advancing.

A certain great prince*° raised a mighty army, filled his coffers with infinite treasures, provided an invincible fleet, and all this without giving the least part of his design to his greatest ministers or his nearest favourites. Immediately the whole world was alarmed; the neighbouring crowns in trembling expectation towards what point the storm would burst; the small politicians everywhere forming profound conjectures. Some believed he had laid a scheme for universal monarchy; others, after much insight, determined the matter to be a project for pulling down the pope and setting up the *reformed* religion, which had once been his own.

* This was Harry the Great of France.

Some again, of a deeper sagacity, sent him into Asia to subdue the Turk and recover Palestine. In the midst of all these projects and preparations, a certain *state-surgeon** gathering the nature of the disease by these symptoms, attempted the cure, at one blow performed the operation, broke the bag, and out flew the *vapour*; nor did anything want to render it a complete remedy, only that the prince unfortunately happened to die in the performance. Now, is the reader exceeding curious to learn from whence this *vapour* took its rise, which had so long set the nations at a gaze? What secret wheel, what hidden spring, could put into motion so wonderful an engine? It was afterwards discovered that the movement of this whole machine had been directed by an absent *female* whose eyes had raised a protuberancy, and before emission, she was removed into an enemy's country. What should an unhappy prince do in such ticklish circumstances as these? He tried in vain the poet's never-failing receipt of *corpora quæque*;° for

> Idque petit corpus mens unde est saucia amore:
> Unde feritur, eo tendit, gestitque coire.°   LUCR.

Having to no purpose used all peaceable endeavours, the collected part of the semen, raised and inflamed, became adust, converted to choler, turned head upon the spinal duct, and ascended to the brain. The very same principle that influences a *bully* to break the windows of a whore who has jilted him, naturally stirs up a great prince to raise mighty armies and dream of nothing but sieges, battles, and victories.

> [Cunnus] teterrima belli
> Causa ——— °

The other instance† is what I have read somewhere in a very ancient author, of a mighty king,° who, for the space of above thirty years, amused himself to take and lose towns; beat armies, and be beaten; drive princes out of their dominions; fright children from their bread and butter; burn, lay waste, plunder, dragoon,° massacre subject and stranger, friend and foe, male and female. 'Tis recorded that the philosophers of each country were in grave dispute upon causes natural, moral, and political, to find out where they should assign an original solution of this *phenomenon*. At last, the *vapour* or *spirit* which animated the hero's brain, being in perpetual circulation, seized upon that region of the human body so renowned for furnishing the *zibeta occidentalis*,‡ and gathering

---

* Ravillac, who stabbed Henry the Great in his coach.

† This is meant of the present French king.

‡ Paracelsus, who was so famous for chemistry, tried an experiment upon human

there into a tumour, left the rest of the world for that time in peace. Of such mighty consequence it is where those exhalations fix, and of so little from whence they proceed. The same spirits which, in their superior progress, would conquer a kingdom, descending upon the *anus* conclude in a *fistula*.

Let us next examine the great introducers of new schemes in philosophy, and search till we can find from what faculty of the soul the disposition arises in mortal man, of taking it into his head to advance new systems with such an eager zeal, in things agreed on all hands impossible to be known; from what seeds this disposition springs, and to what quality of human nature these grand innovators have been indebted for their number of disciples. Because it is plain that several of the chief among them, both *ancient* and *modern*, were usually mistaken by their adversaries, and indeed by all except their own followers, to have been persons crazed, or out of their wits; having generally proceeded in the common course of their words and actions, by a method very different from the vulgar dictates of *unrefined* reason, agreeing for the most part in their several models with their present undoubted successors in the *academy* of *modern Bedlam*° (whose merits and principles I shall further examine in due place). Of this kind were *Epicurus, Diogenes, Apollonius,*° *Lucretius, Paracelsus, Des Cartes*, and others, who if they were now in the world, tied fast, and separate from their followers, would in this our undistinguishing age incur manifest danger of *phlebotomy*, and *whips*, and *chains*, and *dark chambers*, and *straw*. For what man in the natural state or course of thinking, did ever conceive it in his power to reduce the notions of all mankind exactly to the same length, and breadth, and height of his own? Yet this is the first humble and civil design of all innovators in the empire of reason. Epicurus modestly hoped that, one time or other, a certain fortuitous concourse of all men's opinions, after perpetual justlings, the sharp with the smooth, the light and the heavy, the round and the square, would by certain *clinamina*° unite in the notions of *atoms* and *void*, as these did in the originals of all things. Cartesius reckoned to see, before he died, the sentiments of all philosophers, like so many lesser stars in his *romantic* system, wrapped and drawn within his own *vortex*.° Now I would gladly be informed, how it is possible to account for such imaginations as these in particular men without recourse to my *phenomenon* of *vapours*, ascending from the lower faculties to overshadow the brain, and thence distilling into conceptions for which the

excrement to make a perfume of it; which, when he had brought to perfection, he called *zibeta occidentalis*, or *western civet*; the back parts of man (according to his division mentioned by the author, page [134]), being the *west*.

narrowness of our mother tongue has not yet assigned any other name besides that of *madness* or *phrenzy*. Let us therefore now conjecture how it comes to pass, that none of these great prescribers do ever fail providing themselves and their notions with a number of implicit disciples. And I think the reason is easy to be assigned: for there is a peculiar *string* in the harmony of human understanding which, in several individuals, is exactly of the same tuning. This, if you can dexterously screw up to its right key and then strike gently upon it, whenever you have the good fortune to light among those of the same pitch they will, by a secret necessary sympathy, strike exactly at the same time. And in this one circumstance lies all the skill or luck of the matter; for if you chance to jar the string among those who are either above or below your own height, instead of subscribing to your doctrine they will tie you fast, call you mad, and feed you with bread and water. It is therefore a point of the nicest conduct to distinguish and adapt this noble talent, with respect to the differences of persons and times. Cicero understood this very well, when writing to a friend in England with a caution, among other matters, to beware of being cheated by our *hackney-coachmen* (who it seems, in those days were as arrant rascals as they are now) has these remarkable words, *Est quod gaudeas te in ista loca venisse, ubi aliquid sapere viderere.**° For, to speak a bold truth, it is a fatal miscarriage so ill to order affairs as to pass for a *fool* in one company, when in another you might be treated as a *philosopher*. Which I desire *some certain gentlemen of my acquaintance* to lay up in their hearts as a very seasonable *innuendo*.

This, indeed, was the fatal mistake of that worthy gentleman, my most ingenious friend Mr. W[o]tt[o]n: a person, in appearance, ordained for great designs as well as performances, whether you will consider his *notions* or his *looks*. Surely no man ever advanced into the public with fitter qualifications of body and mind for the propagation of a new religion. Oh, had those happy talents, misapplied to vain philosophy, been turned into their proper channels of *dreams* and *visions*, where *distortion* of mind and countenance are of such sovereign use, the base detracting world would not then have dared to report that something is amiss, that his brain hath undergone an unlucky shake, which even his brother *modernists* themselves, like ungrates, do whisper so loud that it reaches up to the very garret I am now writing in.

Lastly, whoever pleases to look into the fountains of *enthusiasm*, from whence in all ages have eternally proceeded such fattening streams, will find the spring head to have been as *troubled* and *muddy* as the current. Of such great emolument is a tincture of this *vapour* which the world calls

* Epist. ad Fam. Trebatio.

madness, that without its help the world would not only be deprived of those two great blessings, *conquests* and *systems*, but even all mankind would unhappily be reduced to the same belief in things invisible. Now, the former *postulatum* being held, that it is of no import from what originals this *vapour* proceeds, but either in what *angles* it strikes and spreads over the understanding or upon what *species* of brain it ascends, it will be a very delicate point to cut the feather,° and divide the several reasons to a nice and curious reader, how this numerical difference in the brain can produce effects of so vast a difference from the same *vapour*, as to be the sole point of individuation between Alexander the Great, Jack of Leyden,° and Monsieur Des Cartes. The present argument is the most abstracted that ever I engaged in; it strains my faculties to their highest stretch; and I desire the reader to attend with the utmost perpensity, for I now proceed to unravel this knotty point.

There is in mankind a certain*   *   *   *   *
*   *   *   *   *   *   *   *

Hic multa   *   *   *   *   *   *
desiderantur.   *   *   *   *   *   *

*   *   *   * And this I take to be a clear solution of the matter.

Having therefore so narrowly passed through this intricate difficulty, the reader will I am sure agree with me in the conclusion, that if the *moderns* mean by *madness*, only a disturbance or transposition of the brain by force of certain *vapours* issuing up from the lower faculties, then has this *madness* been the parent of all those mighty revolutions that have happened in *empire*, in *philosophy*, and in *religion*. For the brain, in its natural position and state of serenity, disposeth its owner to pass his life in the common forms without any thoughts of subduing multitudes to his own *power*, his *reasons*, or his *visions*; and the more he shapes his understanding by the pattern of human learning, the less he is inclined to form parties after his particular notions, because that instructs him in his private infirmities, as well as in the stubborn ignorance of the people. But when a man's fancy gets *astride* on his reason, when imagination is at cuffs with the senses, and common understanding as well as common sense, is kicked out of doors; the first proselyte he makes is himself, and when that is once compassed the difficulty is not so great in bringing over others, a strong delusion always operating from *without* as vigorously as from *within*. For cant and vision are to the ear and the eye, the same that

---

* Here is another defect in the manuscript; but I think the author did wisely, and that the matter which thus strained his faculties was not worth a solution; and it were well if all metaphysical cobweb problems were no otherwise answered.

tickling is to the touch. Those entertainments and pleasures we most value in life are such as *dupe* and play the wag with the senses. For, if we take an examination of what is generally understood by *happiness*, as it has respect either to the understanding or the senses, we shall find all its properties and adjuncts will herd under this short definition: that *it is a perpetual possession of being well deceived*. And first, with relation to the mind or understanding, 'tis manifest what mighty advantages fiction has over truth; and the reason is just at our elbow, because imagination can build nobler scenes and produce more wonderful revolutions than fortune or nature will be at expense to furnish. Nor is mankind so much to blame in his choice thus determining him, if we consider that the debate merely lies between *things past* and *things conceived*; and so the question is only this, whether things that have place in the *imagination*, may not as properly be said to *exist* as those that are seated in the *memory*; which may be justly held in the affirmative, and very much to the advantage of the former since this is acknowledged to be the *womb* of things, and the other allowed to be no more than the *grave*. Again, if we take this definition of happiness and examine it with reference to the senses, it will be acknowledged wonderfully adapt. How fade and insipid do all objects accost us that are not conveyed in the vehicle of *delusion*! How shrunk is everything as it appears in the glass of nature! So that if it were not for the assistance of artificial *mediums*, false lights, refracted angles, varnish, and tinsel, there would be a mighty level in the felicity and enjoyments of mortal men. If this were seriously considered by the world, as I have a certain reason to suspect it hardly will, men would no longer reckon among their high points of wisdom the art of exposing weak sides and publishing infirmities; an employment, in my opinion, neither better nor worse than that of *unmasking*, which I think has never been allowed fair usage, either in the *world* or the *play-house*.

In the proportion that credulity is a more peaceful possession of the mind than curiosity; so far preferable is that wisdom which converses about the surface, to that pretended philosophy which enters into the depth of things, and then comes gravely back with informations and discoveries that in the inside they are good for nothing. The two senses to which all objects first address themselves are the sight and the touch. These never examine further than the colour, the shape, the size, and whatever other qualities dwell, or are drawn by art, upon the outward of bodies; and then comes reason officiously, with tools for cutting, and opening, and mangling, and piercing, offering to demonstrate that they are not of the same consistence quite through. Now I take all this to be the last degree of perverting Nature, one of whose eternal laws it is, to put her best furniture forward. And therefore, in order to save the charges of all such expensive anatomy for the time to come, I do here think fit to inform the reader that in such conclusions as these, reason is certainly in the right, and that in most corporeal beings which have fallen under my cognizance, the *outside* hath been infinitely preferable to the *in*; whereof I have been further convinced from some late experiments. Last week I saw a woman *flayed*, and you will hardly believe how much it altered her person for the worse. Yesterday I ordered the carcass of a *beau* to be stripped in my presence, when we were all amazed to find so many unsuspected faults under one suit of clothes. Then I laid open his *brain*, his *heart*, and his *spleen*; but I plainly perceived at every operation that the farther we proceeded, we found the defects increase upon us in number and bulk; from all which, I justly formed this conclusion to myself. That whatever philosopher or projector can find out an art to solder and patch up the flaws and imperfections of nature will deserve much better of mankind, and teach us a more useful science than that so much in present esteem, of widening and exposing them (like him who held *anatomy* to be the ultimate end of *physic*). And he whose fortunes and dispositions have placed him in a convenient station to enjoy the fruits of this noble art; he that can with Epicurus content his ideas with the *films* and *images* that fly off upon his senses from the *superficies* of things;° such a man, truly wise, creams off Nature, leaving the sour and the dregs for philosophy and reason to lap up. This is the sublime and refined point of felicity, called *the possession of being well deceived*; the serene peaceful state, of being a fool among knaves.

But to return to *madness*. It is certain that, according to the system I have above deduced, every *species* thereof proceeds from a redundancy of *vapours*; therefore, as some kinds of *phrenzy* give double strength to the sinews, so there are of other *species* which add vigour, and life, and spirit to the brain. Now, it usually happens that these active spirits, getting possession of the brain, resemble those that haunt other waste and empty dwellings, which for want of business, either vanish and carry away a piece of the house, or else stay at home, and fling it all out of the windows. By which are mystically displayed the two principal branches of *madness*, and which some philosophers not considering so well as I, have mistook to be different in their causes, over-hastily assigning the first to deficiency, and the other to redundance.

I think it therefore manifest from what I have here advanced, that the main point of skill and address is to furnish employment for this redundancy of *vapour*, and prudently to adjust the seasons of it; by which means it may certainly become of cardinal and catholic emolument in a commonwealth. Thus one man, choosing a proper juncture, leaps into a gulf,° from thence proceeds a hero and is called the saver of his country; another achieves the same enterprise but, unluckily timing it, has left the brand of *madness* fixed as a reproach upon his memory. Upon so nice a distinction are we taught to repeat the name of Curtius with reverence and love, that of Empedocles° with hatred and contempt. Thus also it is usually conceived that the elder Brutus° only personated the *fool* and *madman* for the good of the public; but that was nothing else than a redundancy of the same *vapour* long misapplied, called by the Latins, *ingenium par negotiis*;*° or, (to translate it as nearly as I can) a sort of *phrenzy*, never in its right element till you take it up in business of the state.

Upon all which and many other reasons of equal weight, though not equally curious, I do here gladly embrace an opportunity I have long sought for, of recommending it as a very noble undertaking to Sir E[dwar]d S[eymou]r,° Sir C[hristophe]r M[usgra]ve, Sir J[oh]n B[ow]ls, J[oh]n H[o]w, Esq. and other patriots concerned, that they would move for leave to bring in a bill for appointing commissioners to inspect into Bedlam,° and the parts adjacent; who shall be empowered to *send for persons, papers, and records*, to examine into the merits and qualifications of every student and professor, to observe with utmost exactness their several dispositions and behaviour, by which means, duly distinguishing and adapting their talents, they might produce admirable instruments for the several offices in a state, [*ecclesiastical*], *civil*, and *military*, proceeding in such methods as I shall here humbly propose. And I hope the gentle reader will give some allowance to my great solicitudes in this important affair, upon account of the high esteem I have borne that honourable society whereof I had some time the happiness to be an unworthy member.

Is any student tearing his straw in piecemeal, swearing and blaspheming, biting his grate, foaming at the mouth, and emptying his piss-pot in the spectators' faces? Let the right worshipful the *commissioners of inspection* give him a regiment of dragoons, and send him into Flanders among the *rest*. Is another eternally talking, sputtering, gaping, bawling in a sound without period or article? What wonderful talents are here mislaid! Let him be furnished immediately with a green bag and papers and *threepence* in his pocket,†° and away with him to Westminster Hall. You will find a third gravely taking the dimensions of his kennel, a person of foresight and insight, though kept quite in the

---

* Tacit. [*Annals* vi, 39 and xvi, 18].
† A lawyer's coach-hire.

dark; for why, like Moses *ecce cornuta* erat ejus facies.*° He walks duly in one pace, entreats your penny with due gravity and ceremony, talks much of hard times, and taxes, and the whore of Babylon, bars up the wooden window of his cell constantly at eight o'clock, dreams of *fire*, and *shoplifters*, and *court-customers*, and *privileged places*. Now what a figure would all these acquirements amount to, if the owner were sent into the *city* among his brethren! Behold a fourth, in much and deep conversation with himself, biting his thumbs at proper junctures, his countenance checkered with business and design; sometimes walking very fast, with his eyes nailed to a paper that he holds in his hands; a great saver of time, somewhat thick of hearing, very short of sight, but more of memory; a man ever in haste, a great hatcher and breeder of business, and excellent at the famous art of *whispering nothing*; a huge idolator of monosyllables and procrastination, so ready to *give* his word to everybody that he never *keeps* it; one that has forgot the common *meaning* of words, but an admirable retainer of the *sound*; extremely subject to the *looseness*, for his *occasions* are perpetually *calling him away*. If you approach his grate in his familiar intervals; 'Sir,' says he, 'give me a penny and I'll sing you a song; but give me the penny first' (hence comes the common saying, and commoner practice, of parting with money for a *song*.) What a complete system of *court skill* is here described in every branch of it, and all utterly lost with wrong application! Accost the hole of another kennel, first stopping your nose, you will behold a surly, gloomy, nasty, slovenly mortal, raking in his own dung and dabbling in his urine. The best part of his diet is the reversion of his own ordure which, expiring into steams, whirls perpetually about and at last reinfunds. His complexion is of a dirty yellow with a thin scattered beard, exactly agreeable to that of his diet upon its first declination; like other insects, who having their birth and education in an excrement, from thence borrow their colour and their smell. The student of this apartment is very sparing of his words, but somewhat over-liberal of his breath. He holds his hand out ready to receive your penny, and immediately upon receipt, withdraws to his former occupations. Now, is it not amazing to think, the society of Warwick Lane° should have no more concern for the recovery of so useful a member who, if one may judge from these appearances, would become the greatest ornament to that illustrious body? Another student struts up fiercely to your teeth, puffing with his lips, half squeezing out his eyes, and very graciously holds you out his hand to kiss. The *keeper* desires you not to be afraid of this professor, for he will do you no hurt; to

---

* *Cornutus* is either horned or shining, and by this term Moses is described in the vulgar Latin of the Bible.

him alone is allowed the liberty of the antechamber, and the *orator* of the place° gives you to understand that this solemn person is a *tailor* run mad with pride. This considerable student is adorned with many other qualities, upon which at present I shall not further enlarge.........*Hark in your ear**.........I am strangely mistaken if all his address, his motions, and his airs, would not then be very natural and in their proper element.

I shall not descend so minutely as to insist upon the vast number of *beaux, fiddlers, poets*, and *politicians*, that the world might recover by such a reformation. But what is more material, besides the clear gain redounding to the commonwealth by so large an acquisition of persons to employ, whose talents and acquirements, if I may be so bold to affirm it, are now buried or at least misapplied; it would be a mighty advantage accruing to the public from this inquiry, that all these would very much excel and arrive at great perfection in their several kinds; which I think is manifest from what I have already shown, and shall enforce by this one plain instance, that even I myself, the author of these momentous truths, am a person whose imaginations are hard-mouthed and exceedingly disposed to run away with his *reason*, which I have observed from long experience to be a very light rider, and easily shook off; upon which account, my friends will never trust me alone without a solemn promise to vent my speculations in this, or the like manner, for the universal benefit of human kind; which perhaps the gentle, courteous, and candid reader, brimful of that *modern* charity and tenderness usually annexed to his *office*, will be very hardly persuaded to believe.

SECT. X.

[*A Further Digression.*]

It is an unanswerable argument of a very refined age, the wonderful civilities that have passed of late years between the nation of *authors* and that of *readers*. There can hardly pop out a *play*, a *pamphlet*, or a *poem*, without a preface full of acknowledgments to the world for the general reception and applause they have given it,† which the Lord knows where, or when, or how, or from whom it received. In due deference to so laudable a custom I do here return my humble thanks to *His Majesty*, and

---

* I cannot conjecture what the author means here, or how this chasm could be filled, though it is capable of more than one interpretation.

† This is literally true, as we may observe in the prefaces to most plays, poems, &c.

both houses of *Parliament*; to the *Lords* of the King's Most Honourable Privy Council; to the reverend the *Judges*; to the *clergy*, and *gentry*, and *yeomanry* of this land; but in a more especial manner to my worthy brethren and friends at Will's Coffee-house, and Gresham College, and Warwick Lane, and Moorfields, and Scotland Yard, and Westminster Hall, and Guildhall;° in short, to all inhabitants and retainers whatsoever, either in court, or church, or camp, or city, or country, for their generous and universal acceptance of this divine treatise. I accept their approbation and good opinion with extreme gratitude, and, to the utmost of my poor capacity, shall take hold of all opportunities to return the obligation.

I am also happy that fate has flung me into so blessed an age for the mutual felicity of *booksellers* and *authors*, whom I may safely affirm to be at this day the two only satisfied parties in England. Ask an *author* how his last piece hath succeeded. Why, truly he thanks his stars, the world has been very favourable, and he has not the least reason to complain; and yet, by G—, he writ it in a week, at bits and starts, when he could steal an hour from his urgent affairs, as it is a hundred to one you may see further in the preface, to which he refers you, and for the rest, to the bookseller. There you go as a customer, and make the same question: he blesses his God the *thing* takes wonderfully, he is just printing a second edition, and has but three left in his shop. You beat down the *price*: 'Sir, we shall not differ'—and, in hopes of your custom another time, lets you have it as reasonable as you please, 'and pray send as many of your acquaintance as you will, I shall, upon your account, furnish them at all the same rate.'

Now, it is not well enough considered to what accidents and occasions the world is indebted for the greatest part of these noble writings which hourly start up to entertain it. If it were not for a *rainy day, a drunken vigil, a fit of the spleen, a course of physic, a sleepy Sunday, an ill run at dice, a long tailor's bill, a beggar's purse, a factious head, a hot sun, costive diet, want of books, and a just contempt of learning*—but for these events, I say, and some others too long to recite (especially *a prudent neglect of taking brimstone inwardly*) I doubt the number of *authors* and of *writings* would dwindle away to a degree most woeful to behold. To confirm this opinion, hear the words of the famous Troglodyte philosopher.° ' 'Tis certain' (said he) 'some grains of folly are of course annexed, as part of the composition of human nature, only the choice is left us whether we please to wear them *inlaid* or *embossed*, and we need not go very far to seek how that is usually determined, when we remember it is with human faculties as with liquors, the lightest will be ever at the top.'

There is in this famous island of Britain a certain paltry *scribbler*, very voluminous, whose character the reader cannot wholly be a stranger to.

He deals in a pernicious kind of writings called *Second Parts*, and usually passes under the name of *The Author of the First*. I easily foresee that as soon as I lay down my pen, this nimble *operator* will have stole it, and treat me as inhumanly as he hath already done Dr. B[lackmo]re,° L[estran]ge,° and many others who shall here be nameless. I therefore fly, for justice and relief, into the hands of that great *rectifier of saddles*,° and *lover of mankind*, Dr. B[en]tly, begging he will take this enormous grievance into his most *modern* consideration; and if it should so happen that the *furniture of an ass*,° in the shape of a *Second Part*, must for my sins be clapped by a mistake upon my back, that he will immediately please, in the presence of the world, to lighten me of the burden, and take it home to *his own house* till the *true beast* thinks fit to call for it.

In the meantime I do here give this public notice, that my resolutions are to circumscribe within this discourse the whole stock of matter I have been so many years providing. Since my *vein* is once opened, I am content to exhaust it all at a running for the peculiar advantage of my dear country, and for the universal benefit of mankind. Therefore, hospitably considering the number of my guests, they shall have my whole entertainment at a meal, and I scorn to set up the *leavings* in the cupboard. What the *guests* cannot eat may be given to the *poor*, and the *dogs** under the table may gnaw the *bones*. This I understand for a more generous proceeding, than to turn the company's stomach by inviting them again tomorrow to a scurvy meal of *scraps*.

If the reader fairly considers the strength of what I have advanced in the foregoing section I am convinced it will produce a wonderful revolution in his notions and opinions; and he will be abundantly better prepared to receive and to relish the concluding part of this miraculous treatise. Readers may be divided into three classes—the *superficial*, the *ignorant*, and the *learned*; and I have with much felicity fitted my pen to the genius and advantage of each. The *superficial* reader will be strangely provoked to *laughter*; which clears the breast and the lungs, is sovereign against the *spleen*, and the most innocent of all *diuretics*. The *ignorant* reader (between whom and the former the distinction is extremely nice) will find himself disposed to *stare*; which is an admirable remedy for ill eyes, serves to raise and enliven the spirits, and wonderfully helps *perspiration*. But the reader truly *learned*, chiefly for whose benefit I wake when others sleep, and sleep when others wake, will here find sufficient matter to employ his speculations for the rest of his life. It were much to be wished, and I do here humbly propose for an experiment, that every

---

* By dogs, the author means common injudicious critics, as he explains it himself before in his *Digression upon Critics*.

prince in Christendom will take seven of the *deepest scholars* in his dominions, and shut them up close for *seven* years in *seven* chambers, with a command to write *seven* ample commentaries on this comprehensive discourse. I shall venture to affirm that whatever difference may be found in their several conjectures, they will be all, without the least distortion, manifestly deducible from the text. Meantime it is my earnest request that so useful an undertaking may be entered upon (if their Majesties please) with all convenient speed; because I have a strong inclination, before I leave the world, to taste a blessing which we *mysterious* writers can seldom reach till we have got into our graves: whether it is that *fame*, being a fruit grafted on the body, can hardly grow and much less ripen till the *stock* is in the earth: or whether she be a bird of prey, and is lured among the rest to pursue after the scent of a *carcass*: or whether she conceives her trumpet sounds best and farthest when she stands on a *tomb*, by the advantage of a rising ground and the echo of a hollow vault.

'Tis true indeed, the republic of *dark* authors, after they once found out this excellent expedient of *dying*, have been peculiarly happy in the variety as well as extent of their reputation. For, *night* being the universal mother of things, wise philosophers hold all writings to be *fruitful*, in the proportion they are *dark*; and therefore, the *true illuminated** (that is to say, the *darkest* of all) have met with such numberless commentators, whose *scholiastic* midwifery hath delivered them of meanings that the authors themselves perhaps never conceived, and yet may very justly be allowed the lawful parents of them; the words of such writers being like seed,† which, however scattered at random, when they light upon a fruitful ground, will multiply far beyond either the hopes or imagination of the sower.

And therefore, in order to promote so useful a work I will here take leave to glance a few *innuendoes*, that may be of great assistance to those sublime spirits who shall be appointed to labour in a universal comment upon this wonderful discourse. And first,‡ I have couched a very profound mystery in the number of O's multiplied by *seven*, and divided by *nine*. Also, if a devout brother of the Rosy Cross will pray fervently for sixty three mornings with a lively faith, and then transpose certain letters and syllables according to prescription in the second and fifth section, they will certainly reveal into a full receipt of the *opus magnum*. Lastly,

---

* A name of the Rosicrucians.°

† Nothing is more frequent than for Commentators to force interpretations, which the authors never meant.

‡ This is what the Cabalists among the Jews have done with the Bible, and pretend to find wonderful mysteries by it.

whoever will be at the pains to calculate the whole number of each letter in this treatise, and sum up the difference exactly between the several numbers, assigning the true natural cause for every such difference, the discoveries in the product will plentifully reward his labour. But then he must beware of *Bythus* and *Sigè*,*° and be sure not to forget the qualities of *Acamoth*; *à cujus lacrymis humecta prodit substantia, à risu lucida, à tristitia solida, et à timore mobilis;*° wherein Eugenius Philalethes† hath committed an unpardonable mistake.

SECT. XI.

A Tale of a Tub.

After so wide a compass as I have wandered, I do now gladly overtake and close in with my subject, and shall henceforth hold on with it an even pace to the end of my journey, except some beautiful prospect appears within sight of my way; whereof though at present I have neither warning nor expectation, yet upon such an accident, come when it will, I shall beg my reader's favour and company, allowing me to conduct him through it along with myself. For in *writing* it is as in *travelling*: if a man is in haste to be at home (which I acknowledge to be none of my case, having never so little business as when I am there) if his *horse* be tired with long riding and ill ways or be naturally a jade, I advise him clearly to make the straightest and the commonest road, be it ever so dirty. But then surely we must own such a man to be a scurvy companion at best; he *spatters* himself and his fellow-travellers at every step; all their thoughts, and wishes, and

---

* I was told by an eminent divine, whom I consulted on this point, that these two barbarous words, with that of *Acamoth* and its qualities, as here set down, are quoted from Irenæus. This he discovered by searching that ancient writer for another quotation of our author, which he has placed in the title-page, and refers to the book and chapter; the curious were very inquisitive whether those barbarous words, *basima eacabasa, &c.* are really in Irenæus, and upon inquiry, 'twas found they were a sort of cant or jargon of certain heretics, and therefore very properly prefixed to such a book as this of our author.

† *Vid. Anima Magica Abscondita.*°

Ibid. To the above-mentioned treatise, called *Anthroposophia Theomagica*, there is another annexed, called *Anima Magica Abscondita*, written by the same author, Vaughan, under the name of Eugenius Philalethes, but in neither of those treatises is there any mention of *Acamoth*, or its qualities, so that this is nothing but amusement, and a ridicule of dark, unintelligible writers; only the words, *à cujus lacrymis, &c.* are, as we have said, transcribed from Irenæus, though I know not from what part. I believe one of the author's designs was to set curious men a-hunting through *indexes*, and inquiring for books out of the common road.

conversation, turn entirely upon the subject of their journey's end; and at every splash, and plunge, and stumble they heartily wish one another at the devil.

On the other side, when a traveller and his *horse* are in heart and plight, when his purse is full and the day before him, he takes the road only where it is clean or convenient; entertains his company there as agreeably as he can; but upon the first occasion carries them along with him to every delightful scene in view, whether of art, of nature, or of both; and if they chance to refuse out of stupidity or weariness, let them jog on by themselves and be d—n'd; he'll overtake them at the next town, at which arriving, he rides furiously through; the men, women, and children run out to gaze, a hundred* *noisy curs* run *barking* after him, of which if he honours the boldest with a *lash of his whip*, it is rather out of sport than revenge; but should some *sourer mongrel* dare too near an approach, he receives a *salute* on the chops by an accidental stroke from the courser's heels (nor is any ground lost by the blow) which sends him yelping and limping home.

I now proceed to sum up the singular adventures of my renowned Jack, the state of whose dispositions and fortunes the careful reader does, no doubt, most exactly remember as I last parted with them in the conclusion of a former section. Therefore, his next care must be, from two of the foregoing, to extract a scheme of notions that may best fit his understanding for a true relish of what is to ensue.

Jack had not only calculated the first revolution of his brain so prudently as to give rise to that epidemic sect of Æolists, but succeeding also into a new and strange variety of conceptions, the fruitfulness of his imagination led him into certain notions which, although in appearance very unaccountable, were not without their mysteries and their meanings, nor wanted followers to countenance and improve them. I shall therefore be extremely careful and exact in recounting such material passages of this nature as I have been able to collect, either from undoubted tradition, or indefatigable reading; and shall describe them as graphically as it is possible, and as far as notions of that height and latitude can be brought within the compass of a pen. Nor do I at all question, but they will furnish plenty of noble matter for such whose converting imaginations dispose them to reduce all things into *types*;° who can make *shadows*, no thanks to the sun, and then mould them into substances, no thanks to philosophy; whose peculiar talent lies in fixing tropes and allegories to the *letter*, and refining what is literal into figure and mystery.

* By these are meant what the author calls the *true critics*.

Jack had provided* a fair copy of his father's Will engrossed in form upon a large skin of parchment, and resolving to act the part of a most dutiful son, he became the fondest creature of it imaginable. For although, as I have often told the reader, it consisted wholly in certain plain, easy directions about the management and wearing of their coats, with legacies and penalties in case of obedience or neglect, yet he began to entertain a fancy that the matter was *deeper* and *darker*, and therefore must needs have a great deal more of mystery at the bottom. 'Gentlemen,' said he, 'I will prove this very skin of parchment to be meat, drink, and cloth, to be the philosopher's stone, and the universal medicine.' In consequence of which raptures he resolved to make use of it in the necessary, as well as the most paltry occasions of life. He had a way of working it into any shape he pleased, so that it served him for a nightcap when he went to bed, and for an umbrella in rainy weather. He would lap a piece of it about a sore toe, or when he had fits burn two inches under his nose; or if anything lay heavy on his stomach, scrape off and swallow as much of the powder as would lie on a silver penny. They were all infallible remedies. With analogy to these refinements, his common talk and conversation ran wholly in the phrase of his Will,† and he circumscribed the utmost of his eloquence within that compass, not daring to let slip a syllable without authority from thence. Once at a strange house he was suddenly taken short upon an urgent juncture, whereon it may not be allowed too particularly to dilate; and being not able to call to mind with that suddenness the occasion required, an authentic phrase for demanding the way to the back-side, he chose rather, as the more prudent course, to incur the penalty in such cases usually annexed. Neither was it possible for the united rhetoric of mankind to prevail with him to make himself clean again; because having consulted the Will upon this emergency, he met with a passage‡ near the bottom° (whether foisted in by the transcriber, is not known) which seemed to forbid it.

He made it a part of his religion never to say grace to his meat;§ nor

* The author here lashes those pretenders to purity, who place so much merit in using scripture phrases on all occasions.

† The Protestant dissenters use *scripture phrases* in their serious discourses and composures, more than the Church of England men; accordingly, Jack is introduced making *his common talk and conversation to run wholly in the phrase of his WILL*. W. WOTTON.

‡ I cannot guess the author's meaning here, which I would be very glad to know because it seems to be of importance.

§ The slovenly way of receiving the sacrament among the fanatics.

could all the world persuade him, as the common phrase is, to eat his victuals *like a Christian.**

He bore a strange kind of appetite to *snap-dragon*,† and to the livid snuffs of a burning candle, which he would catch and swallow with an agility wonderful to conceive; and by this procedure, maintained a perpetual flame in his belly, which, issuing in a glowing steam from both his eyes as well as his nostrils and his mouth, made his head appear in a dark night like the skull of an ass wherein a roguish boy hath conveyed a farthing candle, *to the terror of his Majesty's liege subjects*. Therefore, he made use of no other expedient to light himself home, but was wont to say that *a wise man was his own lantern*.

He would shut his eyes as he walked along the streets, and if he happened to bounce his head against a post, or fall into a kennel (as he seldom missed either to do one or both) he would tell the gibing prentices who looked on, that he submitted with entire resignation as to a trip, or a blow of fate, with whom he found by long experience how vain it was either to wrestle or to cuff, and whoever durst undertake to do either would be sure to come off with a swingeing fall or a bloody nose. 'It was ordained',° said he, 'some few days before the Creation, that my nose and this very post should have a rencounter, and therefore nature thought fit to send us both into the world in the same age, and to make us countrymen and fellow-citizens. Now, had my eyes been open it is very likely the business might have been a great deal worse; for how many a confounded slip is daily got by man with all his foresight about him? Besides, the eyes of the understanding see best when those of the senses are out of the way; and therefore blind men are observed to tread their steps with much more caution, and conduct, and judgment, than those who rely with too much confidence upon the virtue of the visual nerve which every little accident shakes out of order, and a drop, or a film, can wholly disconcert; like a lantern among a pack of roaring bullies when they scour the streets, exposing its owner and itself to outward kicks and buffets, which both might have escaped if the vanity of appearing would have suffered them to walk in the dark. But further, if we examine the *conduct* of these boasted lights, it will prove yet a great deal worse than their *fortune*. 'Tis true, I have broke my nose against this post because

---

* This is a common phrase to express eating cleanlily, and is meant for an invective against that undecent manner among some people in receiving the sacrament; so in the lines before, 'tis said, Jack *would never say Grace to his Meat*, which is to be understood of the dissenters refusing to kneel at the sacrament.

† I cannot well find the author's meaning here, unless it be the hot, untimely, blind zeal of Enthusiasts.

fortune either forgot, or did not think it convenient, to twitch me by the elbow and give me notice to avoid it. But let not this encourage either the present age, or posterity, to trust their *noses* into the keeping of their *eyes*, which may prove the fairest way of losing them for good and all. For, O ye eyes, ye blind guides, miserable guardians are ye of our frail noses; ye, I say, who fasten upon the first precipice in view, and then tow our wretched willing bodies after you to the very brink of destruction. But, alas, that brink is rotten, our feet slip, and we tumble down prone into a gulf without one hospitable shrub in the way to break the fall—a fall to which not any nose of mortal make is equal, except that of the giant Laurcalco* who was Lord of the Silver Bridge. Most properly therefore, O eyes, and with great justice may you be compared to those foolish lights which conduct men through dirt and darkness, till they fall into a deep pit or a noisome bog.'

This I have produced as a scantling of Jack's great eloquence and the force of his reasoning upon such abstruse matters.

He was, besides, a person of great design and improvement in affairs of *devotion*, having introduced a new deity who hath since met with a vast number of worshippers, by some called Babel, by others Chaos; who had an ancient temple of Gothic structure° upon Salisbury Plain, famous for its shrine and celebration by pilgrims.

When he had some roguish trick to play† he would down with his knees, up with his eyes, and fall to prayers, though in the midst of the kennel. Then it was that those who understood his pranks would be sure to get far enough out of his way; and whenever curiosity attracted strangers to laugh or to listen, he would of a sudden, with one hand, out with his *gear* and piss full in their eyes, and with the other all to-bespatter them with mud.

In winter he went always loose and unbuttoned‡ and clad as thin as possible, to let *in* the ambient heat; and in summer lapped himself close and thick to keep it *out*.

In all revolutions of government§ he would make his court for the office of *hangman* general, and in the exercise of that dignity, wherein he was very dexterous, would make use of no other *vizard*¶ than a *long prayer*.

He had a tongue so musculous and subtile that he could twist it up into

* *Vide* Don Quixote.°
† The villainies and cruelties committed by Enthusiasts and fanatics among us, were all performed under the disguise of religion and long prayers.
‡ They affect differences in habit and behaviour.
§ They are severe persecutors, and all in a form of cant and devotion.
¶ Cromwell and his confederates went, as they called it, *to seek God*, when they resolved to murder the king.

his nose and deliver a strange kind of speech° from thence. He was also the first in these kingdoms who began to improve the Spanish accomplishment of *braying*;° and having large ears, perpetually exposed and arrect, he carried his art to such a perfection, that it was a point of great difficulty to distinguish either by the view or the sound between the *original* and the *copy*.

He was troubled with a disease reverse to that called the stinging of the *tarantula*,° and would run dog-mad at the noise of *music*,* especially a *pair of bagpipes*. But he would cure himself again by taking two or three turns in Westminster Hall, or Billingsgate, or in a boarding-school, or the Royal Exchange, or a *state coffee-house*.

He was a person that *feared* no *colours*° but mortally *hated* all, and upon that account bore a cruel aversion to *painters*;† insomuch that, in his paroxysms, as he walked the streets he would have his pockets loaden with stones to pelt at the *signs*.

Having from this manner of living, frequent occasions to *wash* himself, he would often leap over head and ears into the water° though it were in the midst of the winter, but was always observed to come out again much *dirtier*, if possible, than he went in.

He was the first that ever found out the secret of contriving a *soporiferous* medicine to be conveyed in at the *ears*;‡ it was a compound of *sulphur* and *balm of Gilead*, with a little *pilgrim's salve*.°

He wore a large plaister of artificial *caustics* on his stomach, with the fervour of which he could set himself a-*groaning*, like the famous *board*° upon application of a red-hot iron.

He would stand in the turning of a street, and calling to those who passed by, would cry to one, 'Worthy sir, do me the honour of a good slap in the chaps.'§ To another, 'Honest friend, pray favour me with a handsome kick on the arse.' 'Madam, shall I entreat a small box in the ear from your ladyship's fair hands?' 'Noble captain, lend a reasonable thwack, for the love of God, with that cane of yours over these poor shoulders.' And when he had, by such earnest solicitations, made a shift to procure a basting sufficient to swell up his fancy and his sides, he

---

* This is to expose our dissenters' aversion to instrumental music in churches. W. WOTTON.

† They quarrel at the most innocent decency and ornament, and defaced the statues and paintings on all the churches in England.

‡ Fanatic preaching, composed either of hell and damnation, or a fulsome description of the joys of heaven; both in such a dirty, nauseous style, as to be well resembled to pilgrim's salve.

§ The fanatics have always had a way of affecting to run into persecution, and count vast merit upon every little hardship they suffer.

would return home extremely comforted, and full of terrible accounts of what he had undergone for the *public good*. 'Observe this stroke,' (said he, showing his bare shoulders) 'a plaguy janissary gave it me this very morning at seven o'clock as, with much ado, I was driving off the Great Turk. Neighbours mine, this broken head deserves a plaster; had poor Jack been tender of his noddle you would have seen the Pope, and the French king, long before this time of day among your wives and your warehouses. Dear Christians, the Great Mogul was come as far as Whitechapel, and you may thank these poor sides that he hath not (God bless us) already swallowed up man, woman, and child.'

It was highly worth observing the singular effects of that aversion* or antipathy which Jack and his brother Peter seemed, even to an affectation, to bear towards each other. Peter had lately done *some rogueries* that forced him to abscond, and he seldom ventured to stir out before night, for fear of bailiffs. Their lodgings were at the two most distant parts of the town from each other; and whenever their occasions or humours called them abroad, they would make choice of the oddest unlikely times, and most uncouth rounds they could invent, that they might be sure to avoid one another: yet, after all this, it was their perpetual fortune to meet. The reason of which is easy enough to apprehend; for the frenzy and the spleen of both having the same foundation, we may look upon them as two pair of compasses, equally extended, and the fixed foot of each remaining in the same centre; which, though moving contrary ways at first, will be sure to encounter somewhere or other in the circumference. Besides, it was among the great misfortunes of Jack to bear a huge personal resemblance with his brother Peter. Their humour and dispositions were not only the same but there was a close analogy in their shape, their size, and their mien. Insomuch, as nothing was more frequent than for a bailiff to seize Jack by the shoulders, and cry 'Mr. Peter, you are the king's prisoner.' Or, at other times, for one of Peter's nearest friends to accost Jack with open arms, 'Dear Peter, I am glad to see thee, pray send me one of your best medicines for the worms.' This we may suppose was a mortifying return of those pains and proceedings Jack had laboured in so long. And finding how directly opposite all his endeavours had answered to the sole end

---

* The papists and fanatics, though they appear the most averse to each other, yet bear a near resemblance in many things, as hath been observed by learned men.

Ibid. The agreement of our dissenters and the papists, in that which Bishop Stillingfleet called *the fanaticism of the Church of Rome*, is ludicrously described for several pages together, by Jack's likeness to Peter, and their being often mistaken for each other, and their frequent meeting when they least intended it. W. WOTTON.

and intention which he had proposed to himself, how could it avoid
having terrible effects upon a head and heart so furnished as his?
However, the poor remainders of his *coat* bore all the punishment; the
orient sun never entered upon his diurnal progress without missing a
piece of it. He hired a tailor to stitch up the collar so close that it was
ready to choke him, and squeezed out his eyes at such a rate as one could
see nothing but the white. What little was left of the main substance of the
coat, he rubbed every day for two hours against a rough-cast wall in order
to grind away the remnants of *lace* and *embroidery*, but at the same time
went on with so much violence that he proceeded a *heathen philosopher*.
Yet after all he could do of this kind, the success continued still to
disappoint his expectation. For, as it is the nature of rags to bear a kind of
mock resemblance to finery, there being a sort of fluttering appearance in
both which is not to be distinguished at a distance, in the dark, or by
short-sighted eyes; so, in those junctures it fared with Jack and his tatters
that they offered to the first view a ridiculous flaunting which, assisting
the resemblance in person and air, thwarted all his projects of separation,
and left so near a similitude between them as frequently deceived the
very disciples and followers of both.

*   *   *   *   *   *   *   *

*   *   *   *   *   *   *   *

Desunt non-   *   *   *   *   *

nulla.   *   *   *   *   *

*   *   *   *   *   *   *   *

*   *   *   *   *   *   *   *

The old Sclavonian proverb said well, that it is with *men* as with *asses*;
whoever would keep them fast, must find a very good hold at their ears.
Yet I think we may affirm, and it hath been verified by repeated
experience, that

Effugiet tamen hæc sceleratus vincula Proteus.°

It is good, therefore, to read the maxims of our ancestors with great
allowances to times and persons; for if we look into primitive records we
shall find that no revolutions have been so great, or so frequent, as those
of human *ears*. In former days there was a curious invention to catch and
keep them, which I think we may justly reckon among the *artes perditæ*;°
and how can it be otherwise when, in these latter centuries, the very
species is not only diminished to a very lamentable degree but the poor
remainder is also degenerated so far as to mock our skilfullest *tenure*?
For, if the only slitting of one *ear* in a stag° hath been found sufficient to
propagate the defect through a whole forest, why should we wonder at

the greatest consequences from so many loppings and mutilations to which the *ears* of our fathers, and our own, have been of late so much exposed? 'Tis true indeed, that while this *island* of ours was under the *dominion of grace*, many endeavours were made to improve the growth of *ears*° once more among us. The proportion of largeness was not only looked upon as an ornament of the *outward* man, but as a type of grace in the *inward*. Besides, it is held by naturalists that if there be a protuberancy of parts in the *superior* region of the body, as in the *ears* and *nose*, there must be a parity also in the *inferior*; and therefore in that truly pious age, the *males* in every assembly, according as they were gifted, appeared very forward in exposing their *ears* to view, and the regions about them; because Hippocrates tells us,* that 'when the vein behind the ear happens to be cut, a man becomes a eunuch'. And the *females* were nothing backwarder in beholding and edifying by them; whereof those who had already *used the means* looked about them with great concern in hopes of conceiving a suitable offspring by such a prospect; others, who stood candidates for *benevolence*, found there a plentiful choice and were sure to fix upon such as discovered the largest *ears*, that the breed might not dwindle between them. Lastly, the devouter sisters, who looked upon all extraordinary dilatations of that member as protrusions of zeal, or spiritual excrescencies, were sure to honour every head they sat upon as if they had been *marks of grace*; but especially that of the preacher, whose *ears* were usually of the prime magnitude, which upon that account, he was very frequent and exact in exposing with all advantages to the people: in his rhetorical *paroxysms* turning sometimes to *hold forth* the one, and sometimes to *hold forth* the other; from which custom the whole operation of preaching is to this very day, among their professors, styled by the phrase of *holding forth*.

Such was the progress of the *saints* for advancing the size of that member. And it is thought the success would have been every way answerable if, in process of time, a cruel king had not arisen† who raised a bloody persecution against all *ears* above a certain standard; upon which, some were glad to hide their flourishing sprouts in a black border, others crept wholly under a periwig; some were slit, others cropped, and a great number sliced off to the stumps. But of this more hereafter in my *General History of Ears*, which I design very speedily to bestow upon the public.

From this brief survey of the falling state of *ears* in the last age, and the

---

* *Lib. de aëre, locis, et aquis* [50, 51].

† This was King Charles the Second, who at his restoration turned out all the dissenting teachers that would not conform.

small care had to advance their ancient growth in the present, it is manifest how little reason we can have to rely upon a hold so short, so weak, and so slippery; and that whoever desires to catch mankind fast must have recourse to some other methods. Now, he that will examine human nature with circumspection enough, may discover several *handles*, whereof the *six** senses° afford one a-piece, beside a great number that are screwed to the passions and some few rivetted to the intellect. Among these last, *curiosity* is one, and of all others affords the firmest grasp; *curiosity*, that spur in the side, that bridle in the mouth, that ring in the nose, of a lazy, an impatient, and a grunting reader. By this *handle* it is that an author should seize upon his readers; which as soon as he hath once compassed, all resistance and struggling are in vain, and they become his prisoners as close as he pleases, till weariness or dulness force him to let go his gripe.

And therefore I, the author of this miraculous treatise, having hitherto beyond expectation maintained, by the aforesaid *handle*, a firm hold upon my gentle readers, it is with great reluctance that I am at length compelled to remit my grasp, leaving them, in the perusal of what remains, to that natural *oscitancy*° inherent in the tribe. I can only assure thee, courteous reader, for both our comforts, that my concern is altogether equal to thine for my unhappiness in losing, or mislaying among my papers, the remaining part of these memoirs; which consisted of accidents, turns, and adventures, both new, agreeable, and surprising, and therefore calculated in all due points to the delicate taste of this our noble age. But, alas, with my utmost endeavours I have been able only to retain a few of the heads. Under which there was a full account, how Peter got a *protection* out of the King's Bench; and of a reconcilement† between Jack and him, upon a design they had, in a certain *rainy night* to trepan brother Martin into a *sponging-house* and there strip him to the skin. How Martin, with much ado, showed them both a fair pair of heels. How a *new warrant* came out against Peter, upon which, how Jack left him in the lurch, *stole his protection, and made use of it himself.* How Jack's tatters came into fashion in *court* and *city*; how *he got upon a great*

* Including Scaliger's.

† In the reign of King James the Second, the Presbyterians, by the king's invitation, joined with the Papists against the Church of England, and addressed him for repeal of the penal laws and Test. The king, by his dispensing power, gave liberty of conscience, which both Papists and Presbyterians made use of; but upon the Revolution, the Papists being down of course, the Presbyterians freely continued their assemblies by virtue of King James's indulgence, before they had a toleration by law. This I believe the author means by Jack's *stealing* Peter's *protection, and making use of it himself.*

horse,* *and eat custard.†* But the particulars of all these, with several others which have now slid out of my memory, are lost beyond all hopes of recovery. For which misfortune, leaving my readers to condole with each other as far as they shall find it to agree with their several constitutions, but conjuring them by all the friendship that hath passed between us, from the title-page to this, not to proceed so far as to injure their healths for an accident past remedy; I now go on to the ceremonial part of an accomplished writer and therefore, by a courtly *modern*, least of all others to be omitted.

THE CONCLUSION.

Going too long is a cause of abortion as effectual, though not so frequent, as *going too short*; and holds true especially in the *labours* of the brain. Well fare the heart of that noble Jesuit‡° who first adventured to confess in print that books must be suited to their several seasons, like dress, and diet, and diversions. And better fare our noble nation for refining upon this among other French modes. I am living fast to see the time when a *book* that misses its tide shall be neglected as the *moon* by day, or like *mackerel* a week after the season. No man hath more nicely observed our climate than the bookseller who bought the copy of this work. He knows to a tittle what subjects will best go off in a *dry year*, and which it is proper to expose foremost when the weather-glass is fallen to *much rain*. When he had seen this treatise and consulted his *almanac* upon it, he gave me to understand that he had maturely considered the two principal things, which were the *bulk* and the *subject*, and found it would never *take* but after a long vacation, and then only in case it should happen to be a hard year for turnips. Upon which I desired to know, *considering my urgent necessities*, what he thought might be acceptable this month. He looked westward and said, 'I doubt we shall have a fit of bad weather. However, if you could prepare some pretty little *banter* (*but not in verse*) or a small treatise upon the ——, it would run like wildfire. But *if it hold up*, I have already hired an author to write something against Dr. B[en]tl[e]y, which I am sure will turn to account.'

At length we agreed upon this expedient; that when a customer comes

---

*   Sir Humphry Edwin, a Presbyterian, was some years ago [1697] Lord Mayor of London, and had the insolence to go in his formalities to a conventicle, with the ensigns of his office.

†   Custard is a famous dish at a Lord Mayor's feast.

‡   Père d'Orleans.

for one of these and desires in confidence to know the author, he will tell him very privately as a friend, naming whichever of the wits shall happen to be that week in the vogue; and if Durfey's last play should be in course, I would as lieve he may be the person as Congreve. This I mention, because I am wonderfully well acquainted with the present relish of courteous readers, and have often observed with singular pleasure, that a *fly* driven from a *honey-pot* will immediately, with very good appetite, alight and finish his meal on an *excrement*.

I have one word to say upon the subject of *profound writers*, who are grown very numerous of late and I know very well the judicious world is resolved to list me in that number. I conceive therefore, as to the business of being *profound*, that it is with *writers* as with *wells*—a person with good eyes may see to the bottom of the deepest provided any *water* be there, and that often when there is nothing in the world at the bottom besides *dryness* and *dirt*, though it be but a yard and half underground it shall pass, however, for wondrous *deep*, upon no wiser a reason than because it is wondrous *dark*.

I am now trying an experiment very frequent among modern authors, which is *to write upon nothing*;° when the subject is utterly exhausted, to let the pen still move on; by some called the ghost of wit, delighting to walk after the death of its body. And to say the truth, there seems to be no part of knowledge in fewer hands than that of discerning *when to have done*. By the time that an author has writ out a book, he and his readers are become old acquaintance and grow very loth to part; so that I have sometimes known it to be in writing as in visiting, where the ceremony of taking leave has employed more time than the whole conversation before. The conclusion of a treatise resembles the conclusion of human life, which hath sometimes been compared to the end of a feast where few are satisfied to depart, *ut plenus vitæ conviva*.° For men will sit down after the fullest meal, though it be only to *doze* or to *sleep* out the rest of the day. But in this latter I differ extremely from other writers, and shall be too proud if by all my labours I can have anyways contributed to the *repose* of mankind, in times* so turbulent and unquiet as these. Neither do I think such an employment so very alien from the office of a *wit* as some would suppose. For, among a very polite nation in Greece,†° there were the same temples built and consecrated to *Sleep* and the *Muses*, between which two deities they believed the strictest friendship was established.

I have one concluding favour to request of my reader; that he will not expect to be equally diverted and informed by every line or every page of

---

* This was writ before the peace of Ryswick.
† Trezenii. Pausan. lib. 2.

this discourse, but give some allowance to the author's spleen and short fits or intervals of dulness, as well as his own; and lay it seriously to his conscience whether, if he were walking the streets in dirty weather or a rainy day, he would allow it fair dealing in folks at their ease from a window to critick his gait, and ridicule his dress at such a juncture.

In my disposure of employments of the brain, I have thought fit to make *invention* the *master*, and to give *method* and *reason* the office of its *lackeys*. The cause of this distribution was, from observing it my peculiar case to be often under a temptation of being *witty* upon occasion where I could be neither *wise*, nor *sound*, nor anything to the matter in hand. And I am too much a servant of the *modern* way to neglect any such opportunities, whatever pains or improprieties I may be at to introduce them. For I have observed that from a laborious collection of seven hundred thirty-eight *flowers* and *shining hints* of the best *modern* authors, digested with great reading into my book of *commonplaces*, I have not been able after five years to draw, hook, or force, into common conversation any more than a dozen. Of which dozen, the one moiety failed of success by being dropped among unsuitable company, and the other cost me so many strains, and traps, and *ambages* to introduce, that I at length resolved to give it over. Now this disappointment (to discover a secret) I must own gave me the first hint of setting up for an *author*; and I have since found, among some particular friends, that it is become a very general complaint and has produced the same effects upon many others. For I have remarked many a *towardly word* to be wholly neglected or despised in *discourse*, which has passed very smoothly, with some consideration and esteem, after its preferment and sanction in *print*. But now, since by the liberty and encouragement of the press, I am grown absolute master of the occasions and opportunities to expose the talents I have acquired, I already discover that the *issues* of my *observanda* begin to grow too large for the *receipts*. Therefore, I shall here pause a while till I find, by feeling the world's pulse and my own, that it will be of absolute necessity (for us both) to resume my pen.

A DISCOURSE Concerning the Mechanical Operation of the SPIRIT. IN A LETTER *To a FRIEND*. A FRAGMENT.

THE BOOKSELLER'S ADVERTISEMENT.

THE *following Discourse came into my hands perfect and entire. But there being several things in it which the present age would not very well bear, I kept it by me some years, resolving it should never see the light. At length, by the advice and assistance of a judicious friend, I retrenched those parts that might give most offence, and have now ventured to publish the remainder. Concerning the author I am wholly ignorant, neither can I conjecture whether it be the same with that of the two foregoing pieces, the original having been sent me at a different time, and in a different hand. The learned reader will better determine; to whose judgement I entirely submit it.*

For T. H. *Esquire,*° *at his Chambers in the Academy of the* Beaux Esprits *in* New Holland.°

Sir,

IT is now a good while since I have had in my head something not only very material, but absolutely necessary to my health, that the world should be informed in. For to tell you a secret, I am able to *contain* it no longer. However, I have been perplexed for some time to resolve what would be the most proper form to send it abroad in. To which end I have three days been coursing through Westminster Hall, and St. Paul's Churchyard, and Fleet Street, to peruse titles, and I do not find any which holds so general a vogue as that of *A Letter to a Friend.* Nothing is more common than to meet with long epistles addressed to persons and places where, at first thinking, one would be apt to imagine it not altogether so necessary or convenient; such as *a Neighbour at next Door, a mortal Enemy, a perfect Stranger,* or *a Person of Quality in the Clouds*; and

This Discourse is not altogether equal to the two former, the best parts of it being omitted; whether the bookseller's account be true, that he durst not print the rest, I know not; nor indeed is it easy to determine whether he may be relied on in anything he says of this or the former treatises, only as to the time they were writ in, which however appears more from the discourses themselves than his relation.

these upon subjects in appearance the least proper for conveyance by the post; as *long schemes in philosophy*; *dark and wonderful mysteries of state*; *laborious dissertations in criticism and philosophy*; *advice to parliaments*, and the like.

Now, Sir, to proceed after the method in present wear—for let me say what I will to the contrary, I am afraid you will publish this letter, as soon as ever it comes to your hands—I desire you will be my witness to the world how careless and sudden a scribble it has been; that it was but yesterday when you and I began accidentally to fall into discourse on this matter; that I was not very well when we parted; that the post is in such haste, I have had no manner of time to digest it into order or correct the style. And if any other modern excuses for haste and negligence shall occur to you in reading, I beg you to insert them, faithfully promising they shall be thankfully acknowledged.

Pray, Sir, in your next letter to the *Iroquois Virtuosi*,° do me the favour to present my humble service to that illustrious body, and assure them I shall send an account of those phenomena, as soon as we can determine them at Gresham.

I have not had a line from the *Literati* of Tobinambou these three last ordinaries.

And now, Sir, having dispatched what I had to say of forms, or of business, let me entreat you will suffer me to proceed upon my subject, and to pardon me if I make no further use of the epistolary style till I come to conclude.

SECTION I.

'Tis recorded of Mahomet that, upon a visit he was going to pay in Paradise, he had an offer of several vehicles to conduct him upwards, as fiery chariots, winged horses, and celestial sedans; but he refused them all and would be borne to Heaven upon nothing but his *ass*. Now this inclination of Mahomet, as singular as it seems, hath been since taken up by a great number of devout Christians, and doubtless with very good reason. For, since that Arabian is known to have borrowed a moiety of his religious system from the Christian faith, it is but just he should pay reprisals to such as would challenge them; wherein the good people of England, to do them all right, have not been backward. For though there is not any other nation in the world so plentifully provided with carriages for that journey, either as to safety or ease, yet there are abundance of us who will not be satisfied with any other machine beside this of Mahomet.

For my own part I must confess to bear a very singular respect to this animal, by whom I take human nature to be most admirably held forth in all its qualities as well as operations. And therefore whatever in my small reading occurs concerning this our fellow creature, I do never fail to set it down by way of commonplace; and when I have occasion to write upon human reason, politics, eloquence, or knowledge, I lay my *memorandums* before me and insert them with a wonderful facility of application. However, among all the qualifications ascribed to this distinguished brute by ancient or modern authors I cannot remember this talent of bearing his rider to Heaven has been recorded for a part of his character, except in the two examples mentioned already. Therefore I conceive the methods of this art to be a point of useful knowledge in very few hands, and which the learned world would gladly be better informed in. This is what I have undertaken to perform in the following discourse. For, towards the operation already mentioned many peculiar properties are required both in the *rider* and the *ass* which I shall endeavour to set in as clear a light as I can.

But, because I am resolved by all means to avoid giving offence to any party whatever, I will leave off discoursing so closely to the *letter* as I have hitherto done, and go on for the future by way of allegory, though in such a manner that the judicious reader may without much straining make his applications as often as he shall think fit. Therefore, if you please, from henceforward instead of the term *ass* we shall make use of *gifted* or *enlightened teacher*; and the word *rider* we will exchange for that of *fanatic auditory*, or any other denomination of the like import. Having settled this weighty point, the great subject of inquiry before us is to examine by what methods this *teacher* arrives at his *gifts*, or *spirit*, or *light*; and by what intercourse between him and his assembly it is cultivated and supported.

In all my writings I have had constant regard to this great end, not to suit and apply them to particular occasions and circumstances of time, of place, or of person; but to calculate them for universal nature and mankind in general. And of such catholic use I esteem this present disquisition; for I do not remember any other temper of body or quality of mind, wherein all nations and ages of the world have so unanimously agreed as that of a *fanatic* strain, or tincture of *enthusiasm*; which, improved by certain persons or societies of men and by them practised upon the rest, has been able to produce revolutions of the greatest figure in history, as will soon appear to those who know anything of Arabia, Persia, India, or China, of Morocco and Peru. Farther, it has possessed as great a power in the kingdom of knowledge, where it is hard to assign one art or science which has not annexed to it some *fanatic* branch: such are the *Philosopher's Stone, The Grand Elixir*,* *The Planetary Worlds*,° *The Squaring of the Circle*,° *The Summum Bonum, Utopian Commonwealths*, with some others of less or subordinate note; which all serve for nothing else but to employ or amuse this grain of *enthusiasm*, dealt into every composition.

But if this plant has found a root in the fields of *empire* and of *knowledge*, it has fixed deeper and spread yet further upon *holy ground*. Wherein, though it hath passed under the general name of *enthusiasm* and perhaps arisen from the same original, yet hath it produced certain branches of a very different nature, however often mistaken for each other. The word in its universal acceptation may be defined, a *lifting up of the soul, or its faculties, above matter*. This description will hold good in general; but I am only to understand it as applied to *religion*, wherein there are three general ways of ejaculating the soul, or transporting it beyond the sphere of matter. The first is the immediate act of God, and is called *prophecy* or *inspiration*. The second is the immediate act of the Devil, and is termed *possession*. The third is the product of natural causes, the effect of strong imagination, spleen, violent anger, fear, grief, pain, and the like. These three have been abundantly treated on by authors and therefore shall not employ my enquiry. But the fourth method of *religious enthusiasm* or launching out the soul, as it is purely an effect of artifice and *mechanic operation*, has been sparingly handled or not at all by any writer; because, though it is an art of great antiquity, yet having been confined to few persons, it long wanted those advancements and refinements which it afterwards met with since it has grown so epidemic and fallen into so many cultivating hands.

It is, therefore, upon this *Mechanical Operation of the Spirit* that I mean to treat, as it is at present performed by our *British Workmen*. I shall deliver to the reader the result of many judicious observations upon the matter, tracing as near as I can the whole course and method of this *trade*, producing parallel instances, and relating certain discoveries that have luckily fallen in my way.

I have said that there is one branch of *religious enthusiasm* which is purely an effect of Nature whereas the part I mean to handle is wholly an effect of art which, however, is inclined to work upon certain natures and constitutions more than others. Besides, there is many an operation which in its original was purely an artifice but through a long succession of ages hath grown to be natural. Hippocrates tells us° that among our ancestors the Scythians there was a nation called *Longheads*,† which at first began, by a custom among midwives and nurses, of moulding, and

* Some writers hold them for the same, others not.   † Macrocephali.

squeezing, and bracing up the heads of infants, by which means Nature, shut out at one passage, was forced to seek another, and finding room above, shot upwards in the form of a sugar-loaf; and being diverted that way for some generations, at last found it out of herself, needing no assistance from the nurse's hand. This was the original of the *Scythian Longheads* and thus did custom, from being a second nature, proceed to be a first. To all which there is something very analogous among us of this nation, who are the undoubted posterity of that refined people. For, in the age of our fathers, there arose a generation of men in this island called *Roundheads*,° whose race is now spread over three kingdoms, yet in its beginning was merely an operation of art, produced by a pair of scissors, a squeeze of the face, and a black cap. These heads thus formed into a perfect sphere in all assemblies were most exposed to the view of the female sort, which did influence their conceptions so effectually that nature at last took the hint and did it of herself; so that a *Roundhead* has been ever since as familiar a sight among us as a *Longhead* among the Scythians.

Upon these examples and others easy to produce, I desire the curious reader to distinguish first, between an effect grown from *Art* into *Nature*, and one that is natural from its beginning; secondly, between an effect wholly natural, and one which has only a natural foundation but where the superstructure is entirely artificial. For the first and the last of these I understand to come within the districts of my subject. And having obtained these allowances, they will serve to remove any objections that may be raised hereafter against what I shall advance.

The practitioners of this famous art proceed in general upon the following fundamental,° that *the corruption of the senses is the generation of the spirit*; because the *senses* in men are so many avenues to the fort of *reason*, which in this operation is wholly blocked up. All endeavours must be therefore used, either to divert, bind up, stupify, fluster, and amuse the *senses*, or else to justle them out of their stations; and while they are either absent or otherwise employed, or engaged in a civil war against each other, the spirit enters and performs its part.

Now the usual methods of managing the senses upon such conjunctures are what I shall be very particular in delivering, as far as it is lawful for me to do; but having had the honour to be initiated into the mysteries of every society, I desire to be excused from divulging any rites wherein the *profane* must have no part.

But here, before I can proceed further, a very dangerous objection must, if possible, be removed: for it is positively denied by certain critics that the *spirit* can by any means be introduced into an assembly of modern saints,° the disparity being so great in many material circumstances, between the primitive way of inspiration and that which is practised in the present age. This they pretend to prove from the second chapter of the *Acts*° where, comparing both, it appears first, that *the apostles were gathered together with one accord, in one place*; by which is meant an universal agreement in opinion and form of worship; a harmony (say they) so far from being found between any two conventicles among us that it is in vain to expect it between any two heads in the same. Secondly, the *spirit* instructed the apostles in the gift of speaking several languages, a knowledge so remote from our dealers in this art that they neither understand propriety of words or phrases in their own. Lastly (say these objectors) the modern artists do utterly exclude all approaches of the *spirit*, and bar up its ancient way of entering, by covering themselves so close and so industriously a-top. For they will needs have it as a point clearly gained that the *Cloven Tongues* never sat upon the apostles' heads while their hats were on.°

Now, the force of these objections seems to consist in the different acceptation of the word *spirit*, which, if it be understood for a supernatural assistance approaching from without, the objectors have reason and their assertions may be allowed; but the *spirit* we treat of here proceeding entirely from within, the argument of these adversaries is wholly eluded. And upon the same account, our modern artificers find it an expedient of absolute necessity to cover their heads as close as they can, in order to prevent perspiration, than which nothing is observed to be a greater spender of Mechanic Light, as we may perhaps further show in convenient place.

To proceed therefore upon the phenomenon of *Spiritual Mechanism*, it is here to be noted that in forming and working up the *spirit*, the assembly has a considerable share as well as the preacher. The method of this *arcanum* is as follows. They violently strain their eyeballs inward, half closing the lids; then, as they sit, they are in a perpetual motion of *see-saw* making long hums at proper periods and continuing the sound at equal height, choosing their time in those intermissions while the preacher is at ebb. Neither is this practice, in any part of it, so singular or improbable as not to be traced in distant regions from reading and observation. For first, the *Jauguis**° or enlightened saints of India see all their visions by help of an acquired straining and pressure of the eyes. Secondly, the art of *see-saw* on a beam and swinging by session upon a cord, in order to raise artificial ecstasies, hath been derived to us from our Scythian† ancestors where it is practised at this day among the women. Lastly, the

* Bernier, *Mem. de Mogol.*   † Guagnini *Hist. Sarmat.*°

whole proceeding as I have here related it is performed by the natives of Ireland with a considerable improvement; and it is granted that this noble nation hath of all others admitted fewer corruptions, and degenerated least from the purity of the old Tartars. Now, it is usual for a knot of Irish, men and women, to abstract themselves from matter, bind up all their senses, grow visionary and spiritual, by influence of a short pipe of tobacco, handed round the company; each preserving the smoke in his mouth till it comes again to his turn to take it in fresh: at the same time there is a consort of a continued gentle hum, repeated and renewed by instinct as occasion requires, and they move their bodies up and down to a degree that sometimes their heads and points lie parallel to the horizon. Meanwhile you may observe their eyes turned up in the posture of one who endeavours to keep himself awake; by which, and many other symptoms among them, it manifestly appears that the reasoning faculties are all suspended and superseded, that imagination hath usurped the seat, scattering a thousand deliriums over the brain. Returning from this digression, I shall describe the methods by which the *spirit* approaches. The eyes being disposed according to art, at first you can see nothing, but after a short pause a small glimmering light begins to appear and dance before you. Then, by frequently moving your body up and down, you perceive the vapours to ascend very fast, till you are perfectly dosed and flustered like one who drinks too much in a morning. Meanwhile the preacher is also at work. He begins a loud hum which pierces you quite through; this is immediately returned by the audience, and you find yourself prompted to imitate them by a mere spontaneous impulse, without knowing what you do. The *interstitia* are duly filled up by the preacher to prevent too long a pause, under which the *spirit* would soon faint and grow languid.

This is all I am allowed to discover about the progress of the *spirit* with relation to that part which is borne by the *assembly*. But in the methods of the preacher to which I now proceed, I shall be more large and particular.

SECTION II.

You will read it very gravely remarked in the books of those illustrious and right eloquent penmen, the modern travellers, that the fundamental difference in point of religion between the wild Indians and us, lies in this; that we worship *God*, and they worship the *devil*. But there are certain critics who will by no means admit of this distinction; rather believing, that all nations whatsoever adore the *true God* because they seem to intend their devotions to some invisible power of greatest *goodness* and *ability* to help them, which perhaps will take in the brightest attributes ascribed to the divinity. Others, again, inform us that those idolators adore two *principles*, the *principle* of *good*, and that of *evil*; which indeed I am apt to look upon as the most universal notion that mankind, by the mere light of nature, ever entertained of things invisible. How this idea hath been managed by the Indians and us, and with what advantage to the understandings of either, may deserve well to be examined. To me, the difference appears little more than this that they are put oftener upon their knees by their *fears*, and we by our *desires*; that the former set them a-*praying*, and us a-*cursing*. What I applaud them for is their discretion in limiting their devotions and their deities to their several districts, nor ever suffering the liturgy of the *white* God to cross or interfere with that of the *black*. Not so with us, who pretending by the lines and measures of our reason to extend the dominion of one invisible power and contract that of the other, have discovered a gross ignorance in the natures of good and evil, and most horribly confounded the frontiers of both. After men have lifted up the throne of their divinity to the *cœlum empyræum*, adorned him with all such qualities and accomplishments as themselves seem most to value and possess: after they have sunk their *principle of evil* to the lowest centre, bound him with chains, loaded him with curses, furnished him with viler dispositions than any *rake-hell* of the town, accoutred him with tail, and horns, and huge claws, and saucer eyes; I laugh aloud to see these reasoners at the same time engaged in wise dispute about certain walks and purlieus, whether they are in the verge of God or the devil, seriously debating whether such and such influences come into men's minds from above or below, or whether certain passions and affections are guided by the evil spirit or the good.

> Dum fas atque nefas exiguo fine libidinum
> Discernunt avidi —°

Thus do men establish a fellowship of Christ with Belial, and such is the analogy they make between *Cloven Tongues* and *Cloven Feet*. Of the like nature is the disquisition before us. It hath continued these hundred years an even debate whether the deportment and the cant of our English enthusiastic preachers were *possession* or *inspiration*, and a world of argument has been drained on either side, perhaps to little purpose. For, I think it is in *life* as in *tragedy*, where it is held a conviction of great defect, both in order and invention, to interpose the assistance of preternatural power without an absolute and last necessity. However, it is a sketch of human vanity for every individual to imagine the whole universe is interessed in his meanest concern. If he hath got cleanly over a kennel, some angel unseen descended on purpose to help him by the hand; if he hath knocked his head against a post, it was the devil, for his sins, let loose from hell on purpose to *buffet* him. Who that sees a little paltry mortal, droning, and dreaming, and drivelling to a multitude, can think it agreeable to common good sense that either Heaven or Hell should be put to the trouble of influence or inspection upon what he is about? Therefore I am resolved immediately to weed this error out of mankind, by making it clear that this mystery of venting spiritual gifts is nothing but a *trade*, acquired by as much instruction and mastered by equal practice and application, as others are. This will best appear by describing and deducing the whole process of the operation, as variously as it hath fallen under my knowledge or experience.

```
*      *      *      *        *        *        *      *
*      *      *      *        *        *        *      *
*      *      *      *        *
*      *      *      *        *   Here the whole scheme of
*      *      *      *        *   spiritual mechanism was de-
*      *      *      *        *   duced and explained, with an
*      *      *      *        *   appearance of great reading
*      *      *      *        *   and observation; but it was
*      *      *      *        *   thought neither safe nor con-
*      *      *      *        *   venient to print it.
*      *      *      *        *        *        *      *
*      *      *      *        *        *        *      *
```

Here it may not be amiss to add a few words upon the laudable practice of wearing *quilted caps*, which is not a matter of mere custom, humour, or fashion, as some would pretend, but an institution of great sagacity and use; these, when moistened with sweat, stop all perspiration, and by reverberating the heat prevent the spirit from evaporating any way but at the mouth: even as a skilful housewife, that covers her still with a wet clout for the same reason, and finds the same effect. For it is the opinion of choice *virtuosi* that the brain is only a crowd of little animals, but with teeth and claws extremely sharp, and therefore cling together in the contexture we behold, like the picture of Hobbes's *Leviathan*,° or like bees in perpendicular swarm upon a tree, or like a carrion corrupted into vermin, still preserving the shape and figure of the mother animal; that all invention is formed by the morsure of two or more of these animals upon certain capillary nerves which proceed from thence, whereof three branches spread into the tongue, and two into the right hand. They hold also, that these animals are of a constitution extremely cold; that their food is the air we attract, their excrement phlegm; and that what we vulgarly call rheums, and colds, and distillations, is nothing else but an epidemical looseness to which that little commonwealth is very subject from the climate it lies under. Further, that nothing less than a violent heat can disentangle these creatures from their hamated station of life, or give them vigour and humour to imprint the marks of their little teeth. That if the morsure be hexagonal, it produces Poetry; the circular gives Eloquence; if the bite hath been conical, the person whose nerve is so affected shall be disposed to write upon Politics; and so of the rest.

I shall now discourse briefly, by what kind of practices the voice is best governed towards the composition and improvement of the *spirit*; for, without a competent skill in tuning and toning each word and syllable and letter to their due cadence, the whole operation is incomplete, misses entirely of its effect on the hearers, and puts the workman himself to continual pains for new supplies without success. For it is to be understood, that in the language of the spirit, *cant* and *droning* supply the place of *sense* and *reason* in the language of men: because in spiritual harangues the disposition of the words according to the art of grammar hath not the least use, but the skill and influence wholly lie in the choice and cadence of the syllables;° even as a discreet *composer*, who in setting a song, changes the words and order so often that he is forced to make it *nonsense* before he can make it *music*. For this reason, it hath been held by some that the Art of Canting is ever in greatest perfection when managed by *ignorance*; which is thought to be enigmatically meant by Plutarch° when he tells us that the best musical instruments were made from the bones of an *ass*. And the profounder critics upon that passage are of opinion, the word in its genuine signification means no other than a jaw-bone, though some rather think it to have been the *os sacrum*; but in so nice a case I shall not take upon me to decide. The curious are at liberty to *pick* from it whatever they please.

The first ingredient towards the Art of Canting is a competent share of *inward light*; that is to say, a large memory plentifully fraught with theological polysyllables and mysterious texts from holy writ, applied and digested by those methods and mechanical operations already related: the bearers of this *light* resembling lanterns compact of leaves from old Geneva Bibles; which invention, Sir H[u]mphrey Edw[i]n,° during his mayoralty, of happy memory, highly approved and advanced, affirming the Scripture to be now fulfilled where it says, *Thy word is a lantern to my feet, and a light to my paths.*°

Now, the Art of *Canting*° consists in skilfully adapting the voice to whatever words the spirit delivers, that each may strike the ears of the audience with its most significant cadence. The force or energy of this eloquence is not to be found, as among ancient orators, in the disposition of words to a sentence or the turning of long periods, but agreeable to the modern refinements in music, is taken up wholly in dwelling and dilating upon syllables and letters. Thus it is frequent for a single *vowel* to draw sighs from a multitude, and for a whole assembly of saints to sob to the music of one solitary *liquid*. But these are trifles, when even sounds inarticulate are observed to produce as forcible effects. A master workman shall *blow his nose so powerfully* as to pierce the hearts of his people, who are disposed to receive the *excrements* of his brain with the same reverence as the *issue* of it. Hawking, spitting, and belching, the defects of other men's rhetoric, are the flowers and figures and ornaments of his. For, the *spirit* being the same in all, it is of no import through what vehicle it is conveyed.

It is a point of too much difficulty to draw the principles of this famous art within the compass of certain adequate rules. However, perhaps I may one day oblige the world with my critical essay upon the Art of *Canting, philosophically, physically, and musically considered.*

But, among all improvements of the *spirit* wherein the voice hath borne a part, there is none to be compared with that of *conveying the sound through the nose*, which under the denomination of *snuffling** hath passed with so great applause in the world. The originals of this institution are very dark, but having been initiated into the mystery of it, and leave being given me to publish it to the world, I shall deliver as direct a relation as I can.

This art, like many other famous inventions, owed its birth or at least improvement and perfection, to an effect of chance, but was established upon solid reasons and hath flourished in this island ever since with great lustre. All agree that it first appeared upon the decay and discouragement of *bagpipes*, which having long suffered under the mortal hatred of the *brethren*, tottered for a time, and at last fell with *monarchy*. The story is thus related.

As yet *snuffling* was not, when the following adventure happened to a *Banbury saint*.° Upon a certain day, while he was far engaged among the tabernacles of the *wicked*, he felt the outward man put into odd commotions, and strangely pricked forward by the inward; an effect very usual among the modern inspired. For, some think that the *spirit* is apt to feed on the *flesh*, like hungry wines upon raw beef. Others rather believe there is a perpetual game at *leap-frog* between both, and sometimes the *flesh* is uppermost, and sometimes the *spirit*; adding that the former,

---

* The *snuffling* of men who have lost their noses by lewd courses is said to have given rise to that tone, which our dissenters did too much affect. W. WOTTON.

while it is in the state of a *rider*, wears huge Rippon spurs,° and when it comes to the turn of being *bearer*, is wonderfully headstrong and hard-mouthed. However it came about, the *saint* felt his *vessel* full *extended* in every part (a very natural effect of strong *inspiration*), and the place and time falling out so unluckily that he could not have the convenience of evacuating upwards by repetition, prayer, or lecture,° he was forced to open an inferior vent. In short, he wrestled with the flesh so long that he at length subdued it, coming off with honourable wounds, all *before*. The surgeon had now cured the parts primarily affected, but the disease, driven from its post, flew up into his head; and, as a skilful general, valiantly attacked in his trenches and beaten from the field, by flying marches withdraws to the capital city, breaking down the bridges to prevent pursuit; so the disease, repelled from its first station, fled before the *Rod* of *Hermes*° to the upper region, there fortifying itself; but finding the foe making attacks at the *nose*, broke down the *bridge*, and retired to the *head*-quarters. Now, the naturalists observe that there is in human noses an *idiosyncrasy*, by virtue of which the more the passage is obstructed, the more our speech delights to go through, as the music of a flageolet is made by the *stops*. By this method the twang of the nose becomes perfectly to resemble the *snuffle* of a bagpipe,° and is found to be equally attractive of British ears; whereof the saint had sudden experience by practising his new faculty with wonderful success in the operation of the *spirit*. For, in a short time, no doctrine passed for sound and orthodox unless it were delivered through the nose. Straight, every pastor copied after this original, and those who could not otherwise arrive to a perfection, spirited by a noble zeal, made use of the same experiment to acquire it. So that I think it may be truly affirmed, the *saints* owe their empire to the *snuffling* of one animal as Darius did his to the *neighing* of another, and both stratagems were performed by the same art; for we read how the *Persian beast* acquired his faculty by *covering a mare* the day before.*°

I should now have done, if I were not convinced that whatever I have yet advanced upon this subject is liable to great exception. For allowing all I have said to be true, it may still be justly objected that there is, in the commonwealth of *artificial enthusiasm*, some real foundation for art to work upon in the temper and complexion of individuals, which other mortals seem to want. Observe but the gesture, the motion, and the countenance, of some choice professors though in their most familiar actions, you will find them of a different race from the rest of human creatures. Remark your commonest pretender to a light *within*, how

* Herodot.

dark, and dirty, and gloomy he is *without*; as lanterns which, the more light they bear in their bodies, cast out so much the more soot and smoke and fuliginous matter to adhere to the sides. Listen but to their ordinary talk, and look on the mouth that delivers it; you will imagine you are hearing some ancient oracle, and your understanding will be *equally* informed. Upon these and the like reasons, certain objectors pretend to put it beyond all doubt that there must be a sort of preternatural *spirit* possessing the heads of the modern saints; and some will have it to be the *heat* of zeal working upon the *dregs* of ignorance, as other *spirits* are produced from *lees* by the force of fire. Some again think that when our earthly tabernacles are disordered and desolate, shaken and out of repair, the *spirit* delights to dwell within them, as houses are said to be haunted when they are forsaken and gone to decay.

To set this matter in as fair a light as possible, I shall here very briefly deduce the history of *Fanaticism* from the most early ages to the present. And if we are able to fix upon any one material or fundamental point wherein the chief professors have universally agreed, I think we may reasonably lay hold on that and assign it for the great seed or principle of the *spirit*.

The most early traces we meet with of *fanatics* in ancient story° are among the Egyptians, who instituted those rites, known in Greece by the names of *Orgia,*° *Panegyres,*° and *Dionysia,*° whether introduced there by Orpheus° or Melampus° we shall not dispute at present, nor in all likelihood at any time for the future.* These feasts were celebrated to the honour of Osiris, whom the Grecians called Dionysius and is the same with Bacchus, which has betrayed some superficial readers to imagine that the whole business was nothing more than a set of roaring, scouring companions, overcharged with wine; but this is a scandalous mistake foisted on the world by a sort of modern authors who have too *literal* an understanding and, because antiquity is to be traced *backwards*, do therefore like Jews begin their books at the wrong end, as if learning were a sort of *conjuring*. These are the men who pretend to understand a book by scouting through the *index,*° as if a traveller should go about to describe a *palace* when he had seen nothing but the privy; or like certain fortune-tellers in North America who have a way of reading a man's destiny by peeping in his *breech*. For, at the time of instituting these mysteries there was not one vine in all Egypt,† the natives drinking nothing but *ale*; which liquor seems to have been far more ancient than wine and has the honour of owing its invention and progress not only to

* Diod. Sic. L. 1.° Plut. *de Iside et Osiride.*
† Herod. L. 2.°

the Egyptian Osiris,* but to the Grecian Bacchus, who in their famous expedition, carried the receipt of it along with them, and gave it to the nations they visited or subdued. Besides, Bacchus himself was very seldom or never drunk; for it is recorded of him that he was the first inventor of the *mitre*,† which he wore continually on his head (as the whole company of bacchanals did) to prevent vapours and the headache after hard drinking. And for this reason (say some) the *Scarlet Whore*,° when she makes the kings of the earth drunk with her cup of abomination, is always sober herself though she never balks the glass in her turn, being it seems kept upon her legs by the virtue of her *triple mitre*. Now, these feasts were instituted in imitation of the famous expedition Osiris made through the world, and of the company that attended him, whereof the bacchanalian ceremonies were so many types and symbols. From which account‡ it is manifest that the fanatic rites of these bacchanals cannot be imputed to intoxications by wine, but must needs have had a deeper foundation. What this was, we may gather large hints from certain circumstances in the course of their mysteries. For, in the first place, there was in their processions an entire *mixture and confusion of sexes*; they affected to ramble about hills and deserts. Their garlands were of *ivy* and *vine*, emblems of cleaving and clinging; or of *fir*, the parent of *turpentine*. It is added that they imitated *satyrs*, were attended by *goats* and rode upon *asses*, all companions of great skill and practice in affairs of gallantry. They bore for their ensigns certain curious figures perched upon long poles, made into the shape and size of the *virga genitalis*, with its *appurtenances*, which were so many shadows and emblems of the whole mystery; as well as trophies set up by the female conquerors. Lastly, in a certain town of Attica, the whole solemnity stripped of all its types§ was performed in *puris naturalibus*, the votaries not flying in coveys but sorted into couples. The same may be farther conjectured from the death of Orpheus, one of the institutors of these mysteries, who was torn in pieces by women because he refused to *communicate his orgies* to them;¶ which others explained by telling us he had castrated himself upon grief for the loss of his wife.

Omitting many others of less note, the next *fanatics* we meet with of any eminence, were the numerous sects of *heretics* appearing in the five first centuries of the *Christian era*, from Simon Magus and his followers to those of Eutyches.° I have collected their systems from infinite reading,

---

* Diod. Sic. L. 1 and 3.   † Id. L. 4.
‡ See the particulars in Diod. Sic. L. 1 and 3.
§ Dionysia Brauronia.°
¶ *Vide* Photium in excerptis è Conone.°

and comparing them with those of their successors in the several ages since, I find there are certain bounds set even to the irregularities of human thought, and those a great deal narrower than is commonly apprehended. For, as they all frequently interfere even in their wildest ravings, so there is one fundamental point wherein they are sure to meet, as lines in a centre, and that is the *community of women*. Great were their solicitudes in this matter, and they never failed of certain articles in their schemes of worship, on purpose to establish it.

The last *fanatics* of note were those which started up in Germany a little after the *reformation* of Luther, springing as *mushrooms* do at the *end of a harvest*; such were John of Leyden, David George, Adam Neuster,° and many others, whose visions and revelations always terminated in *leading about half a dozen sisters apiece*, and making that practice a fundamental part of their system. For human life is a continual navigation, and if we expect our *vessels* to pass with safety through the waves and tempests of this fluctuating world, it is necessary to make a good provision of the *flesh*, as seamen lay in store of *beef* for a long voyage.

Now from this brief survey of some principal sects among the *fanatics* in all ages (having omitted the Mahometans and others, who might also help to confirm the argument I am about) to which I might add several among ourselves, such as the *Family of Love, Sweet Singers of Israel*,° and the like, and from reflecting upon that fundamental point in their doctrines about *women*, wherein they have so unanimously agreed; I am apt to imagine that the seed or principle which has ever put men upon *visions* in things *invisible*, is of a corporeal nature; for the profounder chemists inform us that the strongest *spirits* may be extracted from *human flesh*. Besides, the spinal marrow being nothing else but a continuation of the brain, must needs create a very free communication between the superior faculties and those below: and thus the *thorn in the flesh* serves for a *spur* to the *spirit*. I think it is agreed among physicians that nothing affects the head so much as a tentiginous humour, repelled and elated to the upper region, found by daily practice to run frequently up into madness. A very eminent member of the faculty assured me that when the Quakers first appeared, he seldom was without some female patients among them for the *furor* [*Uterinus*].° Persons of a visionary devotion, either men or women, are in their complexion of all others the most amorous; for *zeal* is frequently kindled from the same spark with other fires, and from inflaming brotherly love will proceed to raise that of a gallant. If we inspect into the usual process of modern courtship, we shall find it to consist in a devout turn of the eyes, called *ogling*; an artificial form of canting and whining by rote, every interval for want of other matter made up with a shrug or a hum, a sigh or a groan; the style compact of insignificant words, incoherences, and repetition. These I take to be the most accomplished rules of address to a mistress; and where are these performed with more dexterity than by the *saints*? Nay, to bring this argument yet closer, I have been informed by certain sanguine brethren of the first class that in the height and *orgasmus* of their spiritual exercise, it has been frequent with them * * * * *; immediately after which they found the *spirit* to relax and flag of a sudden with the nerves, and they were forced to hasten to a conclusion. This may be further strengthened by observing, with wonder, how unaccountably all females are attracted by visionary or enthusiastic preachers, though never so contemptible in their *outward men*; which is usually supposed to be done upon considerations purely spiritual without any carnal regards at all. But I have reason to think the *sex* hath certain characteristics by which they form a truer judgment of human abilities and performings than we ourselves can possibly do of each other. Let that be as it will, thus much is certain that, however spiritual intrigues begin, they generally conclude like all others; they may branch upwards toward heaven but the root is in the earth. Too intense a contemplation is not the business of flesh and blood; it must by the necessary course of things, in a little time let go its hold and fall into *matter*. Lovers, for the sake of celestial converse, are but another sort of *Platonics* who pretend to see stars and heaven in ladies' eyes, and to look or think no lower; but the same *pit* is provided for both; and they seem a perfect moral to the story of that philosopher who, while his thoughts and eyes were fixed upon the *constellations*, found himself seduced by his *lower parts* into a *ditch*.°

I had somewhat more to say upon this part of the subject but the post is just going, which forces me in great haste to conclude,

Sir,

Yours, &c.

*Pray, burn this letter as soon
as it comes to your hands.*

Apothegms and Maxims

WE have just religion enough to make us *hate*, but not enough to make us *love* one another. ['*Various Thoughts* Moral and Diverting', in *Miscellanies in Prose and Verse*, 1711] [1]

When a true genius appears in the world, you may know him by this infallible sign, that the dunces are all in confederacy against him.

[15]

It is pleasant to observe how free the present age is in laying taxes on the next. *Future ages shall talk of this. This shall be famous to all posterity*. Whereas, their time and thoughts will be taken up about present things, as ours are now. [23]

There are but three ways for a man to revenge himself of a censorious world. To despise it; to return the like; or to endeavour to live so as to avoid it. The first of these is usually pretended; the last is almost impossible; the universal practice is for the second. [29]

What they *do* in heaven we are ignorant of; what they do *not* we are told expressly, that they neither marry, nor are given in marriage. [35]

The stoical scheme of supplying our wants by lopping off our desires, is like cutting off our feet, when we want shoes. [38]

The power of fortune is confessed only by the miserable; for the happy impute all their success to prudence or merit. [43]

Ambition often puts men upon doing the meanest offices; so climbing is performed in the same posture with creeping. [44]

Censure is the tax a man pays to the public for being eminent. [46]

Satire is reckoned the easiest of all wit; but I take it to be otherwise in very bad times. For it is as hard to satirize well a man of distinguished vices, as to praise well a man of distinguished virtues. It is easy enough to do either to people of moderate characters. ['*Thoughts on Various Subjects*', in *Miscellanies*, vol. i, 1727] [48]

When the world hath once begun to use us ill, it afterwards continues the same treatment with less scruple or ceremony, as men do a whore.

[53]

Anthony Henley's farmer dying of an asthma, said, 'well, if I can get this breath once *out*, I'll take care it shall never get *in* again'. [57]

Complaint is the largest tribute Heaven receives; and the sincerest part of our devotion.   [59]

Few are qualified to *shine* in company; but it is in most men's power to be *agreeable*. The reason, therefore, why conversation runs so low at present is not the defect of understanding; but pride, vanity, ill-nature, affectation, singularity, positiveness, or some other vice, the effect of a wrong education.   [61]

To be vain, is rather a mark of humility than of pride. Vain men delight in telling what honours have been done them, what great company they have kept, and the like; by which they plainly confess that these honours were more than their due, and such as their friends would not believe if they had not been told: whereas a man truly proud, thinks the greatest honours below his merit, and consequently scorns to boast. I therefore deliver it as a maxim, that whoever desires the character of a proud man, ought to conceal his vanity.   [62]

Law, in a free country, is or ought to be the determination of the majority of those who have property in land.   [63]

The preaching of divines helps to preserve well inclined men in the course of virtue, but seldom or never reclaims the vicious.   [72]

Every man desires to live long; but no man would be old.   [76]

Princes in their infancy, childhood and youth, are said to discover prodigious parts and wit; to speak things that surprise and astonish. Strange, so many *hopeful* princes, and so many *shameful* kings! If they happen to die young, they would have been *prodigies* of wisdom and virtue: if they live, they are often *prodigies* indeed, but of *another sort*.
                                                                      [80]

Venus, a beautiful good-natured lady, was the goddess of love; Juno, a terrible shrew, the goddess of marriage; and they were always mortal enemies.   [83]

A nice man is a man of nasty ideas.   [86]

Most kinds of diversion in men, children, and other animals, are an imitation of fighting.   [91]

Very few men, properly speaking, *live* at present, but are providing to *live* another time.   [96]

As universal a practice as lying is, and as easy a one as it seems, I do not remember to have heard three good lies in all my conversation, even from those who were most celebrated in that faculty.   [97]

Sometimes I read a book with pleasure, and detest the author. ['*Further Thoughts*', in *Miscellanies*, 1745]   [113]

One Dennis, commonly called 'the critic', who had writ a threepenny pamphlet against the power of France, being in the country and hearing of a French privateer hovering about the coast, although he were twenty miles from the sea fled to town, and told his friends they need not wonder at his haste; for the King of France, having got intelligence where he was, had sent a privateer on purpose to catch him.   [115]

I never wonder to see men wicked, but I often wonder to see them not ashamed.   [120]

Eloquence smooth and cutting, is like a razor whetted with oil. [126]

All panegyrics are mingled with an infusion of poppy.   [133]

When I am reading a book, whether wise or silly, it seems to me to be alive and talking to me.   [148]

No man will take counsel, but every man will take money; therefore money is better than counsel.   [156]

To enter into a Party as into an order of *friars*, with so resigned an obedience to superiors, is very unsuitable both with the civil and religious liberties we so zealously assert. [*The Sentiments of a Church-of-England Man with respect to Religion and Government.* Written in the year 1708]

Why, that's a common caution that writing-masters give their scholars; you must have heard it a hundred times. 'Tis this,

> If paper be thin,
> Ink will slip in;
> But if it be thick,
> You may write with a stick.

[*Journal to Stella*, 12 November 1710]

I have heard wise folks say, An ill tongue may do much. And 'tis an old saying,

> Once I guessed right,
> And I got credit by't;
> Thrice I guessed wrong,
> And I kept my credit on.

[25 December 1710]

> Would you answer MD's letter,
> On New-year's-day you'll do it better:
> For when the year with MD 'gins,
> It without MD never lins.

(These proverbs have always old words in them; *lins* is leaves off.)

> But if on New-year you write nones,
> MD then will bang your bones.

[31 December 1710]

It is very ugly walking; a baker's boy broke his thigh yesterday. I walk slow, make short steps, and never tread on my heel. 'Tis a good proverb the Devonshire people have:

> Walk fast in snow,
> In frost walk slow,
> And still as you go,
> Tread on your toe:
> When frost and snow are both together,
> Sit by the fire and spare shoe-leather.

[21 January 1711]

I drink little, miss my glass often, put water in my wine, and go away before the rest, which I take to be a good receipt for sobriety. Let us put it into rhyme, and so make a proverb:

> Drink little at a time:
> Put water with your wine;
> Miss your glass when you can;
> And go off the first man.

[21 April 1711]

I love good creditable acquaintance; I love to be the worst of the company: I am not of those that say, for want of company, welcome trumpery. [17 May 1711]

I dined with him, and we were to do more business after dinner. But after dinner is after dinner—An old saying and a true, Much drinking, little thinking. [26 February 1712]

Proper words in proper places, makes the true definition of a style. [*A Letter to a Young Gentleman, Lately entered into Holy Orders*. Dated January 9, 1720]

And, he gave it for his opinion, that whoever could make two ears of corn, or two blades of grass to grow upon a spot of ground where only one grew before, would deserve better of mankind, and do more essential service to his country than the whole race of politicians put together. [*Gulliver's Travels* (1726), Part II, 'A Voyage to Brobdingnag', chapter VII.]

Poor nations are *hungry*, and *rich* nations are *proud*; and pride and hunger will ever be at variance. [Ibid., Part IV, 'A Voyage to the Houyhnhnms', chapter V.]

It may be prudent in me to act sometimes by other men's reason, but I can think only by my own. ['Thoughts on Religion', in *Works*, vol. xv, 1765]
[R2]

To say a man is bound to believe, is neither truth nor sense.   [R4]

You may force men, by interest or punishment, to say or swear they believe, and to act as if they believed. You can go no further.   [R5]

Every man, as a member of the commonwealth, ought to be content with the possession of his own opinion in private, without perplexing his neighbour or disturbing the public.   [R6]

Violent zeal for truth hath an hundred to one odds to be either petulancy, ambition, or pride.   [R7]

I look upon myself, in the capacity of a clergyman, to be one appointed by Providence for defending a post assigned to me, and for gaining over as many enemies as I can. Although I think my cause is just, yet one great motive is my submitting to the pleasure of Providence, and to the laws of my country.   [R14]

I believe that thousands of men would be orthodox enough in certain points, if divines had not been too curious, or too narrow, in reducing orthodoxy within the compass of subtleties, niceties, and distinctions, with little warrant from Scripture and less from reason or good policy.
[R16]

I never saw, heard, nor read that the clergy were beloved in any nation where Christianity was the religion of the country. Nothing can render them popular but some degree of persecution.   [R17]

It is impossible that anything so natural, so necessary, and so universal as death, should ever have been designed by Providence as an evil to mankind.   [R21]

Although reason were intended by Providence to govern our passions, yet it seems that, in two points of the greatest moment to the being and continuance of the world, God hath intended our passions to prevail over reason. The first is, the propagation of our species, since no wise man ever married from the dictates of reason. The other is, the love of life, which, from the dictates of reason, every man would despise, and wish it at an end, or that it never had a beginning.   [R22]

BAUCIS AND PHILEMON

In ancient time, as story tells,
The saints would often leave their cells
And stroll about, but hide their quality,
To try good people's hospitality.
  It happen'd on a winter's night,
As authors of the legend write,
Two brother-hermits, saints by trade,
Taking their tour in masquerade,
Came to a village hard by Rixham,
Ragged and not a groat betwixt 'em.   10
It rain'd as hard as it could pour,
Yet they were forced to walk an hour
From house to house, wet to the skin,
Before one soul would let 'em in.
They call'd at ev'ry door: 'Good people,
My comrade's blind, and I'm a creeple!
Here we lie starving in the street,
'Twould grieve a body's heart to see't,
No Christian would turn out a beast
In such a dreadful night at least;   20
Give us but straw and let us lie
In yonder barn to keep us dry.'
Thus in the stroller's usual cant
They begg'd relief, which none would grant.
No creature valued what they said:
One family was gone to bed;
The master bawl'd out, half asleep,
'You fellows, what a noise you keep!
So many beggars pass this way,
We can't be quiet, night nor day;   30
We cannot serve you every one;
Pray take your answer, and be gone.'
One swore he'd send 'em to the stocks;
A third could not forbear his mocks,
But bawl'd as loud as he could roar
'You're on the wrong side of the door!'
One surly clown look't out and said,

'I'll fling the p—pot on your head:
You sha'nt come here, nor get a sous!
You look like rogues would rob a house.   40
Can't you go work, or serve the King?
You blind and lame! 'Tis no such thing.
That's but a counterfeit sore leg!
For shame! two sturdy rascals beg!
If I come down, I'll spoil your trick,
And cure you both with a good stick.'

    Our wand'ring saints, in woeful state,
Treated at this ungodly rate,
Having thro' all the village past,
To a small cottage came at last   50
Where dwelt a poor old honest yeoman,
Call'd thereabouts Goodman Philemon;
Who kindly did the saints invite
In his poor house to pass the night;
And then the hospitable sire
Bid Goody Baucis mend the fire;
Whilst he from out the chimney took
A flitch of bacon off the hook,
And freely from the fattest side
Cut off large slices to be fried;   60
Which tost up in a pan with batter,
And served up in an earthen platter,
Quoth Baucis, 'This is wholesome fare,
Eat, honest friends, and never spare,
And if we find our victuals fail,
We can but make it out in ale.'

    To a small kilderkin of beer,
Brew'd for the good time of the year,
Philemon, by his wife's consent,
Stept with a jug, and made a vent,   70
And having fill'd it to the brink,
Invited both the saints to drink.
When they had took a second draught,
Behold, a miracle was wrought;
For, Baucis with amazement found,
Although the jug had twice gone round,
It still was full up to the top,
As if they ne'er had drunk a drop.

You may be sure, so strange a sight
Put the old people in a fright: 80
Philemon whisper'd to his wife,
'These men are Saints, I'll lay my life!'
The strangers overheard, and said,
'You're in the right—but be'nt afraid:
No hurt shall come to you or yours;
But, for that pack of churlish boors,
Not fit to live on Christian ground,
They and their village shall be drown'd;
Whilst you shall see your cottage rise
And grow a church before your eyes.'   90
   Scarce had they spoke, when fair and soft
The roof began to mount aloft;
Aloft rose ev'ry beam and rafter;
The heavy wall went clamb'ring after.
The chimney widen'd and grew higher,
Became a steeple with a spire.
The kettle to the top was hoist,
And there stood fastened to a joist,
But with the upside down, to show
Its inclination for below: 100
In vain; for a superior force
Applied at bottom stops its course:
Doom'd ever in suspense to dwell,
'Tis now no kettle, but a bell.
   The groaning chair began to crawl
Like a huge insect, up the wall;
There stuck, and to a pulpit grew,
But kept its matter and its hue,
And mindful of its ancient state,
Still groans while tattling gossips prate.   110
The mortar only chang'd its name,
In its old shape a font became.
   The porringers, that in a row
Hung high, and made a glitt'ring show,
To a less noble substance changed,
Were now but leathern buckets ranged.
   The ballads, pasted on the wall,
Of Chevy Chase, and English Mall,°
Fair Rosamond, and Robin Hood,

The little Children in the Wood,   120
Enlarged in picture, size, and letter,
And painted, lookt abundance better,
And now the heraldry describe
Of a churchwarden, or a tribe.

    The wooden jack, which had almost
Lost by disuse the art to roast,
A sudden alteration feels,
Increas'd by new intestine wheels;
But what adds to the wonder more,
The number made the motion slower.   130
The flyer, altho't had leaden feet,
Would turn so quick you scarce could see't;
But, now stopt by some hidden powers,
Moves round but twice in twice twelve hours,
While in the station of a jack,
'Twas never known to turn its back,
A friend in turns and windings tried,
Nor ever left the chimney side.
The chimney to a steeple grown,
The jack would not be left alone;   140
But, up against the steeple rear'd,
Became a clock, and still adher'd;
And still its love to household cares,
By a shrill voice at noon declares,
Warning the cookmaid not to burn
That roast meat which it cannot turn.

    A bedstead in the antique mode,
Composed of timber many a load,
Such as our grandfathers did use,
Was metamorphos'd into pews;   150
Which yet their former virtue keep
By lodging folks disposed to sleep.

    The cottage, with such feats as these,
Grown to a church by just degrees,
The holy men desired their host
To ask for what he fancied most.
Philemon, having paused a while,
Replied in complimental style:
'Your goodness, more than my desert,
Makes you take all things in good part: 160

You've raised a church here in a minute,
And I would fain continue in it;
I'm good for little at my days,
Make me the parson if you please.'
    He spoke, and presently he feels
His grazier's coat reach down his heels;
The sleeves new border'd with a list,
Widen'd and gather'd at his wrist,
But, being old, continued just
As threadbare, and as full of dust.   170
A shambling awkward gait he took,
With a demure dejected look,
Talk't of his off'rings, tythes, and dues,
Could smoke and drink and read the news,
Or sell a goose at the next town,
Decently hid beneath his gown;
Contriv'd to preach his sermon next,
Chang'd in the preface and the text.
Carried it to his equals higher,
But most obseqious to the squire.   180
At christ'nings well could act his part,
And had the service all by heart;
Wish'd women might have children fast,
And thought whose sow had farrow'd last;
Against dissenters would repine,
And stood up firm for 'right divine';
Found his head fill'd with many a system;
But classic authors,—he'd ne'er miss'd 'em.
    Thus having furbish'd up a parson,
Dame Baucis next they play'd their farce on: 190
Instead of homespun coif, were seen
Good pinners edg'd with colberteen;
Her petticoat, transform'd apace,
Became black satin, flounced with lace.
Plain 'Goody' would no longer down,
'Twas 'Madam', in her grogram gown.
Philemon was in great surprise,
And hardly could believe his eyes.
Amaz'd to see her look so prim,
And she admir'd as much at him.   200
    Thus happy in their change of life,

Were several years this man and wife:
When on a day, which prov'd their last,
Discoursing o'er old stories past,
They went by chance, amidst their talk,
To the churchyard to take a walk;
When Baucis hastily cried out,
'My dear, I see your forehead sprout!'—
'Sprout?' quoth the man, 'what's this you tell us?
I hope you don't believe me jealous!°   210
But yet, methinks, I feel it true,
And truly yours is budding too—
Nay,—now I cannot stir my foot;
It feels as if 'twere taking root.'

    Description would but tire my Muse.
In short, they both were turn'd to yews.
Old Goodman Dobson of the Green
Remembers he the trees has seen;
He'll talk of them from noon till night,
And goes with folks to show the sight;   220
On Sundays, after ev'ning prayer,
He gathers all the parish there;
Points out the place of either yew:
'Here Baucis, there Philemon, grew;
Till once a parson of our town,
To mend his barn, cut Baucis down;
At which, 'tis hard to be believ'd,
How much the other tree was griev'd,
Grew scrubby, dy'd a-top, was stunted:
So the next parson stubb'd and burnt it.'   230

PREDICTIONS FOR THE YEAR 1708.

Wherein the Month and Day of the Month are set down, the Persons named, and the great Actions and Events of next Year particularly related, as they will come to pass.

Written to prevent the People of England from being further impos'd on by vulgar Almanack-makers.

By ISAAC BICKERSTAFF° *Esq;*

I HAVE long considered the gross abuse of astrology in this kingdom, and upon debating the matter with myself I could not possibly lay the fault upon the art, but upon those gross impostors who set up to be the artists. I know several learned men have contended that the whole is a cheat; that it is absurd and ridiculous to imagine the stars can have any influence at all upon human actions, thoughts, or inclinations; and whoever has not bent his studies that way may be excused for thinking so, when he sees in how wretched a manner that noble art is treated by a few mean, illiterate traders between us and the stars; who import a yearly stock of nonsense, lies, folly, and impertinence which they offer to the world as genuine from the planets, though they descend from no greater a height than their own brains.

I intend in a short time to publish a large and rational defence of this art, and therefore shall say no more in its justification at present than that it hath been in all ages defended by many learned men, and among the rest by Socrates himself whom I look upon as undoubtedly the wisest of uninspired mortals: to which if we add, that those who have condemned this art, though otherwise learned, having been such as either did not apply their studies this way, or at least did not succeed in their applications, their testimony will not be of much weight to its disadvantage, since they are liable to the common objection of condemning what they did not understand.

Nor am I at all offended, or think it an injury to the art, when I see the common dealers in it, the *Students in Astrology*, the *Philomaths*, and the rest of that tribe, treated by wise men with the utmost scorn and contempt; but rather wonder when I observe gentlemen in the country, rich enough to serve the nation in Parliament, poring in Partridge's

Almanac to find out the events of the year at home and abroad nor dare to propose a hunting match till Gadbury or he have fixed the weather.

I will allow either of the two I have mentioned, or any others of the fraternity, to be not only astrologers, but conjurers too, if I do not produce a hundred instances in all their Almanacs to convince any reasonable man, that they do not so much as understand common grammar and syntax; that they are not able to spell any word out of the usual road nor, even in their prefaces, correct common sense or intelligible English. Then, for their observations and predictions, they are such as will equally suit any age or country in the world. 'This month a certain great person will be threatened with death or sickness.' This the newspaper will tell them, for there we find at the end of the year that no month passes without the death of some person of note; and it would be hard if it should be otherwise, when there are at least two thousand persons of note in this kingdom, many of them old, and the Almanac-maker has the liberty of choosing the sickliest season of the year, where he may fix his prediction. Again, 'This month an eminent clergyman will be preferred'; of which there may be some hundreds, half of them with one foot in the grave. Then, 'Such a planet in such a house shows great machinations, plots, and conspiracies, that may in time be brought to light': after which, if we hear of any discovery the astrologer gets the honour; if not, his prediction still stands good. And at last, 'God preserve King William from all his open and secret enemies, Amen.' When, if the king should happen to have died, the astrologer plainly foretold it; otherwise it passes but for the pious ejaculation of a loyal subject; though it unluckily happened in some of their Almanacs that poor King William was prayed for many months after he was dead, because it fell out that he died about the beginning of the year.

To mention no more of their impertinent predictions, what have we to do with their advertisements about pills, and drinks for the venereal disease? or their mutual quarrels in verse and prose of Whig and Tory, wherewith the stars have little to do?

Having long observed and lamented these and a hundred other abuses of this art, too tedious to repeat, I resolved to proceed in a new way, which I doubt not will be to the general satisfaction of the kingdom. I can this year produce but a specimen of what I design for the future, having employed most part of my time in adjusting and correcting the calculations I made for some years past; because I would offer nothing to the world of which I am not as fully satisfied as that I am now alive. For these two last years I have not failed in above one or two particulars, and those of no very great moment. I exactly foretold the miscarriage at

Toulon, with all its particulars; and the loss of Admiral Shovel° though I was mistaken as to the day, placing that accident about thirty six hours sooner than it happened; but upon reviewing my schemes, I quickly found the cause of that error. I likewise foretold the battle at Almanza° to the very day and hour, with the loss on both sides and the consequences thereof. All which I showed to some friends many months before they happened; that is, I gave them papers sealed up, to open in such a time, after which they were at liberty to read them; and there they found my predictions true in every article except one or two, very minute.

As for the few following predictions I now offer the world, I forebore to publish them till I had perused the several Almanacs for the year we are now entered on. I find them all in the usual strain, and I beg the reader will compare their manner with mine. And here I make bold to tell the world that I lay the whole credit of my art upon the truth of these predictions; and I will be content that Partridge and the rest of his clan may hoot me for a cheat and impostor, if I fail in any single particular of moment. I believe any man who reads this paper will look upon me to be at least a person of as much honesty and understanding as a common maker of Almanacs. I do not lurk in the dark; I am not wholly unknown in the world; I have set my name at length to be a mark of infamy to mankind if they shall find I deceive them.

In one thing I must desire to be forgiven, that I talk more sparingly of home affairs. As it would be imprudence to discover secrets of state, so it would be dangerous to my person; but in smaller matters and that are not of public consequence, I shall be very free; and the truth of my conjectures will as much appear from these as the other. As for the most signal events abroad in France, Flanders, Italy, and Spain, I shall make no scruple to predict them in plain terms: some of them are of importance, and I hope I shall seldom mistake the day they will happen; therefore I think good to inform the reader that I all along make use of the Old Style° observed in England, which I desire he will compare with that of the newspapers at the time they relate the actions I mention.

I must add one word more. I know it hath been the opinion of several learned, who think well enough of the true art of astrology, that the stars do only *incline*, and not *force*, the actions or wills of men; and therefore, however I may proceed by right rules, yet I cannot in prudence so confidently assure the events will follow exactly as I predict them.

I hope I have maturely considered this objection, which in some cases is of no little weight. For example a man may by the influence of an over-ruling planet be disposed or inclined to lust, rage, or avarice, and yet by the force of reason overcome that bad influence; and this was the case of Socrates. But the great events of the world usually depending upon numbers of men, it cannot be expected they should all unite to cross their inclinations, from pursuing a general design wherein they unanimously agree. Besides, the influence of the stars reaches to many actions and events which are not any way in the power of reason; as sickness, death, and what we commonly call accidents, with many more needless to repeat.

But it is now time to proceed to my predictions, which I have begun to calculate from the time that the sun enters into Aries.° And this I take to be properly the beginning of the natural year. I pursue them to the time that he enters Libra, or somewhat more, which is the busy period of the year. The remainder I have not yet adjusted, upon account of several impediments needless here to mention: besides, I must remind the reader again that this is but a specimen of what I design in succeeding years to treat more at large, if I may have liberty and encouragement.

My first prediction is but a trifle, yet I will mention it to show how ignorant these sottish pretenders to astrology are in their own concerns: it relates to Partridge the Almanac-maker. I have consulted the star of his nativity by my own rules, and find he will infallibly die upon the 29th of March next, about eleven at night, of a raging fever; therefore I advise him to consider of it and settle his affairs in time.

The month of APRIL will be observable for the death of many great persons. On the 4th will die the Cardinal de Noailles, Archbishop of Paris: on the 11th, the young Prince of Asturias, son to the Duke of Anjou: on the 14th, a great peer of this realm will die at his country house: on the 19th, an old *layman* of great fame for learning: and on the 23d, an eminent goldsmith in Lombard Street. I could mention others, both at home and abroad, if I did not consider it is of very little use or instruction to the reader, or to the world.

As to public affairs: on the 7th of this month there will be an insurrection in Dauphiné, occasioned by the oppressions of the people, which will not be quieted in some months.

On the 15th will be a violent storm on the south-east coast of France, which will destroy many of their ships, and some in the very harbour.

The 19th will be famous for the revolt of a whole province or kingdom, excepting one city, by which the affairs of a certain prince in the alliance will take a better face.

MAY, against common conjectures, will be no very busy month in Europe, but very signal for the death of the Dauphin which will happen on the 7th, after a short sickness and grievous torments with the strangury. He dies less lamented by the court than the kingdom.

On the 9th, a Mareschal of France will break his leg by a fall from his horse. I have not been able to discover whether he will then die or not.

On the 11th will begin a most important siege, which the eyes of all Europe will be upon. I cannot be more particular; for in relating affairs that so nearly concern the confederates, and consequently this kingdom, I am forced to confine myself for several reasons very obvious to the reader.

On the 15th, news will arrive of a very *surprising event*, than which nothing could be more unexpected.

On the 19th, three noble ladies of this kingdom will, against all expectation, prove with child, to the great joy of their husbands.

On the 23d, a famous buffoon of the playhouse will die a ridiculous death, suitable to his vocation.

JUNE. This month will be distinguished at home by the utter dispersing of those ridiculous deluded enthusiasts, commonly called the Prophets;° occasioned chiefly by seeing the time come that many of their prophecies should be fulfilled, and then finding themselves deceived by contrary events. It is indeed to be admired how any deceiver can be so weak to foretell things near at hand, when a very few months must of necessity discover the imposture to all the world; in this point less prudent than common almanac-makers, who are so wise to wander in generals, and talk dubiously, and leave to the reader the business of interpreting.

On the 1st of this month, a French General will be killed by a random shot of a cannon-ball.

On the 6th, a fire will break out in the suburbs of Paris which will destroy above a thousand houses; and seems to be the foreboding of what will happen, to the surprise of all Europe, about the end of the following month.

On the 10th, a great battle will be fought which will begin at four of the clock in the afternoon, and last till nine at night, with great obstinacy but no very decisive event. I shall not name the place, for the reasons aforesaid; but the commanders on each left wing will be killed. - - - - - I see bonfires, and hear the noise of guns for a victory.

On the 14th, there will be a false report of the French King's death.

On the 20th, Cardinal Portocarero will die of a dysentery, with great suspicion of poison; but the report of his intentions to revolt to King Charles will prove false.

JULY. The 6th of this month, a *certain General* will, by a glorious action, recover the reputation he lost by former misfortunes.

On the 12th, a *great commander* will die a prisoner in the hands of his enemies.

On the 14th, a shameful discovery will be made, of a French Jesuit giving poison to a great foreign general; and when he is put to the torture, will make wonderful discoveries.

In short, this will prove a month of great action if I might have liberty to relate the particulars.

At home, the death of an old famous senator will happen on the 15th, at his country house, worn with age and diseases.

But that which will make this month memorable to all posterity, is the death of the French king, Louis the Fourteenth, after a week's sickness, at Marli, which will happen on the 29th, about six o'clock in the evening. It seems to be an effect of the gout in his stomach, followed by a flux. And, in three days after, Monsieur Chamillard will follow his master, dying suddenly of an apoplexy.

In this month likewise an ambassador will die in London, but I cannot assign the day.

AUGUST. The affairs of France will seem to suffer no change for a while under the Duke of Burgundy's administration; but the genius that animated the whole machine being gone, will be the cause of mighty turns and revolutions in the following year. The new King makes yet little change either in the army or the ministry; but the libels against his grandfather, that fly about his very court, give him uneasiness.

I see an express in mighty haste, with joy and wonder in his looks, arriving by break of day on the 26th of this month, having travelled in three days a prodigious journey by land and sea. In the evening I hear bells and guns, and see the blazing of a thousand bonfires.

A young admiral of noble birth does likewise this month gain immortal honour by a great achievement.

The affairs of Poland are this month entirely settled. Augustus resigns his pretensions which he had again taken up for some time: Stanislaus is peaceably possessed of the throne; and the King of Sweden declares for the Emperor.

I cannot omit one particular accident here at home, that near the end of this month much mischief will be done at Bartholomew Fair, by the fall of a booth.

SEPTEMBER. This month begins with a very surprising fit of frosty weather, which will last near twelve days.

The Pope having long languished last month, the swellings in his legs breaking and the flesh mortifying, will die on the 11th instant; and in three weeks' time, after a mighty contest, be succeeded by a Cardinal of the imperial faction, but native of Tuscany, who is now about sixty one years old.

The French army acts now wholly on the defensive, strongly fortified in their trenches; and the young French King sends overtures for a treaty of peace, by the Duke of Mantua; which, because it is a matter of state that concerns us here at home, I shall speak no further of it.

I shall add but one prediction more, and that in mystical terms, which shall be included in a verse out of Virgil—

> *Alter erit jam Tethys, et altera quæ vehat, Argo*
> *Dilectos heroas.*°

Upon the 25th day of this month, the fulfilling of this prediction will be manifest to everybody.

This is the furthest I have proceeded in my calculations for the present year. I do not pretend that these are all the great events which will happen in this period, but that those I have set down will infallibly come to pass. It will perhaps still be objected why I have not spoke more particularly of affairs at home, or of the success of our armies abroad, which I might, and could very largely have done; but those in power have wisely discouraged men from meddling in public concerns, and I was resolved by no means to give the least offence. This I will venture to say, that it will be a glorious campaign for the *Allies*, wherein the English forces, both by sea and land, will have their full share of honour; that Her Majesty Queen ANNE will continue in health and prosperity; and that no ill accident will arrive to any in the chief ministry.

As to the particular events I have mentioned, the readers may judge, by the fulfilling of them, whether I am of the level with common astrologers who, with an old paltry cant and a few pot-hooks for planets to amuse the vulgar, have in my opinion too long been suffered to abuse the world: but an honest physician ought not to be despised because there are such things as mountebanks. I hope I have some share of reputation, which I would not willingly forfeit for a frolic or humour; and I believe no gentleman who reads this paper will look upon it to be of the same last or mould with the common scribbles that are every day hawked about. My fortune has placed me above the little regards of scribbling for a few pence, which I neither value or want: therefore, let not wise men too hastily condemn this essay, intended for a good design to cultivate and improve an ancient art, long in disgrace by having fallen into mean unskilful hands. A little time will determine whether I have deceived others or myself; and I think it is no very unreasonable request that men would please to suspend their judgments till then. I was once of the opinion with those who despise all predictions from the stars, till in the year 1686 a man of quality showed me, written in his album, that the most learned astronomer Captain H[alley]° assured him he would never believe anything of the stars' influence, if there were not a great revolution in England in the year 1688. Since that time I began to have other thoughts, and after eighteen years diligent study and application I think I have no reason to repent of my pains. I shall detain the reader no longer than to let him know that the account I design to give of next year's events shall take in the principal affairs that happen in Europe. And if I be denied the liberty of offering it to my own country, I shall appeal to the learned world by publishing it in Latin, and giving order to have it printed in Holland.

BICKERSTAFF.

Some Reflections upon Mr Bickerstaff's Predictions for the Year MDCCVIII.

BY A PERSON OF QUALITY.

I HAVE not observed for some years past any insignificant paper to have made more noise, or be more greedily bought, than that of these Predictions. They are the wonder of the common people, an amusement for the better sort, and a jest only to the wise: yet among these last, I have heard some very much in doubt whether the author meant to deceive others, or is deceived himself. Whoever he was, he seems to have with great art adjusted his paper both to please the rabble and to entertain persons of condition. The writer is without question a gentleman of wit and learning, although the piece seems hastily written in a sudden frolic, with the scornful thought of the pleasure he will have in putting this great town into a wonderment about nothing: nor do I doubt but he and his friends in the secret laugh often and plentifully in a corner, to reflect how many hundred thousand fools they have already made. And he has them fast for some time: for so they are like to continue until his prophecies begin to fail in the events. Nay, it is a great question whether the miscarriage of the two or three first will so entirely undeceive people as to hinder them from expecting the accomplishing of the rest. I doubt not but some thousands of these papers are carefully preserved by as many persons, to confront with the events and try whether the astrologer exactly keeps the day and hour. And these I take to be Mr Bickerstaff's choicest cullies, for whose sake chiefly he writ his amusement. Meanwhile he has seven weeks good, during which time the world is to be kept in suspense: for it is so long before the almanac maker is to die, which is the first prediction: and if that fellow happens to be a splenetic visionary fop, or has any faith in his own art, the prophecy may punctually come to pass by very natural means. As a gentleman of my acquaintance, who was ill used by a mercer in town, wrote him a letter in an unknown hand to give him notice that care had been taken to convey a slow poison into his drink, which would infallibly kill him in a month; after which the man began in earnest to languish and decay by the mere strength of imagination, and would certainly have died, if care had not been taken to undeceive him before the jest went too far. The like effect upon

Partridge would wonderfully raise Mr Bickerstaff's reputation for a fortnight longer, until we could hear from France whether the Cardinal de Noailles were dead or alive upon the fourth of April, which is the second of his predictions.

For a piece so carelessly written, the observations upon astrology are reasonable and pertinent, the remarks just; and as the paper is partly designed, in my opinion, for a satire upon the credulity of the vulgar and that idle itch of peeping into futurities, so it is no more than what we all of us deserve. And, since we must be teased with perpetual hawkers of *strange and wonderful things*, I am glad to see a man of sense find leisure and humour to take up the trade for his own and our diversion. To speak in the town phrase, it is a *bite*; he has fully had his jest, and may be satisfied.

I very much approve the serious air he gives himself in his introduction and conclusion, which has gone far to give some people, of no mean rank, an opinion that the author believes himself. He tells us, 'He places the whole credit of his art on the truth of these predictions, and will be content to be hooted by Partridge and the rest for a cheat, if he fails in any one particular' with several other strains of the same kind, wherein I perfectly believe him; and that he is very indifferent whether Isaac Bickerstaff be a *mark of infamy* or not. But it seems, although he has joined an odd surname to no very common Christian one, that in this large town there is a man found to own both the names although, I believe, not the paper.

I believe it is no small mortification to this gentleman astrologer, as well as his bookseller, to find their piece which they sent out in a tolerable print and paper, immediately seized on by three or four interloping printers of Grub Street, the title stuffed with an abstract of the whole matter together with the standard epithets of *strange and wonderful*, the price brought down a full half, which was but a penny in its prime, and bawled about by hawkers of the inferior class with the concluding cadence of 'a halfpenny apiece'. But *sic cecidit Phaeton*:° and to comfort him a little, this production of mine will have the same fate. Tomorrow will my ears be grated by the *little boys* and *wenches in straw hats*, and I must a hundred times undergo the mortification to have my own work offered me to sale at an under value. Then, which is a great deal worse, my acquaintance in the coffee-house will ask me whether I have seen the 'Answer to 'Squire Bickerstaff's Predictions' and whether I knew the puppy that writ it; and how to keep a man's countenance in such a juncture is no easy point of conduct. When, in this case, you see a man shy either in praising or condemning, ready to turn off the discourse to another subject, standing as little in the light as he can to hide his blushing, pretending to sneeze or take snuff, or go off as if sudden business called him; then ply him close, observe his looks narrowly, see whether his speech be constrained or affected, then charge him suddenly or whisper and smile, and you will soon discover whether he be guilty. Although this seem not to the purpose I am discoursing on, yet I think it to be so; for I am much deceived if I do not know the true author of Bickerstaff's Predictions, and did not meet with him some days ago in a coffee-house at Covent Garden.

As to the matter of the Predictions themselves, I shall not enter upon the examination of them, but think it very incumbent upon the learned Mr Partridge to take them into his consideration and lay as many errors in astrology as possible to Mr Bickerstaff's account. He may justly I think challenge the 'Squire to publish the calculation he has made of Partridge's nativity, by the credit of which he so determinately pronounces the time and the manner of his death; and Mr Bickerstaff can do no less in honour than give Mr Partridge the same advantage of calculating *his*, by sending him an account of the time and place of his birth, with other particulars necessary for such a work. By which, no doubt, the learned world will be engaged in the dispute, and take part on each side according as they are inclined.

I should likewise advise Mr Partridge to inquire why Mr Bickerstaff does not so much as offer at one prediction to be fulfilled until two months after the time of publishing his paper? This looks a little suspicious, as if he were desirous to keep the world in play as long as he decently could; else it were hard he could not afford us one prediction between this and the 29th of March, which is not so fair dealing as we have, even from Mr Partridge and his brethren who give us their predictions (such as they are indeed) for every month in the year.

There is one passage in Mr Bickerstaff's paper that seems to be as high a strain of assurance as I have any where met with. It is that prediction for the month of June which relates to the French prophets° here in town, where he tells us, 'They will utterly disperse, by seeing the time come wherein their prophecies should be fulfilled and then finding themselves deceived by contrary events.' Upon which he adds, with great reason, 'his wonder how any deceiver can be so weak, to foretell things near at hand when a very few months must discover the imposture to all the world'. This is spoken with a great deal of affected unconcernedness, as if he would have us think himself to be not under the least apprehension that the same in two months will be his own case. With respect to the gentleman, I do not remember to have heard of so refined and pleasant a piece of impudence; which I hope the author will not resent as an uncivil word, because I am sure I enter into his taste and take it as he meant it. However, he half deserves a reprimand for writing with so much scorn and contempt for the understandings of the majority.

For the month of July he tells us 'of a general, who, by a glorious action, will recover the reputation he lost by former misfortunes'. This is commonly understood to be Lord Galway, who if he be already dead, as some newspapers have it, Mr Bickerstaff has made a trip. But this I do not much insist on; for it is hard if *another general* cannot be found under the *same circumstances*, to whom this prediction may be as well applied.

The French King's death is very punctually related; but it was unfortunate to make him die at Marli where he never goes at that season of the year, as I observed myself during three years I passed in that kingdom. And discoursing some months ago with monsieur Tallard, about the French court, I find that the King never goes to Marli for any time but about the season of hunting there, which is not till August. So that there was an unlucky slip of Mr Bickerstaff, for want of foreign education.

He concludes with resuming his promise, of publishing entire predictions for the next year; of which the other astrologers need not be in very much pain. I suppose we shall have them much about the same time with *The General History of Ears*.° I believe we have done with him for ever in this kind, and though I am no astrologer, may venture to prophesy that Isaac Bickerstaff Esquire is now dead, and died just at the time his Predictions were ready for the press: that he dropped out of the clouds about nine days ago, and in about four hours after mounted up thither again like a vapour, and will one day or other, perhaps, descend a second time when he has some new, agreeable, or amusing whimsy to pass upon the town; wherein it is very probable he will succeed as often as he is disposed to try the experiment; that is, as long as he can preserve a thorough contempt for his own time, and other people's understandings, and is resolved not to laugh cheaper than at the expense of a million of people.

An ELEGY on Mr. *PARTRIDGE*, the Almanac-maker, who died on the 29th of this Instant *March*, 1708.

Well; 'tis as Bickerstaff has guess'd,
Though we all took it for a jest:
Partridge is dead; nay more, he died
Ere he could prove the good *'squire* lied.
Strange, an astrologer should die
Without one wonder in the sky!
Not one of all his *crony* stars
To pay their duty at his hearse?
No meteor, no eclipse appear'd?
No comet with a flaming beard?   10
The sun has rose and gone to bed,
Just as if Partridge were not dead;
Nor hid himself behind the moon
To make a dreadful night at noon.
He at fit periods walks through Aries,°
Howe'er our earthly motion varies;
And twice a-year he'll cut th' Equator,
As if there had been no such matter.
   Some wits have wonder'd what analogy
There is 'twixt *cobbling** and *astrology*;   20
How Partridge made his *optics* rise
From a *shoe-sole* to reach the skies.
   A *list* the cobblers' temples ties,
To keep the hair out of their eyes;
From whence 'tis plain, the *diadem*
That princes wear, derives from them;
And therefore *crowns* are now-a-days
Adorn'd with *golden stars* and *rays*;
Which plainly shows the near alliance
'Twixt *cobbling* and the *planet science*.   30
   Besides, that slow-paced sign Boötes°
As 'tis miscall'd, we know not who 'tis;
But Partridge ended all disputes;
He knew his trade, and call'd it *Boots*.†

---

* Partridge was a cobbler.   † See his Almanac.

The *horned moon*, which heretofore
Upon their shoes the Romans wore,
Whose wideness kept their toes from corns
And whence we claim our *shoeing-horns*,
Shows how the art of *cobbling* bears
A near resemblance to the *spheres*.   40

A scrap of *parchment* hung by *geometry*,
(A great refinement in *barometry*)
Can, like the stars, foretell the weather;
And what is *parchment* else but *leather?*
Which an astrologer might use
Either for *almanacs* or *shoes*.

Thus Partridge, by his wit and parts,
At once did practise both these arts:
And as the boding owl (or rather
The bat, because her wings are *leather*)   50
Steals from her private cell by night,
And flies about the candlelight;
So learned Partridge could as well
Creep in the dark from *leathern* cell,
And in his fancy fly as far
To peep upon a twinkling star.

Besides, he could confound the *spheres*,
And set the *planets* by the ears;
To show his skill, he Mars would join
To Venus in *aspect malign*;   60
Then call in *Mercury* for aid,°
And cure the wounds that *Venus* made.

Great scholars have in Lucian read,°
When Philip King of Greece was dead
His *soul* and *spirit* did divide,
And each part took a diff'rent side;
One rose a star; the *other fell*
Beneath, and mended shoes in Hell.

Thus Partridge still shines in each art,
The *cobbling* and *star-gazing* part,   70
And is *install'd* as good a star
As any of the *Caesars* are.

Thou, high exalted in thy sphere,
May'st follow still thy calling there.
To thee the *Bull* will lend his *hide*,

By Phœbus newly tann'd and dried;
For thee they Argo's hulk will tax,°
And scrape her pitchy sides for *wax*:
Then, Ariadne kindly lends
Her braided hair to make thee *ends*;   80
The point of Sagittarius' dart
Turns to an *awl* by heav'nly art;
And Vulcan, wheedled by his wife,
Will forge for thee a *paring-knife*.
For want of room by Virgo's side,°
She'll strain a point, and sit* astride,
To take thee kindly in *between*;
And then the *Signs* will be *Thirteen*.

   Triumphant star! some pity show
On *cobblers militant* below,   90
Whom roguish boys, in stormy nights,
Torment by pissing out their lights,
Or through a chink convey their smoke,
Enclosed *artificers* to choke.

   †But do not shed thy influence down
Upon St. *James*'s end o'th' town;°
Consider where the *Moon* and *Stars*
Have their devoutest worshippers,
Astrologers and *Lunatics*
Have in *Moor Fields* their stations fix,   100
Hither thy gentle aspect bend,
  ‡Nor look asquint on an old friend.

THE EPITAPH

Here, five feet deep, lies on his back
A *cobbler*, *starmonger*, and *quack*;
Who to the stars, in pure good will,
Does to his best look upward still.
Weep, all you customers that use
His *pills*, his *almanacs*, or *shoes*.
And you that did your fortunes seek,
Step to his grave but once a week;   110

* Tibi brachia contrahet Ingens Scorpius°, &c.
† Sed nec in Arctoo sedem tibi legeris Orbe, *&c.*°
‡ Neve tuam videas obliquo sidere Romam.°

This earth, which bears his body's print,
You'll find has so much virtue in't,
That I durst pawn my ears, 'twill tell
Whate'er concerns you full as well,
In *physic*, *stolen goods*, or *love*,
As he himself could, when above.

MR. BICKERSTAFF'S PREDICTIONS.

Being an ACCOUNT of the Death of Mr. PARTRIDGE, the Almanac-maker, Upon the 29th Instant. *In a Letter to a Person of Honour.*

My Lord,

IN obedience to your Lordship's commands, as well as to satisfy my own curiosity, I have for some days past enquired constantly after Partridge the almanac-maker, of whom it was foretold in Mr. Bickerstaff's Predictions, published about a month ago, that he should die the 29th instant, about eleven at night, of a raging fever. I had some sort of knowledge of him when I was employed in the revenue, because he used every year to present me with his almanac, as he did other gentlemen, upon the score of some little gratuity we gave him. I saw him accidentally once or twice about ten days before he died, and observed he began very much to droop and languish, though I hear his friends did not seem to apprehend him in any danger. About two or three days ago he grew ill, was confined first to his chamber, and in a few hours after to his bed; where Dr. Case and Mrs. Kirleus were sent for to visit and to prescribe to him. Upon this intelligence I sent thrice every day one servant or other to inquire after his health; and yesterday about four in the afternoon, word was brought me that he was past hopes; upon which I prevailed with myself to go and see him partly out of commiseration and, I confess, partly out of curiosity. He knew me very well, seemed surprised at my condescension, and made me compliments upon it as well as he could in the condition he was. The people about him said he had been for some hours delirious; but when I saw him he had his understanding as well as ever I knew, and spoke strong and hearty, without any seeming uneasiness or constraint. After I had told him how sorry I was to see him in those melancholy circumstances, and said some other civilities suitable to the occasion, I desired him to tell me freely and ingenuously whether the predictions Mr. Bickerstaff had published relating to his death had not too much affected and worked on his imagination. He confessed he had often had it in his head, but never with much apprehension till about a fortnight before; since which time it had the perpetual possession of his mind and thoughts, and he did verily believe was the true natural cause of his present distemper; for, said he, 'I am thoroughly persuaded, and I think I have very good reasons, that Mr. Bickerstaff spoke altogether by guess, and knew no more what will happen this year than I did myself.' I told him his discourse surprised me, and I would be glad he were in a state of health to be able to tell me what reason he had to be convinced of Mr. Bickerstaff's ignorance. He replied, 'I am a poor ignorant fellow, bred to a mean trade, yet I have sense enough to know that all pretences of foretelling by astrology are deceits, for this manifest reason: because the wise and the learned, who can only know whether there be any truth in this science, do all unanimously agree to laugh at and despise it; and none but the poor ignorant vulgar give it any credit, and that only upon the word of such silly wretches as I and my fellows who can hardly write or read.' I then asked him, why he had not calculated his own nativity to see whether it agreed with Bickerstaff's prediction? At which he shook his head, and said, 'Oh! Sir, this is no time for jesting, but for repenting those fooleries, as I do now from the very bottom of my heart.' 'By what I can gather from you,' said I, 'the observations and predictions you printed with your almanacs were mere impositions on the people.' He replied, 'If it were otherwise, I should have the less to answer for. We have a common form for all those things: as to foretelling the weather, we never meddle with that, but leave it to the printer, who takes it out of any old almanac, as he thinks fit: the rest was my own invention, to make my almanac sell, having a wife to maintain, and no other way to get my bread; for mending old shoes is a poor livelihood; and' (added he, sighing) 'I wish I may not have done more mischief by my physic than my astrology; though I had some good receipts from my grandmother, and my own compositions were such as I thought could at least do no hurt.'

I had some other discourses with him, which now I cannot call to mind; and I fear have already tired your lordship. I shall only add one circumstance, that on his deathbed he declared himself a nonconformist and had a fanatic preacher to be his spiritual guide. After half an hour's conversation I took my leave, being half stifled by the closeness of the room. I imagined he could not hold out long, and therefore withdrew to a little coffee-house hard by, leaving a servant at the house with orders to come immediately and tell me, as near as he could, the minute when Partridge should expire, which was not above two hours after, when looking upon my watch, I found it to be above five minutes after seven: by which it is clear that Mr. Bickerstaff was mistaken almost four hours in his calculation. In the other circumstances he was exact enough. But whether he has not been the cause of this poor man's death, as well as the predictor, may be very reasonably disputed. However, it must be confessed the matter is odd enough, whether we should endeavour to account for it by chance or the effect of imagination: for my own part, though I believe no man has less faith in these matters, yet I shall wait with some impatience, and not without some expectation, the fulfilling of Mr. Bickerstaff's second prediction that the Cardinal de Noailles is to die upon the fourth of April; and if that should be verified as exactly as this of poor Partridge, I must own I should be wholly surprised, and at a loss, and infallibly expect the accomplishment of all the rest.

A

VINDICATION

OF

ISAAC BICKERSTAFF, ESQ.

AGAINST What is Objected to HIM by Mr. *Partridge*, in his Almanac for the present Year 1709. *By the said* ISAAC BICKERSTAFF *Esq.*

MR. PARTRIDGE hath been lately pleased to treat me after a very rough manner in *that which is called* his Almanac for the present year: such usage is very undecent from *one gentleman to another* and does not at all contribute to the discovery of truth, which ought to be the great end in all disputes of the *learned*. To call a man *fool* and *villain* and *impudent fellow*, only for differing from him in a point merely speculative, is in my humble opinion a very improper style for a person of *his education*. I appeal to the *learned world* whether, in my last year's Predictions, I gave him the least provocation for such unworthy treatment. Philosophers have differed in all ages but the discreetest among them have always differed as became philosophers. Scurrility and passion in a controversy among *scholars* is just so much of nothing to the purpose and, at best, a tacit confession of a weak cause. My concern is not so much for my own reputation as that of the *republic of letters*, which Mr. Partridge hath endeavoured to wound through my sides. If men of public spirit must be superciliously treated for their ingenuous attempts, how will true useful knowledge be ever advanced? I wish Mr. Partridge knew the thoughts which *foreign universities* have conceived of his ungenerous proceeding with me; but I am too tender of his reputation to publish them to the world. That spirit of envy and pride which blasts so many rising geniuses in our nation, is yet unknown among *professors* abroad: the necessity of justifying myself will excuse my vanity when I tell the reader, that I have received near a hundred *honorary* letters from several parts of Europe (some as far as Muscovy), in praise of my performance; beside several others, which, as I have been credibly informed, were opened in the p[ost] office and never sent me. 'Tis true, the inquisition in P[ortugal]° was pleased to burn my Predictions and condemn the author and the readers of them: but I hope at the same time it will be considered in how deplorable a state *Learning* lies at present in that kingdom. And with the profoundest veneration for *crowned heads*, I will presume to add that it a little concerned *his Majesty of*

P[ortugal] to interpose his authority in behalf of a *scholar* and a *gentleman*, the subject of a nation with which he is now in so strict an alliance. But the other kingdoms and states of Europe have treated me with more candour and generosity. If I had leave to print the Latin letters transmitted to me from foreign parts, they would fill a volume and be a full defence against all that Mr. Partridge, or his accomplices of the *P[ortugal]inquisition*, will be ever able to object; who, by the way, are the only enemies my Predictions have ever met with at home or abroad. But I hope I know better what is due to the honour of a *learned correspondence*, in so tender a point. Yet some of those illustrious persons will perhaps excuse me, for transcribing a passage or two in my own vindication. The most learned Monsieur Leibnitz thus addresses to me his third letter: '*Illustrissimo Bickerstaffio° astrologico instauratori*', &c. Monsieur Le Clerc, quoting my Predictions in a treatise he published last year, is pleased to say, '*Ità nuperrimè Bickerstaffius magnum illud Angliæ sidus.*' Another great professor writing of me, has these words: '*Bickerstaffius, nobilis Anglus, astrologorum hujusce seculi facilè princeps.*' Signior Magliabecchi, the Great Duke's famous library-keeper, spends almost his whole letter in compliments and praises. 'Tis true, the renowned professor of astronomy at Utrecht seems to differ from me in one article; but it is after the modest manner that becomes a philosopher; as '*pace tanti viri dixerim*': and, page 55, he seems to lay the error upon the printer (as indeed it ought) and says, '*vel forsan error typographi, cum alioquin Bickerstaffius vir doctissimus*', &c.

If Mr. Partridge had followed this example in the controversy between us, he might have spared me the trouble of justifying myself in so public a manner. I believe few men are readier to own their errors than I, or more thankful to those who will please to inform him of them. But it seems this gentleman, instead of encouraging the progress of his own art, is pleased to look upon all attempts of that kind as an invasion of his province. He has been indeed so wise as to make no objection against the truth of my Predictions, except in one single point relating to himself. And to demonstrate how much men are blinded by their own partiality, I do solemnly assure the reader that he is the only person from whom I ever heard that objection offered; which consideration alone, I think, will take off all its weight.

With my utmost endeavours I have not been able to trace above two objections ever made against the truth of my last year's prophecies. The first was of a Frenchman who was pleased to publish to the world 'that the Cardinal de Noailles was still alive, notwithstanding the pretended prophecy of Monsieur Biquerstaffe': but how far a *Frenchman*, a *Papist*, and an *enemy*, is to be believed in his own case against an *English Protestant* who is *true to the government*, I shall leave to the candid and impartial reader.

The other objection is the unhappy occasion of this discourse, and relates to an article in my Predictions which foretold the death of Mr. Partridge to happen on March 29, 1708. This he is pleased to contradict absolutely in the almanac he has published for the present year, and in that ungentlemanly manner (pardon the expression) as I have above related. In that work he very roundly asserts that he 'is not only now alive, but was likewise alive upon that very 29th of March, when I had foretold *he* should die'. This is the subject of the present controversy between us, which I design to handle with all brevity, perspicuity, and calmness. In this dispute I am sensible the eyes not only of England, but of all Europe, will be upon us; and the *learned* in every country will, I doubt not, take part on that side where they find most appearance of reason and truth.

Without entering into criticisms of *chronology* about the hour of his death, I shall only prove that Mr. Partridge is not alive. And my first argument is thus: above a thousand gentlemen having bought his almanac for this year, merely to find what he said against me, at every line they read, they would lift up their eyes, and cry out, betwixt rage and laughter, 'they were sure no man alive ever writ such damned stuff as this'. Neither did I ever hear that opinion disputed; so that Mr. Partridge lies under a *dilemma*, either of disowning his almanac, or allowing himself to be *no man alive*. Secondly, Death is defined by all philosophers, a separation of the soul and body. Now it is certain that the poor woman who has best reason to know, has gone about for some time to every alley in the neighbourhood, and sworn to the gossips that *her husband had neither life nor soul in him*. Therefore, if an *uninformed* carcass walks still about and is pleased to call itself Partridge, Mr. Bickerstaff does not think himself anyway answerable for that. Neither had the said carcass any right to beat the poor boy who happened to pass by it in the street, crying 'A full and true Account of Dr. Partridge's death', &c.

Thirdly, Mr. Partridge pretends to tell fortunes, and recover stolen goods, which all the parish says he must do by conversing with the devil and other evil spirits; and no wise man will ever allow he could converse personally with either, till after he was dead.

Fourthly, I will plainly prove him to be dead, out of his own almanac for this year, and from the very passage which he produces to make us think him alive. He there says, 'he is not only now alive, but was also alive upon that very 29th of March, which I foretold *he* should die on': by this, he declares his opinion that a man may be alive now who was not alive a twelvemonth ago. And indeed, there lies the sophistry of his argument. He dares not assert he was alive ever since that 29th of March, but that he 'is now alive, and was so on that day': I grant the latter, for he did not die till night, as appears by the printed Account of his Death, in a *Letter to a Lord*; and whether he is since revived, I leave the world to judge. This indeed is perfect cavilling, and I am ashamed to dwell any longer upon it.

Fifthly, I will appeal to Mr. Partridge himself, whether it be probable I could have been so indiscreet to begin my Predictions with the *only* falsehood that ever was pretended to be in them, and this in an affair at home, where I had so many opportunities to be exact, and must have given such advantages against me to a person of Mr. Partridge's wit and learning, who, if he could possibly have raised one single objection more against the truth of my prophecies, would hardly have spared me.

And here I must take occasion to reprove the above-mentioned writer of the relation of Mr. Partridge's death, in a *Letter to a Lord*; who was pleased to tax me with a mistake of *four whole hours* in my calculation of that event. I must confess, this censure, pronounced with an air of certainty, in a matter that so nearly concerned me, and by a *grave judicious author*, moved me not a little. But though I was at that time out of town, yet several of my friends whose curiosity had led them to be exactly informed (for as to my own part, having no doubt at all in the matter, I never once thought of it) assured me, I computed to something under half an hour; which (I speak my private opinion) is an error of no very great magnitude, that men should raise a clamour about it. I shall only say it would not be amiss if that author would henceforth be more tender of other men's reputation as well as his own. It is well there were no more mistakes of that kind; if there had, I presume he would have told me of them with as little ceremony.

There is one objection against Mr. Partridge's death which I have sometimes met with, though indeed very slightly offered, that he still continues to write almanacs. But this is no more than what is common to all of that profession; *Gadbury*, *Poor Robin*, *Dove*, *Wing*, and several others, do yearly publish their almanacs, though several of them have been dead since before the *Revolution*. Now, the natural reason of this I take to be, that whereas it is the privilege of other authors *to live after their deaths*, almanac-makers are alone excluded; because their dissertations, treating only upon the minutes as they pass, become useless as those go off. In consideration of which, *Time*, whose *registers* they are, gives them a lease in reversion to continue their works after their death. Or, perhaps, a name can *make* an almanac as well as it can *sell* one. And to strengthen this conjecture, I have heard the booksellers affirm that they have desired

Mr. Partridge to spare himself further trouble and only lend them his name, which could make Almanacs much better than himself.

I should not have given the public, or myself, the trouble of this Vindication, if my name had not been made use of by several persons to whom I never lent it; one of which, a few days ago, was pleased to father on me a new set of Predictions. But I think those are things too serious to be trifled with. It grieved me to the heart when I saw my labours, which had cost me so much thought and watching, bawled about by the common hawkers of Grub Street, which I only intended for the weighty consideration of the gravest persons. This prejudiced the world so much at first, that several of my friends had the assurance to ask me whether I were in jest; to which I only answered coldly, 'that the event would show'. But it is the talent of our age and nation to turn things of the greatest importance into ridicule. When the end of the year had *verified all my Predictions*, out comes Mr. Partridge's almanac disputing the point of his death; so that I am employed like the general who was forced to kill his enemies twice over, whom a *necromancer* had raised to life. If Mr. Partridge has practised the same experiment upon himself, and be again alive, long may he continue so; that does not in the least contradict my veracity; but I think I have clearly proved, *by invincible demonstration*, that he died at furthest within half an hour of the time I foretold.

AN
ARGUMENT
To prove that the *Abolishing of* CHRISTIANITY IN *ENGLAND*, May as things now stand, be attended with some Inconveniences, and perhaps not produce those many good Effects proposed thereby.

I AM very sensible what a weakness and presumption it is, to reason against the general humour and disposition of the world. I remember it was with great justice, and a due regard to the freedom both of the public and the press, forbidden upon severe penalties to write or discourse or lay wagers against the [Union]° even before it was confirmed by parliament, because that was looked upon as a design to oppose the current of the people, which, besides the folly of it, is a manifest breach of the fundamental law that makes this majority of opinion the voice of God. In like manner, and for the very same reasons, it may perhaps be neither safe nor prudent to argue against the abolishing of Christianity, at a juncture when all parties seem so unanimously determined upon the point, as we cannot but allow from their actions, their discourses, and their writings. However, I know not how, whether from the affectation of singularity, or the perverseness of human nature, but so it unhappily falls out that I cannot be entirely of this opinion. Nay, though I were sure an order were issued for my immediate prosecution by the Attorney-General, I should still confess that in the present posture of our affairs at home or abroad, I do not yet see the absolute necessity of extirpating the Christian religion from among us.

This perhaps may appear too great a paradox even for our wise and paradoxical age to endure; therefore I shall handle it with all tenderness, and with the utmost deference to that great and profound majority which is of another sentiment.

And yet the curious may please to observe how much the genius of a nation is liable to alter in half an age. I have heard it affirmed for certain by some very old people, that the contrary opinion was even in their memories as much in vogue as the other is now; and that a project for the abolishing of Christianity would then have appeared as singular, and been thought as absurd, as it would be at this time to write or discourse in its defence.

Therefore I freely own that all appearances are against me. The system of the Gospel, after the fate of other systems, is generally antiquated and exploded, and the mass or body of the common people, among whom it seems to have had its latest credit, are now grown as much ashamed of it as their betters; opinions, like fashions, always descending from those of quality to the middle sort, and thence to the vulgar, where at length they are dropped and vanish.

But here I would not be mistaken, and must therefore be so bold as to borrow a distinction from the writers on the other side, when they make a difference betwixt nominal and real Trinitarians. I hope no reader imagines me so weak to stand up in the defence of real Christianity, such as used in primitive times (if we may believe the authors of those ages) to have an influence upon men's belief and actions. To offer at the restoring of that would indeed be a wild project; it would be to dig up foundations; to destroy at one blow all the wit, and half the learning of the kingdom; to break the entire frame and constitution of things; to ruin trade, extinguish arts and sciences with the professors of them; in short, to turn our courts, exchanges, and shops into deserts; and would be full as absurd as the proposal of Horace,° where he advises the Romans all in a body to leave their city, and seek a new seat in some remote part of the world, by way of a cure for the corruption of their manners.

Therefore I think this caution was in itself altogether unnecessary, (which I have inserted only to prevent all possibility of cavilling) since every candid reader will easily understand my discourse to be intended only in defence of nominal Christianity;° the other having been for some time wholly laid aside by general consent, as utterly inconsistent with all our present schemes of wealth and power.

But why we should therefore cast off the name and title of Christians, although the general opinion and resolution be so violent for it, I confess I cannot (with submission) apprehend the consequence necessary. However, since the undertakers propose such wonderful advantages to the nation by this project, and advance many plausible objections against the systems of Christianity, I shall briefly consider the strength of both, fairly allow them their greatest weight, and offer such answers as I think most reasonable. After which I will beg leave to show what inconveniences may possibly happen by such an innovation, in the present posture of our affairs.

First, one great advantage proposed by the abolishing of Christianity is, that it would very much enlarge and establish liberty of conscience, that great bulwark of our nation and of the Protestant Religion, which is still too much limited by priestcraft, notwithstanding all the good intentions of the legislature, as we have lately found by a severe instance.

For it is confidently reported, that two young gentlemen of real hopes, bright wit, and profound judgment, who upon a thorough examination of causes and effects, and by the mere force of natural abilities, without the least tincture of learning, having made a discovery that there was no God, and generously communicating their thoughts for the good of the public, were some time ago, by an unparalleled severity and upon I know not what obsolete law, broke for blasphemy. And as it hath been wisely observed, if persecution once begins, no man alive knows how far it may reach or where it will end.

In answer to all which, with deference to wiser judgments, I think this rather shows the necessity of a nominal religion among us. Great wits love to be free with the highest objects, and if they cannot be allowed a God to revile or renounce, they will speak evil of dignities, abuse the government, and reflect upon the ministry; which I am sure few will deny to be of much more pernicious consequence, according to the saying of Tiberius, *Deorum offensa diis curæ.*° As to the particular fact related, I think it is not fair to argue from one instance, perhaps another cannot be produced; yet (to the comfort of all those who may be apprehensive of persecution) blasphemy we know is freely spoke a million of times in every coffee-house and tavern, or wherever else good company meet. It must be allowed indeed, that to break an English free-born officer only for blasphemy was, to speak the gentlest of such an action, a very high strain of absolute power. Little can be said in excuse for the general; perhaps he was afraid it might give offence to the allies,° among whom, for aught we know, it may be the custom of the country to believe a God. But if he argued, as some have done, upon a mistaken principle that an officer who is guilty of speaking blasphemy, may some time or other proceed so far as to raise a mutiny, the consequence is by no means to be admitted; for surely, the commander of an English army is like to be but ill obeyed whose soldiers fear and reverence him as little as they do a Deity.

It is further objected against the Gospel System, that it obliges men to the belief of things too difficult for free-thinkers° and such who have shaken off the prejudices that usually cling to a confined education. To which I answer that men should be cautious how they raise objections which reflect upon the wisdom of the nation. Is not everybody freely allowed to believe whatever he pleases and to publish his belief to the world whenever he thinks fit, especially if it serves to strengthen the party which is in the right? Would any indifferent foreigner who should read the trumpery lately written by Asgil, Tindal, Toland, Coward, and forty more, imagine the Gospel to be our rule of faith and to be confirmed by parliaments? Does any man either believe, or say he believes, or desire to have it thought that he says he believes one syllable of the matter? And is any man worse received upon that score, or does he find his want of nominal faith a disadvantage to him in the pursuit of any civil or military employment? What if there be an old dormant statute or two° against him, are they not now obsolete, to a degree that Empson and Dudley° themselves if they were now alive, would find it impossible to put them in execution?

It is likewise urged that there are, by computation, in this kingdom above ten thousand parsons, whose revenues added to those of my lords the bishops would suffice to maintain at least two hundred young gentlemen of wit and pleasure and free-thinking, enemies to priestcraft, narrow principles, pedantry, and prejudices; who might be an ornament to the Court and Town. And then again, so great a number of able [bodied] divines might be a recruit to our fleet and armies. This indeed appears to be a consideration of some weight. But then, on the other side, several things deserve to be considered likewise: as, first, whether it may not be thought necessary that in certain tracts of country, like what we call parishes, there should be one man at least of abilities to read and write. Then it seems a wrong computation that the revenues of the Church throughout this island would be large enough to maintain two hundred young gentlemen or even half that number, after the present refined way of living; that is, to allow each of them such a rent as in the modern form of speech would make them easy. But still there is in this project a greater mischief behind, and we ought to beware of the woman's folly who killed the hen that every morning laid her a golden egg. For, pray what would become of the race of men in the next age if we had nothing to trust to besides the scrofulous, consumptive productions furnished by our men of wit and pleasure, when, having squandered away their vigour, health and estates, they are forced by some disagreeable marriage to piece up their broken fortunes and entail rottenness and politeness on their posterity? Now, here are ten thousand persons reduced by the wise regulations of Henry the Eighth° to the necessity of a low diet and moderate exercise, who are the only great restorers of our breed, without which the nation would in an age or two become one great hospital.

Another advantage proposed by the abolishing of Christianity is the clear gain of one day in seven, which is now entirely lost and consequently the kingdom one seventh less considerable in trade, business, and pleasure; beside the loss to the public of so many stately structures now in the hands of the Clergy, which might be converted into playhouses, exchanges, market-houses, common dormitories, and other public edifices.

I hope I shall be forgiven a hard word if I call this a perfect *cavil*. I readily own there hath been an old custom time out of mind for people to assemble in the churches every *Sunday*, and that shops are still frequently shut in order as it is conceived to preserve the memory of that ancient practice; but how this can prove a hindrance to business or pleasure is hard to imagine. What if the men of pleasure are forced one day in the week to game at home instead of the chocolate-house?° Are not the taverns and coffee-houses open? Can there be a more convenient season for taking a dose of physic? Are fewer claps got upon Sundays than other days? Is not that the chief day for traders to sum up the accounts of the week and for lawyers to prepare their briefs? But I would fain know how it can be pretended that the churches are misapplied? Where are more appointments and rendezvous of gallantry? Where more care to appear in the foremost box with greater advantage of dress? Where more meetings for business? Where more bargains driven of all sorts? And where so many conveniences or incitements to sleep?

There is one advantage greater than any of the foregoing proposed by the abolishing of Christianity: that it will utterly extinguish parties among us, by removing those factious distinctions of High and Low Church, of Whig and Tory, Presbyterian and Church of England, which are now so many mutual clogs upon public proceedings, and are apt to prefer the gratifying themselves or depressing their adversaries, before the most important interest of the state.

I confess, if it were certain that so great an advantage would redound to the nation by this expedient I would submit and be silent. But will any man say that if the words *whoring*, *drinking*, *cheating*, *lying*, *stealing*, were by act of parliament ejected out of the English tongue and dictionaries, we should all awake next morning chaste and temperate, honest and just, and lovers of truth? Is this a fair consequence? Or if the physicians would forbid us to pronounce the words *pox*, *gout*, *rheumatism* and *stone*, would that expedient serve like so many *talismans* to destroy the diseases themselves? Are party and faction rooted in men's hearts no deeper than phrases borrowed from religion, or founded upon no firmer principles? And is our language so poor that we cannot find other terms to express them? Are envy, pride, avarice and ambition such ill nomenclators that they cannot furnish appellations for their owners? Will not *heydukes* and *mamalukes*, *mandarins* and *patshaws*, or any other words formed at pleasure, serve to distinguish those who are in the ministry, from others who would be in it if they could? What, for instance, is easier than to vary the form of speech, and instead of the word church, make it a question in politics whether the Monument° be in danger? Because religion was nearest at hand to furnish a few convenient phrases, is our invention so barren we can find no others? Suppose, for argument sake, that the Tories favoured Margarita, the Whigs Mrs Tofts, and the Trimmers° Valentini; would not *Margaritians*, *Toftians*, and *Valentinians* be very tolerable marks of distinction? The Prasini and Veniti,° two most virulent factions in Italy, began (if I remember right) by a distinction of colours in ribbons, which we might do with as good a grace about the dignity of the *blue* and the *green*, and serve as properly to divide the Court, the Parliament, and the Kingdom between them, as any terms of art whatsoever borrowed from religion. And therefore I think there is little force in this objection against Christianity, or prospect of so great an advantage as is proposed in the abolishing of it.

'Tis again objected as a very absurd ridiculous custom, that a set of men should be suffered, much less employed and hired, to bawl one day in seven against the lawfulness of those methods most in use towards the pursuit of greatness, riches and pleasure, which are the constant practice of all men alive on the other six. But this objection is, I think, a little unworthy so refined an age as ours. Let us argue this matter calmly. I appeal to the breast of any polite free-thinker whether in the pursuit of gratifying a predominant passion, he hath not always felt a wonderful incitement by reflecting it was a thing forbidden; and therefore we see, in order to cultivate this taste, the wisdom of the nation hath taken special care that the ladies should be furnished with prohibited silks, and the men with prohibited wine.° And indeed it were to be wished that some other prohibitions were promoted, in order to improve the pleasures of the town; which for want of such expedients begin already, as I am told, to flag and grow languid, giving way daily to cruel inroads from the spleen.

'Tis likewise proposed as a great advantage to the public, that if we once discard the system of the Gospel, all religion will of course be banished for ever, and consequently, along with it, those grievous prejudices of education which under the names of virtue, conscience, honour, justice, and the like, are so apt to disturb the peace of human minds, and the notions whereof are so hard to be eradicated by right reason or free-thinking, sometimes during the whole course of our lives.

Here first I observe how difficult it is to get rid of a phrase, which the world is once grown fond of, though the occasion that first produced it be entirely taken away. For some years past, if a man had but an ill-favoured nose, the deep thinkers of the age would some way or other contrive to impute the cause to the prejudice of his education. From this fountain were said to be derived all our foolish notions of justice, piety, love of our country, all our opinions of God or a future state, Heaven, Hell, and the like. And there might formerly perhaps have been some pretence for this charge. But so effectual care hath been since taken to remove those prejudices by an entire change in the methods of education, that (with honour I mention it to our polite innovators) the young gentlemen who are now on the scene seem to have not the least tincture of those infusions or string of those weeds; and, by consequence, the reason for abolishing nominal Christianity upon that pretext is wholly ceased.

For the rest, it may perhaps admit a controversy, whether the banishing of all notions of religion whatsoever would be convenient for the vulgar. Not that I am in the least of opinion with those who hold religion to have been the invention of politicians, to keep the lower part of the world in awe by the fear of invisible powers; unless mankind were then very different from what it is now. For I look upon the mass or body of our people here in England, to be as free-thinkers, that is to say, as staunch unbelievers, as any of the highest rank. But I conceive some scattered notions about a superior power to be of singular use for the common people, as furnishing excellent materials to keep children quiet when they grow peevish, and providing topics of amusement in a tedious winter night.

Lastly, 'tis proposed as a singular advantage that the abolishing of Christianity will very much contribute to the uniting of Protestants, by enlarging the terms of communion so as to take in all sorts of dissenters who are now shut out of the pale upon account of a few ceremonies which all sides confess to be things indifferent; that this alone will effectually answer the great ends of a scheme for comprehension,° by opening a large noble gate at which all bodies may enter; whereas the chaffering with dissenters, and dodging about this or t'other ceremony, is but like opening a few wickets and leaving them ajar, by which no more than one can get in at a time, and that not without stooping, and sideling, and squeezing his body.

To all this I answer that there is one darling inclination of mankind, which usually affects to be a retainer to religion, though she be neither its parent, its godmother, nor its friend; I mean the spirit of opposition, that lived long before Christianity and can easily subsist without it. Let us for instance examine wherein the opposition of sectaries among us consists, we shall find Christianity to have no share in it at all. Does the Gospel any where prescribe a starched squeezed countenance, a stiff formal gait, a singularity of manners and habit, or any affected forms and modes of speech different from the reasonable part of mankind? Yet, if Christianity did not lend its name to stand in the gap and to employ or divert these humours, they must of necessity be spent in contraventions to the laws of the land, and disturbance of the public peace. There is a portion of enthusiasm assigned to every nation, which, if it hath not proper objects to work on, will burst out and set all into a flame. If the quiet of a state can be bought by only flinging men a few ceremonies to devour, it is a purchase no wise man would refuse. Let the mastiffs amuse themselves about a sheepskin stuffed with hay, provided it will keep them from worrying the flock. The institution of convents abroad seems in one point a strain of great wisdom, there being few irregularities in human passions which may not have recourse to vent themselves in some of those orders, which are so many retreats for the speculative, the melancholy, the proud, the silent, the politic, and the morose, to spend themselves and evaporate the noxious particles; for each of whom we in this island are forced to provide a several sect of religion to keep them quiet. And whenever Christianity shall be abolished, the legislature must find some other expedient to employ and entertain them. For what imports it how large a gate you open, if there will be always left a number who place a pride and a merit in not coming in?

Having thus considered the most important objections against Christianity and the chief advantages proposed by the abolishing thereof, I shall now with equal deference and submission to wiser judgments as before, proceed to mention a few inconveniences that may happen if the Gospel should be repealed, which perhaps the projectors may not have sufficiently considered.

And first, I am very sensible how much the gentlemen of wit and pleasure are apt to murmur, and be choqued° at the sight of so many daggled-tail parsons that happen to fall in their way, and offend their eyes; but at the same time these wise reformers do not consider what an advantage and felicity it is for great wits to be always provided with objects of scorn and contempt, in order to exercise and improve their talents and divert their ¯spleen from falling on each other or on themselves; especially when all this may be done without the least imaginable danger to their persons.

And to urge another argument of a parallel nature, if Christianity were once abolished how would the free-thinkers, the strong reasoners, and the men of profound learning, be able to find another subject so calculated in all points whereon to display their abilities? What wonderful productions of wit should we be deprived of, from those whose genius by continual practice hath been wholly turned upon raillery and invectives against religion, and would therefore never be able to shine or distinguish themselves upon any other subject? We are daily complaining of the great decline of wit among us, and would we take away the greatest, perhaps the only topic we have left? Who would ever have suspected Asgil for a wit, or Toland for a philosopher, if the inexhaustible stock of Christianity had not been at hand to provide them with materials? What other subject through all art or nature could have produced Tindal for a profound author, or furnished him with readers? It is the wise choice of the subject that alone adorns and distinguishes the writer. For, had a hundred such pens as these been employed on the side of religion, they would have immediately sunk into silence and oblivion.

Nor do I think it wholly groundless, or my fears altogether imaginary, that the abolishing of Christianity may perhaps bring the Church in danger, or at least put the senate to the trouble of another securing vote. I desire I may not be mistaken. I am far from presuming to affirm or think that the Church is in danger at present, or as things now stand, but we know not how soon it may be so when the Christian religion is repealed. As plausible as this project seems, there may a dangerous design lurk under it. Nothing can be more notorious than that the Atheists, Deists, Socinians,° Anti-Trinitarians, and other subdivisions of free-thinkers, are persons of little zeal for the present ecclesiastical establishment. Their declared opinion is for repealing the Sacramental Test; they are very indifferent with regard to ceremonies; nor do they hold the *jus divinum* of Episcopacy.° Therefore this may be intended as one politic step towards altering the constitution of the Church established, and setting up Presbytery in the stead, which I leave to be further considered by those at the helm.

In the last place, I think nothing can be more plain than that by this expedient we shall run into the evil we chiefly pretend to avoid, and that the abolishment of the Christian religion will be the readiest course we can take to introduce popery. And I am the more inclined to this opinion because we know it has been the constant practice of the Jesuits to send over emissaries with instructions to personate themselves members of the several prevailing sects amongst us. So it is recorded that they have at sundry times appeared in the guise of Presbyterians, Anabaptists, Independents, and Quakers, according as any of these were most in credit; so, since the fashion hath been taken up of exploding religion, the popish missionaries have not been wanting to mix with the free-thinkers, among whom Toland, the great oracle of the Antichristians, is an Irish priest, the son of an Irish priest; and the most learned and ingenious author of a book called *The Rights of the Christian Church*,° was in a proper juncture reconciled to the Romish faith, whose true son (as appears by a hundred passages in his treatise) he still continues. Perhaps I could add some others to the number; but the fact is beyond dispute, and the reasoning they proceed by is right. For, supposing Christianity to be extinguished, the people will never be at ease till they find out some other method of worship, which will as infallibly produce superstition, as this will end in popery.

And therefore, if notwithstanding all I have said it still be thought necessary to have a bill brought in for repealing Christianity, I would humbly offer an amendment, that instead of the word Christianity, may be put Religion in general; which I conceive will much better answer all the good ends proposed by the projectors of it. For, as long as we leave in being a God and his Providence, with all the necessary consequences which curious and inquisitive men will be apt to draw from such premises, we do not strike at the root of the evil though we should ever so effectually annihilate the present scheme of the Gospel. For, of what use is freedom of thought if it will not produce freedom of action, which is the sole end, how remote soever in appearance, of all objections against Christianity? And therefore the free-thinkers consider it as a sort of edifice, wherein all the parts have such a mutual dependence on each other that if you happen to pull out one single nail, the whole fabric must fall to the ground. This was happily expressed by him who had heard of a text brought for proof of the Trinity, which in an ancient manuscript was differently read; he thereupon immediately took the hint, and by a sudden deduction of a long sorites° most logically concluded 'Why, if it be as you say, I may safely whore and drink on, and defy the parson.' From which, and many the like instances easy to be produced, I think nothing can be more manifest than that the quarrel is not against any particular points of hard digestion in the Christian system, but against religion in general, which, by laying restraints on human nature, is supposed the great enemy to the freedom of thought and action.

Upon the whole, if it shall still be thought for the benefit of Church and State that Christianity be abolished, I conceive however it may be more convenient to defer the execution to a time of peace, and not venture in this conjuncture to disoblige our allies who, as it falls out, are all Christians, and many of them by the prejudices of their education so bigoted as to place a sort of pride in the appellation. If upon being rejected by them, we are to trust an alliance with the Turk, we shall find ourselves much deceived. For, as he is too remote, and generally engaged in war with the Persian emperor, so his people would be more scandalized at our infidelity than our Christian neighbours. For they are not only strict observers of religious worship, but what is worse, believe a God; which is more than is required of us even while we preserve the name of Christians.

To conclude, whatever some may think of the great advantages to trade by this favourite scheme, I do very much apprehend that in six months time after the Act is passed for the extirpation of the Gospel, the Bank and East India Stock may fall at least one *per cent*. And since that is fifty times more than ever the wisdom of our age thought fit to venture for the preservation of Christianity, there is no reason we should be at so great a loss merely for the sake of destroying it.

[*Answer to Verses from May Fair*]

In pity to the empty'ng Town
   Some god May Fair invented,°
When Nature would invite us down,
   To be by Art prevented.

What a corrupted taste is ours
   When milk maids in mock state
Instead of garlands made of flow'rs
   Adorn their pails with plate.

So are the joys which Nature yields
   Inverted in May Fair,   10
In painted cloth we look for fields,
   And step in booths for air.

Here a dog dancing on his hams
   And puppets mov'd by wire,
Do far exceed your frisking lambs,
   Or song of feather'd quire.

Howe'er, such verse as yours I grant
   Would be but too inviting:
Were fair Ardelia not my Aunt,°
   Or were it Worsley's writing.   20

Dear Aunt, think this a lucky hit,
   Nor e'er expect another,
For Cousin Harry is no wit
   Tho' he's a younger brother.

A Description of the Morning

Now hardly here and there an hackney-coach
Appearing, show'd the ruddy morn's approach.
Now Betty from her master's bed had flown,
And softly stole to discompose her own.
The slip-shod 'prentice from his master's door
Had pared the street, and sprinkled round the floor.
Now Moll had whirl'd her mop with dext'rous airs,
Prepared to scrub the entry and the stairs.
The youth with broomy stumps began to trace
The kennel edge, where wheels had worn the place.°   10
The small-coal man was heard with cadence deep,°
Till drown'd in shriller notes of '*chimney-sweep*'.
Duns at his lordship's gate began to meet;
And brickdust Moll had scream'd through half a street.°
The turnkey now his flock returning sees,
Duly let out a-nights to steal for fees.°
The watchful bailiffs take their silent stands;
And schoolboys lag with satchels in their hands.

Journal to Stella

[LETTER VI.]

Swift to Esther Johnson and Rebecca Dingley

London, Oct. 10, 1710.

SO, as I told you just now in the letter I sent half an hour ago, I dined with Mr Harley today, who presented me to the Attorney-General, Sir Simon Harcourt, with much compliment on all sides, etc. Harley told me he had shown my memorial° to the Queen, and seconded it very heartily; and he desires me to dine with him again on Sunday, when he promises to settle it with her majesty, before she names a governor; and I protest I am in hopes it will be done, all but the forms, by that time, for he loves the church: this is a popular thing, and he would not have a governor share in it; and, besides, I am told by all hands, he has a mind to gain me over. But in the letter I writ last post (yesterday) to the Archbishop,° I did not tell him a syllable of what Mr Harley said to me last night, because he charged me to keep it secret; so I would not tell it to you, but that before this goes, I hope the secret will be over. I am now writing my poetical *Description of a Shower*° in London, and will send it to the *Tatler*. This is the last sheet of a whole quire I have written since I came to town. Pray, now it comes into my head, will you, when you go to Mrs Walls, contrive to know whether Mrs Wesley be in town, and still at her brother's, and how she is in health, and whether she stays in town. I writ to her from Chester, to know what I should do with her note; and I believe the poor woman is afraid to write to me; so I must go to my business, &c.

11. Today at last I dined with Lord Montrath, and carried Lord Mountjoy and Sir Andrew Fountain with me; and was looking over them at ombre till eleven this evening like a fool: they played running ombre half crowns; and Sir Andrew Fountain won eight guineas of Mr Coote: so I am come home late, and will say but little to MD this night. I have gotten half a bushel of coals, and Patrick, the extravagant whelp,° had a fire ready for me; but I picked off the coals before I went to bed. It is a sign London is now an empty place, when it will not furnish me with matter for above five or six lines in a day. Did you smoke in my last how I told you the very day and the place you were playing at ombre? But I interlined and altered a little, after I had received a letter from Mr Manley, that said you were at it in his house, while he was writing to me; but without his help I guessed within one day. Your town is certainly much more sociable than ours. I have not seen your mother yet, &c.

12. I dined today with Dr Garth and Mr. Addison, at the Devil Tavern by Temple Bar, and Garth treated; and 'tis well I dine every day, else I should be longer making out my letters: for we are yet in a very dull state, only inquiring every day after new elections, where the Tories carry it among the new members six to one. Mr. Addison's election° has passed easy and undisputed; and I believe if he had a mind to be chosen king he would hardly be refused. An odd accident has happened at Colchester: one Captain Lavallin° coming from Flanders or Spain, found his wife with child by a clerk of Doctors' Commons,° whose trade, you know, it is to prevent fornications; and this clerk was the very same fellow that made the discovery of Dyet's counterfeiting the stamp paper. Lavallin has been this fortnight hunting after the clerk to kill him; but the fellow was constantly employed at the Treasury about the discovery he made: the wife had made a shift to patch up the business, alleging that the clerk had told her her husband was dead, and other excuses; but t'other day somebody told Lavallin his wife had intrigues before he married her: upon which he goes down in a rage, shoots his wife through the head, then falls on his sword; and, to make the matter sure, at the same time discharges a pistol through his own head, and died on the spot, his wife surviving him about two hours; but in what circumstances of mind and body is terrible to imagine. I have finished my poem on the *Shower*, all but the beginning, and am going on with my *Tatler*.° They have fixed about fifty things on me since I came: I have printed but three. One advantage I get by writing to you daily, or rather you get, is, that I shall remember not to write the same things twice; and yet I fear I have done it often already: but I'll mind and confine myself to the accidents of the day; and so get you gone to ombre, and be good girls, and save your money, and be rich against Presto° comes, and write to me now and then: I am thinking it would be a pretty thing to hear sometimes from saucy MD; but do not hurt your eyes, Stella, I charge you.

13. O Lord, here is but a trifle of my letter written yet; what shall Presto do for prittle prattle to entertain MD? The talk now grows fresher of the Duke of Ormond for Ireland, though Mr Addison says he hears it will be in commission, and Lord Gallaway one. These letters of mine are a sort of journal, where matters open by degrees; and, as I tell true or false, you will find by the event whether my intelligence be good; but I don't care twopence whether it be or no.—At night. Today I was all about St. Paul's and up at the top, like a fool, with Sir Andrew Fountain and two more; and spent seven shillings for my dinner like a puppy: this is the second time he has served me so; but I'll never do it again, though all mankind should persuade me, unconsidering puppies! There's a young

fellow here in town we are all fond of, and about a year or two come from the university, one Harrison, a little pretty fellow, with a great deal of wit, good sense, and good nature; has written some mighty pretty things; that in your 6th 'Miscellanea',° about the *Sprig of an Orange*, is his: he has nothing to live on but being governor to one of the Duke of Queensbury's sons for forty pounds a year. The fine fellows are always inviting him to the tavern, and make him pay his club. Henley is a great crony of his: they are often at the tavern at six or seven shillings reckoning, and always make the poor lad pay his full share. A colonel and a lord were at him and me by the same way tonight: I absolutely refused, and made Harrison lag behind, and persuaded him not to go to them. I tell you this, because I find all rich fellows have that humour of using all people without any consideration of their fortunes; but I'll see them rot before they shall serve me so. Lord Halifax is always teazing me to go down to his country house,° which will cost me a guinea to his servants, and twelve shillings coach hire; and he shall be hanged first. Is not this a plaguy silly story? But I am vexed at the heart; for I love the young fellow, and am resolved to stir up people to do something for him: he is a Whig, and I'll put him upon some of my cast Whigs; for I have done with them, and they have, I hope, done with this kingdom for our time. They were sure of the four members for London above all places, and they have lost three in the four. Sir Richard Onslow, we hear, has lost for Surrey: and they are overthrown in most places. Lookee, gentlewomen, if I write long letters I must write you news and stuff, unless I send you my verses; and some I dare not; and those on the *Shower in London* I have sent to the *Tatler*, and you may see them in Ireland. I fancy you'll smoke me in the *Tatler* I am going to write; for I believe I have told you the hint. I had a letter sent me tonight from Sir Matthew Dudley, and found it on my table when I came in. Because it is extraordinary I will transcribe it from beginning to end. It is as follows—'Is the devil in you? Oct. 13, 1710.' I would have answered every particular passage in it, only I wanted time. Here's enough for tonight, such as it is, &c.

14. Is that tobacco at the top of the paper, or what? I don't remember I slobbered. Lord, I dreamed of Stella, &c. so confusedly last night, and that we saw Dean Bolton and Sterne go into a shop; and she bid me call them to her, and they proved to be two parsons I know not; and I walked without till she was shifting, and such stuff, mixed with much melancholy and uneasiness, and things not as they should be, and I know not how; and it is now an ugly gloomy morning—At night. Mr Addison and I dined with Ned Southwell, and walked in the Park; and at the coffee-house I found a letter from the Bishop of Clogher, and a packet from MD. I

opened the Bishop's letter; but put up MD's, and visited a lady just come
to town,° and am now got into bed, and going to open your little letter:
and God send I may find MD well, and happy, and merry, and that they
love Presto as they do fires. Oh, I won't open it yet! yes I will! no I won't; I
am going; I can't stay till I turn over:° what shall I do? my fingers itch; and
now I have it in my left hand; and now I'll open it this very moment.—I
have just got it, and am cracking the seal, and can't imagine what's in it; I
fear only some letter from a Bishop, and it comes too late: I shall employ
no body's credit but my own. Well, I see though—Pshaw, 'tis from Sir
Andrew Fountain: what, another! I fancy this is from Mrs Barton; she
told me she would write to me; but she writes a better hand than this: I
wish you would inquire; it must be at Dawson's office at the Castle.° I
fear this is from Patty Rolt, by the scrawl. Well, I'll read MD's letter. Ah,
no; it is from poor Lady Berkeley,° to invite me to Berkeley Castle this
winter; and now it grieves my heart: she says she hopes my lord is in a fair
way of recovery; poor lady. Well, now I go to MD's letter: faith, 'tis all
right; I hoped it was wrong. Your letter, N. 3, that I have now received, is
dated Sept. 26, and Manley's letter, that I had five days ago, was dated
Oct. 3, that's a fortnight difference: I doubt it has lain in Steele's office,
and he forgot. Well, there's an end of that: he is turned out of his place;
and you must desire those who send me packets, to enclose them in a
paper, directed to Mr Addison, at St James's Coffee-house: not common
letters, but packets: the Bishop of Clogher may mention it to the
Archbishop when he sees him. As for your letter, it makes me mad:
sliddikins, I have been the best boy in Christendom, and you come with
your two eggs a penny.—Well; but stay, I'll look over my book: adad, I
think there was a *chasm* between my N. 2 and N. 3. Faith, I won't promise
to write to you every week; but I'll write every night, and when it is full I
will send it; that will be once in ten days, and that will be often enough:
and if you begin to take up the way of writing to Presto, only because it is
Tuesday, a Monday bedad, it will grow a task; but write when you have a
mind.—No, no, no, no, no, no, no, no,—Agad, agad, agad, agad, agad,
agad; no, poor Stellakins.° Slids, I would the horse were in
your—chamber. Have I not ordered Parvisol to obey your directions
about him? and han't I said in my former letters that you may pickle him,
and boil him, if you will? What do you trouble me about your horses for?
Have I any thing to do with them!—Revolutions a hindrance to me in my
business; revolutions—to me in my business? If it were not for the
revolutions, I could do nothing at all; and now I have all hopes possible,
though one is certain of nothing; but tomorrow I am to have an answer,
and am promised an effectual one. I suppose I have said enough in this

and a former letter how I stand with new people; ten times better than ever I did with the old; forty times more caressed. I am to dine tomorrow at Mr Harley's; and if he continues as he has begun, no man has been ever better treated by another. What you say about Stella's mother, I have spoken enough to it already. I believe she is not in town; for I have not yet seen her. My lampoon° is cried up to the skies; but nobody suspects me for it, except Sir Andrew Fountain: at least they say nothing of it to me. Did not I tell you of a great man who received me very coldly? That's he; but say nothing; 'twas only a little revenge. I'll remember to bring it over. The Bishop of Clogher has smoked my *Tatler* about shortening of words,° &c. But, God so! &c.

15. I will write plainer, if I can remember it; for Stella must not spoil her eyes, and Dingley can't read my hand very well; and I am afraid my letters are too long: then you must suppose one to be two, and read them at twice. I dined today with Mr Harley: Mr Prior dined with us. He has left my memorial with the Queen, who has consented to give the First-Fruits and Twentieth Parts, and will, we hope, declare it to-morrow in the cabinet. But I beg you to tell it to no person alive; for so I am ordered, till in public; and I hope to get something of greater value. After dinner came in Lord Peterborow: we renewed our acquaintance, and he grew mightily fond of me. They began to talk of a paper of verses called *Sid Hamet*. Mr Harley repeated part, and then pulled them out, and gave them to a gentleman at the table to read, though they had all read them often: Lord Peterborow would let nobody read them but himself: so he did; and Mr Harley bobbed° me at every line to take notice of the beauties. Prior rallied Lord Peterborow for author of them; and Lord Peterborow said, he knew them to be his; and Prior then turned it upon me, and I on him. I am not guessed at all in town to be the author; yet so it is: but that is a secret only to you. Ten to one whether you see them in Ireland; yet here they run prodigiously. Harley presented me to Lord President of Scotland,° and Mr Benson, Lord of the Treasury. Prior and I came away at nine, and sat at the *Smyrna°* till eleven, receiving acquaintance.

16. This morning early I went in a chair, and Patrick before it, to Mr Harley, to give him another copy of my memorial, as he desired; but he was full of business, going to the Queen, and I could not see him; but he desired I would send up the paper, and excused himself upon his hurry. I was a little baulked, but they tell me it is nothing. I shall judge by next visit. I tipped his porter with a half crown; and so I am well there for a time at least; I dined at Stratford's in the city, and had burgundy and tokay: came back afoot like a scoundrel; then went with Mr Addison and

supped with Lord Mountjoy, which made me sick all night. I forgot that I bought six pounds of chocolate for Stella, and a little wooden box; and I have a great piece of Brazil tobacco° for Dingley, and a bottle of palsy water for Stella; all which, with the two handkerchiefs that Mr Sterne° has bought, and you must pay him for, will be put in the box directed to Mrs Curry's, and se[n]t by Dr Hawkshaw, whom I have not seen; but Sterne has undertaken it. The chocolate is a present, madam, for Stella. Don't read this, you little rogue, with your little eyes; but give it to Dingley, pray now; and I'll write as plain as the skies: and let Dingley write Stella's part, and Stella dictate to her, when she apprehends her eyes, &c.

17. This letter should have gone this post, if I had not been taken up with business, and two nights being late out; so it must stay till Thursday. I dined today with your Mr Sterne, by invitation, and drank Irish wine;° but, before we parted, there came in that prince of puppies, Colonel Edgworth, so I went away. This day came out the *Tatler*, made up wholly of my *Shower*, and a preface to it. They say 'tis the best thing I ever writ, and I think so too. I suppose the Bishop of Clogher will show it you. Pray tell me how you like it. Tooke is going on with my *Miscellany*.° I'd give a penny the letter to the Bishop of Killaloe° was in it: 'twould do him honour. Could not you contrive to say you hear they are printing my *Things* together; and that you wish the bookseller had that letter among the rest: but don't say anything of it as from me. I forgot whether it was good or no; but only having heard it much commended, perhaps it may deserve it. Well, I have tomorrow to finish this letter in, and then I'll send it next day. I am so vexed that you should write your third to me, when you had but my second, and I had written five, which now I hope you have all: and so I tell you, you are saucy, little, pretty, dear rogues, &c.

18. Today I dined, by invitation, with Stratford and others, at a young merchant's in the city, with hermitage and tokay, and stayed till nine, and am now come home. And that dog Patrick is abroad, and drinking, and I can't get my nightgown. I have a mind to turn that puppy away: he has been drunk ten times in three weeks. But I han't time to say more; so good night, &c.

19. I am come home from dining in the city with Mr Addison, at a merchant's: and just now, at the coffee-house, we have notice that the Duke of Ormond was this day declared Lord Lieutenant, at Hampton Court, in Council. I have not seen Mr Harley since; but hope the affair is done about First-Fruits. I will see him, if possible, tomorrow morning; but this goes tonight. I have sent a box to Mr Sterne, to send to you by some friend; I have directed it for Mr Curry, at his house; so you have

warning when it comes, as I hope it will soon. The handkerchiefs will be put in some friend's pocket, not to pay custom. And so here ends my sixth, sent when I had but three of MD's: now I am beforehand, and will keep so; and God Almighty bless dearest MD, &c.

A Short
CHARACTER
OF
His Ex. *T.* E. of *W.*
L.L. of *I*——

An Account of some smaller Facts, during His Government, which will not be put into the Articles of Impeachment.

[*London*,] August 30, 1710.

THE kingdom of Ir[elan]d being governed by deputation from hence, its annals since the English establishment are usually digested under the heads of the several governors. But the affairs and events in that island for some years past have been either so insignificant, or so annexed to those of England, that they have not furnished matter of any great importance to history. The share of honour which the gentlemen from thence have had by their conduct and employments in the army, turns all to the article of this kingdom; the rest, which relates to politics or the art of government, is inconsiderable to the last degree, however it may be represented at court by those who preside there and would value themselves upon every step they make towards finishing the slavery of that people, as if it were gaining a mighty point to the advantage of England.

Generally speaking, the times which afford most plentiful matter for story are those wherein a man would least choose to live; such as the various events and revolutions of war, the intrigues of a ruined faction, or the violence of a prevailing one, and lastly, the arbitrary unlawful acts of oppressing governors. In the war, Ir[elan]d has no share but in subordination to us; the same may be said of their factions, which at present are but imperfect transcripts of ours. But the third subject for history, which is arbitrary power and oppression, as it is that whereby the people of Ir[elan]d have for some time been distinguished from all Her Majesty's subjects, so being now at its greatest height under his Ex[cellency] T[homas] E[arl] of W[harton], a short account of his government may be of some use or entertainment to the present age, though I hope it will be incredible to the next.

And because the relation I am going to make, may be judged rather a history of his Excellency than of his government, I must here declare that I have not the least view of his person in any part of it: I have had the honour of much conversation with his lordship, and am thoroughly convinced how indifferent he is to applause and how insensible of reproach; which is not a humour put on to serve a turn or keep a countenance, not arising from the consciousness of his innocence or any grandeur of mind, but the mere unaffected bent of his nature. He is without the sense of shame or glory, as some men are without the sense of smelling; and therefore a *good name* to him is no more than a *precious ointment* would be to those. Whoever were to describe the nature of a serpent, a wolf, a crocodile, or a fox, must be understood to do it for the sake of others, without any personal love or hatred for the animals themselves.

In the same manner, his Excellency is one whom I neither personally love or hate; I see him at court, at his own house, and sometimes at mine (for I have the honour of his visits); and when these papers are public, 'tis odds but he will tell me, as he once did upon a like occasion, that 'he is damnably mauled'; and then with the easiest transition in the world, ask about the weather or time of the day; so that I enter on the work with more cheerfulness because I am sure neither to make him angry, nor any way hurt his reputation; a pitch of happiness and security his excellency has arrived to, which no philosopher before him could ever reach.

I intend to execute this performance by first giving a character of his Excellency and then relating some facts during his government in Ir[elan]d, which will serve to confirm it.

I know very well that men's characters are best learnt from their actions; but these being confined to his administration in that kingdom, his character may perhaps take in something more, which the narrowness of the time or the scene hath not given him opportunity to exert.

T[homas] E[arl] of W[harton], L[ord] L[ieutanant] of I[reland], by the force of a wonderful constitution hath passed some years his grand climacteric,° without any visible effects of old age either on his body or his mind, and in spite of a continual prostitution to those vices which usually wear out both. His behaviour is in all the forms of a young man at five-and-twenty. Whether he walks, or whistles, or swears, or talks bawdy, or calls names, he acquits himself in each beyond a Templar of three years standing. With the same grace and in the same style, he will rattle his coachman in the midst of the street, where he is governor of the kingdom: and all this is without consequence, because it is in his character and what every body expects. He seems to be but an ill dissembler and an ill liar, though they are the two talents he most practises and most values himself upon. The ends he has gained by lying appear to be more owing to the frequency than the art of them, his lies being sometimes detected in an hour, often in a day, and always in a week. He tells them freely in mixed companies, though he knows half of those that hear him to be his enemies and is sure they will discover them the moment they leave him. He swears solemnly he loves and will serve you, and your back is no sooner turned but he tells those about him, you are a dog and a rascal. He goes constantly to prayers in the forms of his place and will talk bawdy and blasphemy at the chapel door. He is a Presbyterian in politics, and an atheist in religion, but he chooses at present to whore with a *Papist*. In his commerce with mankind his general rule is to endeavour imposing on their understandings, for which he has but one reciept, a composition of lies and oaths; and this he applies indifferently to a freeholder of forty shillings and a Privy Councillor, by which the easy and the honest are often either deceived or amused; and either way he gains his point. He will openly take away your employment today, because you are not of his party; tomorrow he will meet or send for you as if nothing at all had passed, lay his hands with much friendliness on your shoulders, and with the greatest ease and familiarity in the world tell you that *the faction* are driving at something in the House; that you must be sure to attend, and to speak to all your friends to be there, though he knows at the same time that you and your friends are against him in that very point he mentions. And however absurd, ridiculous, and gross this may appear, he has often found it successful; some men having such an awkward bashfulness they know not how to refuse upon a sudden, and every man having something to fear or to hope, which often hinders them from driving things to extremes with persons of power, whatever provocations they may have received. He hath sunk his fortunes by endeavouring to ruin one kingdom, and hath raised them by going far in the ruin of another.° With a good natural understanding, a great fluency in speaking, and no ill taste of wit, he is generally the worst companion in the world; his thoughts being wholly taken up between vice and politics, so that bawdy, prophaneness, and business fill up his whole conversation. To gratify himself in the two first, he makes choice of suitable favourites whose talent reaches no higher than to entertain him with all the lewdness that passes in town. As for business, he is said to be very dexterous at that part of it which turns upon intrigue, and he seems to have transferred the talents of his youth for intriguing with women, into public affairs. For, as some vain young fellows, to make a gallantry appear of consequence, will choose to venture their necks by climbing up a wall or window at midnight to a common wench, where they might as freely have gone at the door and at noonday; so his excellency, either to keep himself in practice, or to advance the fame of his politics, affects the most obscure, troublesome, and winding paths, even in the commonest affairs, those which would as well be brought about in the ordinary forms or which would proceed of course whether he intervened or no.

He bears the gallantries of his L[ad]y with the indifference of a *Stoic*, and thinks them well recompensed by a return of children to support his family, without the fatigues of being a father.

He has three predominant passions which you will seldom observe united in the same man, as arising from different dispositions of mind, and naturally thwarting each other; these are love of power, love of money, and love of pleasure. They ride him sometimes by turns and sometimes all together. Since he went into that kingdom he seems most disposed to the second and has met with great success, having gained by his government of under two years, five-and-forty thousand pounds by the most favourable computation, half in the regular way, and half in the prudential.

He was never yet known to refuse or keep a promise, as I remember he told a lady, but with an exception to the promise he then made (which was to get her a pension), yet he broke even that, and I confess, deceived us both. But here I desire to distinguish between a promise and a bargain; for he will be sure to keep the latter when he has had the fairest offer.

Thus much for his Ex[cellenc]y's character. I shall now proceed to his actions, only during the time he was gov[erno]r of Ir[elan]d, which were transmitted to me by an eminent person in business there, who had all opportunities of being well informed and whose employment did not lie at his Ex[cellency]'s mercy.

This intelligence being made up of several facts independent of each other, I shall hardly be able to relate them in due order of time, my correspondent omitting that circumstance and transmitting them to me as they came into his memory. So that the gentlemen of that kingdom now in town, I hope will pardon me any slips I shall make in that or any other kind, while I keep exactly to the truth.

Thomas Proby, Esq., Surgeon-General of Ireland, a person universally esteemed, and whom I have formerly seen here, had built a country house half a mile from Dublin, adjoining to the Park. In a corner of the Park, just under his house, he was much annoyed with a dog-kennel which belonged to the government; upon which he applied to Thomas Earl of Pembroke, then L—d L——t, and to the commissioners of the revenue, for a lease of about five acres of that part of the Park. His petition was referred to the L[or]d T[reasure]r here, and sent back for a report, which was in his favour and the bargain so hard that the L[or]d T[reasure]r struck off some part of the rent. He had a lease granted him for which he was to build another kennel, provide ice yearly for the government, and pay a certain rent; the land might be worth about thirty shillings an acre. His Ex[cellenc]y, soon after his arrival in I[relan]d, was told of this lease and by his absolute authority commanded Mr. Proby to surrender up the land, which he was forced to do after all the expense he had been at or else must have expected to lose his employment; at the same time he is under obligation to pay his rent, and I think he does it to this day. There are several circumstances in this story which I have forgot, having not been sent me with the rest, but I had it from a gentleman of that kingdom who some time ago was here in Town.

Upon his Ex[cellenc]y's being declared L—d L——t there came over to make his court one Dr. L[loy]d, Fellow of Dublin College, noted in that kingdom for being the only clergyman that declared for taking off the sacramental test, as he did openly in their Convocation where he was a member. The merit of this and some other principles suitable to it recommended by Tom Br[o]dr[ic]k, so far ingratiated him with his Ex[cellenc]y, that being provided of a *proper chaplain* already, he took him however into a great degree of favour. The Doctor attended his Ex[cellenc]y to Ireland, and observing a cast wench in the family to be in much confidence with my L[ad]y, he thought by addressing there, to have a short open passage to preferment. He met with great success in his amour, and walking one day with his mistress after my L[or]d and L[ad]y in the Castle Garden, my L[ad]y said to his Ex[cellenc]y 'What do you think? We are going to lose poor Foidy' (a name of fondness they usually gave her). 'How do you mean?' said my Lord. 'Why, the doctor behind us is resolved to take her from us.' 'Is he, by G–d? Why then, G–d d–m me, he shall have the first bishopric that falls.'* The doctor thus encouraged, grew a most violent lover, returned with his Ex[cellenc]y for England, and soon after, the bishopric of Cork falling void, to show he meant fair, he married his damosel publicly here in London, and his Ex[cellenc]y as honourably engaged his credit to get him the bishopric; but the matter was reckoned so infamous that both the archbishops here, especially his Grace of York, interposed with the Qu[ee]n to hinder so great a scandal

---

* It was confidently reported, as a conceit of his Ex[cellenc]y's, that talking upon this subject, he once said, with great pleasure, that he hoped to make his wh[o]re a bishop.

to the church, and Dr. Brown, Provost of Dublin College, being then in town, Her Majesty was pleased to nominate him; so that Dr. L[loy]d was forced to sit down with a moderate deanery° in the northern parts of that kingdom, and the additional comfort of a sweet lady who brought this her first husband no other portion than a couple of olive branches for his table, though she herself hardly knows by what hand they were planted.

The Queen reserves all the great employments of Ireland to be given by herself, though often by the recommendation of the chief governor according to his credit at court. The provostship of Dublin College is of this number, which was now vacant upon the promotion of Dr. Brown. Dr. Benjamin Pratt, a Fellow of that college, and chaplain to the House of Commons of that kingdom, as well as domestic chaplain to the Duke of Ormonde, was at that time here in attendance upon the duke. He is a gentleman of good birth and fortune in Ireland, [and] lived here in a very decent figure. He is a person of wit and learning, has travelled and conversed in the best company, and was very much esteemed among us here, where I had the pleasure of his acquaintance. But he had the original sin of being a reputed *Tory*, and a dependant on the Duke of Ormonde. However, he had many friends among the bishops and other nobility to recommend him to the Queen. At the same time there was another Fellow of that college, one Dr. Hall, who had much the advantage of Pratt in point of seniority. This gentleman had very little produced himself into the world, but lived retired, though otherwise said to be an excellent person and very deserving for his learning and sense. He had been recommended from Ireland by several persons; and his Ex[cellenc]y, who had never seen nor thought on him in his life, after having tried to injure the college by recommending persons from this side, at last set up Hall with all imaginable zeal against Pratt. I tell this story the more circumstantially, because it is affirmed by his Ex[cellenc]y's friends, that he never made more use of his court skill than at this time to hinder Dr. Pratt from the provostship; not only from the personal hatred he had to the man upon the account of his patron and principles, but that he might return to Ireland with some little opinion of his credit at court, which had mightily suffered by many disappointments, especially the last of his chaplain Dr. L[loy]d. It would be incredible to relate the many artifices he used to this end, of which the Doctor had daily intelligence, and would fairly tell his Ex[cellenc]y so at his levees; who sometimes could not conceal his surprise, and then would promise with half a dozen oaths never to concern himself one way or other; these were broke every day, and every day detected. One morning, after some expostulations between his Ex[cellenc]y and the

Doctor, and a few additional oaths that he would never oppose him any more, his Ex[cellenc]y went immediately to the Bishop of E[l]y, and prevailed on him to go to the Qu[ee]n from him and let her know, that he never could consent as long as he lived that Dr. Pratt should be provost, which the bishop barely complied with and delivered his message, though at the same time he did the Doctor all the good offices he could. The next day the Doctor was again with his Ex[cellenc]y and gave him thanks for so open a proceeding; the affair was now past dissembling and his Ex[cellenc]y confessed that he did not *directly* oppose him, but *collaterally* he did. The Doctor a little warmed, said, 'No, my lord, you mean *directly* you did not, but *indirectly* you did.' The conclusion was that the Queen named the Doctor to the place, and as a further mortification, just upon the day of his Ex[cellenc]y's departure for Ireland.

But here I must desire the reader's pardon if I cannot digest the following facts in so good a manner as I intended, because it is thought expedient, for some reasons, that the world should be informed of his Ex[cellency]'s merits as soon as possible. I will therefore only transcribe the several passages as they were sent me from Dublin, without either correcting the style or adding any remarks of my own. As they are, they may serve for hints to any person who may hereafter have a mind to write memoirs of his Ex[cellency]'s life.

A relation of several facts, exactly as they were transmitted to me from Ireland about three months ago, and at several times, from a person of quality, and in employment there.

The Earl of Rochford's regiment of dragoons was embarked for Her Majesty's service abroad on the 27th of August, 1709, and left their horses behind them, which were subsisted, in order to mount another regiment to fill up their room, as the horses of Lieutenant-General Harvey's regiment had formerly mounted a regiment raised and still commanded by the D[uke] of O[rmonde]; on which occasion the duke had Her Majesty's order only for as much money as would supply the charge of the horses till the regiment was raised, which was soon after, and then it was put on the establishment as other regiments; but that which was to supply the Earl of Rochford's, had not a commission granted till the 29th of April, 1710, and all the pay, from the 27th of August, to that time, being above 5700*l*. was taken under pretence of keeping the horses, buying new ones in the room of such as should be wanting or unserviceable, and for providing accoutrements for the men and horses. As for the last use, those are always provided out of the funds for providing clothing, and the D[uke] of O[rmonde] did so. As for horses wanting, they are very few, and the captains have orders to provide them another way, and the keeping the horses did not come to 700*l*. by the accounts laid before the committee of parliament; so there was at least 5000*l*. charged to the nation more than the actual charge could amount to.

Mrs. L[loy]d, at first coming over, expected the benefit of the box-money,° and accordingly talked of selling it for about 200*l*. but at last was told, she must expect but part of it, and that the grooms of the chamber and other servants would deserve a consideration for their attendance. Accordingly his Ex[cellency] had it brought to him every night, and to make it worth his receiving, my L[ad]y gave great encouragement to play, so that by moderate computation, it amounted to near 1000*l*. of which a small share was given to the grooms of the chamber, and the rest made a perquisite to his Ex[cellency], for Mrs. L[loy]d having a husband and a bishopric promised her, the other pretensions were cut off.

He met Lieutenant-General Langston in the Court of Requests, and presented a gentleman to him, saying, 'This is a particular friend of mine, he tells me he is a l[ieutenan]t in your regiment; I must desire you will take the first opportunity you can to give him a troop, and you will oblige me mightily.' The Lieutenant-General answered, 'He had served very well, and had very good pretensions to a troop, and that he would give him the first that fell' with which the gentleman was mighty well satisfied, so returned thanks and withdrew; upon which, his Ex[cellenc]y immediately said, 'I was forced to speak for him, because a great many of his friends have votes in elections, but damn him, he's a rogue, therefore take no care for him.'

He brought one May to the D[uke] of O[rmonde] and recommended him as a very honest gentleman, and desired his grace would provide for him, which his grace promised, so May withdrew; as soon as he was gone, his l[ordshi]p immediately said to the duke, 'That fellow is the greatest rogue in Christendom.'

Colonel C[o]w[a]rd having for some time received pay in two or three regiments of the army, as captain, but never done any other service to the crown, except eating and drinking in the expedition to Cadiz,° under the D[uke] of O[rmonde], finding he had not pretensions enough to rise, after he had sold the last employment he had, applies to his Ex[cellenc]y, who gave him so favourable a report that he got above 900*l*. as an arrear of half-pay, which he had no title to, and a pension of 10*s*. a day, which he reckoning as much too little for his wants, as every body else did too much for his pretensions, gave in a second petition to the Q[uee]n for 10s. a day more to be added; which being referred to his Ex[cellenc]y, he gave him a favourable report, by means whereof 'tis hoped his merit will be farther rewarded.

He turned out the poor gatekeeper at Chapelizod gate,° though he and his wife were each above sixty years old, without assigning any cause, and they are now starving.

As to the business of the Arsenal, it was the product of chance, and never so much as thought of by the persons who of late have given so many good reasons for the building it, till upon enquiring into the funds they were found to hold out so well, that there was an absolute necessity of destroying about sixty or seventy thousand pounds, otherwise his Ex[cellenc]y for that time could hardly have the credit of taxing the kingdom. Upon this occasion many projects were proposed, all which at last, gave way to a proposal of a worthy person, who had often persuaded the nation to do itself a great deal of harm, by attempting to do itself a little good, which was, That forty thousand arms should be provided for the militia, and ammunition in proportion, to be kept in four arsenals to be built for that purpose; which was accordingly put into the heads of a bill, and then this worthy patriot, in his usual sincerity, declared he would not consent to the giving money for any other use, as every body thought by the words he spoke, though afterwards he showed them that his meaning was not to be known by the vulgar acceptation of words; for he not only gave his consent to the bill, but used all the art and industry he was master of to have it pass, though the money was applied in it to the building one arsenal, and ammunition and other stores proportionable, without one word of the militia. So the arsenal was conceived, and afterwards formed in a proper manner; but when it came to be brought forth, his Ex. took it out of the hands that had formed it, as far as he could, and contrary to all precedents, put it out of the care of the ordnance board, who were an office to have taken care of the receipt and payment of the money, without any farther charge to the public; and appointed his second secretary, Mr. Denton, to be paymaster, whose salary was a charge of above five hundred pounds in the whole; then thinking this too small a charge to put the public to for nothing, he made an establishment for that work, consisting of one superintendent at three pounds per week, eight overseers at seven pounds four shillings a week, and sixteen assistants at seven pounds four shillings a week, making in all seventeen pounds eight shillings a week, and these were almost all persons that had no knowledge of such business; and their honesty was equal to their knowledge, as it hath since appeared by the notorious cheats and neglects that have been made out against them; insomuch that the work that they have overseen, which, with their salaries, has cost near three thousand pounds, might have been done for less than eighteen hundred pounds, if it had been agreed for by the yard, which is the usual method, and was so proposed in the estimate; and this is all a certainty, because all that has been done, is only removing earth, which has been exactly computed by the yard, and might have been so agreed for.

Philip S[a]v[a]ge, Esq., as chancellor of the exchequer, demanded fees of the commissioners of the revenue, for sealing writs in the Queen's business, and showed them for it some sort of precedents; but they not being well satisfied with them, wrote to Mr. South, one of the commissioners (then in London) to enquire the practice there; he sent them word upon enquiry, that fees were paid in the like cases there; so they adjudged it for him, and constantly paid him fees. If therefore that was a fault, it must lie at their door, for he never offered to stop the business; yet his Ex[cellenc]y knew so well how to choose an attorney and solicitor-general, that when the case was referred to them, they gave it against the chancellor, and said, he had forfeited his place by it, and ought to refund the money (being about two hundred pounds *per annum*). But never found any fault in the commissioners who adjudged the case for him, and might have refused him the money if they had thought fit.

Captain Robert F[itz]gerald, father to the present Earl of Kildare, had a grant from King Charles the Second of the office of comptroller of the musters, during the lives of Captain Chambers Brabazon, now Earl of Meath, and George F[itz]gerald, elder brother to the present Earl of Kildare, which the said Robert F[itz]gerald enjoyed, with a salary of three hundred pounds *per annum*; and after his death, his son George enjoyed it, till my Lord Galway did, by threats, compel him to surrender the said patent, for a pension of two hundred pounds *per annum*, which he enjoyed during his life. Some time ago the present Earl of Kildare, as heir to his father and brother, looked upon himself to be injured by the surrender of the said patent, which should have come to him, the Earl of Meath being still alive; therefore, in order to right himself, did petition Her Majesty, which petition, as usual, was referred to the E[arl] of W[harton], the L[or]d L[ieutenan]t, who being then in London, according to the common method on such occasions, referred it to the Lord Chancellor and Lieutenant-General Ingoldsby, the then Lords Justices of this kingdom, who, for their information, ordered the attorney-general to inquire whether the E[arl] of K[ildare] had any legal title to the said patent, which he in a full report said he had: And they referred it to the deputy vice-treasurer to inquire into the nature of the office, and to give them his opinion, whether he thought it useful and necessary for Her Majesty's service; he gave in his report, and said, he thought it was both useful and necessary, and with more honesty than wit, gave the following reasons: first, that the muster-master-general computed the pay of the whole military list, which is above 200,000*l. per annum*, so having no check on him, might commit mistakes, to the great prejudice of the crown; and secondly, because he had himself found out several of those mistakes, which a comptroller might prevent. The lords justices approved of these reasons, and so sent over their report to my L[or]d-L[ieutenan]t, that they thought the office useful and necessary. But Colonel P[ennyfathe]r the muster-master-general being then in London, and having given my L[or]d-L[ieutenan]t one thousand pounds for his consent to enjoy that office, after he had got Her Majesty's orders for a patent, thought a check upon his office would be a troublesome spy upon him, so he pleaded the merit of his thousand pounds, and desired, that in consideration thereof his Ex. would free him from an office that would put it out of his power to wrong the crown; and to strengthen his pretensions, put my L[ad]y in mind of what money he had lost to her at play; who immediately, out of a grateful sense of benefits received, railed as much against the lords justices' report, as ever she had done against the Tories; and my L[or]d-L[ieutenan]t prompted by the same virtue, made his report, that there needed no comptroller to that office, because he controlled it himself, which (now having given his word for it) he will beyond all doubt effectually do for the future; though since, it plainly has been made appear, that for want of some control on that office, Her Majesty has been wronged of many hundred pounds by the roguery of a clerk; and that during the time of his Ex[cellenc]y's government, of which there has been but a small part refunded, and the rest has not been inquired after, for fear it should make it plainly appear that a comptroller in that office is absolutely necessary.

His Ex[cellenc]y being desirous, for a private reason, to provide for the worthless son of a worthless father, who had lately sold his company, and of course all pretensions to preferment in the army, took this opportunity. A captain in the oldest regiment in the kingdom, being worn out with service, desired leave to sell, which was granted him, and accordingly for a consideration agreed upon, he gave a resignation of his company to a person approved of by the commander of the regiment, who at the same time applied to his Ex[cellenc]y for leave for another captain of his regiment, who is an engineer in Her Majesty's service in Spain, and absent by Her Majesty's licence; his Ex[cellenc]y hearing that, said they might give him a company in Spain, for he would dispose of his here; and so notwithstanding all the commander of the regiment could urge, he gave the company that was regularly surrendered, to his worthy favourite; and the other company, that was a disputable title, to the gentleman that had paid his money for that which was surrendered.

Talking one morning as he was dressing (at least a dozen people present) of the debates in council about the affair of Trim,° he said the Lord Chief Justice D[oyne] had laid down as law, a thing for which a man ought to have his gown stript off, and be whipt at the cart-arse; and in less than a quarter of an hour repeated the expression again; yet some days after, sent Dr. L[a]mb[e]rt° to assure his Lordship he said no such thing. Some time after while he was in England, he made it his utmost efforts with the Queen to turn him out, but could not. So when he came once again he took an opportunity (when the judges were to wait on him) to say to them, particularly Lord Chief Justice D[oyne], that perhaps some officious persons would spread stories that he had endeavoured to do some of 'em a prejudice in England, which he assured them he never had; but on the contrary, would always, without distinction, show every body his favours as they behaved themselves, which the Lord Chief Justice Br[o]dr[ic]k was pleased to approve of, by saying, 'That was very honourable, that was very gracious', though he knew the contrary himself.

In England he bid Mr. Deering assure all his friends and acquaintance here, that they and every body, without distinction, might depend on his favour as they behaved themselves; with which Mr. D. was much pleased, and wrote over to his friends accordingly. And as soon as his back was turned, he jeeringly said, 'D[a]mn me, how easily he is bit!'

When the D[uke] of O[rmonde] was in the government, he gave to Mr. Anderson Saunders the government of Wicklow Castle, which has no salary, but a perquisite of some land worth about 12l. *per annum*, which Mr. Saunders gave to the free-school of the town; but his Ex[cellenc]y not liking either the person or the use, without any ceremonies or reason given, superseded him, by giving a commission for it to Jennings the horse-courser, who lies under several odious and scandalous reflections, particularly of very narrowly escaping the gallows for coining.

Some time after his Ex[cellenc]y's landing the second time, he sent for Mr. Saunders among others, desiring their good offices in the ensuing session, and that Mr. Saunders would not take amiss his giving that place to Jennings, for he assured him he did not know it belonged to him; which is highly probable, because men of his knowledge use to give away things without enquiring how they are in their disposal. Mr. Saunders answered him, 'He was very glad to find what was done, was not out of any particular displeasure to him, because Mr. Whitshed° had said at Wicklow (by way of apology for what his Ex[cellenc]y had done) that it was occasioned by Mr. Saunders's having it; and seeing his Ex[cellenc]y had no ill intention against him, was glad he could tell his Ex— it was not legally given away (for he had a *custodium* for the land out of the Court of Exchequer); so his Ex[cellenc]y's commission to Jennings could do him no prejudice.'

Lieutenant-General Echlin had pay on this Establishment as Brigadier, to the middle of October, 1708, at which time he was removed from it by his Ex[cellenc]y, because his regiment went away at that time, and Lieutenant-General Gorges was put in his room. Some time after Major-General Rooke, considering the reason why Echlin was removed, concluded that Gorges could not come on till some time in February after, because his regiment also was out of the kingdom till that time; and that therefore he being the eldest general officer that had no pay as such, was entitled to the brigadier's pay, from the time Echlin was not qualified to receive it till Gorges was qualified to receive it, he having done the duty. His Ex[cellenc]y upon hearing the reason, owned it to be a very good one, and told him if the money were not paid to Gorges he should have it; so bid him go see, which he did, and found it was; then his Ex[cellenc]y told him, he would refer his case to the court of general officers to give their opinion in it, which he said must needs be in his favour, and upon that ground he would find a way to do him right; yet when the general officers sat he sent for several of them, and made them give the case against Rooke.

When the prosecution against the dissenting ministers at Drogheda was depending, one Stevens a lawyer in this town (Dublin), sent his Ex[cellenc]y, then in London, a petition in the name of the said dissenting minister, in behalf of himself and others, who lay under any such prosecution; and in about a fortnight's time his Ex[cellenc]y sent over a letter to the then Lords Justices, to give the attorney and solicitor-general orders, to enter *nolle prosequi*'s to all such suits; which was done accordingly, though he never so much as inquired into the merits of the cause, or referred the petition to any body, which is a justice done to all men, let the case be never so light. He said he had Her Majesty's orders for it, but they did not appear under her hand, and it is generally affirmed he never had any.

That his Ex[cellenc]y can descend to small gains, take this instance. There was 850*l*. ordered by Her Majesty to buy liveries for the state-trumpets, messengers, &c.; but with great industry he got them made cheaper by 200*l*. which he saved out of that sum; and 'tis reported that his steward got a handsome consideration out of the undertaker besides.

The agent to his regiment being so also to others, bought a Lieutenant's commission in a regiment of foot, for which he never was to do any duty, which service pleased his Ex[cellenc]y so well that he gave him leave to buy a company, and would have had him [keep] both; but before his pleasure was known, the former was disposed of.

The Ld-L[ieutenan]t has no power to remove or put in a solicitor-general without a Q[ueen]'s letter, it being one of those employments excepted out of his commission; yet because Sir Richard L[e]v[i]ng disobliged him by voting according to his opinion, he removed him, and put in Mr. Forster, though he had no Q[ueen]'s letter for so doing; only a letter from Mr. Secretary Boyle that Her Majesty designed to remove him.

The Privy Council in Ireland have a great share of the administration; all things being carried by the consent of a majority, and they sign all orders and proclamations made there, as well as the chief governor; but his Ex[cellenc]y disliked so much share of power in any beside himself, and when matters were debated in council otherwise than he approved, he would stop them and say, 'Come, my lords, I see how your opinions are, and therefore I will not take your votes'; and so would put an end to the dispute.

One of his chief favourites was a scandalous clergyman, a constant companion of his pleasures, who appeared publicly with his Ex[cellenc]y but never in his habit, and who was a hearer and sharer of all the lewd and blasphemous discourses of his Ex[cellenc]y and his cabal. His Ex[cellenc]y presented this worthy divine to one of the bishops with the following recommendation: 'My lord, Mr. —— is a very honest fellow, and has no fault but that he is a little too immoral.' He made this man chaplain to his regiment, though he had been so infamous that a bishop in England refused to admit him to a living that he was presented to, till the patron forced him to it by law.

His Ex[cellenc]y recommended the E[arl] of In[chiquin] to be one of the Lords Justices in his absence, and was much mortified when he found Lieutenant-General Ing[oldsby] appointed, without any regard to his recommendations; particularly, because the usual salary to a lord justice in the L[or]d-L[ieutenan]t's absence is 100*l*. per month, and he had bargained with the Earl to be content with 40*l*.

I will send you, in a packet or two, some particulars of his Ex[cellenc]y's usage of the Convocation; of his infamous intrigues with

Mrs. C[oni]ngsby; an account of his arbitrary proceedings about the election of a mayor in Trim; his selling the place of a privy councillor and commissioner of the revenue to Mr. C[o]n[o]lly; his barbarous injustice to Dean Jephson, and poor Will. Crow; his deciding a case at hazard to get my Lady 20 guineas, but in so scandalous and unfair a manner that the arrantest sharper would be ashamed of; the common custom of playing on Sunday in my L[a]dy's closet; the *partie carrée* between her La[dyshi]p and Mrs. Fl[oy]d,° and two young fellows dining privately and frequently at Clontarf, where they used to go in a hackney coach; and his Ex[cellenc]y making no scruple of dining in a hedge tavern whenever he was invited; with some other passages, which I hope you will put into some method, and correct the style, and publish as speedily as you can.

Note, Mr. S[a]v[a]ge, besides the persecution about his fees before-mentioned, was turned out of the Council for giving his vote in parliament, in a case where his Ex[cellenc]y's own friends were of the same opinion, till they were wheedled or threatened out of it by his Ex[cellenc]y.

The particulars before-mentioned I have not yet received; whenever they come, I shall publish them in a Second Part.

The TATLER.

FROM TUESDAY SEPTEMBER 26, TO THURSDAY
SEPTEMBER 28. 1710.

From my own Apartment, September 27.

THE following letter has laid before me many great and manifest evils in the world of letters which I had overlooked; but they open to me a very busy scene, and it will require no small care and application to amend errors which are become so universal. The affectation of politeness is exposed in this epistle with a great deal of wit and discernment; so that whatever discourses I may fall into hereafter upon the subjects the writer treats of, I shall at present lay the matter before the World without the least alteration from the words of my correspondent.

'To Isaac Bickerstaff Esq;

'SIR,

'There are some abuses among us of great consequence, the reformation of which is properly your province, though, as far as I have been conversant in your papers, you have not yet considered them. These are, the deplorable ignorance that for some years hath reigned among our English writers, the great depravity of our taste, and the continual corruption of our style. I say nothing here of those who handle particular sciences, divinity, law, physic, and the like; I mean, the traders in history and politics, and the *belles lettres*; together with those by whom books are not translated, but (as the common expressions are) "done out of French, Latin", or other language, and "made English". I cannot but observe to you, that till of late years a Grub Street book was always bound in sheepskin, with suitable print and paper, the price never above a shilling, and taken off wholly by common tradesmen, or country pedlars; but now they appear in all sizes and shapes, and in all places. They are handed about from lapfuls in every coffee-house to persons of quality, are shown in Westminster Hall and the Court of Requests. You may see them gilt, and in royal paper, of five or six hundred pages, and rated accordingly. I would engage to furnish you with a catalogue of English books published within the compass of seven years past, which at the first hand would cost you a hundred pounds, wherein you shall not be able to find ten lines together of common grammar or common sense.

'These two evils, ignorance and want of taste, have produced a third; I mean, the continual corruption of our English tongue, which, without some timely remedy, will suffer more by the false refinements of twenty years past, than it hath been improved in the foregoing hundred. And this is what I design chiefly to enlarge upon, leaving the former evils to your animadversion.

'But instead of giving you a list of the late refinements crept into our language, I here send you the copy of a letter I received some time ago from a most accomplished person in this way of writing, upon which I shall make some remarks. It is in these terms.

' "Sir,

' "I *cou'dn't* get the things you sent for all *about Town.*—I *thôt* to *ha'* come down myself, and then *I'd ha' brôut 'um*; but I *han't don't*, and I believe I *can't do't*, that's *pozz.*—*Tom* begins to *g'imself airs* because *he's* going with the *plenipo's*.°—'Tis said, the French King will *bamboozl' us agen*, which *causes many speculations*. The *Jacks*,° and others of that *kidney*, are very *uppish*, and *alert upon't*, as you may see by their *phizz's*.—Will Hazzard has got the *hipps*, having lost *to the tune of* five *hundr'd* pound, *thô* he understands play very well, *nobody better.* He has promis't me upon *rep*, to leave off play; but you know 'tis a weakness *he's* too apt to *give into*, *thô* he has as much wit as any man, *nobody more.* He has lain *incog* ever since.—The *mobb's* very quiet with us now.—I believe you *thôt* I *banter'd* you in my last like a *country put.*—I *sha'n't* leave Town this month, *&c.*"

'This letter is in every point an admirable pattern of the present polite way of writing; nor is it of less authority for being an epistle. You may gather every flower in it, with a thousand more of equal sweetness, from the books, pamphlets, and single papers, offered us every day in the coffee-houses. And these are the beauties introduced to supply the want of wit, sense, humour, and learning, which formerly were looked upon as qualifications for a writer. If a man of wit, who died forty years ago, were to rise from the grave on purpose, how would he be able to read this letter? And after he had got through that difficulty, how would he be able to understand it? The first thing that strikes your eye is the *breaks* at the end of almost every sentence; of which I know not the use, only that it is a refinement, and very frequently practised. Then you will observe the abbreviations and elisions, by which consonants of most obdurate sound are joined together, without one softening vowel to intervene; and all this only to make one syllable of two, directly contrary to the example of the Greeks and Romans; altogether of the Gothic strain, and a natural tendency towards relapsing into barbarity, which delights in monosyllables, and uniting of mute consonants; as it is observable in all the Northern languages. And this is still more visible in the next refinement, which consists in pronouncing the first syllable in a word that has many, and dismissing the rest; such as *phizz*, *hipps*, *mobb*, *poz.*, *rep.* and many more; when we are already overloaded with monosyllables, which are the disgrace of our language. Thus we cram one syllable, and cut off the rest; as the owl fattened her mice, after she had bit off their legs to prevent them from running away; and if ours be the same reason for maiming our words, it will certainly answer the end; for I am sure no other Nation will desire to borrow them. Some words are hitherto but fairly split, and therefore only in their way to perfection, as *incog* and *plenipo*. But in a short time it is to be hoped they will be further docked to *inc* and *plen*. This reflection has made me of late years very impatient for a Peace, which I believe would save the lives of many brave words, as well as men. The war has introduced abundance of polysyllables, which will never be able to live many more campaigns. *Speculations*, *operations*, *preliminaries*, *ambassadors*, *palisadoes*, *communication*, *circumvallation*, *battalions*, as numerous as they are, if they attack us too frequently in our coffee-houses, we shall certainly put them to flight, and cut off the rear.

'The third refinement observable in the letter I send you, consists in the choice of certain words invented by some *pretty fellows*; such as *banter*, *bamboozle*, *country put*, and *kidney*, as it is there applied; some of which are now struggling for the vogue, and others are in possession of it. I have done my utmost for some years past to stop the progress of *mobb* and *banter*, but have been plainly borne down by numbers, and betrayed by those who promised to assist me.

'In the last place you are to take notice of certain choice phrases scattered through the letter; some of them tolerable enough, till they were worn to rags by servile imitators. You might easily find them, though they were not in a different print, and therefore I need not disturb them.

'These are the false refinements in our style which you ought to correct: first, by argument and fair means; but if those fail, I think you are to make use of your authority as Censor, and by an annual *index expurgatorius* expunge all words and phrases that are offensive to good sense, and condemn those barbarous mutilations of vowels and syllables. In this last point the usual pretence is, that they spell as they speak. A noble standard for language! to depend upon the caprice of every coxcomb, who, because words are the clothing of our thoughts, cuts them out, and shapes them as he pleases, and changes them oftener than his dress. I believe, all reasonable people would be content that such refiners were more sparing in their words, and liberal in their syllables. And upon this head I should be glad you would bestow some advice upon several young readers in our churches, who coming up from the University, full fraight with admiration of our Town politeness, will needs correct the style of their Prayer Books. In reading the absolution, they are very careful to say "*pardons* and *absolves*"; and in the Prayer for the Royal Family, it must be, "*endue'um, enrich'um, prosper'um,* and *bring'um*". Then in their sermons they use all the modern terms of art, *sham, banter, mob, bubble, bully, cutting, shuffling,* and *palming*, all which, and many more of the like stamp, as I have heard them often in the pulpit from such young sophisters, so I have read them in some of *those sermons that have made most noise of late*. The design, it seems, is to avoid the dreadful imputation of pedantry, to show us, that they know the Town, understand men and manners, and have not been poring upon old unfashionable books in the University.

'I should be glad to see you the instrument of introducing into our style that simplicity which is the best and truest ornament of most things in life, which the politer ages always aimed at in their building and dress (*simplex munditiis*)° as well as their productions of wit. 'Tis manifest, that all new, affected modes of speech, whether borrowed from the Court, the Town, or the theatre, are the first perishing parts in any language, and, as I could prove by many hundred instances, have been so in ours. The writings of Hooker,° who was a country clergyman, and of Parsons the Jesuit,° both in the reign of Queen Elizabeth, are in a style that, with very few allowances, would not offend any present reader; much more clear and intelligible than those of Sir H. Wotton, Sir Robert Naunton, Osborn, Daniel the historian,° and several others who writ later; but being men of the Court, and affecting the phrases then in fashion, they are often either not to be understood, or appear perfectly ridiculous.

'What remedies are to be applied to these evils I have not room to consider, having, I fear, already taken up most of your paper. Besides, I think it is our office only to represent abuses, and yours to redress them.

'I am, with great respect,
'Sir,
'Your, &c.'

A Description of a City Shower

OCTOBER 1710.

Careful observers may foretell the hour
(By sure prognostics) when to dread a show'r:
While rain depends, the pensive cat gives o'er
Her frolics, and pursues her tail no more.
Returning home at night, you'll find the sink
Strike your offended sense with double stink.
If you be wise, then go not far to dine:
You'll spend in coach-hire more than save in wine.
A coming show'r your shooting corns presage,
Old a-ches throb, your hollow tooth will rage.°   10
Saunt'ring in coffeehouse is Dulman seen;
He damns the climate, and complains of *spleen*.
 Meanwhile the *South*, rising with dabbled wings,
A sable cloud athwart the welkin flings
That swill'd more liquor than it could contain,
And, like a drunkard, gives it up again.
Brisk Susan whips her linen from the rope,
While the first drizzling show'r is borne aslope;
Such is that sprinkling which some careless quean
Flirts on you from her mop, but not so clean: 20
You fly, invoke the gods; then turning, stop
To rail; she singing, still whirls on her mop.
Not yet the dust had shunn'd th'unequal strife,
But, aided by the wind, fought still for life,
And wafted with its foe by violent gust,
'Twas doubtful which was rain, and which was dust.
Ah! where must needy poet seek for aid,
When dust and rain at once his coat invade?
His only coat, where dust confus'd with rain
Roughen the nap, and leave a mingled stain.   30
 Now in contiguous drops the flood comes down,
Threat'ning with deluge this *devoted* town.
To shops in crowds the daggled females fly,
Pretend to cheapen goods, but nothing buy.
The Templar spruce, while ev'ry spout's abroach,
Stays till 'tis fair, yet *seems* to call a coach.
The tuck'd-up sempstress walks with hasty strides,

While streams run down her oil'd umbrella's sides.°
Here various kinds, by various fortunes led,
Commence acquaintance underneath a shed: 40
Triumphant Tories, and desponding Whigs,°
Forget their feuds, and join to save their wigs.
Box'd in a chair the beau impatient sits,
While spouts run clatt'ring o'er the roof by fits,
And ever and anon with frightful din
The leather sounds; he trembles from within.
So when Troy chairmen bore the wooden steed,
Pregnant with Greeks impatient to be freed
(Those bully Greeks, who, as the moderns do,
Instead of paying chairmen, run them thro'), 50
Laoco'n struck the outside with his spear,°
And each imprison'd hero quaked for fear.
  Now from all parts the swelling kennels flow,
And bear their trophies with them, as they go:
Filth of all hues and odours seem to tell
What street they sail'd from, by their sight and smell.
They, as each torrent drives with rapid force,
From Smithfield, or St. 'Pulchre's shape their course,°
And in huge confluent join'd at Snow Hill ridge,
Fall from the Conduit prone to Holborn-bridge. 60
Sweepings from butchers' stalls, dung, guts, and blood,° ⎫
Drown'd puppies, stinking sprats, all drench'd in mud, ⎬
Dead cats, and turnip-tops, come tumbling down the flood. ⎭

The EXAMINER.

FROM THURSDAY

NOVEMBER 16, TO THURSDAY NOVEMBER 23. 1710.

Qui sunt boni cives? Qui belli, qui domi de patriâ bene merentes, nisi qui patriae beneficia meminerunt?°

I WILL employ this present paper upon a subject which of late hath very much affected me, which I have considered with a good deal of application and made several enquiries about among those persons who I thought were best able to inform me; and if I deliver my sentiments with some freedom, I hope it will be forgiven while I accompany it with that tenderness which so nice a point requires.

I said in a former paper (Numb. 14) that one specious objection to the late removals at court was the fear of giving uneasiness to a general who has been long successful abroad. And accordingly, the common clamour of tongues and pens for some months past has run against the baseness, the inconstancy and ingratitude of the whole kingdom to the Duke of M[arlborough], in return of the most eminent services that ever were performed by a subject to his country; not to be equalled in history. And then to be sure some bitter stroke of detraction against Alexander and Cæsar, who never did us the least injury. Besides, the people that read Plutarch come upon us with parallels drawn from the Greeks and Romans who ungratefully dealt with I know not how many of their most deserving generals; while the profounder politicians have seen pamphlets where Tacitus and Machiavel have been quoted to shew the danger of too resplendent a merit. Should a stranger hear these furious outcries of ingratitude against our general, without knowing the particulars, he would be apt to enquire where was his tomb or whether he were allowed Christian burial, not doubting but we had put him to some ignominious death. Or, has he been tried for his life, and very narrowly escaped? Has he been accused of high crimes and misdemeanours? Has the prince seized on his estate, and left him to starve? Has he been hooted at as he passed the streets, by an ungrateful mob? Have neither honours, offices nor grants, been conferred on him or his family? Have not he and they been barbarously stripped of them all? Have not he and his forces been ill paid abroad? And does not the prince by a scanty, limited commission, hinder him from pursuing his own methods in the conduct of the war? Has he no power at all of disposing commissions as he pleases? Is he not severely used by the Ministry or Parliament, who yearly call him to a strict account? Has the senate ever thanked him for good success, and have they not always publicly censured him for the least miscarriage? Will the accusers of the nation join issue upon any of these particulars, or tell us in what point our damnable sin of ingratitude lies? Why, 'tis plain and clear; for while he is commanding abroad, the Queen dissolves her Parliament and changes her ministry at home: in which *universal calamity*, no less than *two persons* allied by marriage to the general° have lost their places. Whence came this wonderful sympathy between the civil and military powers? Will the troops in Flanders refuse to fight unless they can have *their own* lord keeper, *their own* lord president of the council, *their own* chief Governor of Ireland, and *their own* Parliament? In a kingdom where the people are free, how came they to be so fond of having their councils under the influence of their army, or those that lead it, who in all well instituted states had no commerce with the civil power, further than to receive their orders and obey them without reserve?

When a general is not so popular, either in his army or at home, as one might expect from a long course of success, it may perhaps be ascribed to his *wisdom*, or perhaps to his complexion. The possession of some one *quality*, or a defect in *some other*, will extremely damp the people's favour as well as the love of the soldiers. Besides, this is not an age to produce favourites of the people, while we live under a Queen who engrosses all our love and all our veneration, and where the only way for a great general or minister to acquire any degree of subordinate affection from the public, must be by all marks of the most *entire submission and respect* to her sacred person and commands; otherwise, no pretence of great services, either in the field or the cabinet, will be able to screen them from universal hatred.

But the late ministry was closely joined to the general by friendship, interest, alliance, inclination and opinion, which cannot be affirmed of the present; and the ingratitude of the nation lies in the people's *joining as one man*, to wish that such a ministry should be changed. Is it not at the same time notorious to the whole kingdom that nothing but a tender regard to the general was able to preserve that ministry so long, till neither God nor man could suffer their continuance? Yet in the highest ferment of things we heard few or no reflections upon this great commander, but all seemed unanimous in wishing he might still be at the head of the confederate forces; only at the same time, in case he were resolved to resign, they chose rather to turn their thoughts somewhere else than throw up all in despair. And this I cannot but add in defence of the people, with regard to the person we are speaking of, that in the high station he has been for many years past, his *real defects* (as nothing human is without them) have in a detracting age been very sparingly mentioned either in libels or conversation, and all his *successes* very freely and universally applauded.

There is an active and a passive ingratitude. Applying both to this occasion, we may say the first is when a prince or people returns good services with cruelty or ill usage: the other is when good services are not at all, or very meanly rewarded. We have already spoke of the former; let us therefore in the second place examine how the services of our general have been rewarded, and whether upon that article either prince or people have been guilty of ingratitude?

Those are the most valuable rewards which are given to us from the certain knowledge of the donor, that they *fit our temper best*. I shall therefore say nothing of the title of *Duke*, or the *Garter* which the Queen bestowed the general in the beginning of her reign; but I shall come to *more substantial* instances and mention nothing which has not been given in the face of the world. The lands of Woodstock° may, I believe, be reckoned worth 40,000*l*. On the building of Blenheim Castle 200,000*l*. have been already expended, though it be not yet near finished. The grant of 5,000*l*. *per ann*. on the post office is richly worth 100,000*l*. His principality in Germany may be computed at 30,000*l*. Pictures, jewels, and other gifts from foreign princes, 60,000*l*. The grant at the Pall Mall, the rangership,° &c. for want of more certain knowledge, may be called 10,000*l*. His own and his duchess's employments at five years value, reckoning only the known and avowed salaries, are very low rated at 100,000*l*. Here is a good deal above half a million of money, and I dare say those who are loudest with the clamour of ingratitude will readily own that all this is but a trifle in comparison of what is *untold*.

The reason of my stating this account is only to convince the world that we are not quite so ungrateful either as the Greeks or the Romans. And in order to adjust this matter with all fairness I shall confine myself to the latter, who were much the more generous of the two. A victorious general of Rome in the height of that empire, having *entirely subdued his enemy*, was rewarded with the larger triumph; and perhaps a statue in the Forum, a bull for a sacrifice, an embroidered garment to appear in: a crown of laurel, a monumental trophy with inscriptions; sometimes five hundred or a thousand copper coins were struck on occasion of the victory, which doing honour to the general, we will place to his account;

and lastly, sometimes, though not very frequently, a triumphal arch. These are all the rewards that I can call to mind which a victorious general received after his return from the most glorious expedition, conquered some great kingdom, brought the king himself, his family and nobles to adorn the triumph in chains, and made the kingdom either a Roman province, or at best a poor depending state, in humble alliance to that empire. Now of all these rewards I find but two which were of real profit to the general; the *laurel crown*, made and sent him at the charge of the public, and the embroidered garment; but I cannot find whether this last were paid for by the senate, or the general: however, we will take the more favourable opinion, and in all the rest admit the whole expense, as if it were ready money in the general's pocket. Now according to these computations on both sides, we will draw up two fair accounts, the one of Roman gratitude and the other of British ingratitude, and set them together in balance.

A BILL OF ROMAN GRATITUDE.

	l.	s.	d.
Imprimis for frankincense and earthen pots to burn it in	4	10	0
A bull for sacrifice	8	0	0
An embroidered garment	50	0	0
A crown of laurel	0	0	2
A statue	100	0	0
A trophy	80	0	0
A thousand copper medals value half pence a piece	2	1	8
A triumphal arch	500	0	0
A triumphal car, valued as a modern coach	100	0	0
Casual charges at the triumph	150	0	0
Sum total	994	11	10

A BILL OF BRITISH INGRATITUDE.

	l.	s.	d.
Imprimis Woodstock	40,000	0	0
Blenheim	200,000	0	0
Post-office grant	100,000	0	0
Mildenheim	30,000	0	0
Pictures, jewels, &c.	60,000	0	0
Pall Mall grant, &c.	10,000	0	0
Employments	100,000	0	0
Sum total	540,000	0	0

This is an account of the visible profits on both sides; and if the Roman general had any *private perquisites* they may be easily discounted, and by more probable computations, and differ yet more upon the balance, if we consider that all the gold and silver for *safeguards* and *contributions*, also all *valuable prizes* taken in the war were openly exposed in the triumph and then lodged in the Capitol for the public service.

So that upon the whole, we are not yet quite so bad at *worst* as the Romans were at *best*. And I doubt, those who raise this hideous cry of ingratitude may be mightily mistaken in the consequence they propose from such complaints. I remember a saying of Seneca,° *Multos ingratos invenimus, plures facimus*. 'We find many ungrateful persons in the world, but we *make* more', by setting too high a rate upon our pretensions and undervaluing the rewards we receive. When unreasonable bills are brought in, they ought to be taxed or cut off in the middle. Where there have been long accounts between two persons I have known one of them perpetually making large demands and pressing for payments, who when the accounts were cast up on both sides was found to be debtor for some hundreds. I am thinking if a proclamation were issued out for every man to send in his *bill of merits* and the lowest price he set them at, what a pretty sum it would amount to, and how many such islands as this must be sold to pay them. I form my judgment from the practice of those who sometimes happen to *pay themselves*, and I dare affirm, would not be so unjust to take a farthing more than they think is due to their deserts. I will instance only in one article. A lady of my acquaintance appropriated twenty six pounds a year out of her allowance for certain uses, which her woman received and was to pay to the lady or her order, as it was called for. But after eight years, it appeared upon the strictest calculation that the woman had paid but four pound a year, and sunk two-and-twenty for her own pocket. It is but supposing instead of twenty six pound, twenty six thousand, and by that you may judge what the pretensions of *modern merit* are, where it happens to be its own paymaster.

𝕹𝖚𝖒𝖇. 32.

The EXAMINER.

FROM THURSDAY MARCH 1, TO THURSDAY MARCH 8.

1710–11.

—— *Garrit aniles*
Ex re fabellas.°

I HAD last week sent me by an unknown hand, a passage out of Plato°
with some hints how to apply it. That author puts a fable into the mouth
of Aristophanes, with an account of the original of *Love*. That, mankind
was at first created with four arms and legs, and all other parts double to
what they are now, till Jupiter, as a punishment for his sins, cleft him in
two with a thunderbolt, since which time we are always looking for our
other half; and this is the cause of *Love*. But Jupiter threatened that if they
did not mend their manners, he would give them t'other slit and leave
them to hop about in the shape of figures in *basso relievo*. The effect of this
last threatening, my correspondent imagines, is now come to pass, and
that as the first splitting was the original of love by inclining us to search
for our t'other half, so the second was the cause of *hatred*, by prompting
us to fly from our *other side* and dividing the same *body* into two, gave each
slice the name of a party.

I approve the fable and application, with this refinement upon it. For
parties do not only *split* a nation but every individual among them, leaving
each but *half* their strength, and wit, and honesty, and good nature; but
one eye and ear for their sight and hearing, and equally lopping the rest of
the senses. Where *parties* are pretty equal in a state, no man can perceive
one bad quality in his own or good one in his adversaries. Besides, *party*
being a dry disagreeable subject, it renders conversation insipid or sour
and confines invention. I speak not here of the leaders, but the
insignificant crowd of followers in a *party*, who have been the instruments
of mixing it in every condition and circumstance of life. As the *zealots*
among the *Jews* bound the *law* about their foreheads, and wrists, and
hems of their garments, so the *women* among us have got the
distinguishing marks of *party* in their *muffs*, their *fans*, and their *furbelows*.
The Whig ladies put on their patches in a different manner from the
Tories. They have made *schisms* in the *playhouse*, and each have their
particular sides at the *opera*: and when a man changes his *party*, he must

infallibly count upon the loss of his *mistress*. I asked a gentleman t'other day, how he liked such a *lady*? But he would not give me his opinion till I had answered him whether she were a Whig or a Tory. Mr. ———° since he is known to visit the present m[inist]ry, and lay some time under a suspicion of writing the 'Examiner', is no longer a man of *wit*; his very *poems* have contracted a *stupidity* many years after they were printed.

Having lately ventured upon a metaphorical genealogy of *Merit*, I thought it would be proper to add another of *Party*, or rather of *Faction* (to avoid mistake) not telling the reader whether it be my own or a quotation till I know how it is approved; but whether I read or dreamed it, the fable is as follows.

Liberty, *the daughter of* Oppression, *after having brought forth several fair children, as* Riches, Arts, Learning, Trade, *and many others, was at last delivered of her youngest daughter, called* FACTION; *whom Juno, doing the office of the midwife, distorted in its birth, out of envy to the mother, from whence it derived its* peevishness *and* sickly constitution. *However, as it is often the nature of parents to grow most fond of their youngest and disagreeablest children, so it happened with* Liberty, *who doted on this daughter to such a degree that by her good will she would never suffer the girl to be out of her sight. As Miss* Faction *grew up, she became so termagant and froward that there was no enduring her any longer in Heaven. Jupiter gave her warning to be gone, and her mother rather than forsake her, took the whole family down to earth. She landed at first in Greece, was expelled by degrees through all the Cities by her daughter's ill conduct; fled afterwards to Italy, and being banished thence, took shelter among the Goths with whom she passed into most parts of Europe; but driven out every where, she began to lose esteem, and her daughter's faults were imputed to herself. So that at this time, she has hardly a place in the world to retire to. One would wonder what strange qualities this daughter must possess, sufficient to blast the influence of so divine a mother and the rest of her children. She always affected to keep mean and scandalous company; valuing nobody but just as they agreed with her in every capricious opinion she thought fit to take up; and rigorously exacting compliance though she changed her sentiments ever so often. Her great employment was to breed* discord *among friends and relations, and make up monstrous alliances between those whose dispositions least resembled each other. Whoever offered to contradict her, though in the most insignificant trifle, she would be sure to distinguish by some ignominious* appellation *and allow them to have neither honour, wit, beauty, learning, honesty or common sense. She intruded into all companies at the most unseasonable times, mixed at balls, assemblies, and other parties of pleasure; haunted every coffee-house and bookseller's shop, and by her perpetual talking filled all places with disturbance and confusion. She buzzed about the* merchant *in the Exchange, the* divine *in his pulpit, and the* shopkeeper *behind his counter. Above all, she frequented* public assemblies *where she sat in the shape of an* obscene, ominous bird, *ready to prompt her friends as they spoke.*

If I understand this fable of *Faction* right, it ought to be applied to those who set themselves up against the true interest and constitution of their country; which I wish the *undertakers* for the late m[inistr]y° would please to take notice of, or tell us by what figure of speech they pretend to call so great and *unforced* a majority, with the Qu[een] at the head, by the name of 'the Faction'; which is not unlike the phrase of the Nonjurors,° who dignifying one or two deprived bishops and half a score clergymen of the same stamp, with the title of the 'Church of England,' exclude all the rest as *schismatics*; or like the Presbyterians laying the same accusation, with equal justice, against the *Established Religion*.

And here it may be worth inquiring what are the true characteristics of a *faction*, or how it is to be distinguished from that great body of the people who are friends to the constitution? The *heads* of a *faction* are usually a set of *upstarts*, or men ruined in their fortunes, whom some great change in a government did at first, out of their obscurity, produce upon the stage. They associate themselves with those who dislike the old establishment, religious and civil. They are full of new schemes in politics and divinity; they have an incurable hatred against the old nobility, and strengthen their party by dependants raised from the lowest of the people; they have several ways of working themselves into power; but they are sure to be *called* when a *corrupt administration* wants to be supported against those who are endeavouring at a *reformation*; and they firmly observe that celebrated maxim of preserving power by the same arts it is attained. They act with the spirit of those who believe their *time is but short*, and their first care is to heap up immense riches at the public expense; in which they have two ends beside that common one of insatiable avarice, which are, to make themselves necessary and to keep the Commonwealth in dependence. Thus they hope to compass their design which is, instead of fitting their principles to the constitution, to alter and adjust the constitution to their own pernicious principles.

'Tis easy determining by this test to which side the name of *faction* most properly belongs. But however, I will give them any system of law or regal government from William the Conqueror to this present time, to try whether they can *tally* it with their late *models*; excepting only that of Cromwell whom perhaps they will reckon for a *monarch*.

If the present ministry and so great a majority in the Parliament and Kingdom be only a *faction*, it must appear by some actions which answer the idea we usually conceive from that word. Have they abused the prerogatives of the prince, or invaded the rights and liberties of the subject? Have they offered at any dangerous innovations in Church or State? Have they broached any doctrines of heresy, rebellion or tyranny? Have any of them treated their sovereign with insolence, engrossed and sold all her favours, or deceived her by base, gross misrepresentations of her most faithful servants? These are the arts of a *faction*, and whoever has practised them, they and their followers must take up with the *name*.

It is usually reckoned a Whig principle to appeal to *the people*; but that is only when they have been so wise as to poison their understandings beforehand. Will they now stand to this appeal, and be determined by their *vox populi* to which side their title of *faction* belongs? And that the *people* are now left to the natural freedom of their understanding and choice, I believe our adversaries will hardly deny. They will now refuse this *appeal*, and it is reasonable they should; and I will further add that if our *people* resembled the old Grecians, there might be danger in such a trial. A pragmatical orator told a great man at Athens that whenever the *people* were *in their rage*, they would certainly tear him to pieces. 'Yes,' says the other, 'and they will do the same by you, whenever they are *in their wits*.' But God be thanked, *our populace* is more merciful in their nature, and *at present* under better direction; and the *orators* among us have attempted to confound both *prerogative* and *law*, in their *sovereign's presence* and before the *highest court of judicature*, without any hazard to their persons.

The EXAMINER.

FROM THURSDAY APRIL 19, TO THURSDAY APRIL 26, 1711.

Indignum est in eâ civitate, quæ legibus continetur, discedi a legibus.°

I HÁVE been often considering how it comes to pass that the dexterity of mankind in evil should always outgrow, not only the prudence and caution of private persons, but the continual expedients of the wisest laws contrived to prevent it. I cannot imagine a knave to possess a greater share of natural wit or genius than an honest man. I have known very notable sharpers at play, who upon all other occasions were as great dunces as human shape can well allow, and I believe the same might be observed among the other knots of thieves and pickpockets about this town. The proposition however is certainly true and to be confirmed by an hundred instances. A scrivener, an attorney, a stockjobber, and many other *retailers of fraud*, shall not only be able to overreach others much wiser than themselves, but find out new inventions to elude the force of any law made against them. I suppose the reason of this may be that as the *aggressor* is said to have generally the advantage of the *defender*, so the makers of the law, which is to defend our rights, have usually not so much industry or vigour as those whose interest leads them to attack it. Besides, it rarely happens that men are rewarded by the public for their justice and virtue; neither do those who act upon such principles expect any recompense till the next world; whereas fraud, where it succeeds, gives present pay, and this is allowed the greatest spur imaginable both to labour and invention. When a law is made to stop some growing evil, the wits of those whose interest it is to break it with secrecy or impunity, are immediately at work; and even among those who pretend to fairer characters, many would gladly find means to avoid what they would not be thought to violate. They desire to reap the advantage, if possible, without the shame, or at least without the danger. This art is what I take that dexterous race of men sprung up soon after the Revolution, to have studied with great application ever since, and to have arrived at great perfection in it. According to the doctrine of some Romish casuists, they have found out *quam prope ad peccatum sine peccato possint accedere.*° They can tell how to go within an inch of an impeachment, and yet come back untouched. They know what degree of corruption will just forfeit an employment, and whether the bribe you receive be sufficient to set you right and put something in your pocket besides; how much to a penny you may safely cheat the Qu[ee]n, whether forty, fifty or sixty *per cent*. according to the station you are in, and the dispositions of the persons in office, below and above you. They have computed the price you may securely take or give for a place, or what part of the salary you ought to reserve. They can discreetly distribute five hundred pounds in a small borough, without any danger from the statutes against bribing elections. They can manage a bargain for an office by a third, fourth or fifth hand, so that you shall not know whom to accuse; and win a thousand guineas at play, in spite of the dice, and send away the loser satisfied. They can pass the most exorbitant accounts, overpay the creditor with half his demands, and sink the rest.

It would be endless to relate, or rather indeed impossible to discover, the several arts which curious men have found out to enrich themselves by defrauding the public in defiance of the law. The military men, both by sea and land, have equally cultivated this most useful science: neither hath it been altogether neglected by the other sex, of which, on the contrary, I could produce an instance° that would make ours blush to be so far outdone.

Besides, to confess the truth, our laws themselves are extremely defective in many articles, which I take to be one ill effect of our best possession, liberty. Some years ago, the ambassador of a great prince° was arrested and outrages committed on his person in our streets, without any possibility of redress from Westminster Hall or the prerogative of the sovereign; and the legislature was forced to provide a remedy against the like evil in times to come. A commissioner of the stamped paper° was lately discovered to have notoriously cheated the public of great sums for many years by counterfeiting the stamps, which the law had made capital. But the aggravation of his crime proved to be the cause that saved his life, and that additional heightening circumstance of betraying his trust was found to be a legal defence. I am assured that the notorious cheat of the brewers at Portsmouth,° detected about two months ago in Parliament, cannot by any law now in force be punished in any degree equal to the guilt and infamy of it. Nay, what is almost incredible, had Guiscard survived his detestable attempt upon Mr. Harley's person, all the inflaming circumstances of the fact would not have sufficed, in the opinion of many lawyers, to have punished him with death; and the public must have lain under this *dilemma*, either to condemn him by a law *ex post facto* (which would have been of dangerous consequence, and form an ignominious precedent) or undergo the mortification to see the greatest villain upon earth escape unpunished, to the infinite triumph and delight of *Popery* and *faction*. But even this is not to be wondered at when we consider that of all the insolences offered to the Qu[een] since the Act of Indemnity° (at least, that ever came to my ears) I can hardly instance above two or three which by the letter of the law could amount to high treason.

From these defects in our laws, and the want of some discretionary power safely lodged to exert upon emergencies, as well as from the great acquirements of able men to elude the penalties of those laws they break, it is no wonder the injuries done to the public are so seldom redressed. But besides, no individual suffers by any wrong he does to the commonwealth, in proportion to the advantage he gains by doing it. There are seven or eight millions who contribute to the loss, while the whole gain is sunk among a few. The damage suffered by the public is not so immediately or heavily felt by particular persons, and the zeal of prosecution is apt to drop and be lost among numbers.

But imagine a set of politicians for many years at the head of affairs, the game visibly their own, and by consequence acting with great security: may not these be sometimes tempted to forget their caution by length of time, by excess of avarice and ambition, by the insolence or violence of their nature, or perhaps by a mere contempt for their adversaries? May not such motives as these, put them often upon actions directly against the law, such as no evasions can be found for, and which will lay them fully open to the vengeance of a prevailing interest, whenever they are out of power? 'Tis answered in the affirmative. And here we cannot refuse the late m[inistr]y their due praises, who foreseeing a storm, provided for their own safety by two admirable expedients, by which, with great prudence, they have escaped the punishments due to pernicious counsels and corrupt management. The first was to procure under pretences hardly specious a general Act of Indemnity, which cuts off all impeachments. The second was yet more refined: suppose, for instance, a counsel is to be pursued which is necessary to carry on the dangerous designs of a prevailing party, to preserve them in power, to gratify the unmeasurable appetites of a few *leaders*, civil and military, though by hazarding the ruin of the whole nation: this counsel, desperate in itself, unprecedented in the nature of it, they procure a majority to form into an address, which makes it look like the sense of the nation. Under that shelter they carry on their work and lie secure against after-reckonings.

I must be so free to tell my meaning in this, that among other things I understand it of the address made to the Qu[een] about three years ago,° to desire that her M[ajest]y would not consent to a peace without the entire restitution of Sp[ai]n. A proceeding, which to people abroad, must look like the highest strain of temerity, folly, and gasconade. But we at home, who allow the promoters of that advice to be no fools, can easily comprehend the depth and mystery of it. They were assured by this means to pin down the war upon us, consequently to increase their own power and wealth, and multiply difficulties on the Qu[een] and kingdom till they had fixed their party too firmly to be shaken whenever they should find themselves disposed to reverse their address, and give us leave to wish for a peace.

If any man entertains a more favourable opinion of this monstrous step in politics, I would ask him what we must do in case we find it impossible to recover Spain? Those among the *Whigs* who believe a GOD, will confess that the events of war lie in his Hands; and the rest of them who acknowledge no such power, will allow that *Fortune* hath too great a share in the good or ill success of military actions to let a wise man reason upon them as if they were entirely in his power. If Providence shall think fit to refuse success to our arms, with how ill a grace, with what shame and confusion, shall we be obliged to recant that precipitate address, unless the world will be so charitable to consider that parliaments among us differ as much as princes, and that by the fatal conjunction of many unhappy circumstances it is very possible for our island to be represented sometimes by those who have the least pretensions to it. So little truth or justice there is in what some pretend to advance, that the actions of former senates ought always to be treated with respect by the latter; that those assemblies are all equally venerable, and no one to be preferred before another; by which argument the Parliament that began the rebellion against King Charles the First, voted his trial, and appointed his murderers, ought to be remembered with respect.

But to return from this digression; 'tis very plain, that considering the defectiveness of our laws, the variety of cases, the weakness of the prerogative, the power or the cunning of ill-designing men, it is possible that many great abuses may be visibly committed which cannot be legally punished: especially if we add to this that some enquiries might probably involve those whom upon other accounts it is not thought convenient to disturb. Therefore it is very false reasoning, especially in the management of public affairs, to argue that men are innocent because the law hath not pronounced them guilty.

I am apt to think it was to supply such defects as these, that Satire was first introduced into the world, whereby those whom neither religion, nor natural virtue, nor fear of punishment, were able to keep within the bounds of their duty, might be withheld by the shame of having their crimes exposed to open view in the strongest colours, and themselves rendered odious to mankind. Perhaps all this may be little regarded by such hardened and abandoned natures as I have to deal with; but, next to taming or binding a savage animal, the best service you can do the neighbourhood is to give them warning, either to arm themselves or not come in its way.

Could I have hoped for any signs of remorse from the leaders of that faction, I should very gladly have changed my style and forgot or passed by their million of enormities. But they are every day more fond of discovering their impotent zeal and malice: witness their conduct in the City about a fortnight ago,° which had no other end imaginable beside that of perplexing our affairs, and endeavouring to make things desperate that themselves may be thought necessary. While they continue in this frantic mood, I shall not forbear to treat them as they deserve; that is to say, as the inveterate, irreconcilable enemies to our country and its constitution.

[LETTER XXX.]

Swift to Esther Johnson and Rebecca Dingley

Windsor, Sept. 8, 1711.

I MADE the coachman stop, and put in my twenty-ninth at the post office at two o'clock today, as I was going to Lord Treasurer,° with whom I dined, and came here by a quarter past eight; but the *moon* shone, and so we were not in much danger of overturning; which, however, he values not a straw, and only laughs when I chide at him for it. There was nobody but he and I, and we supped together, with Mr Masham° and Dr Arbuthnot, the Queen's favourite physician, a Scotchman. I could not keep myself awake after supper, but did all I was able to disguise it, and thought I came off clear; but at parting he told me, I had got my nap already. It is now one o'clock; but he loves sitting up late.

9. The Queen is still in the gout, but recovering; she saw company in her bedchamber after church; but the crowd was so great, I could not see her. I dined with my brother, Sir William Wyndham, and some others of our Society,° to avoid the great tables on Sunday at Windsor, which I hate. The usual company supped tonight at Lord Treasurer's, which was Lord Keeper, Mr Secretary,° George Granville, Masham, Arbuthnot and I. But showers have hindered me from walking today, and that I don't love.—Noble fruit, and I dare not eat a bit.° I ate one fig today, and sometimes a few mulberries, because it is said they are wholesome, and you know, a good name does much. I shall return to town tomorrow, though I thought to have stayed a week, to be at leisure for something I am doing.° But I have put it off till next; for I shall come here again next Saturday, when our society are to meet at supper at Mr Secretary's. My life is very regular here: on Sunday morning I constantly visit Lord Keeper, and sup at Lord Treasurer's with the same set of company. I was not sleepy tonight; I resolved I would not; yet it is past midnight at this present writing.

London, 10. Lord Treasurer and Masham and I left Windsor at three this afternoon: we dropped Masham at Kensington with his lady, and got home by six. It was seven before we sat down to dinner, and I stayed till past eleven. Patrick came home with the Secretary: I am more plagued with Patrick and my portmantua than with myself. I forgot to tell you, that when I went to Windsor on Saturday, I overtook Lady Giffard and Mrs Fenton° in a chariot going, I suppose, to Sheen. I was then in a chariot too, of Lord Treasurer's brother, who had business with the Treasurer; and my lord came after, and overtook me at Turnham Green, four miles from London, and then the brother went back, and I went in the coach with Lord Treasurer: so it happened that those people saw me, and not with Lord Treasurer. Mrs F. was to see me about a week ago; and desired I would get her son into the Charterhouse.

11. This morning the printer sent me an account of Prior's *Journey*;° it makes a twopenny pamphlet; I suppose you will see it, for I dare engage it will run; 'tis a formal grave lie, from the beginning to the end. I writ all but about the last page; that I dictated, and the printer writ. Mr Secretary sent to me to dine where he did; it was at Prior's; when I came in Prior showed me the pamphlet, seemed to be angry, and said, here is our English liberty: I read some of it, and said I liked it mightily, and envied the rogue the thought: for had it come into my head, I should have certainly done it myself. We stayed at Prior's till past ten, and then the Secretary received a packet with the news of Bouchain being taken,° for which the guns will go off tomorrow. Prior owned his having been in France, for it was past denying; it seems he was discovered by a rascal at Dover, who had positive orders to let him pass. I believe we shall have a peace.

12. It is terrible rainy weather, and has cost me three shillings in coaches and chairs today, yet I was dirty into the bargain. I was three hours this morning with the Secretary about some business of moment, and then went into the city to dine. The printer tells me he sold yesterday a thousand of Prior's *Journey*, and had printed five hundred more. It will do rarely, I believe, and is a pure bite. And what is MD doing all this while? got again to their cards, their Walls, their deans, their Stoytes, and their claret? Pray present my service to Mr Stoyte and Catherine. Tell Goody Stoyte she owes me a world of dinners, and I will shortly come over and demand them.—Did I tell you of the Archbishop of Dublin's° last letter? He had been saying in several of his former that he would shortly write to me something about myself, and looked to me as if he intended something for me: at last out it comes, and consists of two parts. First, he advises me to strike in for some preferment now I have friends; and secondly, he advises me, since I have parts, and learning, and a happy pen, to think of some new subject in *divinity* not handled by others, which I should manage better than any body. A rare spark this, with a pox! but I shall answer him as rarely. Methinks he should have invited me over, and given me some hopes or promises. But, hang him! and so good night, &c.

13. It rained most furiously all this morning till about twelve, and sometimes thundered; I trembled for my shillings,° but it cleared up, and

I made a shift to get a walk in the Park, and then went with the Secretary to dine with Lord Treasurer. Upon Thursdays there is always a select company; we had the Duke of Shrewsbury, Lord Rivers, the two Secretaries,° Mr Granville, and Mr Prior. Half of them went to council at six; but Rivers, Granville, Prior and I, stayed till eight. Prior was often affecting to be angry at the account of his journey to Paris; and indeed the two last pages, which the printer got somebody to add, are so romantic, they spoil all the rest. Dilly Ashe pretended to me that he was only going to Oxford and Cambridge for a fortnight, and then would come back. I could not see him as I appointed t'other day; but some of his friends tell me, he took leave of them as going to Ireland; and so they say at his lodging. I believe the rogue was ashamed to tell me so, because I advised him to stay the winter, and he said he would. I find he had got into a good set of scrub acquaintance, and I thought passed his time very merrily; but I suppose he languished after Balderig, and the claret of Dublin: and, after all, I think he is in the right; for he can eat, drink, and converse better there than here. Bernage° was with me this morning: he calls now and then; he is in terrible fear of a Peace. He said, he never had his health so well as in Portugal. He is a favourite of his colonel.

14. I was mortified enough today, not knowing where in the world to dine, the town is so empty; I met H. Coote, and thought he would invite me, but he did not: Sir John Stanley did not come into my head; so I took up with Mrs Van,° and dined with her and her damned landlady, who I believe, by her eyebrows, is a bawd. This evening I met Addison and Pastoral Philips in the Park, and supped with them at Addison's lodgings; we were very good company; and yet know no man half so agreeable to me as he is. I sat with them till twelve, so you may think 'tis late, young women; however, I would have some little conversation with MD before your Presto goes to bed, because it makes me sleep and dream, and so forth. Faith this letter goes on slowly enough, sirrahs, but I can't write much at a time till you are quite settled after your journey you know, and have gone all your visits, and lost your money at ombre. You never play at chess now, Stella. That puts me in mind of Dick Tighe; I fancy I told you, he used to beat his wife here: and she deserved it; and he resolves to part with her; and they went to Ireland in different coaches. O Lord, I said all this before, I'm sure. Go to bed, sirrahs.

Windsor, 15. I made the Secretary stop at Brentford, because we set out at two this afternoon, and fasting would not agree with me. I only designed to eat a bit of bread and butter, but he would light, and we ate roast beef like dragons. And he made me treat him and two more gentlemen; faith it cost me a guinea: I don't like such jesting, yet I was mightily pleased with it too. Tonight our Society met at the Secretary's, there were nine of us; and we have chosen a new member, the Earl of Jersey, whose father died lately. 'Tis past one, and I have stolen away.

16. I design to stay here this week by myself, about some business° that lies on my hands, and will take up a great deal of time. Dr Adams, one of the canons, invited me today to dinner. The tables are so full here on Sunday, that it is hard to dine with a few, and Dr Adams knows I love to do so; which is very obliging. The Queen saw company in her bedchamber; she looks very well, but she sat down. I supped with Lord Treasurer as usual, and stayed till past one as usual, and with our usual company, except Lord Keeper, who did not come this time to Windsor. I hate these suppers mortally; but I seldom eat any thing.

17. Lord Treasurer and Mr Secretary stay here till tomorrow; some business keeps them, and I am sorry for it, for they hinder me a day. Mr Lewis and I were going to dine soberly with a little court friend at one. But Lord Harley and Lord Dupplin° kept me by force, and said we should dine at Lord Treasurer's, who intended to go at four to London; I stayed like a fool, and went with the two young lords to Lord Treasurer; who very fairly turned us all three out of doors. They both were invited to the Duke of Somerset, but he was gone to a horse race, and would not come till five: so we were forced to go to a tavern, and sent for wine from Lord Treasurer's, who at last we were told did not go to town till the morrow, and at Lord Treasurer's we supped again; and I desired him to let me add four shillings to the bill I gave him. We sat up till two, yet I must write to little MD.

18. They are all gone early this morning; and I am alone to seek my fortune; but Dr Arbuthnot engages me for my dinners; and he yesterday gave me my choice of place, person and victuals for today. So I chose to dine with Mrs Hill, who is one of the dressers° and Mrs Masham's sister; no company but us three, and to have a shoulder of mutton, a small one, which was exactly, only there was too much victuals besides; and the Dr's wife was of the company. And tomorrow Mrs Hill and I are to dine with the Doctor. I have seen a fellow often about court, whom I thought I knew; I asked who he was, and they told me it was the gentleman porter; then I called him to mind; he was Killy's acquaintance (I won't say yours), I think his name is Lovet, or Lovel, or something like it. I believe he does not know me, and in my present posture I shall not be fond of renewing old acquaintance; I believe I used to see him with the Bradleys; and by the way, I have not seen Mrs Bradley since I came to England. I left your letter in London, like a fool; and cannot answer it till I go back, which will

not be until Monday next: so this will be above a fortnight from my last; but I will fetch it up in my next, so go and walk to the Dean's for your health this fine weather.

19. The Queen designs to have cards and dancing here next week, which makes us think she will stay here longer than we believed. Mrs Masham is not well after her lying-in: I doubt she got some cold: she is lame in one of her legs with a rheumatic pain. Dr Arbuthnot and Mrs Hill go tomorrow to Kensington to see her, and return the same night. Mrs Hill and I dined with the Doctor today. I rode out this morning with the Doctor to see Cranburn,° a house of Lord Ranelagh's, and the Duchess of Marlborough's lodge, and the Park; the finest places they are for nature, and plantations, that ever I saw; and the finest riding upon artificial roads, made on purpose for the Queen. Arbuthnot made me draw up a sham subscription for a book, called *A History of the Maids of Honour since Harry the Eighth*, showing they make the best wives, with a list of all the Maids of Honour since, &c.: to pay a crown in hand, and t'other crown upon delivery of the book; and all in the common forms of those things. We got a gentleman to write it fair, because my hand is known, and we sent it to the maids of honour when they came to supper. If they bite at it, 'twill be a very good court jest; and the queen will certainly have it; we did not tell Mrs Hill.

20. Today I was invited to the Green Cloth° by Colonel Godfrey, who married the Duke of Marlborough's sister, mother to the Duke of Berwick by King James: I must tell you those things that happened before you were born: but I made my excuses, and young Harcourt (Lord Keeper's son) and I dined with my next neighbour Dr Adams. Mrs Masham is better, and will be here in three or four days. She had need; for the Duchess of Somerset is thought to gain ground daily.°—We have not yet sent you over all your bills;° and I think we have altered your money-bill. The Duke of Ormond is censured here by those in power for very wrong management in the affair of the mayoralty.° He is governed by fools; and has usually much more sense than his advisers, but never proceeds by it. I must know how your health continues after Wexford. Walk and use exercise, sirrahs both; and get somebody to play at shuttlecock with you, Madam Stella, and walk to the Dean's and Donnybrook.

21. Colonel Godfrey sent to me again today; so I dined at the Green Cloth, and we had but eleven at dinner, which is a small number there, the court being always thin of company till Saturday night. This new ink and pen makes a strange figure; *I must write larger, yes, I must, or* Stella *won't be able to read this*.° S. S. S. there's your S s for you, Stella. The

maids of honour are bit, and have all contributed their crowns, and are teazing others to subscribe for the book. I will tell Lord Keeper and Lord Treasurer tomorrow; and I believe the Queen will have it. After a little walk this evening, I squandered away the rest of it in sitting at Lewis's lodging, while he and Dr Arbuthnot played at picquet. I have that foolish pleasure, which I believe nobody has beside me, except old Lady Berkeley. But I fretted when I came away; I will loiter so no more, for I have a plaguy deal of business upon my hands, and very little time to do it. The pamphleteers begin to be very busy against the ministry: I have begged Mr Secretary to make examples of one or two of them; and he assures me he will. They are very bold and abusive.

22. This being the day the ministry comes to Windsor, I ate a bit or two at Mr Lewis's lodgings, because I must sup with Lord Treasurer; and at half an hour after one, I led Mr Lewis a walk up the avenue, which is two miles long: we walked in all about five miles, but I was so tired with his slow walking, that I left him here, and walked two miles towards London, hoping to meet Lord Treasurer, and return with him, but it grew darkish, and I was forced to walk back, so I walked nine miles in all, and Lord Treasurer did not come till after eight, which is very wrong, for there was no *moon*, and I often tell him how ill he does to expose himself so, but he only makes a jest of it. I supped with him, and stayed till now, when it is half an hour after two. He is as merry, and careless, and disengaged as a young heir at one-and-twenty. 'Tis late indeed.

23. The Secretary did not come last night, but at three this afternoon; I have not seen him yet; but I verily think they are contriving a Peace as fast as they can, without which it will be impossible to subsist. The Queen was at church today, but was carried in a chair. I and Mr. Lewis dined privately with Mr. Lowman, clerk of the kitchen. I was to see Lord Keeper this morning, and told him the jest of the maids of honour, and Lord Treasurer had it last night. That rogue Arbuthnot puts it all upon me. The court was very full today; I expected Lord Treasurer would have invited me to supper; but he only bowed to me, and we had no discourse in the drawing-room. 'Tis now seven at night, and I am at home; and I hope Lord Treasurer will not send for me to supper; if he does not, I will reproach him, and he will pretend to chide me for not coming. So farewell till I go to bed, for I am going to be busy.—'Tis now past ten, and I went down to ask the servants about Mr Secretary; they tell me the queen is yet at council, and that she went to supper, and came out to the council afterwards. 'Tis certain they are managing a Peace. I will go to bed, and there's an end.—'Tis now eleven, and a messenger is come from Lord Treasurer to sup with them; but I have excused myself, and

am glad I am in bed; for else I should sit up till two, and drink till I was hot. Now I'll go sleep.

London, 24. I came to town by six with Lord Treasurer, and have stayed till ten. That of the Queen's going out to sup, and coming in again, is a lie, as the Secretary told me this morning: but I find the ministry are very busy with Mr Prior, and I believe he will go again to France. I am told so much, that we shall certainly have a Peace very soon. I had charming weather all last week at Windsor; but we have had a little rain today, and yesterday was windy. Prior's *Journey* sells still; they have sold two thousand, although the town is empty. I found a letter from Mrs Fenton here, desiring me, in Lady Giffard's name, to come and pass a week at Sheen, while she is at Moor Park. I will answer it with a vengeance; and now you talk of answering, there is MD's N. 20 is yet to be answered: I had put it up so safe I could hardly find it; but here it is, faith, and I am afraid I cannot send this till Thursday, for I must see the Secretary tomorrow morning, and be in some other place in the evening.

25. Stella writes like an emperor, and gives such an account of her journey, never saw the like. Let me see; stand away, let us compute; you stayed four days at Inish-Corthy; two nights at Mrs Proby's mother's; and yet was but six days in journey; for your words are, 'We left Wexford this day se'ennight, and came here last night.' I have heard them say that travellers may lie by authority. Make up this, if you can. How far is it from Wexford to Dublin? how many miles did you travel in a day? Let me see—thirty pounds in two months, is nine score pounds a year; a matter of nothing in Stella's purse. I dreamed Billy Swift° was alive, and that I told him, you writ me word he was dead, and that you had been at his funeral, and I admired at your impudence, and was in mighty haste to run and let you know what lying rogues you were. Poor lad, he is dead of his mother's former folly and fondness, and yet now I believe as you say, that her grief will soon wear off.—O yes, Madam Dingley, mightily tired of the company, no doubt of it, at Wexford! And your description of it is excellent; clean sheets, but bare walls; I suppose then you lay upon the walls.—Mrs Walls has got her tea, but who pays me the money? Come, I shall never get it, so I make a present of it to stop some gaps, &c. Where's the thanks of the house? So, that's well; why, it cost four-and-thirty shillings English.—You must adjust that with Mrs Walls; I think that is so many pence more with you.—No, Leigh and Sterne,° I suppose, were not at the waterside; I fear Sterne's business will not be done; I have not seen him this good while. I hate him for the management of that box; and I was the greatest fool in nature for trusting to such a young jackanapes; I will speak to him once more about it, when I see him. Mr Addison and I

met once more since, and I supped with him: I believe I told you so somewhere in this letter. The Archbishop chose an admirable messenger in Walls to send to me, yet I think him fitter for a messenger than any thing. The d— she has! I did not observe her looks. Will she rot out of modesty with Lady Giffard? I pity poor Jenny°—but her husband is a dunce, and with respect to him, she loses little by her deafness. I believe, Madam Stella, in your accounts you mistook one liquor for another, and it was a hundred and forty quarts of wine, and thirty-two of water.—This is all written in the morning, before I go to the Secretary, as I am now doing. I have answered your letter a little shorter than ordinary; but I have a mind it should go today, and I will give you my journal at night in my next, for I'm so afraid of another letter before this goes: I will never have two together again unanswered. What care I for Dr Tisdall and Dr Raymond, or how many children they have? I wish they had a hundred apiece. Lord Treasurer promises me to answer the bishops' letter tomorrow, and show it me; and I believe it will confirm all I said, and mortify those that threw the merit on the Duke of Ormond.° For I have made him jealous of it; and t'other day talking of the matter, he said, I am your witness you got it for them before the Duke was Lord Lieutenant. My humble service to Mrs Walls, Mrs. Stoyte, and Catherine. Farewell, &c.

What do you do when you see any literal mistakes in my letters? how do you set them right? for I never read them over to correct them. Farewell again.

Pray send this note to Mrs Brent, to get the money when Parvisol comes to town, or she can send to him.

THE
CONDUCT
OF THE
ALLIES,
AND OF THE
Late Ministry,
IN
Beginning and Carrying on
THE
Present War.

—— *Partem tibi Gallia nostri*
Eripuit: partem duris Hispania bellis:
Pars jacet Hesperia: totoq; exercitus orbe
Te vincente perit ——°

Odimus accipitrem quia semper vivit in armis.°

—— *Victrix Provincia plorat.*°

THE PREFACE

I CANNOT *sufficiently admire the industry of a sort of men, wholly out of favour with the prince and people, and openly professing a separate interest from the bulk of the landed men, who yet are able to raise, at this juncture, so great a clamour against a peace without offering one single reason but what we find in their* ballads. *I lay it down for a maxim, That no reasonable man whether Whig or Tory (since it is necessary to use those foolish terms) can be of opinion for continuing the war upon the foot it now is, unless he be a gainer by it, or hopes it may occasion some new turn of affairs at home to the advantage of his party; or lastly, unless he be very ignorant of the kingdom's condition, and by what means we have been reduced to it. Upon the two first cases, where interest is concerned, I have nothing to say. But as to the last, I think it highly necessary that the public should be freely and impartially told what circumstances they are in, after what manner they have been treated by those whom they trusted so many years with the disposal of their blood and treasure, and what the consequences of this management are like to be upon themselves and their posterity.*

Those who, either by writing or discourse, have undertaken to defend the proceedings of the late ministry in the management of the war, and of the treaty at Gertruydenburg,° have spent time in celebrating the conduct and valour of our leaders and their troops, in summing up the victories they have gained, and the towns they have taken. Then they tell us what high articles were insisted on by our ministers and those of the confederates,° and what pains both were at in persuading France to accept them. But nothing of this can give the least satisfaction to the just complaints of the kingdom. As to the war, our grievances are, that a greater load has been laid on us than was either just or necessary or than we have been able to bear; that the grossest impositions have been submitted to for the advancement of private wealth and power or in order to forward the more dangerous designs of a faction, *to both which a peace would have put an end; and that the part of the war which was chiefly our province, which would have been most beneficial to us, and destructive to the enemy, was wholly neglected. As to a peace, we complain of being deluded by a* mock treaty; *in which those who negotiated, took care to make such demands as they knew were impossible to be complied with, and therefore might securely press every article as if they were in earnest.*

These are some of the points I design to treat of in the following discourse; with several others which I thought it necessary, at this time, for the kingdom to be informed of. I think I am not mistaken in those facts I mention, at least not in any circumstance so material as to weaken the consequences I draw from them.

After ten years war with perpetual success, to tell us it is yet impossible to have a good peace is very surprising, and seems so different from what hath ever happened in the world before that a man of any party may be allowed suspecting we have either been ill used, or have not made the most of our victories, and might therefore desire to know where the difficulty lay. Then it is natural to enquire into our present condition; how long we shall be able to go on at this rate; what the consequences may be upon the present and future ages; and whether a peace without that impracticable point which some people do so much insist on, be really ruinous in itself, or equally so with the continuance of the war.

THE *CONDUCT* OF THE ALLIES, *&c.*

THE motives that may engage a wise prince or state in a war, I take to be [A] one or more of these. Either to check the overgrown power of some ambitious neighbour; to recover what hath been unjustly taken from them; to revenge some injury they have received (which all political casuists allow); to assist some ally in a just quarrel; or lastly, to defend themselves when they are invaded. In all these cases the writers upon politics admit a war to be justly undertaken. The last is what hath been usually called *pro aris et focis*;° where no expense or endeavour can be too great because all we have is at stake, and consequently our utmost force to be exerted; and the dispute is soon determined either in safety or utter destruction. But in the other four, I believe it will be found that no monarch or commonwealth did ever engage beyond a certain degree; never proceeding so far as to exhaust the strength and substance of their country by anticipations and loans, which in a few years must put them in a worse condition than any they could reasonably apprehend from those evils for the preventing of which they first entered into the war; because this would be to run into real infallible ruin, only in hopes to remove what might perhaps but appear so by a probable speculation.

And, as a war should be undertaken upon a just and prudent motive, so it is still more obvious that a prince ought maturely to consider the condition he is in when he enters on it. Whether his coffers be full, his revenues clear of debts, his people numerous and rich by a long peace and free trade, not overpressed with many burthensome taxes; no violent faction ready to dispute his just prerogative, and thereby weaken his authority at home and lessen his reputation abroad. For, if the contrary of all this happen to be his case, he will hardly be persuaded to disturb the world's quiet and his own while there is any other way left of preserving the latter with honour and safety.

Supposing the war to have commenced upon a just motive, the next thing to be considered is, when a prince ought in prudence to receive the overtures of a peace: which I take to be either when the enemy is ready to yield the point originally contended for, or when that point is found impossible to be ever obtained; or when contending any longer, though with probability of gaining that point at last, would put such a prince and his people in a worse condition than the present loss of it. All which considerations are of much greater force where a war is managed by an alliance of many confederates, which in the variety of interests among the several parties, is liable to so many unforeseen accidents.

In a confederate war it ought to be considered which party has the deepest share in the quarrel: for though each may have their particular reasons, yet one or two among them will probably be more concerned than the rest and therefore ought to bear the greatest part of the burthen in proportion to their strength. For example, two princes may be competitors for a kingdom, and it will be your interest to take the part of him who will probably allow you good conditions of trade, rather than of the other who possibly may not. However, that prince whose cause you espouse, though never so vigorously, is the principal in that war, and you, properly speaking, are but a second. Or a commonwealth may lie in danger to be overrun by a powerful neighbour, which in time may produce very bad consequences upon your trade and liberty. 'Tis therefore necessary, as well as prudent, to lend them assistance and help them to win a strong secure frontier; but, as they must in course be the first and greatest sufferers, so in justice they ought to bear the greatest weight. If a house be on fire, it behoves all in the neighbourhood to run with buckets to quench it; but the owner is sure to be undone first; and it is not impossible that those at next door may escape, by a shower from Heaven, or the stillness of the weather, or some other favourable accident.

But if an ally who is not so immediately concerned in the good or ill fortune of the war, be so generous as to contribute more than the principal party, and even more in proportion to his abilities, he ought at least to have his share in what is conquered from the enemy: or, if his romantic disposition transports him so far as to expect little or nothing of this, he might, however, hope that the principals would make it up in dignity and respect; and he would surely think it monstrous to find them intermeddling in his domestic affairs, prescribing what servants he should keep or dismiss, pressing him perpetually with the most unreasonable demands, and at every turn threatening to break the alliance if he will not comply.

From these reflections upon war in general, I descend to consider those wars wherein England hath been engaged since the Conquest. In the civil wars of the barons, as well as those between the houses of York and Lancaster, great destruction was made of the nobility and gentry, new families raised and old ones extinguished, but the money spent on both sides was employed and circulated at home; no public debts contracted; and a very few years of peace quickly set all right again.

The like may be affirmed even of that unnatural rebellion against King Charles I. The usurpers maintained great armies in constant pay, had almost continual war with Spain or Holland, but managing it by their fleets they increased very much the riches of the kingdom instead of exhausting them.

Our foreign wars were generally against Scotland or France; the first being upon our own continent, carried no money out of the kingdom, and were seldom of long continuance. During our first wars with France we possessed great dominions in that country, where we preserved some footing till the reign of Queen Mary; and though some of our latter princes made very chargeable expeditions thither, a subsidy, and two or three fifteenths, cleared all the debt. Beside, our victories were then of some use as well as glory; for we were so prudent to fight, and so happy to conquer, only for ourselves.

The Dutch wars in the reign of King Charles II, though begun and carried on under a very corrupt administration, and much to the dishonour of the crown, did indeed keep the king needy and poor, by discontinuing or discontenting his parliament when he most needed their assistance; but neither left any debt upon the nation nor carried any money out of it.

At the Revolution a general war broke out in Europe, wherein many princes joined in an alliance against France to check the ambitious designs of that monarch; and here the emperor, the Dutch, and England were principals. About this time the custom first began among us of borrowing millions upon funds of interest. It was pretended that the war could not possibly last above one or two campaigns and that the debts contracted might be easily paid in a few years by a gentle tax, without burthening the subject. But the true reason for embracing this expedient was the security of a new prince, not firmly settled on the throne. People were tempted to lend, by great premiums and large interest, and it concerned them nearly to preserve that government which they trusted with their money. The person said to have been author of so detestable a project° is still living, and lives to see some of its fatal consequences whereof his grandchildren will not see an end. And this pernicious counsel closed very well with the posture of affairs at that time. For a set of upstarts, who had little or no part in the Revolution, but valued themselves by their noise and pretended zeal when the work was over, were got into credit at court by the merit of becoming undertakers and projectors of loans and funds. These, finding that the gentlemen of estates were not willing to come into their measures, fell upon those new schemes of raising money, in order to create a monied interest that might in time vie with the landed, and of which they hoped to be at the head.

[B]   The ground of the first war, for ten years after the Revolution, as to the part we had in it, was to make France acknowledge the late king° and to recover Hudson's Bay. But during that whole war the sea was almost entirely neglected, and the greatest part of six millions annually employed to enlarge the frontier of the Dutch. For the king was a general but not an admiral, and although King of England, was a native of Holland.

After ten years fighting to little purpose; after the loss of above an hundred thousand men and a debt remaining of twenty millions, we at length hearkened to the terms of a peace,° which was concluded with great advantages to the empire and Holland but none at all to us, and clogged soon after by the famous treaty of partition,° by which Naples, Sicily, and Lorrain, were to be added to the French dominions. Or if that crown should think fit to set aside the treaty upon the Spaniards refusing to accept it, as they declared they would to the several parties at the very time of transacting it, then the French would have pretensions to the whole monarchy. And so it proved in the event; for, the late King of Spain° reckoning it an indignity to have his territories cantoned out into parcels by other princes, during his own life and without his consent, rather chose to bequeath the monarchy entire to a younger son of France. And this prince was acknowledged for King of Spain both by us and Holland.

It must be granted, that the counsels of entering into [the present] war were violently opposed by the church-party, who first advised the late king to acknowledge the Duke of Anjou; and particularly, 'tis affirmed that a certain great person, who was then in the church interest,° told the king in November 1701 that since His Majesty was determined to engage in a war so contrary to his private opinion, he could serve him no longer, and accordingly gave up his employment; though he happened afterwards to change his mind when he was to be at the head of the Treasury and have the sole management of affairs at home, while those abroad were to be in the hands of one whose advantage, by all sorts of ties, he was engaged to promote.°

The declarations of war against France and Spain, made by us and Holland, are dated within a few days of each other. In that published by the States, they say very truly, that 'they are nearest, and most exposed to the fire; that they are blocked up on all sides, and actually attacked by the Kings of France and Spain; that their declaration is the effect of an urgent and pressing necessity'; with other expressions to the same purpose. They 'desire the assistance of all kings and princes', &c. The grounds of their quarrel with France are such as only affect themselves, or at least more immediately than any other prince or state; such as, 'the French refusing to grant the Tariff promised by the treaty of Ryswick; the loading the Dutch inhabitants settled in France with excessive duties, contrary to the said treaty; the violation of the Partition Treaty, by the French accepting the King of Spain's will, and threatening the States if they would not comply; the seizing the Spanish Netherlands by the French troops, and turning out the Dutch, who by permission of the late King of Spain were in garrison there; by which means that republic was deprived of her barrier, contrary to the treaty of partition, where it was particularly stipulated that the Spanish Netherlands should be left to the archduke.' They alleged that 'the French king governed Flanders as his own, though under the name of his grandson, and sent great numbers of troops thither to fright them: that he had seized the city and citadel of Liège, had possessed himself of several places in the archbishopric of Cologne, and maintained troops in the country of Wolfenbuttel, in order to block up the Dutch on all sides; and caused his Resident to give in a memorial, wherein he threatened the States to act against them if they refused complying with the contents of that memorial.'

The Queen's declaration of war is grounded upon the Grand Alliance, as this was upon the unjust usurpations and encroachments of the French king; whereof the instances produced are, 'his keeping in possession a great part of the Spanish dominions, seizing Milan and the Spanish Low Countries, making himself master of Cadiz, &c. And instead of giving satisfaction in these points, his putting an indignity and affront on Her Majesty and kingdoms, by declaring the pretended Prince of Wales K. of England, &c.' which last was the only personal quarrel we had in the war; and even this was positively denied by France, that king being [then] willing to acknowledge Her Majesty.

I think it plainly appears by both declarations, that England ought no more to have been a principal in this war than Prussia, or any other power who came afterwards into that alliance. Holland was first in danger, the French troops being at that time just at the gates of Nimeguen. But the complaints made in our declaration do all, except the last, as much or more concern almost every prince in Europe.

For, among the several parties who came first or last into this confederacy, there were few but who in proportion had more to get or to lose, to hope or to fear from the good or ill success of this war, than we. The Dutch took up arms to defend themselves from immediate ruin, and by a successful war they proposed to have a larger extent of country, and a better frontier against France. The emperor hoped to recover the monarchy of Spain or some part of it, for his younger son, chiefly at the expense of us and Holland. The King of Portugal had received intelligence that Philip designed to renew the old pretensions of Spain upon that kingdom, which is surrounded by the other on all sides except towards the sea, and could therefore only be defended by maritime powers. This, with the advantageous terms offered by K. Charles,° as well as by us, prevailed with that prince to enter into the alliance. The Duke of Savoy's temptations and fears were yet greater. The main charge of the war on that side was to be supplied by England, and the profit to redound to him. In case Milan should be conquered it was stipulated that his highness should have the Duchy of Montferrat, belonging to the Duke of Mantua, the provinces of Alexandria and

Valencia, and Lomellino, with other lands between the Po and the Tanaro, together with the Vigevenasco, or in lieu of it an equivalent out of the province of Novara, adjoining to his own state; beside whatever else could be taken from France on that side by the confederate forces. Then, he was in terrible apprehensions of being surrounded by France, who had so many troops in the Milanese and might have easily swallowed up his whole duchy.

The rest of the allies came in purely for subsidies, whereof they sunk considerable sums into their own coffers, and refused to send their contingent to the emperor, alleging their troops were already hired by England and Holland.

Some time after the Duke of Anjou's succeeding to the monarchy of Spain in breach of the Partition Treaty, the question here in England was, whether the peace should be continued, or a new war begun. Those who were for the former alleged the debts and difficulties we laboured under; that both we and the Dutch had already acknowledged Philip for King of Spain; that the inclinations of the Spaniards to the house of Austria, and their aversion for that of Bourbon, were not so surely to be reckoned upon as some would pretend; that we thought it a piece of insolence, as well as injustice, in the French to offer putting a king upon us, and the Spaniards would conceive we had as little reason to force one upon them; that it was true the nature and genius of those two people differed very much, and so would probably continue to do as well under a king of French blood as one of Austrian; but that if we should engage in a war for dethroning the D. of Anjou, we should certainly effect what, by the progress and operations of it, we endeavoured to prevent, I mean an union of interest and affections between the two nations; for the Spaniards must of necessity call in French troops to their assistance. This would introduce French counsellors into King Philip's court; and this, by degrees, would habituate and reconcile the two nations. That to assist King Charles by English or Dutch forces would render him odious to his new subjects, who have nothing in so great an abomination as those whom they hold for heretics. That the French would by this means become masters of the treasures in the Spanish West Indies. That, in the last war when Spain, Cologne, and Bavaria were in our alliance, and by a modest computation brought sixty thousand men into the field against the common enemy; when Flanders, the seat of war, was on our side, and His Majesty, a prince of great valour and conduct, at the head of the whole confederate army; yet we had no reason to boast of our success. How then should we be able to oppose France with those powers against us, which would carry sixty thousand men from us to the enemy, and so make us, upon the balance, weaker by one hundred and twenty thousand men at the beginning of this war, than of that in 1688?

On the other side, those whose opinion or some private motives inclined them to give their advice for entering into a new war, alleged how dangerous it would be for England that Philip should be King of Spain; that we could have no security for our trade while that kingdom was subject to a prince of the Bourbon family; nor any hopes of preserving the balance of Europe, because the grandfather would, in effect, be king while his grandson had but the title, and thereby have a better opportunity than ever of pursuing his design for universal monarchy. These and the like arguments prevailed; and so, without offering at any other remedy, without taking time to consider the consequences, or to reflect on our own condition, we hastily engaged in a war which hath cost us sixty millions; and after repeated, as well as unexpected success in arms, hath put us and our posterity in a worse condition not only than any of our allies, but even our conquered enemies themselves.

[C]   The part we have acted in the conduct of this whole war, with reference to our allies abroad, and to a prevailing faction at home, is what I shall now particularly examine; where I presume it will appear, by plain matters of fact, that no nation was ever so long or so scandalously abused by the folly, the temerity, the corruption, the ambition of its domestic enemies; or treated with so much insolence, injustice and ingratitude by its foreign friends.

This will be manifest by proving the three following points.

First, That against all manner of prudence, or common reason, we engaged in this war as principals, when we ought to have acted only as auxiliaries.

Secondly, That we spent all our vigour in pursuing that part of the war which could least answer the end we proposed by beginning of it; and made no efforts at all where we could have most weakened the common enemy, and at the same time enriched ourselves.

Lastly, That we suffered each of our allies to break every article in those treaties and agreements by which they were bound, and to lay the burthen upon us.

UPON the first of these points, That we ought to have entered into this war only as auxiliaries. Let any man reflect upon our condition at that time: just come out of the most tedious, expensive and unsuccessful war that ever England had been engaged in; sinking under heavy debts of a nature and degree never heard of by us or our ancestors; the bulk of the gentry and people heartily tired of the war, and glad of a peace, though it brought no other advantage but itself; no sudden prospect of lessening our taxes, which were grown as necessary to pay our debts as to raise armies: a sort of artificial wealth of funds and stocks in the hands of those who for ten years before had been plundering the public: many corruptions in every branch of our government that needed reformation. Under these difficulties, from which twenty years peace and the wisest management could hardly recover us, we declare war against France, fortified by the accession and alliance of those powers I mentioned before, and which in the former war, had been parties in our confederacy. It is very obvious what a change must be made in the balance by such weights taken out of our scale and put into theirs; since it was manifest by ten years experience that France without those additions of strength, was able to maintain itself against us. So that human probability ran with mighty odds on the other side; and in that case, nothing under the most extreme necessity should force any state to engage in a war. We had already acknowledged Philip for King of Spain; neither does the Queen's declaration of war take notice of the Duke of Anjou's succession to that monarchy, as a subject of quarrel; but the French king's governing it as if it were his own; his seizing Cadiz, Milan, and the Spanish Low Countries, with the indignity of proclaiming the Pretender. In all which we charge that prince with nothing directly relating to us, excepting the last: and this, although indeed a great affront, might have easily been redressed without a war; for the French court declared they did not acknowledge the Pretender but only gave him the title of king, which was allowed to Augustus by his enemy of Sweden, who had driven him out of Poland and forced him to acknowledge Stanislaus.°

'Tis true indeed, the danger of the Dutch, by so ill a neighbourhood in Flanders, might affect us very much in the consequences of it; and the loss of Spain to the house of Austria, if it should be governed by French influence and French politics, might in time be very pernicious to our trade. It would therefore have been prudent as well as generous and charitable to help our neighbour; and so we might have done without injuring ourselves. For by an old treaty with Holland, we were bound to assist that republic with ten thousand men whenever they were attacked by the French; whose troops, upon the King of Spain's death, taking possession of Flanders in right of Philip and securing the Dutch garrisons till they would acknowledge him, the States-General, by memorials from their envoy here, demanded only the ten thousand men we were obliged to give them by virtue of that treaty. And I make no doubt but Holland would have exerted themselves so vigorously as to be able, with that assistance alone, to defend their frontiers. Or, if they had been forced to a peace, the Spaniards who abhor dismembering their monarchy would never have suffered the French to possess themselves of Flanders. At that time they had none of those endearments to each other which this war hath created; and whatever hatred and jealousy were natural between the two nations, would then have appeared. So that there was no sort of necessity for us to proceed further, although we had been in a better condition. But our politicians at that time had other views; and a new war must be undertaken upon the advice of those who with their partisans and adherents were to be the sole gainers by it. A grand alliance was therefore made between the Emperor, England, and the States-General; by which, if the injuries complained of from France were not remedied in two months, the parties concerned were obliged mutually to assist each other *with their whole strength*.

Thus we became principal in a war, in conjunction with two allies whose share in the quarrel was beyond all proportion greater than ours. However, I can see no reason from the words of the grand alliance by which we were obliged to make those prodigious expenses we have since been at. By what I have always heard and read I take the 'whole strength of the nation', as understood in that treaty, to be the utmost that a prince can raise annually from his subjects; if he be forced to mortgage and borrow, whether at home or abroad, it is not, properly speaking, *his own strength* or that of the nation, but the entire substance of particular persons, which not being able to raise out of the annual income of his kingdom, he takes upon security, and can only pay the interest; and by this method one part of the nation is pawned to the other, with hardly a possibility left of being ever redeemed.

Surely it would have been enough for us to have suspended the payment of our debts contracted in the former war, and to have continued our land and malt tax, with those others which have since been mortgaged. These, with some additions, would have made up such a sum as, with prudent management, might I suppose have maintained an hundred thousand men by sea and land; a reasonable quota in all conscience for that ally who apprehended least danger and expected least advantage. Nor can we imagine that either of the confederates, when the war began, would have been so unreasonable as to refuse joining with us upon such a foot, and expect that we should every year go between three and four millions in debt (which hath been our case); because the French could hardly have contrived any offers of a peace so ruinous to us as such a war. Posterity will be at a loss to conceive what kind of spirit could possess their ancestors, who after ten years suffering, by the unexampled politics of a nation maintaining a war by annually pawning itself; and during a short peace, while they were looking back with horror on the heavy load of debts they had contracted; universally condemning those pernicious counsels which had occasioned them; racking their invention for some remedies or expedients to mend their shattered condition—That these very people, without giving themselves time to breathe, should again enter into a more dangerous, chargeable and extensive war for the same or perhaps a greater period of time and without any apparent necessity. It is obvious in a private fortune, that whoever annually runs out and continues the same expenses must every year mortgage a greater quantity of land than he did before; and as the debt doubles and trebles upon him, so doth his inability to pay it. By the same proportion we have suffered twice as much by this last ten years war as we did by the former; and if it were possible to continue it five years longer at the same rate, it would be as great a burthen as the whole twenty. This computation, so easy and trivial as it is almost a shame to mention, posterity will think that those who first advised the war, had either not the sense or the honesty to consider.

And as we have wasted our strength and vital substance in this profuse manner, so we have shamefully misapplied it to ends at least very different from those for which we undertook the war, and often to effect others which after peace we may severely repent. This is the second article I proposed to examine.

WE have now for ten years together turned the whole force and expense of the war where the enemy was best able to hold us at a bay; where we could propose no manner of advantage to ourselves; where it was highly impolitic to enlarge our conquests; utterly neglecting that part which would have saved and gained us many millions, which perpetual maxims of our government teach us to pursue; which would have soonest weakened the enemy, and must either have promoted a speedy peace, or enabled us to continue the war.

Those who are fond of continuing the war cry up our constant success at a most prodigious rate, and reckon it infinitely greater than in all human probability we had reason to hope. Ten glorious campaigns are passed, and now at last, like the sick man, we are just expiring with all sorts of good symptoms. Did the advisers of this war suppose it would continue ten years, without expecting the successes we have had; and yet at the same time determine that France must be reduced, and Spain subdued, by employing our whole strength upon Flanders? Did they believe the last war left us in a condition to furnish such vast supplies for so long a period, without involving us and our posterity in unextricable debts? If after such miraculous *doings*, we are not yet in a condition of bringing France to our terms nor can tell when we shall be so, though we should proceed without any reverse of fortune; what could we look for in the ordinary course of things, but a Flanders war of at least twenty years longer? Do they indeed think a town taken for the Dutch is a sufficient recompense to us for six millions of money? which is of so little consequence to the determining the war that the French may yet hold out a dozen years more, and afford a town every campaign at the same price.

I say not this, by any means, to detract from the army or its leaders. Getting into the enemy's lines, passing rivers, and taking towns, may be actions attended with many glorious circumstances. But when all this brings no real solid advantage to us, when it hath no other end than to enlarge the territories of the Dutch and increase the fame and wealth of our general,° I conclude, however it comes about, that things are not as they should be, and that surely our forces and money might be better employed, both towards reducing our enemy and working out some benefit to ourselves. But the case is still much harder. We are destroying many thousand lives, exhausting all our substance, not for our own interest, which would be but common prudence; not for a thing indifferent, which would be sufficient folly, but perhaps to our own destruction, which is perfect madness. We may live to feel the effects of our valour more sensibly than all the consequences we imagine from the dominions of Spain in the Duke of Anjou. We have conquered a noble territory for the States,° that will maintain sufficient troops to defend itself, feed many hundred thousand inhabitants, where all encourage-ment will be given to introduce and improve manufactures, which was the only advantage they wanted; and which, added to their skill, industry and parsimony, will enable them to undersell us in every market of the world.

Our supply of forty thousand men, according to the first stipulation, added to the quotas of the emperor and Holland, which they were obliged to furnish, would have made an army of near two hundred thousand, exclusive of garrisons; enough to withstand all the power that France could bring against it; and we might have employed the rest much better, both for the common cause and our own advantage.

The war in Spain must be imputed to the credulity of our ministers, who suffered themselves to be persuaded by the imperial court that the Spaniards were so violently affected to the house of Austria, as upon the first appearance there, with a few troops under the archduke, the whole kingdom would immediately revolt. This we tried, and found the emperor to have deceived either us or himself. Yet there we drove on the war at a prodigious disadvantage, with great expense; and by a most corrupt management, the only general° who by a course of conduct and fortune almost miraculous had nearly put us into possession of the kingdom, was left wholly unsupported, exposed to the envy of his rivals, disappointed by the caprices of a young unexperienced prince under the guidance of a rapacious German ministry, and at last called home in discontent. By which our armies, both in Spain and Portugal, were made a sacrifice to avarice, ill conduct, or treachery.

In common prudence, we should either have pushed that war with the utmost vigour in so fortunate a juncture, especially since the gaining that kingdom was the great point for which we pretended to continue the war; or at least, when we had *found* or *made* that design impracticable, we should not have gone on in so expensive a management of it, but have kept our troops on the defensive in Catalonia, and pursued some other way more effectual for distressing the common enemy and advantaging ourselves.

And what a noble field of honour and profit had we before us, wherein to employ the best of our strength which, against all the maxims of British policy, we suffered to lie wholly neglected? I have sometimes wondered how it came to pass, that the style of 'maritime powers', by which our allies, in a sort of contemptuous manner, usually couple us with the Dutch, did never put us in mind of the sea; and while some politicians were showing us the way to Spain by Flanders, others by Savoy or Naples, that the West Indies should never come into their heads. With half the charge we have been at, we might have maintained our original quota of forty thousand men in Flanders, and at the same time, by our fleets and naval forces, have so distressed the Spaniards in the north and south seas of America, as to prevent any returns of money from thence, except in our own bottoms. This is what best became us to do as a maritime power. This, with any common degree of success, would soon have compelled France to the necessities of a peace, and Spain to acknowledge the archduke. But while we for ten years have been squandering away our money upon the continent, France hath been wisely engrossing all the trade of Peru, going directly with their ships to Lima and other ports, and there receiving ingots of gold and silver for French goods of little value; which, beside the mighty advantage to their nation at present, may divert the channel of that trade for the future, so beneficial to us, who used to receive annually such vast sums at Cadiz for our goods sent thence to the Spanish West Indies. All this we tamely saw and suffered without the least attempt to hinder it; except what was performed by some private men at Bristol,° who inflamed by a true spirit of courage and industry, did, about three years ago, with a few vessels fitted out at their own charge, make a most successful voyage into those parts, took one of the Acapulco ships, very narrowly missed of the other, and are lately returned laden with unenvied wealth; to show us what might have been done with the like management, by a public undertaking. At least we might easily have prevented those great returns of money to France and Spain, though we could not have taken it ourselves. And if it be true, as the advocates for war would have it, that the French are now so impoverished; in what condition must they have been if that issue of wealth had been stopped?

But great events often turn upon very small circumstances. It was the kingdom's misfortune that the sea was not the Duke of Marlborough's element, otherwise the whole force of the war would infallibly have been bestowed there, infinitely to the advantage of his country which would then have gone hand in hand with his own. But it is very truly objected that if we alone had made such an attempt as this, Holland would have been jealous; or if we had done it in conjunction with Holland, the house of Austria would have been discontented. This hath been the style of late years; which whoever introduced among us, they have taught our allies to speak after them. Otherwise it could hardly enter into any imagination that while we are confederates in a war, with those who are to have the whole profit, and who leave a double share of the burthen upon us, we dare not think of any design, though against the common enemy, where there is the least prospect of doing good to our own country for fear of giving umbrage and offence to our allies; while we are ruining ourselves to conquer provinces and kingdoms for them. I therefore confess with shame that this objection is true. For it is very well known that while the design of Mr. Hill's expedition° remained a secret, it was suspected in Holland and Germany to be intended against Peru; whereupon the Dutch made every where their public complaints, and the ministers at Vienna talked of it as 'an insolence in the Qu— to attempt such an undertaking'; which, however it has failed, partly by the accidents of a storm and partly by the stubbornness or treachery of some in that colony, for whose relief and at whose entreaty it was in some measure designed, is no objection at all to an enterprise so well concerted, and with such fair probability of success.

It was something singular that the States should express their uneasiness when they thought we intended to make some attempt in the

Spanish West Indies; because it is agreed between us that whatever is conquered there by us or them shall belong to the conqueror, which is the only article that I can call to mind in all our treaties or stipulations, with any view of interest to this kingdom; and for that very reason, I suppose, among others, hath been altogether neglected. Let those who think this too severe a reflection examine the whole management of the present war by sea and land with all our alliances, treaties, stipulations and conventions, and consider whether the whole does not look as if some particular care and industry had been used to prevent any benefit or advantage that might possibly accrue to Britain.

This kind of treatment from our two principal allies hath taught the same dialect to all the rest; so that there is hardly a petty prince whom we half maintain by subsidies and pensions, who is not ready upon every occasion to threaten us that he will recall his troops (though they must rob or starve at home) if we refuse to comply with him in any demand, however so unreasonable.

UPON the third head I shall produce some instances, to show how tamely we have suffered each of our allies to infringe every article in those treaties and stipulations by which they were bound, and to lay the load upon us.

But before I enter upon this, which is a large subject, I shall take leave to offer a few remarks on certain articles in three of our treaties, which may let us perceive how much those ministers valued or understood the true interest, safety or honour of their country.

We have made two alliances with Portugal,° an offensive and defensive. The first is to remain in force only during the present war; the second to be perpetual. In the offensive alliance, the emperor, England and Holland are parties with Portugal; in the defensive only we and the States.

Upon the first article of the offensive alliance it is to be observed that although the grand alliance, as I have already said, allows England and Holland to possess for their own whatever each of them shall conquer in the Spanish West Indies; yet here we are quite cut out, by consenting that the archduke shall possess the dominions of Spain in as full a manner as their late King Charles. And what is more remarkable, we broke this very article in favour of Portugal by subsequent stipulations, where we agree that K. Charles shall deliver up Estremadura, Vigo and some other places to the Portuguese, as soon as we can conquer them from the enemy. They who were guilty of so much folly and contradiction, know best whether it proceeded from corruption or stupidity.

By two other articles (beside the honour of being convoys and guards in ordinary to the Portuguese ships and coasts) we are to guess the enemy's thoughts, and to take the King of Portugal's word whenever he has a fancy that he shall be invaded. We are also to furnish him with a strength superior to what the enemy intends to invade any of his dominions with, let that be what it will. And, till we know what the enemy's forces are, His Portuguese Majesty is sole judge what strength is superior and what will be able to prevent an invasion; and may send our fleets, whenever he pleases, upon his errands to some of the furthest parts of the world, or keep them attending upon his own coasts till he thinks fit to dismiss them. These fleets must likewise be subject in all things not only to the king, but to his viceroys, admirals and governors in any of his foreign dominions, when he is in a humour to apprehend an invasion; which I believe is an indignity that was never offered before, except to a conquered nation.

In the defensive alliance with that crown, which is to remain perpetual, and where only England and Holland are parties with them, the same care in almost the same words is taken for our fleet to attend their coasts and foreign dominions, and to be under the same obedience. We and the States are likewise to furnish them with twelve thousand men at our own charge, which we are constantly to recruit, and these are to be subject to the Portuguese generals.

In the offensive alliance we took no care of having the assistance of Portugal, whenever we should be invaded. But in this, it seems, we were wiser; for that king is obliged to make war on France or Spain, whenever we or Holland are invaded by either; but before this, we are to supply them with the same forces, both by sea and land, as if he were invaded himself. And this must needs be a very prudent and safe course for a maritime power to take upon a sudden invasion; by which, instead of making use of our fleets and armies for our own defence, we must send them abroad for the defence of Portugal.

By the thirteenth article we are told what this assistance is which the Portuguese are to give us, and upon what conditions. They are to furnish ten men of war; and when England or Holland shall be invaded by France and Spain together, or by Spain alone; in either of these cases, those ten Portuguese men of war are to serve only upon their own coasts, where no doubt they will be of mighty use to their allies, and terror to the enemy.

How the Dutch were drawn to have a part in either of these two alliances, is not very material to enquire since they have been so wise as never to observe them, nor, I suppose, ever intended it, but resolved as they have since done to shift the load upon us.

Let any man read these two treaties from the beginning to the end, he will imagine that the King of Portugal and his ministers sat down and made them by themselves, and then sent them to their allies to sign; the whole spirit and tenor of them, quite through, running only upon this single point, what we and Holland are to do for Portugal, without any mention of an equivalent except those ten ships, which at the time when we have greatest need of their assistance, are obliged to attend upon their own coasts.

The barrier treaty° between Great Britain and Holland, was concluded at the Hague on the 29th of October in the year 1709. In this treaty, neither Her Majesty nor her kingdoms have any interest or concern, farther than what is mentioned in the second and the twentieth articles. By the former, the States are to assist the Queen in defending the act of succession; and by the other, not to treat of a peace till France acknowledges the Queen and the succession of Hanover, and promises to remove the Pretender out of his dominions.

As to the first of these, it is certainly for the safety and interest of the States-General that the Protestant succession should be preserved in England; because such a popish prince as we apprehend would infallibly join with France in the ruin of that republic. And the Dutch are as much bound to support our succession as they are tied to any part of a treaty of league offensive and defensive, against a common enemy, without any separate benefit upon that consideration. Her Majesty is in the full peaceable possession of her kingdoms, and of the hearts of her people; among whom hardly one in five hundred are in the Pretender's interest. And whether the assistance of the Dutch to preserve a right so well established, be an equivalent to those many unreasonable exorbitant articles in the rest of the treaty, let the world judge. What an impression of our settlement must it give abroad to see our ministers offering such conditions to the Dutch, to prevail on them to be guarantees of our acts of parliament! Neither perhaps is it right, in point of policy or good sense, that a foreign power should be called in to confirm our succession by way of guarantee; but only to acknowledge it. Otherwise we put it out of the power of our own legislature to change our succession without the consent of that prince or state who is guarantee, how much soever the necessities of the kingdom may require it.

As to the other article, it is a natural consequence that must attend any treaty of peace we can make with France; being only the acknowledgment of Her Majesty as queen of her own dominions, and the right of succession by our own laws, which no foreign power hath any pretence to dispute.

However, in order to deserve these mighty advantages from the States, the rest of the treaty is wholly taken up in directing what we are to do for them.

By the grand alliance, which was the foundation of the present war, the Spanish Low Countries were to be recovered and delivered to the King of Spain. But by this treaty, that prince is to possess nothing in Flanders during the war; and after a peace, the States are to have the military command of about twenty towns with their dependencies, and four hundred thousand crowns a year from the King of Spain to maintain their garrisons. By which means they will have the command of all Flanders, from Nieuport on the Sea to Namur on the Meuse, and be entirely masters of the Pays de Waas, the richest part of those provinces. Further, they have liberty to garrison any place they shall think fit in the Spanish Low Countries, whenever there is an appearance of war; and consequently to put garrisons into Ostend, or where else they please, upon a rupture with England.

By this treaty likewise, the Dutch will, in effect, be entire masters of all the Low Countries, may impose duties, restrictions in commerce, and prohibitions at their pleasure; and in that fertile country may set up all sorts of manufactures, particularly the woollen, by inviting the disobliged manufacturers in Ireland, and the French refugees° who are scattered all over Germany. And as this manufacture increases abroad, the clothing people of England will be necessitated, for want of employment, to follow; and in few years, by help of the low interest of money in Holland, Flanders may recover that beneficial trade which we got from them. The landed men of England will then be forced to re-establish the staples of wool abroad; and the Dutch, instead of being only the carriers, will become the original possessors of those commodities, with which the greatest part of the trade of the world is now carried on. And as they increase their trade, it is obvious they will enlarge their strength at sea, and that ours must lessen in proportion.

All the ports in Flanders are to be subject to the like duties the Dutch shall lay upon the Scheldt, which is to be closed on the side of the States. Thus all other nations are, in effect, shut out from trading with Flanders. Yet in the very same article it is said that the States shall be 'favoured in all the Spanish dominions as much as Great Britain, or as the people most favoured'. We have conquered Flanders for them, and are in a worse condition as to our trade there than before the war began. We have been the great support of the King of Spain, to whom the Dutch have hardly contributed any thing at all; and yet 'they are to be equally favoured with us in all his dominions'. Of all this, the Queen is under the unreasonable obligation of being guarantee, and that they shall possess their barrier, and their four hundred thousand crowns a year, even before a peace.

It is to be observed, that this treaty was only signed by one of our plenipotentiaries:° And I have been told that the other was heard to say, he would rather lose his right hand than set it to such a treaty. Had he spoke those words in due season, and loud enough to be heard on this side the water, considering the credit he then had at court he might have saved much of his country's honour, and got as much to himself. Therefore, if the report be true, I am inclined to think he only *said* it. I have been likewise told, that some very necessary circumstances were wanting in the entrance upon this treaty; but the ministers here rather chose to sacrifice the honour of the crown and the safety of their country, than not ratify what one of their favourites had transacted.

Let me now consider in what manner our allies have observed those treaties they made with us, and the several stipulations and agreements pursuant to them.

By the grand alliance between the Empire, England and Holland, we were to assist the other two, *totis viribus*, by sea and land. By a convention subsequent to this treaty, the proportions which the several parties should contribute towards the war were adjusted in the following manner. The emperor was obliged to furnish ninety thousand men against France, either in Italy, or upon the Rhine: Holland to bring sixty thousand into the field in Flanders, exclusive of garrisons; and we forty thousand. In winter, 1702, which was the next year, the Duke of Marlborough proposed the raising of ten thousand men more, by way of augmentation, and to carry on the war with greater vigour; to which the parliament agreed, and the Dutch were to raise the same number. This was upon a *par*, directly contrary to the former stipulation whereby our part was to be a third less than theirs; and therefore it was granted with a condition that Holland should break off all trade and commerce with France. But this condition was never executed, the Dutch only amusing us with a specious declaration till our session of parliament was ended; and the following year it was taken off, by concert between our general and the States, without any reason assigned for the satisfaction of the kingdom. The next and some ensuing campaigns, further additional forces were allowed by parliament for the war in Flanders; and in every new supply, the Dutch gradually lessened their proportions; though the parliament addressed the Queen that the States might be desired to observe them according to agreement; which had no other effect than to teach them to elude it, by making their troops nominal corps, as they did by keeping up the numbers of regiments, but sinking a fifth part of the men and money. So that now things are just inverted, and in all new levies we contribute a third more than the Dutch, who at first were obliged to the same proportion more than us.

Besides, the more towns we conquer for the States the worse condition we are in towards reducing the common enemy, and consequently of putting an end to the war. For they make no scruple of employing the troops of their quota towards garrisoning every town as fast as it is taken, directly contrary to the agreement between us, by which all garrisons are particularly excluded. This is at length arrived by several steps to such a height that there are at present in the field not so many forces under the Duke of Marlborough's command in Flanders, as Britain alone maintains for that service, nor have been for some years past. [And it is well known, that the battles of Hochstet and Ramillies° were fought with not above fifty thousand men on a side.]

The Duke of Marlborough having entered the enemy's lines and taken Bouchain,° formed the design of keeping so great a number of troops, and particularly of cavalry, in Lille, Tournay, Douay, and the country between, as should be able to harass all the neighbouring provinces of France during the winter, prevent the enemy from erecting their magazines, and by consequence from subsisting their forces next spring, and render it impossible for them to assemble their army another year without going back behind the Somme to do it. In order to effect this project, it was necessary to be at an expense extraordinary of forage for the troops, of building stables, finding fire and candle for the soldiers, with other incident charges. The Queen readily agreed to furnish her share of the first article, that of the forage, which only belonged to her. But the States insisting that Her Majesty should likewise come into a proportion of the other articles, which in justice belonged totally to them, She agreed even to that, rather than a design of this importance should fail. And yet we know it hath failed, and that the Dutch refused their consent till the time was past for putting it in execution, even in the opinion of those who proposed it. Perhaps a certain article in the treaties of contributions, submitted to by such of the French dominions as pay them to the States, was the principal cause of defeating this project; since one great advantage to have been gained by it was, as before is mentioned, to have hindered the enemy from erecting their magazines; and one article in those treaties of contributions is that the product of those countries shall pass free and unmolested. So that the question was reduced to this short issue, whether the Dutch should lose this paltry benefit, or the common cause an advantage of such mighty importance.

The sea being the element where we might most probably carry on the war with any advantage to ourselves, it was agreed that we should bear five-eighths of the charge in that service, and the Dutch the other three. And by the grand alliance, whatever we or Holland should conquer in the Spanish West Indies, was to accrue to the conquerors. It might therefore have been hoped that this maritime ally of ours would have made up in their fleet what they fell short in their army; but quite otherwise, they never once furnished their quota either of ships or men; or if some few of their fleet now and then appeared, it was no more than appearing for they immediately separated to look to their merchants and protect their trade. And we may remember very well when these guarantees of our succession, after having not one ship for many months together in the Mediterranean, sent that part of their quota thither, and furnished nothing to us, at the same time that they alarmed us with the rumour of an invasion. And last year when Sir James Wishart was dispatched into Holland to expostulate with the States, and to desire they would make good their agreements in so important a part of the service, he met with such a reception as ill became a republic to give that lies under so many great obligations to us; in short, such a one as those only deserve who are content to take.

It hath likewise been no small inconvenience to us that the Dutch are always slow in paying their subsidies, by which means the weight and pressure of the payment lies upon the Queen, as well as the blame, if Her Majesty be not very exact; nor will even this always content our allies. For in July 1711, the King of Spain was paid all his subsidies to the first of January next; nevertheless he hath since complained for want of money; and his secretary threatened, that if we would not further supply His Majesty, he could not answer for what might happen, although King Charles had not at that time one third of the troops for which he was paid; and even those he had, were neither paid nor clothed. [I shall add one example more to show how this prince has treated the Queen, to whom he owes such infinite obligations. Her Majesty borrowed two hundred thousand pounds from the Genoese, and sent it to Barcelona for the payment of the Spanish army. This money was to be recoined into the current species of Catalonia, which by the alloy is lower in value 25*l. per cent*. The Queen expected, as she had reason, to have the benefit of this re-coinage, offering to apply it all to the use of the war; but King Charles, instead of consenting to this, made a grant of the coinage to one of his courtiers; which put a stop to the work. And when it was represented that the army would starve by this delay, His Majesty only replied, 'Let them starve!' and would not recall his grant.]

I cannot forbear mentioning here another passage concerning subsidies to show what opinion foreigners have of our easiness, and how much they reckon themselves masters of our money whenever they think fit to call for it. The Queen was by agreement to pay two hundred thousand crowns a year to the Prussian troops, the States one hundred thousand, and the emperor only thirty thousand, for recruiting, which his Imperial Majesty never paid. Prince Eugene happening to pass by Berlin, the ministers of that court applied themselves to him for redress in this particular; and His Highness very frankly promised them, that in consideration of this deficiency, Britain and the States should increase their subsidies to seventy thousand crowns more between them, and that the emperor should be punctual for the time to come. This was done by that prince, without any orders or power whatsoever. The Dutch very reasonably refused consenting to it; but the Prussian minister here, making his applications at our court, prevailed on us to agree to our proportion, before we could hear what resolution would be taken in Holland. It is therefore to be hoped that his Prussian Majesty, at the end of this war, will not have the same cause of complaint which he had at the close of the last; that his military chest was emptier by twenty thousand crowns, than at the time that war began.

The emperor, as we have already said, was by stipulation to furnish ninety thousand men against the common enemy, as having no fleets to maintain, and in right of his family being most concerned in the success of the war. However, this agreement hath been so ill observed that from the beginning of the war to this day, neither of the two last emperors° had ever twenty thousand men on their own account in the common cause, excepting once in Italy, when the imperial court exerted itself in a point they have much more at heart than that of gaining Spain or the Indies to their family. When they had succeeded in their attempts on the side of Italy, and observed our blind zeal for pushing on the war at all adventures, they soon found out the most effectual expedient to excuse themselves. They computed easily that it would cost them less to make large presents to one single person° than to pay an army, and turn to as good account. They thought they could not put their affairs into better hands; and therefore wisely left us to fight their battles.

Besides, it appeared by several instances how little the emperor regarded his allies, or the cause they were engaged in, when once he thought the empire itself was secure. 'Tis known enough, that he might several times have made a peace with his discontented subjects in Hungary, upon terms not at all unbefitting either his dignity or interest. But he rather chose to sacrifice the whole alliance to his private passion, by entirely subduing and enslaving a miserable people, who had but too much provocation to take up arms to free themselves from the oppressions under which they were groaning. Yet this must serve as an excuse for breaking his agreement, and diverting so great a body of troops which might have been employed against France.

Another instance of the emperor's indifference, or rather dislike to the common cause of the allies is the business of Toulon.° This design was indeed discovered here at home by a person whom every body knows to be the creature of a certain *great man*,° at least as much noted for his skill in gaming as in politics, upon the base mercenary end of getting money by wagers; which was then so common a practice that I remember a gentleman in business who having the curiosity to enquire how wagers went upon the Exchange, found some people, deep in the secret, to have been concerned in that kind of traffic, as appeared by premiums named for towns, which nobody but those behind the curtain could suspect. However, although this project had gotten wind by so scandalous a proceeding, yet Toulon might probably have been taken, if the emperor had not thought fit in that very juncture to detach twelve or fifteen thousand men to seize Naples, as an enterprise that was more his private and immediate interest. But it was manifest that his Imperial Majesty had no mind to see Toulon in possession of the allies; for even with these discouragements the attempt might have yet succeeded, if Prince Eugene had not thought fit to oppose it; which cannot be imputed to his own judgment, but to some politic reasons of his court. The Duke of Savoy was for attacking the enemy as soon as our army arrived; but when the Maréchal de Tessé's troops° were all come up, to pretend to besiege the place in the condition we were at that time was a farce and a jest. Had Toulon fallen then into our hands, the maritime power of France would, in a great measure, have been destroyed.

But a much greater instance than either of the foregoing how little the emperor regarded us or our quarrel, after all we had done to save his imperial crown and to assert the title of his brother to the monarchy of Spain, may be brought from the proceedings of that court not many months ago. It was judged that a war carried on upon the side of Italy would cause a great diversion of the French forces, wound them in a very tender part, and facilitate the progress of our arms in Spain, as well as Flanders. It was proposed to the Duke of Savoy to make this diversion; and not only a diversion during the summer, but the winter too, by taking quarters on this side of the hills. Only in order to make him willing and able to perform this work, two points were to be settled. First, it was necessary to end the dispute between the imperial court and his Royal Highness; which had no other foundation than the emperor's refusing to make good some articles of that treaty, on the faith of which the Duke engaged in the present war, and for the execution whereof Britain and Holland became guarantees at the request of the late Emperor Leopold. To remove this difficulty, the Earl of Peterborough was dispatched to Vienna, got over some parts of those disputes to the satisfaction of the Duke of Savoy, and had put the rest in a fair way of being accommodated at the time the emperor Joseph died. Upon which great event the Duke of Savoy took the resolution of putting himself immediately at the head of the army, though the whole matter was not finished, since the common cause required his assistance; and that until a new emperor were elected it was impossible to make good the treaty to him. In order to enable him, the only thing he asked was that he should be reinforced by the imperial court with eight thousand men before the end of the campaign. Mr. Whitworth was sent to Vienna to make this proposal; and it is credibly reported that he was empowered, rather than fail, to offer forty thousand pounds for the march of those eight thousand men, if he found it was want of ability and not inclination that hindered the sending them. But he was so far from succeeding that it was said the ministers of that court did not so much as give him an opportunity to tempt them with any particular sums; but cut off all his hopes at once by alleging the impossibility of complying with the Queen's demands upon any consideration whatsoever. They could not plead their old excuse of the war in Hungary, which was then brought to an end. They had nothing to offer but some general speculative reasons which it would expose them to repeat; and so, after much delay and many trifling pretences, they utterly refused so small and seasonable an assistance; to the ruin of a project that would have more terrified France and caused a greater diversion of their forces, than a much more numerous army in any other part. Thus, for want of eight thousand men, for whose winter campaign the Queen was willing to give forty thousand pounds; and for want of executing the design I lately mentioned of hindering the enemy from erecting magazines, towards which Her Majesty was ready not only to bear her own proportion, but a share of that which the States were obliged to; our hopes of taking winter quarters in the north and south parts of France are eluded, and the war left in that method which is like to continue it longest. Can there an example be given in the whole course of this war, where we have treated the pettiest prince with whom we had to deal, in so contemptuous a manner? Did we ever once consider what we could afford or what we were obliged to, when our assistance was desired, even while we lay under immediate apprehensions of being invaded?

When Portugal came as a confederate into the grand alliance, it was stipulated that the empire, England and Holland, should each maintain four thousand men of their own troops in that kingdom, and pay between them a million of patacoons° to the King of Portugal for the support of twenty-eight thousand Portuguese; which number of forty thousand was to be the confederate army against Spain on the Portugal side. This treaty was ratified by all the three powers. But in a short time after, the emperor declared himself unable to comply with his part of the agreement, and so left the two-thirds upon us; who very generously undertook that burthen and at the same time two-thirds of the subsidies for maintenance of the Portuguese troops. But neither is this the worst part of the story: for, although the Dutch did indeed send their own particular quota of four thousand men to Portugal (which however they would not agree to, but upon condition that the other two-thirds should be supplied by us), yet they never took care to recruit them. For in the year 1706, the Portuguese, British and Dutch forces, having marched with the Earl of Galway into Castile, and by the noble conduct of that general being forced to retire into Valencia,° it was found necessary to raise a new army on the Portugal side; where the Queen hath, at several times, increased her establishment to ten thousand five hundred men and the Dutch never replaced one single man nor paid one penny of their subsidies to Portugal in six years.

The Spanish army on the side of Catalonia is, or ought to be, about fifty thousand men (exclusive of Portugal). And here the war hath been carried on almost entirely at our cost. For this whole army is paid by the Queen, excepting only seven battalions and fourteen squadrons of Dutch and Palatines;° and even fifteen hundred of these are likewise in our pay; besides the sums given to King Charles for subsidies and the maintenance of his court. Neither are our troops at Gibraltar included within this number. And further, we alone have been at all the charge of transporting the forces first sent from Genoa to Barcelona; and of all the imperial recruits from time to time, and have likewise paid vast sums as levy-money for every individual man and horse so furnished to recruit, though the horses were scarce worth the price of transportation. But this hath been almost the constant misfortune of our fleet during the present war: instead of being employed on some enterprise for the good of the nation, or even for the protection of our trade, to be wholly taken up in transporting soldiers.

We have actually conquered all Bavaria, Ulm, Augsburg, Landau, and a great part of Alsace, for the emperor; and by the troops we have furnished, the armies we have paid, and the diversions we have given to the enemies' forces, have chiefly contributed to the conquests of Milan, Mantua and Mirandola, and to the recovery of the dutchy of Modena. The last emperor drained the wealth of those countries into his own coffers, without increasing his troops against France by such mighty acquisitions or yielding to the most reasonable requests we have made.

Of the many towns we have taken for the Dutch, we have consented by the barrier treaty that all those which were not in possession of Spain, upon the death of the late Catholic king, shall be part of the States dominions and that they shall have the military power in the most considerable of the rest; which is, in effect, to be the absolute sovereigns of the whole. And the Hollanders have already made such good use of their time, that in conjunction with our general the oppressions of Flanders are much greater than ever.

And this treatment, which we have received from our two principal allies, hath been pretty well copied by most other princes in the confederacy with whom we have any dealings. For instance, seven Portuguese regiments after the battle of Almanza° went off with the rest of that broken army to Catalonia; the King of Portugal said he was not able to pay them, while they were out of his country; the Queen consented therefore to do it herself, provided the king would raise as many more to supply their place. This he engaged to do but never performed. Notwithstanding which, his subsidies were constantly paid him by my Lord Godolphin for almost four years, without any deduction upon account of those seven regiments; directly contrary to the seventh article of our offensive alliance with that crown, where it is agreed that a deduction shall be made out of those subsidies, in proportion to the number of men wanting in that complement which the king is to maintain. But whatever might have been the reasons for this proceeding, it seems they are above the understanding of the present Lord Treasurer; who not entering into those refinements, of paying the *public* money upon *private* considerations, hath been so uncourtly as to stop it. This disappointment I suppose hath put the court of Lisbon upon other expedients of raising the price of forage, so as to force us either to lessen our number of troops or be at double expense in maintaining them; and this at a time when their own product, as well as the import of corn, was never greater; and of demanding a duty upon the soldiers' clothes we carry over for those troops which have been their sole defence against an inveterate enemy, and whose example might have infused courage as well as taught them discipline, if their spirits had been capable of receiving either.

In order to augment our forces every year, in the same proportion as those for whom we fight diminish theirs, we have been obliged to hire troops from several princes of the empire, whose ministers and residents here have perpetually importuned the court with unreasonable demands, under which our late ministers thought fit to be passive. For those demands were always backed with a threat to recall their soldiers, which was a thing not to be heard of because it might *discontent the Dutch*. In the meantime those princes never sent their contingent to the emperor as by the laws of the empire they are obliged to do, but gave for their excuse that we had already hired all they could possibly spare.

BUT if all this be true—If, according to what I have affirmed, we [D] began this war contrary to reason: If, as the other party themselves, upon all occasions, acknowledge, the success we have had was more than we could reasonably expect: If, after all our success, we have not made that use of it which in reason we ought to have done: If we have made weak and foolish bargains with our allies, suffered them tamely to break every article even in those bargains to our disadvantage, and allowed them to treat us with insolence and contempt, at the very instant when we were gaining towns, provinces, and kingdoms for them, at the price of our ruin and without any prospect of interest to ourselves: If we have consumed all our strength in attacking the enemy on the strongest side, where (as the old Duke of Schomberg expressed it) 'to engage with France, was to take a bull by the horns' and left wholly unattempted that part of the war which could only enable us to continue or to end it: If all this, I say, be our case, it is a very obvious question to ask by what motives, or what management, we are thus become the *dupes* and *bubbles* of Europe? Surely it cannot be owing to the stupidity arising from the coldness of our climate, since those among our allies who have given us most reason to complain, are as far removed from the sun as ourselves.

If in laying open the real causes of our present misery I am forced to speak with some freedom, I think it will require no apology. Reputation is the smallest sacrifice those can make us, who have been the instruments of our ruin; because it is that for which in all probability they have the least value. So that in exposing the actions of such persons I cannot be said, properly speaking, to do them an injury. But as it will be some satisfaction to the people, to know by whom they have been so long abused, so it may be of great use to us and our posterity, not to trust the safety of their country in the hands of those who act by such principles, and from such motives.

I have already observed that when the counsels of this war were debated in the late king's time, a certain *great man* was then so averse from entering into it that he rather chose to give up his employment and tell the king he could serve him no longer. Upon that prince's death, although the grounds of our quarrel with France had received no manner of addition yet this lord thought fit to alter his sentiments; for the scene was quite changed; his lordship, and the family with whom he was engaged by so complicated an alliance, were in the highest credit possible with the Queen. The treasurer's staff was ready for his lordship, the Duke was to command the army, and the Duchess by her employments and the favour she was possessed of, to be always nearest Her Majesty's person; by which the whole power at home and abroad would be devolved upon the family.° This was a prospect so very inviting that, to confess the truth, it could not be easily withstood by any who have so keen an appetite for wealth or ambition. By an agreement subsequent to the grand alliance, we were to assist the Dutch with forty thousand men, all to be commanded by the D[uke] of M[arlborough]. So that whether this war were prudently begun or not, it is plain that the true spring or motive of it was the aggrandizing a particular family, and in short, a war of the *general* and the *ministry* and not of the *prince* or *people*; since those very persons were against it when they knew the power, and consequently the profit, would be in other hands.

With these measures fell in all that set of people who are called the *monied men*; such as had raised vast sums by trading with stocks and funds, and lending upon great interest and premiums; whose perpetual harvest is war and whose beneficial way of traffic must very much decline by a peace.

In that whole chain of encroachments made upon us by the Dutch which I have above deduced, and under those several gross impositions from other [powers], if any one should ask why our g[enera]l continued so easy to the last, I know no other way probable or indeed so charitable to account for it, as by that unmeasurable love of wealth which his best friends allow to be his predominant passion. However, I shall waive any thing that is personal upon this subject. I shall say nothing of those great presents made by several princes, which the soldiers used to call 'winter foraging', and said it was better than that of the summer; of two and an half *per cent*. subtracted out of all the subsidies we pay in those parts, which amounts to no inconsiderable sum; and lastly, of the grand perquisites in a long successful war, which are so amicably adjusted between him and the States.

But when the war was thus begun, there soon fell in other incidents here at home which made the continuance of it necessary for those who were the chief advisers. The Whigs were at that time out of all credit or consideration. The reigning favourites had always carried what was called the Tory principle at least as high as our constitution could bear; and most others in great employments were wholly in the church interest. These last, among whom several were persons of the greatest merit, quality and consequence, were not able to endure the many instances of pride, insolence, avarice and ambition which those favourites began so early to discover, nor to see them presuming to be the sole dispensers of the royal favour. However, their opposition was to no purpose; they wrestled with too great a power and were soon crushed under it. For those in possession finding they could never be quiet in their usurpations, while others had any credit who were at least upon an equal foot of merit, began to make overtures to the discarded Whigs, who would be content with any terms of accommodation. Thus commenced this *solemn league and covenant* which hath ever since been cultivated with so much application. The great traders in money were wholly devoted to the Whigs who had first raised them. The army, the court, and the treasury, continued under the old *despotic* administration. The Whigs were received into employment, left to manage the parliament, cry down the landed interest, and worry the church. Meantime our allies, who were not ignorant that all this artificial structure had no true foundation in the hearts of the people, resolved to make their best use of it as long as it should last. And the general's credit being raised to a great height at home by our success in Flanders, the Dutch began their gradual impositions; lessening their quotas, breaking their stipulations, garrisoning the towns we took for them, without supplying their troops; with many other infringements. All which we were forced to submit to, because the general was *made easy*; because the monied men at home were fond of the war; because the Whigs were not yet firmly settled; and because that exorbitant degree of power which was built upon a supposed necessity of employing particular persons, would go off in a peace. It is needless to add that the emperor, and other princes, followed the example of the Dutch, and succeeded as well for the same reasons.

I have here imputed the continuance of the war to the mutual indulgence between our general and allies, wherein they both so well found their accounts; to the fears of the *money-changers*, lest their *tables should be overthrown*;° to the designs of the Whigs, who apprehended the loss of their credit and employments in a peace; and to those at home who held their immoderate engrossments of power and favour by no other tenure than their own presumption upon the necessity of affairs. The truth of this will appear indisputable by considering with what unanimity and concert these several parties acted towards that great end.

When the vote passed in the House of Lords against any peace without Spain being restored to the Austrian family, the Earl of W[harto]n told the House that it was indeed impossible and impracticable to recover Spain; but however, there were *certain reasons* why such a vote should be made at that time; which reasons wanted no explanation, for the general and the ministry having refused to accept very advantageous offers of a peace after the battle of Ramillies,° were forced to take in a set of men with a previous bargain to screen them from the consequences of that miscarriage. And accordingly upon the first succeeding opportunity that fell, which was that of the Prince of Denmark's death,° the chief leaders of the party were brought into several great employments.

So when the Queen was no longer able to bear the tyranny and insolence of those ungrateful servants, who as they *waxed the fatter* did but *kick the more*,° our two great allies abroad, and our stock-jobbers at home, took immediate alarm; applied the nearest way to the throne by memorials and messages,° jointly directing Her Majesty not to change her secretary or treasurer; who for the true reasons that these officious intermeddlers demanded their continuance, ought never to have been admitted into the least degree of trust, since what they did was nothing less than betraying the interest of their native country to those princes, who in their turns, were to do what they could to support them in power at home.

Thus it plainly appears that there was a conspiracy on all sides to go on with those measures which must perpetuate the war; and a conspiracy founded upon the interest and ambition of each party; which begat so firm a union that instead of wondering why it lasted so long, I am astonished to think how it came to be broken. The prudence, courage, and firmness of Her Majesty in all the steps of that great change, would if the particulars were truly related make a very shining part in her story.° Nor is her judgment less to be admired which directed her in the choice of perhaps the only persons who had skill, credit, and resolution enough to be her instruments in overthrowing so many difficulties.

Some would pretend to lessen the merit of this by telling us that the rudeness, the tyranny, the oppression, the ingratitude of the late favourites towards their mistress were no longer to be borne. They produce instances to show how Her M[ajest]y was pursued through all her retreats, particularly at Windsor; where, after the enemy had possessed themselves of every inch of ground, they at last attacked and stormed the castle, forcing the Q[uee]n to fly to an adjoining cottage, pursuant to the advice of Solomon° who tells us, 'It is better to live on the house-tops, than with a scolding woman in a large house.' They would have it that such continued ill usage was enough to inflame the meekest spirit. They blame the favourites in point of policy, and think it nothing extraordinary that the Queen should be at an end of her patience, and resolve to discard them. But I am of another opinion and think their proceedings were right. For nothing is so apt to break even the bravest spirits, as a continual chain of oppressions. One injury is best defended by a second, and this by a third. By these steps, the *old masters of the palace* in France° became *masters of the kingdom*; and by these steps, a *g[enera]l during pleasure*, might have grown into a *general for life*, and a *g[enera]l for life* into a *king*.° So that I still insist upon it as a wonder how Her M[ajest]y, thus besieged on all sides, was able to extricate herself.

HAVING thus mentioned the real causes, though disguised under [E] specious pretences, which have so long continued the war, I must beg leave to reason a little with those persons who are against any peace but what they call a *good one*, and explain themselves, that no peace can be *good* without an entire restoration of Spain to the House of Austria. It is to be supposed that what I am to say upon this part of the subject will have little influence on those whose particular ends or designs of any sort lead them to wish the continuance of the war. I mean the general and our allies abroad; the knot of late favourites at home; the body of such as traffic in stocks; and lastly, that set of factious politicians who were so violently bent, at least, upon *clipping* our constitution in church and state. Therefore I shall not apply myself to any of those, but to all others indifferently, whether Whig or Tory, whose private interest is best answered by the welfare of their country. And if among these there be any who think we ought to fight on till King Charles is quietly settled in the monarchy of Spain, I believe there are several points which they have not thoroughly considered.

For, first, it is to be observed that this resolution against any peace without Spain is a new incident, grafted upon the original quarrel by the intrigues of a faction among us, who prevailed to give it the sanction of a vote in both Houses of Parliament to justify those whose interest lay in perpetuating the war. And, as this proceeding was against the practice of all princes and states whose intentions were fair and honourable; so is it contrary to common prudence as well as justice. I might add that it was impious too, by presuming to control events which are only in the hands of God. Ours and the States' complaint against France and Spain are deduced in each of our declarations of war, and our pretensions specified in the eighth article of the grand alliance; but there is not in any of these the least mention of demanding Spain for the House of Austria, or of refusing any peace without that condition. Having already made an extract from both declarations of war, I shall here give a translation of the eighth article in the grand alliance, which will put this matter out of dispute.

The Eighth ARTICLE Of The GRAND ALLIANCE.

When the war is once undertaken, none of the parties shall have the liberty to enter upon a treaty of peace with the enemy, but jointly, and in concert with the others. Nor is peace to be made, without having first obtained a just and reasonable satisfaction for his Cæsarean Majesty, and for his Royal Majesty of Great Britain, and a particular security to the lords the States-General, of their dominions, provinces, titles, navigation, and commerce, and a sufficient provision, that the kingdoms of France and Spain be never united, or come under the government of the same person, or that the same man may never be king of both kingdoms; and particularly, that the French may never be in possession of the Spanish West Indies; and that they may not have the liberty of navigation, for conveniency of trade, under any pretence whatsoever, neither directly nor indirectly; except it is agreed, that the subjects of Great Britain and Holland, may have full power to use and enjoy all the same privileges, rights, immunities and liberties of commerce, by land and sea, in Spain, in the Mediterranean, and in all the places and countries, which the late King of Spain, at the time of his death, was in possession of, as well in Europe, as elsewhere, as they did then use and enjoy; or which the subjects of both, or each nation, could use and enjoy, by virtue of any right, obtained before the death of the said King of Spain, either by treaties, conventions, custom, or any other way whatsoever.

HERE, we see the demands intended to be insisted on by the allies upon any treaty of peace, are a just and reasonable satisfaction for the emperor and King of Great Britain, a security to the States-General for their dominions, &c. and a sufficient provision that France and Spain be never united under the same man as king of both kingdoms. The rest relates to the liberty of trade and commerce for us and the Dutch; but not a syllable of engaging to dispossess the Duke of Anjou.°

But to know how this new language of 'no peace without Spain' was first introduced and at last prevailed among us, we must begin a great deal higher.

It was the partition treaty° which begot the Will in favour of the Duke of Anjou. For this naturally led the Spaniards to receive a prince supported by a great power, whose interest as well as affection engaged them to preserve that monarchy entire, rather than to oppose him in favour of another family, who must expect assistance from a number of confederates whose principal members had already disposed of what did not belong to them, and by a previous treaty parcelled out the monarchy of Spain.

Thus the Duke of Anjou got into the full possession of all the kingdoms and states belonging to that monarchy, as well in the old world as the new. And whatever the House of Austria pretended from their memorials to us and the States, it was at that time but too apparent that the inclinations of the Spaniards were on the Duke's side.

However, a war was resolved, and in order to carry it on with greater vigour, a grand alliance formed, wherein the ends proposed to be obtained are plainly and distinctly laid down, as I have already quoted them. It pleased God in the course of this war to bless the armies of the allies with remarkable successes by which we were soon put into a condition of demanding and expecting such terms of a peace as we proposed to ourselves when we began the war. But instead of this, our victories only served to lead us on to further visionary prospects. Advantage was taken of the sanguine temper which so many successes had wrought the nation up to; new romantic views were proposed and the old, reasonable, sober design was forgot.

This was the artifice of those here who were sure to grow richer as the public became poorer, and who after the resolutions which the two houses were prevailed upon to make, might have carried on the war with safety to themselves till malt and land were mortgaged, till a general excise were established, and the *dixième denier*° raised by *collectors in red coats*. And this was just the circumstance which it suited their interests to be in.

The House of Austria approved this scheme with reason, since whatever would be obtained by the blood and treasure of others was to accrue to that family, and they only lent their name to the cause.

The Dutch might perhaps have grown resty under their burthen; but care was likewise taken of that by a barrier-treaty made with the States, which deserves such epithets as I care not to bestow, but may perhaps consider it at a proper occasion, in a *discourse* by itself.°

By this treaty, the condition of the war with respect to the Dutch, was widely altered. They fought no longer for security, but for grandeur; and we instead of labouring to make them safe, must beggar ourselves to render them formidable.

Will any one contend that if at the treaty of Gertruydenberg° we could have been satisfied with such terms of a peace as we proposed to ourselves by the grand alliance, the French would not have allowed them? 'Tis plain they offered many more, and much greater, than ever we thought to insist on when the war began. And they had reason to grant as well as we to demand them, since conditions of peace do certainly turn upon events of war. But surely there is some measure to be observed in this. Those who have defended the proceedings of our negotiators at the treaty of Gertruydenberg, dwell very much upon their zeal and patience in endeavouring to work the French up to their demands, but say nothing to justify those demands, or the probability that France would ever accept them. Some of the [preliminary] articles in that treaty were so very extravagant that in all human probability we could not have obtained them by a successful war of forty years. One of them was inconsistent with common reason; wherein the confederates reserved to themselves full liberty of demanding what further conditions they should think fit; and in the meantime, France was to deliver up several of their strongest towns in a month. These articles were very gravely signed by our plenipotentiaries and those of Holland, but not by the French, though it ought to have been done interchangeably; nay they were brought over by the secretary of the embassy,° and the ministers here prevailed upon the Queen to execute a ratification of articles, which only one part had signed. This was an absurdity in form as well as in reason, because the usual form of a ratification is with a preamble showing that 'whereas our ministers, and those of the allies, and of the enemy, have signed, &c. We ratify, &c.' The person who brought over the articles said in all companies (and perhaps believed) that it was a pity we had not demanded more, for the French were in a disposition to refuse us nothing we would ask. One of our plenipotentiaries affected to have the same concern, and particularly, that we had not obtained some further security for the empire on the Upper Rhine.

What could be the design of all this grimace but to amuse the people, and to raise stocks for their friends in the secret to sell to advantage? I have too great a respect for the abilities of those who acted in this negotiation, to believe they hoped for any other issue from it than what we found by the event. Give me leave to suppose the continuance of the war was the thing at heart among those in power, both abroad and at home, and then I can easily show the consistency of their proceedings; otherwise they are wholly unaccountable and absurd. Did those who insisted on such wild demands, ever sincerely intend a peace? Did they really think that going on with the war was more eligible for their country than the least abatement of those conditions? Was the smallest of them worth six millions a year and an hundred thousand men's lives? Was there no way to provide for the safety of Britain, or the security of its trade, but by the French king's turning his own arms to beat his grandson out of Spain? If these able statesmen were so truly concerned for our trade, which they made the pretence of the war's beginning as well as continuance, why did they so neglect it in those very preliminaries where the enemy made so many concessions, and where all that related to the advantage of Holland or the other confederates was expressly settled? But whatever concerned us was to be left to a general treaty; no tariff agreed on with France or the Low Countries, only the Scheldt was to remain shut which ruins our commerce with Antwerp. Our trade with Spain was referred the same way; but this they will pretend to be of no consequence because that kingdom was to be under the House of Austria; and we had already made a treaty with King Charles. I have indeed heard of a treaty made by Mr. Stanhope with that prince, for settling our commerce with Spain. But whatever it were, there was another between us and Holland which went hand in hand with it, I mean that of barrier, wherein a clause was inserted by which all advantages proposed for Britain are to be in common with Holland.

ANOTHER point which, I doubt, those have not considered who are against any peace without Spain, is that the face of affairs in Christendom since the emperor's death° hath been very much changed. By this accident the views and interests of several princes and states in the alliance have taken a new turn, and I believe it will be found that ours ought to do so too. We have sufficiently blundered once already by changing our measures with regard to a peace, while our affairs continued in the same posture; and it will be too much in conscience to blunder again by *not* changing the first, when the others are so much altered.

To have a prince of the Austrian family on the throne of Spain is undoubtedly more desirable than one of the House of Bourbon; but to have the empire and Spanish monarchy united in the same person is a dreadful consideration, and directly opposite to that wise principle on which the eighth article of the [Grand] Alliance is founded.*

* We and Holland, as well as Portugal, were so apprehensive of this, that, by the

To this perhaps it will be objected that the indolent character of the Austrian princes, the wretched economy of that government, the want of a naval force, the remote distance of their several territories from each other, would never suffer an emperor though at the same time King of Spain to become formidable. On the contrary, that his dependence must continually be on Great Britain; and the advantages of trade, by a peace founded upon that condition, would soon make us amends for all the expenses of the war.

In answer to this, let us consider the circumstances we must be in before such a peace could be obtained, if it were at all practicable. We must become not only poor for the present, but reduced by further mortgages to a state of beggary for endless years to come. Compare such a weak condition as this with so great an accession of strength to Austria, and then determine how much an emperor in such a state of affairs would either fear or need Britain.

Consider, that the comparison is not formed between a prince of the House of Austria, Emperor and King of Spain, and between a prince of the Bourbon family, King of France and Spain; but between a prince of the latter only King of Spain, and one of the former, uniting both crowns in his own person.

What returns of gratitude can we expect, when we are no longer wanted? Has all that we have hitherto done for the imperial family been taken as a favour, or only received as the due of the *augustissima casa*?°

Will the House of Austria yield the least acre of land, the least article of strained and even usurped prerogative, to resettle the minds of those princes in the alliance who are alarmed at the consequences of this turn of affairs occasioned by the emperor's death? We are assured it never will. Do we then imagine that those princes who dread the overgrown power of the Austrian as much as that of the Bourbon family, will continue in our alliance upon a system contrary to that which they engaged with us upon? For instance, what can the Duke of Savoy expect in such a case? Will he have any choice left him but that of being a slave and a frontier to France; or a *vassal*, in the utmost extent of the word, to the imperial court? Will he not therefore, of the two evils choose the least, by submitting to a master who has no immediate claim upon him, and to whose family he is nearly allied; rather than to another who hath already revived several claims upon him and threatens to revive more?

Nor are the Dutch more inclined than the rest of Europe, that the

twenty-fifth article of the offensive alliance, his Portuguese Majesty was not to acknowledge the Archduke for King of Spain, till the two late emperors had made a cession to Charles of the said monarchy. [*Note in second edition.*]

empire and Spain should be united in King Charles, whatever they may now pretend. *On the contrary, 'tis known to several persons, that upon the death of the late Emperor Joseph, the State resolved, that those two powers should not be joined in the same person*; and this they determined as a fundamental maxim, by which they intended to proceed. So that Spain was first given up by *them*; and since they maintain no troops in that kingdom, it should seem that they understand the Duke of Anjou to be lawful monarch.

THIRDLY, Those who are against any peace without Spain, if they be such as no way find their private account by the war, may perhaps change their sentiments if they will reflect a little upon our present condition.

I had two reasons for not sooner publishing this discourse. The first was, because I would give way to others, who might argue very well upon the same subject from general topics and reason, though they might be ignorant of several facts which I had the opportunity to know. The second was, because I found it would be necessary in the course of this argument to say something of the state to which this war hath reduced us. At the same time I knew that such a discovery ought to be made as late as possible, and at another juncture would not only be very indiscreet but might perhaps be dangerous.

It is the folly of too many to mistake the echo of a London coffee-house for the voice of the kingdom. The city coffee-houses have been for some years filled with people whose fortunes depend upon the Bank, East India, or some other stock. Every new fund to these is like a new mortgage to an usurer, whose compassion for a young heir is exactly the same with that of a stock-jobber to the landed gentry. At the court end of the town, the like places of resort are frequented either by men out of place and consequently enemies to the present ministry, or by officers of the army. No wonder then if the general cry, in all such meetings, be against any peace either *with* Spain or *without*; which, in other words, is no more than this, that discontented men desire another change of ministry; that soldiers would be glad to keep their commissions; and that the creditors have money still, and would have the debtors borrow on at the old extorting rates while they have any security to give.

Now, to give the most ignorant reader some idea of our present circumstances without troubling him or myself with computations in form. Every body knows that our land and malt tax amount annually to about two millions and an half. All other branches of the revenue are mortgaged to pay interest for what we have already borrowed. The yearly charge of the war is usually about six millions; to make up which sum we are forced to take up, on the credit of new funds, about three millions and an half. This last year the computed charge of the war came to above a million more than all the funds the parliament could contrive would pay interest for; and so we have been forced to divide a deficiency of twelve hundred thousand pounds among the several branches of our expense. This is a demonstration that if the war lasts another campaign, it will be impossible to find funds for supplying it without mortgaging the malt tax, or by some other method equally desperate.

If the peace be made this winter, we are then to consider what circumstances we shall be in towards paying a debt of about fifty millions, which is a fourth part of the purchase of the whole island, if it were to be sold.

Towards clearing ourselves of this monstrous incumbrance, some of these annuities will expire or pay off the principal in thirty, forty, or an hundred years; the bulk of the debt must be lessened gradually by the best management we can, out of what will remain of the land and malt taxes, after paying guards and garrisons, and maintaining and supplying our fleet in the time of peace. I have not skill enough to compute what will be left after these necessary charges towards annually clearing so vast a debt, but believe it must be very little. However, it is plain that both these taxes must be continued, as well for supporting the government as because we have no other means for paying off the principal. And so likewise must all the other funds remain for paying the interest. How long a time this must require, how steady an administration, and how undisturbed a state of affairs both at home and abroad, let others determine.

However, some people think all this very reasonable, and that since the struggle hath been for peace and safety, posterity, who is to partake the benefit, ought to share in the expense; as if at the breaking out of this war there had been such a conjunction of affairs as never happened before, nor would ever happen again. 'Tis wonderful that our ancestors in all their wars, should never fall under such a necessity; that we meet no examples of it in Greece and Rome; that no other nation in Europe ever knew anything like it, except Spain about an hundred and twenty years ago, which they drew upon themselves by their own folly and have suffered for it ever since. No doubt we shall teach posterity wisdom, but they will be apt to think the purchase too dear, and I wish they may stand to the bargain we have made in their names.

'Tis easy to entail debts on succeeding ages and to hope they will be able and willing to pay them; but how to ensure peace for any term of years is difficult enough to apprehend. Will human nature ever cease to have the same passions, princes to entertain designs of interest or ambition, and occasions of quarrel to arise? May not we ourselves, by the variety of events and incidents which happen in the world, be under a necessity of recovering towns out of the very hands of those for whom we are now ruining our country to take them? Neither can it be said that those States with whom we may probably differ will be in as bad a condition as ourselves; for, by the circumstances of our situation, and the impositions of our allies, we are more exhausted than either they or the enemy; and by the nature of our government, the corruption of our manners, and the opposition of factions, we shall be more slow in recovering.

It will, no doubt, be a mighty comfort to our grandchildren when they see a few rags hang up in Westminster Hall, which cost an hundred millions whereof they are paying the arrears, and boasting, as beggars do, that their grandfathers were rich and great.

I have often reflected on that mistaken notion of credit, so boasted of by the advocates of the late ministry. Was not all that credit built upon funds raised by the landed men, whom they so much hate and despise? Are not the greatest part of those funds raised from the growth and product of land? Must not the whole debt be entirely paid and our fleets and garrisons be maintained, by the land and malt tax, after a peace? If they call it credit to run ten millions in debt without parliamentary security by which the public is defrauded of almost half, I must think such credit to be dangerous, illegal, and perhaps treasonable. Neither hath anything gone further to ruin the nation than their boasted credit. For my own part, when I saw this false credit sink upon the change of the ministry, I was singular enough to conceive it a good omen. It seemed as if the young extravagant heir had got a new steward and was resolved to look into his estate before things grew desperate, which made the usurers forbear feeding him with money, as they used to do.

Since the monied men are so fond of war, I should be glad they would furnish out one campaign at their own charge. It is not above six or seven millions; and I dare engage to make it out that when they have done this, instead of contributing equal to the landed men, they will have their full principal and interest at 6 *per cent.* remaining of all the money they ever lent to the government.

Without this resource, or some other equally miraculous, it is impossible for us to continue the war upon the same foot. I have already observed that the last funds of interest fell short above a million, though the persons most conversant in ways and means employed their utmost invention; so that of necessity we must be still more defective next campaign. But perhaps our allies will make up this deficiency on our side by greater efforts on their own. Quite the contrary. Both the emperor and Holland failed this year in several articles, and signified to us, some time ago, that they cannot keep up to the same proportions in the next. We have gained a noble barrier for the latter, and they have nothing more to demand or desire. The emperor, however sanguine he may now affect to appear, will I suppose be satisfied with Naples, Sicily, Milan, and his other acquisitions, rather than engage in a long hopeless war for the recovery of Spain, to which his allies the Dutch will neither give their assistance nor consent. So that since we have done their business, since they have no further service for our arms and we have no more money to give them; and lastly, since we neither desire any recompense nor expect any thanks, we ought in pity to be dismissed and have leave to shift for ourselves. They are ripe for a peace, to enjoy and cultivate what we have conquered for them; and so are we, to recover, if possible, the effects of their hardships upon us. The first overtures from France are made to England, upon safe and honourable terms. We who bore the burthen of the war ought in reason to have the greater share in making the peace. If we do not hearken to a peace, others certainly will, and get the advantage of us there as they have done in the war. We know the Dutch have perpetually threatened us that they would enter into separate measures of a peace; and by the strength of that argument, as well as by *other powerful motives*, prevailed on those who were then at the helm, to comply with them on any terms rather than put an end to a war, which every year brought them such great accessions to their wealth and power. Whoever falls off, a peace will follow; and then we must be content with such conditions as our allies out of their great concern for our safety and interest will please to choose. They have no further occasion for fighting; they have gained their point, and they now tell us, it is *our war*; so that in common justice, it ought to be *our peace*.

All we can propose, by the desperate steps of pawning our land or malt tax, or erecting a general excise, is only to raise a fund of interest for running us annually four millions further in debt, without any prospect of ending the war so well as we can do at present. And when we have sunk the only unengaged revenues we had left, our incumbrances must of necessity remain perpetual.

We have hitherto lived upon *expedients*, which in time will certainly destroy any constitution whether civil or natural; and there was no country in Christendom had less occasion for them than ours. We have dieted a healthy body into a consumption by plying it with physic instead of food. Art will help us no longer; and if we cannot recover by letting the remains of nature work, we must inevitably die.

What arts have been used to possess the people with a *strong delusion* that Britain must infallibly be ruined without the recovery of Spain to the House of Austria?—making the safety of a great and powerful kingdom, as ours was then, to depend upon an event which even after a war of miraculous successes proves impracticable; as if princes and great ministers could find no way of settling the public tranquillity, without changing the possessions of kingdoms and forcing sovereigns upon a people against their inclinations. Is there no security for the Island of Britain unless a King of Spain be dethroned by the hands of his grandfather? Has the enemy no cautionary towns and seaports to give us for securing trade? Can he not deliver us possession of such places as would put him in a worse condition whenever he should perfidiously renew the war? The present King of France has but few years to live° by the course of nature, and doubtless would desire to end his days in peace. Grandfathers in private families are not observed to have great influence on their grandsons, and I believe they have much less among princes. However, when the authority of a parent is gone, is it likely that Philip will be directed by a brother against his own interest and that of his subjects? Have not those two realms their separate maxims of policy which must operate in times of peace? These at least are probabilities, and cheaper by six millions a year than recovering Spain or continuing the war, both which seem absolutely impossible.

But the common question is, if we must now surrender Spain, what have we been fighting for all this while? The answer is ready. We have been fighting for the ruin of the public interest, and the advancement of a private. We have been fighting to raise the wealth and grandeur of a particular family; to enrich usurers and stockjobbers; and to cultivate the pernicious designs of a faction by destroying the landed interest. The nation begins now to think these *blessings* are not worth fighting for any longer, and therefore desires a peace.

But the advocates on the other side cry out that we might have had a better peace than is now in agitation, above two years ago. Supposing this to be true, I do assert that by parity of reason we must expect one just so much worse, about two years hence. If those in power could then have given us a better peace, more is their infamy and guilt that they did it not; why did they insist upon conditions which they were certain would never be granted? We allow it was in their power to have put a good end to the war and left the nation in some hope of recovering itself. And this is what we charge them with as answerable to God, their country, and posterity, that the bleeding condition of their fellow-subjects was a feather in the balance with their private ends.

When we offer to lament the heavy debts and poverty of the nation, 'tis pleasant to hear some men answer all that can be said, by crying up the power of England, the courage of England, the inexhaustible riches of England. I have heard a man very sanguine upon this subject, with a good employment for life and a hundred thousand pounds in the funds, bidding us 'take courage', and 'warranting, that all would go well'. This is the style of men at ease, *who lay heavy burthens upon others, which they will not touch with one of their fingers*.° I have known some people such ill computers as to imagine the many millions in stocks and annuities are so much real wealth in the nation; whereas every farthing of it is entirely lost to us, scattered in Holland, Germany, and Spain; and the landed men, who now pay the interest, must at last pay the principal.

FOURTHLY, those who are against any peace without Spain, have I doubt been ill informed as to the low condition of France, and the mighty consequences of our successes. As to the first, it must be confessed that after the battle of Ramillies° the French were so discouraged with their frequent losses, and so impatient for a peace that their king was resolved to comply on any reasonable terms. But when his subjects were informed of our exorbitant demands, they grew jealous of his honour and were unanimous to assist him in continuing the war at any hazard rather than submit. This fully restored his authority; and the supplies he hath received from the Spanish West Indies, which in all are computed since the war to amount to four hundred millions of livres (and all in specie), have enabled him to pay his troops. Besides, the money is spent in his own country; and he hath since waged war in the most thrifty manner by acting on the defensive, compounding with us every campaign for a town, which costs us fifty times more than it is worth either as to the value or the consequences. Then he is at no charge of a fleet further than providing privateers wherewith his subjects carry on a piratical war at their own expense, and he shares in the profit, which hath been very considerable to France, and of infinite disadvantage to us, not only by the perpetual losses we have suffered to an immense value, but by the general discouragement of trade on which we so much depend. All this considered, with the circumstances of that government where the prince is master of the lives and fortunes of so mighty a kingdom, shows that monarch to be not so sunk in his affairs as we have imagined and have long flattered ourselves with the hopes of. [For an absolute government may endure a long war, but it hath generally been ruinous to free countries.]

Those who are against *any peace without Spain* seem likewise to have been mistaken in judging our victories and other successes to have been of greater consequence than they really were.

When our armies take a town in Flanders, the Dutch are immediately put into *possession*, and we at home make *bonfires*. I have sometimes pitied the deluded people to see them squandering away their fuel to so little purpose. For example, what is it to us that Bouchain is taken, about which the warlike politicians of the coffee-house make such a clutter? What though the garrison surrendered prisoners of war, and in sight of the enemy? We are not now in a condition to be fed with points of honour. What advantage have we but that of spending three or four millions more to get another town for the States, which may open them a new country for *contributions*, and increase the perquisites of the g[enera]l?

In that war of ten years under the late King, when our commanders and soldiers were raw and unexperienced in comparison of what they are at present, we lost battles and towns, as well as we gained them of late, since those gentlemen have better learned their trade; yet we bore up then as the French do now. Nor was there any thing decisive in their successes: they grew weary as well as we, and at last consented to a peace under which we might have been happy enough if it had not been followed by that wise Treaty of Partition, which revived the flame that hath lasted ever since. I see nothing else in the modern way of making war, but that the side which can hold out longest, will end it with most advantage. In such a close country as Flanders where it is carried on by sieges, the army that acts offensively is at a much greater expense of men and money; and there is hardly a town taken in the common forms where the besiegers have not the worse of the bargain. I never yet knew a soldier who would not affirm that any town might be taken if you were content to be at the charge. If you will count upon sacrificing so much blood and treasure, the rest is all a regular, established method which cannot fail. When the King of France, in the times of his grandeur, sat down before a town, his generals and engineers would often fix the day when it should surrender. The enemy, sensible of all this, hath for some years past avoided a battle where he hath so ill succeeded, and taken a surer way to consume us by letting our courage evaporate against stones and rubbish, and sacrificing a single town to a campaign, which he can so much better afford to lose than we to take.

LASTLY, those who are so violent against *any* peace without Spain being restored to the House of Austria, have not I believe cast their eye upon a cloud gathering in the north, which we have helped to raise and may quickly break in a storm upon our heads.

The northern war hath been on foot almost ever since our breach with France. The success of it various; but one effect to be apprehended was always the same, that sooner or later it would involve us in its consequences and that, whenever this happened, let our success be never so great against France, from that moment France would have the advantage.

By our guarantee of the treaty of Travendal,° we were obliged to hinder the King of Denmark from engaging in a war with Sweden. It was at that time understood by all parties, and so declared, even by the British ministers, that this engagement specially regarded Denmark's not assisting King Augustus. But however, if this had not been so, yet our obligation to Sweden stood in force by virtue of former treaties with that crown, which were all revived and confirmed by a subsequent one concluded at the Hague by Sir Joseph Williamson and Monsieur Lilienroot,° about the latter end of the late King's reign.

However, the war in the north proceeded, and our not assisting Sweden was at least as well excused by the war which we were entangled in, as his not contributing his contingent to the empire whereof he is a member was excused by the pressures he lay under, having a confederacy to deal with.

In this war the King of Sweden was victorious, and what dangers were we not then exposed to? What fears were we not in? He marched into Saxony, and if he had really been in the French interest, might at once have put us under the greatest difficulties. But the torrent turned another way and he contented himself with imposing on his enemy the treaty of Alt Rastadt;° by which King Augustus makes an absolute cession of the crown of Poland, renounces any title to it, acknowledges Stanislaus, and then both he and the King of Sweden join in desiring the guarantee of England and Holland. The Q[uee]n did, indeed, not give this guarantee in form; but as a step towards it, the title of King was given to Stanislaus by a letter from Her Majesty; and the strongest assurances were given to the Swedish minister, in Her Majesty's name and in a committee of council, that the guarantee should speedily be granted; and that in the meanwhile, it was the same thing as if the forms were passed.

In 1708, King Augustus made the campaign in Flanders; what measures he might at that time take, or of what nature the arguments might be that he made use of, is not known. But immediately after, he breaks through all he had done, marches into Poland, and reassumes the crown.

After this we apprehended that the peace of the empire might be endangered; and therefore entered into an act of guarantee for the neutrality of it. The King of Sweden refused upon several accounts to submit to the terms of this treaty; particularly, because we went out of the empire to cover Poland and Jutland but did not go out of it to cover the territories of Sweden.

Let us therefore consider what is our case at present. If the King of Sweden returns° and gets the better, he will think himself under no obligation of having any regard to the interests of the allies; but will naturally pursue, according to his own expression, 'his enemy, wherever he finds him'. In this case the corps of the neutrality is obliged to oppose him, and so we are engaged in a second way before the first is ended.

If the northern confederates succeed against Sweden, how shall we be able to preserve the balance of power in the north so essential to our trade, as well as in many other respects? What will become of that great support of the *Protestant interest* in Germany, which is the footing that the Swedes now have in the empire? Or, who shall answer that these princes, after they have settled the north to their minds, may not take a fancy to look southward and make our peace with France according to their own schemes?

And lastly, if the King of Prussia, the Elector of Hanover, and other princes whose dominions lie contiguous, are forced to draw from those armies which act against France, we must live in hourly expectation of having those troops recalled which they now leave with us; and this recall may happen in the midst of a siege or on the eve of a battle. Is it therefore our interest to toil on in a ruinous war for an impracticable end till one of these cases shall happen, or to get under shelter before the storm?

There is no doubt but the present ministry (provided they could get over the obligations of honour and conscience) might find their advantage in advising the continuance of the war, as well as the last did though not in the same degree, after the kingdom has been so much exhausted. They might prolong it till the parliament desire a peace; and in the mean time leave them in full possession of power. Therefore it is plain that their proceedings at present are meant to serve their country, directly against their private interest, whatever clamour may be raised by those who for the vilest ends would remove heaven and earth to oppose their measures. But they think it infinitely better to accept such terms as will secure our trade, find a sufficient barrier for the States, give *reasonable satisfaction* to the emperor, and restore the tranquillity of

Europe, though without adding Spain to the empire: rather than go on in a languishing way upon the vain expectation of some improbable turn for the recovery of that monarchy out of the Bourbon family; and at last be forced to a worse peace, by some of the allies falling off, upon our utter inability to continue the war.

POSTSCRIPT:

[to the Fourth Edition.]

I have in this edition° explained three or four lines in the thirty-eighth page, which mentions the *succession*, to take off, if possible, all manner of cavil; though, at the same time, I cannot but observe how ready the adverse party is to make use of any objections, even such as destroy their own principles. I put a distant case of the possibility that our *succession*, through extreme necessity, might be changed by the legislature in future ages; and it is pleasant to hear those people quarrelling at this, who profess themselves for changing it as often as they please and that even without the consent of the entire legislature.

[The reading (on p. 297) of the first three editions, 'how much soever the necessities of the kingdom may require it', was altered in the fourth edition to 'however our posterity may hereafter, by the tyranny and oppression of succeeding princes, be reduced to the fatal necessity of breaking in upon the excellent and happy settlement now in force'.]

Dunkirk *to be Let*, Or, *A Town Ready Furnish'd*

WITH

A Hue-and-Cry after Dismal

Being a full and true Account, how a Whig *Lord was taken at* Dunkirk, *in the Habit of a Chimney-Sweeper, and carryed before General* Hill. *To which is added the Copy of a* PAPER *that was found in his Pocket.*

WE have an old Saying, *That it is better to play at a small Game than to stand out*: And it seems, the Whigs practise accordingly, there being nothing so little or so base, that they will not attempt, to recover their Power. On Wednesday Morning the 9th Instant, we are certainly informed, that Collonell Killegrew (who went to France with Generall Hill) walking in Dunkirk Streets met a Tall Chimney-Sweeper, with his Brooms and Poles, and a Bunch of Holly upon his Shoulders, who was followed by another of a shorter Size. The Tall Fellow cry'd in the French Language (which the Collonel understands) *Sweep, Sweep*; The Collonell thought he knew the Voice, and that the Tone of it was like one of your fine Speakers. This made him follow the Chimney-Sweeper, and examine nicely his Shape and Countenance. Besides, he conceived also that the Chimney-Sweeper's Man was not altogether unknown to him, so the Collonel went to wait on the Generall who is Governor of Dunkirk for Her Majesty, and told his Honor, that he had a strong Suspicion that he had seen Dismal in the Streets of Dunkirk. (Now you must know, that our Courtiers call a certain great Whig Lord by the Name of Dismal; belike, by reason of his Dark and Dismal Countenance). This is impossible sure, said the Governor. I am confident of it said the Collonel; nay, and what is more, the Fellow that followed him was Mr. *Squash*,° tho' the Master was as black as his Man; and if your Honor pleases, I will bring them both to you immediately, for I observed the House they went in. So, away went the Collonel with a File of Musquiteers, and found them both in an Ale-house, that was kept by a Dutch-man. He could see nothing of the Master, but a Leg upon each Hobb, the rest of the Body being out of sight; the Collonel ordered him to come down, which he did, with a great deal of Soot after him. Master and Man were immediately conducted through the Town, with a great Mob at their Heels to the Governor's Castle, where his Honor was sitting in a Chair, with his English and French Nobles about him.

It is said, that he had the following Verses found in his Pocket, which he scatter'd up and down the Town.

> *Old* Lewis *thus the Terms of Peace to Burnish,*
> *Has lately let out* Dunkirk *Ready Furnish'd;*
> *But whether 'tis by* Lease, *or* Coppy-hold,
> *Or* Tenure in Capite, *we've not been told:*
> *But this we hope, if yet he pulls his Horns in,*
> *He'll be obliged to give his Tenants Warning.*

The Governor with a stern Countenance asked the tall Man who he was! He answered he was a Savoyard (for beyond Sea, all the Chimney-Sweepers came from Savoy, a great Town in Italy) and he spoke a sort of Gibberish like broken French. But the French Mounseers that were by, assured the Governor, he could be no French-man, no nor Savoyard neither. So then the Governor spoke to him in English, said there was Witnesses ready to prove, that under pretence of sweeping Chimnyes cheaper than other People, he endeavored to persuade the Townsfolks not to let the English come into the Town, and how as that he should say, that the English would cut all the French-mens Throats, and that his Honor believed he was no Chimny-Sweeper, but some Whiggish English Traitor.

The Governor then gave Command, that both of them should be washed in his Presence by two of his Guards. And first they began with the Man, and spent a whole Pail-full of Water in vain: They then used Soap and Suds, but all to no Purpose; at last they found he was a Black-a-more, and that they had been acting the Labor-in-vain. Then the Collonel whispered the Governor, your Honor may plainly see that this is *Squash.* (Now you must know, that *Squash* is the Name of a Blackamore that waits upon the Lord whom the Courtiers call **Dismal**). Then with a fresh Pail they began to wash the Master; but for a while, all their Scrubbing did no good, so that they thought he was a Black-a-moor too. At last they perceived some dawning of a dark sallow Brown, and the Governor immediately knew it was the Lord **Dismal**, which the other, after some shuffling Excuses, confessed. Then the Governor said, *I am very sorry to see your Lordship in such a Condition, but you are Her Majesty's Prisoner, and I will send you immediately to England, where the Queen my Liege may dispose of you according to Her Royal Pleasure.* Then his Honor ordered new Cloaths to be made both for Master and Man, and sent them on Shipboard: From whence in a few Hours they landed in England.

IT is observed, that the Lord's Face, which at best is very Black and Swarthy, hath been much darker ever since, and all the Beauty-washes he uses, it is thought will never be able to restore it. Which wise Men reckon to be a just Judgement on him for his late Apostacy.

The Seventh
EPISTLE
Of the first Book of
HORACE
Imitated.

And Addressed to a Noble Lord.

Harley, the nation's great support,
Returning home one day from court,
(His mind with public cares possest,
All Europe's business in his breast)
Observed a *parson* near Whitehall,
Cheap'ning *old* authors on a stall.
The priest was pretty well in case,
And show'd some humour in his face;
Look'd with an easy, careless mien,
A perfect stranger to the spleen;   10
Of size that might a pulpit fill,
But more inclining to sit still.
My lord (who, as a man may say't,
Loves mischief better than his meat)
Was now dispos'd to crack a jest,
And bid friend Lewis go in quest
(This Lewis was a cunning shaver,
And very much in Harley's favour)—
In quest who might this *parson* be,
What was his name, of what degree;   20
If possible, to learn his story,
And whether he were *Whig* or *Tory*.

  Lewis his patron's humour knows;
Away upon his errand goes,
And quickly did the matter sift;
Found out that it was Doctor Swift,
A clergyman of special note
For shunning those of his own coat;
Which made his brethren of the gown
Take care betimes to run him down: 30
No libertine, nor over-nice,

Addicted to no sort of vice;
Went where he pleas'd, said what he thought;
Not rich, but owed no man a groat;
In state opinions *à la mode*,
But hated Wharton like a toad;
Had giv'n the *Faction* many a wound,°
And libell'd all the *Junto* round;°
Kept company with men of wit,
Who often father'd what he writ: 40
His works were hawk'd in ev'ry street,
But seldom rose above a sheet:
Of late, indeed, the paper-*stamp*°
Did very much his genius cramp;
And, since he could not spend his fire,
Is now contented to retire.
   Said Harley, 'I desire to know
From his own mouth, if this be so:
Step to the doctor straight, and say,
I'd have him dine with me today.'   50
Swift seem'd to wonder what he meant,
Nor could believe my lord had sent;
So never offer'd once to stir,
But coldly said, 'Your servant, sir.'
'Does he refuse me?' Harley cry'd.
'He does; with insolence and pride.'
   Some few days after, Harley spies
The doctor fasten'd by the eyes
At Charing Cross, among the rout,
Where painted monsters are hung out: 60
He pull'd the string, and stopt the coach,
Beck'ning the doctor to approach.
Swift, who would neither fly nor hide,
Came sneaking by the chariot's side,
And offer'd many a lame excuse:
He never meant the least abuse—
'My lord—the honour you design'd—
Extremely proud—but I had dined—
I am sure I never should neglect—
No man alive has more respect'—   70
'Well, I shall think of that no more,
If you'll be sure to come at *four*.'

    The doctor now obeys the summons,
Likes both his company and commons;
Displays his talent, sits till ten;
Next day invited, comes again;
Soon grows domestic, seldom fails,
Either at morning or at meals;
Came early, and departed late;
In short, the gudgeon took the bait.   80
My lord would carry on the jest,
And down to WINDSOR takes his guest.
Swift much admires the place and air,
And longs to be a *Canon* there;
In summer round the Park to ride,
In winter—never to reside.
'A *Canon*!—that's a place too mean:
No, doctor, you shall be a *Dean*;
Two dozen *canons* round your stall,
And you the tyrant o'er them all: 90
You need but cross the Irish seas,
To live in plenty, power, and ease.'
Poor Swift departed, and, what's worse,
With borrow'd money in his purse,°
Travels at least a hundred leagues,
And suffers numberless fatigues.

    Suppose him now a *Dean* complete,
Devoutly lolling in his seat,
And silver verge, with decent pride,°
Stuck underneath his cushion side.   100
Suppose him gone through all vexations,
Patents, Instalments, Abjurations,
First-fruits, and Tenths, and Chapter-treats;
Dues, Payments, Fees, Demands, and 'Cheats°
(The wicked *laity's* contriving
To hinder clergymen from thriving).
Now all the doctor's money's spent,
His tenants wrong him in his rent,
The farmers, spitefully combin'd,
Force him to take his tithes in kind,   110
And Parvisol* discounts arrears,
By bills, for taxes and repairs.

           * The Doctor's Proctor.

Poor Swift, with all his losses vex'd,
Not knowing where to turn him next,
Above a thousand pounds in debt,
Takes horse, and in a mighty fret
Rides day and night at such a rate,
He soon arrives at Harley's gate;
But was so dirty, pale and thin,
Old Read* would hardly let him in.°   120

   Said Harley, 'Welcome, rev'rend Dean!
What makes your worship look so lean?
Why, sure you won't appear in town
In that old wig and rusty gown!
I doubt your heart is set on pelf
So much that you neglect yourself.
What! I suppose, now stocks are high,
You've some good purchase in your eye?
Or is your money out at use?'—

   'Truce, good my lord, I beg a truce!'   130
The doctor in a passion cried,
'Your raillery is misapplied;
I have experience dearly bought;
You know I am not worth a groat:
But you're resolved to have your jest,
And 'twas a folly to contest.
Then, since you now have done your worst,
Pray leave me where you found me first.'

        * The porter.

Cadenus and Vanessa

The *shepherds* and the *nymphs* were seen
Pleading before the Cyprian queen:°
The counsel for the fair began,
Accusing that false creature, *Man*.
The brief with weighty crimes was charged
On which the pleader much enlarged;
That, Cupid now has lost his art,
Or blunts the point of ev'ry dart;
His altar now no longer smokes,°
His mother's aid no youth invokes: 10
This tempts free-thinkers to refine,
And bring in doubt their pow'r divine;
Now, love is dwindled to intrigue,
And marriage grown a money-league;
Which crimes aforesaid (*with her leave*)
Were (*as he humbly did conceive*)
Against our sov'reign lady's peace,
Against the statutes in that case,
Against her dignity and crown:°
Then pray'd an answer, and sat down.   20
   The *nymphs* with scorn beheld their foes;
When the defendant's counsel rose,
And, what no lawyer ever lack'd,
With impudence own'd all the fact;
But, what the gentlest heart would vex,
Laid all the fault on t'other sex.
That, modern love is no such thing
As what those ancient poets sing:
A fire celestial, chaste, refined,
Conceived and kindled in the mind;   30
Which, having found an equal flame,
Unites, and both become the same:
In diff'rent breasts together burn,
Together both to ashes turn.
But women now feel no such fire,
And only know the gross desire.
Their passions move in lower spheres,
Where'er caprice or folly steers:

A dog, a parrot, or an ape,
(Or a worse brute in human shape)   40
Engross the fancies of the fair,
The few soft moments they can spare
From visits to receive and pay,
From scandal, politics, and play;
From fans, and flounces, and brocades,
From equipage and park parades,°
From all the thousand female toys,
From ev'ry trifle that employs
The out or in-side of their heads,
Between their toilets and their beds.   50
  In a dull stream, which moving slow,
You hardly see the current flow;
If a small breeze obstructs the course,
It whirls about for want of force,
And in its narrow circle gathers
Nothing but chaff and straws, and feathers.
The current of a female's mind
Stops thus, and turns with ev'ry wind:
Thus whirling round, together draws
Fools, fops, and rakes, for chaff and straws.   60
Hence we conclude, no women's hearts
Are won by virtue, wit, and parts:
Nor are the men of sense to blame
For breasts uncapable of flame;
The fault must on the *nymphs* be plac'd,
Grown so corrupted in their taste.
  The pleader having spoke his best,
Had witness ready to attest,
Who fairly could on oath depose
When questions on the fact arose,   70
That ev'ry article was true;
Nor further those deponents knew.
Therefore he humbly would insist,
The bill might be with costs dismiss'd.
  The cause appear'd of so much weight
That Venus, from her judgment seat,
Desired them not to talk so loud,
Else she must interpose a cloud:
For if the heav'nly folks should know

These pleadings in the courts below,   80
That mortals here disdain to love,
She ne'er could show her face above;
For gods, their betters, are too wise
To value that which men despise.
And then, said she, my son and I
Must stroll in air 'twixt land and sky;
Or else, shut out from heav'n and earth,
Fly to the sea, my place of birth:
There live with daggled *mermaids* pent,
And keep on fish perpetual *Lent*.   90

    But since the case appear'd so nice,
She thought it best to take advice.
The Muses, by their king's permission,°
Though foes to love, attend the session,
And on the right hand took their places
In order; on the left, the Graces:°
To whom she might her doubts propose
On all emergencies that rose.
The Muses oft were seen to frown;
The Graces, half ashamed, look'd down;   100
And 'twas observed, there were but few ⎫
Of either sex, among the crew,   ⎬
Whom she or her assessors knew.   ⎭
The goddess soon began to see
Things were not ripe for a decree;
And said, she must consult her books,
The lovers' Fletas, Bractons, Cokes.°
First to a dapper clerk she beckon'd
To turn to Ovid, Book the Second:°
She then referr'd them to a place   110
In Virgil (*vide* Dido's case):°
As for Tibullus's Reports,°
They never pass'd for law in courts:
For Cowley's briefs, and pleas of Waller,°
Still their authority was smaller.

    There was on both sides much to say:
She'd hear the Cause another day;
And so she did, and then a third;
She heard it—there she kept her word.
But, with rejoinders or replies,   120

Long bills, and answers stuff'd with lies,
Demur, imparlance, and essoign,°
The parties ne'er could issue join:
For sixteen years the cause was spun,
And then stood where it first begun.
  —Now, gentle Clio, sing or say°
What Venus meant by this delay.
The goddess, much perplex'd in mind
To see her empire thus declin'd,
When first this grand debate arose   130
Above her wisdom to compose,
Conceived a project in her head
To work her ends; which, if it sped,
Would show the merits of the cause
Far better than consulting laws.
  In a glad hour Lucina's aid°
Produced on earth a wondrous maid,
On whom the Queen of Love was bent
To try a new experiment.
She threw her law-books on the shelf,   140
And thus debated with herself.
  'Since men allege they ne'er can find
Those beauties in a female mind,
Which raise a flame that will endure
For ever uncorrupt and pure;
If 'tis with reason they complain,
This infant shall restore my reign.
I'll search where ev'ry virtue dwells,
From courts inclusive down to cells:
What preachers talk, or sages write—   150
These will I gather and unite,
And represent them to mankind
Collected in that infant's mind.'
  This said, she plucks from Heaven's high bow'rs
A sprig of amaranthine flow'rs.
In nectar thrice infuses bays,
Three times refined in Titan's rays;
Then calls the Graces to her aid,
And sprinkles thrice the newborn maid:
From whence the tender skin assumes   160
A sweetness above all perfumes;

From whence a cleanliness remains,
Incapable of outward stains;
From whence that decency of mind,
So lovely in the female kind,
Where not a careless thought intrudes
Less modest than the speech of prudes,
Where never blush was call'd in aid,
That spurious virtue in a maid
(A virtue but at second-hand;   170
They blush because they understand).

   The Graces next would act their part,
And show'd but little of their art;
Their work was half already done,
The child with native beauty shone;
The outward form no help required:
Each, breathing on her thrice, inspired
That gentle, soft, engaging air,
Which in old times adorn'd the fair,
And said, 'Vanessa be the name   180
By which thou shalt be known to fame;
Vanessa, by the gods enroll'd:
Her name on earth—shall not be told.'

   But still the work was not complete,
When Venus thought on a deceit:
Drawn by her doves, away she flies
And finds out Pallas in the skies.°
'Dear Pallas, I have been this morn
To see a lovely infant born:
A boy in yonder isle below,   190
So like my own, without his bow;
By beauty could your heart be won,
You'd swear it is Apollo's son.
But it shall ne'er be said, a child
So hopeful, has by me been spoil'd;
I have enough besides to spare,
And give him wholly to your care.'

   Wisdom's above suspecting wiles;
The Queen of Learning gravely smiles,
Down from Olympus comes with joy,   200
Mistakes Vanessa for a boy;
Then sows within her tender mind

Seeds long unknown to womankind:
For manly bosoms chiefly fit,
The seeds of knowledge, judgment, wit.
Her soul was suddenly endu'd
With justice, truth, and fortitude;
With honour, which no breath can stain,
Which malice must attack in vain;
With open heart and bounteous hand.   210
But Pallas here was at a stand;
She knew, in our degen'rate days
Bare virtue could not live on praise;
That meat must be with money bought.
She therefore, upon second thought,
Infused, yet as it were by stealth,
Some small regard for state and wealth
(Of which, as she grew up, there stayed
A tincture in the prudent maid:
She managed her estate with care,   220
Yet liked three footmen to her chair);
But, lest he should neglect his studies
Like a young heir, the thrifty goddess
(For fear young master should be spoil'd)
Would use him like a younger child;
And, after long computing, found
'Twould come to just five thousand pound.
    The Queen of Love was pleased and proud
To see Vanessa thus endow'd:
She doubted not but such a dame   230
Through ev'ry breast would dart a flame;
That ev'ry rich and lordly swain
With pride would drag about her chain;
That scholars would forsake their books
To study bright Vanessa's looks;
As she advanced, that womankind
Would by her model form their mind,
And all their conduct should be tried
By her, as an unerring guide;
Offending daughters oft would hear   240
Vanessa's praise rung in their ear:
Miss Betty, when she does a fault,
Lets fall her knife, or spills the salt,

Will thus be by her mother chid,
' 'Tis what Vanessa never did!'
Thus by the nymphs and swains adored,
My pow'r shall be again restored,
And happy lovers bless my reign—
So Venus hoped, but hoped in vain.

 For when in time the Martial Maid   250
Found out the trick that Venus play'd,
She shakes her helm, she knits her brows,
And, fired with indignation, vows,
Tomorrow ere the setting sun,
She'd all undo that she had done.

 But gods, we are by poets taught,
Must stand to what themselves have wrought.
For in their old records we find
A *wholesome law*, time out of mind,
Confirmed long since by Fate's decree,   260
That gods, of whatsoe'er degree,
Resume not what themselves have giv'n,
Or any brother god in Heav'n:
Which keeps the peace among the gods,
Else they must always be at odds:
And Pallas, if she broke the laws,
Must yield her foe the stronger cause;
A shame to one so much ador'd
For wisdom at Jove's council board.
Besides, she fear'd the Queen of Love   270
Would meet with better friends above.
And though she must with grief reflect,
To see a mortal virgin deck'd
With graces hitherto unknown
To female breasts, except her own;
Yet she would act as best became
A goddess of unspotted fame.
She knew, by augury divine,
Venus would fail in her design:
She studied well the point, and found   280
Her foe's conclusions were not sound,
From premisses erroneous brought,
And therefore the deduction's naught;
And must have contrary effects

To what her treach'rous foe expects.
   In proper season Pallas meets
The Queen of Love, whom thus she greets,
(For gods, we are by Homer told,
Can in celestial language scold)—
'Perfidious goddess! but in vain 290
You form'd this project in your brain;
A project for thy talents fit,
With much deceit and little wit.
Thou hast, as thou shalt quickly see,
Deceived thyself, instead of me;
For how can heav'nly wisdom prove
An instrument to earthly love?
Knows't thou not yet, that men commence
Thy votaries for want of sense?
Nor shall Vanessa be the theme 300
To manage thy abortive scheme:
She'll prove the greatest of thy foes;
And yet I scorn to interpose,
But, using neither skill nor force,
Leave all things to their nat'ral course.'
   The goddess thus pronounced her doom,
When, lo! Vanessa in her bloom
Advanced, like Atalanta's star,°
But rarely seen, and seen from far:
In a new world with caution stepped, 310
Watch'd all the company she kept,
Well knowing, from the books she read,
What dang'rous paths young virgins tread:
Would seldom at the Park appear,
Nor saw the playhouse twice a year;
Yet, not uncurious, was inclin'd
To know the converse of mankind.
   First issued from perfumers' shops
A crowd of fashionable fops:
They ask'd her how she liked the play, 320
Then told the tattle of the day:
A duel fought last night at two,
About a lady—you know who;
Talk'd of a new Italian, come°
Either from Muscovy or Rome;

Gave hints of who and who's together;
Then fell to talking of the weather,
'Last night was so extremely fine,
The ladies walk'd till after nine.'
Then, in soft voice and speech absurd,   330
With nonsense ev'ry second word,
With fustian from exploded plays,
They celebrate her beauty's praise;
Run o'er their cant of stupid lies,
And tell the murders of her eyes.
　　With silent scorn Vanessa sat,
Scarce list'ning to their idle chat;
Further than sometimes by a frown,
When they grew pert, to pull them down.
At last she spitefully was bent   340
To try their wisdom's full extent;
And said, she valued nothing less
Than titles, figure, shape and dress;
That, merit should be chiefly placed
In judgment, knowledge, wit, and taste;
And these, she offer'd to dispute,
Alone distinguished man from brute:
With her a wealthy fool could pass
At best, but for a golden ass.
That present times have no pretence   350
To virtue, in the noblest sense
By Greeks and Romans understood,
To perish for our country's good.
She named the ancient heroes round,
Explain'd for what they were renown'd;
Then spoke with censure or applause
Of foreign customs, rites, and laws;
Through nature and through art she ranged
And gracefully her subjects changed;
In vain! her hearers had no share   360
In all she spoke, except to stare.
Their judgment was, upon the whole,
'That lady is the dullest soul!'
Then tipt their foreheads in a jeer,
As who should say—'She wants it here!
She may be handsome, young, and rich,

But none will burn her for a witch!'°
   A party next, of glitt'ring dames
From round the purlieus of St. James,°
Came early, out of pure good will,   370
To see the girl in deshabille.
Their clamour, 'lighting from their chairs,
Grew louder all the way up stairs;
At entrance loudest, where they found
The room with volumes litter'd round:
Vanessa held Montaigne, and read,
While Mrs. Susan comb'd her head.
They call'd for tea and chocolate,
And fell into their usual chat,
Discoursing with important face,   380
On ribbons, fans, and gloves and lace;
Show'd patterns just from India brought,
And gravely ask'd her what she thought:
Whether the red or green were best,
And what they cost. Vanessa guess'd
As came into her fancy first,
Named half the rates, and liked the worst.
To scandal next—'What awkward thing
Was that, last Sunday in the Ring?'°
'I'm sorry Mopsa breaks so fast: 390
I said her face would never last.'
'Corinna, with that youthful air,
Is thirty, and a bit to spare:
Her fondness for a certain earl
Began when I was but a girl!'
'Phyllis, who but a month ago
Was married to the Tunbridge beau,°
I saw coquetting t'other night
In public with that odious knight!'
   They rallied next Vanessa's dress: 400
'That gown was made for old Queen Bess.'
'Dear madam, let me see your head:
Don't you intend to put on red?'
'A petticoat without a hoop!
Sure, you're not ashamed to stoop!
With handsome garters at your knees,
No matter what a fellow sees.'

Fill'd with disdain, with rage inflamed,
Both of herself and sex ashamed,
The nymph stood silent out of spite,   410
Nor would vouchsafe to set them right.
Away the fair detractors went,
And gave by turns their censures vent:
'She's not so handsome in my eyes;
For wit, I wonder where it lies?
She's fair and clean, and that's the most,
But why proclaim her for a toast?'
'A baby-face; no life, no airs,
But what she learn'd at country fairs;
Scarce knows what diff'rence is between   420
Rich Flanders lace and Colberteen.'
'I'd undertake, my little Nancy
In flounces has a better fancy.
With all her wit, I would not ask
Her judgment how to buy a mask.'
'We begg'd her but to patch her face,°
She never hit one proper place;
Which ev'ry girl at five years old
Can do as soon as she is told.'
'I own, that out-of-fashion stuff   430
Becomes the *creature* well enough.
The girl might pass, if we could get her
To know the world a little better.'
('To know the world'! a modern phrase
For visits, ombre, balls, and plays.)
    Thus, to the world's perpetual shame,
The Queen of Beauty lost her aim;
Too late with grief she understood
Pallas had done more harm than good;
For great examples are in vain,   440
Where ignorance begets disdain.
Both sexes, arm'd with guilt and spite,
Against Vanessa's pow'r unite:
To copy her, few nymphs aspired,
Her virtues fewer swains admired.
So stars, beyond a certain height,
Give mortals neither heat nor light.
    Yet some of either sex, endow'd

With gifts superior to the crowd,
With virtue, knowledge, taste and wit,   450
She condescended to admit:
With pleasing art she could reduce
Men's talents to their proper use;
And with address each genius held
To that wherein it most excell'd;
Thus, making others' wisdom known,
Could please them, and improve her own.
A modest youth said something new;
She placed it in the strongest view.
All humble worth she strove to raise,   460
Would not be praised, yet loved to praise.
The learned met with free approach,
Although they came not in a coach:
Some clergy too she would allow,
Nor quarrell'd at their awkward bow;
But this was for Cadenus' sake,°
A gownman of a diff'rent make;
Whom Pallas, once Vanessa's tutor,
Had fix'd on for her coadjutor.

But Cupid, full of mischief, longs   470
To vindicate his mother's wrongs.
On Pallas all attempts are vain.
One way he knows to give her pain:
Vows on Vanessa's heart to take
Due vengeance, for her patron's sake.
Those early seeds by Venus sown,
In spite of Pallas now were grown;
And Cupid hoped they would improve
By time, and ripen into love.
The boy made use of all his craft,   480
In vain discharging many a shaft,
Pointed with col'nels, lords, and beaus:
Cadenus warded off the blows.
For, placing still some book betwixt,
The darts were in the cover fix'd,
Or, often blunted and recoil'd,
On Plutarch's *Morals* struck, were spoil'd.°
The Queen of Wisdom could foresee,
But not prevent, the Fates' decree:

And human caution tries in vain   490
To break that adamantine chain.
Vanessa, though by Pallas taught,
By Love invulnerable thought,
Searching in books for wisdom's aid,
Was, in the very search, betray'd.
   Cupid, though all his darts were lost,
Yet still resolv'd to spare no cost:
He could not answer to his fame
The triumphs of that stubborn dame,
A nymph so hard to be subdued,   500
Who neither was coquette nor prude.
I find, said he, she wants a Doctor,
Both to adore her and instruct her:
I'll give her what she most admires
Among those venerable sires.
Cadenus is a subject fit,
Grown old in politics and wit;
Caress'd by ministers of state,
Of half mankind the dread or hate.
Whate'er vexations love attend,   510
She need no rivals apprehend.
Her sex, with universal voice,
Must laugh at her capricious choice.
   Cadenus many things had writ:
Vanessa much esteem'd his wit,
And call'd for his *Poetic Works*:
Meantime the boy in secret lurks;
And while the book was in her hand,
The urchin from his private stand
Took aim, and shot with all his strength   520
A dart of such prodigious length,
It pierced the feeble volume through
And deep transfix'd her bosom too.
Some lines, more moving than the rest,
Stuck to the point that pierced her breast,
And, borne directly to her heart,
With pains unknown increased the smart.
   Vanessa, not in years a score,
Doats on a gown of forty-four;
Imaginary charms can find   530

In eyes with reading almost blind:
Cadenus now no more appears
Declined in health, advanc'd in years.
She fancies music in his tongue;
Nor further looks, but thinks him young.
What mariner is not afraid
To venture in a ship decay'd?
What planter will attempt to yoke
A saplin with a falling oak?
As years increase, she brighter shines; 540
Cadenus with each day declines:
And he must fall a prey to time,
While she continues in her prime.
　　Strange, that a nymph by Pallas nursed,
In love should make advances first.
Cadenus, common forms apart,
In ev'ry scene had kept his heart;
Had sigh'd and languished, vow'd, and writ,
For pastime, or to show his wit,
But time, and books, and state affairs 550
Had spoil'd his fashionable airs:
He now could praise, esteem, approve,
But understood not what was love.
His conduct might have made him styled
A father, and the nymph his child.
That innocent delight he took
To see the virgin mind her book,
Was but a master's secret joy
In schools to hear the finest boy.
Her knowledge with her fancy grew; 560
She hourly press'd for something new;
Ideas came into her mind
So fast, his lessons lagg'd behind;
She reason'd without plodding long,
Nor ever gave her judgment wrong.
　　But now a sudden change was wrought;
She minds no longer what he taught.
She wished her tutor were her lover;
Resolved she would her flame discover.
And when Cadenus would expound 570
Some notion subtle or profound,

The nymph would gently press his hand
As if she seemed to understand;
Or dext'rously dissembling chance,
Would sigh and steal a secret glance.
   Cadenus was amazed to find
Such marks of a distracted mind:
For, though she seem'd to listen more
To all he spoke, then e'er before,
He found her thoughts would absent range,   580
Yet guess'd not whence could spring the change.
And first he modestly conjectures
His pupil might be tired with lectures;
Which help'd to mortify his pride,
Yet gave him not the heart to chide.
But in a mild dejected strain,
At last he ventured to complain:
Said, she should be no longer teased,
Might have her freedom when she pleased;
Was now convinced he acted wrong   590
To hide her from the world so long,
And in dull studies to engage
One of her tender sex and age;
That ev'ry nymph with envy own'd
How she might shine in the *grand monde*:
And ev'ry shepherd was undone
To see her cloister'd like a nun.
His was a visionary scheme:
He waked, and found it but a dream;
A project far above his skill,   600
For Nature must be Nature still.
If he was bolder than became
A scholar to a courtly dame,
She might excuse a man of letters;
Thus tutors often treat their betters;
But since his talk offensive grew,
He came to take his last adieu.
   Vanessa, fill'd with just disdain,
Would still her dignity maintain,
Instructed from her early years   610
To scorn the art of female tears.
   Had he employ'd his time so long

To teach her what was right and wrong,
Yet could such notions entertain
That all his lectures were in vain?
She own'd the wand'ring of her thoughts;
But he must answer for her faults.
She well remember'd to her cost,
That all his lessons were not lost.
Two maxims she could still produce,   620
And sad experience taught their use:
That virtue, pleased with being shown,
Knows nothing which it dares not own,
Can make us without fear disclose
Our inmost secrets to our foes;
That common forms were not design'd
Directors to a noble mind.
'Now', said the nymph, 'to let you see
My actions with your rules agree;
That I can vulgar forms despise,   630
And have no secrets to disguise;
I'll fully prove your maxims true
By owning here my love for you.
I knew, by what you said and writ,
How dangerous things were men of wit;
You caution'd me against their charms,
But never gave me equal arms;
Your lessons found the weakest part,
Aim'd at the head, but reach'd the heart.'
   Cadenus felt within him rise   640
Shame, disappointment, grief, surprise.
He knew not how to reconcile
Such language, with her usual style:
And yet her words were so expressed,
He could not hope she spoke in jest.
His thoughts had wholly been confined
To form and cultivate her mind.
He hardly knew, till he was told,
Whether the nymph were young or old;
Had met her in a public place   650
Without distinguishing her face;
Much less should his declining age
Vanessa's earliest thoughts engage;

And, if her youth indiff'rence met,
His person must contempt beget;
Or, grant her passion be sincere,
How shall his innocence be clear?
Appearances were all so strong,
The world must think him in the wrong;
Would say, he made a treach'rous use   660
Of wit, to flatter and seduce;
The town would swear he had betray'd
By magic spells the harmless maid:
And ev'ry beau would have his jokes,
That scholars were like other folks;
That, when Platonic heights were over,
The tutor turn'd a mortal lover.
So tender of the young and fair!
It show'd a true paternal care—
'Five thousand guineas in her purse?   670
The doctor might have fancied worse.'

    Hardly at length he silence broke,
And falter'd every word he spoke;
Interpreting her complaisance,
Just like a man *sans consequence*.
She rallied well, he always knew:
Her manner now was something new;
And what she spoke was in an air
As serious as a tragic player.
But those who aim at ridicule   680
Should fix upon some certain rule
Which fairly hints they are in jest,
Else he must enter his protest.
For let a man be ne'er so wise,
He may be caught with sober lies;
A science which he never taught,
And, to be free, was dearly bought;
For, take it in its proper light,
'Tis just what coxcombs call *a bite*.

    But, not to dwell on things minute,   690
Vanessa finish'd the dispute;
Brought weighty arguments to prove
That reason was her guide in love.
She thought he had himself described,

His doctrines when she first imbibed;
From him transfused into her breast
With pleasure not to be expressed.
What he had planted, now was grown;
His virtues she may call her own;
As he approves, as he dislikes,   700
Love or contempt her fancy strikes.
Self-love, in Nature rooted fast,
Attends us first, and leaves us last;
Why she loves him, admire not at her;
She loves herself, and that's the matter.
How was her tutor wont to praise
The geniuses of ancient days!
(Those authors he so oft had named,
For learning, wit, and wisdom, famed);
Was struck with love, esteem, and awe,   710
For persons whom he never saw.
Suppose Cadenus flourish'd then,
He must adore such god-like men.
If one short volume could comprise
All that was witty, learn'd and wise,
How would it be esteem'd and read,
Although the writer long were dead!
If such an author were alive,
How all would for his friendship strive,
Would come in crowds to see his face!   720
And this she takes to be her case.
Cadenus answers ev'ry end,
The book, the author, and the friend.
The utmost her desires will reach,
Is but to learn what he can teach:
His converse is a system, fit
Alone to fill up all her wit;
While ev'ry passion of her mind
In him is centred and confined.

   Love can with speech inspire a mute,   730
And taught Vanessa to dispute.
This topic, never touch'd before,
Display'd her eloquence the more:
Her knowledge, with such pains acquired,
By this new passion grew inspired;

Through Love she made all objects pass,
Which gave a tincture o'er the mass;
As rivers, though they bend and twine,
Still to the sea their course incline:
Or, as philosophers, that find   740
Some fav'rite system to their mind,
In ev'ry point to make it fit,
Will force all Nature to submit.
    Cadenus, who could ne'er suspect
His lessons would have this effect,
Or be so artfully applied,
Insensibly came on her side.
It was an unforeseen event,
Things took a turn he never meant.
Who'er excels in what we prize,   750
Appears a hero in our eyes;
Each girl, when pleased with what is taught,
Will have the teacher in her thought.
When Miss delights in her spinet,
A fiddler may a fortune get;
A blockhead with melodious voice,
In boarding-schools can have his choice;
And oft the dancing-master's art
Climbs from the toe to reach the heart.
In learning let a nymph delight,   760
The pedant gets a mistress by't.
Cadenus, to his grief and shame,
Could scarce oppose Vanessa's flame;
But though her arguments were strong,
At least could hardly wish them wrong.
Howe'er it came, he could not tell,
But, sure, she never talk'd so well.
His pride began to interpose;
Preferr'd before a crowd of beaus!
So bright a nymph to come unsought,   770
Such wonders by his merit wrought!
'Tis merit must with her prevail:
He never knew her judgment fail!
She noted all she ever read,
And had a most discerning head!
    'Tis an old maxim in the schools,

That Vanity's the food of fools;
Yet now and then your men of wit
Will condescend to taste a bit.
   So when Cadenus could not hide,   780
He chose to justify his pride;
Constr'ing the passion she had shown,°
Much to her praise, more to his own;
Nature in him had merit placed,
In her, a most judicious taste.
Love, hitherto a transient guest,
Ne'er held possession of his breast;
So long attending at the gate,
Disdain'd to enter in so late.
Love why do we one passion call,   790
When 'tis a compound of them all?
Where hot and cold, where sharp and sweet,
In all their equipages meet;
Where pleasures mix'd with pains appear,
Sorrow with joy, and hope with fear;
Wherein his dignity and age
Forbid Cadenus to engage.
But friendship, in its greatest height
A constant, rational delight,
On virtue's basis fix'd, to last   800
When love's allurements long are past,
Which gently warms, but cannot burn,
He gladly offers in return;
His want of passion will redeem
With gratitude, respect, esteem:
With that devotion we bestow
When goddesses appear below.
   While thus Cadenus entertains
Vanessa in exalted strains,
The nymph in sober words entreats   810
A truce with all sublime conceits.
For, why such raptures, flights, and fancies,
To her who durst not read romances?
In lofty style to make replies
Which he had taught her to despise?
But when her tutor will affect
Devotion, duty, and respect,

He fairly abdicates the throne:
The government is now her own;
He has a forfeiture incurr'd;   820
She vows to take him at his word,
And hopes he will not think it strange
If both should now their stations change.
The nymph will have her turn, to be
The tutor; and the pupil, he;
Though she already can discern
Her scholar is not apt to learn;
Or wants capacity to reach
The science she designs to teach;
Wherein his genius was below   830
The skill of ev'ry common beau;
Who, though he cannot spell, is wise
Enough to read a lady's eyes,
And will each accidental glance
Interpret for a kind advance.

    But what success Vanessa met,
Is to the world a secret yet.
Whether the nymph, to please her swain,
Talks in a high romantic strain;
Or whether he at last descends   840
To love with less seraphic ends;
Or to compound the business, whether
They temper love and books together;
Shall never to mankind be told,
Nor dares the conscious Muse unfold.

    Meantime the mournful Queen of Love
Led but a weary life above.
She ventures now to leave the skies,
Grown by Vanessa's conduct wise.
For, though by one perverse event   850
Pallas had cross'd her first intent,
Though her design was not obtain'd,
Yet had she much experience gain'd,
And, by the project vainly tried,°
Could better now the Cause decide.
She gave due notice that both parties,
Coram Regina, prox. die Martis,°
Should at their peril, without fail,

Come and appear, and save their bail.
    All met; and, Silence thrice proclaim'd,   860
One lawyer to each side was named.
The judge discover'd in her face
Resentments for her late disgrace;
And full of anger, shame, and grief,
Directed them to mind their brief;
Nor spend the time to show their reading:
She'd have a summary proceeding.
She gather'd under ev'ry head
The sum of what each lawyer said,
Gave her own reasons last, and then   870
Decreed the Cause against the *Men*.
    But in a weighty case like this,
To show she did not judge amiss,
Which evil tongues might else report,
She made a speech in open court:
Wherein she grievously complains,
'How she was cheated by the swains;
On whose petition (humbly showing
That women were not worth the wooing
And that, unless the sex would mend,   880
The race of lovers soon must end)
She was at Lord knows what expense
To form a nymph of wit and sense,
A model for her sex design'd,
Who never could one lover find.
She saw her favour was misplaced;
The fellows had a wretched taste;
She needs must tell them to their face,
They were a stupid, senseless race;
And, were she to begin again,   890
She'd study to reform the *Men*;
Or add some grains of folly more
To *Women*, than they had before,
To put them on an equal foot;
And this, or nothing else, would do't.
This might their mutual fancy strike;
Since ev'ry being loves its *like*.
    'But now, repenting what was done,
She left all business to her son.

She puts the world in his possession,   900
And let him use it at discretion.'
    The crier was order'd to dismiss
The court, so made his last *O yes!*°
The goddess would no longer wait,
But, rising from her chair of state,
Left all below at six and sev'n,°
Harness'd her doves, and flew to Heav'n.

Swift to Miss Esther Vanhomrigh

Laracor, *July* 8, 1713.

I stayed but a fortnight in Dublin, very sick, and returned not one visit of a hundred that were made me, but all to the Dean and none to the Doctor. I am riding here for life, and think I am something better, and hate the thoughts of Dublin, and prefer a field-bed and an earthen floor before the great house there, which they say is mine. I had your last splenetic letter. I told you when I left England, I would endeavour to forget everything there, and would write as seldom as I could. I did, indeed, design one general round of letters to my friends, but my health has not yet suffered me. I design to pass the greatest part of the time I stay in Ireland here in the cabin where I am now writing, neither will I leave the kingdom till I am sent for, and if they have no further service for me, I will never see England again. At my first coming I thought I should have died with discontent, and was horribly melancholy while they were installing me, but it begins to wear off, and change to dulness. My river walk is extremely pretty, and my canal in great beauty, and I see trouts playing in it.

I know not any one thing in Dublin, but Mr. Ford is very kind, and writes to me constantly what passes among you. I find you are likewise a good politician, and I will say so much to you that I verily think, if the thing you know of had been published° just upon the Peace, the Ministry might have avoided what hath since happened. But I am now fitter to look after willows, and to cut hedges, than meddle with affairs of state. I must order one of the workmen to drive those cows out of my island, and make up the ditch again; a work much more proper for a country vicar than driving out factions and fencing against them. And I must go and take my bitter draught to cure my head, which is spoilt by the bitter draughts the public hath given me.

How does Davila go on?° Johnny Clark is chosen portreeve of our town of Trim, and we shall have the assizes there next week, and fine doings, and I must go and borrow a horse to meet the judges, and Joe Beaumont and all the boys that can get horses will go too. Mr. Warburton has but a thin school. Mr. Percival has built up the other side of his house, but people whisper that it is but scurvily built. Mr. Steers is come to live in Mr. Melthorp's house, and it is thought the widow Melthorp will remove to Dublin.—Nay, if you do not like this sort of news, I have no better. So go to your Dukes and Duchesses, and leave me to Goodman Bomford, and Patrick Dolan of Clanduggan. Adieu.

THE
IMPORTANCE
OF THE
GUARDIAN
Considered, in a Second
LETTER
TO THE
Bailiff of *Stockbridge*.

By a Friend of Mr. St[ee]le.

THE PREFACE.

MR. *Steele, in his* Letter to the Bailiff of Stockbridge, *has given us leave to 'treat him as we think fit, as he is our brother scribbler; but not to attack him as an honest man'. That is to say, he allows us to be his* critics, *but not his* answerers; *and he is altogether in the right, for there is in his letter much to be* criticised *and little to be* answered. *The situation and importance of Dunkirk are pretty well known; Mons. Tugghe's Memorial, published and handed about by the Whigs, is allowed to be a very trifling paper. And as to the immediate demolishment of that town, Mr. Steele pretends to offer no other argument but the* Expectations *of the people, which is a figurative speech, naming the tenth part for the whole: as Bradshaw told King Charles I. that the people of England expected justice against him. I have therefore entered very little into the subject he pretends to treat, but have considered his pamphlet partly as a* critic, *and partly as a* commentator, *which, I think, is 'to treat him only as my brother scribbler', according to the permission he has graciously allowed me.*

TO

THE WORSHIPFUL

MR. JOHN SNOW,

BAILIFF OF STOCKBRIDGE.

SIR,

I have just been reading a twelvepenny pamphlet about Dunkirk, addressed to your worship from one of your intended representatives;

and I find several passages in it which want explanation, especially to you in the country: for we in town have a way of talking and writing, which is very little understood beyond the bills of mortality. I have therefore made bold to send you here a second letter, by way of comment upon the former.

In order to this, *You* Mr. Bailiff, *and at the same time the whole borough*, may please to take notice, that London writers often put titles to their papers and pamphlets which have little or no reference to the main design of the work. So, for instance, you will observe in reading, that the letter called, *The Importance of Dunkirk*, is chiefly taken up in showing you the Importance of Mr. Steele; wherein it was indeed reasonable your borough should be informed, which had chosen him to represent them.

I would therefore place the *importance* of this gentleman before you in a clearer light than he has given himself the trouble to do; without running into his early history, because I owe him no malice.

Mr. Steele is author of two tolerable plays° (or at least of the greatest part of them) which, added to the company he kept, and to the continual conversation and friendship of Mr. Addison, hath given him the character of a wit. To take the height of his learning, you are to suppose a lad just fit for the university, and sent early from thence into the wide world, where he followed every way of life that might least improve or preserve the rudiments he had got. He hath no invention, nor is master of a tolerable style; his chief talent is humour, which he sometimes discovers both in writing and discourse; for after the first bottle he is no disagreeable companion. I never knew him taxed with ill-nature, which hath made me wonder how ingratitude came to be his prevailing vice; and I am apt to think it proceeds more from some unaccountable sort of instinct, than premeditation. Being the most imprudent man alive, he never follows the advice of his friends, but is wholly at the mercy of fools or knaves, or hurried away by his own caprice; by which he hath committed more absurdities in economy, friendship, love, duty, good manners, politics, religion and writing, than ever fell to one man's share. He was appointed Gazetteer° by Mr. Harley (then Secretary of State) at the recommendation of Mr. Mainwaring, with a salary of three hundred pounds; was a commissioner of stamped-paper of equal profit, and had a pension of a hundred pounds *per annum*, as a servant to the late Prince George.

This gentleman, whom I have now described to you, began between four and five years ago to publish a paper thrice a week, called *The Tatler*. It came out under the borrowed name of Isaac Bickerstaff, and by contribution of his ingenious friends, grew to have a great reputation, and was equally esteemed by both parties because it meddled with neither. But some time after Sacheverell's trial,° when things began to change their aspect, Mr. Steele, whether by the command of his superiors, his own inconstancy, or the absence of his assistants, would needs corrupt his paper with politics; published one or two most virulent libels, and chose for his subject even that individual Mr. Harley,° who had made him Gazetteer. But his finger and thumb not proving strong enough to stop the general torrent, there was an universal change made in the Ministry; and the two new Secretaries, not thinking it decent to employ a man in their office who had acted so infamous a part; Mr. Steele, to avoid being discarded, thought fit to resign his place of Gazetteer. Upon which occasion I cannot forbear relating a passage 'to you, Mr. Bailiff, and the rest of the borough', which discovers a very peculiar turn of thought in this gentleman you have chosen to represent you. When Mr. Mainwaring recommended him to the employment of Gazetteer, Mr. Harley, out of an inclination to encourage men of parts, raised that office from fifty pounds to three hundred pounds a year; Mr. Steele according to form, came to give his new patron thanks; but the Secretary, who had rather confer a hundred favours than receive acknowledgments for one, said to him in a most obliging manner, 'Pray Sir, do not thank me, but thank Mr. Mainwaring.' Soon after Mr. Steele's quitting that employment, he complained to a gentleman in office, of the hardship put upon him in being forced to quit his place; that he knew Mr. Harley was the cause; that he never had done Mr. Harley any injury, nor received any obligation from him. The gentleman, amazed at this discourse, put him in mind of those libels published in his *Tatlers*: Mr. Steele said he was only the publisher, for they had been sent him by other hands. The gentleman thinking this a very monstrous kind of excuse, and not allowing it, Mr. Steele then said, 'Well, I have libelled him and he has turned me out, and so we are equal.' But neither would this be granted. And he was asked whether the place of Gazetteer were not an obligation? 'No,' said he, 'not from Mr. Harley; for when I went to thank him he forbade me, and said I must only thank Mr. Mainwaring.'

But I return, Mr. Bailiff, to give you a further account of this gentleman's Importance. In less, I think, than two years, the town and he grew weary of the *Tatler*: he was silent for some months; and then a daily paper came from him and his friends, under the name of *Spectator*, with good success. This being likewise dropped after a certain period, he hath of late appeared under the style of *Guardian*, which he hath now likewise quitted for that of *Englishman*;° but having chosen other assistance, or trusting more to himself, his papers have been very coldly received, which hath made him fly for relief to the never-failing source of faction.

On the —— of August last, Mr. Steele writes a letter to Nestor Ironside, Esq. and subscribes it with the name of 'English Tory'. On the 7th the said Ironside publishes this letter in the *Guardian*. How shall I explain this matter to you, Mr. Bailiff, and your brethren of the borough? You must know then, that Mr. Steele and Mr. Ironside are the same persons, because there is a great relation between Iron and Steel; and 'English Tory' and Mr. Steele are the same persons, because there is no relation at all between Mr. Steele and an English Tory; so that to render this matter clear to the very meanest capacities, Mr. English Tory, the very same person with Mr. Steele, writes a letter to Nestor Ironside, Esq. who is the same person with English Tory, who is the same person with Mr. Steele. And Mr. Ironside, who is the same person with English Tory, publishes the letter written by English Tory, who is the same person with Mr. Steele, who is the same person with Mr. Ironside. This letter written and published by these three gentlemen who are *one* of your representatives, complains of a printed paper in French and English, lately handed about the town, and given *gratis* to passengers in the streets at noonday; the title whereof is 'A most humble Address or Memorial presented to Her Majesty the Queen of Great Britain, by the Deputy of the Magistrates of Dunkirk'. This deputy, it seems, is called the Sieur Tugghe. Now, the remarks made upon this memorial by Mr. English Tory, in his letter to Mr. Ironside, happening to provoke the *Examiner*, and another pamphleteer,° they both fell hard upon Mr. Steele, charging him with insolence and ingratitude towards the Queen. But Mr Steele nothing daunted, writes a long letter 'to you Mr. Bailiff, and at the same time to the whole borough', in his own vindication. But there being several difficult passages in this letter, which may want clearing up, I here send you and the borough my annotations upon it.

Mr. Steele in order to display his *importance* to your borough, begins his letter by letting you know 'he is no small man', because in the pamphlets he hath sent you down you will 'find him spoken of more than once in print'. It is indeed a great thing to be 'spoken of in print', and must needs make a mighty sound at Stockbridge among the electors. However, if Mr. Steele has really sent you down all the pamplets and papers printed since the dissolution, you will find he is not the only person of importance; I could instance Abel Roper,° Mr. Marten the surgeon, Mr. John Moore the apothecary at the Pestle and Mortar, Sir William Read, Her Majesty's oculist, and of later name and fame, Mr. John Smith the corn-cutter, with several others who are 'spoken of more than once in print'. Then he recommends to your perusal, and sends you a copy of a printed paper given *gratis* about the streets, which is the Memorial of Monsieur Tugghe (above mentioned) 'Deputy of the magistrates of Dunkirk', to desire Her Majesty not to demolish the said town. He tells you how insolent a thing it is, that such a paper should be publicly distributed, and he tells you true; but these insolences are very frequent among the Whigs. One of their present topics for clamour is Dunkirk. Here is a memorial said to be presented to the Queen by an obscure Frenchman. One of your party gets a copy, and immediately prints it by contribution, and delivers it *gratis* to the people; which answers several ends. *First*, it is meant to lay an odium on the Ministry. *Secondly*, if the town be soon demolished, Mr. Steele and his faction have the merit, their arguments and threatenings have frightened my Lord Treasurer. *Thirdly*, if the demolishing should be further deferred, the nation will be fully convinced of his lordship's intention to bring over the Pretender.

Let us turn over fourteen pages, which contain the memorial itself, and which is indeed as idle a one as ever I read; we come now to Mr. Steele's letter under the name of English Tory, to Mr. Ironside. In the preface to this letter, he hath these words, 'It is certain there is not much danger in delaying the demolition of Dunkirk during the life of his present Most Christian Majesty, who is renowned for the most inviolable regard to treaties; but that pious prince is aged, and in case of his decease', &c. This preface is in the words of Mr. Ironside, a professed Whig, and perhaps you in the country will wonder to hear a zealot of your own party celebrating the French king for his piety and his religious performance of treaties. For this I can assure you is not spoken in jest, or to be understood by contrary. There is a wonderful resemblance between that prince and the party of Whigs among us. Is he for arbitrary government? So are they. Hath he persecuted Protestants? So have the Whigs. Did he attempt to restore King James and his pretended son? They did the same. Would he have Dunkirk surrendered to him? This is what they desire. Does he call himself the Most Christian? The Whigs assume the same title, though their leaders deny Christianity. Does he break his promises? Did they ever keep theirs?

From the 16th to the 38th page Mr. Steele's pamphlet is taken up with a copy of his letter to Mr. Ironside, the remarks of the *Examiner*, and another author upon that letter; the hydrography of some French and English ports, and his answer to Mr. Tugghe's Memorial. The bent of his discourse is in appearance to show of what prodigious consequence to the welfare of England, the surrendry of Dunkirk was. But here, Mr.

Bailiff, you must be careful; for all this is said in raillery; for you may easily remember that when the town was first yielded to the Queen, the Whigs declared it was of no consequence at all, that the French could easily repair it after the demolition, or fortify another a few miles off, which would be of more advantage to them. So that what Mr. Steele tells you of the prodigious benefit that will accrue to England by destroying this port, is only suited to present junctures and circumstances. For if Dunkirk should now be represented as insignificant as when it was first put into Her Majesty's hands, it would signify nothing whether it were demolished or no, and consequently one principal topic of clamour would fall to the ground.

In Mr. Steele's answer to Monsieur Tugghe's arguments against the demolishing of Dunkirk, I have not observed any thing that so much deserves your peculiar notice as the great eloquence of your new member, and his wonderful faculty of varying his style, which he calls, 'proceeding like a man of great gravity and business'. He has ten arguments of Tugghe's to answer; and because he will not go in the old beaten road, like a parson of a parish, *first*, *secondly*, *thirdly*, &c. his manner is this,

> In answer to the sieur's *first*.
> As to the sieur's *second*.
> As to his *third*.
> As to the sieur's *fourth*.
> As to Mr. Deputy's *fifth*.
> As to the sieur's *sixth*.
> As to this agent's *seventh*.
> As to the sieur's *eighth*.
> As to his *ninth*.
> As to the memorialist's *tenth*.

You see every second expression is more or less diversified to avoid the repetition of, 'As to the sieur's' &c. and there is the tenth into the bargain. I could heartily wish Monsieur Tugghe had been able to find ten arguments more, and thereby given Mr. Steele an opportunity of showing the utmost variations our language would bear in so momentous a trial.

Mr. Steele tells you, that having now done 'with his foreign enemy Monsieur Tugghe, he must face about to his domestic foes, who accuse him of ingratitude and insulting his prince, while he is eating her bread'.

To do him justice, he acquits himself pretty tolerably of this last charge. For he assures you, he gave up his stamped-paper office, and pension as gentleman-usher, before he writ that letter to himself in the

Guardian, so that he had already received his salary, and spent the money, and consequently the bread was eaten at least a week before he would offer to insult his prince. So that the folly of the *Examiner*'s objecting ingratitude to him upon this article, is manifest to all the world.

But he tells you he has quitted those employments to render him more useful to his queen and country in the station you have honoured him with. That, no doubt, was the principal motive; however I shall venture to add some others. *First*, the *Guardian* apprehended it impossible that the ministry would let him keep his place much longer, after the part he had acted for above two years past. *Secondly*, Mr. Ironside said publicly that he was ashamed to be obliged any longer to a person (meaning Lord Treasurer) whom he had used so ill. For it seems, a man ought not to use his benefactors ill above two years and a half. *Thirdly*, the *Sieur* Steele appeals for protection to you, Mr. Bailiff, from *others* of your *denomination*, who would have carried him *somewhere else*, if you had not relieved him by your *habeas corpus* to St. Stephen's Chapel.° *Fourthly*, Mr. English Tory found by calculating the life of a Ministry, that it hath lasted above three years and is near expiring; he resolved therefore to 'strip off the very garments spotted with the flesh',° and be wholly regenerate against the return of his old masters.

In order to serve all these ends, your borough hath honoured him (as he expresses it) with choosing him to represent you in parliament, and it must be owned, he hath equally honoured you. Never was borough more happy in suitable representatives, than you are in Mr. Steele and his colleague,° nor were ever representatives more happy in a suitable borough.

When Mr. Steele talked of 'laying before Her Majesty's Ministry, that the nation hath a strict eye upon their behaviour with relation to Dunkirk', did not you, Mr. Bailiff, and your brethren of the borough presently imagine he had drawn up a sort of counter-memorial to that of Monsieur Tugghe's, and presented it in form to my Lord Treasurer, or a Secretary of State? I am confident you did; but this comes by not understanding the town. You are to know then that Mr. Steele publishes every day a penny paper to be read in coffee-houses, and get him a little money. This by a figure of speech, he calls, 'laying things before the Ministry', who seem at present a little too busy to regard such memorials; and, I dare say, never saw his paper, unless he sent it by the penny-post.

Well, but he tells you, 'he cannot offer against the *Examiner*, and his other adversary, reason and argument without appearing void of both'. What a singular situation of the mind is this! How glad should I be to hear a man 'offer reasons and argument, and yet at the same time appear void of both'! But this whole paragraph is of a peculiar strain; the consequences so just and natural, and such a propriety in thinking, as few authors ever arrived to. 'Since it has been the fashion to run down men of much greater consequence than I am, I will not bear the accusation.' This I suppose is 'to offer reasons and arguments, and yet appear void of both'. And in the next lines, 'These writers shall treat me as they think fit, as I am their brother-scribbler, but I shall not be so unconcerned when they attack me as an honest man.' And how does he defend himself? 'I shall therefore inform them that it is not in the power of a private man to hurt the prerogative' &c. Well, I shall 'treat him only as a brother scribbler'. And I guess he will hardly be attacked as an honest man. But if his meaning be that his honesty ought not to be attacked because he 'has no power to hurt the honour and prerogative of the crown without being punished', he will make an admirable reasoner in the House of Commons.

But all this wise argumentation was introduced only to close the paragraph by haling in a fact, which he relates to you and your borough, in order to quiet the minds of the people and express his duty and gratitude to the Queen. The fact is this, 'That Her Majesty's honour is in danger of being lost by her ministers tolerating villains without conscience to abuse the greatest instruments of honour and glory to our country, the most wise and faithful managers, and the most pious, disinterested, generous, and self-denying patriots.' And the instances he produces, are the Duke of Marlborough, the late Earl of Godolphin, and about two-thirds of the bishops.

Mr. Bailiff, I cannot debate this matter at length without putting you and the rest of my countrymen who will be at the expense, to sixpence charge extraordinary. The Duke and Earl were both removed from their employments; and I hope you have too great a respect for the Queen to think it was done for nothing. The former was *at the head* of many great actions; and he has received plentiful oblations of praise and profit. Yet having read all that ever was objected against him by the *Examiner*, I will undertake to prove every syllable of it true, particularly that famous attempt to be General for life. The Earl of Godolphin is dead, and his faults may sojourn with him in the grave till some historian shall think fit to revive part of them for instruction and warning to posterity. But it grieved me to the soul to see so many good epithets bestowed by Mr. Steele upon the bishops. Nothing has done more hurt to that sacred order for some years past, than to hear some prelates extolled by Whigs, Dissenters, Republicans, Socinians,° and in short by all who are enemies to episcopacy. God in His mercy for ever keep our prelates from deserving the praises of such panegyrists!

Mr. Steele is discontented that the Ministry have not 'called the *Examiner* to account as well as the *Flying Post*'. I will inform you, Mr. Bailiff, how that matter stands. The author of the *Flying Post* has thrice a week, for above two years together, published the most impudent reflections upon all the present Ministry, upon all their proceedings, and upon the whole body of Tories. The *Examiner* on the other side, writing in defence of those whom Her Majesty employs in her greatest affairs, and of the cause they are engaged in, hath always borne hard upon the Whigs, and now and then upon some of their leaders. Now, Sir, we reckon here that supposing the persons on both sides to be of equal intrinsic worth, it is more impudent, immoral, and criminal to reflect on a *majority* in power, than a *minority* out of power. Put the case, that an odd rascally Tory in your borough should presume to abuse your worship who, in the language of Mr. Steele, is first minister, and the majority of your brethren, for sending two such Whig representatives up to parliament. And on the other side, that an honest Whig should stand in your defence, and fall foul on the Tories. Would you equally resent the proceedings of both, and let your friend and enemy sit in the stocks together? Hearken to another case, Mr. Bailiff. Suppose your worship, during your annual administration, should happen to be kicked and cuffed by a parcel of Tories, would not the circumstance of your being a magistrate make the crime the greater, than if the like insults were committed on an ordinary Tory shopkeeper by a company of honest Whigs? What bailiff would venture to arrest Mr. Steele, now he has the honour to be your representative? and what bailiff ever scrupled it before?

You must know, Sir, that we have several ways here of abusing one another, without incurring the danger of the law. First, we are careful never to print a man's name out at length, but as I do that of Mr. St—le. So that although every body alive knows whom I mean, the plaintiff can have no redress in any court of justice. Secondly, by putting cases. Thirdly, by insinuations. Fourthly, by celebrating the actions of others, who acted directly contrary to the persons we would reflect on. Fifthly, by nicknames, either commonly known or stamped for the purpose, which every body can tell how to apply. Without going on further, it will be enough to inform you that by some of the ways I have already mentioned, Mr. Steele gives you to understand that the Queen's honour is blasted by the actions of her present ministers; That 'her prerogative is disgraced by erecting a dozen peers, who, by their votes, turned a point upon which your all depended; That these ministers made the Queen lay down her conquering arms, and deliver herself up to be vanquished; That they made Her Majesty betray her allies, by ordering her army to face about, and leave them in the moment of distress; That the present ministers are men of poor and narrow conceptions, self-interested, and without benevolence to mankind; and were brought into Her Majesty's favour for the sins of a nation, and only think what they may do, not what they ought to do.' This is the character given by Mr. Steele of those persons, whom Her Majesty has thought fit to place in the highest stations of the kingdom, and to trust them with the management of her most weighty affairs. And this is the gentleman who cries out, 'Where is honour? where is government? where is prerogative?', because the *Examiner* has sometimes dealt freely with those whom the Queen has thought fit to discard, and the parliament to censure.

But Mr. Steele thinks it highly dangerous to the prince, 'that any man should be hindered from offering his thoughts upon public affairs' and resolves to do it, 'though with the loss of Her Majesty's favour'. If a clergyman offers to preach obedience to the higher powers, and proves it by Scripture, Mr. Steele and his fraternity immediately cry out, 'What have parsons to do with politics?' I ask, what shadow of a pretence has he to offer his crude thoughts in matters of state? To print and publish them? 'To lay them before the queen and ministry?' and to reprove both for maladministration? How did he acquire these abilities of directing in the counsels of princes? Was it from **publishing**° *Tatlers* and *Spectators*, and writing now and then a *Guardian*? Was it from his being a soldier, alchemist,° gazetteer, commissioner of stamped-papers, or gentleman usher? No; but he insists it is every man's right to find fault with the administration in print, whenever they please. And therefore you, Mr. Bailiff, and as many of your brethren in the borough as can write and read, may publish pamphlets, and 'lay them before the queen and ministry', to show your utter dislike of all their proceedings; and for this reason, because you 'can certainly see and apprehend with your own eyes and understanding, those dangers which the ministers do not'.

One thing I am extremely concerned about, that Mr. Steele resolves as he tells you, when he comes into the House, 'to follow no leaders, but vote according to the dictates of his conscience'. He must, at that rate, be a very useless member to his party unless his conscience be already cut out and shaped for their service, which I am ready to believe it is, if I may have leave to judge from the whole tenor of his life. I would only have his friends be cautious not to reward him too liberally. For, as it was said of Cranmer, 'Do the archbishop an ill turn, and he is your friend for ever', so I do affirm of your member, 'Do Mr. Steele a good turn, and he is your enemy for ever.'

I had like to let slip a very trivial matter (which I should be sorry to have done). In reading this pamphlet, I observed several mistakes, but knew not whether to impute them to the author or printer, till turning to the end, I found there was only one *erratum*, thus set down, 'Pag. 45, line 28, for *admonition* read *advertisement*.' This (to imitate Mr. Steele's propriety of speech) is a very *old* practice among *new* writers, to make a wilful mistake and then put it down as an *erratum*. The word is brought in upon this occasion. To convince all the world that he was not guilty of ingratitude, by reflecting on the Queen when he was actually under salary, as the *Examiner* affirms, he assures you he 'had resigned and divested himself of all, before he would presume to write any thing which was so apparently an admonition to those employed in Her Majesty's service'. In case the *Examiner* should find fault with this word, he might appeal to the *erratum*; and having formerly been Gazetteer, he conceived he might very safely venture to advertise.

You are to understand, Mr. Bailiff, that in the great rebellion against King Charles I. there was a distinction found out between the *personal* and *political* capacity of the prince; by the help of which, those rebels professed to fight for the king, while the great guns were discharging against Charles Stuart. After the same manner Mr. Steele distinguishes between the *personal* and *political* prerogative. He does not care to trust this jewel 'to the will, and pleasure, and passion of Her Majesty'. If I am not mistaken, the crown jewels cannot be alienated by the prince; but I always thought the prince could *wear* them during his reign, else they had as good be in the hands of the subject. So, I conceive, Her Majesty may and ought to *wear* the prerogative; that it is hers during life; and she ought to be so much the more careful neither to soil nor diminish it for that very reason, because it is by law unalienable. But what must we do with this prerogative, according to the notion of Mr. Steele? It must not be trusted with the queen, because Providence has given her *will, pleasure, and passion*. Her ministers must not act by the authority of it; for then Mr. Steele will cry out, 'What? Are Majesty and Ministry consolidated? And must there be no distinction between the one and the other?' He tells you, 'The prerogative attends the crown' and therefore, I suppose, must lie in the Tower to be shown for twelvepence, but never produced except at a coronation or passing an Act. Well, but says he, 'A whole Ministry may be impeached and condemned by the House of Commons, without the prince's suffering by it.' And what follows? Why, therefore a single burgess of Stockbridge, before he gets into the House, may at any time revile a whole Ministry in print, before he knows whether they are guilty of any one neglect of duty, or breach of trust.

I am willing to join issue with Mr. Steele in one particular, which perhaps may give you some diversion. He is taxed by the *Examiner* and others for an insolent expression, that the British nation *expects* the immediate demolition of Dunkirk. He says, the word EXPECT was meant to the Ministry, and not to the queen, 'but that however, for argument sake, he will suppose those words were addressed immediately to the queen'. Let me then likewise for argument sake, suppose a very ridiculous thing, that Mr. Steele were admitted to her Majesty's sacred person, to tell his own story, with his letter to you, Mr. Bailiff, in his hand to have recourse to upon occasion. I think his speech must be in these terms.

'*Madam,*

'*I Richard Steele publisher of the "Tatler" and "Spectator", late Gazetteer, commissioner of stamped-papers, and pensioner to your Majesty, now burgess elect of Stockbridge, do see and apprehend with my own eyes and understanding, the imminent danger that attends the delay of the demolition of Dunkirk, which I believe your ministers, whose greater concern it is, do not. For, Madam, the thing is not done. My Lord Treasurer and Lord Bolingbroke, my fellow-subjects, under whose immediate direction it is, are careless, and overlook it, or something worse; I mean, they design to sell it to France, or make use of it to bring in the Pretender. This is clear from their suffering Mr. Tugghe's memorial to be published without punishing the printer. Your Majesty has told us that the equivalent for Dunkirk is already in the French King's hands; therefore all obstacles are removed on the part of France; and I, though a mean fellow, give your Majesty to understand in the best method I can take, and from the sincerity of my GRATEFUL heart, that the British nation EXPECTS the IMMEDIATE demolition of Dunkirk; as you hope to preserve your person, crown and dignity, and the safety and welfare of the people committed to your charge.*'

I have contracted such a habit of treating princes familiarly, by reading the pamphlets of Mr. Steele and his fellows, that I am tempted to suppose Her Majesty's answer to this speech might be as follows.

'*Mr. Richard Steele, late Gazetteer, &c. I do not conceive that any of your titles empower you to be My director, or to report to Me the expectations of My people. I know their expectations better than you; they love Me, and will trust*

Me. My ministers were of My own free choice; I have found them wise and faithful; and whoever calls them fools or knaves, designs indirectly an affront to Myself. I am under no obligations to demolish Dunkirk, but to the Most Christian King; if you come here as an orator from that prince to demand it in his name, where are your powers? If not, let it suffice you to know, that I have My reasons for deferring it; and that the clamours of a faction *shall not be a rule by which I or My servants are to proceed.'*

Mr. Steele tells you, 'his adversaries are so unjust, they will not take the least notice of what led him into the necessity of writing his letter to the *Guardian.*' And how is it possible, any mortal should know all his necessities? Who can guess whether this necessity were imposed on him by his superiors, or by the itch of party, or by the mere want of other matter to furnish out a *Guardian*?

But Mr. Steele has 'had a liberal education, and knows the world as well as the Ministry does, and will therefore speak on, whether he offends them or no, and though their clothes be ever so new, when he thinks his queen and country is' (or as a Grammarian would express it, *are*) 'ill treated'.

It would be good to hear Mr. Steele explain himself upon this phrase of 'knowing the world', because it is a science which maintains abundance of pretenders. Every idle young rake who understands how to pick up a wench, or bilk a hackney coachman, or can call the players by their names, and is acquainted with five or six faces in the chocolate-house, will needs pass for a man that 'knows the world'. In the like manner Mr. Steele who from some few sprinklings of rudimental literature, proceeded a gentleman of the horse-guards, thence by several degrees to be an ensign and an alchemist, where he was wholly conversant with the lower part of mankind, thinks he 'knows the world' as well as the Prime Minister; and upon the strength of that knowledge, will needs direct Her Majesty in the weightiest matters of government.

And now Mr. Bailiff, give me leave to inform you that this long letter of Mr. Steele filled with quotations and a clutter about Dunkirk was wholly written for the sake of the six last pages, taken up in vindicating himself directly, and vilifying the queen and ministry by innuendoes. He apprehends that 'some representations have been given of *him* in your town, as, that a man of so small a fortune as he, must have secret views or supports which could move him to leave his employments', &c. He answers, by owning he 'has indeed very particular views; for he is animated in his conduct by justice and truth, and benevolence to mankind'. He has given up his employments, because he 'values no advantages above the conveniences of life but as they tend to the service of the public'. It seems, he could not 'serve the public' as a pensioner, or commissioner of stamped-paper, and therefore gave them up to sit in parliament out of 'charity to his country, and to contend for liberty'. He has transcribed the commonplaces of some canting moralist *de contemptu mundi, et fuga seculi*,° and would put them upon you as rules derived from his own practice.

Here is a most miraculous and sudden reformation, which I believe can hardly be matched in history or *legend*. And Mr. Steele, not unaware how slow the world was of belief, has thought fit to anticipate all objections; he foresees that 'prostituted pens will entertain a pretender to such reformations with a recital of his own faults and infirmities, but he is prepared for such usage, and gives himself up to all nameless authors, to be treated as they please'.

It is certain, Mr. Bailiff, that no man breathing can pretend to have arrived at such a sublime pitch of virtue as Mr. Steele, without some tendency in the world to suspend at least their belief of the fact, till time and observation shall determine. But I hope few writers will be so 'prostitute' as to trouble themselves with 'the faults and infirmities' of Mr. Steele's past life, with what he somewhere else calls 'the sins of his youth'° and in one of his late papers confesses to have been *numerous* enough. A shifting scambling scene of youth, attended with poverty and ill company, may put a man of no ill inclinations upon many extravagances, which as soon as they are left off are easily pardoned and forgot. Besides, I think, popish writers tell us that the greatest sinners make the greatest saints; but so very quick a sanctification, and carried to so prodigious a height, will be apt to rouse the suspicion of infidels, especially when they consider that this pretence of his to so romantic a virtue, is only advanced by way of solution to that difficult problem, *Why he has given up his employments?* And according to the new philosophy, they will endeavour to solve it by some easier and shorter way. For example, the question is put, Why Mr. Steele gives up his employment and pension at this juncture? I must here repeat with some enlargement what I said before on this head. These unbelieving gentlemen will answer, First, That a new commission was every day expected for the stamped-paper, and he knew his name would be left out; and therefore his resignation would be an appearance of virtue cheaply bought.

Secondly, He dreaded the violence of creditors, against which his employments were no manner of security.

Thirdly, Being a person of great sagacity, he hath some foresight of a change from the usual age of a ministry, which is now almost expired;

from the little misunderstandings that have been reported sometimes to happen among the men in power; from the bill of commerce being rejected,° and from some *horrible expectations*,° wherewith his party have been deceiving themselves and their friends *abroad* for about two years past.

Fourthly, He hopes to come into all the perquisites of his predecessor Ridpath,° and be the principal writer of his faction, where everything is printed by subscription, which will amply make up the loss of his place.

But it may be still demanded, Why he affects those exalted strains of piety and resignation? To this I answer with great probability, That he hath resumed his old pursuits after the *philosopher's stone*, towards which it is held by all *adepts* for a most essential ingredient, that a man must seek it merely for the glory of God, and without the least desire of being rich.

Mr. Steele is angry, that some of our friends have been reflected on in a pamphlet, because they left us in a point of the greatest consequence; and upon that account he runs into their panegyric against his conscience, and the interest of his cause, without considering that those gentlemen have reverted to us again. The case is thus: He never would have praised them, if they had remained firm, nor should we have railed at them. The one is full as honest, and as natural as the other. However, Mr. Steele hopes (I beg you Mr. Bailiff to observe the consequence) that notwithstanding this pamphlet's reflecting on some Tories who opposed the treaty of commerce, 'the ministry will see Dunkirk effectually demolished'.

Mr. Steele says something in commendation of the Queen, but stops short, and tells you (if I take his meaning right) that he 'shall leave what he has to say on this topic, till he and Her Majesty are both dead'. Thus, he defers his praises as he does his debts, after the manner of the Druids, to be paid in another world. If I have ill interpreted him, it is his own fault for studying cadence instead of propriety, and filling up niches with words before he has adjusted his conceptions to them. One part of the Queen's character is this, 'that all the hours of her life are divided between the exercises of devotion, and taking minutes of the sublime affairs of her government'. Now, if the business of Dunkirk be one of the 'sublime affairs of Her Majesty's government', I think we ought to be at ease, or else she 'takes her minutes' to little purpose. No, says Mr. Steele, the Queen is a *Lady*, and unless a prince will now and then get drunk with his ministers, 'he cannot learn their interests or humours': but this being by no means proper for a *Lady*, she can know nothing but what they think fit to tell her when they are sober. And therefore 'all the fellow subjects' of these ministers must watch their motions and 'be very solicitous for what passes beyond the ordinary rules of government'. For while we are foolishly 'relying upon Her Majesty's virtues', these ministers are 'taking the advantage of increasing the power of France'.

There is a very good maxim, I think it is neither Whig nor Tory, 'that the prince can do no wrong', which I doubt is often applied to very ill purposes. A monarch of Britain is pleased to create *a dozen peers*, and to make a peace; both these actions are (for instance) within the undisputed prerogative of the crown, and are to be reputed and submitted to as the actions of the prince. But as a king of England is supposed to be guided in matters of such importance by the advice of those he employs in his councils, whenever a parliament thinks fit to complain of such proceedings, as a public grievance, then this maxim takes place, that the prince can do no wrong, and the advisers are called to account. But shall this empower such an individual as Mr. Steele, in his *tatling* or *pamphleteering* capacity, to fix 'the ordinary rules of government' or to affirm that 'her ministers, upon the security of Her Majesty's goodness, are labouring for the grandeur of France'? What ordinary rule of government is transgressed by the Queen's delaying the demolition of Dunkirk? Or what addition is thereby made to the grandeur of France? Every tailor in your corporation is as much a fellow subject as Mr. Steele, and do you think in your conscience that every tailor of Stockbridge is fit to direct Her Majesty and her ministers in 'the sublime affairs of her government'?

But he 'persists in it, that it is no manner of diminution of the wisdom of a prince, that he is obliged to act by the information of others'. The sense is admirable; and the interpretation is this, that what a man is forced to 'is no diminution of his wisdom'. But if he would conclude from this sage maxim that because a prince 'acts by the information of others', therefore those actions may lawfully be traduced in print by every fellow subject, I hope there is no man in England so much a Whig, as to be of his opinion.

Mr. Steele concludes his letter to you with a story about King William and his 'French dog-keeper, who gave that prince a gun loaden only with powder, and then pretended to wonder how His Majesty could miss his aim: which was no argument against the King's reputation for shooting very finely'. This he would have you apply, by allowing Her Majesty to be a wise prince, but deceived by wicked counsellors, who are in the interest of France. Her Majesty's aim was peace, which I think she hath not missed; and, God be thanked, she hath got it without any more expense, either of *shot* or *powder*. Her *dog-keepers*, for some years past, had directed her *gun* against her *friends*, and at last *loaded* it so deep, that it was in danger to *burst* in her hands.

You may please to observe, that Mr. Steele calls this *dog-keeper* a 'minister', which, with humble submission, is a gross impropriety of speech. The word is derived from Latin, where it properly signifies a *servant*; but in English is never made use of otherwise than to denominate those who are employed in the service of church or state. So that the appellation, as he directs it, is no less absurd than it would be for you, Mr. Bailiff, to send your 'prentice for a pot of ale, and give him the title of your *envoy*; to call a petty constable a *magistrate*, or the common hangman a *minister* of justice. I confess, when I was choqued° at this word in reading the paragraph, a gentleman offered his conjecture that it might possibly be intended for a reflection or a jest. But if there be any thing further in it than a want of understanding our language, I take it to be only a refinement upon the old levelling principle of the Whigs. Thus, in their opinion, a *dog-keeper* is as much a *minister* as any Secretary of State. And thus Mr. Steele and my Lord Treasurer are both *fellow subjects*. I confess I have known some *ministers* whose birth, or qualities, or both, were such that nothing but the capriciousness of fortune, and the iniquity of the times, could ever have raised them above the station of *dog-keepers*, and to whose administration I should be loth to entrust a dog I had any value for. Because, by the rule of proportion, they who treated their *prince* like a *slave*, would have used their *fellow subjects* like *dogs*; and how they would treat a *dog*, I can find no similitude to express; yet I well remember they maintained a large number, whom they taught to *fawn* upon themselves, and *bark* at their mistress. However, while they were in service, I wish they had only kept Her Majesty's DOGS, and not been trusted with her GUNS. And thus much by way of comment upon this worthy story of King William and his *dog-keeper*.

I have now, Mr. Bailiff, explained to you all the difficult parts in Mr. Steele's letter. As for the importance of Dunkirk, and when it shall be demolished, or whether it shall be demolished or not, neither he, nor you, nor I, have anything to do in the matter. Let us all say what we please, Her Majesty will think herself the best *judge*, and her ministers the best *advisers*; neither hath Mr. Steele pretended to prove that any law ecclesiastical or civil, statute or common, is broken by keeping Dunkirk undemolished, as long as the Queen shall think it best for the service of herself and her kingdoms; and it is not altogether impossible that there may be some few reasons of state, which have not been yet communicated to Mr. Steele. I am, with respect to the borough and yourself,

Sir,

Your most humble
and most obedient servant,
&c.

The Author upon Himself

A few of the first lines were wanting in the copy sent us by a friend of the Author's from London.

    *   *   *   *   *   *

    *   *   *   *   *   *

    *   By an old red-pate, murd'ring hag* pursued,
A crazy prelate,† and a royal prude;‡°
By dull divines, who look with envious eyes
On ev'ry genius that attempts to rise,
And pausing o'er a pipe, with doubtful nod
Give hints that poets ne'er believe in God.
So, clowns on scholars as on wizards look,
And take a folio for a conj'ring book.

   Swift had the sin of wit, no venial crime;
Nay, 'twas affirm'd he sometimes dealt in rhyme.   10
Humour and mirth had place in all he writ,
He reconcil'd divinity and wit:
He moved and bow'd, and talk'd with too much grace,
Nor show'd the parson in his gait or face;
Despised luxurious wines and costly meat,
Yet still was at the tables of the great.
Frequented lords; *saw those that saw the queen*;
At Child's or Truby's,§ never once had been,
Where town and country vicars flock in tribes,
Secured by numbers from the laymen's gibes,   20
And deal in vices of the graver sort,
Tobacco, censure, coffee, pride, and port.

   But, after sage monitions from his friends,
His talents to employ for nobler ends;
To better judgments willing to submit,
He turns to politics his dang'rous wit.

   And now, the public Int'rest to support,
By Harley Swift invited comes to court;
In favour grows with ministers of state;
Admitted private, when superiors wait: 30

* The late Duchess of Somerset.
† Dr. Sharpe, Archbishop of York.
‡ Her late Majesty.
§ A coffee-house and tavern near St. Paul's, much frequented by the clergy.

And Harley, not ashamed his choice to own,
Takes him to Windsor in his coach, alone.
At Windsor Swift no sooner can appear,
But St. John* comes, and whispers in his ear;
The waiters stand in ranks: the yeomen cry
Make room, as if a duke were passing by.

    Now Finch† alarms the lords: he hears for certain
This dang'rous priest is got behind the curtain;
Finch, famed for tedious elocution, proves
That Swift oils many a spring which Harley moves.   40
Walpole and Aislaby,‡ to clear the doubt,°
Inform the Commons that the secret's out:
'A *certain* doctor is observed of late
To haunt a *certain* minister of state:
From whence with half an eye we may discover
The Peace is made, and Perkin must come over.'°

    York is from Lambeth sent, to show the queen°
A dang'rous treatise writ against the spleen;°
Which, by the style, the matter, and the drift,
'Tis thought could be the work of none but Swift.   50
Poor York! the harmless tool of others' hate;
He sues for pardon,§ and repents too late.°

    Now Madam Coningsmark¶ her vengeance vows°
On Swift's reproaches for her murder'd spouse:
From her red locks her mouth with venom fills,
And thence into the royal ear instils.
The queen incensed, his services forgot,
Leaves him a victim to the vengeful Scot.‖°
Now through the realm a proclamation spread,
To fix a price on his devoted head;   60

    * Then Secretary of State, now Lord Bolingbroke, the most universal genius in Europe.

    † Late Earl of Nottingham, who made a speech in the House of Lords against the Author.

    ‡ Those two made speeches in the House of Commons against the Author, although the latter professed much friendship for him.

    § It is known that his Grace sent a message to the Author, to desire his pardon, and that he was very sorry for what he had said and done.

    ¶ The Lady hinted at before. There was a short severe satire writ against her, which she charged on the Author, and did him ill offices by her great credit with the Queen.

    ‖ The proclamation was against the Author of a pamphlet, called, *The Publick Spirit of the Whigs*, against which the Scotch lords complained.

While innocent, he scorns ignoble flight:
His watchful friends preserve him by a sleight.
　　By Harley's favour once again he shines;
Is now caress'd by candidate divines
Who change opinions with the changing scene:
Lord! how were they mistaken in the Dean!
Now Delawar* again familiar grows;
And in Swift's ear thrusts half his powder'd nose.
The Scottish nation, whom he durst offend,
Again apply that Swift would be their friend†　　　　70
　　By faction tired, with grief he waits awhile,
His great contending friends to reconcile;
Performs what friendship, justice, truth require:
What could he more, but decently retire?‡

* Lord Delawere, then Treasurer of the Household, always caressing the Author at court. But during the trial of the printers before the House of Lords, and while the proclamation hung over the Author, his Lordship would not seem to know him, till the danger was past.

† The Scotch Lords treated and visited the Author more after the proclamation than before, except the Duke of Argyle, who would never be reconciled.

‡ The Author retired to a friend in Berkshire, ten weeks before the Queen died: and never saw the Ministry after.

Swift to Joseph Addison

Sir,

I should be much concerned if I did not think you were a little angry with me for not congratulating you upon being Secretary.° But I choose my time as I would to visit you, when all your company is gone. I am confident you have given ease of mind to many thousand people, who will never believe any ill can be intended to the constitution in Church or State while you are in so high a trust, and I should have been of the same opinion though I had not the happiness to know you.

I am extremely obliged for your kind remembrance some months ago by the Bishop of Derry, and for your generous intentions if you had come to Ireland, to have made party give way to friendship by continuing your acquaintance.

I examine my heart, and can find no other reason why I write to you now, beside that great love and esteem I have always had for you. I have nothing to ask you either for any friend or for myself. When I conversed among Ministers, I boasted of your acquaintance, but I feel no vanity from being known to a Secretary of State. I am only a little concerned to see you stand single, for it is a prodigious singularity in any Court to owe one's rise entirely to merit. I will venture to tell you a secret, that three or four more such choices, would gain more hearts in three weeks than all the methods hitherto practised have been able to do in as many years.

It is now time for me to recollect that I am writing to a Secretary of State, who has little time allowed him for trifles; I therefore take my leave with assurances of my being ever with the truest respect, Sir,

Your most obedient and most humble servant,

JONATH. SWIFT.

THE
TESTIMONY OF CONSCIENCE

2 CORINTHIANS, I. 12. PART OF IT.

'—— For our rejoicing is this, the testimony of our conscience.'

THERE is no word more frequently in the mouths of men than that of *conscience*, and the meaning of it is in some measure generally understood. However, because it is likewise a word extremely abused by many people who apply other meanings to it which God Almighty never intended, I shall explain it to you in the clearest manner I am able. The word *conscience* properly signifies that knowledge which a man hath within himself of his own thoughts and actions. And because if a man judgeth fairly of his own actions by comparing them with the law of God, his mind will either approve or condemn him according as he hath done good or evil; therefore this knowledge or conscience may properly be called both an accuser and a judge. So that whenever our conscience accuseth us, we are certainly guilty; but we are not always innocent when it doth not accuse us. For very often through the hardness of our hearts, or the fondness and favour we bear to ourselves, or through ignorance or neglect, we do not suffer our conscience to take any cognizance of several sins we commit. There is another office likewise belonging to conscience, which is that of being our director and guide; and the wrong use of this hath been the occasion of more evils under the sun than almost all other causes put together. For, as conscience is nothing else but the knowledge we have of what we are thinking and doing; so it can guide us no farther than that knowledge reacheth. And therefore God hath placed conscience in us to be our director only in those actions which Scripture and reason plainly tell us to be good or evil. But in cases too difficult or doubtful for us to comprehend or determine, there conscience is not concerned; because it cannot advise in what it doth not understand nor decide where it is itself in doubt: but by God's great mercy, those difficult points are never of absolute necessity to our salvation. There is likewise another evil, that men often say a thing is against their conscience when really it is not. For instance, ask any of those who differ from the worship established, why they do not come to church? They will say they dislike the ceremonies, the prayers, the habits, and the like, and therefore it goes against their conscience. But they are mistaken, their teacher hath put those words into their mouth; for a man's conscience can go no higher than his knowledge, and therefore till he has thoroughly examined by

Scripture and the practice of the ancient church, whether those points are blameable or no, his conscience cannot possibly direct him to condemn them. Hence have likewise arisen those mistakes about what is usually called Liberty of Conscience; which, properly speaking, is no more than a liberty of knowing our own thoughts; which liberty no one can take from us. But those words have obtained quite different meanings. Liberty of Conscience is nowadays not only understood to be the liberty of believing what men please, but also of endeavouring to propagate the belief as much as they can and to overthrow the faith which the laws have already established, to be rewarded by the public for those wicked endeavours. And this is the liberty of conscience which the fanatics are now openly in the face of the world endeavouring at with their utmost application. At the same time it cannot but be observed, that those very persons who under a pretence of a public spirit and tenderness towards their Christian brethren are so jealous for such a liberty of conscience as this, are of all others the least tender to those who differ from them in the smallest point relating to government; and I wish I could not say that the Majesty of the living God may be offended with more security than the memory of a dead prince. But the wisdom of the world at present seems to agree with that of the heathen Emperor who said,° if the gods were offended, it was their own concern and they were able to vindicate themselves.

But although conscience hath been abused to those wicked purposes which I have already related, yet a due regard to the directions it plainly gives us, as well as to its accusations, reproaches, and advices, would be of the greatest use to mankind, both for their present welfare and future happiness.

Therefore my discourse at this time shall be directed to prove to you that there is no solid, firm foundation for virtue but on a conscience which is guided by religion.

In order to this, I shall first show you the weakness and uncertainty of two false principles which many people set up in the place of conscience, for a guide to their actions.

The first of these principles is what the world usually calls *Moral Honesty*. There are some people who appear very indifferent as to religion, and yet have the repute of being just and fair in their dealings; and these are generally known by the character of good moral men. But now, if you look into the grounds and the motives of such a man's actions, you shall find them to be no other than his own ease and interest. For example, you trust a moral man with your money in the way of trade; you trust another with the defence of your cause at law, and perhaps they both deal justly with you. Why? Not from any regard they have for justice, but because their fortune depends upon their credit, and a stain of open public dishonesty must be to their disadvantage. But let it consist with such a man's interest and safety to wrong you, and then it will be impossible you can have any hold upon him; because there is nothing left to give him a check, or to put in the balance against his profit. For if he hath nothing to govern himself by but the opinion of the world, as long as he can conceal his injustice from the world, he thinks he is safe.

Besides, it is found by experience that those men who set up for morality without regard to religion, are generally but virtuous in part; they will be just in their dealings between man and man; but if they find themselves disposed to pride, lust, intemperance, or avarice, they do not think their morality concerned to check them in any of these vices, because it is the great rule of such men that they may lawfully follow the dictates of nature wherever their safety, health, and fortune are not injured. So that upon the whole, there is hardly one vice which a mere moral man may not upon some occasions allow himself to practise.

The other false principle, which some men set up in the place of conscience to be their director in life, is what those who pretend to it call *Honour*.

This word is often made the sanction of an oath; it is reckoned a great commendation to be a man of strict honour; and it is commonly understood that a man of honour can never be guilty of a base action. This is usually the style of military men; of persons with titles; and of others who pretend to birth and quality. 'Tis true indeed, that in ancient times it was universally understood that honour was the reward of virtue; but if such honour as is nowadays going will not permit a man to do a base action, it must be allowed there are very few such things as base actions in nature. No man of honour, as that word is usually understood, did ever pretend that his honour obliged him to be chaste or temperate; to pay his creditors; to be useful to his country; to do good to mankind; to endeavour to be wise or learned; to regard his word, his promise, or his oath; or if he hath any of these virtues, they were never learned in the catechism of honour, which contains but two precepts, the punctual payment of debts contracted at play, and the right understanding the several degrees of an affront, in order to revenge it by the death of an adversary.

But suppose this principle of honour, which some men so much boast of, did really produce more virtues than it ever pretended to; yet since the very being of that honour dependeth upon the breath, the opinion, or the fancy of the people, the virtues derived from it could be of no long or certain duration. For example, suppose a man from a principle of honour should resolve to be just, or chaste, or temperate, and yet the censuring world should take a humour of refusing him those characters, he would then think the obligation at an end. Or on the other side, if he thought he could gain honour by the falsest and vilest actions (which is a case that very often happens), he would then make no scruple to perform it. And God knows, it would be an unhappy state to have the religion, the liberty, or the property of a people lodged in such hands, which however hath been too often the case.

What I have said upon this principle of honour may perhaps be thought of small concernment to most of you who are my hearers. However, a caution was not altogether unnecessary; since there is nothing by which not only the vulgar, but the honest tradesman hath been so much deceived, as this infamous pretence to honour in too many of their betters.

Having thus shown you the weakness and uncertainty of those principles which some men set up in the place of conscience to direct them in their actions, I shall now endeavour to prove to you that there is no solid, firm foundation of virtue but in a conscience directed by the principles of religion.

There is no way of judging how far we may depend upon the actions of men otherwise than by knowing the motives, and grounds, and causes of them; and if the motives of our actions be not resolved and determined into the law of God, they will be precarious and uncertain, and liable to perpetual changes. I will show you what I mean by an example. Suppose a man thinks it his duty to obey his parents, because reason tells him so, because he is obliged by gratitude, and because the laws of his country command him to do so; but if he stops here, his parents can have no lasting security; for an occasion may happen wherein it may be extremely his interest to be disobedient, and where the laws of the land can lay no hold upon him: therefore, before such a man can safely be trusted, he must proceed farther and consider that his reason is the gift of God; that God commanded him to be obedient to the laws, and did moreover in a particular manner enjoin him to be dutiful to his parents; after which, if he lays a due weight upon those considerations, he will probably continue in his duty to the end of his life, because no earthly interest can ever come in competition to balance the danger of offending his Creator, or the happiness of pleasing him. And of all this his conscience will certainly inform him, if he hath any regard to religion.

Secondly, fear and hope are the two greatest natural motives of all men's actions. But neither of these passions will ever put us in the way of virtue unless they be directed by conscience. For although virtuous men do sometimes accidentally make their way to preferment, yet the world is so corrupted that no man can reasonably hope to be rewarded in it merely upon account of his virtue. And consequently, the fear of punishment in this life will preserve men from very few vices since some of the blackest and basest do often prove the surest steps to favour; such as ingratitude, hypocrisy, treachery, malice, subornation, atheism, and many more which human laws do little concern themselves about. But when conscience placeth before us the hopes of everlasting happiness and the fears of everlasting misery, as the reward and punishment of our good or evil actions, our reason can find no way to avoid the force of such an argument otherwise than by running into infidelity.

Lastly, conscience will direct us to love God, and to put our whole trust and confidence in him. Our love of God will inspire us with a detestation for sin, as what is of all things most contrary to his divine nature; and if we have an entire confidence in him, *that* will enable us to subdue and despise all the allurements of the world.

It may here be objected, if conscience be so sure a director to us Christians in the conduct of our lives, how comes it to pass that the ancient heathens, who had no other lights but those of nature and reason, should so far exceed us in all manner of virtue, as plainly appears by many examples they have left on record?

To which it may be answered; first, those heathens were extremely strict and exact in the education of their children; whereas among us this care is so much laid aside that the more God hath blessed any man with estate or quality, just so much the less in proportion is the care he takes in the education of his children, and particularly of that child which is to inherit his fortune; of which the effects are visible enough among the great ones of the world. Again, those heathens did in a particular manner instil the principle into their children of loving their country; which is so far otherwise nowadays that, of the several parties among us, there is none of them that seem to have so much as heard whether there be such a virtue in the world; as plainly appears by their practices, and especially when they are placed in those stations where they can only have opportunity of showing it. Lastly, the most considerable among the heathens did generally believe rewards and punishments in a life to come; which is the great principle for conscience to work upon. Whereas too many of those who would be thought the most considerable among us, do, both by their practices and their discourses, plainly affirm that they believe nothing at all of the matter.

Wherefore, since it hath manifestly appeared that a religious conscience is the only true solid foundation upon which virtue can be built, give me leave before I conclude, to let you see how necessary such a conscience is to conduct us in every station and condition of our lives.

That a religious conscience is necessary in any station, is confessed even by those who tell us that all religion was invented by cunning men in order to keep the world in awe. For if religion, by the confession of its adversaries, be necessary towards the well-governing of mankind, then every wise man in power will be sure not only to choose out for every station under him such persons as are most likely to be kept in awe by religion, but likewise to carry some appearance of it himself, or else he is a very weak politician. And accordingly in any country where great persons affect to be open despisers of religion, their counsels will be found at last to be fully as destructive to the state as to the church.

It was the advice of Jethro to his son-in-law Moses,° to 'provide able men, such as fear God, men of truth, hating covetousness', and to place such over the people; and Moses, who was as wise a statesman at least as any in this age, thought fit to follow that advice. Great abilities without the fear of God are most dangerous instruments when they are trusted with power. The laws of man have thought fit that those who are called to any office of trust should be bound by an oath to the faithful discharge of it. But an oath is an appeal to God, and therefore can have no influence except upon those who believe that he is, and that he is a rewarder of those that seek him, and a punisher of those who disobey him. And therefore we see the laws themselves are forced to have recourse to conscience in these cases, because their penalties cannot reach the arts of cunning men, who can find ways to be guilty of a thousand injustices without being discovered, or at least without being punished. And the reason why we find so many frauds, abuses, and corruptions where any trust is conferred, can be no other than that there is so little conscience and religion left in the world, or at least that men in their choice of instruments have private ends in view, which are very different from the service of the public. Besides, it is certain that men who profess to have no religion are full as zealous to bring over proselytes as any Papist or fanatic can be. And therefore, if those who are in station high enough to be of influence or example to others; if those (I say) openly profess a contempt or disbelief of religion, they will be sure to make all their dependants of their own principles; and what security can the public expect from such persons, whenever their interests or their lusts come into competition with their duty? It is very possible for a man who hath the appearance of religion, and is a great pretender to conscience, to be wicked and an hypocrite; but it is impossible for a man who openly declares against religion to give any reasonable security that he will not be false and cruel, and corrupt, whenever a temptation offers which he values more than he does the power wherewith he was trusted. And if such a man doth not betray his cause and his master, it is only because the temptation was not properly offered, or the profit was too small, or the danger was too great. And hence it is that we find so little truth or justice among us, because there are so very few who either in the service of the public, or in common dealings with each other, do ever look farther than their own advantage and how to guard themselves against the laws of the country; which a man may do by favour, by secrecy, or by cunning, though he breaks almost every law of God.

Therefore to conclude, it plainly appears that unless men are guided by the advice and judgment of a conscience founded on religion, they can give no security that they will be either good subjects, faithful servants of the public, or honest in their mutual dealings; since there is no other tie through which the pride, or lust, or avarice, or ambition of mankind will not certainly break one time or other.

Consider what has been said, &c.

Stella's Birthday

March 13, 1718-19

Stella this day is thirty-four°
(We shan't dispute a year or more).
However, Stella, be not troubled,
Although thy size and years are doubled
Since first I saw thee at sixteen,
The brightest virgin on the green;
So little is thy form declined,
Made up so largely in thy mind.
  O, would it please the gods to *split*
Thy beauty, size, and years, and wit,   10
No age could furnish out a pair
Of nymphs so graceful, wise, and fair;
With half the lustre of your eyes,
With half your wit, your years and size.
And then, before it grew too late,
How should I beg of gentle Fate,
(That either nymph might have her swain)
To split my worship too in twain.

Swift to Bishop Evans

I had an express sent to me yesterday by some friends, to let me know that you refused to accept my proxy,° which I think was in a legal form, and with all the circumstances it ought to have. I was likewise informed of some other particulars, relating to your displeasure for my not appearing. You may remember, if you please, that I promised last year never to appear again at your visitations; and I will most certainly keep my word, if the law will permit me, not from any contempt of your Lordship's jurisdictions, but that I would not put you under the temptation of giving me injurious treatment, which no wise man, if he can avoid it, will receive above once from the same person.

I had the less apprehension of any hard dealing from your Lordship, because I had been more than ordinary officious in my respects to you from your first coming over.° I waited on you as soon as I knew of your landing. I attended on you in your first journey to Trim. I lent you a useful book relating to your diocese; and repeated my visits, till I saw you never intended to return them. And I could have no design to serve myself, having nothing to hope or fear from you. I cannot help it, if I am called of a different party from your Lordship; but that circumstance is of no consequence with me, who respect good men of all parties alike.

I have already nominated a person to be my curate, and did humbly recommend him to your Lordship to be ordained, which must be done by some other bishop, since you were pleased, as I am told, to refuse it; and I am apt to think you will be of opinion, that when I have a lawful curate, I shall not be under the necessity of a personal appearance, from which I hold myself excused by another station. If I shall prove to be mistaken, I declare my appearance will be extremely against my inclinations. However, I hope that in such a case your Lordship will please to remember in the midst of your resentments that you are to speak to a clergyman, and not to a footman. I am,

Your Lordship's most obedient, humble servant,

JON. SWIFT.

Phyllis

OR, THE PROGRESS OF LOVE

Desponding Phyllis was endued
With ev'ry talent of a prude:
She trembled when a man drew near;
Salute her, and she turn'd her ear:
If o'er against her you were placed,
She durst not look above your waist:
She'd rather take you to her bed
Than let you see her dress her head.
In church you heard her, thro' the crowd,
Repeat the *absolution* loud: 10
In church, secure behind her fan,
She durst behold that monster, man:
There practis'd how to place her head,
And bit her lips to make them red;
Or, on the mat devoutly kneeling,
Would lift her eyes up to the ceiling,
And heave her bosom unaware
For neighb'ring beaux to see it bare.

   At length a lucky lover came,
And found admittance from the dame.   20
Suppose all parties now agreed,
The writings drawn, the lawyer fee'd,
The vicar and the ring bespoke:
Guess, how could such a match be broke?
See then what mortals place their bliss in!
Next morn betimes the bride was missing:
The mother scream'd, the father chid—
Where can this idle wench be hid?
No news of Phyl! The bridegroom came,
And thought his bride had skulk'd for shame,   30
Because her father used to say
The girl *had such a bashful way*.

   Now John the butler must be sent
To learn the way that Phyllis went:
The groom was *wish'd** to saddle Crop;
For John must neither light nor stop,

      * A tradesman's phrase.

But find her, where soe'er she fled,
And bring her back alive or dead.
   See here again the dev'l to do!
For, truly, John was missing too: 40
The horse and pillion both were gone—
Phyllis, it seems, was fled with John.
   Old Madam, who went up to find
What papers Phyl had left behind,
A letter on the toilet sees:
'To my much honour'd father, these—'
('Tis always done, romances tell us,
When daughters run away with fellows)
Fill'd with the choicest commonplaces,
By others used in the like cases;   50
That, long ago a *fortune-teller*
Exactly said, what now befell her;
And in a *glass* had made her see
A *serving-man of low degree*.
It was *her fate*, must be forgiven;
For *marriages are made in Heaven.*°
His pardon begg'd: but, to be plain,
She'd *do't,* if *'twere to do again*:
Thank God, 'twas *neither shame nor sin,*
For John was come of *honest kin*.   60
Love never thinks of rich and poor;
She'd beg with John from door to door.
Forgive her, if it be a crime;
She'll never do't *another time*.
She ne'er before in all her life
Once disobey'd him, *maid nor wife*.
One argument she summ'd up all in:
The thing was done and past recalling;
And therefore hoped she would recover
His favour, when his *passion's over*.   70
She valued not what others thought her,
And was—his *most obedient daughter*.
   Fair maidens all, attend the Muse,
Who now the wand'ring pair pursues.
Away they rode in homely sort,
Their journey long, their money short;
The loving couple well bemir'd;

The horse and both the riders tir'd:
Their victuals bad, their lodgings worse.
Phyl cried, and John began to curse.   80
Phyl wish'd that she had strain'd a limb,
When first she ventured out with him;
John wish'd that he had broke a leg,
When first for her he quitted Peg.

But what adventures more befell 'em,
The Muse has now not time to tell 'em;
How Johnny wheedled, threaten'd, fawn'd,
Till Phyllis all her trinkets pawn'd:
How oft she broke her marriage vows
In kindness to maintain her spouse,
Till swains unwholesome spoil'd the trade;   90
For now the surgeon must be paid,
To whom those perquisites are gone
In Christian justice due to John.

When food and raiment now grew scarce,
Fate put a period to the farce,
And with exact poetic justice;
For John is landlord, Phyllis hostess:
They keep, at Staines, the Old Blue Boar,
Are cat and dog, and rogue and whore.   100

The Progress of Beauty

When first Diana leaves her bed,
  Vapours and steams her looks disgrace,
A frowzy dirty-colour'd red
  Sits on her cloudy wrinkled face:

But by degrees, when mounted high,
  Her artificial face appears
Down from her window in the sky.
  Her spots are gone, her visage clears.

'Twixt earthly females and the moon,
  All parallels exactly run;   10
If Celia should appear too soon,
  Alas, the nymph would be undone!

To see her from her pillow rise,
  All reeking in a cloudy steam,
Crack'd lips, foul teeth, and gummy eyes,
  Poor Strephon, how would he blaspheme!

The soot or powder which was wont
  To make her hair look black as jet,
Falls from her tresses on her front,
  A mingled mass of dirt and sweat.   20

Three colours, black, and red, and white,
  So graceful in their proper place,
Remove them to a diff'rent light,
  They form a frightful hideous face:

For instance, when the lily skips
  Into the precincts of the rose,
And takes possession of the lips,
  Leaving the purple to the nose:

So, Celia went entire to bed,
  All her complexions safe and sound;   30
But when she rose, the black and red,
  Though still in sight, had changed their ground.

The black, which would not be confined,
   A more inferior station seeks,
Leaving the fiery red behind,
   And mingles in her muddy cheeks.

The paint by perspiration cracks,
   And falls in rivulets of sweat,
On either side you see the tracks
   While at her chin the confluents met.   40

A skilful housewife thus her thumb
   With spittle, while she spins, anoints;
And thus the brown meanders come
   In trickling streams betwixt her joints.

But Celia can with ease reduce,
   By help of pencil, paint and brush,
Each colour to its place and use,
   And teach her cheeks again to blush.

She knows her *early* self no more,
   But fill'd with admiration stands;   50
As *other* painters oft adore
   The workmanship of their own hands.°

Thus, after four important hours,
   Celia's the wonder of her sex;
Say, which among the heav'nly pow'rs
   Could cause such marvellous effects?

Venus, indulgent to her kind,
   Gave women all their hearts could wish,
When first she taught them where to find
   White lead, and Lusitanian dish.°   60

Love with white lead cements his wings;
   White lead was sent us to repair
Two brightest, brittlest, earthly things,
   A lady's face, and China-ware.

She ventures now to lift the sash;
   The window is her proper sphere;
Ah, lovely nymph! be not too rash,
   Nor let the beaux approach too near.

Take pattern by your *sister* star;
   Delude at once, and bless our sight;   70
When you are seen, be seen from far,
   And chiefly choose to shine by night.

In the Pell-Mell when passing by,°
   Keep up the glasses of your chair,°
Then each transported fop will cry,
   'G–d d—n me Jack, she's wondrous fair!'

But, art no longer can prevail
   When the materials all are gone;
The best mechanic hand must fail,
   Where nothing's left to work upon.   80

Matter, as wise logicians say,
   Cannot without a *form* subsist;
And *form*, say I as well as they,
   Must fail, if *matter* brings no grist.

And this is fair Diana's case;
   For, all astrologers maintain,
Each night a bit drops off her face
   When mortals say she's in her wane:

While Partridge wisely shows the cause
   Efficient, of the moon's decay,°   90
That Cancer with his pois'nous claws
   Attacks her in the *milky way*:°

But Gadbury, in art profound,°
   From her pale cheeks pretends to show
That swain Endymion is not sound,°
   Or else, that *Mercury*'s her foe.°

But let the cause be what it will,
   In half a month she looks so thin
That Flamsteed can, with all his skill,°
   See but her forehead and her chin.   100

Yet, as she wastes, she grows discreet;
   Till midnight never shows her head;
So rotting Celia strolls the street,
   When sober folks are all a-bed:

For sure, if this be Luna's fate,
   Poor Celia, but of mortal race,
In vain expects a longer date
   To the materials of *her* face.

When Mercury her tresses mows,
   To think of oil and soot is vain: 110
No painting can restore a *nose*,
   Nor will her *teeth* return again.

Two balls of glass may serve for eyes,
   White lead can plaister up a cleft;
But these alas, are poor supplies
   If neither cheeks nor lips be left.

Ye pow'rs who over love preside!
   Since mortal beauties drop so soon,
If you would have us well supplied,
   Send us *new* nymphs with each *new* moon.   120

To Stella,

As, when a lofty pile is raised,
We never hear the workmen praised
Who bring the lime, or place the stones—
But all admire Inigo Jones:°
So, if this pile of scatter'd rhymes
Should be approved in after-times;
If it both pleases and endures,
The merit and the praise are yours.

   Thou, Stella, wert no longer young
When first for thee my harp I strung,   10
Without one word of Cupid's darts,
Of killing eyes, or bleeding hearts.
With friendship and esteem possessed,
I ne'er admitted Love a guest.

   In all the habitudes of life,
The friend, the mistress, and the wife,
Variety we still pursue,
In pleasure seek for something new;
Or else, comparing with the rest,
Take comfort that our own is best   20
(The best we value by the worst,
As tradesmen show their trash at first):
But his pursuits are at an end,
Whom Stella chooses for a *friend.*

   A poet starving in a garret,
Conning all topics like a parrot,
Invokes his Mistress and his Muse,
And stays at home for want of shoes:
Should but his Muse, descending, drop
A slice of bread and mutton chop;   30
Or kindly, when his credit's out,
Surprise him with a pint of stout;
Or patch his broken stocking soles;
Or send him in a peck of coals;
Exalted in his mighty mind
He flies, and leaves the stars behind;

Counts all his labours amply paid,
Adores her for the timely aid.
 Or should a porter make inquiries
For Chloe, Sylvia, Phyllis, Iris;   40
Be told the lodging, lane, and sign,
The bow'rs that hold those nymphs divine;
Fair Chloe would perhaps be found
With footmen tippling under ground;°
The charming Sylvia beating flax,
Her shoulders marked with bloody tracks;°
Bright Phyllis mending ragged smocks,
And radiant Iris in the pox.
These are the goddesses enroll'd
In Curll's collections, new and old,°   50
Whose scoundrel fathers would not know 'em,
If they should meet 'em in a poem.
 True poets can depress and raise,
Are lords of infamy and praise;
They are not scurrilous in satire,
Nor will in panegyric flatter.
Unjustly poets we asperse:
Truth shines the brighter, clad in verse,
And all the fictions they pursue
Do but insinuate what is true.   60
 Now, should my praises owe their truth
To beauty, dress, or paint, or youth,
What stoics call *without our power*,°
They could not be ensur'd an hour;
'Twere grafting on an annual stock,
That must our expectation mock
And, making one luxuriant shoot,
Die the next year for want of root:
Before I could my verses bring,
Perhaps you're quite another thing.   70
 So Mævius, when he drain'd his skull°
To celebrate some suburb trull,°
His similes in order set,
And ev'ry crambo he could get;°
Had gone through all the commonplaces
Worn out by wits, who rhyme on faces;
Before he could his poem close

The lovely nymph had lost her nose.°
   Your virtues safely I commend,
They on no accidents depend: 80
Let malice look with all her eyes,
She dares not say the poet lies.
   Stella, when you these lines transcribe,
Lest you should take them for a bribe,
Resolved to mortify your pride
I'll here expose your weaker side.
   Your spirits kindle to a flame,
Moved with the lightest touch of blame;
And when a friend in kindness tries
To show you where your error lies,   90
Conviction does but more incense;
Perverseness is your whole defence;
Truth, judgment, wit, give place to spite,
Regardless both of wrong and right;
Your virtues, all suspended, wait
Till time hath open'd reason's gate;
And what is worse, your passion bends
Its force against your nearest friends;
Which manners, decency, and pride,
Have taught you from the world to hide.   100
In vain; for see, your friend hath brought
To public light your *only* fault;
And yet a fault we often find
Mix'd in a noble, gen'rous mind:
And may compare to Ætna's fire
Which, though with trembling, all admire;
The heat that makes the summit glow,
Enriching all the vales below.
Those who in warmer climes complain
From Phœbus' rays they suffer pain,   110
Must own that pain is largely paid
By gen'rous wines beneath a shade.
   Yet, when I find your passions rise,
And anger sparkling in your eyes,
I grieve those spirits should be spent,
For nobler ends by Nature meant.
One passion, with a diff'rent turn,
Makes wit inflame, or anger burn:

So the sun's heat, with different pow'rs,
Ripens the grape, the liquor sours.   120
Thus Ajax, when with rage possessed,°
By Pallas breathed into his breast,
His valour would no more employ,
Which might alone have conquer'd Troy;
But, blinded by resentment, seeks
For vengeance on his friends the Greeks.
    You think this turbulence of blood
From stagnating preserves the flood,
Which thus fermenting, by degrees
Exalts the spirits, sinks the lees.   130
    Stella, for once you reason wrong;
For should this ferment last too long,
By time subsiding, you may find
Nothing but acid left behind.
From passion you may then be freed,
When peevishness and spleen succeed.
    Say, Stella, when you copy next,
Will you keep strictly to the text?
Dare you let these reproaches stand,
And to your failing set your hand?   140
Or, if these lines your anger fire,
Shall they in baser flames expire?
Whene'er they burn, if burn they must,
They'll prove my accusation just.

A PROPOSAL FOR THE UNIVERSAL USE OF IRISH MANUFACTURE, IN CLOTHES AND FURNITURE OF HOUSES, &c.

UTTERLY REJECTING AND RENOUNCING EVERY THING WEARABLE THAT COMES FROM ENGLAND.

IT is the peculiar felicity and prudence of the people in this kingdom, that whatever commodities or productions lie under the greatest discouragements from England, those are what we are sure to be most industrious in cultivating and spreading. *Agriculture*, which hath been the principal care of all wise nations, and for the encouragement whereof there are so many statute laws in England, we countenance so well that the landlords are everywhere by *penal clauses* absolutely prohibiting their tenants from ploughing;° not satisfied to confine them within certain limitations, as it is the practice of the English; one effect of which is already seen in the prodigious dearness of corn, and the importation of it from London, as the cheaper market. And because people are the *riches of a country*, and that our *neighbours* have done, and are doing all that in them lie to make our wool a drug to us,° and a monopoly to them; therefore the politic gentlemen of Ireland have depopulated vast tracts of the best land, for the feeding of sheep.

I could fill a volume as large as the *History of the Wise Men of Gotham* with a catalogue only of some *wonderful* laws and customs we have observed within thirty years past. 'Tis true indeed, our beneficial traffic of wool with France hath been our only support for several years past, furnishing us all the little money we have to pay our rents and go to market. But our merchants assure me, 'This trade hath received a great damp by the present fluctuating condition of the coin in France; and that most of their wine is paid for in specie, without carrying thither any commodity from hence.'

However, since we are so universally bent upon enlarging our *flocks*, it may be worth enquiring what we shall do with our wool, in case Barnstaple should be overstocked,° and our French commerce should fail?

I could wish the Parliament had thought fit to have suspended their regulation of *church* matters and enlargements of the *prerogative* till a more convenient time, because they did not appear very pressing (at least to the persons *principally concerned*) and instead of those great refinements in *politics* and *divinity*, had *amused* themselves and their committees a little with the *state of the nation*. For example: What if the House of Commons had thought fit to make a resolution *nemine contradicente* against wearing any cloth or stuff in their families, which were not of the growth and manufacture of this kingdom? What if they had extended it so far as utterly to exclude all silks, velvets, calicoes, and the whole *lexicon* of female fopperies; and declared that whoever acted otherwise, should be deemed and reputed *an enemy to the nation*? What if they had sent up such a resolution to be agreed to by the House of Lords, and by their own practice and encouragement spread the execution of it in their several countries? What if we should agree to make *burying in woollen* a *fashion*, as our neighbours have made it a *law*? What if the ladies would be content with Irish stuffs for the furniture of their houses, for gowns and petticoats to themselves and their daughters? Upon the whole, and to crown all the rest; Let a firm resolution be taken by *male* and *female*, never to appear with one single *shred* that comes from England; 'And let all the people say, AMEN.'

I hope and believe nothing could please His Majesty better than to hear that his loyal subjects of both sexes in this kingdom celebrated his *birthday* (now approaching) *universally* clad in their own manufacture. Is there virtue enough left in this deluded people to save them from the brink of ruin? If the men's opinion may be taken, the ladies will look as handsome in stuffs as brocades; and since all will be equal, there may be room enough to employ their wit and fancy in choosing and matching of patterns and colours. I heard the late Archbishop of Tuam° mention a pleasant observation of somebody's, 'that Ireland would never be happy till a law were made for *burning* everything that came from England, except their *people* and their *coals*'. Nor am I *even yet* for lessening the number of those exceptions.

Non tanti mitra est, non tanti Judicis ostrum.°

But I should rejoice to see a *staylace* from England be thought *scandalous*, and become a topic for *censure* at *visits* and *tea-tables*.

If the unthinking shopkeepers in this town had not been *utterly* destitute of common sense, they would have made some *Proposal to the Parliament*, with a *petition* to the purpose I have mentioned, promising to improve the 'cloths and stuffs of the nation into all possible degrees of fineness and colours, and engaging not to play the knave according to their custom by exacting and imposing upon the nobility and gentry either as to the prices or the goodness'. For I remember in London upon a general mourning, the *rascally mercers* and *woollen-drapers* would in four-and-twenty hours raise their *cloths* and *silks* to above a double price; and if the mourning continued long, then come whining with *petitions* to the *court, that they were ready to starve, and their fineries lay upon their hands*.

I could wish our shopkeepers would immediately think on this *proposal*, addressing it to all persons of quality and others; but first be sure to get somebody who can write sense, to put it into form.

I think it needless to exhort the *clergy* to follow this good example, because *in a little time, those among them who are so unfortunate to have had their birth and education in this country, will think themselves abundantly happy when they can afford* Irish *crape, and an* Athlone *hat*; and as to the others *I shall not presume* to direct them. I have indeed seen the present Archbishop of Dublin° clad from head to foot in our own manufacture; and yet, under the rose be it spoken, *his Grace deserves as good a gown as any prelate in Christendom*.

I have not courage enough to offer *one syllable* on this subject to *their honours* of the army. Neither have I sufficiently considered the great importance of *scarlet* and *gold lace*.

The fable in Ovid of Arachne and Pallas,° is to this purpose. The goddess had heard of one Arachne a young virgin, very famous for *spinning* and *weaving*. They both met upon a trial of skill; and Pallas finding herself almost equalled in her own art, stung with rage and envy, knocked her *rival* down, turned her into a *spider*, enjoining her to *spin* and *weave* for ever, *out of her own bowels*, and *in a very narrow compass*. I confess that from a boy I always pitied poor Arachne, and could never heartily love the goddess on account of *so cruel and unjust a sentence*; which however is *fully executed* upon *us* by England, with further additions of *rigour* and *severity*. For the greatest part of *our bowels and vitals* are extracted without allowing us the liberty of *spinning* and *weaving* them.

The Scripture tells us, that 'oppression makes a wise man mad'.° Therefore, consequently speaking, the reason why some men are not *mad* is because they are not *wise*. However, it were to be wished that *oppression* would in time teach a little *wisdom* to *fools*.

I was much delighted with a person who hath a great estate in this kingdom, upon his complaints to me, 'how grievously POOR England suffers by impositions from Ireland. That we convey our own wool to France in spite of all the *harpies* at the custom-house. That Mr. Shuttleworth, and others on the Cheshire coasts are such fools to sell us their *bark* at a good price for tanning *our own hides* into leather; with other enormities of the like weight and kind.' To which I will venture to add some more: 'That the mayoralty of this city is always executed by an *inhabitant*, and often by a *native*, which might as well be done by a *deputy*, with a moderate salary, whereby POOR England loses at least one thousand pounds a year upon the balance. That the governing of this kingdom costs the lord lieutenant two thousand four hundred pounds a year, so much *net* loss to POOR England. That the people of Ireland presume to dig for coal *in their own grounds*; and the farmers in the county of Wicklow send their turf to the very market of Dublin, to the great discouragement of the coal trade at Mostyn and Whitehaven.° That the revenues of the *post-office* here, so righteously belonging to the English treasury, as arising chiefly from our own commerce with each other, should be remitted to London clogged with that grievous burthen of exchange, and the pensions paid out of the Irish revenues to English *favourites* should lie under the same disadvantage, to the great loss of the grantees. When a *divine* is sent over to a *bishopric* here, with the hopes of five-and-twenty hundred pounds a year; upon his arrival, he finds, alas! a dreadful discount of ten or twelve *per cent*. A *judge* or a *commissioner* of the revenue has the same cause of complaint.' Lastly, 'The ballad upon Cotter is vehemently suspected to be Irish manufacture; and yet is allowed to be sung in our open streets, under the very *nose* of the *government*.'

These are a few among the many hardships we put upon that POOR kingdom of England; for which I am confident every *honest* man wishes a *remedy*. And I hear there is a project *on foot* for transporting our best wheaten *straw* by sea and land carriage to Dunstable, and *obliging us by a law* to take off yearly so many *ton of straw hats* for the use of our women; which will be a *great encouragement* to the manufacture of that industrious town.

I should be glad to learn among the divines, whether a law *to bind men without their own consent*, be obligatory *in foro conscientia*; because I find Scripture, Sanderson and Suarez° are wholly silent in the matter. The oracle of *reason*, the great *law of nature*, and general opinion of *civilians*, wherever they treat of *limited governments*, are indeed decisive enough.

It is wonderful to observe the bias among our people in favour of *things*, *persons*, and *wares* of all kinds that come from England. The *printer* tells his *hawkers* that he has got 'an excellent new song just brought from London'. I have somewhat of a tendency that way myself; and upon hearing a *coxcomb* from thence displaying himself with great volubility upon the *park*, the *playhouse*, the *opera*, the *gaming ordinaries*, it was apt to beget in me a kind of veneration for his parts and accomplishments. 'Tis not many years since I remember a *person* who by his style and literature° seems to have been *corrector* of a hedge-press in some *blind alley* about

Little Britain,° proceed *gradually* to be an *author*, at least a *translator* of a lower rate, though somewhat of a larger bulk than any that now *flourishes* in Grub Street; and upon the strength of this foundation, come over *here*, *erect* himself up into an *orator* and *politician*, and lead a *kingdom* after him. This, I am told, was the *very motive* that prevailed on the *author* of a play,° called 'Love in a hollow Tree', to do us the *honour* of a visit; presuming with very good reason, *that he was a writer of a superior class*. I know *another*, who for thirty years past, hath been the *common standard of stupidity* in England, where he was never heard a minute in any *assembly*, or by any *party* with *common Christian treatment*; yet upon his arrival hither could put on a *face of importance and authority*, talked more than six, without either *gracefulness*, *propriety*, or *meaning*; and at the same time be admired and followed as the pattern of *eloquence* and *wisdom*.

Nothing hath humbled me so much or shown a greater disposition to a *contemptuous* treatment of Ireland in some Ministers, than that high style of several speeches from the *throne*, delivered, as usual, after the *royal assent*, in *some periods* of the two last *reigns*. Such high exaggerations of the prodigious *condescensions* in the prince, to pass *those good laws*, would have but an odd sound at Westminster. Neither do I apprehend how any *good law* can pass wherein the *king*'s interest is not as much concerned as that of the *people*. I remember after a speech on the like occasion delivered by my L[or]d W[harton], (I think it was his last) he desired Mr. Addison to *ask my opinion of it*. My answer was, 'That his Excellency had very honestly forfeited his head on account of one paragraph; wherein he asserted by plain consequence, *a dispensing power* in the Queen.'° His Lordship owned *it was true*, but *swore* the words were *put into his mouth* by direct orders from Court. From whence it is clear, that some *ministries* in those times were apt, from their *high* elevation, to look *down* upon this kingdom as if it had been one of their *colonies* of *outcasts* in America. And I observed a little of the same turn of spirit in *some great men*, from whom I expected better; although to do them justice, it proved no point of difficulty to make them *correct their idea*, whereof the *whole nation* quickly found the benefit—But that is forgotten. How the style hath since run, I am wholly a stranger, having never seen a speech since the last of the Queen.

I would now expostulate a little with our country landlords, who by unmeasurable *screwing* and *racking* their tenants all over the kingdom, have already reduced the miserable *people* to a *worse condition* than the *peasants* in France, or the *vassals* in Germany and Poland; so that the whole *species* of what we call *substantial farmers*, will in a very few years be utterly at an end. It was pleasant to observe these gentlemen *labouring* with all their *might* for preventing the *bishops* from letting their revenues at a moderate half value, (whereby the whole *order* would in an age have been reduced to manifest beggary) at the very instant when they were everywhere *canting* their own lands° upon short leases, and sacrificing their *oldest tenants for a penny an acre advance*. I know not how it comes to pass, (and yet perhaps I know well enough) that *slaves* have a natural disposition to be *tyrants*; and that when my *betters* give me a kick, I am apt to revenge it with six upon my *footman*, although perhaps he may be an honest and diligent fellow. I have heard *great* divines affirm that 'nothing is so likely to call down an universal judgment from Heaven upon a nation as universal oppression'; and whether this be not already verified in part, *their worships* the landlords are *now* at full leisure to consider. Whoever travels this country, and observes the *face* of nature or the *faces*, and habits, and dwellings of the *natives*, will hardly think himself in a land where either *law*, *religion*, or *common humanity* is professed.

I cannot forbear saying one word upon a *thing* they call a *Bank*,° which I hear is projecting in this town. I never saw the *proposals*, nor understand any one particular of their scheme. What I wish for at present is only a sufficient provision of *hemp*, and *caps*, and *bells*, to distribute according to the several degrees of *honesty* and *prudence* in *some persons*. I *hear* only of a monstrous sum already named; and if OTHERS do not soon hear of it too, and *hear* it with a *vengeance*, then am I a gentleman of less sagacity, than myself and very few besides, take me to be. And the jest will be still the better, if it be true, as judicious persons have assured me, that one half of this money will be *real*, and the other half only *Gasconnade*. The matter will be likewise much mended if the merchants continue to carry off our gold, and our goldsmiths to melt down our heavy silver.

An Excellent New Song

ON A SEDITIOUS PAMPHLET.

To the tune of 'Packington's Pound'.

The Author having wrote a treatise advising the people of Ireland to wear their own manufactures, a prosecution was set on foot against Waters the printer thereof, which was carried on with so much violence, that one Whitshed, their Chief Justice, thought proper, in a manner the most extraordinary, to keep the Grand Jury above twelve hours and to send them eleven times out of court, until he had wearied them into a special verdict.

Brocados, and damasks, and tabbies, and gauzes,
   Are, by Robert Ballentine, lately brought over,
With forty things more: Now hear what the law says,
   Whoe'er will not wear them is not the king's lover.
         Though a printer and Dean
         Seditiously mean
Our true Irish hearts from Old England to wean,
We'll buy English silks for our wives and our daughters,
In spite of his Deanship and Journeyman Waters.°

In England the dead in woollen are clad,°   10
   The Dean and his printer then let us cry Fie on;
To be clothed like a carcass would make a Teague mad,
   Since a living dog better is than a dead lion.°
         Our wives they grow sullen
         At wearing of woollen,
And all we poor shopkeepers must our horns pull in.
Then we'll buy English silks for our wives and our daughters,
In spite of his Deanship and Journeyman Waters.

Whoever our trading with England would hinder,
   To *inflame* both the nations do plainly conspire,   20
Because Irish linen will soon turn to tinder,
   And wool it is greasy, and quickly takes fire.
         Therefore, I assure ye,
         Our noble grand jury,
When they saw the Dean's book they were in a great fury;
They would buy English silks for their wives and their daughters,
In spite of his Deanship and Journeyman Waters.

This wicked rogue Waters, who always is sinning,
  And before *coram nobis* so oft has been call'd,°
Henceforward shall print neither pamphlets nor linen,   30
  And if swearing can do't, shall be swingeingly maul'd:
        And as for the Dean,
        You know whom I mean,
If the printer will 'peach him, he'll scarce come off clean.
Then we'll buy English silks for our wives and our daughters,
In spite of his Deanship and Journeyman Waters.

The Run upon the Bankers

This poem was printed some years ago, and it should seem, by the late failure of two bankers, to be somewhat prophetic. It was therefore thought fit to be reprinted.

The bold encroachers on the deep
    Gain by degrees huge tracts of land,
Till Neptune, with a gen'ral sweep,
    Turns all again to barren strand.

The multitude's capricious pranks°
    Are said to represent the seas,
Breaking the *bankers* and the *banks*,
    Resume *their own* whene'er they please.

Money, the *life-blood* of the nation,
    Corrupts and stagnates in the veins,   10
Unless a proper *circulation*
    Its motion and its heat maintains.

Because 'tis *lordly* not to pay,
    Quakers and *aldermen*, in state,°
Like *peers*, have *levees* ev'ry day
    Of duns attending at their gate.

We want our money on the nail;
    The banker's ruin'd if he pays:
They seem to act an ancient tale,
    The *birds* are met to strip the *jays*.   20

'Riches', the wisest monarch sings,°
    'Make pinions for themselves to fly';
They fly like bats, on *parchment* wings,
    And *geese* their *silver* plumes supply.

No money left for squand'ring heirs!
    Bills turn the lenders into debtors:
The wish of Nero now is theirs,°
    That they *had never known their letters*.

Conceive the works of midnight hags,
    Tormenting fools behind their backs: 30
Thus bankers, o'er their bills and bags,
    Sit squeezing *images of wax.*°

Conceive the whole enchantment broke;
    The witches left in open air,
With pow'r no more than other folk,
    Exposed with all their *magic* ware.

So pow'rful are a banker's bills
    When creditors demand their due;
They break up counters, doors, and tills,
    And leave his empty chests in view.   40

Thus when an earthquake lets in light
    Upon the god of *gold* and *hell*,°
Unable to endure the sight,
    He hides within his darkest cell.

As when a conj'rer takes a lease
    From Satan for a term of years,
The *tenant*'s in a dismal case
    Whene'er the *bloody bond* appears.°

A *baited* banker thus desponds,°
    From his own hand foresees his fall;   50
They have his *soul* who have his *bonds*;
    'Tis like the *writing on the wall.*°

How will the caitiff wretch be scared,
    When first he finds himself awake
At the last trumpet, unprepared,
    And all his *grand account* to make!

For in that universal *call*,°
    Few bankers will to Heav'n be mounters;
They'll cry, 'Ye *shops*, upon us fall!
    Conceal and cover us, ye *counters*!'   60

When *other* hands the *scales* shall hold,
    And they, in *men and angels' sight*
Produced with all their bills and gold,
    Weigh'd in the balance, and found light!°

Swift to Alexander Pope*

Dublin, *January* 10, 1721.

A thousand things have vexed me of late years, upon which I am determined to lay open my mind to you. I rather choose to appeal to you than to my Lord Chief Justice [Whitshed], under the situation I am in. For I take this cause properly to lie before you. You are a much fitter judge of what concerns the credit of a writer, the injuries that are done him, and the reparations he ought to receive. Besides, I doubt whether the arguments I could suggest to prove my own innocence would be of much weight from the gentlemen of the long robe to those in furs,° upon whose decision about the difference of style or sentiments, I should be very unwilling to leave the merits of my cause.

Give me leave then to put you in mind (although you cannot easily forget it) that about ten weeks before the Queen's death, I left the town, upon occasion of that incurable breach among the great men at Court, and went down to Berkshire, where you may remember that you gave me the favour of a visit. While I was in that retirement, I writ a discourse° which I thought might be useful in such a juncture of affairs, and sent it up to London; but upon some difference in opinion between me and a certain great Minister° now abroad, the publishing of it was deferred so long that the Queen died, and I recalled my copy, which hath been ever since in safe hands. In a few weeks after the loss of that excellent Princess, I came to my station here, where I have continued ever since in the greatest privacy, and utter ignorance of those events which are most commonly talked of in the world. I neither know the names nor number of the family which now reigns, further than the Prayer Book informs me. I cannot tell who is Chancellor, who are Secretaries, nor with what nations we are in peace or war. And this manner of life was not taken up out of any sort of affectation, but merely to avoid giving offence, and for fear of provoking party zeal.

I had indeed written some Memorials of the four last years of the Queen's reign,° with some other informations which I received as necessary materials to qualify me for doing something in an employment then designed me. But as it was at the disposal of a person who had not the smallest share of steadiness or sincerity, I disdained to accept it.

These papers, at my few hours of health and leisure, I have been digesting into order by one sheet at a time, for I dare not venture any further, lest the humour of searching and seizing papers should revive;

* This letter Mr. Pope never received.

not that I am in pain of any danger to myself, (for they contain nothing of present times or persons, upon which I shall never lose a thought while there is a cat or a spaniel in the house) but to preserve them from being lost among Messengers and Clerks.

I have written in this kingdom, a discourse° to persuade the wretched people to wear their own manufactures instead of those from England. This treatise soon spread very fast, being agreeable to the sentiments of the whole nation, except of those gentlemen who had employments, or were expectants, upon which a person in great office here° immediately took the alarm; he sent in haste for the Chief Justice, and informed him of a seditious, factious and virulent pamphlet, lately published with a design of setting the two kingdoms at variance, directing at the same time that the printer should be prosecuted with the utmost rigour of law. The Chief Justice had so quick an understanding, that he resolved if possible to outdo his orders. The Grand Juries of the county and city were practised effectually with, to present the said pamphlet with all aggravating epithets, for which they had thanks sent them from England, and their presentments published for several weeks in all the newspapers. The printer was seized, and forced to give great bail. After his trial the jury brought him in not guilty, though they had been culled with the utmost industry. The Chief Justice sent them back nine times, and kept them eleven hours, until being perfectly tired out, they were forced to leave the matter to the mercy of the judge, by what they call a special verdict. During the trial, the Chief Justice among other singularities, laid his hand on his breast, and protested solemnly that the author's design was to bring in the Pretender, although there was not a single syllable of party in the whole treatise, and although it was known that the most eminent of those who professed his own principles, publicly disallowed his proceedings. But the cause being so very odious and impopular, the trial of the verdict was deferred from one term to another, till upon the Duke of Grafton's arrival, his Grace after mature advice, and permission from England, was pleased to grant a *noli prosequi*.°

This is the more remarkable, because it is said that the man is no ill decider in common cases of property, where party is out of the question; but when that intervenes, with ambition at heels to push it forward, it must needs confound any man of little spirit, and low birth, who hath no other endowment than that sort of knowledge, which however possessed in the highest degree, can possibly give no one good quality to the mind.

'Tis true, I have been much concerned, for several years past, upon account of the public as well as of myself, to see how ill a taste for wit and sense prevails in the world, which politics and South Sea, and party, and operas and masquerades have introduced. For besides many insipid papers which the malice of some hath entitled me to, there are many persons appearing to wish me well, and pretending to be judges of my style and manner, who have yet ascribed some writings to me, of which any man of common sense and literature would be heartily ashamed. I cannot forbear instancing a treatise° called a Dedication upon Dedications, which many would have to be mine, although it be as empty, dry, and servile a composition, as I remember at any time to have read. But above all, there is one circumstance which makes it impossible for me to have been author of a treatise, wherein there are several pages containing a panegyric upon King George, of whose character and person I am utterly ignorant, nor ever had once the curiosity to inquire into either, living at so great a distance as I do, and having long done with whatever can relate to public matters.

Indeed, I have formerly delivered my thoughts very freely, whether I were asked or no, but never affected to be a counsellor, to which I had no manner of call. I was humbled enough to see myself so far outdone by the Earl of Oxford in my own trade as a scholar, and too good a courtier not to discover his contempt of those who would be men of importance out of their sphere. Besides, to say the truth, although I have known many great ministers ready enough to hear opinions, yet I have hardly seen one that would ever descend to take advice; and this pedantry arises from a maxim themselves do not believe at the same time they practise by it, that there is something profound in politics, which men of plain honest sense cannot arrive to.

I only wish my endeavours had succeeded better in the great point I had at heart, which was that of reconciling the ministers to each other. This might have been done, if others who had more concern and more influence would have acted their parts; and if this had succeeded, the public interest both of Church and State would not have been the worse, nor the Protestant succession endangered.

But whatever opportunities a constant attendance of four years might have given me for endeavouring to do good offices to particular persons, I deserve at least to find tolerable quarter from those of the other party; for many of which I was a constant advocate with the Earl of Oxford, and for this I appeal to his Lordship. He knows how often I pressed him in favour of Mr. Addison, Mr. Congreve, Mr. Rowe, and Mr. Steele; although I freely confess that his Lordship's kindness to them was altogether owing to his generous notions, and the esteem he had for their wit and parts, of which I could only pretend to be a remembrancer. For I can never forget the answer he gave to the late Lord Halifax, who upon the first change of the Ministry interceded with him to spare Mr. Congreve. It was by repeating these two lines of Virgil,

> Non obtusa adeo gestamus pectora Pœni,
> Nec tam aversus equos Tyria Sol jungit ab urbe.°

Pursuant to which, he always treated Mr. Congreve with the greatest personal civilities, assured him of his constant favour and protection, adding that he would study to do something better for him.

I remember it was in those times a usual subject of raillery towards me among the Ministers, that I never came to them without a Whig in my sleeve; which I do not say with any view towards making my court. For the new principles fixed to those of that denomination, I did then, and do now from my heart abhor, detest, and abjure, as wholly degenerate from their predecessors. I have conversed in some freedom with more Ministers of State of all parties than usually happens to men of my level; and I confess, in their capacity as Ministers, I look upon them as a race of people whose acquaintance no man would court, otherwise than upon the score of vanity or ambition. The first quickly wears off (and is the vice of low minds, for a man of spirit is too proud to be vain) and the other was not my case. Besides, having never received more than one small favour, I was under no necessity of being a slave to men in power, but chose my friends by their personal merit, without examining how far their notions agreed with the politics then in vogue. I frequently conversed with Mr. Addison, and the others I named (except Mr. Steele) during all my Lord Oxford's ministry, and Mr. Addison's friendship to me continued inviolable, with as much kindness as when we used to meet at my Lord Somers or Halifax, who were leaders of the opposite party.

I would infer from all this, that it is with great injustice I have these many years been pelted by your pamphleteers, merely upon account of some regard which the Queen's last Ministers were pleased to have for me. And yet in my conscience I think I am a partaker in every ill design they had against the Protestant succession, or the liberties and religion of their country; and can say with Cicero, that I should be proud to be included with them in all their actions, *tanquam in equo Trojano*.° But if I have never discovered by my words, writings, or actions, any party virulence, or dangerous designs against the present powers; if my friendship and conversation were equally shown among those who liked or disapproved the proceedings then at Court, and if I was known to be a common friend of all deserving persons of the latter sort when they were in distress; I cannot but think it hard that I am not suffered to run quietly among the common herd of people whose opinions unfortunately differ from those which lead to favour and preferment.

I ought to let you know, that the thing we called a Whig in England is a creature altogether different from those of the same denomination here, at least it was so during the reign of her late Majesty. Whether those on your side have changed or no, it hath not been my business to inquire. I remember my excellent friend Mr. Addison, when he first came over hither Secretary° to the Lieutenant, was extremely offended at the conduct and discourse of the chief manager[s] here. He told me they were a sort of people who seemed to think, that the principles of a Whig consisted in nothing else but damning the Church, reviling the clergy, abetting Dissenters, and speaking contemptibly of revealed religion.

I was discoursing some years ago with a certain Minister, about that Whiggish or fanatical genius so prevalent among the English of this kingdom. His Lordship accounted for it by that number of Cromwell's soldiers, adventurers established here, who were all of the sourest leaven and the meanest birth, and whose posterity are now in possession of their lands and their principles. However, it must be confessed that of late some people in this country are grown weary of quarrelling, because interest, the great motive of quarrelling is at an end; for it is hardly worth contending who shall be an exciseman, a country vicar, a crier in the courts, or an under-clerk.

You will perhaps be inclined to think, that a person so ill treated as I have been, must at some time or other have discovered very dangerous opinions in government; in answer to which, I will tell you what my political principles were in the time of her late glorious Majesty, which I never contradicted by any action, writing, or discourse.

First, I always declared myself against a Popish successor to the crown, whatever title he might have by the proximity of blood. Neither did I ever regard the right line, except upon two accounts; first as it was established by law, and secondly as it hath much weight in the opinions of the people. For necessity may abolish any law, but cannot alter the sentiments of the vulgar; right of inheritance being perhaps the most popular of all topics; and therefore in great changes when that is broke, there will remain much heart-burning and discontent among the meaner people; which (under a weak prince and corrupt administration) may have the worst consequences upon the peace of any state.

As to what is called a revolution principle, my opinion was this; that whenever those evils which usually attend and follow a violent change of government, were not in probability so pernicious as the grievances we suffer under a present power, then the public good will justify such a revolution. And this I took to have been the case in the Prince of Orange's expedition, although in the consequences it produced some very bad effects, which are likely to stick long enough by us.

I had likewise in those days a mortal antipathy against standing armies in times of peace; because I always took standing armies to be only servants hired by the master of the family, for keeping his own children in slavery. And because I conceived that a prince who could not think himself secure without mercenary troops, must needs have a separate interest from that of his subjects—although I am not ignorant of those artificial necessities which a corrupted ministry can create, for keeping up forces to support a faction against the public interest.

As to Parliaments, I adored the wisdom of that gothic institution, which made them annual: and I was confident our liberty could never be placed upon a firm foundation till that ancient law were restored among us. For, who sees not, that while such assemblies are permitted to have a longer duration, there grows up a commerce of corruption between the ministry and the deputies, wherein they both find their accounts to the manifest danger of liberty—which traffic would neither answer the design nor expense, if Parliaments met once a year.

I ever abominated that scheme of politics (now about thirty years old) of setting up a moneyed interest in opposition to the landed. For I conceived there could not be a truer maxim in our government than this, that the possessors of the soil are the best judges of what is for the advantage of the kingdom. If others had thought the same way, funds of credit and South Sea projects would neither have been felt nor heard of.

I could never discover the necessity of suspending any law upon which the liberty of the most innocent persons depended: neither do I think this practice hath made the taste of arbitrary power so agreeable as that we should desire to see it repeated.° Every rebellion subdued and plot discovered, contributes to the firmer establishment of the Prince. In the latter case, the knot of conspirators is entirely broke, and they are to begin their work anew under a thousand disadvantages; so that those diligent inquiries into remote and problematical guilt, with a new power of enforcing them by chains and dungeons to every person whose face a minister thinks fit to dislike, are not only opposite to that maxim, which declares it better that ten guilty men should escape, than one innocent suffer, but likewise leave a gate wide open to the whole tribe of informers; the most accursed, prostitute, and abandoned race that God ever permitted to plague mankind.

'Tis true, the Romans had a custom of choosing a dictator, during whose administration the power of other magistrates was suspended;

but this was done upon the greatest emergencies—a war near their doors, or some civil dissension; for armies must be governed by arbitrary power. But when the virtue of that commonwealth gave place to luxury and ambition, this very office of dictator became perpetual in the persons of the Caesars and their successors, the most infamous tyrants that have anywhere appeared in story.

These are some of the sentiments I had relating to public affairs while I was in the world; what they are at present, is of little importance either to that or myself; neither can I truly say I have any at all, or if I had, I dare not venture to publish them; for however orthodox they may be while I am now writing, they may become criminal enough to bring me into trouble before midsummer. And indeed I have often wished for some time past, that a political catechism might be published by authority four times a year, in order to instruct us how we are to speak, and write, and act, during the current quarter. I have by experience felt the want of such an instructor; for, intending to make my court to some people on the prevailing side, by advancing certain old Whiggish principles, which it seems had been exploded about a month before, I have passed for a disaffected person. I am not ignorant how idle a thing it is for a man in obscurity to attempt defending his reputation as a writer, while the spirit of faction so hath universally possessed the minds of men, that they are not at leisure to attend to anything else. They will just give themselves time to libel and accuse me, but cannot spare a minute to hear my defence. So in a plot-discovering age, I have often known an innocent man seized and imprisoned,° and forced to lie several months in chains, while the Ministers were not at leisure to hear his petition, till they had prosecuted and hanged the number they proposed.

All I can reasonably hope for by this letter, is to convince my friends and others who are pleased to wish me well, that I have neither been so ill a subject, nor so stupid an author, as I have been represented by the virulence of libellers; whose malice hath taken the same train in both, by fathering dangerous principles in government upon me which I never maintained, and insipid productions which I am not capable of writing. For however I may have been soured by personal ill treatment, or by melancholy prospects for the public, I am too much a politician to expose my own safety by offensive words. And if my genius and spirit be sunk by increasing years, I have at least enough discretion left, not to mistake the measure of my own abilities by attempting subjects where those talents are necessary, which perhaps I may have lost with my youth.

A Satirical Elegy

ON THE DEATH OF A LATE FAMOUS GENERAL

His Grace! impossible! what, dead!
Of old age too, and in his bed!
And could that Mighty Warrior fall?
And so inglorious, after all!
Well, since he's gone, no matter how,
The last loud trump must wake him now;°
And, trust me, as the noise grows stronger,
He'd wish to sleep a little longer.
And could he be indeed so old
As by the newspapers we're told?   10
Threescore, I think, is pretty high;
'Twas time in conscience he should die.
This world he cumber'd long enough;
He burnt his candle to the snuff;
And that's the reason, some folks think,
He left behind *so great a stink*.
Behold his funeral appears,°
Nor widow's sighs, nor orphan's tears,
Wont at such times each heart to pierce,
Attend the progress of his hearse.   20
But what of that? his friends may say
He had those honours in his day.
True to his profit and his pride,
He made them weep before he died.

  Come hither, all ye empty things,
Ye bubbles raised by breath of kings
Who float upon the tide of state;
Come hither, and behold your fate!
Let Pride be taught by this rebuke,
How very mean a thing's a duke;   30
From all his ill-got honours flung,
Turn'd to that dirt from whence he sprung.

Upon the Horrid Plot

DISCOVERED BY HARLEQUIN, THE BISHOP OF ROCHESTER'S FRENCH DOG. IN A DIALOGUE BETWEEN A WHIG AND A TORY

I ask'd a *Whig* the other night,
How came this wicked plot to light?
He answer'd that a *dog* of late
Inform'd a minister of state.
Said I, from thence I nothing know,
For are not all informers so?
A villain who his friend betrays,
We style him by no other phrase;
And so a perjured *dog* denotes
Porter, and Prendergast, and Oates,°   10
And forty others I could name—
   WHIG. But you must know this dog was lame.°
   TORY. A weighty argument indeed!
Your *evidence* was *lame*,—proceed;
Come, help your *lame dog o'er the stile.*°
   WHIG. Sir, you mistake me all this while:
I mean a *dog* (without a joke)
Can howl, and bark, but never spoke.
   TORY. I'm still to seek which *dog* you mean;
Whether cur Plunkett, or whelp Skean,°   20
An English or an Irish hound;
Or t'other *puppy* that was drown'd,°
Or Mason, that abandon'd bitch.°
Then pray be free, and tell me which:
For every stander-by was marking
That all the noise they made was *barking*.
You pay them well, the *dogs* have got
Their *dogs-heads in a porridge-pot*:°
And 'twas but just; for wise men say
That *every dog must have his day*.°   30
Dog Walpole laid a quart of *nog* on't,
He'd either *make a hog or dog on't*;°
And look'd, since he has got his wish,
As if he had *thrown down a dish*.

Yet this I dare foretell you from it,
He'll soon *return to his own vomit*.
   WHIG. Besides, this horrid plot was found
By Neynoe, after he was drown'd.
   TORY. Why then the proverb is not right,
Since you can teach *dead dogs to bite*.°   40
   WHIG. I proved my proposition full:
But Jacobites are strangely dull.
Now, let me tell you plainly, sir,
Our witness is a real *cur*,
A *dog* of spirit for his years;
Has twice two legs, two hanging ears;
His name is *Harlequin*, I wot,
And that's a name in every *plot*:
Resolv'd to save the British nation,
Though French by birth and education;   50
His correspondence plainly dated,
Was all *deciphered*, and *translated*.°
His answers were exceeding pretty
Before the secret wise Committee;°
Confess'd as plain as he could bark,
Then with his fore-foot set his *mark*.°
   TORY. Then all this while have I been bubbled,
I thought it was a *dog in doublet*:°
The matter now no longer sticks,
For statesmen never want *dog-tricks*.   60
But since it was a real *cur*,
And not a *dog* in metaphor,
I give you joy of the report
That he's to have a place at court.
   WHIG. Yes, and a place he will grow rich in;
A turnspit in the royal kitchen.
Sir, to be plain, I tell you what,
We had occasion for a plot;
And when we found the *dog* begin it,
We guess'd the bishop's *foot was in it*.   70
   TORY. I own it was a dang'rous project,
And you have proved it by *dog-logic*.
Sure such intelligence between
A *dog* and *bishop* ne'er was seen
Till you began to change the breed;
Your *bishops* are all *dogs* indeed.

Swift to Bishop Stearne

Deanery House, [Friday,] *February* 28, 1723–4.

My Lord,

If you do not appoint tomorrow, Monday, Tuesday, Wednesday, or Thursday to dine at the Deanery with the old club° of the Walls and ladies, I believe there may be a mutiny; therefore pray fix the matter for your own sake. I am

Your Lordship's most dutiful,

JONATH. SWIFT.

Addressed—To the Right Reverend the Lord Bishop of Clogher.

A
LETTER
TO THE SHOP-KEEPERS, TRADESMEN, FARMERS, AND COMMON-PEOPLE IN GENERAL, OF THE KINGDOM OF IRELAND,

Concerning the Brass Half-Pence Coined by M^r 𝕸𝖔𝖔𝖉𝖘, WITH A DESIGN to have them Pass in this KINGDOM. By M. B. *Drapier*.

Brethren, Friends, Countrymen
and Fellow-Subjects

WHAT I intend now to say to you, is, next to your duty to God, and the care of your salvation, of the greatest concern to yourselves, and your children; your *bread* and *clothing*, and every common necessary of life entirely depend upon it. Therefore I do most earnestly exhort you as *men*, as *Christians*, as *parents*, and as *lovers of your country*, to read this paper with the utmost attention, or get it read to you by others; which that you may do at the less expense, I have ordered the printer to sell it at the lowest rate.°

It is a great fault among you, that when a person writes with no other intention than *to do you good, you will not be at the pains to read his advices*. One copy of this paper may serve a dozen of you, which will be less than a farthing a-piece. It is your folly that you have no common or general interest in your view, not even the wisest among you; neither do you know or enquire, or care who are your friends, or who are your enemies.

About three years ago, a little book° was written, to advise all people to wear the *manufactures of this our own dear country*. It had no other design, said nothing against the *King* or *Parliament*, or *any man*, yet the POOR PRINTER was prosecuted two years, with the utmost violence; and even some WEAVERS themselves, for whose sake it was written, being upon the JURY, FOUND HIM GUILTY. This would be enough to discourage any man from endeavouring to do you good, when you will either neglect him or fly in his face for his pains, and when he must expect only *danger to himself* and *loss of money*, perhaps to his ruin.

However I cannot but warn you once more of the manifest destruction before your eyes, if you do not behave yourselves as you ought.

I will therefore first tell you the *plain story of the fact*; and then I will lay before you how you ought to act in common prudence, and according to the *laws of your country*.

The fact is thus: It having been many years since COPPER HALF-PENCE or FARTHINGS were last coined in this *kingdom*, they have been for some time very scarce, and many *counterfeits* passed about under the name of RAPS, several applications were made to England, that we might have liberty to *coin new ones*, as in former times we did; but they did not succeed. At last one Mr. WOOD, a *mean ordinary man*, *a hardware dealer*, procured a *patent* under his MAJESTY'S BROAD SEAL to coin FOURSCORE AND TEN THOUSAND POUNDS° in *copper* for this *kingdom*, which patent however did not oblige any one here to take them, unless they pleased. Now you must know, that the HALFPENCE and FARTHINGS in *England* pass for very little more than they are worth. And if you should beat them to pieces, and sell them to the *brazier* you would not lose above a penny in a shilling. But Mr. WOOD made his HALFPENCE of such *base metal*, and so much smaller than the English ones, that the *brazier* would not give you above a *penny* of good money for a *shilling* of his; so that this sum of *fourscore* and *ten thousand pounds* in good gold and silver, must be given for TRASH that will not be worth above *eight* or *nine thousand pounds* real value. But this is not the worst; for Mr. WOOD when he pleases may by stealth send over *another* and *another fourscore and ten thousand pounds*, and buy *all our goods for eleven parts in twelve*, under the value. For example, if a *hatter* sells a dozen of *hats* for *five shillings* a-piece, which amounts to *three pounds*, and receives the payment in Mr. WOOD's coin, he really receives only the value of *five shillings*.

Perhaps you will wonder how such *an ordinary fellow* as this Mr. WOOD could have so much interest as to get His MAJESTY's broad seal for so great a sum of bad money, to be sent to this poor country, and that all the *nobility* and *gentry* here could not obtain the same favour, and let us make our own *halfpence*, as we used to do. Now I will make that matter very plain. We are at a great distance from the *King's court*, and have nobody there to solicit for us, although a great number of *lords* and *squires*, whose estates are here, and are our countrymen, spend all their *lives* and *fortunes* there. But this same Mr. WOOD was able to attend constantly, for his own interest; he is an ENGLISHMAN and had GREAT FRIENDS, and it seems knew very well *where to give money*, to those that would speak to OTHERS that could speak to the KING and could tell A FAIR STORY. And HIS MAJESTY, and perhaps the great lord or lords who advised him, might think it was for our *country's good*; and so, as the lawyers express it, 'the KING was deceived in his grant', which often happens in *all reigns*. And I am sure if His MAJESTY knew that such a patent, if it should take effect according to the desire of Mr. WOOD, would utterly ruin this kingdom, which hath given such great proof of its *loyalty*, he would immediately recall it, and perhaps show his displeasure to SOMEBODY OR OTHER. *But a word to the wise is enough*. Most of you must have heard, with what anger our *honourable House of Commons* received an account of this WOOD's PATENT. There were several *fine speeches* made upon it, and plain proofs that it was all A WICKED CHEAT from the *bottom to the top*, and several *smart votes* were printed, which that same WOOD had the assurance to answer likewise in *print*, and in so confident a way, as if he were *a better man than our whole Parliament* put together.

This WOOD, as soon as his *patent* was passed, or soon after, sends over a great many *barrels of these HALFPENCE*, to Cork and other *sea-port towns*, and to get them off offered an *hundred pounds* in his coin for *seventy* or *eighty* in *silver*. But the *collectors* of the KING's customs very honestly refused to take them, and so did almost everybody else. And since the *Parliament* hath condemned them, and desired the KING that they might be stopped, all the *kingdom* do abominate them.

But WOOD is still working *underhand* to force his HALFPENCE upon us, and if he can by help of his *friends* in England prevail so far as to get an order that the *commissioners* and *collectors* of the KING's money shall receive them, and that the ARMY is to be paid with them, then he thinks *his work shall be done*. And this is the difficulty you will be under in such a *case*. For the common soldier when he goes to the *market* or *alehouse* will offer this money, and if it be refused, perhaps he will SWAGGER and HECTOR, and *threaten* to *beat* the BUTCHER or *alewife*, or take the goods by force, and throw them the bad HALFPENCE. In this and the like cases, the *shopkeeper*, or *victualler*, or *any other tradesman* has no more to do than to demand ten times the price of his goods, if it is to be paid in WOOD's money; for example, twenty pence of that money for A QUART OF ALE, and so in all things else, and not part with his goods till he gets the *money*.

For suppose you go to an ALEHOUSE with that base money, and the landlord gives you a quart for four of these HALFPENCE, what must the *victualler* do? His BREWER will not be paid in that coin, or if the BREWER should be such a fool, the *farmers* will not take it from them for their *bere*, because they are bound by their leases to pay their rents in good and lawful money of England, which this is not, nor of Ireland neither, and the *'squire their landlord* will never be so bewitched to take such *trash* for his land; so that it must certainly stop somewhere or other, and wherever it stops it is the same thing, and we are all undone.

The common weight of these HALFPENCE is between four and five to an *ounce*; suppose five, then three shillings and fourpence will weigh a pound, and consequently *twenty shillings* will weigh *six pound butter weight*. Now there are many hundred *farmers* who pay two hundred pound a year rent. Therefore when one of these farmers comes with his half-year's rent, which is one hundred pound, it will be at least six hundred pound weight, which is three horse load.

If a *'squire* has a mind to come to town to buy clothes and wine and spices for himself and family, or perhaps to pass the winter here; he must bring with him five or six horses loaden with *sacks* as the farmers bring their corn; and when his lady comes in her coach to our shops, it must be followed by a car loaden with Mr. WOOD's money. And I hope we shall have the grace to take it for no more than it is worth.

They say 'SQUIRE C——Y° has *sixteen thousand pounds a year*, now if he sends for his *rent* to town, *as it is likely he does*, he must have *two hundred and forty horses* to bring up his *half-year's rent*, and two or three great *cellars* in his house for stowage. But what the bankers will do I cannot tell. For I am assured, that some great bankers keep by them *forty thousand pounds* in ready cash to answer all payments, which sum, in Mr. WOOD's money, would require twelve hundred horses to carry it.

For my own part, I am already resolved what to do; I have a pretty good shop of *Irish stuffs* and *silks*, and instead of taking Mr. WOOD's bad copper, I intend to truck with my neighbours the BUTCHERS, and *bakers*, and *brewers*, and the rest, *goods for goods*, and the little *gold* and *silver* I have, I will keep by me like my *heart's blood* till better times, or till I am just ready to starve, and then I will buy Mr. WOOD's money as my father did the brass money in K. JAMES's time;° who could buy *ten pound* of it with a *guinea*, and I hope to get as much for a *pistole*, and so purchase *bread* from those who will be such fools as to sell it me.

These HALFPENCE, if they once pass, will soon be COUNTER-FEIT, because it may be cheaply done, the *stuff* is so *base*. The DUTCH likewise will probably do the same thing, and send them over to us to pay for our *goods*. And Mr. WOOD will never be at rest but coin on: so that in some years we shall have at least five times fourscore and ten thousand pounds of this *lumber*. Now the current money of this kingdom is not reckoned to be above *four hundred thousand pounds* in all; and while there is a *silver* sixpence left these BLOOD-SUCKERS will never be quiet.

When once the *kingdom* is reduced to such a condition, I will tell you what must be the end: The *gentlemen of estates* will all turn off their *tenants* for want of payment, because as I told you before, the *tenants* are obliged by their leases to pay *sterling* which is lawful current money of England; then they will turn their own *farmers*, AS TOO MANY OF THEM DO ALREADY, run *all* into *sheep°* where they can, keeping only such other *cattle* as are necessary, then they will be their own *merchants* and send their *wool* and *butter* and *hides* and *linen* beyond sea for ready *money* and *wine* and *spices* and *silks*. They will keep only a few miserable *cottiers*. The *farmers* must *rob* or *beg*, or leave their *country*. The *shopkeepers* in this and every other town, must *break* and *starve*; for it is the *landed man* that maintains the *merchant*, and *shopkeeper*, and *handicraftsman*.

But when the *'squire* turns *farmer* and *merchant* himself, all the good money he gets from abroad, he will hoard up or send for England, and keep some poor *tailor* or *weaver* and the like in his own house, who will be glad to get bread at any rate.

I should never have done if I were to tell you all the miseries that we shall undergo, if we be so *foolish* and *wicked* as to take this CURSED COIN. It would be very hard if all Ireland should be put into *one scale*, and *this sorry fellow* WOOD *into the other*, that Mr. WOOD should weigh down *this whole kingdom*, by which England gets above a million of good money every year clear into their *pockets*, and that is more than the English do by *all the world besides*.

But your *great comfort is*, that as His MAJESTY's *patent* does not oblige you to take this *money*, so the *laws* have not given the *crown* a power of forcing the *subjects* to take what *money* the *KING* pleases: for then by the same reason we might be bound to take PEBBLE-STONES or *cockle-shells* or *stamped leather* for *current coin*, if ever we should happen to live under an ill PRINCE; who might likewise by the same power make a *guinea* pass for ten pounds, a *shilling* for twenty shillings, and so on, by which he would in a short time get all the *silver* and *gold* of the *kingdom* into his own hands, and leave us nothing but *brass* or *leather* or what he pleased. Neither is anything reckoned more *cruel* or *oppressive* in the French *government* than their common practice of calling in all their money after they have sunk it very low, and then coining it anew at a much higher value, which however is not the thousandth part so wicked as this *abominable project* of Mr. WOOD. For the French give their subjects *silver* for *silver* and *gold* for *gold*, but *this fellow* will not so much as give us good *brass* or *copper* for our *gold* and *silver*, nor even a twelfth part of their worth.

Having said thus much, I will now go on to tell you the judgments of some great *lawyers* in this matter, whom I fee'd on purpose for your sakes, and got their *opinions* under their *hands*, that I might be sure I went upon good grounds.

A famous law-book, called 'The Mirror of Justice',° *discoursing of the articles (or laws) ordained by our* ancient kings *declares the* law *to be as follows*: 'It was ordained that no *king* of this realm should *change, impair* or *amend* the *money* or make any other *money* than of *gold* or *silver without the assent of all the counties'*, that is, as my Lord Coke says,* *without the assent of* Parliament.

This book is very ancient, and of great authority for the time in which it was wrote, and with that character is often quoted by that great lawyer my Lord Coke.† By the law of England, the several metals are divided into *lawful* or *true metal* and *unlawful* or *false metal*; the former comprehends *silver* or *gold*; the latter all *baser metals*. That the former is only to pass in payments appears by an act of *Parliament*‡ made the twentieth year of Edward the First, called the 'Statute concerning the Passing of Pence', which I give you here as I got it translated into English, for some of our *laws* at that time, were, as I am told, writ in Latin: 'Whoever in buying or selling presumeth to refuse an halfpenny or farthing of lawful money, bearing the stamp which it ought to have, let him be seized on as a contemner of the King's majesty, and cast into prison.'

By this *statute*, no person is to be reckoned a *contemner* of the KING's *majesty*, and for that crime to be *committed to prison*; but he who refuses to accept the KING's coin made of *lawful metal*, by which, as I observed before, *silver* and *gold* only are intended.

That this is the true *construction* of the *Act*, appears not only from the plain meaning of the words, but from my Lord Coke's observation upon it. 'By this Act' (says he) 'it appears, that no subject can be forced to take in *buying* or *selling* or other *payments*, any money made but of lawful metal; that is, of *silver* or *gold*.'§

The law of England gives the KING all mines of *gold* and *silver*, but not the mines of other *metals*, the reason of which *prerogative* or *power*, as it is given by my Lord Coke¶ is, because money can be made of *gold* and *silver*, but not of other metals.

Pursuant to this opinion *halfpence* and *farthings* were anciently made of *silver*, which is most evident from the Act of Parliament of Henry the 4th. chap. 4.° by which it is enacted as follows: 'Item, for the great scarcity that is at present within the realm of England of halfpence and farthings of *silver*, it is ordained and established that the third part of all the money of

* 2 Inst. 576.   † 2 Inst. 576–577.   ‡ 2 Inst. 577.
§ 2 Inst. 577.   ¶ 2 Inst. 577.

silver plate which shall be brought to the *bullion*, shall be made in *halfpence* and *farthings*.' This shows that by the word 'halfpenny' and 'farthing' of lawful money in that statute concerning the passing of *pence*, are meant a small coin in halfpence and farthings of *silver*.

This is further manifest from the statute of the ninth year of Edward the 3d, chap. 3. which enacts, 'That no sterling HALFPENNY or FARTHING be molten for to make vessel, nor any other thing by the goldsmiths, nor others, upon forfeiture of the *money* so molten' (or melted).

By another Act in this *King's* reign° *black money* was not to be current in England, and by an Act made in the eleventh year of his reign chap. 5. *galley halfpence* were not to pass. What kind of *coin* these were I do not know, but I presume they were made of *base metal*, and that these Acts were no new *laws*, but farther declarations of the old *laws* relating to the *coin*.

Thus the *law* stands in relation to *coin*, nor is there any example to the contrary, except one in Davis's *Reports*,° who tells us that in the time of Tyrone's rebellion QUEEN ELIZABETH ordered *money of mixed metal* to be coined in the Tower of London, and sent over hither for payment of the ARMY, obliging all people to receive it and commanding that all silver money should be taken only as *bullion*, that is, for as much as it weighed. Davis tells us several particulars in this matter too long here to trouble you with, and that the *privy-council* of this *kingdom* obliged a *merchant* in England to receive this mixed money for goods transmitted hither.

But this proceeding is rejected by all the best lawyers as contrary to law, the *privy-council* here having no such power. And besides it is to be considered, that the *Queen* was then under great difficulties by a rebellion in this *kingdom* assisted from *Spain*, and whatever is done in great exigences and dangerous times should never be an example to proceed by in seasons of *peace* and *quietness*.

I will now, my dear friends, to save you the trouble, set before you in short, what the *law* obliges you *to do*, and what it does *not* oblige you to.

First, You are obliged to take all money in payments which is coined by the KING and is of the English standard or weight, provided it be of *gold* or *silver*.

Secondly, You are not obliged to take any money which is not of *gold* or *silver*, no not the HALFPENCE, or FARTHINGS of England, or of any other country, and it is only for convenience, or ease, that you are content to take them, because the custom of coining *silver* HALFPENCE &

FARTHINGS hath long been left off, I will suppose on account of their being subject to be lost.

Thirdly, Much less are you obliged to take those *vile halfpence* of that same WOOD, by which you must lose almost eleven-pence in every shilling.

Therefore my *friends*, stand to it one and all, refuse this *filthy trash*. It is no treason to rebel against Mr. WOOD. His MAJESTY in his patent obliges nobody to take these halfpence,° our GRACIOUS PRINCE hath no so ill advisers about him; or if he had, yet you see the laws have not left it in the KING's power, to force us to take any coin but what is lawful, of right standard *gold* and *silver*, therefore you have nothing to fear.

And let me in the next place apply myself particularly to you who are the poor sort of *tradesmen*: perhaps you may think you will not be so great losers as the rich, if these *halfpence* should pass, because you seldom see any *silver*, and your *customers* come to your *shops* or *stalls* with nothing but brass, which you likewise find hard to be got. But you may take my word, whenever this money gains footing among you, you will be utterly undone. If you carry these *halfpence* to a shop for *tobacco* or *brandy*, or *any other thing* you want, the *shopkeeper* will advance his goods accordingly, or else he must break, and leave the *key under the door*. Do you think I will sell you a yard of tenpenny stuff for twenty of Mr. WOOD's *halfpence*? No, not under two hundred at least, neither will I be at the trouble of counting, but weigh them in a lump. I will tell you one thing further, that if Mr. WOOD's project should take, it will ruin even our beggars. For when I give a *beggar* an halfpenny, it will quench his thirst, or go a good way to fill his belly, but the twelfth part of a halfpenny will do him no more service than if I should give him three pins out of my sleeve.

In short these HALFPENCE are like 'the accursed thing,° which' *as the* Scripture *tells us,* 'the children of Israel were forbidden to touch'. *They will run about like the* plague *and destroy every one who lays his hands upon them. I have heard scholars talk of a man who told a king that he had invented a way to torment people by putting them into a* bull of brass° *with fire under it, but the* prince *put the* projector *first into his own* brazen bull *to make the experiment; this very much resembles the project of Mr. WOOD, and the like of this may possibly be Mr. WOOD's fate, that the brass he contrived to torment this* kingdom *with, may prove his own torment, and his destruction at last.*

N.B. The AUTHOR of this paper is informed by persons who have made it their business to be exact in their observations on the true value of these HALFPENCE, that any person may expect to get a quart of twopenny ale for thirty-six of them.

I desire all persons may keep this paper carefully by them to refresh their memories whenever they shall have farther notice of Mr. WOOD's halfpence, or any other the like imposture.

Swift to Lord Carteret

April 28th, 1724.

My Lord,

Many of the principal persons in this kingdom, distinguished for their loyalty to his present Majesty, hearing that I had the honour to be known to your Excellency, have for some time pressed me very earnestly, since you were declared Lord-Lieutenant of this kingdom, to represent to your Excellency the apprehensions they are under concerning Mr. Wood's patent for coining halfpence to pass in Ireland. Your Excellency knows the unanimous sentiments of the Parliament here upon that matter: and, upon inquiry, you will find that there is not one person of any rank or party in this whole kingdom, who does not look upon that patent as the most ruinous project that ever was contrived against any nation. Neither is it doubted, that when your Excellency shall be thoroughly informed, your justice and compassion for an injured people will force you to employ your credit for their relief.

I have made bold to send you enclosed two small tracts° on this subject, one written (as it is supposed) by the Earl of Abercorn; the other is entitled to a weaver, and suited to the vulgar, but thought to be the work of a better hand.

I hope your Excellency will forgive an old humble servant, and one who always loved and esteemed you, for interfering in matters out of his province; which he would never have done, if many of the greatest persons here had not, by their importunity, drawn him out of his retirement to venture giving you a little trouble, in hopes to save their country from utter destruction; for which the memory of your government will be blessed by posterity.

I hope to have the honour of seeing your Excellency here, and do promise neither to be a frequent visitor nor troublesome solicitor; but ever, with the greatest respect, &c.

Addressed—To his Excellency the Lord Carteret, Lord-Lieutenant of Ireland.

Swift to Lord Carteret

June 9th, 1724

My Lord,

It is above a month since I took the boldness of writing to your Excellency, upon a subject wherein the welfare of this kingdom is highly concerned.

I writ at the desire of several considerable persons here, who could not be ignorant that I had the honour of being well known to you.

I could have wished your Excellency had condescended so far, as to let one of your under-clerks have signified to me that a letter was received.

I have been long out of the world, but have not forgotten what used to pass among those I lived with, while I was in it, and I can say, that during the experience of many years, and many changes in affairs, your Excellency, and one more, who is not worthy to be compared to you, are the only great persons that ever refused to answer a letter from me, without regard to business, party, or greatness; and if I had not a peculiar esteem for your personal qualities, I should think myself to be acting a very inferior part in making this complaint.

I never was so humble, as to be vain upon my acquaintance with men in power, and always rather chose to avoid it when I was not called. Neither were their power or titles sufficient, without merit, to make me cultivate them; of which I have witnesses enough left, after all the havoc made among them, by accidents of time, or by changes of persons, measures, and opinions.

I know not how your conceptions of yourself may alter, by every new high station, but mine must continue the same, or alter for the worse. I often told a great Minister,° whom you well know, that I valued him for being the same man through all the progress of power and place. I expected the like in your Lordship, and still hope that I shall be the only person who will ever find it otherwise.

I pray God to direct your Excellency in all your good undertakings, and especially in your government of this kingdom.

I shall trouble you no more; but remain, with great respect, my Lord, Your Excellency's most obedient and most humble servant.

Swift to Lord Carteret

July 9th, 1724.

My Lord,

I humbly claim the privilege of an inferior, to be the last writer; yet with great acknowledgements for your condescension in answering my letters, I cannot but complain of you for putting me in the wrong. I am in the circumstances of a waiting-woman, who told her lady, that nothing vexed her more than to be caught in a lie. But what is worse, I have discovered in myself somewhat of the bully; and that, after all my rattling, you have brought me down to be as humble as the most distant attender at your levee. It is well your Excellency's talents are in few hands; for, if it were otherwise, we who pretend to be free speakers, in quality of philosophers, should be utterly cured of our forwardness; at least I am afraid there will be an end of mine, with regard to your Excellency. Yet, my Lord, I am ten years older than I was when I had the honour to see you last, and consequently ten times more testy. Therefore I foretell that you, who could so easily conquer so captious a person, and of so little consequence, will quickly subdue this whole kingdom to love and reverence you. I am, with the greatest respect, my Lord, &c.

A LETTER TO THE WHOLE PEOPLE OF IRELAND. By M. B. *Drapier*. AUTHOR of the LETTER to the SHOP-KEEPERS, &c.

My Dear Countrymen,

HAVING already written three *letters* upon so disagreeable a subject as Mr. *Wood* and his *halfpence*; I conceived my task was at an end. But I find that cordials must be frequently applied to weak constitutions, *political* as well as *natural*. A people long used to hardships lose by degrees the very notions of liberty; they look upon themselves as creatures at mercy, and that all impositions laid on them by a stronger hand, are, in the phrase of the *Report*, *legal* and *obligatory*. Hence proceeds that *poverty* and *lowness of spirit*, to which a *kingdom* may be subject as well as a *particular person*. And when *Esau came fainting from the field at the point to die*, it is no wonder that he *sold his birthright for a mess of pottage*.°

I thought I had sufficiently shown to all who could want instruction, by what methods they might safely proceed whenever this *coin* should be offered to them; and I believe there hath not been for many ages an example of any kingdom so firmly united in a point of great importance, as this of ours is at present against that detestable fraud. But however, it so happens that some weak people begin to be alarmed anew, by rumours industriously spread. *Wood* prescribes to the newsmongers in London what they are to write. In one of their papers published here by some obscure printer (and probably with no good design) we are told that 'the Papists in Ireland have entered into an association against his coin', although it be notoriously known that they never once offered to stir in the matter; so that the two Houses of Parliament, the privy-council, the great number of corporations, the lord mayor and aldermen of Dublin, the grand juries, and principal gentlemen of several counties, are stigmatized in a lump under the name of 'Papists'.

This impostor and his crew do likewise give out that, by refusing to receive his dross for sterling, we 'dispute the King's prerogative, are grown ripe for rebellion, and ready to shake off the dependency of Ireland upon the crown of England'. To countenance which reports he hath published a paragraph in another newspaper to let us know that 'the Lord Lieutenant is ordered to come over immediately to settle his halfpence'.

I entreat you, my dear countrymen, not to be under the least concern upon these and the like rumours, which are no more than the last howls of a dog dissected alive, as I hope he hath sufficiently been. These calumnies are the only reserve that is left him. For surely our continued and (almost) unexampled loyalty will never be called in question for not suffering ourselves to be robbed of all that we have, by one obscure *ironmonger*.

As to disputing the King's *prerogative*, give me leave to explain to those who are ignorant, what the meaning of that word *prerogative* is.

The Kings of these realms enjoy several powers wherein the laws have not interposed. So they can make war and peace without the consent of Parliament; and this is a very great *prerogative*. But if the Parliament doth not approve of the war, the King must bear the charge of it out of his own purse, and this is as great a check on the crown. So the King hath a *prerogative* to coin money without consent of Parliament. But he cannot compel the subject to take that money except it be sterling, gold or silver; because herein he is limited by law. Some princes have indeed extended their *prerogative* further than the law allowed them: wherein however, the lawyers of succeeding ages, as fond as they are of *precedents*, have never dared to justify them. But to say the truth, it is only of late times that *prerogative* hath been fixed and ascertained. For whoever reads the histories of England will find that some former Kings, and these none of the worst, have upon several occasions ventured to control the laws with very little ceremony or scruple, even later than the days of Queen Elizabeth. In her reign that pernicious counsel of sending *base money* hither,° very narrowly failed of losing the kingdom, being complained of by the lord-deputy, the council, and the whole body of the English here. So that soon after her death it was recalled by her successor, and lawful money paid in exchange.

Having thus given you some notion of what is meant by the King's *prerogative*, as far as a *tradesman* can be thought capable of explaining it, I will only add the opinion of the great Lord Bacon,° that 'as God governs the world by the settled laws of nature which he hath made, and never transcends these laws, but upon high important occasions; so among earthly princes, those are the wisest and the best who govern by the known laws of the country, and seldomest make use of their *prerogative*'.

Now, here you may see that the vile accusation of *Wood* and his accomplices, charging us with 'disputing the King's prerogative' by refusing his brass, can have no place, because compelling the subject to take any coin which is not sterling, is no part of the King's *prerogative*, and I am very confident if it were so, we should be the last of his people to dispute it, as well from that inviolable loyalty we have always paid to His Majesty, as from the treatment we might in such a case justly expect from some, who seem to think we have neither *common sense* nor *common senses*. But God be thanked, the best of them are only our *fellow-subjects*, and not our *masters*. One great merit I am sure we have, which those of English birth° can have no pretence to; that our ancestors reduced this kingdom to the obedience of ENGLAND; for which we have been rewarded with a worse climate, the privilege of being governed by laws to which we do not consent, a ruined trade, a House of *Peers* without *jurisdiction*, almost an incapacity for all employments; and the dread of *Wood*'s halfpence.

But we are so far from disputing the King's *prerogative* in coining, that we own he has power to give a patent to any man for setting his royal image and superscription upon whatever materials he pleases; and liberty to the patentee to offer them in any country from England to Japan, only attended with one small limitation, That *nobody alive is obliged to take them*.

Upon these considerations I was ever against all recourse to England for a remedy against the present impending evil, especially when I observed that the addresses of both Houses, after long expectance, produced nothing but a REPORT altogether in favour of *WOOD*; upon which I made some observations in a former letter,° and might at least have made as many more; for it is a paper of as singular a nature as I ever beheld.

But I mistake; for before this *Report* was made, His Majesty's *most gracious answer* to the House of Lords was sent over and printed, wherein there are these words, 'granting the patent for coining halfpence and farthings AGREEABLE TO THE PRACTICE OF HIS ROYAL PREDECESSORS, &c.' That King Charles 2d. and King James 2d. (AND THEY ONLY) did grant patents for this purpose, is indisputable, and I have shown it at large.° Their patents were passed under the great seal of IRELAND by references to IRELAND, the copper to be coined in IRELAND, the patentee was bound on demand to receive his coin back in IRELAND, and pays silver and gold in return. *Wood*'s patent was made under the great seal of ENGLAND, the brass coined in ENGLAND, not the least reference made to IRELAND, the sum immense, and the patentee under no obligation to receive it again and give good money for it. This I only mention, because in my private thoughts I have sometimes made a query, whether the *penner* of those words in His Majesty's *most gracious answer*, 'agreeable to the practice of his royal predecessors', had maturely considered the several circumstances which, in my poor opinion, seem to make a difference.

Let me now say something concerning the other great cause of some people's fear, as *Wood* has taught the London newswriter to express it, that 'his Excellency the Lord Lieutenant is coming over to settle *Wood*'s halfpence'.

We know very well that the Lords Lieutenants for several years past have not thought this kingdom *worthy the honour of their residence* longer than was absolutely necessary for the King's business, which consequently *wanted no speed in the dispatch*; and therefore it naturally fell into most men's thoughts, that a new governor coming at an *unusual* time must portend some *unusual* business to be done, especially if the common report be true, that the Parliament prorogued to I know not when, is by a new summons (revoking that prorogation) to assemble° soon after his arrival. For which extraordinary proceeding the lawyers on t'other side the water have, by great good fortune, found two precedents.

All this being granted, it can never enter into my head that *so little a creature* as *Wood* could find credit enough with the King and his ministers, to have the Lord Lieutenant of Ireland sent hither in a hurry upon his errand.

For let us take the whole matter nakedly as it lies before us, without the refinements of some people, with which we have nothing to do. Here is a patent granted under the great seal of England, upon false suggestions, to one *William Wood* for coining copper halfpence for Ireland. The *Parliament* here, upon apprehensions of the worst consequences from the said patent, address the King to have it recalled; this is refused, and a committee of the privy-council *report* to His Majesty that *Wood* has performed the conditions of his patent. He then is left to do the best he can with his halfpence, no man being obliged to receive them; the people here, being likewise left to themselves, unite as one man, resolving they will have nothing to do with his ware. By this plain account of the fact it is manifest that the King and his ministry are wholly out of the case, and the matter is left to be disputed between him and us. Will any man therefore attempt to persuade me that a Lord Lieutenant is to be dispatched over in great haste, before the ordinary time, and a Parliament summoned by anticipating a prorogation, merely to put an hundred thousand pounds into the pocket of a *sharper*, by the ruin of a most loyal kingdom?

But supposing all this to be true. By what arguments could a Lord Lieutenant prevail on the same Parliament which addressed with so much zeal and earnestness against this evil, to pass it into a law? I am sure their opinion of *Wood* and his project is not mended since the last prorogation. And supposing those *methods* should be used which *detractors* tell us have been sometimes put in practice for *gaining votes*, it is well known that in this kingdom there are few employments to be given, and if there were more, it is *as well known* to whose share they must fall.

But because great numbers of you are altogether ignorant in the affairs of your country, I will tell you some reasons why there are so few employments to be disposed of in this kingdom. All considerable offices for life here are possessed by those to whom the reversions were granted, and these have been generally followers of the chief governors,° or persons who had interest in the Court of England. So the Lord Berkeley of Stratton holds that great office of *master of the rolls*; the Lord Palmerstown is *first remembrancer* worth near 2000*l. per ann.* One Dodington, secretary to the Earl of Pembroke, *begged* the reversion of *clerk of the pells* worth 2500*l.* a year, which he now enjoys by the death of the Lord Newtown. Mr. Southwell is secretary of state, and the Earl of Burlington lord high treasurer of Ireland by inheritance. These are only a few among many others which I have been told of, but cannot remember. Nay the reversion of several employments during pleasure° are granted the same way. This among many others, is a circumstance whereby the kingdom of Ireland is distinguished from all other nations upon earth; and makes it so difficult an affair to get into a civil employ that Mr. Addison was forced to purchase an old obscure place, called *keeper of the records of* Bermingham's *Tower*, of ten pounds a year, and to get a salary of 400*l.* annexed to it, though all the records there are not worth half-a-crown, either for curiosity or use. And we lately saw a *favourite secretary*° descend to be *master of the revels*, which by his *credit and extortion* he hath made *pretty considerable*. I say nothing of the under-treasurership worth about 8000*l.* a year, nor the commissioners of the revenue, four of whom generally live in England; for I think none of these are granted in reversion. But the jest is, that I have known upon occasion some of these absent officers as *keen* against the interest of Ireland, as if they had never been indebted to her for a *single groat*.

I confess, I have been sometimes tempted to wish that this project of *Wood* might succeed; because I reflected with some pleasure what a *jolly crew* it would bring over among us of *lords* and *squires*, and *pensioners* of *both sexes*, and officers *civil* and *military*, where we should live together as merry and sociable as beggars; only with this one abatement, that we should neither have *meat* to feed, nor *manufactures* to clothe us, unless we could be content to *prance* about in *coats of mail*, or eat brass as ostriches do iron.

I return from this digression to that which gave me the occasion of making it. And I believe you are now convinced, that if the Parliament of Ireland were as *temptable* as any *other* assembly *within a mile of* Christendom (which God forbid) yet the *managers* must of necessity fail for want of *tools* to work with. But I will yet go one step further, by supposing that a hundred new employments were erected on purpose to gratify *compliers*. Yet still an insuperable difficulty would remain; for it happens, I know not how, that *money* is neither *Whig* nor *Tory*, neither of *town* nor *country party*; and it is not improbable that a gentleman would rather choose to live upon his *own estate* which brings him *gold* and *silver*, than with the addition of an *employment*, when his *rents* and *salary* must both be paid in *Wood*'s brass at above eighty *per cent*. discount.

For these and many other reasons, I am confident you need not be under the least apprehensions from the sudden expectation of the *Lord Lieutenant*, while we continue in our present hearty disposition; to alter which there is no suitable temptation can possibly be offered. And if, as I have often asserted from the best authority, the *law* hath not left a *power* in the *crown* to force any money except sterling upon the subject, much less can the crown *devolve* such a *power* upon *another*.

This I speak with the utmost respect to the *person* and *dignity* of his Excellency the Lord Carteret, whose character hath been given me by a gentleman that hath known him from his first appearance in the world. That gentleman describes him as a young nobleman of great accomplishments, excellent learning, regular in his life, and of much spirit and vivacity. He hath since, as I have heard, been employed abroad, was principal secretary of state; and is now about the 37th year of his age appointed Lord Lieutenant of Ireland. From such a governor this kingdom may reasonably hope for as much prosperity as, *under so many discouragements*, it can be capable of receiving.

It is true indeed, that within the memory of man, there have been governors of so much dexterity as to carry points of terrible consequence to this kingdom, by their power with *those who were in office* and by their arts in managing or deluding others with *oaths*, *affability*, and even with *dinners*. If *Wood*'s brass had in those times been upon the *anvil*, it is obvious enough to conceive what methods would have been taken. *Depending* persons would have been told in plain terms, that it was a 'service expected from them, under pain of the public business being put into more complying hands'. Others would be allured by *promises*. To the *country gentlemen* (besides *good words*) *burgundy* and *closeting*.° It would perhaps have been hinted how 'kindly it would be taken to comply with a royal patent, though it were not compulsory', that if any inconveniences ensued, it might be made up with other 'graces or favours hereafter'. That 'gentlemen ought to consider whether it were prudent or safe to disgust England'. They would be desired to 'think of some good bills for encouraging of trade, and setting the poor to work, some further acts against Popery and for uniting Protestants'. There would be solemn engagements that we should 'never be troubled with above forty thousand pounds in his coin, and all of the best and weightiest sort, for which we should only give our manufactures in exchange, and keep our gold and silver at home'. Perhaps a 'seasonable report of some invasion would have been spread in the most proper juncture', which is a great smoother of rubs in public proceedings; and we should have been told that 'this was no time to create differences when the kingdom was in danger'.

These, I say, and the like methods would in corrupt times have been taken to let in this deluge of brass among us; and I am confident would even then have not succeeded, much less under the administration of so excellent a person as the Lord Carteret, and in a country where the people of all ranks, parties and denominations are convinced to a man, that the utter undoing of themselves and their posterity for ever, will be dated from the admission of that execrable coin; that if it once enters, it can be no more confined to a small or moderate quantity, than the *plague* can be confined to a few families, and that no *equivalent* can be given by any earthly power, any more than a dead carcass can be recovered to life by a cordial.

There is one comfortable circumstance in this universal opposition to Mr. *Wood*, that the people sent over hither from England to *fill up our vacancies ecclesiastical, civil and military*, are all on our side. *Money*, the great *divider* of the world, hath by a strange revolution been the great *uniter* of a most *divided* people. Who would leave a hundred pounds a year in England (*a country of freedom*) to be paid a thousand in Ireland out of *Wood*'s exchequer? The *gentleman they* have lately made *primate*° would never quit his seat in an English House of Lords, and his preferments at Oxford and Bristol, worth twelve hundred pounds a year , for four times the denomination here, but not half the value; therefore I expect to hear he will be as good an Irishman, upon *this article*, as any of his brethren, or even of *us* who have had the *misfortune* to be born in this island. For those, who, in the common phrase, do not 'come hither to learn the language', would never change a better country for a worse, to receive *brass* instead of *gold*.

Another slander spread by *Wood* and his emissaries is that by opposing him, we discover an inclination to 'shake off our dependence upon the crown of England'. Pray observe how important a person is this same *William Wood*, and how the public weal of two kingdoms is involved in his private interest. First, all those who refuse to take his coin *are Papists*, for he tells us that 'none but Papists are associated against him'. Secondly, they 'dispute the King's prerogative'. Thirdly, 'they are ripe for rebellion'. And fourthly, they are going to 'shake off their dependence upon the crown of England'. That is to say, 'they are going to choose another king'. For there can be no other meaning in this expression, however some may pretend to strain it.

And this gives me an opportunity of explaining to those who are ignorant, another point which hath often *swelled in my breast*. Those who come over hither to us from England, and some *weak* people among ourselves, whenever in discourse we make mention of *liberty* and *property*, shake their heads and tell us that Ireland is a 'depending kingdom',° as if they would seem, by this phrase, to intend that the people of Ireland is in some state of slavery or dependence different from those of England. Whereas a 'depending kingdom' is a *modern term of art*, unknown, as I have heard, to all ancient *civilians* and *writers upon government*; and Ireland is on the contrary called in some statutes an 'imperial crown', as held only from God; which is as high a style as any kingdom is capable of receiving. Therefore by this expression, a 'depending kingdom', there is no more understood than that by a statute made here in the 33d year of Henry 8th°, 'The King and his successors are to be kings imperial of this realm as united and knit to the imperial crown of England.' I have looked over all the English and Irish statutes without finding any law that makes Ireland *depend* upon England, any more than England does upon Ireland. We have indeed obliged ourselves to have the *same king with them*, and consequently they are obliged to have the *same king with us*. For the law was made by *our own Parliament*, and our ancestors then were not such *fools (whatever they were in the preceding reign)* to bring themselves under I know not what *dependence*, which is now talked of without any ground of *law, reason* or *common sense*.

Let whoever think otherwise, I *M. B. Drapier*, desire to be excepted, for I declare, next under God, I *depend* only on the King my sovereign, and on the laws of my own country; and I am so far from *depending* upon the people of England, that if they should ever *rebel* against my sovereign (which God forbid) I would be ready at the first command from His Majesty to take arms against them, as some of *my* countrymen did against *theirs* at Preston.° And if such a rebellion should prove so successful as to fix the *Pretender* on the throne of England, I would venture to transgress that *statute* so far as to lose every drop of my blood to hinder him from being *King* of Ireland.

'Tis true indeed, that within the memory of man, the Parliaments of England° have *sometimes* assumed the power of binding this kingdom by laws enacted there, wherein they were at first openly opposed (as far as *truth, reason* and *justice* are capable of *opposing*) by the famous Mr.

Molineux, an English gentleman born here, as well as by several of the greatest patriots and *best Whigs* in England. But the *love and torrent* of power prevailed. Indeed the arguments on both sides were invincible. For in *reason*, all *government* without the consent of the *governed* is the *very definition of slavery*. But in *fact, eleven men well armed will certainly subdue one single man in his shirt*. But I have done. For those who have used *power* to cramp *liberty* have gone so far as to resent even the *liberty* of *complaining*, although a man upon the rack was never known to be refused the liberty of *roaring* as loud as he thought fit.

And as we are apt to *sink* too *much* under *unreasonable* fears, so we are too soon inclined to be *raised* by groundless hopes (according to the nature of all *consumptive* bodies like ours). Thus, it hath been given about for several days past that *somebody* in England° empowered a second *somebody* to write to a third *somebody* here, to assure us that we 'should no more be troubled with those halfpence'. And this is reported to have been done by the *same person*, who was said to have sworn some months ago that he would 'ram them down our throats' (though I doubt they would *stick in our stomachs*); but whichever of these reports is true or false, it is no concern of ours. For *in this point* we have nothing to do with English *ministers*, and I should be sorry it lay in their power to *redress* this grievance or to *enforce* it; for the 'Report of the Committee' hath given me a *surfeit*. The remedy is wholly in your own hands; and therefore I have digressed a little in order to refresh and continue that *spirit* so seasonably raised amongst you, and to let you see, that by the laws of GOD, of NATURE, of NATIONS, and of your own Country, you ARE and OUGHT to be as FREE a people as your brethren in England.

If the pamphlets published at London by *Wood* and his *journeymen* in defence of his cause were reprinted here, and that our countrymen could be persuaded to read them, they would convince you of his wicked design more than all I shall ever be able to say. In short, I make him a perfect *saint* in comparison of what he appears to be from the writings of those whom he *hires* to justify his *project*. But he is so far *master of the field* (*let others guess the reason*) that no London printer dare publish any paper written in favour of Ireland, and here nobody hath yet been so *bold* as to publish anything in *favour* of *him*.

There was a few days ago a pamphlet sent me of near 50 pages° written in favour of Mr. *Wood* and his coinage, printed in London; it is not worth answering, because probably it will never be published here. But it gave me an occasion to reflect upon an unhappiness we lie under, that the people of England are utterly ignorant of our case; which however is no wonder since it is a point they do not in the least concern themselves about, farther than perhaps as a subject of discourse in a coffee-house when they have nothing else to talk of. For I have reason to believe that no minister ever gave himself the trouble of reading any papers written in our defence, because I suppose *their opinions are already determined*, and are formed wholly upon the reports of *Wood* and his accomplices; else it would be impossible that any man could have the impudence to write such a pamphlet as I have mentioned.

Our *neighbours, whose understandings are just upon a level with ours* (which perhaps are none of the *brightest*) have a strong contempt for most nations, but especially for Ireland. They look upon us as a sort of *savage* Irish, whom our ancestors conquered several hundred years ago, and if I should describe the Britons to you as they were in Cæsar's time, when they *painted their bodies, or clothed themselves with the skins of beasts*, I would act full as reasonably as they do. However they are so far to be excused in relation to the present subject, that, hearing only *one side of the cause*, and having neither opportunity nor curiosity to examine the *other*, they *believe a lie* merely for their ease, and conclude because Mr. *Wood* pretends to have *power*, he hath also *reason* on his side.

Therefore to let you see how this case is represented in England by *Wood* and his adherents, I have thought it proper to extract out of that pamphlet a few of those notorious falsehoods in point of *fact* and *reasoning* contained therein; the knowledge whereof will confirm my countrymen in their *own* right sentiments, when they will see by comparing both, how much their *enemies are in the wrong*.

First, the writer positively asserts, 'That *Wood*'s halfpence were current among us for several months with the universal approbation of all people, without one single gainsayer, and we all to a man thought ourselves happy in having them.'

Secondly, he affirms, 'That we were drawn into a dislike of them only by some cunning evil-designing men among us, who opposed this patent of *Wood* to get another for themselves.'

Thirdly, That 'those who most declared at first against *Wood*'s patent were the very men who intended to get another for their own advantage.'

Fourthly, That 'our Parliament and privy-council, the Lord Mayor and aldermen of Dublin, the grand juries and merchants, and in short the whole kingdom, nay the very dogs' (as he expresseth it) 'were fond of those halfpence, till they were inflamed by those few designing persons aforesaid.'

Fifthly, he says directly, That 'all those who opposed the halfpence were Papists and enemies to King George.'

Thus far I am confident the most ignorant among you can safely swear from your own knowledge, that the author is a most notorious liar in every article; the direct contrary being so manifest to the whole kingdom that if occasion required, we might get it confirmed *under five hundred thousand hands*.

Sixthly, he would persuade us, that 'if we sell five shillings worth of our goods or manufactures for two shillings and fourpence worth of copper, although the copper were melted down, and that we could get five shillings in gold or silver for the said goods; yet to take the said two shillings and fourpence in copper would be greatly for our advantage.'

And Lastly, he makes us a very fair offer, as empowered by *Wood*, that 'if we will take off two hundred thousand pounds in his halfpence for our goods, and likewise pay him three *per cent.* interest for thirty years for an hundred and twenty thousand pounds (at which he computes the coin-age above the intrinsic value of the copper) for the loan of his coin, he will after that time give us good money for what halfpence will be then left.'

Let me place this offer in as clear a light as I can, to show the unsupportable villainy and impudence of that incorrigible wretch. First (says he) 'I will send two hundred thousand pounds of my coin into your country; the copper I compute to be in real value eighty thousand pounds, and I charge you with an hundred and twenty thousand pounds for the coinage; so that you see, I lend you an hundred and twenty thousand pounds for thirty years, for which you shall pay me three *per cent.* That is to say three thousand six hundred pounds *per ann.* which in thirty years will amount to an hundred and eight thousand pounds. And when these thirty years are expired, return me my copper and I will give you good money for it.'

This is the proposal made to us by *Wood* in that pamphlet written by one of his *commissioners*; and the author is supposed to be the same infamous Coleby one of his *underswearers* at the *committee of council*, who was tried for *robbing the treasury here*, where he was an under-clerk.

By this proposal he will first receive two hundred thousand pounds, in goods or sterling, for as much copper as he values at eighty thousand pounds, but in reality not worth thirty thousand pounds. Secondly, he will receive for interest an hundred and eight thousand pounds. And when our children come thirty years hence to return his halfpence upon his executors (for before that time he will be probably gone *to his own place*) those executors will very reasonably reject them as raps and counterfeits, which probably they will be, and millions of them of his own coinage.

Methinks I am fond of such a *dealer* as this who mends every day upon our hands, like a Dutch reckoning,° where if you dispute the unreasonableness and exorbitance of the bill, the landlord shall bring it up every time with new additions.

Although these and the like pamphlets published by *Wood* in London be altogether unknown here, where nobody could read them without as much *indignation* as *contempt* would allow, yet I thought it proper to give you a specimen how the *man* employs his time, where he rides alone without one creature to contradict him; while OUR FEW FRIENDS there wonder at our silence, and the English in general, if they think of this matter at all, impute our refusal to *wilfulness* or *disaffection* just as *Wood* and his *hirelings* are pleased to represent.

But although our arguments are not suffered to be printed in England, yet the consequence will be of little moment. Let *Wood* endeavour to *persuade* the people *there* that we ought to *receive* his coin, and let me *convince* our people *here* that they ought to *reject* it under pain of our utter undoing. And then let him do his *best* and his *worst*.

Before I conclude, I must beg leave in all humility to tell Mr. *Wood*, that he is guilty of great *indiscretion*, by causing so honourable a name as that of Mr. W[alpole] to be mentioned so often, and in such a manner, upon his occasion. A short paper printed at Bristol° and reprinted here reports Mr. *Wood* to say, that he 'wonders at the impudence and insolence of the Irish in refusing his coin, and what he will do when Mr. W[alpole] comes to town'. Where, by the way, he is mistaken, for it is the *true English people* of Ireland° who refuse it, although we take it for granted that the Irish will do so too whenever they are asked. He orders it to be printed in another paper, that 'Mr. W[alpole] will cram this brass down our throats'. Sometimes it is given out that we must 'either take these halfpence or eat our brogues'. And, in another newsletter but of yesterday° we read that the same great man 'hath sworn to make us swallow his coin in fire-balls'.

This brings to my mind the known story of a Scotchman, who receiving sentence of death, with all the circumstances of *hanging, beheading, quartering, embowelling* and the like, cried out, 'What need all this COOKERY?' And I think we have reason to ask the same question; for if we believe *Wood*, here is a *dinner* getting ready for us, and you see the *bill of fare*, and I am sorry the drink was forgot, which might easily be supplied with *melted lead* and *flaming pitch*.

What vile words are these to put into the mouth of a great councillor, in high trust with His Majesty, and looked upon as a prime minister. If Mr. *Wood* hath no better a manner of representing his patrons, when I come to be a *great man* he shall never be suffered to attend at my *levee*. This is not the style of a great minister, it savours too much of the *kettle* and the *furnace*, and came entirely out of Mr. *Wood*'s *forge*.

As for the threat of making us *eat our brogues*, we need not be in pain; for if his coin should pass, that *unpolite covering for the feet* would no longer be a *national reproach*; because then we should have neither *shoe* nor *brogue* left in the kingdom. But here the falsehood of Mr. *Wood* is fairly detected; for I am confident Mr. W[alpole] never heard of a *brogue* in his whole life.

As to 'swallowing these halfpence in fire-balls', it is a story equally improbable. For to execute this *operation* the whole stock of Mr. *Wood*'s coin and metal must be melted down and moulded into hollow *balls* with *wild-fire*, no bigger than a *reasonable* throat can be able to swallow. Now the metal he hath prepared, and already coined, will amount to at least fifty millions of halfpence to be *swallowed* by a million and a half of people; so that allowing two halfpence to each *ball*, there will be about seventeen *balls* of *wild-fire* a-piece to be swallowed by every person in this kingdom. And to administer this dose there cannot be conveniently fewer than fifty thousand *operators*,° allowing one *operator* to every thirty, which, considering the *squeamishness* of some stomachs and the *peevishness* of *young children*, is but reasonable. Now, under correction of better judgments, I think the trouble and charge of such an experiment would exceed the profit; and therefore I take this *report* to be *spurious*, or at least only a new *scheme* of Mr. *Wood* himself, which to make it pass the better in Ireland he would father upon a *minister of state*.

But I will now demonstrate beyond all contradiction that Mr. W[alpole] is against this project of Mr. *Wood*, and is an entire friend to Ireland, only by this one invincible argument, That he has the universal opinion of being a wise man, an able minister, and in all his proceedings pursuing the *true interest* of the *King his master*; and that, as his *integrity* is above all *corruption*, so is his *fortune* above all *temptation*. I reckon therefore we are perfectly safe from that *corner*, and shall never be under the necessity of contending with so *formidable a power*, but be left to possess our *brogues* and *potatoes* in *peace*, as *remote from thunder as we are from* Jupiter.°

                    I am,
                 My dear countrymen,
                    Your loving fellow-subject,
                       fellow-sufferer, and humble servant.
                                                    M. B.

Oct. 13. 1724.

Advertisement to the *Reader.*

THE former of the two following Papers is dated Oct. [2]6th. 1724, *by which it appears to be written a little after the Proclamation against the author of the* Drapier'*s fourth Letter. It is delivered with much caution, because the Author confesseth himself to be* D— *of St.* P——k's; *and I could discover his name subscribed at the end of the original, although blotted out by some other hand. I can tell no other reason why it was not printed, than what I have heard; that the writer finding how effectually the* Drapier *had succeeded, and at the same time how highly the people in power seemed to be displeased, thought it more prudent to keep the paper in his cabinet. However, having received some encouragement to collect into one volume all papers relating to* Ireland, *supposed to be written by the* Drapier; *and knowing how favourably that author's writings in this kind have been received by the publick; to make the volume more compleat, I procured a copy of the following Letter from one of the author's friends, with whom it was left, while the author was in* England; *and I have printed it as near as I could in the order of time.*

A LETTER TO THE *LORD CHANCELLOR* MIDDLETON.

My Lord,

I DESIRE you will consider me as a member who comes in at the latter end of a debate; or as a lawyer who speaks to a cause, when the matter hath been almost exhausted by those who spoke before.

I remember some months ago I was at your house upon a commission, where I am one of the governors. But I went thither not so much on account of the commission, as to ask you some questions concerning Mr. Wood's patent to coin halfpence for Ireland; where you very freely told me, in a mixed company, how much you had been always against that wicked project, which raised in me an esteem for you so far, that I went in a few days to make you a visit, after many years' intermission.° I am likewise told, that your son wrote two letters from London, (one of which I have seen) empowering those to whom they were directed, to assure his friends, that whereas there was a malicious report spread of his engaging himself to Mr. Walpole for forty thousand pounds of Wood's coin, to be received in Ireland, the said report was false and groundless; and he had never discoursed with that minister on the subject; nor would ever give his consent to have one farthing of the said coin current here. And although it be long since I have given myself the trouble of conversing with people of titles or stations; yet I have been told by those who can take up with such amusements, that there is not a considerable person of the kingdom, scrupulous in any sort to declare his opinion. But all this is needless to allege, when we consider that the ruinous consequences of Wood's patent have been so strongly represented by both Houses of Parliament; by the privy-council; the Lord Mayor and Aldermen of Dublin; by so many corporations; and the concurrence of the principal gentlemen in most counties at their quarter-sessions, without any regard to party, religion, or nation.

I conclude from hence that the currency of these halfpence would, in the universal opinion of our people, be utterly destructive to this kingdom; and consequently that it is every man's duty, not only to refuse this coin himself, but as far as in him lies, to persuade others to do the like. And whether this be done in private or in print is all a case; as no layman is forbid to write, or to discourse upon religious or moral subjects, although he may not do it in a pulpit (at least in our church). Neither is this an affair of state° until authority shall think fit to declare it so. Or if you should understand it in that sense, yet you will please to consider that I am not now a preaching.

Therefore, I do think it my duty, since the Drapier will probably be no more heard of, so far to supply his place as not to incur his fortune. For I have learnt from old experience that there are times wherein a man ought to be cautious as well as innocent. I therefore hope that preserving both those characters, I may be allowed, by offering new arguments or enforcing old ones, to refresh the memory of my fellow-subjects, and keep up that good spirit raised among them, to preserve themselves from utter ruin by lawful means, and such as are permitted by his Majesty.

I believe you will please to allow me two propositions. First, that we are a most loyal people; and secondly, that we are a free people, in the common acceptation of that word applied to a subject under a limited monarch. I know very well, that you and I did many years ago in discourse differ much, in the presence of Lord Wharton, about the meaning of that word *liberty*, with relation to Ireland. But if you will not allow us to be a free people, there is only another appellation left; which I doubt my Lord Chief Justice Whitshed° would call me to an account for, if I venture to bestow. For, I observed, and I shall never forget upon what occasion, the device upon his coach to be *Libertas et natale solum*; at the very point of time when he was sitting in his court, and perjuring himself to betray both.

Now, as for our loyalty to His present Majesty; if it hath ever been equalled in any other part of his dominions, I am sure it hath never been exceeded. And I am confident he hath not a minister in England who could ever call it once in question. But that some hard rumours at least have been transmitted from t'other side the water, I suppose you will not doubt, and rumours of the severest kind; which many good people have imputed to the indirect proceeding of Mr. Wood and his emissaries; as if he endeavoured it should be thought that our loyalty depended upon the test of refusing or taking his copper. Now, as I am sure you will admit us to be a loyal people; so you will think it pardonable in us to hope for all proper marks of favour and protection from so gracious a King that a loyal and free people can expect. Among which, we all agree in reckoning this to be one; that Wood's halfpence may never have entrance into this kingdom. And this we shall continue to *wish*, when we dare no longer express our wishes; although there were no such mortal as a *Drapier* in the world.

I am heartily sorry, that any writer should, in a cause so generally approved, give occasion to the government and council to charge him with *paragraphs 'highly reflecting upon His Majesty and his ministers; tending to alienate the affections of his good subjects in England and Ireland from each other; and to promote sedition among the people'. I must confess, that with many others, I thought he meant well; although he might have the failing of better writers, to be not always fortunate in the manner of expressing himself.

However, since the Drapier is but one man, I shall think I do a public service by asserting that the rest of my countrymen are wholly free from learning out of *his* pamphlets to reflect on the King or his ministers, to breed sedition.

I solemnly declare, that I never once heard the least reflection cast upon the King, on the subject of Mr. Wood's coin; for in many discourses on this matter, I do not remember His Majesty's name to be so much as mentioned. As to the ministry in England, the only two persons hinted at were the Duke of Grafton, and Mr. Walpole.° The former, as I have heard you and a hundred others affirm, declared that he never saw the patent in favour of Mr. Wood, before it was passed, although he were then lord lieutenant. And therefore I suppose everybody believes that his grace hath been wholly unconcerned in it since.

Mr. Walpole was indeed supposed to be understood by the letter *W.* in several newspapers; where it is said that some expressions fell from him

---

* *Taken out of the* Drapier's *4th Letter, for which the Printer was prosecuted; and a Proclamation published against the Author, offering* 300l. *Reward for discovering him.*

not very favourable to the people of Ireland; for the truth of which the kingdom is not to answer, any more than for the discretion of the publishers. You observe, the Drapier wholly clears Mr. Walpole of this charge, by very strong arguments; and speaks of him with civility. I cannot deny myself to have been often present where the company gave their opinion that Mr. Walpole favoured Mr. Wood's project, which I always contradicted; and for my own part, never once opened my lips against that minister either in mixed or particular meetings. And my reason for this reservedness was; because it pleased him, in the Queen's time (I mean Queen Anne of ever blessed memory) to make a speech directly against me,° by name, in the House of Commons, as I was told a very few minutes after, in the Court of Requests, by more than fifty members.

But you who are in a great station here (if anything here may be called great) cannot be ignorant, that whoever is understood by public voice to be chief minister, will among the general talkers share the blame whether justly or no of every thing that is disliked; which I could easily make appear in many instances from my own knowledge, while I was in the world; and particularly in the case of the *greatest, the wisest, and the most uncorrupt minister, I ever conversed with.

But, whatever unpleasing opinion some people might conceive of Mr. Walpole on account of those halfpence, I dare boldly affirm, it was entirely owing to Mr. Wood. Many persons of credit, come from England, have affirmed to me and others, that they have seen letters under his hand full of arrogance and insolence towards Ireland; and boasting of his favour with Mr. Walpole; which is highly probable, because he reasonably thought it for his interest to spread such a report, and because it is the known talent of low and little spirits, to have a great man's name perpetually in their mouths.

Thus I have sufficiently justified the people of Ireland, from learning any bad lessons out of the Drapier's pamphlets, with regard to His Majesty and his ministers. And therefore, if those papers were intended to sow sedition among us, GOD be thanked the seeds have fallen upon a very improper soil.

As to alienating the affections of the people of England and Ireland from each other, I believe the Drapier, whatever his intentions were, hath left that matter just as he found it.

I have lived long in both kingdoms, as well in country as in town, and therefore take myself to be as well informed as most men, in the dispositions of each people toward the other. By the people, I understand

* *Supposed to be the Lord Treasurer* Oxford.

here only the bulk of the common people; and I desire no lawyer may distort or extend my meaning.

There is a vein of industry and parsimony that runs through the whole people of England, which, added to the easiness of their rents, makes them rich and sturdy. As to Ireland, they know little more than they do of Mexico, further than that it is a country subject to the King of England, full of bogs, inhabited by wild Irish Papists, who are kept in awe by mercenary troops sent from thence. And their general opinion is, that it were better for England if this whole island were sunk into the sea; for they have a tradition, that every forty years there must be a rebellion in Ireland. I have seen the grossest suppositions pass upon them; that the wild Irish were taken in toils, but that, in some time, they would grow so tame as to eat out of your hands. I have been asked by hundreds, and particularly by my neighbours, your tenants at Pepper-harrow,° whether I had come from Ireland by sea. And upon the arrival of an Irishman to a country town, I have known crowds coming about him, and wondering to see him look so much better than themselves.

A gentleman now in Dublin affirms, that passing some months ago through Northampton, and finding the whole town in a lurry, with bells, bonfires, and illuminations; upon asking the cause, was told it was for joy, that the Irish had submitted to receive Wood's halfpence. This, I think, plainly shows what sentiments that large town hath of us, and how little they made it their own case; although they lie directly in our way to London, and therefore cannot but be frequently convinced that we have human shapes.

As to the people of this kingdom, they consist either of Irish Papists, who are as inconsiderable, in point of power, as the women and children; or of English Protestants, who love their brethren of that kingdom, although they may possibly sometimes complain when they think they are hardly used. However, I confess I do not see any great consequence, how their personal affections stand to each other while the sea divides them, and while they continue in their loyalty to the same prince. And yet, I will appeal to you, whether those from England have reason to complain, when they come hither in pursuit of their fortunes? Or, whether the people of Ireland have reason to boast when they go to England on the same design?

My second proposition was, that we of Ireland are a free people. This, I suppose, you will allow, at least with certain limitations remaining in your own breast. However, I am sure it is not criminal to affirm; because the words 'liberty' and 'property' as applied to the subject are often mentioned in both houses of Parliament, as well as in yours and other courts below; from whence it must follow, that the people of Ireland do or ought to enjoy all the benefits of the common and statute law; such as to be tried by juries, to pay no money without their own consent, as represented in Parliament; and the like. If this be so, and if it be universally agreed that a free people cannot, by law, be compelled to take any money in payment except gold and silver; I do not see why any man should be hindered from cautioning his countrymen against this coin of William Wood; who is endeavouring by fraud to rob us of that property which the laws have secured. If I am mistaken, and that this copper can be obtruded on us, I would put the Drapier's case in another light, by supposing that a person going into his shop should agree for thirty shillings' worth of goods, and force the seller to take his payment in a parcel of copper pieces, intrinsically not worth above a crown. I desire to know, whether the Drapier would not be actually robbed of five and twenty shillings, and how far he could be said to be master of his property? The same question may be applied to rents and debts, on bond or mortgage, and to all kind of commerce whatsoever.

Give me leave to do what the Drapier hath done more than once before me; which is, to relate the naked fact as it stands in the view of the world.

One William Wood, Esq; and hardware-man, obtains, by fraud, a patent in England to coin 108,000*l.* in copper, to pass in Ireland; leaving us liberty to take or to refuse. The people here, in all sorts of bodies and representatives, do openly and heartily declare that they will not accept this coin. To justify these declarations they generally offer two reasons; first, because by the words of the patent, they are left to their own choice, and secondly, because they are not obliged by law. So that here you see there is, *bellum atque virum,*° a kingdom on one side, and William Wood on the other. And if Mr. Wood gets the victory, at the expense of Ireland's ruin and the profit of one or two hundred thousand pounds (I mean by continuing, and counterfeiting as long as he lives) for himself; I doubt both present and future ages will, at least, think it a very singular scheme.

If this fact be truly stated, I must confess I look upon it as my duty, so far as God hath enabled me, and as long as I keep within the bounds of truth, of duty, and of decency, to warn my fellow-subjects, as they value their King, their country, and all that ought or can be dear to them, never to admit this pernicious coin; no not so much as one single halfpenny. For if one single thief forces the door, it is in vain to talk of keeping out the whole crew behind.

And while I shall be thus employed, I will never give myself leave to suppose that what I say can either offend my *Lord Lieutenant, whose person and great qualities I have always highly respected (as I am sure his excellency will be my witness) or the ministers in England, with whom I have nothing to do, or they with me; much less the privy-council here, who as I am informed did send an address to His Majesty against Mr. Wood's coin; which, if it be a mistake, I desire I may not be accused for a spreader of false news. But, I confess, I am so great a stranger to affairs that for anything I know the whole body of the council may since have been changed. And, although I observed some of the very same names in a late declaration against that coin, which I saw subscribed to the proclamation against the Drapier; yet possibly they may be different persons, for they are utterly unknown to me, and are like to continue so.

In this controversy, where the reasoners on each side are divided by St. George's Channel, His Majesty's prerogative perhaps would not have been mentioned, if Mr. Wood, and his advocates, had not made it necessary by giving out that the currency of his coin should be enforced by a proclamation. The traders and common people of the kingdom were heartily willing to refuse this coin; but the fear of a proclamation brought along with it most dreadful apprehensions. It was therefore absolutely necessary for the Drapier to remove this difficulty; and accordingly in one of his former pamphlets,° he hath produced invincible arguments (wherever he picked them up) that the King's prerogative was not at all concerned in the matter; since the law had sufficiently provided against any coin to be imposed upon the subject, except gold and silver; and that copper is not money, but as it hath been properly called, *nummorum famulus*.°

The three former letters from the Drapier having not received any public censure, I look upon them to be without exception, and that the good people of the kingdom ought to read them often, in order to keep up that spirit raised against this destructive coin of Mr. Wood. As for this last letter, against which a proclamation is issued, I shall only say that I could wish it were stripped of all that can be any way exceptionable; which I would not think it below me to undertake if my abilities were equal. But being naturally somewhat slow of comprehension, no lawyer, and apt to believe the best of those who profess good designs without any visible motive either of profit or honour, I might pore for ever without distinguishing the cockle from the corn.

That which I am told gives greatest offence in this last letter is where the Drapier affirms, 'that if a rebellion should prove so successful, as to fix the Pretender on the throne of England, he would venture so far to

* *Lord* Carteret.

transgress the Irish statute (which unites Ireland to England under one King) as to lose every drop of his blood, to hinder him from being King of Ireland.'

I shall not presume to vindicate any man who openly declares he would transgress a statute, and a statute of such importance. But with the most humble submission, and desire of pardon for a very innocent mistake, I should be apt to think that the loyal intention of the writer might be at least some small extenuation of his crime. For, in this I confess myself to think with the Drapier.

I have not hitherto been told of any other objections against that pamphlet, but I suppose they will all appear at the prosecution of the Drapier. And I think whoever in his own conscience believes the said pamphlet to be 'wicked and malicious, seditious and scandalous, highly reflecting upon His Majesty and his ministers, &c.' would do well to discover the author (as little a friend as I am to the trade of informers) although the reward of 300*l*. had not been tacked to the discovery. I own it would be a great satisfaction to me to hear the arguments not only of judges, but of lawyers, upon this case. Because you cannot but know there often happens occasions, wherein it would be very convenient that the bulk of the people should be informed how they ought to conduct themselves; and therefore, it hath been the wisdom of the English Parliaments to be very reserved in limiting the press. When a bill is debating in either House of Parliament there, nothing is more usual than to have the controversy handled by pamphlets on both sides, without the least animadversion upon the authors.

So here, in the case of Mr. Wood and his coin; since the two Houses gave their opinion by addresses how dangerous the currency of that copper would be to Ireland, it was, without all question, both lawful and convenient that the bulk of the people should be let more particularly into the nature of the danger they were in; and of the remedies that were in their own power, if they would have the sense to apply them; and this cannot be more conveniently done than by particular persons to whom GOD hath given zeal and understanding sufficient for such an undertaking. Thus it happened in the case of that destructive project for a bank in Ireland,° which was brought into Parliament a few years ago; and it was allowed that the arguments and writings of some without doors, contributed very much to reject it.

Now, I should be heartily glad if some able lawyers would prescribe the limits, how far a private man may venture in delivering his thoughts upon public matters. Because a true lover of his country may think it hard to be a quiet stander-by, and an indolent looker-on, while a public error prevails, by which a whole nation may be ruined. Every man who enjoys property hath some share in the public, and therefore the care of the public is, in some degree, every such man's concern.

To come to particulars, I could wish to know whether it be utterly unlawful in any writer so much as to mention the prerogative; at least so far as to bring it into doubt, upon any point whatsoever? I know it is often debated in Westminster Hall; and Sir Edward Coke,° as well as other eminent lawyers, do frequently handle that subject in their books.

Secondly, how far the prerogative extends to force coin upon the subject, which is not sterling; such as lead, brass, copper, mixt metal, shells, leather, or any other material; and fix upon it whatever denomination the crown shall think fit?

Thirdly, what is really and truly meant by that phrase of 'a depending kingdom' as applied to Ireland, and wherein that dependency consisteth?

Lastly, in what points relating to *liberty* and *property* the people of Ireland differ, or at least ought to differ, from those of England?

If these particulars were made so clear that none could mistake them, it would be of infinite ease and use to the kingdom, and either prevent or silence all discontents.

My Lord Somers, the greatest man I ever knew of your robe,° and whose thoughts of Ireland differed as far as heaven and earth from those of some others among his brethren here; lamented to me that the prerogative of the Crown, or the privileges of Parliament, should ever be liable to dispute in any single branch of either; by which means, he said, the public often suffered great inconveniences, whereof he gave me several instances. I produce the authority of so eminent a person to justify my desires that some high points might be cleared.

For want of such known ascertainment, how far a writer may proceed in expressing his good wishes for his country, a person of the most innocent intentions may possibly by the oratory and comments of lawyers, be charged with many crimes which from his very soul he abhors; and consequently may be ruined in his fortunes, and left to rot among thieves in some stinking jail, merely for mistaking the purlieus of the law. I have known in my lifetime a printer prosecuted° and convicted for publishing a *pamphlet, where the author's intentions, I am confident, were as good and innocent as those of a martyr at his last prayers. I did very lately, as I thought it my duty, preach° to the people under my inspection upon the subject of Mr. Wood's coin, and although I never heard that my sermon gave the least offence, as I am sure none

* *Supposed to be*, A Proposal for the universal Use of Irish Manufacture, *written by the Author.*

was intended, yet if it were now printed and published, I cannot say I would ensure it from the hands of the common hangman, or my own person from those of a Messenger.

I have heard the late Chief Justice Holt affirm, that in all criminal cases the most favourable interpretation should be put upon words that they can possibly bear. You meet the same position asserted in many trials for the greatest crimes; though often very ill practised by the perpetual corruption of judges. And I remember at a trial in Kent, where Sir George Rook° was indicted for calling a gentleman knave and villain, the lawyer for the defendant brought off his client by alleging that the words were not injurious; for *knave* in the old and true signification, imported only a servant; and *villain* in Latin is *villicus*, which is no more than a man employed in country labour, or rather a bailiff.

If Sir John Holt's opinion were a standard maxim for all times and circumstances, any writer, with a very small measure of discretion, might easily be safe; but I doubt in practice it hath been frequently controlled,° at least before his time, for I take it to be an old rule in law.

I have read, or heard, a passage of Signor Leti,° an Italian, who being in London busying himself with writing the History of England, told King Charles the Second that he endeavoured as much as he could to avoid giving offence, but found it a thing impossible, although he should have been as wise as Solomon. The King answered that if this were the case, he had better employ his time in writing proverbs as Solomon did. But Leti lay under no public necessity of writing; neither would England have been one halfpenny the better, or the worse, whether he writ or no.

This I mention, because I know it will readily be objected, 'What have private men to do with the public? What call had a *Drapier* to turn politician, to meddle in matters of state? Would not his time have been better employed in looking to his shop, or his pen in writing proverbs, elegies, ballads, garlands,° and wonders? He would then have been out of all danger of proclamations and prosecutions. Have we not able magistrates and counsellors, hourly watching over the public weal?' All this may be true. And yet when the addresses from both Houses of Parliament against Mr. Wood's halfpence failed of success, if some pen had not been employed to inform the people how far they might legally proceed in refusing that coin, to detect the fraud, the artifice, and insolence of the coiner, and to lay open the most ruinous consequences to the whole kingdom, which would inevitably follow from the currency of the said coin; I might appeal to many hundred thousand people, whether any one of them would ever have had the courage or sagacity to refuse it.

If this copper should begin to make its way among the common, ignorant people, we are inevitably undone; it is they who give us the greatest apprehension, being easily frightened and greedy to swallow misinformations. For, if every man were wise enough to understand his own interest, which is every man's principal study, there would be no need of pamphlets upon this occasion. But as things stand I have thought it absolutely necessary, from my duty to God, my King, and my country, to inform the people that the proclamation lately issued against the Drapier, doth not in the least affect the case of Mr. Wood and his coin; but only refers to certain paragraphs in the Drapier's last pamphlet (not immediately relating to his subject, nor at all to the merits of the cause) which the government was pleased to dislike; so that any man has the same liberty to reject, to write, and to declare against this coin, which he had before. Neither is any man obliged to believe that those honourable persons (whereof you are the first) who signed that memorable proclamation against the Drapier, have at all changed their opinions with regard to Mr. Wood or his coin.

Therefore concluding myself to be thus far upon a safe and sure foot, I shall continue, upon any proper occasion, as God enables me, to revive and preserve that spirit raised in the nation (whether the real author were a real Drapier or no is little to the purpose) against this horrid design of Mr. Wood; at the same time carefully watching every stroke of my pen, and venturing only to incur the public censure of the world as a writer, not of my Lord Chief Justice Whitshed as a criminal. Whenever an order shall come out by authority, forbidding all men upon the highest penalties to offer anything in writing or discourse against Mr. Wood's halfpence; I shall certainly submit. However, if that should happen I am determined to be somewhat more than the last man in the kingdom to receive them, because I will never receive them at all. For, although I know how to be silent, I have not yet learned to pay active obedience against my conscience and the public safety.

I desire to put a case which I think the Drapier, in some of his books, hath put before me, although not so fully as it requires.

You know the copper halfpence in England are coined by the public, and every piece worth pretty tolerably near the value of the copper. Now suppose that, instead of the public coinage, a patent had been granted to some private, obscure person for coining a proportionable quantity of copper in that kingdom to what Mr. Wood is preparing in this; and all of it at least five times below the intrinsic value. The current money of England is reckoned to be twenty millions and ours under *five hundred

*It is since sunk to 200,000l.

thousand pounds. By this computation, as Mr. Wood hath power to give us 108,000 pound, so the patentee in England by the same proportion might circulate four millions three hundred and twenty thousand pounds, besides as much more by stealth and counterfeits. I desire to know from you whether the Parliament might not have addressed upon such an occasion; what success they probably would have had; and how many Drapiers would have risen to pester the world with pamphlets. Yet that kingdom would not be so great a sufferer as ours in the like case, because their cash would not be conveyed into foreign countries, but lie hid in the chests of cautious, thrifty men, until better times. Then I desire for the satisfaction of the public that you will please to inform me why this country is treated in so very different a manner in a point of such high importance; whether it be on account of Poining's act;° of subordination; dependence; or any other term of art; which I shall not contest, but am too dull to understand.

I am very sensible that the good or ill success of Mr. Wood will affect you less than any person of consequence in the kingdom, because I hear you are so prudent as to make all your purchases° in England; and truly so would I, if I had money, although I were to pay a hundred years' purchase; because I should be glad to possess a freehold that could not be taken from me by any law to which I did not give my own consent, and where I should never be in danger of receiving my rents in mixed copper, at the loss of sixteen shillings in the pound. You can live in ease and plenty at Pepper-harrow, in Surrey, and therefore I thought it extremely generous and public-spirited in you to be of the kingdom's side in this dispute, by showing without reserve your disapprobation of Mr. Wood's design; at least if you have been so frank to others as you were to me, which indeed I could not but wonder at, considering how much we differ in other points; and therefore I could get but few believers, when I attempted to justify you in this article from your own words.

I would humbly offer another thought, which I do not remember to have fallen under the Drapier's observation. If these halfpence should once gain admittance, it is agreed that in no long space of time, what by the clandestine practices of the coiner, what by his own counterfeits, and those of others, either from abroad or at home, his limited quantity would be trebled upon us, until there would not be a grain of gold or silver visible in the nation. This, in my opinion would lay a heavy charge upon the crown, by creating a necessity of transmitting money from England to pay the salaries at least of the principal civil officers. For I do not conceive how a judge (for instance) could support his dignity with a thousand pounds a year in Wood's coin, which would not intrinsically be worth near two hundred. To argue that these halfpence, if no other coin were current, would answer the general ends of commerce among ourselves, is a great mistake; and the Drapier hath made that matter too clear to admit an answer, by showing us what every owner of land must be forced to do with the products of it in such a distress. You may read his remarks at large in his second and third letter, to which I refer you.

Before I conclude, I cannot but observe that for several months past there have more papers been written in this town, such as they are, all upon the best public principle, the love of our country, than perhaps hath been known in any other nation and in so short a time. I speak in general, from the Drapier down to the maker of ballads;° and all without any regard to the common motives of writers, which are profit, favour, and reputation. As to profit, I am assured by persons of credit that the best ballad upon Mr. Wood will not yield above a groat to the author; and the unfortunate adventurer Harding, declares he never made the Drapier any present, except one pair of scissors. As to favour, whoever thinks to make his court by opposing Mr. Wood is not very deep in politics. And as to reputation, certainly no man of worth and learning would employ his pen upon so transitory a subject, and in so obscure a corner of the world, to distinguish himself as an author. So that I look upon myself, the Drapier, and my numerous brethren, to be all true patriots in our several degrees.

All that the public can expect for the future is only to be sometimes warned to beware of Mr. Wood's halfpence; and refer them for conviction to the Drapier's reasons. For, a man of the most superior understanding will find it impossible to make the best use of it while he writes in constraint, perpetually softening, correcting, or blotting out expressions, for fear of bringing his printer, or himself, under a prosecution from my Lord Chief Justice Whitshed. It calls to my remembrance the madman in *Don Quixote*,° who being soundly beaten by a weaver for letting a stone (which he always carried on his shoulder) fall upon a spaniel, apprehended that every cur he met was of the same species.

For these reasons, I am convinced that what I have now written will appear low and insipid; but if it contributes, in the least, to preserve that union among us for opposing this fatal project of Mr. Wood, my pains will not be altogether lost.

I sent these papers to an eminent lawyer (and yet a man of virtue and learning into the bargain) who, after many alterations returned them back, with assuring me that they are perfectly innocent, without the least mixture of treason, rebellion, sedition, malice, disaffection, reflection, or wicked insinuation whatsoever.

If the *bellman* of each parish, as he goes his circuit, would cry out every night, 'Past twelve o'clock—Beware of Wood's halfpence' it would probably cut off the occasion for publishing any more pamphlets; provided that in country towns it were done upon market-days. For my own part, as soon as it shall be determined that it is not against law, I will begin the experiment in the liberty of St. Patrick's, and hope my example may be followed in the whole city. But if authority shall think fit to forbid all writings or discourses upon this subject, except such as are in favour of Mr. Wood, I will obey as it becomes me; only when I am in danger of bursting, I will go and whisper among the reeds,° not any reflection upon the wisdom of my countrymen, but only these few words, *BEWARE OF WOOD's HALFPENCE*.

I am,
With due Respect,
Your Most Obedient,
Humble Servant,
J.S.

Deanery House,
    Oct. 26, 1724.

Horace, Book I, Ode xiv

PARAPHRASED AND INSCRIBED TO IRELAND

The INSCRIPTION°

> *Poor floating isle, tossed on ill fortune's waves,*
> *Ordain'd by Fate to be the land of slaves,*
> *Shall moving Delos now deep-rooted stand?°*
> *Thou, fixed of old, be now the moving land?*
> *Although the metaphor be worn and stale,*
> *Betwixt a state and vessel under sail,*
> *Let me suppose thee for a ship awhile*
> *And thus address thee in the sailor style.*

Unhappy ship, thou art return'd in vain;
New waves shall drive thee to the deep again.   10
Look to thyself, and be no more the sport
Of giddy winds, but make some friendly port.
Lost are thy oars, that used thy course to guide
Like faithful counsellors, on either side.
Thy mast, which like some aged patriot stood,
The single pillar for his country's good,
To lead thee as a staff directs the blind,
Behold, it cracks by yon rough *eastern* wind;
Your cables burst, and you must quickly feel
The waves impetuous ent'ring at your keel;   20
Thus, commonwealths receive a foreign yoke,
When the strong cords of union once are broke.
Torn by a sudden tempest is thy sail,
Expanded to invite a milder gale.
   As when some writer in a public cause
His pen, to save a sinking nation, draws,
While all is calm, his arguments prevail;
The people's voice expand his paper sail:
Till pow'r, discharging all her stormy bags,
Flutters the feeble pamphlet into rags.   30
The nation scared, the author doom'd to death,
Who fondly put his trust in pop'lar breath.
   A larger sacrifice in vain you vow;

There's not a pow'r above will help you now:
A nation thus, who oft Heav'n's call neglects,
In vain from injured Heav'n relief expects.
  'Twill not avail, when thy strong sides are broke,
That thy descent is from the British oak,
Or, when your name and family you boast,
From fleets triumphant o'er the Gallic coast.   40
Such was Ierne's claim, as just as thine,°
Her sons descended from the British line;
Her matchless sons, whose valour still remains
On French records for twenty long campaigns;°
Yet, from an empress now a captive grown,
She saved Britannia's rights, and lost her own.
  In ships decay'd no mariner confides,
Lured by the gilded stern and painted sides:
Yet, at a ball, unthinking fools delight
In the gay trappings of a birthday night: 50
They on the gold brocades and satins raved,
And quite forgot their country was enslaved.
  Dear vessel, still be to thy steerage just,
Nor change thy course with ev'ry sudden gust;
Like supple patriots of the modern sort,
Who turn with ev'ry gale that blows from court.
  Weary and sea-sick when in thee confined,
Now, for thy safety, cares distract my mind;
As those who long have stood the storms of state
Retire, yet still bemoan their country's fate.   60
Beware, and when you hear the surges roar,
Avoid the rocks on Britain's angry shore.
They lie, alas, too easy to be found;
For thee alone they lie the island round.

On Dreams

AN IMITATION OF PETRONIUS

'Somnia quae mentes ludunt volitantibus umbris, &c.'

Those dreams that on the silent night intrude,
And with false flitting shades our minds delude,
Jove never sends us downward from the skies;
Nor can they from infernal mansions rise;
But all are mere productions of the brain,
And fools consult interpreters in vain.

For, when in bed we rest our weary limbs,
The mind, unburthen'd, sports in various whims;
The busy head with mimic art runs o'er
The scenes and actions of the day before.   10

The drowsy tyrant, by his minions led,
To regal rage devotes some patriot's head.
With equal terrors, not with equal guilt,
The murd'rer dreams of all the blood he spilt.

The soldier smiling hears the widow's cries,
And stabs the son before the mother's eyes.
With like remorse his *brother* of the *trade*,
The butcher, feels the lamb beneath his blade.

The statesman rakes the town to find a plot,
And dreams of forfeitures by treason got.   20
Nor less *Tom-turd-man*, of *true statesman* mould,
Collects the city filth in search of gold.

Orphans around his bed the lawyer sees,
And takes the plaintiff's and defendant's fees.
His *fellow pick-purse*, watching for a job,
Fancies his fingers in the cully's fob.

The kind physician grants the husband's prayers,
Or gives relief to long-expecting heirs.
The sleeping hangman ties the fatal noose,
Nor unsuccessful waits for dead men's shoes.°   30

The grave divine, with knotty points perplexed,
As if he were awake, nods o'er his text:
While the sly mountebank attends his trade,
Harangues the rabble, and is better paid.

The hireling senator of modern days
Bedaubs the guilty great with nauseous praise:
And *Dick* the scavenger, with equal grace,
Flirts from his cart the mud in *Walpole*'s face.

Swift to Charles Ford

Dublin. Mar. 11th 1724–5

I have been resolving for some time past to go to England about the End of this month, and have lately communicated my Intention to five or six Friends, who are all dissuading me with the greatest Violence, and desire that I would at least defer it till next Year. Their Reasons I do not all approve; because I know very well how apt the People of Ireland are to think that their little Affairs are regarded in England. They would have it that what has been lately written about the Drapier has given great Offence on your side, that the private Malice of the Projector and those who were examined in his Behalf might tempt them to some violent Action of Revenge, and that M^r W—— thinks himself personally offended, and that somebody for whose Advantage° that Project was contrived would use all means to prosecute whoever has opposed it, which may end in Messengers hands, Accusations, Imprisonments &c. Now in my own Mind I am quite of another Opinion. I do not think the thing is of Weight enough for a Ministry to trouble themselves about, and as for the Malice of mean paltry Rascals it may be avoyded by common Care. There was a Time when in England some great Friends looked on me as in Danger, and used to warn me against Night walking &c.; but I thought it was a shame to be afraid of such Accidents and looked as if a man affected to be thought of Importance. Neither do I find that Assassinations are things in fashion at present; and in my Opinion a Secretary of State is a much more terrible animal, when he has a mind to be malicious. Our Friend in Grafton Street swears it is a Fatality upon me. In order to their Satisfaction I desire to know your Opinion, whether I may be in any Danger of being teazed at Whitehall, or have Searches for Papers &c. for as to private malice, I very little apprehend it. Pray write me your Thoughts as soon as you can, that I may take my Measures.

Our Friend with the weak Stomack° eats less than ever, and I am in pain about her, and would fain persuade her to go for England, but she will not. Your People are well, I dined with them very lately—

Y^{rs}

Address: To Charles Ford Esqr | to be left at the Coco-tree | in Pell-mell | London
Postmarks: DUBLIN *and* 19 MR

Swift to Charles Ford

Our Method about Letters here, is this, Every Saterday we send 8 miles to Kells for Vittells, the Messenger carryes thither what Letters we write, and brings back whatever Letters are sent us to Kells. Thus our Letters often lye at Kells a week, and we are very indifferent, or rather vexed when we see any Letters come to us, unless from particular Friends. Thus it happened that the Messenger of Saterday last carryed a Letter to Kells directed to You in London, and brought one from you dated at Dublin. If your coming be sufficiently known, perhaps the Post master may send it to you, or if the Packet be not gone, you may send a servant for it, rather than let it have two Voyages by Sea. The Letter you gave Sheridan for me, is in ill Hands, for I hear nothing of his coming down to Quilca, and if he does, it is great Odds he will leave it behind, or lose it, or forget to give it me. I find you have been a better Manager than usuall, by making your Money hold out almost two years, unless you have mangè votre bled en herbe; and in that Case you will be punished with a longer Stay in Ireland. I hope you will, or rather your Friends will have one Advantage by our Absence, that it will force you to cotton a little better with the Country and the People; for upon your old System it will be impossible for you to live in it without Spleen. No men in Dublin go to Taverns who are worth sitting with, and to ask others, is just to desire them to throw away half a Crown for bad wine, (which they can ill spare), when they know where to get good, for nothing, and among Company where they can amuse themselves with Play or trifling; and this you must do, or get you gone back to England. For we know it is not Love that sends you to us, and that nothing keeps you here an hour but Joyntures and old Leases.

The Razors will be a great Treasure to me, for want of good ones I pass one hour in eight and fourty very miserably.

In my Letter to you I desired Your Assistance in getting the Ring and Picture from Lᵈ Oxford,° but fearing you might be out of Town, (though not in Ireland) I writt the same Post to Mʳ Charleton from whom I lately had a Letter; since I knew not what else to do. But if Mʳ Lewis° will take that Trouble, it will be much better.

Our Scheme was to stay till Michaelmas, but our Return must depend upon our Health. Mʳˢ Johnson is much better and walks three or four Irish Miles a day over Bogs and mountain. But I have generally every month a Return of my Deafness, though the Fits do not last so long as usuall. But I have some Reasons not to be in Dublin° till the Parliament here has sate a good while. Neither am I willing to see Mr Prat while he is in Prison. I believe I shall not lose above 100^ll Interest by him. But I despaired of every Penny, and yet I have legall Witness that I was a great Philosopher in that Matter.

We live here among a Million of wants, and where ever[y] body is a Thief. I am amusing my self in the Quality of Bayliff to Sheridan, among Bogs and Rocks, overseeing and ranting at Irish Laborers, reading Books twice over for want of fresh ones, and fairly correcting and transcribing my Travells,° for the Publick. Any thing rather than the Complaint of being Deaf in Dublin.

I hope to see you well settled in a Kind of Acquaintance, and tallying with the usuall way of Life, else it had been better you had contrived to pass the Summer here, and kept London for Winter. This is an Irish Holyday when our Scoundrels will not work, else perhaps my Letter would have been shorter.

My most humble Service to the Ladyes where you Live. Adieu.

The Ladyes here assure me they are your humble Servants.

Address: To Charles Ford Esqr at | Mrs Ford's House in Dawson Street | Dublin. *Postmarks*: [Kells] *and* 20 AU

Swift to the Rev. Thomas Sheridan

If you are indeed a discarded courtier,° you have reason to complain, but none at all to wonder; you are too young for many experiences to fall in your way, yet you have read enough to make you know the nature of man. It is safer for a man's interest to blaspheme God than to be of a party out of power or even to be thought so. And since the last was the case, how could you imagine that all mouths would not be open when you were received, and in some manner preferred by the government, though in a poor way? I tell you there is hardly a Whig in Ireland who would allow a potato and butter-milk to a reputed Tory. Neither is there anything in your countrymen, upon this article, more than what is common in all other nations, only quoad magis et minus. Too much advertency is not your talent, or else you had fled from that text as from a rock. For as Don Quixote said to Sancho,° what business had you to speak of a halter, in a family where one of it was hanged? And your innocence is a protection that wise men are ashamed to rely on, further than with God. It is indeed against common sense to think that you should choose such a time, when you had received a favour from the Lord Lieutenant, and had reason to expect more, to discover your disloyalty in the pulpit. But what will that avail? Therefore sit down and be quiet, and mind your business, as you do, and contract your friendships, and expect no more from man than such an animal is capable of, and you will every day find my description of Yahoos more resembling. You should think and deal with every man as a villain, without calling him so, or flying from him, or valuing him less. This is an old true lesson. You believe every one will acquit you of any regard to temporal interest; and how came you to claim an exception from all mankind? I believe you value your temporal interest as much as anybody, but you have not the arts of pursuing it. You are mistaken. Domestic evils are no more within a man than others; and he who cannot bear up against the first, will sink under the second, and in my conscience I believe this is your case; for being of a weak constitution, in an employment precarious and tiresome, loaden with children, cum uxore neque leni neque commoda, a man of intent and abstracted thinking, enslaved by mathematics, and complaint of the world, this new weight of party malice hath struck you down, like a feather on a horse's back already loaden as far as he is able to bear. You ought to change the apostle's expression,° and say, I will strive to learn in whatever state, &c.

I will bear none of your visions; you shall live at Quilca but three fortnights and a month in the year; perhaps not so much. You shall make no entertainments but what are necessary to your interests; for your true friends would rather see you over a piece of mutton and a bottle once a quarter; you shall be merry at the expense of others; you shall take care of your health, and go early to bed, and not read late at night; and laugh with all men, without trusting any, and then a fig for the contrivers of your ruin, who now have no further thoughts than to stop your progress, which perhaps they may not compass, unless I am deceived more than is usual. All this you will do si mihi credis, and not dream of printing your sermon, which is a project abounding with objections unanswerable, and with which I could fill this letter. You say nothing of having preached before the Lord Lieutenant, nor whether he is altered towards you; for you speak nothing but generals. You think all the world has now nothing to do but to pull Mr. Sheridan down, whereas it is nothing but a slap in your turn, and away. Lord Oxford said once to me, on an occasion, 'these fools, because they hear a noise about their ears of their own making, think the whole world is full of it'. When I come to town we will change all this scene, and act like men of the world. Grow rich, and you will have no enemies. Go sometimes to the Castle, keep fast Mr. Tickell and Balaguer; frequent those on the right side, friends to the present powers; drop those who are loud on the wrong party, because they know they can suffer nothing by it.

Swift to Alexander Pope

September 29, 1725.

Sir,

I cannot guess the reason of Mr. Stopford's management° but impute it
at a venture either to haste or bashfulness, in the latter of which he is
excessive to a fault, although he had already gone the tour of Italy and
France, to harden him: perhaps this second journey and for a longer time
may amend him. He treated you just as he did Lord Carteret, to whom I
recommended him. My letter you saw to Lord Bolingbroke has shown
you the situation I am in, and the company I keep, if I do not forget some
of its contents. But I am now returning to the noble scene of Dublin into
the Grand Monde, for fear of burying my parts, to signalise myself
among curates and vicars, and correct all corruptions crept in relating to
the weight of bread and butter through those dominions where I govern.°
I have employed my time (besides ditching) in finishing, correcting,
amending, and transcribing my Travels,° in four parts complete, newly
augmented, and intended for the press when the world shall deserve
them, or rather when a printer shall be found brave enough to venture his
ears. I like your schemes of our meeting after distresses and dispersions;
but the chief end I propose to myself in all my labours is to vex the world
rather than divert it, and if I could compass that design without hurting
my own person or fortune I would be the most indefatigable writer you
have ever seen, without reading. I am exceedingly pleased that you have
done with translations.° Lord Treasurer Oxford often lamented that a
rascally world should lay you under a necessity of misemploying your
genius for so long a time. But since you will now be so much better
employed, when you think of the world give it one lash the more at my
request. I have ever hated all nations, professions, and communities, and
all my love is toward individuals; for instance, I hate the tribe of lawyers,
but I love Counsellor Such-a-one, Judge Such-a-one: so with
physicians—I will not speak of my own trade—soldiers, English, Scotch,
French, and the rest. But principally I hate and detest that animal called
man, although I heartily love John, Peter, Thomas, and so forth. This is
the system upon which I have governed myself many years (but do not
tell) and so I shall go on till I have done with them. I have got materials
toward a treatise proving the falsity of that definition *animal rationale*; and
to show it should be only *rationis capax*. Upon this great foundation of
misanthropy (though not in Timon's manner)° the whole building of my
Travels is erected; and I never will have peace of mind till all honest men

are of my opinion. By consequence you are to embrace it immediately and procure that all who deserve my esteem may do so too. The matter is so clear that it will admit little dispute; nay I will hold a hundred pounds that you and I agree in the point.

I did not know your Odyssey was finished, being yet in the country, which I shall leave in three days. I shall thank you kindly for the present, but shall like it three fourths the less from the mixture you mention of another hand; however, I am glad you saved yourself so much drudgery. I have been long told by Mr. Ford of your great achievements in building and planting and especially of your subterranean passage to your garden, whereby you turned a blunder° into a beauty, which is a piece of ars poetica.

I have almost done with harridans and shall soon become old enough to fall in love with girls of fourteen. The lady whom you describe to live at court,° to be deaf and no party woman, I take to be mythology but know not how to moralise it. She cannot be Mercy, for Mercy is neither deaf nor lives at Court. Justice is blind and perhaps deaf but neither is she a Court lady. Fortune is both blind and deaf and a Court lady, but then she is a most damnable party woman, and will never make me easy as you promise. It must be Riches which answers all your description. I am glad she visits you, but my voice is so weak that I doubt she will never hear me.

Mr. Lewis sent me an account of Dr. Arbuthnot's illness which is a very sensible affliction to me, who by living so long out of the world have lost that hardness of heart contracted by years and general conversation. I am daily losing friends, and neither seeking nor getting others. Oh, if the world had but a dozen Arbuthnots in it I would burn my Travels, but however he is not without fault. There is a passage in Bede° highly commending the piety and learning of the Irish in that age, where after abundance of praises he overthrows them all by lamenting that, Alas, they kept Easter at a wrong time of the year. So our Doctor has every quality and virtue that can make a man amiable or useful, but alas he hath a sort of slouch in his walk. I pray God protect him for he is an excellent Christian though not a Catholic, and as fit a man either to die or live as ever I knew.

I hear nothing of our friend Gay, but I find the Court keeps him at hard meat. I advised him to come over here with a Lord Lieutenant. Mr. Tickell is in a very good office. I have not seen Philips, though formerly we were so intimate. He has got nothing and by what I find will get nothing though he writes little flams (as Lord Leicester called those sort of verses) on Miss Carteret and others. It is remarkable and deserves recording that a Dublin blacksmith, a great poet, hath imitated his manner in a poem to the same Miss. Philips is a complainer, and on this occasion I told Lord Carteret that complainers never succeed at Court though railers do.

Are you altogether a country gentleman that I must address to you out of London, to the hazard of your losing this precious letter, which I will now conclude, although so much paper is left. I have an ill name and therefore shall not subscribe it; but you will guess it comes from one who esteems and loves you about half as much as you deserve; I mean as much as he can.

I am in great concern at what I am just told in some newspaper, that Lord Bolingbroke is much hurt by a fall in hunting. I am glad he has so much youth and vigour left, of which he hath not been thrifty, but I wonder he has no more discretion.

Address: For Mr. Pope at his House at Twickenham near Hampton Court. By London.

Swift to the Earl of Peterborough

April 28, 1726.

My Lord,

Your Lordship having, at my request, obtained for me an hour from Sir Robert Walpole, I accordingly attended him yesterday at eight o'clock in the morning, and had somewhat more than an hour's conversation with him. Your Lordship was this day pleased to inquire what passed between that great Minister and me, to which I gave you some general answers from whence you said you could comprehend little or nothing.

I had no other design in desiring to see Sir Robert Walpole than to represent the affairs of Ireland to him in a true light, not only without any view to myself but any party whatsoever; and because I understood the affairs of that kingdom tolerably well, and observed the representations he had received were such as I could not agree to, my principal design was to set him right not only for the service of Ireland, but likewise of England and of his own administration.

I failed very much in my design; for I saw he had conceived opinions from the example and practices of the present and some former governors, which I could not reconcile to the notions I had of liberty, a possession always understood by the British nation to be the inheritance of a human creature.

Sir Robert Walpole was pleased to enlarge very much upon the subject of Ireland, in a manner so alien from what I conceived to be rights and privileges of a subject of England that I did not think proper to debate the matter with him so much as I otherwise might, because I found it would be in vain. I shall, therefore, without entering into dispute make bold to mention to your Lordship some few grievances of that kingdom, as it consists of a people who beside a natural right of enjoying the privileges of subjects, have also a claim of merit from their extraordinary loyalty to the present King and his family:—

First, that all persons born in Ireland are called and treated as Irishmen, although their fathers and grandfathers were born in England; and their predecessors having been conquerors of Ireland, it is humbly conceived they ought to be on as good a foot as any subjects of Britain, according to the practice of all other nations, and particularly of the Greeks and Romans.

Secondly, that they are denied the natural liberty of exporting their manufactures to any country which is not engaged in a war with England.

Thirdly, that whereas there is a University in Ireland,° founded by Queen Elizabeth, where youth are instructed with a much stricter discipline than either in Oxford or Cambridge, it lies under the greatest discouragements, by filling all the principal employments, civil and ecclesiastical, with persons from England who have neither interest, property, acquaintance, nor alliance in that kingdom; contrary to the practice of all other States in Europe which are governed by viceroys, at least what hath never been used without the utmost discontents of the people.

Fourthly, that several of the bishops sent over to Ireland, having been clergymen of obscure condition and without other distinction than that of chaplains to the governors, do frequently invite over their old acquaintance or kindred, to whom they bestow the best preferments in their gift. The like may be said of the judges, who take with them one or two dependants to whom they give their countenance, and who consequently, without other merit, grow immediately into the chief business of their courts. The same practice is followed by all others in civil employments, if they have a cousin, a valet, or footman, in their family born in England.

Fifthly, that all civil employments grantable in reversion are given to persons who reside in England.

The people of Ireland, who are certainly the most loyal subjects in the world, cannot but conceive that most of these hardships have been the consequence of some unfortunate representations (at least) in former times; and the whole body of the gentry feel the effects in a very sensible part, being utterly destitute of all means to make provision for their younger sons, either in the Church, the law, the revenue, or (of late) in the army: and, in the desperate condition of trade, it is equally vain to think of making them merchants. All they have left is, at the expiration of leases, to rack their tenants, which they have done to such a degree that there is not one farmer in a hundred through the kingdom who can afford shoes or stockings to his children, or to eat flesh, or drink anything better than sour milk or water, twice in a year; so that the whole country, except the Scotch plantation in the north, is a scene of misery and desolation hardly to be matched on this side Lapland.

The rents of Ireland are computed to about a million and a half, whereof one half million at least is spent by lords and gentlemen residing in England, and by some other articles too long to mention.

About three hundred thousand pounds more are returned thither on other accounts; and, upon the whole, those who are the best versed in that kind of knowledge, agree that England gains annually by Ireland a million at least, which even I could make appear beyond all doubt.

But, as this mighty profit would probably increase, with tolerable treatment, to half a million more; so it must of necessity sink, under the hardships that kingdom lies at present.

And whereas Sir Robert Walpole was pleased to take notice how little the King gets by Ireland, it ought perhaps to be considered that the revenues and taxes, I think, amount to above four hundred thousand pounds a year; and reckoning the riches of Ireland, compared with England, to be as one to twelve, the King's revenues there would be equal to more than five millions here; which, considering the bad payment of rents from such miserable creatures as most of the tenants in Ireland are, will be allowed to be as much as such a kingdom can bear.

The current coin of Ireland is reckoned, at most, but five hundred thousand pounds; so that above four fifths are paid every year into the exchequer.

I think it manifest that whatever circumstances can possibly contribute to make a country poor and despicable, are all united with respect to Ireland. The nation controlled by laws to which they do not consent, disowned by their brethren and countrymen, refused the liberty not only of trading with their own manufactures but even their native commodities, forced to seek for justice many hundred miles by sea and land, rendered in a manner incapable of serving their King and country in any employment of honour, trust, or profit; and all this without the least demerit: while the governors sent over thither can possibly have no affection to the people, further than what is instilled into them by their own justice and love of mankind (which do not always operate) and whatever they please to represent hither is never called in question.

Whether the representatives of such a people, thus distressed and laid in the dust, when they meet in a Parliament, can do the public business with that cheerfulness which might be expected from free-born subjects, would be a question in any other country, except that unfortunate island, the English inhabitants whereof have given more and greater examples of their loyalty and dutifulness than can be shown in any other part of the world.

What part of these grievances may be thought proper to be redressed by so wise and great a minister as Sir Robert Walpole, he perhaps will please to consider; especially because they have been all brought upon that kingdom since the Revolution, which, however, is a blessing annually celebrated there with the greatest zeal and sincerity.

I most humbly entreat your Lordship to give this paper to Sir Robert Walpole, and desire him to read it, which he may do in a few minutes. I am, with the greatest respect, my Lord,

Your Lordship's most obedient servant,

JON. SWIFT.

'Richard Sympson' to Benjamin Motte

London, *August* 8, 1726.

Sir,

My cousin Mr. Lemuel Gulliver entrusted me some years ago with a copy of his Travels, whereof that which I here send you is about a fourth part, for I shortened them very much as you will find in my Preface to the Reader. I have shown them to several persons of great judgement and distinction, who are confident they will sell very well. And although some parts of this and the following volumes may be thought in one or two places to be a little satirical, yet it is agreed they will give no offence, but in that you must judge for yourself, and take the advice of your friends, and if they or you be of another opinion, you may let me know it when you return these papers, which I expect shall be in three days at furthest. The good report I have received of you makes me put so great a trust into your hands, which I hope you will give me no reason to repent, and in that confidence I require that you will never suffer these papers to be once out of your sight.

As the printing these Travels will probably be of great value to you, so as a manager for my friend and cousin I expect you will give a due consideration for it, because I know the author intends the profit for the use of poor seamen, and I am advised to say that two hundred pounds is the least sum I will receive on his account; but if it shall happen that the sale will not answer as I expect and believe, then whatever shall be thought too much, even upon your own word, shall be duly repaid.

Perhaps you may think this a strange way of proceeding to a man of trade, but since I begin with so great a trust to you, whom I never saw, I think it not hard that you should trust me as much. Therefore, if after three days reading and consulting these papers, you think it proper to stand to my agreement, you may begin to print them, and the subsequent parts shall be all sent you one after another in less than a week, provided that immediately upon your resolution to print them, you do within three days deliver a bank bill of two hundred pounds wrapped up so as to make a parcel to the hand from whence you receive this, who will come in the same manner exactly at nine o'clock at night on Thursday which will be the 11th instant.

If you do not approve of this proposal, deliver these papers to the person who will come on Thursday.

If you choose rather to send the papers make no other proposal of your own but just barely write on a piece of paper that you do not accept my offer. I am, Sir,

Your humble servant,

Richard Sympson

For Mr. Motte.

Stella's Birthday

March 13, 1726–7

This day, whate'er the Fates decree,
Shall still be kept with joy by me:
This day then, let us not be told
That you are sick, and I grown old;
Nor think on our approaching ills,
And talk of spectacles and pills.
Tomorrow will be time enough
To hear such mortifying stuff.
Yet, since from reason may be brought
A better and more pleasing thought,   10
Which can, in spite of all decays,
Support a few remaining days—
From not the gravest of divines
Accept, for once, some serious lines.

   Although we now can form no more
Long schemes of life, as heretofore;
Yet you, while time is running fast,
Can look with joy on what is past.

   Were future happiness and pain
A mere contrivance of the brain,   20
As *atheists* argue, to entice
And fit their proselytes for vice
(The only comfort they propose,
To have companions in their woes):
Grant this the case, yet sure 'tis hard
That virtue, styled its own reward,°
And by all sages understood
To be the chief of human good,
Should acting die; nor leave behind
Some lasting pleasure in the mind,   30
Which, by remembrance, will assuage
Grief, sickness, poverty, and age;
And strongly shoot a radiant dart
To shine through life's declining part.

   Say, Stella, feel you no content,
Reflecting on a life well spent?
Your skilful hand employ'd to save

Despairing wretches from the grave;
And then supporting with your store
Those whom you dragg'd from death before?   40
(So Providence on mortals waits,
Preserving what it first creates.)
Your gen'rous boldness to defend
An innocent and absent friend;
That courage which can make you just
To merit humbled in the dust;
The detestation you express
For vice in all its glitt'ring dress;
That patience under torturing pain,
Where stubborn stoics would complain.   50
    Must these like empty shadows pass,
Or forms reflected from a glass?
Or mere chimeras in the mind,
That fly, and leave no marks behind?
Does not the body thrive and grow
By food of twenty years ago?
And, had it not been still supplied,
It must a thousand times have died.
Then, who with reason can maintain
That no effects of food remain?   60
And is not virtue in mankind
The nutriment that feeds the mind,
Upheld by each good action past
And still continued by the last?
Then, who with reason can pretend
That all effects of virtue end?
    Believe me, Stella, when you show
That true contempt for things below,
Nor prize your life for other ends
Than merely to oblige your friends;   70
Your former actions claim their part,
And join to fortify your heart.
For Virtue, in her daily race,
Like Janus, bears a double face;
Looks back with joy where she has gone
And therefore goes with courage on.
She at your sickly couch will wait,
And guide you to a better state.

O then, whatever Heav'n intends,
Take pity on your pitying friends!   80
Nor let your ills affect your mind
To fancy they can be unkind.
Me, surely me, you ought to spare,
Who gladly would your suff'rings share,
Or give my scrap of life to you,
And think it far beneath your due:
You, to whose care so oft I owe
That I'm alive to tell you so.

Desire and Possession

'Tis strange what diff'rent thoughts inspire
In Man, *Possession* and *Desire!*
Think what they wish so great a blessing,
So disappointed when possessing!
　A moralist profoundly sage
(I know not in what book or page,
Or whether o'er a pot of ale)
Related thus the following tale:
　Possession, and *Desire*, his brother,
But still at variance with each other,　　　　　　10
Were seen contending in a race,
And kept at first an equal pace.
'Tis said, their course continued long,
For this was active, that was strong:
Till Envy, Slander, Sloth, and Doubt,
Misled them many a league about;
Seduced by some deceiving light,
They take the wrong way for the right;
Through slipp'ry by-roads, dark and deep,
They often climb, and oft'ner creep.　　　　　　20
　Desire, the swifter of the two,
Along the plain like lightning flew:
Till, ent'ring on a broad highway,
Where *Power* and *Titles* scatter'd lay,
He strove to pick up all he found,
And by excursions lost his ground.
No sooner got, than with disdain
He threw them on the ground again;
And hasted forward to pursue
Fresh objects, fairer to his view,　　　　　　30
In hope to spring some nobler game;
But all he took was just the same:
Too scornful now to stop his pace,
He spurn'd them in his rival's face.
　Possession kept the beaten road,
And gather'd all his brother strow'd;
But overcharged, and out of wind,
Though strong in limbs, he lagg'd behind.

Desire had now the goal in sight.
It was a tow'r of monstrous height, 40
Where on the summit *Fortune* stands,
A crown and sceptre in her hands;
Beneath, a chasm as deep as Hell,
Where many a bold advent'rer fell.
Desire, in rapture gazed awhile,
And saw the treach'rous goddess smile;
But, as he climbed to grasp the crown
She knock'd him with the sceptre down.
He tumbled in the gulf profound,
There doom'd to whirl an endless round. 50
   Possession's load was grown so great,
He sunk beneath the cumbrous weight;
And, as he now expiring lay,
Flocks ev'ry ominous bird of prey;
The raven, vulture, owl, and kite,
At once upon his carcass light
And strip his hide, and pick his bones,
Regardless of his dying groans.

On the Death of Mrs. Johnson [Stella].

THIS day, being Sunday, January 28th, 1727–8, about eight o'clock at night, a servant brought me a note with an account of the death of the truest, most virtuous, and valuable friend, that I, or perhaps any other person ever was blessed with. She expired about six in the evening of this day; and as soon as I am left alone, which is about eleven at night, I resolve for my own satisfaction to say something of her life and character.

She was born at Richmond, in Surrey, on the thirteenth day of March, in the year 1681. Her father was a younger brother of a good family in Nottinghamshire, her mother of a lower degree: and indeed she had little to boast of her birth. I knew her from six years old, and had some share in her education by directing what books she should read, and perpetually instructing her in the principles of honour and virtue; from which she never swerved in any one action or moment of her life. She was sickly from her childhood until about the age of fifteen; but then grew into perfect health, and was looked upon as one of the most beautiful, graceful, and agreeable young women in London, only a little too fat. Her hair was blacker than a raven, and every feature of her face in perfection. She lived generally in the country with a family, where she contracted an intimate friendship with another lady° of more advanced years. I was then (to my mortification) settled in Ireland; and about a year after, going to visit my friends in England, I found she was a little uneasy upon the death of a person° on whom she had some dependance. Her fortune, at that time, was in all not above fifteen hundred pounds, the interest of which was but a scanty maintenance, in so dear a country, for one of her spirit. Upon this consideration, and indeed very much for my own satisfaction, who had few friends or acquaintance in Ireland, I prevailed with her and her dear friend and companion, the other lady, to draw what money they had into Ireland, a great part of their fortune being in annuities upon funds. Money was then at ten *per cent.* in Ireland, besides the advantage of returning it, and all necessaries of life at half the price. They complied with my advice, and soon after came over; but, I happening to continue some time longer in England, they were much discouraged to live in Dublin, where they were wholly strangers. She was at that time about nineteen years old, and her person was soon distinguished. But the adventure looked so like a frolic the censure held, for some time, as if there were a secret history in such a removal; which, however, soon blew off by her excellent conduct. She came over with her friend on the ——— in the year 170–; and they both lived together until this day, when death removed her from us. For some years past, she had been visited with continual ill-health; and several times, within these two years, her life was despaired of. But, for this twelvemonth past, she never had a day's health; and, properly speaking, she hath been dying six months, but kept alive almost against nature by the generous kindness of two physicians and the care of her friends. Thus far I writ the same night between eleven and twelve.

Never was any of her sex born with better gifts of the mind, or more improved them by reading and conversation. Yet her memory was not of the best, and was impaired in the latter years of her life. But I cannot call to mind that I ever once heard her make a wrong judgment of persons, books, or affairs. Her advice was always the best, and with the greatest freedom, mixed with the greatest decency. She had a gracefulness somewhat more than human, in every motion, word, and action. Never was so happy a conjunction of civility, freedom, easiness and sincerity. There seemed to be a combination among all that knew her, to treat her with a dignity much beyond her rank: yet people of all sorts were never more easy than in her company. Mr. Addison, when he was in Ireland, being introduced to her, immediately found her out; and, if he had not soon after left the kingdom, assured me he would have used all endeavours to cultivate her friendship. A rude or conceited coxcomb passed his time very ill, upon the least breach of respect; for in such a case she had no mercy, but was sure to expose him to the contempt of the standers-by; yet in such a manner as he was ashamed to complain, and durst not resent. All of us who had the happiness of her friendship, agreed unanimously, that, in an afternoon or evening's conversation, she never failed before we parted of delivering the best thing that was said in the company. Some of us have written down several of her sayings, or what the French call *bon mots*,° wherein she excelled almost beyond belief. She never mistook the understanding of others; nor ever said a severe word, but where a much severer was deserved.

Her servants loved and almost adored her at the same time. She would upon occasions treat them with freedom; yet her demeanour was so awful that they durst not fail in the least point of respect. She chid them seldom, but it was with severity, which had an effect upon them for a long time after.

January 29th, My head aches, and I can write no more.

January 30th, Tuesday.

This is the night of the funeral, which my sickness will not suffer me to attend. It is now nine at night, and I am removed into another apartment, that I may not see the light in the church, which is just over against the window of my bedchamber.

With all the softness of temper that became a lady, she had the personal courage of a hero. She and her friend having removed their lodgings to a new house which stood solitary, a parcel of rogues, armed, attempted the house, where there was only one boy. She was then about four and twenty; and having been warned to apprehend some such attempt, she learned the management of a pistol; and the other women and servants being half dead with fear, she stole softly to her dining-room window, put on a black hood to prevent being seen, primed the pistol fresh, gently lifted up the sash; and taking her aim with the utmost presence of mind, discharged the pistol loaden with the bullets into the body of one villain, who stood the fairest mark. The fellow, mortally wounded, was carried off by the rest and died the next morning; but his companions could not be found. The Duke of Ormond hath often drank her health to me upon that account, and had always an high esteem of her. She was indeed under some apprehensions of going in a boat, after some danger she had narrowly escaped by water, but she was reasoned thoroughly out of it. She was never known to cry out or discover any fear in a coach or on horseback, or any uneasiness by those suddent accidents with which most of her sex, either by weakness or affectation, appear so much disordered.

She never had the least absence of mind in conversation, nor given to interruption, or appeared eager to put in her word by waiting impatiently until another had done. She spoke in a most agreeable voice, in the plainest words, never hesitating, except out of modesty before new faces, where she was somewhat reserved: nor, among her nearest friends, ever spoke much at a time. She was but little versed in the common topics of female chat; scandal, censure, and detraction, never came out of her mouth. Yet, among a few friends, in private conversation, she made little ceremony in discovering her contempt of a coxcomb, and describing all his follies to the life; but the follies of her own sex she was rather inclined to extenuate or to pity.

When she was once convinced, by open facts of any breach of truth or honour, in a person of high station, especially in the Church, she could not conceal her indignation nor hear them named without showing her displeasure in her countenance; particularly one or two of the latter sort, whom she had known and esteemed, but detested above all mankind when it was manifest that they had sacrificed those two precious virtues to their ambition, and would much sooner have forgiven them the common immoralities of the laity.

Her frequent fits of sickness, in most parts of her life, had prevented her from making that progress in reading which she would otherwise have done. She was well versed in the Greek and Roman story, and was not unskilled in that of France and England. She spoke French perfectly, but forgot much of it by neglect and sickness. She had read carefully all the best books of travels, which serve to open and enlarge the mind. She understood the Platonic and Epicurean philosophy, and judged very well of the defects of the latter. She made very judicious abstracts of the best books she had read. She understood the nature of government, and could point out all the errors of Hobbes, both in that and religion. She had a good insight into physic, and knew somewhat of anatomy, in both which she was instructed in her younger days by an eminent physician, who had her long under his care, and bore the highest esteem for her person and understanding. She had a true taste of wit and good sense, both in poetry and prose, and was a perfect good critic of style: neither was it easy to find a more proper or impartial judge, whose advice an author might better rely on if he intended to send a thing into the world, provided it was on a subject that came within the compass of her knowledge. Yet, perhaps, she was sometimes too severe, which is a safe and pardonable error. She preserved her wit, judgment, and vivacity to the last, but often used to complain of her memory.

Her fortune with some accession could not, as I have heard say, amount to much more than two thousand pounds, whereof a great part fell with her life, having been placed upon annuities in England, and one in Ireland.

In a person so extraordinary, perhaps it may be pardonable to mention some particulars, although of little moment further than to set forth her character. Some presents of gold pieces being often made to her while she was a girl, by her mother and other friends, on promise to keep them, she grew into such a spirit of thrift that in about three years, they amounted to above two hundred pounds. She used to show them with boasting; but her mother, apprehending she would be cheated of them, prevailed, in some months, and with great importunities, to have them put out to interest. When the girl lost the pleasure of seeing and counting her gold, which she never failed of doing many times in a day, and despaired of heaping up such another treasure, her humour took the quite contrary turn. She grew careless and squandering of every new acquisition, and so continued till about two and twenty; when, by advice of some friends, and the fright of paying large bills of tradesmen who enticed her into their debt, she began to reflect upon her own folly, and was never at rest until she had discharged all her shop-bills, and refunded herself a considerable sum she had run out. After which, by the addition of a few years, and a superior understanding, she became and continued all her life a most prudent economist; yet still with a strong bent to the liberal side, wherein she gratified herself by avoiding all expense in clothes (which she ever despised) beyond what was merely decent. And, although her frequent returns of sickness were very chargeable, except fees to physicians of which she met with several so generous that she could force nothing on them (and indeed she must otherwise have been undone), yet she never was without a considerable sum of ready money. Insomuch that, upon her death, when her nearest friends thought her very bare, her executors found in her strong box about a hundred and fifty pounds in gold. She lamented the narrowness of her fortune in nothing so much as that it did not enable her to entertain her friends so often and in so hospitable a manner as she desired. Yet they were always welcome, and while she was in health to direct, were treated with neatness and elegance, so that the revenues of her and her companion passed for much more considerable than they really were. They lived always in lodgings, their domestics consisted of two maids and one man. She kept an account of all the family expenses from her arrival in Ireland to some months before her death; and she would often repine, when looking back upon the annals of her household bills, that everything necessary for life was double the price, while interest of money was sunk almost to one half; so that the addition made to her fortune was indeed grown absolutely necessary.

[I since writ as I found time.]

But her charity to the poor was a duty not to be diminished, and therefore became a tax upon those tradesmen who furnish the fopperies of other ladies. She bought clothes as seldom as possible, and those as plain and cheap as consisted with the situation she was in; and wore no lace for many years. Either her judgment or fortune was extraordinary in the choice of those on whom she bestowed her charity; for it went further in doing good than double the sum from any other hand. And I have heard her say, she always met with gratitude from the poor; which must be owing to her skill in distinguishing proper objects as well as her gracious manner in relieving them.

But she had another quality that much delighted her, although it may be thought a kind of check upon her bounty; however, it was a pleasure she could not resist: I mean that of making agreeable presents, wherein I never knew her equal, although it be an affair of as delicate a nature as most in the course of life. She used to define a present, that it was a gift to a friend of something he wanted or was fond of, and which could not be easily gotten for money. I am confident during my acquaintance with her, she hath, in these and some other kinds of liberality, disposed of to the value of several hundred pounds. As to presents made to herself she received them with great unwillingness, but especially from those to whom she had ever given any; being on all occasions the most disinterested mortal I ever knew or heard of.

From her own disposition, at least as much as from the frequent want of health, she seldom made any visits; but her own lodgings, from before twenty years old, were frequented by many persons of the graver sort, who all respected her highly upon her good sense, good manners, and conversation. Among these were the late Primate Lindsay, Bishop Lloyd, Bishop Ashe, Bishop Brown, Bishop Stearne, Bishop Pulleyn, with some others of later date; and indeed the greatest number of her acquaintance was among the clergy. Honour, truth, liberality, good nature, and modesty, were the virtues she chiefly possessed and most valued in her acquaintance; and where she found them, would be ready to allow for some defects, nor valued them less, although they did not shine in learning or in wit; but would never give the least allowance for any failures in the former, even to those who made the greatest figure in either of the two latter. She had no use of any person's liberality, yet her detestation of covetous people made her uneasy if such a one was in her company; upon which occasion she would say many things very entertaining and humorous.

She never interrupted any person who spoke; she laughed at no mistakes they made, but helped them out with modesty; and if a good thing were spoken but neglected, she would not let it fall, but set it in the best light to those who were present. She listened to all that was said, and had never the least distraction or absence of thought.

It was not safe nor prudent, in her presence, to offend in the least word against modesty; for she then gave full employment to her wit, her contempt and resentment, under which even stupidity and brutality were forced to sink into confusion; and the guilty person, by her future avoiding him like a bear or a satyr, was never in a way to transgress a second time.

It happened one single coxcomb, of the pert kind, was in her company among several other ladies; and in his flippant way began to deliver some double meanings; the rest flapped their fans, and used the other common expedients practised in such cases, of appearing not to mind or comprehend what was said. Her behaviour was very different, and perhaps may be censured. She said thus to the man: 'Sir, all these ladies and I understand your meaning very well, having, in spite of our care, too often met with those of your sex who wanted manners and good sense. But believe me, neither virtuous nor even vicious women love such kind of conversation. However, I will leave you and report your behaviour: and whatever visit I make, I shall first enquire at the door whether you are in the house, that I may be sure to avoid you.' I know not whether a majority of ladies would approve of such a proceeding; but I believe the practice of it would soon put an end to that corrupt conversation, the worst effect of dullness, ignorance, impudence, and vulgarity, and the highest affront to the modesty and understanding of the female sex.

By returning very few visits, she had not much company of her own sex, except those whom she most loved for their easiness, or esteemed for their good sense; and those, not insisting on ceremony, came often to her. But she rather chose men for her companions, the usual topics of ladies discourse being such as she had little knowledge of, and less relish. Yet no man was upon the rack to entertain her, for she easily descended to anything that was innocent and diverting. News, politics, censure, family management, or town-talk, she always diverted to something else; but these indeed seldom happened, for she chose her company better. And therefore many, who mistook her and themselves, having solicited her acquaintance, and finding themselves disappointed, after a few visits dropped off; and she was never known to enquire into the reason, or ask what was become of them.

She was never positive in arguing, and she usually treated those who were so, in a manner which well enough gratified that unhappy disposition; yet in such a sort as made it very contemptible, and at the same time did some hurt to the owners. Whether this proceeded from her easiness in general, or from her indifference to persons, or from her despair of mending them, or from the same practice which she much liked in Mr. Addison, I cannot determine; but when she saw any of the company very warm in a wrong opinion, she was more inclined to confirm them in it than oppose them. The excuse she commonly gave, when her friends asked the reason, was that it prevented noise and saved time. Yet I have known her very angry with some whom she much esteemed for sometimes falling into that infirmity.

She loved Ireland much better than the generality of those who owe both their birth and riches to it; and having brought over all the fortune she had in money, left the reversion of the best part of it, one thousand pounds, to Dr. Stephens's Hospital.° She detested the tyranny and injustice of England in their treatment of this kingdom. She had indeed reason to love a country, where she had the esteem and friendship of all who knew her, and the universal good report of all who ever heard of her without one exception, if I am told the truth by those who keep general conversation. Which character is the more extraordinary, in falling to a person of so much knowledge, wit, and vivacity, qualities that are used to create envy, and consequently censure; and must be rather imputed to her great modesty, gentle behaviour, and inoffensiveness, than to her superior virtues.

Although her knowledge, from books and company, was much more extensive than usually falls to the share of her sex; yet she was so far from making a parade of it, that her female visitants, on their first acquaintance, who expected to discover it by what they call hard words and deep discourse, would be sometimes disappointed, and say, they found she was like other women. But wise men, through all her modesty, whatever they discoursed on, could easily observe that she understood them very well, by the judgment shown in her observations as well as in her questions.

A

MODEST PROPOSAL

FOR PREVENTING THE CHILDREN OF POOR
PEOPLE FROM BEING A 𝕭𝖀𝕽𝕿𝕳𝕰𝕹 𝕿𝕺 𝕿𝕳𝕰𝕴𝕽
𝕻𝕬𝕽𝕰𝕹𝕿𝕾 OR THE COUNTRY, AND FOR
MAKING THEM BENEFICIAL TO THE PUBLIC.

IT is a melancholy object to those who walk through this great town,° or travel in the country, when they see the *streets*, the *roads*, and *cabin-doors* crowded with *beggars* of the female sex, followed by three, four, or six children, *all in rags*, and importuning every passenger for an alms. These *mothers* instead of being able to work for their honest livelihood, are forced to employ all their time in strolling° to beg sustenance for their *helpless infants* who, as they grow up, either turn *thieves* for want of work, or leave their *dear Native Country to fight for the Pretender* in Spain,° or sell themselves to the Barbadoes.

I think it is agreed by all parties that this prodigious number of children, in the arms, or on the backs, or at the *heels* of their *mothers*, and frequently of their fathers, is *in the present deplorable state of the kingdom*, a very great additional grievance; and therefore whoever could find out a fair, cheap and easy method of making these children sound useful members of the commonwealth would deserve so well of the public, as to have his statue set up for a preserver of the nation.

But my intention is very far from being confined to provide only for the children of *professed beggars*, it is of a much greater extent, and shall take in the whole number of infants at a certain age, who are born of parents in effect as little able to support them as those who demand our charity in the streets.

As to my own part, having turned my thoughts for many years upon this important subject, and maturely weighed the several *schemes of other projectors*, I have always found them grossly mistaken in their computation. It is true a child *just dropped from its dam* may be supported by her milk for a solar year with little other nourishment, at most not above the value of two shillings, which the mother may certainly get, or the value in *scraps*, by her lawful occupation of *begging*. And it is exactly at one year old that I propose to provide for them in such a manner as, instead of being a charge upon their *parents*, or the *parish*, or *wanting food and raiment* for the rest of their lives, they shall, on the contrary, contribute to the feeding and partly to the clothing of many thousands.

There is likewise another great advantage in my scheme, that it will prevent those *voluntary abortions*, and that horrid practice of *women murdering their bastard children*, alas! too frequent among us, sacrificing the *poor innocent babes*, I doubt, more to avoid the expense than the shame, which would move tears and pity in the most savage and inhuman breast.

The number of souls in this kingdom being usually reckoned one million and a half, of these I calculate° there may be about two hundred thousand couple whose wives are breeders, from which number I subtract thirty thousand couples who are able to maintain their own children, although I apprehend there cannot be so many under *the present distresses of the kingdom*, but this being granted, there will remain an hundred and seventy thousand breeders. I again subtract fifty thousand for those women who miscarry, or whose children die by accident, or disease within the year. There only remain an hundred and twenty thousand children of poor parents annually born. The question therefore is, how this number shall be reared and provided for, which, as I have already said, under the present situation of affairs is utterly impossible by all the methods hitherto proposed, for we can *neither employ them in handicraft*, or *agriculture*; we neither build houses (I mean in the country) nor cultivate land:° they can very seldom pick up a livelihood *by stealing* till they arrive at six years old, except where they are of towardly parts, although I confess they learn the rudiments much earlier, during which time they can however be properly looked upon only as *probationers*, as I have been informed by a principal gentleman in the County of Cavan, who protested to me that he never knew above one or two instances under the age of six, even in a part of the kingdom *so renowned for the quickest proficiency in that art.*

I am assured by our merchants that a boy or a girl, before twelve years old, is no saleable commodity, and even when they come to this age, they will not yield above three pounds, or three pounds and half-a-crown at most on the Exchange, which cannot turn to account either to the parents or the kingdom, the charge of nutriment and rags having been at least four times that value.

I shall now therefore humbly propose my own thoughts, which I hope will not be liable to the least objection.

I have been assured by a very knowing American of my acquaintance in London, that a young healthy child, well nursed, is at a year old a most delicious, nourishing, and wholesome food, whether *stewed, roasted, baked*, or *boiled*, and I make no doubt that it will equally serve in a *fricassee*, or a *ragout*.

I do therefore humbly offer it to *public consideration*, that of the hundred and twenty thousand children, already computed, twenty thousand may be reserved for breed, whereof only one fourth part to be males, which is more than we allow to *sheep*, *black-cattle*, or *swine*; and my reason is that these children are seldom the fruits of marriage, *a circumstance not much regarded by our savages*; therefore *one male* will be sufficient to serve *four females*. That the remaining hundred thousand may at a year old be offered in sale to the *persons of quality* and *fortune*, through the kingdom, always advising the mother to let them suck plentifully of the last month, so as to render them plump and fat for a good table. A child will make two dishes at an entertainment for friends, and when the family dines alone the fore or hind quarter will make a reasonable dish, and seasoned with a little pepper or salt will be very good boiled on the fourth day, especially in *winter*.

I have reckoned upon a medium,° that a child just born will weigh 12 pounds, and in a solar year if tolerably nursed increaseth to 28 pounds.

I grant this food will be somewhat dear, and therefore very *proper for landlords*, who, as they have already devoured most of the parents, seem to have the best title to the children.

Infants' flesh will be in season throughout the year, but more plentiful in *March*, and a little before and after, for we are told by a grave author,° an eminent French physician, that *fish being a prolific diet*, there are more children born in *Roman Catholic countries* about nine months after *Lent*, than at any other season; therefore reckoning a year after *Lent*, the markets will be more glutted than usual, because the number of *Popish infants* is at least three to one in this kingdom, and therefore it will have one other collateral advantage by lessening the number of *Papists* among us.

I have already computed the charge of nursing a beggar's child (in which list I reckon all *cottagers*, *labourers*, and four fifths of the *farmers*) to be about two shillings *per annum*, rags included, and I believe no gentleman would repine to give ten shillings for the *carcass of a good fat child*, which, as I have said, will make four dishes of excellent nutritive meat, when he hath only some particular friend, or his own family to dine with him. Thus the Squire will learn to be a good landlord, and grow popular among his tenants, the mother will have eight shillings net profit, and be fit for work till she produces another child.

Those who are more thrifty (*as I must confess the times require*) may flay the carcass; the skin of which, artificially dressed, will make admirable *gloves for ladies,* and *summer boots for fine gentlemen.*

As to our City of Dublin, shambles may be appointed for this purpose in the most convenient parts of it, and butchers we may be assured will not be wanting, although I rather recommend buying the children alive, and dressing them hot from the knife, as we do *roasting pigs.*

A very worthy person, *a true lover of his country,* and whose virtues I highly esteem, was lately pleased in discoursing on this matter, to offer a refinement upon my scheme. He said that many gentlemen of this kingdom, having of late destroyed their deer, he conceived that the want of venison might be well supplied by the bodies of young lads and maidens not exceeding fourteen years of age, nor under twelve, so great a number of both sexes in every country being now ready to starve for want of work and service: and these to be disposed of by their parents if alive, or otherwise by their nearest relations. But with due deference to so excellent a friend and so deserving a patriot, I cannot be altogether in his sentiments; for as to the males, my American acquaintance assured me from frequent experience that their flesh was generally tough and lean, like that of our schoolboys, by continual exercise, and their taste disagreeable, and to fatten them would not answer the charge. Then as to the females, it would I think with humble submission, *be a loss to the public,* because they soon would become breeders themselves. And besides, it is not improbable that some scrupulous people might be apt to censure such a practice (although indeed very unjustly) as a little bordering upon cruelty, which, I confess, hath always been with me the strongest objection against any project, however so well intended.

But in order to justify my friend, he confessed that this expedient was put into his head by the famous *Psalmanazar,*° a native of the island Formosa, who came from thence to London above twenty years ago, and in conversation told my friend that in his country when any young person happened to be put to death, the executioner sold the carcass to *persons of quality,* as a prime dainty, and that in his time, the body of a plump girl of fifteen, who was crucified for an attempt to poison the emperor, was sold to his Imperial *Majesty's Prime Minister of State,* and other great *Mandarins* of the Court, *in joints from the gibbet,* at four hundred crowns. Neither indeed can I deny, that if the same use were made of several plump young girls in this town, who, without one single groat to their fortunes, cannot stir abroad without a chair, and appear at the *playhouse* and *assemblies* in foreign fineries which they never will pay for, the kingdom would not be the worse.

Some persons of a desponding spirit are in great concern about that vast number of poor people who are aged, diseased, or maimed, and I have been desired to employ my thoughts what course may be taken to ease the nation of so grievous an encumbrance. But I am not in the least pain upon that matter, because it is very well known that they are every day *dying*, and *rotting*, by *cold* and *famine*, and *filth*, and *vermin*, as fast as can be reasonably expected. And as to the younger labourers they are now in almost as hopeful a condition. They cannot get work, and consequently pine away for want of nourishment, to a degree that if at any time they are accidentally hired to common labour, they have not strength to perform it; and thus the country and themselves are happily delivered from the evils to come.

I have too long digressed, and therefore shall return to my subject. I think the advantages by the proposal which I have made are obvious and many, as well as of the highest importance.

For *first*, as I have already observed, it would greatly lessen the *number of Papists*, with whom we are yearly over-run, being the principal breeders of the nation as well as our most dangerous enemies, and who stay at home on purpose with a design to *deliver the kingdom to the Pretender*, hoping to take their advantage by the absence of *so many good Protestants*, who have chosen rather to leave their country than stay at home and pay tithes against their conscience to an *Episcopal curate*.

Secondly, the poorer tenants will have something valuable of their own, which by law may be made liable to distress, and help to pay their landlord's rent, their corn and cattle being already seized, and *money a thing unknown*.

Thirdly, whereas the maintenance of an hundred thousand children, from two years old and upwards, cannot be computed at less than ten shillings a piece *per annum*, the nation's stock will be thereby increased fifty thousand pounds *per annum*, besides the profit of a new dish introduced to the tables of all *gentlemen of fortune* in the kingdom who have any refinement in taste; and the money will circulate among ourselves, the goods being entirely of our own growth and manufacture.

Fourthly, the constant breeders, besides the gain of eight shillings *sterling per annum* by the sale of their children, will be rid of the charge of maintaining them after the first year.

Fifthly, this food would likewise bring great *custom to taverns*, where the vintners will certainly be so prudent as to procure the best receipts for dressing it to perfection, and consequently have their houses frequented by all the *fine gentlemen*, who justly value themselves upon their knowledge in good eating; and a skilful cook, who understands how to oblige his guests, will contrive to make it as expensive as they please.

Sixthly, this would be a great inducement to marriage, which all wise nations have either encouraged by rewards, or enforced by laws and penalties. It would increase the care and tenderness of mothers toward their children, when they were sure of a settlement for life to the poor babes, provided in some sort by the public to their annual profit instead of expense. We should see an honest emulation among the married women, *which of them could bring the fattest child to the market*. Men would become as *fond* of their wives, during the time of their pregnancy, as they are now of their *mares* in foal, their *cows* in calf, or *sows* when they are ready to farrow; nor offer to beat or kick them (as it is too *frequent* a practice) for fear of a miscarriage.

Many other advantages might be enumerated. For instance, the addition of some thousand carcasses in our exportation of barrelled beef; the propagation of *swine's flesh* and improvement in the art of making good *bacon*, so much wanted among us by the great destruction of *pigs*, too frequent at our tables, which are no way comparable in taste, or magnificence to a well-grown, fat yearling child, which roasted whole will make a considerable figure at a *Lord Mayor's feast*, or any other public entertainment. But this and many others I omit, being studious of brevity.

Supposing that one thousand families in this city, would be constant customers for infants' flesh, besides others who might have it at *merry-meetings*, particularly *weddings* and *christenings*, I compute that Dublin would take off annually about twenty thousand carcasses, and the rest of the kingdom (where probably they will be sold somewhat cheaper) the remaining eighty thousand.

I can think of no one objection that will possibly be raised against this proposal, unless it should be urged that the number of people will be thereby much lessened in the kingdom. This I freely own, and it was indeed one principal design in offering it to the world. I desire the reader will observe, that I calculate my remedy *for this one individual Kingdom of IRELAND, and for no other that ever was, is, or, I think, ever can be upon earth*. Therefore let no man talk to me of other expedients:° *Of taxing our absentees at five shillings a pound: Of using neither clothes, nor household furniture, except what is of our own growth and manufacture: Of utterly rejecting the materials and instruments that promote foreign luxury: Of curing the expensiveness of pride, vanity, idleness, and gaming in our women: Of introducing a vein of parsimony, prudence and temperance: Of learning to love our Country, wherein we differ even from LAPLANDERS, and the inhabitants of TOPINAMBOO:° Of quitting our animosities and factions, nor act any longer like the Jews, who were murdering one another at the very*

*moment their city was taken:° Of being a little cautious not to sell our country
and consciences for nothing:° Of teaching landlords to have at least one degree of
mercy toward their tenants. Lastly of putting a spirit of honesty, industry and
skill into our shopkeepers, who, if a resolution could now be taken to buy only our
native goods, would immediately unite to cheat and exact upon us in the price,
the measure, and the goodness, nor could ever yet be brought to make one fair
proposal of just dealing, though often and earnestly invited to it.*

Therefore I repeat, let no man talk to me of these and the like
expedients, till he hath at least some glimpse of hope that there will ever
be some hearty and sincere attempt to put them in practice.

But as to myself, having been wearied out for many years with offering
vain, idle, visionary thoughts, and at length utterly despairing of success,
I fortunately fell upon this proposal, which as it is wholly new, so it hath
something solid and real, of no expense and little trouble, full in our own
power, and whereby we can incur no danger in *disobliging England*. For
this kind of commodity will not bear exportation, the flesh being of too
tender a consistence to admit a long continuance in salt, *although perhaps
I could name a country which would be glad to eat up our whole nation without
it.*

After all, I am not so violently bent upon my own opinion as to reject
any offer proposed by wise men, which shall be found equally innocent,
cheap, easy and effectual. But before something of that kind shall be
advanced in contradiction to my scheme, and offering a better, I desire
the author, or authors, will be pleased maturely to consider two points.
First, as things now stand, how they will be able to find food and raiment
for an hundred thousand useless mouths and backs. And *secondly*, there
being a round million of creatures in human figure throughout this
kingdom, whose whole subsistence put into a common stock would
leave them in debt two millions of pounds *sterling*; adding those who are
beggars by profession, to the bulk of farmers, cottagers and labourers
with their wives and children, who are beggars in effect; I desire those
politicians who dislike my overture and may perhaps be so bold to attempt
an answer, that they will first ask the parents of these mortals, whether
they would not at this day think it a great happiness to have been sold for
food at a year old, in the manner I prescribe; and thereby have avoided
such a perpetual scene of misfortunes as they have since gone through,
by the *oppression of landlords*, the impossibility of paying rent without
money or trade, the want of common sustenance, with neither house nor
clothes to cover them from the inclemencies of the weather, and the most
inevitable prospect of entailing the like, or greater miseries upon their
breed for ever.

I profess in the sincerity of my heart that I have not the least personal interest in endeavouring to promote this necessary work, having no other motive than the *public good of my country, by advancing our trade, providing for infants, relieving the poor, and giving some pleasure to the rich.* I have no children, by which I can propose to get a single penny; the youngest being nine years old, and my wife past child-bearing.

THE GRAND QUESTION DEBATED:

WHETHER HAMILTON'S BAWN* SHOULD BE TURNED INTO A BARRACK OR A MALT-HOUSE.

THE PREFACE TO THE ENGLISH EDITION

THE author of the following poem is said to be Dr. J. S. D. S. P. D. who writ it, as well as several other copies of verses of the like kind, by way of amusement, in the family of an honourable gentleman in the north of Ireland, where he spent a summer about two or three years ago.

A certain very great person, then in that kingdom, having heard much of this poem, obtained a copy from the gentleman, or, as some say, the lady in whose house it was written, from whence (I know not by what accident) several other copies were transcribed, full of errors. As I have a great respect for the supposed author, I have procured a true copy of the poem, the publication whereof can do him less injury than printing any of those incorrect ones which run about in manuscript, and would infallibly be soon in the press, if not thus prevented. Some expressions being peculiar to Ireland, I have prevailed on a gentleman of that kingdom to explain them, and I have put the several explanations in their proper places.

> Thus spoke to my lady, the knight full of care,
> 'Let me have your advice in a weighty affair.
> This Hamilton's *bawn*†, while it sticks on my hand
> I lose by the house what I get by the land;
> But how to dispose of it to the best bidder,
> For a *barrack*‡ or *malt-house*, we now must consider.
>
> 'First, let me suppose I make it a *malt-house*,
> Here I have computed the profit will fall t' us:
> There's nine hundred pounds for labour and grain,
> I increase it to twelve, so three hundred remain;   10
> A handsome addition for wine and good cheer,
> Three dishes a day, and three hogsheads a year;
> With a dozen large vessels my vault shall be stor'd;
> No little scrub joint shall come on my board;
> And you and the *Dean* no more shall combine

---

* A bawn was a place near the house, enclosed with mud or stone walls, to keep the cattle from being stolen in the night. They are now little used.

† A large old house two miles from Sir Arthur Acheson's seat.

‡ The army in Ireland, is lodged in strong buildings over the whole kingdom, called barracks.

To stint me at night to one bottle of wine;
Nor shall I, for his humour, permit you to purloin
A stone and a half of good beef from my sirloin.
　'If I make it a *barrack*, the crown is my tenant.
My dear, I have ponder'd again and again on't:　　　　　　20
In poundage and drawbacks I lose half my rent,°
And whatever they give me, I must be content,
Or join with the court in ev'ry debate;
And rather than that, I would lose my estate.'
　Thus ended the knight; thus began his *meek* wife:
'It *must*, and it *shall* be a *barrack*, my life.
I'm grown a mere mopus; no company comes
But a rabble of tenants, and rusty dull *rums*.*
With *parsons* what lady can keep herself clean?
I'm all over daub'd when I sit by the *Dean*.　　　　　　30
But if you will give us a *barrack*, my dear,
The *captain*, I'm sure, will always come here;
I then shall not value his Deanship a straw,
For the Captain, I warrant, will keep him in awe;
Or, should he pretend to be brisk and alert,
Will tell him that chaplains must not be so pert;
That men of his coat should be minding their pray'rs,
And, not among ladies to give themselves airs.'
　Thus argued my lady, but argued in vain;
The knight his opinion resolv'd to maintain.　　　　　　40
　But Hannah,† who listn'd to all that had past,
And could not endure so vulgar a taste,
As soon as her ladyship call'd to be dressed,
Cried, 'Madam, why sure my master's possessed,
Sir Arthur the maltster! how fine it will sound!
I'd rather the *bawn* were sunk under ground.
But, madam, I guess'd there would never come good
When I saw him so often with Darby and Wood.‡
And now my dream's out; for I was a-dream'd°
That I saw a huge rat,—O dear, how I scream'd!　　　　　　50
And after, methought, I lost my new shoes;
And Molly, she said I should hear some ill news.
　'Dear Madam, had you but the spirit to tease,

---

* A cant-word in Ireland for a poor country clergyman.
† My lady's waiting-woman.
‡ Two of Sir Arthur's managers.

You might have a *barrack* whenever you please:
And madam, I always believed you so stout,
That for twenty denials you would not give out.
If I had a husband like him, I *purtest*,
Till he gave me my will, I would give him no rest;
And, rather than come in the same pair of sheets
With such a cross man, I would lie in the streets.   60
But madam, I beg you, contrive and invent,
And worry him out till he gives his consent.

  'Dear madam, whene'er of a *barrack* I think,
An I were to be hang'd I can't sleep a wink:
For, if a new crotchet comes into my brain,
I can't get it out, though I'd never so fain.
I fancy already a *barrack* contrived
At Hamilton's *bawn*, and the troop is arrived;
Of this, to be sure, Sir Arthur has warning,
And waits on the Captain betimes the next morning.   70

  'Now see, when they meet, how their Honours behave:
"Noble Captain, your servant"—"Sir Arthur, your slave;
You honour me much"—"The honour is mine."—
"'Twas a sad rainy night"—"But the morning is fine."—
"Pray, how does my lady?"—"My wife's at your service."—
"I think I have seen her picture by Jervis."—°
"Good morrow, good Captain, I'll wait on you down"—
"You shan't stir a foot, you'll think me a clown."—
"For all the world, Captain, not half an inch farther,
You must be obey'd:"—"Your servant, Sir Arthur,   80
My humble respects to my lady unknown."—
"I hope you will use my house as your own."'

  'Go bring me my smock, and leave off your prate;
Thou hast certainly gotten a cup in thy pate.'°

  'Pray, madam, be quiet: what was it I said?
You had like to have put it quite out of my head.

  'Next day to be sure, the Captain will come
At the head of his troop, with trumpet and drum.
Now madam, observe how he marches in state:
The man with the kettle-drum enters the gate,   90
Dub, dub, adub, dub. The trumpeters follow,
Tantara, tantara; while all the boys halloo.
See now comes the Captain all daub'd with gold lace:
O law, the sweet gentleman! look in his face;

And see how he rides like a lord of the land,
With the fine flaming sword that he holds in his hand;
And his horse, the dear *creter*, it prances and rears,
With ribbins in knots at its tail and its ears.
At last comes the troop, by word of command
Drawn up in our court; till the Captain cries, STAND!   100
Your ladyship lifts up the sash to be seen
(For sure, I had *dizen'd* you out like a *Queen*).
The Captain, to show he is proud of the favour,
Looks up to your *window*, and cocks up his beaver.
(His beaver is cock'd: pray, madam, mark that,
For, a captain of horse never takes off his hat;
Because he has never a hand that is idle,
For the right holds his sword, and the left holds his bridle.)
Then flourishes thrice his sword in the air,
As a compliment due to a lady so fair;   110
(How I tremble to think of the blood it hath spilt!)
Then he low'rs down the point, and kisses the hilt.
Your ladyship smiles, and thus you begin:
"Pray, Captain, be pleased to 'light and walk in."
The Captain salutes you with *congé* profound,
And your ladyship curchies half way to the ground.°
"Kit, run to your master, and bid him come to us;°
I'm sure he'll be proud of the honour you do us;
And, Captain, you'll do us the favour to stay,
And take a short dinner here with us today.   120
You're heartily welcome; but as for good cheer,
You come in the very worst time of the year.
If I had expected so worthy a guest—"
"Lord, madam! your ladyship sure is in jest.
You *banter* me, madam; the kingdom must grant—"
"You officers, Captain, are so complaisant!"'—
  'Hist, hussy, I think I hear somebody coming'—
'No madam: 'tis only Sir Arthur a-humming.
  'To shorten my tale, (for I hate a long story)
The Captain at dinner appears in his glory.   130
The Dean and the Doctor* have humbled their pride,.
For the Captain's entreated to sit by your side.
And, because he's their betters, you carve for him first;
The *parsons* for envy are ready to burst.
  * Dr. Jenny, a clergyman in the neighbourhood.

The servants, amazed, are scarce ever able
To keep off their eyes as they wait at the table.
And Molly and I have thrust in our nose
To peep on the Captain, in all his fine *clo'es*.
Dear madam, be sure he's a fine-spoken man,
Do but hear on the clergymen how his tongue ran;   140
And, "madam," says he, "if such dinners you give,
You'll never want *parsons* as long as you live.
I ne'er knew a *parson* without a good nose;
But the devil's as welcome, wherever he goes.
G–d d—n me, they bid us reform and repent,
But, zounds! by their looks they never keep Lent.
Mister *Curate*, for all your grave looks, I'm afraid
You cast a sheep's eye on her ladyship's maid:°
I wish she would lend you her pretty white hand
In mending your gown, and smoothing your band":   150
(For the *Dean* was so shabby, and looked like a *ninny*,
That the Captain supposed he was *curate* to Jinny)°
"Whenever you see a cassock and gown,
A hundred to one but it covers a clown.
Observe how a *parson* comes into a room.
G–d d—n me, he hobbles as bad as my groom.
A *scholard*, when just from his college broke loose,
Can hardly tell how to cry *Bo* to a goose;°
Your *Noveds*, and *Blutracks*, and *Omurs*,* and stuff,
By G—, they don't signify this pinch of snuff.   160
To give a young gentleman right education,
The army's the only good school in the nation:
My schoolmaster call'd me a dunce and a fool,
But at cuffs I was always the cock of the school.
I never could take to my book for the blood o' me,
And the puppy confess'd he expected no good o' me.
He caught me one morning coquetting his wife, ⎫
But he maul'd me, I ne'er was so maul'd in my life: ⎬ †
So I took to the road, and, what's very odd, ⎪
The first man I robb'd was a parson, by G—. ⎭   170
Now, madam, you'll think it a strange thing to say,
But the sight of a book makes me sick to this day."

---

* Ovids, Plutarchs, Homers.
† [Lines 167–70 were added by Swift in his own copy of *Miscellanies, The Third Volume*, 1732.]

'Never since I was born did I hear so much wit,
And, madam, I laugh'd till I thought I should split.
So then you look'd scornful, and sniffed at the Dean,
As who should say, "Now, am I *skinny and lean**?
But he durst not so much as once open his lips,
And the Doctor was plaguily down in the hips."°
 Thus, merciless Hannah ran on in her talk,
Till she heard the Dean call, 'Will your ladyship walk?' 180
Her ladyship answers, 'I'm just coming down.'
Then, turning to Hannah, and forcing a frown,
Although it was plain in her heart she was glad,
Cried, 'Hussy, why sure the wench is gone mad:
How could these chimeras get into your brains?—
Come hither, and take this old gown for your pains.
But the Dean, if this secret should come to his ears,
Will never have done with his gibes and his jeers.
For your life, not a word of the matter, I charge ye:
Give me but a *barrack*, a fig for the *clergy*.' 190

---

* Nicknames for my lady.

Swift to Lord Carteret

[*April*, 1730.]

My Lord,

I told your Excellency that you were to run on my errands. My Lord Burlington hath a very fine monument of his ancestor, the Earl of Cork,° in my Cathedral, which your Excellency hath seen. I and the Chapter have written to him in a body to have it repaired, and I in person have desired he would do it. And I desired likewise, that he would settle a parcel of land, worth five pounds a year, (not an annuity) to keep it always in repair. He said he would do anything to oblige me, but was afraid that, in future times, the five pounds a year would be misapplied, and secured by the Dean and Chapter to their own use. I answered that a Dean and twenty-four members of so great a Chapter, who, in livings, estates, &c. had about four thousand pounds a year amongst them, would hardly divide four shillings among them to cheat his posterity; and that we could have no view but to consult the honour of his family. I therefore command your Excellency to lay this before him, and the affront he hath put upon us, in not answering a letter written to him by the Dean and Chapter in a body.

The great Duke of Schomberg° is buried under the altar in my Cathedral. My Lady Holderness is my old acquaintance, and I writ to her about a small sum to make a monument for her grandfather. I writ to her myself; and also, there was a letter from the Dean and Chapter to desire she would order a monument to be raised for him in my Cathedral. It seems Mildmay, now Lord Fitzwalter, her husband, is a covetous fellow; or whatever is the matter, we have had no answer. I desire you will tell Lord Fitzwalter that if he will not send fifty pounds to make a monument for the old Duke, I and the Chapter will erect a small one of ourselves for ten pounds, wherein it shall be expressed, That the posterity of the Duke, naming particularly Lady Holderness and Mr. Mildmay, not having the generosity to erect a monument, we have done it of ourselves. And if, for an excuse, they pretend they will send for his body, let them know it is mine; and rather than send it, I will take up the bones, and make of it a skeleton, and put it in my registry-office, to be a memorial of their baseness to all posterity. This I expect your Excellency will tell Mr. Mildmay, or, as you now call him, Lord Fitzwalter; and I expect likewise, that he will let Sir Conyers Darcy know how ill I take his neglect in this matter; although, to do him justice, he averred that Mildmay was so avaricious a wretch, that he would let his own father be buried without a coffin, to save charges.

I expect likewise, that if you are acquainted with your successor,° you will let him know how impartial I was in giving you characters of clergymen, without regard to party, and what weight you laid on them. And that having but one clergyman who had any relation to me, I let him pass unpreferred.° And lastly, that you will let your said successor know, that you lament the having done nothing for Mr. Robert Grattan, and give him such a recommendation, that he may have something to mend his fortune.

These are the matters I leave in charge to your Excellency. And I desire that I, who have done with Courts, may not be used like a courtier. For, as I was a courtier when you were a schoolboy, I know all your arts. And so God bless you, and all your family, my old friends. And remember, I expect you shall not dare to be a courtier to me. I am, &c.

Death and Daphne

TO AN AGREEABLE YOUNG LADY, BUT
EXTREMELY LEAN.

Death went, upon a solemn day,
At Pluto's hall his court to pay;°
The phantom, having humbly kiss'd
His grisly monarch's sooty fist,
Presented him the weekly bills°
Of doctors, fevers, plagues, and pills.
Pluto, observing since the Peace°
The burial article decrease,
And, vex'd to see affairs miscarry,
Declared in council *Death* must marry;   10
Vow'd, he no longer could support
Old bachelors about his court;
The interest of his realm had need
That *Death* should get a num'rous breed;
Young *deathlings*, who, by practice made
Proficients in their father's trade,
With colonies might stock around
His large dominions under ground.
    A consult of coquettes below
Was call'd, to rig him out a beau;   20
From her own head, Megaera takes°
A periwig of twisted snakes:
Which in the nicest fashion curl'd,
(Like *toupees* of this upper world)°
With flower of sulphur powder'd well,
That graceful on his shoulders fell;
An adder of the sable kind,
In line direct, hung down behind:
The owl, the raven, and the bat,
Clubb'd for a feather to his hat: 30
His coat, an usurer's velvet pall,
Bequeath'd to Pluto, corpse and all.
But, loath his person to expose
Bare, like a carcass pick'd by crows,
A lawyer, o'er his hands and face,

Stuck artfully a parchment case.
No new-flux'd rake show'd fairer skin;°
Nor Phyllis after lying-in.
With snuff was fill'd his ebon box,
Of shin-bones rotted by the pox. 40
Nine spirits of blaspheming fops,
With aconite anoint his chops,°
And give him words of dreadful sounds,
G–d d—n his blood! and Bloods and Wounds!
    Thus furnish'd out, he sent his train
To take a house in Warwick Lane:
The *faculty*, his humble friends,°
A complimental message sends:
Their president in scarlet gown
Harangued, and welcom'd him to town. 50
    But, *Death* had business to dispatch;
His mind was running on his match.
And hearing much of Daphne's fame,
His Majesty of Terrors came,
Fine as a col'nel of the Guards,
To visit where she sat at cards;
She, as he came into the room,
Thought him Adonis in his bloom.°
And now her heart with pleasure jumps,
She scarce remembers what is trumps; 60
For, such a shape of skin and bone
Was never seen, except her own.
Charm'd with his eyes, and chin, and snout,
Her pocket-glass drew slily out;
And grew enamour'd with her phiz,
As just the counterpart of his.
She darted many a private glance,
And freely made the first advance;
Was of her beauty grown so vain,
She doubted not to win the *swain*. 70
Nothing, she thought, could sooner gain him,
Than with her wit to entertain him.
She ask'd about her friends below,
This meagre fop, that batter'd beau;
Whether some late departed toasts
Had got gallants among the ghosts?

If Chloe were a sharper still,
As great as ever, at quadrille?
(The ladies there must needs be rooks,°
For cards, we know, are Pluto's books.)°   80
If Florimel had found her love,
For whom she hang'd herself above?
How oft a-week was kept a ball
By Proserpine at Pluto's hall?°
She fancied those Elysian shades°
The sweetest place for masquerades;
How pleasant on the banks of Styx,°
To troll it in a coach and six!
   What pride a female heart inflames!
How endless are ambition's aims!   90
Cease, haughty nymph; the Fates decree
Death must not be a spouse for thee;
For, when by chance the meagre shade
Upon thy hand his finger laid,
Thy hand as dry and cold as lead,
His matrimonial spirit fled;
He felt about his heart a damp
That quite extinguish'd Cupid's lamp.
Away the frighted spectre scuds,
And leaves my lady in the suds.°   100

An Excellent New Ballad

OR, THE TRUE ENGLISH DEAN TO BE HANGED FOR A RAPE.

Our brethren of England who love us so dear,
  And in all they do for us, so kindly do mean,
(A blessing upon them) have sent us this year,
  For the good of our church, a true English dean.
A holier priest ne'er was wrapt up in crape,
The worst you can say, he committed a rape.

In his journey to Dublin, he lighted at Chester,
  And there he grew fond of another man's wife;
Burst into her chamber, and would have caress'd her;
  But she valued her honour much more than her life. 10
She bustled and struggled, and made her escape
To a room full of guests, for fear of a rape.

The dean he pursued, to recover his game;
  And now to attack her again he prepares:
But the company stood in defence of the dame,
  They cudgell'd and cuff'd him, and kick'd him
    downstairs.
His deanship was now in a damnable scrape,
And this was no time for committing a rape.

To Dublin he comes, to the *bagnio* he goes,
  And orders the landlord to bring him a whore; 20
No scruple came on him his gown to expose,
  'Twas what all his life he had practis'd before.
He made himself drunk with the juice of the grape,
And got a good *clap*, but commited no rape.

The dean, and his landlord, a jolly comrade,
  Resolved for a fortnight to swim in delight;
For why, they had both been brought up to the trade
  Of drinking all day, and of whoring all night.
His landlord was ready his deanship to ape
In ev'ry debauch, but committing a rape. 30

This *Protestant* zealot, this *English* divine,
   In church and in state was of principles sound;
Was truer than Steele to the Hanover line,
   And griev'd that a *Tory* should live above ground.
Shall a subject so loyal be hang'd by the nape,
For no other crime but committing a rape?

By old Popish canons, as wise men have penn'd 'em,
   Each priest had a concubine, *jure ecclesiae*;
Who'd be Dean of Ferns without a *commendam*?°
   And precedents we can produce, if it please ye: 40
Then, why should the dean, when whores are so cheap,
Be put to the peril and toil of a rape?

If fortune should please but to take such a crotchet,
   (To thee I apply, great Smedley's successor)°
To give thee *lawn sleeves*, a *mitre* and *rochet*,
   Whom wouldst thou resemble? I leave thee a guesser;
But I only behold thee in Atherton's shape,°
For *sodomy* hang'd; as thou for a rape.

Ah! dost thou not envy the brave Colonel Chartres,°
   Condemn'd for thy crime, at threescore and ten?   50
To hang him, all England would lend him their garters,
   Yet he lives, and is ready to ravish again.
Then throttle thyself with an ell of strong tape,
For thou has not a groat to atone for a rape.

The dean he was vex'd that his whores were so willing,
   He long'd for a girl that would struggle and squall;
He ravish'd her fairly, and saved a good shilling;
   But here was to pay the devil and all.°
His troubles and sorrows now come in a heap,
And hang'd he must be, for committing a rape.   60

If maidens are ravish'd, it is their own choice:
   Why are they so wilful to struggle with men?
If they would but lie quiet, and stifle their voice,
   No devil, nor dean could ravish 'em then.
Nor would there be need of a strong hempen cape,
Tied round the dean's neck, for committing a rape.

Our church and our state dear England maintains,
    For which all true Protestant hearts should be glad:
She sends us our bishops and judges and deans,
    And better would give us, if better she had.   70
But, lord! how the rabble will stare and will gape,
When the good English dean is hang'd up for a rape!

VERSES ON THE DEATH OF DR. *SWIFT*, D.S.P.D.

Occasioned by reading a Maxim in *Rochefoucault*°

Dans l'adversité de nos meilleurs amis, nous trouvons quelque chose, qui ne nous deplaist pas.

In the adversity of our best friends, we find something that doth not displease us.

Written by Himself, November 1731

As Rochefoucault his maxims drew
From nature, I believe 'em true:
They argue no corrupted mind
In him; the fault is in mankind.

This maxim more than all the rest
Is thought too base for human breast:
'In all distresses of our friends
We first consult our private ends,
While nature, kindly bent to ease us,
Points out some circumstance to please us.'   10

If this perhaps your patience move,°
Let reason and experience prove.

We all behold with envious eyes
Our *equal* rais'd above our *size*;
Who would not at a crowded show
Stand high himself, keep others low?
I love my friend as well as you,
But why should he obstruct my view?
Then let me have the higher post;
Suppose it but an inch at most.   20

If, in a battle you should find
One, whom you love of all mankind,
Had some heroic action done,
A champion kill'd, or trophy won;
Rather than thus be over-topped,
Would you not wish his laurels cropped?

Dear honest Ned is in the gout,
Lies racked with pain, and you without:
How patiently you hear him groan!
How glad the case is not your own!   30

What poet would not grieve to see
His brother write as well as he?
But rather than they should excel,
He'd wish his rivals all in Hell.

Her end when emulation misses,
She turns to envy, stings and hisses:
The strongest friendship yields to pride,
Unless the odds be on our side.

Vain human kind! fantastic race!
Thy various follies, who can trace?   40
Self-love, ambition, envy, pride,
Their empire in our hearts divide:
Give others riches, pow'r, and station,
'Tis all on me an usurpation.
I have no title to aspire;
Yet when you sink, I seem the higher.
In Pope, I cannot read a line
But with a sigh, I wish it mine:
When he can in one couplet fix
More sense, than I can do in six,   50
It gives me such a jealous fit,
I cry, 'pox take him and his wit.'

I grieve to be outdone by Gay
In my own hum'rous, biting way.

Arbuthnot is no more my friend,
Who dares to irony pretend;
Which I was born to introduce,
Refined it first, and show'd its use.

St. John, as well as Pultney, knows
That I had some repute for prose;   60

And, till they drove me out of date,°
Could maul a minister of state.
If they have mortified my pride
And made me throw my pen aside,
If with such talents Heav'n hath blest 'em,
Have I not reason to detest 'em?

To all my foes, dear Fortune, send
Thy gifts, but never to my friend:
I tamely can endure the first,
But, this with envy makes me burst.   70

Thus much may serve by way of proem;
Proceed we therefore to our poem.

The time is not remote, when I
Must by the course of nature die:
When I foresee, my special friends
Will try to find their private ends.
And tho' 'tis hardly understood
Which way my death can do them good,
Yet thus, methinks, I hear 'em speak:
'See, how the Dean begins to break!   80
Poor gentleman, he droops apace,
You plainly find it in his face:
That old vertigo in his head
Will never leave him, till he's dead:
Besides, his memory decays,
He recollects not what he says;
He cannot call his friends to mind;
Forgets the place where last he din'd:
Plies you with stories o'er and o'er,
He told them fifty times before.   90
How does he fancy, we can sit
To hear his out-of-fashion'd wit?
But he takes up with younger folks,
Who, for his wine, will bear his jokes.
Faith, he must make his stories shorter,
Or change his comrades once a quarter.
In half the time, he talks them round;
There must another set be found.

'For poetry, he's past his prime,
He takes an hour to find a rhyme: 100
His fire is out, his wit decay'd,
His fancy sunk, his muse a jade.
I'd have him throw away his pen;
But there's no talking to some men.'

And then, their tenderness appears
By adding largely to my years:
'He's older than he would be reckon'd,
And well remembers Charles the Second.

'He hardly drinks a pint of wine;
And that, I doubt, is no good sign.   110
His stomach too begins to fail:
Last year we thought him strong and hale,
But now, he's quite another thing;
I wish he may hold out till spring.'

Then hug themselves, and reason thus:
'It is not yet so bad with us.'

In such a case they talk in tropes,°
And, by their fears express their hopes:
Some great misfortune to portend,
No enemy can match a friend.   120
With all the kindness they profess,
The merit of a lucky guess
(When daily Howd'y's come of course,°
And servants answer, *worse and worse*)
Would please 'em better, than to tell
That, God be prais'd, the Dean is well.
Then he, who prophesied the best,
Approves his judgement to the rest:
'You know, I always feared the worst,
And often told you so at first'.   130
He'd rather choose that I should die,
Than his prediction prove a lie.
Not one foretells I shall recover;
But all agree to give me over.

Yet should some neighbour feel a pain,
Just in the parts where I complain;
How many a message would he send!
What hearty prayers that I should mend!
Enquire what regimen I kept;
What gave me ease, and how I slept?   140
And more lament when I was dead,
Than all the sniv'llers round my bed.

My good companions, never fear;
For though you may mistake a year,
Though your prognostics run too fast,
They must be verified at last.

Behold the fatal day arrive!
'How is the Dean?'—'He's just alive.'
Now the departing pray'r is read.
He hardly breathes. The Dean is dead.   150
Before the passing-bell begun,
The news thro' half the town has run.
'O, may we all for death prepare!
What has he left? And who's his heir?
I know no more than what the news is,
'Tis all bequeath'd to public uses.
To public uses! There's a whim!
What had the public done for him?
Mere envy, avarice, and pride!
He gave it all,—but first he died.   160
And had the Dean, in all the nation,
No worthy friend, no poor relation?
So ready to do strangers good,
Forgetting his own flesh and blood?'

Now Grub-street wits are all employed,
With elegies, the town is cloyed:
Some paragraph in ev'ry paper
To *curse* the Dean, or *bless* the Drapier.*

* The author imagines that the scribblers of the prevailing party, which he always
opposed, will libel him after his death; but that others will remember him with
gratitude, who consider the service he had done to Ireland, under the name of M. B.
Drapier, by utterly defeating the destructive project of Wood's half-pence, in five
Letters to the People of Ireland, at that time read universally and convincing every
reader.

The doctors, tender of their fame,
Wisely on me lay all the blame: 170
'We must confess his case was nice:
But he would never take advice.
Had he been rul'd, for aught appears,
He might have lived these twenty years:
For when we open'd him, we found
That all his vital parts were sound.'

From Dublin soon to London spread,
'Tis told at Court, the Dean is dead.*
And Lady Suffolk† in the spleen
Runs laughing up to tell the Queen.   180
The Queen so gracious, mild, and good,
Cries, 'Is he gone? 'Tis time he should.
He's dead you say? Why, let him rot;
I'm glad the medals were forgot.‡
I promis'd him, I own, but when?
I only was the Princess then;°
But now as consort of a king,
You know 'tis quite a diff'rent thing.'

Now Chartres§ at Sir Robert's levee,
Tells with a sneer the tidings heavy: 190

* The Dean supposeth himself to die in Ireland.
† Mrs. Howard, afterwards Countess of Suffolk, then of the Bedchamber to the Queen, professed much friendship for the Dean. The Queen then Princess, sent a dozen times to the Dean (then in London) with her command to attend her; which at last he did, by advice of all his friends. She often sent for him afterwards, and always treated him very graciously. He taxed her with a present worth ten pounds, which she promised before he should return to Ireland, but on his taking leave, the medals were not ready.
‡ The medals were to be sent to the Dean in four months, but she forgot, or thought them too dear. The Dean being in Ireland sent Mrs. Howard a piece of plaid made in that kingdom, which the Queen seeing took from her and wore it herself, and sent to the Dean for as much as would clothe herself and children, desiring he would send the charge of it. He did the former; it cost 35l. but he said he would have nothing except the medals. He was the summer following in England, was treated as usual, and she being then Queen, the Dean was promised a settlement in England but returned as he went, and, instead of favour or medals, hath been ever since under her Majesty's displeasure.
§ Chartres is a most infamous, vile scoundrel, grown from a foot-boy, or worse, to a prodigious fortune both in England and Scotland: he had a way of insinuating himself into all Ministers under every change, either as pimp, flatterer, or informer. He was

'Why, if he died without his shoes'°
(Cries Bob*) 'I'm sorry for the news;
Oh, were the wretch but living still,
And in his place my good friend Will;†
Or, had a mitre on his head
Provided Bolingbroke‡ were dead!'

Now, Curl§ his shop from rubbish drains
Three genuine tomes of *Swift's Remains*!
And then, to make them pass the glibber,
Revised by Tibbalds, Moore, and Cibber.¶   200
He'll treat me as he does my betters,
Publish my *Will*, my *Life*, my *Letters*;‖
Revive the libels born to die,
Which Pope must bear, as well as I.

tried at seventy for a rape, and came off by sacrificing a great part of his fortune (he is
since dead, but this poem still preserves the scene and time it was writ in).

   * Sir Robert Walpole, Chief Minister of State, treated the Dean in 1726, with great
distinction, invited him to dinner at Chelsea, with the Dean's friends chosen on
purpose; appointed an hour to talk with him of Ireland, to which kingdom and people
the Dean found him no great friend; for he defended Wood's project of half-pence,
&c. The Dean would see him no more; and upon his next year's return to England, Sir
Robert on an accidental meeting, only made a civil compliment, and never invited him
again.

   † Mr. William Pultney, from being Mr. Walpole's intimate friend, detesting his
administration, became his mortal enemy, and joyned with my Lord Bolingbroke, to
expose him in an excellent paper, called the *Craftsman*, which is still continued.

   ‡ Henry St. John, Lord Viscount Bolingbroke, Secretary of State to Queen Anne of
blessed memory. He is reckoned the most universal genius in Europe; Walpole
dreading his abilities, treated him most injuriously, working with King George who
forgot his promise of restoring the said lord, upon the restless importunity of Sir
Robert Walpole.

   § Curl hath been the most infamous bookseller of any age or country; his character
in part may be found in Mr. Pope's *Dunciad*. He published three volumes all charged
on the Dean, who never writ three pages of them; he hath used many of the Dean's
friends in almost as vile a manner.

   ¶ Three stupid verse writers in London, the last to the shame of the Court, and the
highest disgrace to wit and learning, was made Laureate. Moore, commonly called
Jemmy Moore, son of Arthur Moore, whose father was jaylor of Monaghan in Ireland.
See the character of Jemmy Moore, and Tibbalds (Theobald), in the *Dunciad*.

   ‖ Curl is notoriously infamous for publishing the Lives, Letters, and last Wills and
Testaments of the nobility and Ministers of State, as well as of all the rogues, who are
hanged at Tyburn. He hath been in custody of the House of Lords for publishing or
forging the letters of many peers; which made the Lords enter a resolution in their
Journal Book, that no life or writings of any lord should be published without the
consent of the next heir at law, or licence from their House.

Here shift the scene, to represent
How those I love, my death lament.
Poor Pope will grieve a month; and Gay
A week, and Arbuthnot a day.

St. John himself will scarce forbear
To bite his pen, and drop a tear.   210
The rest will give a shrug, and cry
'I'm sorry; but we all must die!'

Indiff'rence, clad in wisdom's guise,
All fortitude of mind supplies:
For how can stony bowels melt
In those who never pity felt?
When *We* are lash'd, *They* kiss the rod,
Resigning to the will of God.

The fools, my juniors by a year,
Are tortured with suspence and fear;   220
Who wisely thought my age a screen,
When death approach'd, to stand between:
The screen remov'd, their hearts are trembling;
They mourn for me without dissembling.

My female friends, whose tender hearts
Have better learned to act their parts,
Receive the news in *doleful dumps,*°
'The Dean is dead, (*pray what is trumps?*)
Then Lord have mercy on his soul.
(Ladies, I'll venture for the *vole.*)°   230
Six deans, they say, must bear the pall.
(I wish I knew what *king* to call.)'
'Madam, your husband will attend
The fun'ral of so good a friend?'
'No, madam, 'tis a shocking sight,
And he's engag'd tomorrow night!
My Lady *Club* wou'd take it ill,
If he should fail her at *quadrille.*
He loved the Dean—(*I lead a heart*)
But dearest friends, they say, must part.°   240
His time was come, he ran his race;°
We hope he's in a better place.'

Why do we grieve that friends should die?
No loss more easy to supply.
One year is past; a different scene;
No further mention of the Dean;
Who now, alas, no more is missed
Than if he never did exist.
Where's now the fav'rite of Apollo?
Departed; *and his works must follow*:   250
Must undergo the common fate.
His kind of wit is out of date.

Some country squire to Lintot* goes,
Enquires for SWIFT in Verse and Prose:
Says Lintot, 'I have heard the name:
He died a year ago.' 'The same.'
He searches all his shop in vain;
'Sir, you may find them in Duck-lane:†°
I sent them with a load of books,
Last Monday, to the pastry-cook's.°   260
To fancy they could live a year!
I find you're but a stranger here.
The Dean was famous in his time,
And had a kind of knack at rhyme:
His way of writing now is past;
The town has got a better taste.
I keep no antiquated stuff,
But, spick and span I have enough.
Pray, do but give me leave to show 'em:
Here's Colley Cibber's Birthday poem.   270
This ode you never yet have seen,
By Stephen Duck, upon the Queen.
Then, here's a Letter finely penn'd
Against the *Craftsman* and his friend;°
It clearly shows that all reflection
On ministers, is disaffection.
Next, here's Sir Robert's *Vindication*,‡

---

* Bernard Lintot, a bookseller in London. *Vide* Mr. Pope's *Dunciad*.

† A place in London where old books are sold.

‡ Walpole hires a set of party scribblers, who do nothing else but write in his defence.

And Mr. Henly's last Oration:*°
The hawkers have not got 'em yet,
Your Honour please to buy a set?   280
Here's Woolston's† tracts, the twelfth edition;
'Tis read by ev'ry politician:
The country members, when in town,
To all their boroughs send them down:
You never met a thing so smart;
The courtiers have them all by heart:
Those Maids of Honour (who can read)
Are taught to use them for their creed.
The rev'rend author's good intention
Hath been rewarded with a pension: 290
He doth an honour to his gown,
By bravely running *priest-craft* down:
He shows, as sure as God's in Glo'ster,°
That [Jesus] was a grand impostor,
That all his miracles were cheats,
Performed as jugglers do their feats.
The Church had never such a writer:
A shame, he hath not got a mitre!'

    Suppose me dead; and then suppose
A club assembled at the Rose;°   300
Where, from discourse of this and that,
I grow the subject of their chat:
And while they toss my name about,
With favour some, and some without—
One quite indiff'rent in the cause,
My character impartial draws:

    'The Dean, if we believe report,
Was never ill receiv'd at Court.

---

    * Henly is a clergyman who, wanting both merit and luck to get preferment, or even
to keep his curacy in the Established Church, formed a new conventicle, which he calls
an Oratory. There, at set times, he delivereth strange speeches compiled by himself
and his associates, who share the profit with him: every hearer pays a shilling each day
for admittance. He is an absolute dunce, but generally reputed crazy.

    † Woolston was a clergyman, but for want of bread, hath in several treatises, in the
most blasphemous manner, attempted to turn Our Saviour and his miracles into
ridicule. He is much caressed by many great courtiers, and by all the infidels, and his
books read generally by the Court Ladies.

As for his Works in Verse or Prose,
I own myself no judge of those: 310
Nor can I tell what critics thought 'em;
But this I know, all people bought 'em,
As with a moral view design'd
To cure the vices of mankind.
Although ironically grave,
He shamed the fool, and lashed the knave.
To steal a hint was never known,
But what he writ, was all his own.°

 'He never thought an honour done him
Because a peer was proud to own him: 320
Would rather slip aside, and choose
To talk with wits in dirty shoes:
And scorn the tools with Stars and Garters,°
So often seen caressing Chartres.*
He never courted men in station,
Nor persons had in admiration;°
Of no man's greatness was afraid,
Because he sought for no man's aid.
Though trusted long in great affairs,
He gave himself no haughty airs: 330
Without regarding private ends,
Spent all his credit for his friends:
And only chose the wise and good,
No flatt'rers, no allies in blood;
But succoured virtue in distress,
And seldom failed of good success;
As numbers in their hearts must own,
Who, but for him, had been unknown.

 'He kept with princes due decorum,
Yet never stood in awe before 'em: 340
He follow'd David's lesson just,
In princes never put his trust.°
And, would you make him truly sour,
Provoke him with *a slave in power*:

---

 * See the notes before on Chartres.

The Irish Senate* if you nam'd,
With what impatience he declaim'd!
Fair LIBERTY was all his cry;
For her he stood prepared to die;
For her he boldly stood alone;
For her he oft exposed his own.   350
Two kingdoms, just as faction led,
Had set a price upon his head;†°
But not a traitor could be found,
To sell him for six hundred pound.

'Had he but spared his tongue and pen,
He might have rose like other men:
But, power was never in his thought,
And wealth he valu'd not a groat.
Ingratitude he often found,
And pitied those who meant the wound: 360
But kept the tenor of his mind,
To merit well of human kind;
Nor made a sacrifice of those
Who still were true, to please his foes.
He laboured many a fruitless hour
To reconcile his friends in pow'r;‡

* [The Irish parliament are reduced to the utmost degree of slavery, flattery, corruption, and meanness of spirit, and the worse they are treated, the more fawning and servile they grow; under the greatest and most contemptuous grievances they dare not complain; by which baseness and tameness, unworthy human creatures, the kingdom is irrecoverably ruined.]

† In the Year 1713, the late Queen was prevailed with by an Address of the House of Lords in England, to publish a Proclamation, promising three hundred pounds to whatever person would discover the author of a pamphlet called *The Publick Spirit of the Whigs*; and in Ireland, in the year 1724, my Lord Carteret at his first coming into the Government, was prevailed on to issue a Proclamation for promising the like reward of three hundred pounds, to any person who could discover the author of a pamphlet called, *The Drapier's Fourth Letter*, &c. writ against that destructive project of coining half-pence for Ireland; but in neither kingdom was the Dean discovered.

‡ Queen Anne's Ministry fell to variance from the first year after their Ministry began: Harcourt the Chancellor, and Lord Bolingbroke the Secretary, were discontented with the Treasurer Oxford, for his too much mildness to the Whig Party; this quarrel grew higher every day till the Queen's death. The Dean, who was the only person that endeavoured to reconcile them, found it impossible; and thereupon retired to the country about ten weeks before that fatal event: upon which he returned to his Deanery in Dublin, where for many years he was worried by the new people in power, and had hundreds of libels writ against him in England.

Saw mischief by a faction brewing,
While they pursued each other's ruin.
But, finding vain was all his care,
He left the court in mere despair.°   370

'And, O! how short are human schemes!
Here ended all our golden dreams.
What St. John's skill in state affairs,
What Ormond's *valour*, Oxford's cares,
To save their sinking country lent,
Was all destroyed by one event.
Too soon that precious life was ended,*
On which alone, our weal depended.
When up a dangerous faction starts,†
With wrath and vengeance in their hearts;   380
By solemn League and Cov'nant bound,°
To ruin, slaughter, and confound;
To turn religion to a fable,
And make the Government a *Babel*:
Pervert the law, disgrace the gown,
Corrupt the senate, rob the crown;
To sacrifice old England's glory,
And make her infamous in story.°
When such a tempest shook the land,
How could unguarded virtue stand?   390

'With horror, grief, despair, the Dean
Beheld the dire destructive scene:
His friends in exile, or the Tower,
Himself within the frown of power;‡

* In the height of the quarrel between the Minister, the Queen died.

† Upon Queen Anne's death the Whig faction was restored to power, which they exercised with the utmost rage and revenge; impeached and banished the chief leaders of the Church party, and stripped all their adherents of what employments they had, after which England was never known to make so mean a figure in Europe. The greatest preferments in the Church in both kingdoms were given to the most ignorant men. Fanatics were publicly caressed; Ireland utterly ruined and enslaved; only great Ministers heaping up millions; and so affairs continue until this present 3rd. day of May 1732, and are likely to go on in the same manner.

‡ Upon the Queen's death, the Dean returned to live in Dublin, at his Deanery-house. Numberless libels were writ against him in England, as a Jacobite; he was insulted in the street, and at nights he was forced to be attended by his servants armed.

Pursued by base envenom'd pens,
Far to the land of slaves and fens;*
A servile race in folly nurs'd,
Who truckle most, when treated worst.

'By innocence and resolution,
He bore continual persecution;   400
While numbers to preferment rose
Whose merits were, to be his foes;
When, *ev'n his own familiar friends*°
Intent upon their private ends,
Like renegadoes now he feels,
Against him lifting up their heels.

'The Dean did by his pen defeat
An infamous destructive cheat;†
Taught fools their int'rest how to know;
And gave them arms to ward the blow.   410
Envy hath owned it was his doing,
To save that helpless land from ruin;
While they who at the steerage stood
And reaped the profit, sought his blood.

'To save them from their evil fate,
In him was held a crime of state.
A wicked monster on the bench,‡
Whose fury blood could never quench;
As vile and profligate a villain,
As modern Scroggs, or old Tressilian;§°   420

* The Land of slaves and fens, is Ireland.

† One Wood, a hardware-man from England, had a patent for coining copper
half-pence in Ireland, to the sum of 108,000l. which in the consequence, must leave
that kingdom without gold or silver. (See *Drapier's Letters*.)

‡ One Whitshed was then Chief Justice. He had some years before prosecuted a
printer for a pamphlet writ by the Dean, to persuade the people of Ireland to wear their
own manufactures. Whitshed sent the jury down eleven times, and kept them nine
hours, until they were forced to bring in a special verdict. He sat as judge afterwards on
the trial of the printer of the *Drapier's Fourth Letter*; but the jury, against all he could say
or swear, threw out the bill. All the kingdom took the Drapier's part, except the
courtiers, or those who expected places. The Drapier was celebrated in many poems
and pamphlets: his sign was set up in most streets of Dublin (where many of them still
continue) and in several country towns.

§ Scroggs was Chief Justice under King Charles the Second. His judgment always

Who long all justice had discarded,
Nor fear'd he GOD, *nor man regarded*;°
Vow'd on the Dean his rage to vent,
And make him of his zeal repent.
But Heav'n his innocence defends,
The grateful people stand his friends:
Not strains of law, nor judge's frown,
Nor topics brought to please the crown,°
Nor witness hir'd, nor jury pick'd,
Prevail to bring him in convict.   430

   'In exile* with a steady heart,
He spent his life's declining part;
Where folly, pride, and faction sway,
Remote from St. John,† Pope, and Gay.

   'His friendship still to few confin'd,‡
Were always of the middling kind:
No fools of rank or mongrel breed
Who fain would pass for Lords indeed.
Where titles give no right or power
And peerage is a wither'd flower,§   440
He would have deem'd it a disgrace
If such a wretch had known his face.
On rural squires, that kingdom's bane,
He vented oft his wrath in vain:
Biennial squires, to market brought,¶
Who sell their souls and votes for naught;

varied in state trials, according to directions from Court. Tressilian was a wicked judge, hanged above three hundred years ago.

  * In Ireland, which he had reason to call a place of exile; to which country nothing could have driven him, but the Queen's death, who had determined to fix him in England, in spite of the Duchess of Somerset, &c.

  † Henry St. John, Lord Viscount Bolingbroke, mentioned before.

  ‡ In Ireland the Dean was not acquainted with one single Lord Spiritual or Temporal. He only conversed with private gentlemen of the clergy or laity, and but a small number of either.

  § The peers of Ireland lost a great part of their jurisdiction by one single Act,° and tamely submitted to this infamous mark of slavery without the least resentment, or remonstrance.

  ¶ The Parliament (as they call it) in Ireland meet but once in two years, and after giving five times more than they can afford, return home to reimburse themselves by all country jobs and oppressions, of which some few only are here mentioned.

The nation stripp'd, go joyful back
To rob the Church, their tenants rack,
Go snacks with thieves and rapparees*°
And keep the peace, to pick up fees: 450
In every job to have a share,
A jail or barrack to repair;†
And turn the ways for public roads
Commodious to their own abodes.

'Perhaps I may allow, the Dean
Had too much satire in his vein,
And seemed determin'd not to starve it,
Because no age could more deserve it.
Yet, malice never was his aim;
He lash'd the vice, but spared the name.   460
No individual could resent
Where thousands equally were meant.
His satire points at no defect,
But what all mortals may correct;
For he abhorr'd that senseless tribe
Who call it humour when they jibe:
He spar'd a hump, or crooked nose,
Whose owners set not up for beaux,
True genuine dullness moved his pity,
Unless it offered to be witty.   470
Those who their ignorance confess'd
He ne'er offended with a jest;
But laughed to hear an idiot quote
A verse from Horace, learned by rote.

'He knew an hundred pleasant stories,
With all the turns of *Whigs* and *Tories*:
Was cheerful to his dying day,
And friends would let him have his way.

* The highwaymen in Ireland, are, since the late wars there, usually called Rapparees, which was a name given to those Irish soldiers who in small parties used, at that time, to plunder the Protestants.

† The army in Ireland is lodged in barracks, the building and repairing whereof, and other charges, have cost a prodigious sum to that unhappy kingdom.

'He gave the little wealth he had,
To build a house for fools and mad:°   480
To show, by one satiric touch,
No nation wanted it so much:
That kingdom* he hath left his debtor,
I wish it soon may have a better.'

* Meaning Ireland, where he now lives, and probably may die.

The Place of the Damned

All folks who pretend to *Religion* and *Grace*,
Allow there's a HELL, but dispute of the place:
But, if HELL may by logical rules be defined
The place of the *damn'd*,—I'll tell you my mind.
   Wherever the damn'd do chiefly abound,
Most certainly there is HELL to be found:
Damn'd *poets*, damn'd *critics*, damn'd *blockheads*, damn'd *knaves*,
Damn'd *senators* bribed, damn'd prostitute *slaves*;
Damn'd *lawyers* and *judges*, damn'd *lords* and damn'd *squires*,
Damn'd *spies* and *informers*, damn'd *friends* and damn'd *liars*;   10
Damn'd *villains*, corrupted in every *station*;
Damn'd *time-serving priests* all over the *nation*.
And into the bargain, I'll readily give ye
Damn'd ignorant *prelates*, and *Counsellors Privy*.
Then let us no longer by *parsons* be flamm'd,
For we know by these *marks*, the place of the damn'd:
And HELL to be sure is at Paris or Rome—
How happy for *us* that it is not at *home*!

[THE
DAY OF JUDGEMENT.]

Dooms-day

Once, with a whirl of Thought opprest,
I sunk from Reverie, to rest—
An horrid vision seizd my Head:
I saw the Graves give up their dead;
Jove arm'd with terror burst the skies;
The thunder roars, the Lightning flies!
Confused, Amazed, its Fate unknown
The world stands trembling at his throne.
While each pale sinner hangs his head,
Jove nodding shook the Heav'ns & said   10
'Offending race of human kind,
By nature, custom, learning blind;
You who, thro *Frailty* slip'd aside
And you who never fell, thro *Pride*;
And you, by differing churches shamm'd
Who come to see each other damn'd!
(—So some Folks told you—but they knew
No more of Joves designs than you)—
The worlds mad business now is o'er
And I resent those Pranks no more.   20
I to such Blockheads set my Wit!
I damn such Fools!—Go, go, you're bit.'

A BEAUTIFUL YOUNG NYMPH
GOING TO BED.

WRITTEN FOR THE HONOUR OF THE *FAIR SEX*.

Pars minima est ipsa Puella sui.° Ovid Remed. Amoris.

Corinna, pride of Drury Lane,°
For whom no shepherd sighs in vain;
Never did Covent Garden boast
So bright a batter'd, strolling toast!
No drunken rake to pick her up,
No cellar where on tick to sup;
Returning at the midnight hour,
Four stories climbing to her bow'r;
Then, seated on a three-legg'd chair,
Takes off her artificial hair;   10
Now picking out a crystal eye,
She wipes it clean, and lays it by.
Her eyebrows from a mouse's hide,
Stuck on with art on either side,
Pulls off with care, and first displays 'em,
Then in a play-book smoothly lays 'em.
Now dext'rously her plumpers draws,
That serve to fill her hollow jaws,
Untwists a wire, and from her gums
A set of teeth completely comes;   20
Pulls out the rags contrived to prop
Her flabby dugs, and down they drop.
Proceeding on, the lovely goddess
Unlaces next her steel-ribb'd bodice,
Which, by the operator's skill,
Press down the lumps, the hollows fill.
Up goes her hand, and off she slips
The bolsters that supply her hips;
With gentlest touch, she next explores
Her chancres, issues, running sores,   30
Effects of many a sad disaster;
And then to each applies a plaster:
But must, before she goes to bed,
Rub off the daubs of white and red,

And smooth the furrows in her front
With greasy paper stuck upon't.
She takes a *bolus* ere she sleeps,
And then between two blankets creeps.
With pains of love tormented lies;
Or, if she chance to close her eyes,   40
Of Bridewell and the Compter dreams,°
And feels the lash, and faintly screams;
Or, by a faithless bully drawn,
At some hedge-tavern lies in pawn;
Or to Jamaica seems transported,
*Alone, and by no planter courted;
Or, near Fleet-ditch's oozy brinks,°
Surrounded with a hundred stinks;
Belated, seems on watch to lie,
And snap some cully passing by;   50
Or, struck with fear, her fancy runs
On watchmen, constables and duns,
From whom she meets with frequent rubs;
But never from religious clubs;°
Whose favour she is sure to find
Because she pays 'em all in kind.

  Corinna wakes. A dreadful sight!
Behold the ruins of the night!
A wicked rat her plaster stole,
Half eat, and dragg'd it to his hole.   60
The crystal eye, alas, was miss'd;
And puss had on her plumpers p—st,
A pigeon pick'd her issue-peas:°
And Shock her tresses fill'd with fleas.

  The nymph, though in this mangled plight,
Must ev'ry morn her limbs unite.
But how shall I describe her arts
To re-collect the scatter'd parts?
Or show the anguish, toil, and pain,
Of gath'ring up herself again?   70
The bashful Muse will never bear
In such a scene to interfere.
Corinna, in the morning dizen'd,
Who sees, will spew; who smells, be poison'd.

* ——— Et longam incomitata videtur | Ire viam ——.

On Poetry

A RHAPSODY.

All human race would fain be *wits*.
And millions miss, for one that hits.
Young's universal passion, *pride*,°
Was never known to spread so wide.
Say, Britain, could you ever boast
Three *poets* in an age at most?
Our chilling climate hardly bears
A *sprig* of bays in fifty years;
While ev'ry fool his claim alleges,
As if it grew in common hedges.   10
What reason can there be assign'd
For this perverseness in the mind?
Brutes find out where their talents lie:
A *bear* will not attempt to fly;
A founder'd *horse* will oft debate
Before he tries a five-barr'd gate;
A *dog* by instinct turns aside,
Who sees the ditch too deep and wide.
But *Man* we find the only creature
Who, led by *Folly*, fights with *Nature*;   20
Who, when *she* loudly cries, *Forbear*,
With obstinacy fixes there;
And, where his *genius* least inclines,
Absurdly bends his whole designs.

  Not *empire* to the rising sun
By valour, conduct, fortune won;
Not highest *wisdom* in debates,
For framing laws to govern states;
Not skill in sciences profound
So large to grasp the circle round,   30
Such heav'nly influence require,
As how to strike the *Muse's lyre*.

  Not beggar's brat, on bulk begot;
Not bastard of a pedlar Scot;
Not boy brought up to cleaning shoes,
The spawn of Bridewell, or the stews;°

Not infants dropp'd, the spurious pledges
Of gipsies litt'ring under hedges;
Are so disqualified by fate
To rise in *church*, or *law*, or *state*,   40
As he whom Phœbus in his ire
Hath *blasted* with poetic fire.

What hope of custom in the *fair*,
While not a soul demands your ware?
Where you have nothing to produce
For private life, or public use?
Court, *city*, *country*, want you not;
You cannot bribe, betray, or plot.
For poets, law makes no provision;
The wealthy have you in derision.°   50
Of state affairs you cannot smatter,
Are awkward when you try to flatter;
Your portion, taking Britain round,
Was just one annual hundred pound;*°
Now not so much as in remainder
Since Cibber brought in an attainder;
For ever fix'd by right divine
(A monarch's right) on Grub Street line.
Poor starv'ling bard, how small thy gains!
How unproportion'd to thy pains!   60

And here a *simile* comes pat in:
Though *chickens* take a month to fatten,
The guests in less than half an hour
Will more than half a score devour.
So, after toiling twenty days,
To earn a stock of pence and praise,
Thy labours, grown the critic's prey,
Are swallow'd o'er a dish of tea;
Gone, to be never heard of more,
Gone where the *chickens* went before.   70

How shall a new attempter learn
Of diff'rent spirits to discern,°
And how distinguish which is which,
The poet's vein, or scribbling itch?
Then hear an old experienced sinner
Instructing thus a young beginner.

* Paid to the Poet Laureate, which place was given to one Cibber, a player.

  Consult yourself; and if you find
A pow'rful impulse urge your mind,
Impartial judge within your breast
What subject you can manage best;   80
Whether your genius most inclines
To satire, praise, or hum'rous lines,
To elegies in mournful tone,
Or prologue sent from hand unknown.
Then, rising with Aurora's light,
The Muse invoked, sit down and write;
Blot out, correct, insert, refine,
Enlarge, diminish, interline;
Be mindful, when invention fails,
To scratch your head, and bite your nails.   90
  Your poem finish'd, next your care
Is needful to transcribe it fair.
In modern wit all printed trash is
Set off with num'rous *breaks*—and *dashes*—
To statesmen would you give a wipe,
You print it in *Italic type.*
When letters are in vulgar shapes,
'Tis ten to one the wit escapes:
But when in CAPITALS express'd,
The dullest reader smokes the jest: 100
Or else perhaps he may invent
A better than the poet meant;
As learned commentators view
In Homer more than Homer knew.
  Your poem in its modish dress,
Correctly fitted for the press,
Convey by penny-post to Lintot,*
But let no friend alive look into't.
If Lintot thinks 'twill quit the cost,
You need not fear your labour lost: 110
And how agreeably surprised
Are you to see it advertised!
The hawker shows you one in print,
As fresh as farthings from the mint:
The product of your toil and sweating,
A bastard of your own begetting.

    * A bookseller in London.

　　Be sure at Will's,* the following day,°
Lie snug, to hear what critics say;
And, if you find the general vogue
Pronounces you a stupid rogue,   120
Damns all your thoughts as low and little,
Sit still, and swallow down your spittle.°
Be silent as a politician,
For talking may beget suspicion;
Or praise the judgment of the town,
And help, yourself, to run it down.
Give up your fond paternal pride,
Nor argue on the weaker side:
For, poems read without a name
We justly praise, or justly blame;   130
And critics have no partial views,
Except they know whom they abuse.
And since you ne'er provok'd their spite,
Depend upon't their judgment's right.
But if you blab, you are undone;
Consider what a risk you run.
You lose your credit all at once;
The town will mark you for a dunce;
The vilest dogg'rel Grub Street sends,
Will pass for yours with foes and friends;   140
And you must bear the whole disgrace
Till some fresh blockhead takes your place.

　　Your secret kept, your poem sunk,
And sent in quires to line a trunk,
If still you be disposed to rhyme,
Go try your hand a second time.
Again you fail; yet *Safe*'s the word;
Take courage and attempt a third.
But first with care employ your thoughts
Where critics mark'd your former faults: 150
The trivial turns, the borrow'd wit,
The *similes* that nothing fit;
The *cant* which every fool repeats,
Town jests and coffee-house conceits,
Descriptions tedious, flat and dry,
And introduced the Lord knows why:

* The poets' coffee-house.

Or, where we find your fury set
Against the harmless alphabet;
On A's and B's your malice vent,
While readers wonder whom you meant: 160
A public or a private *robber*,
A *statesman*, or a South Sea *jobber*;°
A *prelate*, who no God believes;
A parliament, or den of thieves;
⌈A House of Peers, or gaming crew,
A griping monarch, or a Jew;⌉
A pickpurse at the bar, or bench,
A duchess, or a suburb wench.
Or oft, when epithets you link,
In gaping lines to fill a chink;
Like stepping-stones, to save a stride
In streets where kennels are too wide;   170
Or like a heel-piece, to support
A cripple with one foot too short;
Or like a bridge, that joins a marish
To moorlands of a diff'rent parish.
So have I seen ill-coupled hounds
Drag diff'rent ways on miry grounds.
So geographers, in Afric maps,
With savage pictures fill their gaps,
And o'er unhabitable downs
Place elephants for want of towns.   180
     But, though you miss your third essay,
You need not throw your pen away.
Lay now aside all thoughts of fame,
To spring more profitable game.
From party merit seek support;
The vilest verse thrives best at court.
⌈And may you ever have the luck
To rhyme almost as ill as Duck;
And, though you never learn'd to scan verse,
Come out with some lampoon on D'Anvers.⌉°
A pamphlet in Sir Bob's defence°
Will never fail to bring in pence:
Nor be concern'd about the sale,
He pays his workmen on the nail.   190
⌈Display the blessings of the nation,

And praise the whole administration.
Extol the bench of bishops round,
Who at them rail, bid God confound:
To bishop-haters answer thus
(The only logic used by us)
What though they don't believe in [Christ],
Deny them Protestants—thou ly'st.¹

    A prince, the moment he is crown'd,
Inherits ev'ry virtue round,
As emblems of the sov'reign pow'r,
Like *other* baubles in the Tower;°
Is gen'rous, valiant, just, and wise,
And so continues till he dies.
His humble *senate* this professes,
In all their *speeches, votes, addresses.*
But once you fix him in a tomb,
His virtue fades, his vices bloom;   200
And each perfection, wrong imputed,
Is fully at his death confuted.
The loads of poems in his praise,
Ascending, make one fun'ral blaze:
⌈His panegyrics then are ceased,
He's grown a tyrant, dunce, and beast.⌉
As soon as you can hear his knell,
This god on earth turns *dev'l* in hell:
And lo! his ministers of state,
Transform'd to imps, his levee wait;
Where, in the scenes of endless woe,°
They ply their former arts below: 210
And as they sail in Charon's boat,
Contrive to bribe the judge's vote.
To Cerberus they give a sop,
His triple-barking mouth to stop;
Or, in the iv'ry gate of dreams,*°
Project excise and South-Sea schemes;°
Or hire their party pamphleteers
To set Elysium by the ears.
    Then, poet, if you mean to thrive,

* Sunt geminae Somni portae—— | Altera candenti perfecta nitens elephanto.
—Virg., *Aen.*, vi. ['There are two gates of sleep—the one shining with the gleam of polished ivory.']

Employ your muse on kings alive; 220
With prudence gath'ring up a cluster
Of all the virtues you can muster,
Which, form'd into a garland sweet,
Lay humbly at your monarch's feet:
Who, as the odours reach his throne,
Will smile, and think 'em all his own;
For *law* and *gospel* both determine
All virtues lodge in royal ermine
(I mean the oracles of both,
Who shall depose it upon oath). 230
Your garland, in the following reign,
Change but the names, will do again.
　　But, if you think this trade too base,
(Which seldom is the dunce's case)
Put on the critic's brow, and sit
At Will's, the puny judge of wit.°
A nod, a shrug, a scornful smile,
With caution used, may serve awhile.
Proceed no further in your part,
Before you learn the terms of art 240
(For you can never be too far gone
In all our modern critics' jargon).
Then talk with more authentic face
Of *unities, in time and place*:
Get scraps of Horace from your friends,
And have them at your fingers' ends;
Learn Aristotle's rules by rote,
And at all hazards boldly quote;
Judicious Rymer oft review,°
Wise Dennis, and profound Bossu. 250
Read all the prefaces of Dryden,
For these our critics much confide in,
Though merely writ at first for filling,
To raise the volume's price a shilling.
　　A forward critic often dupes us
With sham quotations *peri hupsous*:*°
And if we have not read Longinus,
Will magisterially outshine us.
Then, lest with Greek he overrun ye,

　　* A famous treatise of Longinus.

Procure the book for love or money,   260
Translated from Boileau's translation,*
And quote *quotation* on *quotation*.
  At Will's you hear a poem read,
Where Battus from the table head,°
Reclining on his elbow-chair,
Gives judgment with decisive air;
To whom the tribe of circling wits,
As to an oracle, submits.
He gives directions to the town,
To cry it up, or run it down   270
(Like *courtiers*, when they send a note,
Instructing *members* how to vote).
He sets the stamp of bad and good,
Though not a word be understood.
Your lesson learn'd, you'll be secure
To get the name of *connoisseur*.
And, when your merits once are known,
Procure disciples of your own.
  Our poets (you can never want 'em,
Spread through Augusta Trinobantum)†°   280
Computing by their pecks of coals,
Amount to just nine thousand souls.
These o'er their proper districts govern,
Of wit and humour judges sov'reign.
In ev'ry street a city bard
Rules, like an alderman, his ward;
His indisputed rights extend
Through all the *lane*, from end to end;
The neighbours round admire his *shrewdness*
For songs of *loyalty* and *lewdness*;   290
Outdone by none in rhyming well,
Although he never learn'd to spell.
  Two bord'ring wits contend for glory;
And one is *Whig*, and one is *Tory*:
And this, for epics claims the bays,
And that, for elegiac lays:
Some famed for numbers soft and smooth,
By lovers spoke in Punch's booth;
And some as justly Fame extols

* By Mr. Welsted.   † The ancient name of London.

For lofty lines in Smithfield drolls.° 300
Bavius in Wapping gains renown,
And Mævius reigns o'er Kentish Town:°
Tigellius, placed in Phœbus' car,
From Ludgate shines to Temple Bar.°
Harmonious Cibber entertains
The court with annual birthday strains;
Whence Gay was banish'd in disgrace,
Where Pope will never show his face,
Where Young must torture his invention
To flatter *knaves*, or lose his *pension*. 310
  But these are not a thousandth part
Of jobbers in the poet's art,
Attending each his proper station,
And all in due subordination;
Through ev'ry alley to be found,
In garrets high, or under ground:
And when they join their *pericranies*,
Out skips a *book of miscellanies*.
  Hobbes clearly proves that ev'ry creature
Lives in a state of war by nature.° 320
The greater for the smaller watch,
But meddle seldom with their match.
A whale of mod'rate size will draw
A shoal of herrings down her maw;
A fox with geese his belly crams;
A wolf destroys a thousand lambs.
But search among the rhyming race,
The *brave* are worried by the *base*.
If on Parnassus' top you sit,
You rarely bite, are always bit: 330
Each poet of inferior size
On you shall rail and criticise,
And strive to tear you limb from limb;
While others do as much for him.
The vermin only teaze and pinch
Their foes superior by an inch.
So, nat'ralists observe, a flea
Hath smaller fleas that on him prey;
And these have smaller yet to bite 'em,
And so proceed *ad infinitum*. . 340

Thus ev'ry poet, in his kind,
Is bit by him that comes behind:
Who, though too little to be seen,
Can teaze, and gall, and give the spleen;
Call 'dunces', 'fools', and 'sons of whores',
Lay *Grub Street* at each other's doors;
Extol the Greek and Roman masters,
And curse our modern poetasters;
Complain, as many an ancient bard did,
How genius is no more rewarded;   350
How wrong a taste prevails among us;
How much our ancestors out-sung us:
Can personate an awkward scorn
For those who are not poets born;
And all their brother dunces lash
Who crowd the press with hourly trash.

  O Grub Street! how do I bemoan thee,
Whose graceless children scorn to own thee!
Their filial piety forgot,
Deny their country, like a Scot;   360
Though by their idiom and grimace
They soon betray their native place:
Yet *thou* hast greater cause to be
Ashamed of them, than they of thee;
Degen'rate from their ancient brood
Since first the court allow'd them food.

  Remains a difficulty still,
To purchase fame by writing ill.
From Flecknoe down to Howard's time,°
How few have reach'd the *low sublime*!   370
For when our high-born Howard died,
Blackmore alone his place supplied:
And lest a chasm should intervene,
When death had finish'd Blackmore's reign,
The *leaden crown* devolved to thee,
Great poet* of the 'Hollow Tree'.
But O! how unsecure thy throne!
Ten thousand bards thy right disown:
They plot to turn, in factious zeal,
Duncenia to a common-weal;   380

                    * Lord Grimston.

And with rebellious arms pretend
An equal priv'lege to *descend*.
   In bulk there are not more degrees
From *elephants* to *mites* in cheese,
Than what a curious eye may trace
In creatures of the rhyming race.
From bad to worse, and worse, they fall,
But who can reach the worst of all?
For though in nature, depth and height
Are equally held infinite,   390
In poetry, the height we know;
'Tis only infinite below.
For instance: when you rashly think,*
No rhymer can like Welsted sink—
His merits balanced, you shall find
The Laureate leaves him far behind.
Concanen, more aspiring bard,
Climbs *downwards* deeper by a yard.
Smart Jemmy Moore with vigour drops,°
The rest pursue as thick as hops: 400
With heads to points the gulf they enter,
Link'd perpendic'lar to the centre;
And as their heels elated rise,
Their heads attempt the nether skies.
   O, what indignity and shame,
To prostitute the Muse's name!
By flatt'ring kings, whom Heaven design'd
The plague and scourges of mankind;
Bred up in ignorance and sloth,
And ev'ry vice that nurses both.   410
  Perhaps you say Augustus shines
Immortal made in Virgil's lines,
And Horace brought the tuneful quire
To sing his virtues on the lyre,
Without reproach for flattery; true,
Because their praises were his due.
For in those ages kings, we find,
Were *animals* of human kind.
But now, go search all Europe round
Among the *savage monsters* crown'd,   [10]

* Vide *The Treatise on the Profound*, and Mr. Pope's *Dunciad*.

With vice polluting every throne
(I mean all kings except our own).
In vain you make the strictest view
To find a king in all the crew,
With whom a footman out of place
Would not conceive a high disgrace,
A burning shame, a crying sin,
To take his morning's cup of gin.
    Thus, all are destined to obey
Some beast of burthen, or of prey.   [20]
    'Tis sung, Prometheus, forming man,
Through all the brutal species ran,
Each proper quality to find
Adapted to a human mind:
A mingled mass of good and bad,
The worst and best that could be had;
Then from a clay of mixture base
He shaped a king to rule the race,
Endow'd with gifts from every brute,
That best the regal nature suit.   [30]
Thus, think on kings: the name denotes
Hogs, asses, wolves, baboons, and goats;
To represent in figure just,
Sloth, folly, rapine, mischief, lust;
Oh, were they all but Neb-cadnezers,°
What herds of kings would turn to grazers![1]
    Fair Britain, in thy monarch blest,°
Whose virtues bear the strictest test;
Whom never *faction* could bespatter,
Nor *minister* nor *poet* flatter;
What justice in rewarding merit!
What magnanimity of spirit!
⌐How well his public thrift is shown!
All coffers full, except his own.⌐
What lineaments divine we trace
Through all his figure, mien, and face!
Though peace with olive binds his hands,
Confess'd the conqu'ring hero stands.   420
Hydaspes, Indus, and the Ganges,
Dread from his arm impending changes.
From him the Tartar and Chinese,

Short by the knees,* entreat for peace.°
The *consort* of his throne and bed,°
A perfect goddess born and bred,
Appointed sov'reign judge to sit
On learning, eloquence and wit.
Our eldest hope, divine Iülus,°
(Late, very late, O may he rule us!)
What early manhood has he shown,   430
Before his downy beard was grown!
Then think, what wonders will be done
By going on as he begun,
An heir for Britain to secure
As long as sun and moon endure.

   The remnant of the royal blood
Comes pouring on me like a flood.
Bright goddesses, in number five;
Duke William, sweetest prince alive.°   440
   Now sing the *minister of state,*°
Who shines alone, without a mate.
Observe with what majestic port
This *Atlas* stands to prop the court:
Intent the public debts to pay,
Like prudent Fabius,† by *delay*.°
Thou great vicegerent of the king,
Thy praises ev'ry Muse shall sing!
In all affairs thou sole director,
Of wit and learning chief protector;   450
Though small the time thou hast to spare,
The church is thy peculiar care.
Of pious prelates what a stock
You choose, to rule the sable flock!
You raise the honour of the peerage,
Proud to attend you at the steerage;
You dignify the noble race,
Content yourself with humbler place.
Now Learning, Valour, Virtue, Sense,
To titles give the sole pretence.   460
St. George beheld thee with delight°
Vouchsafe to be an azure knight,

* —— genibus minor.
  † Unus homo nobis cunctando restituis rem.

When on thy breast and sides Herculean
He fix'd the *star* and *string cerulean*.
    Say, poet, in what other nation
Shone ever such a constellation!
Attend, ye Popes, and Youngs, and Gays,
And tune your harps, and strew your bays.
Your panegyrics here provide,
You cannot err on flatt'ry's side: 470
Above the stars exalt your style,
You still are low ten thousand mile.
On Lewis all his bards bestow'd°
Of incense many a thousand load;
But Europe mortified his pride,
And swore the fawning rascals lied.
Yet what the world refused to Lewis,
Applied to George, exactly true is.
'Exactly true'? invidious poet!
'Tis fifty thousand times below it.   480
    Translate me now some lines, if you can,
From Virgil, Martial, Ovid, Lucan.
They could all pow'r in Heav'n divide,
And do no wrong to either side;
They teach you how to split a hair,
Give *George* and *Jove* an equal share.*
Yet why should we be laced so strait?
I'll give my sov'reign *butter-weight*.
And reason good; for many a year
[*Christ*] never intermeddled here: 490
Nor, though his priests be duly paid,
Did ever we *desire* his aid:
We now can better do without him,
Since Woolston gave us arms to rout him.°

        Caetera desiderantur.°

* Divisum imperium cum Jove Caesar habet.°

DIRECTIONS TO SERVANTS.

RULES THAT CONCERN ALL SERVANTS IN GENERAL.

When your master or lady calls a servant by name, if that servant be not in the way, none of you are to answer, for then there will be no end of your drudgery: and masters themselves allow, that if a servant comes when he is called, it is sufficient.

When you have done a fault, be always pert and insolent, and behave yourself as if you were the injured person; this will immediately put your master or lady off their mettle.

If you see your master wronged by any of your fellow-servants, be sure to conceal it, for fear of being called a tell-tale. However, there is one exception, in case of a favourite servant, who is justly hated by the whole family; who therefore are bound, in prudence, to lay all the faults they can upon the favourite.

The cook, the butler, the groom, the market-man, and every other servant who is concerned in the expenses of the family, should act as if his master's whole estate ought to be applied to that servant's particular business. For instance, if the cook computes his master's estate to be a thousand pounds a year, he reasonably concludes that a thousand pounds a year will afford meat enough, and therefore he need not be saving; the butler makes the same judgment, so may the groom and the coachman, and thus every branch of expense will be filled to your master's honour.

When you are chid before company (which, with submission to our masters and ladies, is an unmannerly practice) it often happens that some stranger will have the good nature to drop a word in your excuse; in such a case you have a good title to justify yourself, and may rightly conclude, that whenever he chides you afterwards on other occasions, he may be in the wrong; in which opinion you will be the better confirmed by stating the case to your fellow-servants in your own way, who will certainly decide in your favour: therefore, as I have said before, whenever you are chidden, complain as if you were injured.

It often happens, that servants sent on messages are apt to stay out somewhat longer than the message requires, perhaps two, four, six, or eight hours, or some such trifle, for the temptation to be sure was great, and flesh and blood cannot always resist. When you return, the master storms, the lady scolds; stripping, cudgelling, and turning off is the word.

But here you ought be provided with a set of excuses, enough to serve on all occasions. For instance, your uncle came fourscore miles to town this morning, on purpose to see you, and goes back by break of day tomorrow; a brother-servant, that borrowed money of you when he was out of place, was running away to Ireland; you were taking leave of an old fellow-servant, who was shipping for Barbados: your father sent a cow for you to sell, and you could not find a chapman till nine at night; you were taking leave of a dear cousin who is to be hanged next Saturday; you wrenched your foot against a stone, and were forced to stay three hours in a shop before you could stir a step; some nastiness was thrown on you out of a garret-window, and you were ashamed to come home before you were cleaned, and the smell went off; you were pressed for the sea-service, and carried before a justice of peace, who kept you three hours before he examined you, and you got off with much a-do; a bailiff, by mistake, seized you for a debtor, and kept you the whole evening in a sponging-house; you were told your master had gone to a tavern, and came to some mischance, and your grief was so great, that you inquired for his honour in a hundred taverns between Pall Mall and Temple Bar.

Take all trademen's parts against your master, and when you are sent to buy any thing, never offer to cheapen it, but generously pay the full demand. This is highly for your master's honour; and may be some shillings in your pocket; and you are to consider, if your master hath paid too much, he can better afford the loss than a poor tradesman.

Never submit to stir a finger in any business, but that for which you were particularly hired. For example, if the groom be drunk or absent, and the butler be ordered to shut the stable door, the answer is ready, 'An please your honour, I don't understand horses.' If a corner of the hanging wants a single nail to fasten it, and the footman be directed to tack it up, he may say he doth not understand that sort of work, but his honour may send for the upholsterer.

Masters and ladies are usually quarrelling with the servants for not shutting the doors after them; but neither masters nor ladies consider that those doors must be open before they can be shut, and that the labour is double to open and shut the doors; therefore the best, the shortest, and easiest way is to do neither. But if you are so often teased to shut the door, that you cannot easily forget it, then give the door such a clap at your going out, as will shake the whole room, and make everything rattle in it, to put your master and lady in mind that you observe their directions.

If you find yourself to grow into favour with your master or lady, take some opportunity in a very mild way to *give them warning*; and when they ask the reason, and seem loth to part with you, answer, that you would rather live with them than any body else, but a poor servant is not to be blamed if he strives to better himself; that service is no inheritance; that your work is great, and your wages very small. Upon which, if your master hath any generosity, he will add five or ten shillings a quarter rather than let you go. But if you are baulked, and have no mind to go off, get some fellow-servant to tell your master that he had prevailed upon you to stay.

Whatever good bits you can pilfer in the day, save them to junket with your fellow-servants at night, and take in the butler, provided he will give you drink.

Write your own name and your sweetheart's, with the smoke of a candle, on the roof of the kitchen or the servants' hall, to show your learning.

If you are a young, sightly fellow, whenever you whisper your mistress at the table, run your nose full in her cheek, or if your breath be good, breathe full in her face; this I know to have had very good consequences in some families.

Never come till you have been called three or four times; for none but dogs will come at the first whistle; and when the master calls 'Who's there?' no servant is bound to come; for *Who's there* is no body's name.

When you have broken all your earthen drinking-vessels below stairs (which is usually done in a week) the copper pot will do as well; it can boil milk, heat porridge, hold small beer, or, in case of necessity, serve for a jordan; therefore apply it indifferently to all these uses; but never wash or scour it, for fear of taking off the tin.

Although you are allowed knives for the servants' hall at meals, yet you ought to spare them, and make use only of your master's.

Let it be a constant rule, that no chair, stool, or table in the servants' hall or the kitchen, shall have above three legs, which hath been the ancient and constant practice in all the families I ever knew, and is said to be founded upon two reasons; first, to show that servants are ever in a tottering condition; secondly, it was thought a point of humility, that the servants' chairs and tables should have at least one leg fewer than those of their masters. I grant there hath been an exception to this rule with regard to the cook, who, by old custom, was allowed an easy chair to sleep in after dinner; and yet I have seldom seen them with above three legs. Now this epidemical lameness of servants' chairs is, by philosophers, imputed to two causes, which are observed to make the greatest revolutions in states and empires; I mean love and war. A stool, a chair, or a table is the first weapon taken up in a general romping or skirmish; and after a peace, the chairs, if they be not very strong, are apt to suffer in the conduct of an amour, the cook being usually fat and heavy, and the butler a little in drink.

I could never endure to see maid-servants so ungenteel as to walk the streets with their petticoats pinned up; it is a foolish excuse to allege their petticoats will be dirty, when they have so easy a remedy as to walk three or four times down a clean pair of stairs after they come home.

When you step to tattle with some crony servant in the same street, leave your own street-door open, that you may get in without knocking when you come back; otherwise your mistress may know you are gone out, and you will be chidden.

I do most earnestly exhort you all to unanimity and concord. But mistake me not: you may quarrel with each other as much as you please, only bear in mind that you have a common enemy, which is your master and lady, and you have a common cause to defend. Believe an old practitioner; whoever, out of malice to a fellow-servant, carries a tale to his master, should be ruined by a general confederacy against him.

The general place of rendezvous for all servants, both in winter and summer, is the kitchen; there the grand affairs of the family ought to be consulted, whether they concern the stable, the dairy, the pantry, the laundry, the cellar, the nursery, the dining-room, or my lady's chamber: there, as in your own proper element, you can laugh, and squall, and romp, in full security.

When any servant comes home drunk, and cannot appear, you must all join in telling your master that he is gone to bed very sick; upon which your lady will be so good-natured as to order some comfortable thing for the poor man or maid.

When your master and lady go abroad together, to dinner, or on a visit for the evening, you need leave only one servant in the house, unless you have a black-guard boy to answer at the door, and attend the children, if there be any. Who is to stay at home is to be determined by short and long cuts, and the stayer at home may be comforted by a visit from a sweetheart, without danger of being caught together. These opportunities must never be missed, because they come but sometimes; and you are always safe enough while there is a servant in the house.

When your master or lady comes home, and wants a servant who happens to be abroad, your answer must be, that he is just that minute stept out, being sent for by a cousin who is dying.

If your master calls you by name, and you happen to answer at the fourth call, you need not hurry yourself; and if you be chidden for staying, you may lawfully say, you came no sooner, because you did not know what you were called for.

When you are chidden for a fault, as you go out of the room, and down stairs, mutter loud enough to be plainly heard; this will make him believe you are innocent.

Whoever comes to visit your master or lady when they are abroad, never burthen your memory with the person's name, for indeed you have too many other things to remember. Besides, it is a porter's business, and your master's fault that he doth not keep one; and who can remember names? and you will certainly mistake them, and you can neither write nor read.

If it be possible, never tell a lie to your master or lady, unless you have some hopes that they cannot find it out in less than half an hour.

When a servant is turned off, all his faults must be told, although most of them were never known by his master or lady; and all mischiefs done by others, charge to him. And when they ask any of you why you never acquainted them before, the answer is, 'Sir, (or Madam) really I was afraid it would make you angry; and besides, perhaps you might think it was malice in me.' Where there are little masters and misses in a house, they are usually great impediments to the diversions of the servants; the only remedy is to bribe them with *goody goodies*, that they may not tell tales to papa and mamma.

I advise you of the servants, whose masters live in the country, and who expect vales, always to stand rank and file when a stranger is taking his leave; so that he must of necessity pass between you; and he must have more confidence, or less money than usual, if any of you let him escape; and according as he behaves himself, remember to treat him the next time he comes.

If you be sent with ready money to buy any thing at a shop, and happen at that time to be out of pocket (which is very usual), sink the money and take up the goods on your master's account. This is for the honour of your master and yourself; for he becomes a man of credit at your recommendation.

When your lady sends for you up to her chamber, to give you any orders, be sure to stand at the door, and keep it open, fiddling with the lock all the while she is talking to you, and keep the button in your hand, for fear you should forget to shut the door after you.

If your master or lady happen once in their lives to accuse you wrongfully, you are a happy servant; for you have nothing more to do, than for every fault you commit while you are in their service, to put them in mind of that false accusation, and protest yourself equally innocent in the present case.

When you have a mind to leave your master, and are too bashful to break the matter for fear of offending him, your best way is to grow rude and saucy of a sudden, and beyond your usual behaviour, till he finds it necessary to turn you off; and when you are gone, to revenge yourself, give him and his lady such a character to all your brother servants who are out of place, that none will venture to offer their service.

Some nice ladies who are afraid of catching cold, having observed that the maids and fellows below stairs often forget to shut the door after them, as they come in or go out into the back yards, have contrived that a pulley and rope with a large piece of lead at the end, should be so fixed, as to make the door shut of itself, and require a strong hand to open it; which is an immense toil to servants whose business may force them to go in and out fifty times in a morning. But ingenuity can do much, for prudent servants have found out an effectual remedy against this insupportable grievance, by tying up the pulley in such a manner that the weight of the lead shall have no effect; however, as to my own part, I would rather choose to keep the door always open, by laying a heavy stone at the bottom of it.

The servants' candlesticks are generally broken, for nothing can last for ever. But you may find out many expedients; you may conveniently stick your candle in a bottle, or with a lump of butter against the wainscot, or in a powder-horn, or in an old shoe, or in a cleft stick, or in the barrel of a pistol, or upon its own grease on a table, in a coffeecup or a drinking-glass, a horn can, a teapot, a twisted napkin, a mustard-pot, an ink-horn, a marrowbone, a piece of dough, or you may cut a hole in the loaf, and stick it there.

When you invite the neighbouring servants to junket with you at home in an evening, teach them a peculiar way of tapping or scraping at the kitchen-window, which you may hear, but not your master or lady, whom you must take care not to disturb or frighten at such unseasonable hours.

Lay all faults on a lap-dog, a favourite cat, a monkey, a parrot, a child, or on the servant who was last turned off; by this rule you will excuse yourself, do no hurt to any body else, and save your master or lady from the trouble and vexation of chiding.

When you want proper instruments for any work you are about, use all expedients you can invent rather than leave your work undone. For instance, if the poker be out of the way, or broken, stir up the fire with the tongs; if the tongs be not at hand, use the muzzle of the bellows, the wrong end of the fire-shovel, the handle of the fire-brush, the end of a mop, or your master's cane. If you want paper to singe a fowl, tear the first book you see about the house. Wipe your shoes, for want of a clout, with the bottom of a curtain, or a damask napkin. Strip your livery lace for garters. If the butler wants a jordan, in case of need he may use the great silver cup.

There are several ways of putting out candles, and you ought to be instructed in them all. You may run the candle end against the wainscot, which puts the snuff out immediately; you may lay it on the floor, and tread the snuff out with your foot; you may hold it upside down, until it is choked with its own grease; or cram it into the socket of the candlestick; you may whirl it round in your hand till it goes out: when you go to bed, after you have made water, you may dip your candle end into the chamber-pot: you may spit on your finger and thumb, and pinch the snuff until it goes out. The cook may run the candle's nose into the meal-tub, or the groom into a vessel of oats, or a lock of hay, or a heap of litter; the housemaid may put out her candle by running it against a looking-glass, which nothing cleans so well as candle-snuff; but the quickest and best of all methods is to blow it out with your breath, which leaves the candle clear, and readier to be lighted.

There is nothing so pernicious in families as a tell-tale, against whom it must be the principal business of you all to unite: whatever office he serves in, take all opportunities to spoil the business he is about, and to cross him in every thing. For instance, if the butler be the tell-tale, break his glasses whenever he leaves the pantry door open; or lock the cat or the mastiff in it, who will do as well: mislay a fork or a spoon so as he may never find it. If it be the cook, whenever she turns her back, throw a lump of soot or a handful of salt in the pot, or smoking coals into the dripping-pan, or daub the roast meat with the back of the chimney, or hide the key of the jack. If a footman be suspected, let the cook daub the back of his new livery; or when he is going up with a dish of soup, let her follow him softly with a ladleful, and dribble it all the way up stairs to the dining-room, and then let the housemaid make such a noise that her lady may hear it. The waiting-maid is very likely to be guilty of this fault, in hopes to ingratiate herself: in this case the laundress must be sure to tear her smocks in the washing, and yet wash them but half; and when she complains, tell all the house that she sweats so much, and her flesh is so nasty, that she fouls a smock more in one hour, than the kitchen-maid does in a week.

A CHARACTER, PANEGYRIC, AND DESCRIPTION OF THE *LEGION CLUB*

As I stroll the city, oft I
See a building large and lofty,°
Not a bow-shot from the college;
Half the globe from sense and knowledge;
By the prudent architect
Placed against the church direct,°
Making good my grandam's jest,°
Near the church—you know the rest.
   Tell us what this pile contains?
Many heads that hold no brains.   10
These demoniacs let me dub
With the name of *Legion Club*.
Such assemblies, you would swear,
Meet when butchers bait a bear:
Such a noise and such haranguing,
When a brother thief is hanging:
Such a rout and such a rabble
Run to hear Jackpudden gabble:°
Such a crowd their ordure throws
On a far less villain's nose.°   20
   Could I from the building's top
Hear the rattling thunder drop,
While the devil upon the roof
(If the devil be thunder-proof)
Should, with poker fiery-red,
Crack the stones, and melt the lead;
Drive them down on ev'ry skull,
While the den of thieves is full;°
Quite destroy that harpies' nest—
How might then our isle be blest!   30
For divines allow, that God
Sometimes makes the devil his rod;
And the gospel will inform us,
He can punish crimes enormous.
   Yet should Swift endow the schools°
For his *lunatics* and *fools*,
With a rood or two of land,

I allow the pile may stand.
You perhaps will ask me, 'Why so?'
But it is with this proviso: 40
Since the House is like to last,
Let the royal grant be pass'd,
That the Club have leave to dwell
Each within his proper cell,
With a passage left to creep in
And a hole above for peeping.
   Let them, when they once get in,
Sell the nation for a pin;
While they sit a-picking straws,
Let them rave at making laws;   50
While they never hold their tongue,
Let them dabble in their dung:°
Let them form a grand committee
How to plague and starve the city;°
Let them stare and storm and frown
When they see a clergy-gown;
Let them, ere they crack a louse,
Call for th' Orders of the House;
Let them, with their gosling quills
Scribble senseless heads of bills;°   60
We may, while they strain their throats,
Wipe our arses with their Votes.°
   Let Sir Tom, that rampant ass,
Stuff his guts with flax and grass;°
But before the priest he fleeces,
Tear the Bible all to pieces:
At the parsons, Tom, 'Halloo-Boy',°
Worthy offspring of a shoe-boy,
Footman, traitor, vile seducer,
Perjur'd rebel, bribed accuser.   70
Lay thy paltry priv'lege aside,
From Papist sprung, and regicide;
Fall a-working like a mole,
Raise the dirt about your hole.
   Come, assist me, Muse obedient!
Let us try some new expedient;
Shift the scene for half an hour,
Time and place are in thy pow'r.

Thither, gentle Muse, conduct me;
I shall ask, and you instruct me.   80
    See, the Muse unbars the gate;
Hark, the monkeys, how they prate!
    All ye gods who rule the soul:*
Styx, through Hell whose waters roll!
Let me be allow'd to tell
What I heard in yonder Hell.
    Near the door an entrance gapes,†
Crowded round with antic shapes,
Poverty, and *Grief*, and *Care*,
Causeless *Joy*, and true *Despair*;   90
Discord periwigg'd with snakes,‡
See the dreadful strides she takes!
    By this odious crew beset,§
I began to rage and fret,
And resolv'd to break their pates,
Ere we enter'd at the gates;
Had not Clio in the nick¶
Whisper'd me, *Let down your stick.*
What! said I, is this the *mad-house*?
These, she answer'd are but shadows,   100
Phantoms bodiless and vain,
Empty visions of the brain.
    In the porch Briareus stands,‖
Shows a bribe in all his hands:
Briareus the Secretary,
But we mortals call him Cary.
When the rogues their country fleece,
They may hope for pence apiece.
    Clio, who had been so wise
To put on a fool's disguise,   110

* Di quibus imperium est animarum, &c.
  Sit mihi fas audita loqui &c.°
† Vestibulum ante ipsum primisque in faucibus Orci
  Luctus et ultrices, &c.°
‡ ——Discordia demens,
  Vipereum crinem vittis innexa cruentis.°
§ Corripit hic subita trepidus, &c.
  ——strictamque aciem venientibus offert.°
¶ Et ni docta comes tenues sine corpore vitas.°
‖ Et centumgeminus Briareus.°

To bespeak some approbation
And be thought a near relation,
When she saw three hundred brutes°
All involved in wild disputes,
Roaring, till their lungs were spent,
PRIVILEGE OF PARLIAMENT,
Now a new misfortune feels,
Dreading to be laid by th' heels.
Never durst a Muse before   120
Enter that infernal door;
Clio, stifled with the smell,
Into spleen and vapours fell,
By the Stygian steams that flew
From the dire infectious crew.
Not the stench of Lake Avernus°
Could have more offended her nose;
Had she flown but o'er the top,
She must feel her pinions drop.
And by exhalations dire,
Though a goddess, must expire.   130
In a fright she crept away,
Bravely I resolved to stay.
When I saw the Keeper frown,
Tipping him with half-a-crown,
Now, said I, we are alone,
Name your heroes one by one.

Who is that hell-featured brawler,
Is it Satan? No; 'tis Waller.
In what figure can a bard dress
Jack, the grandson of Sir Hardress?   140
Honest keeper, drive him further,
In his looks are Hell and murther;
See his scowling visage drop,
Just as when he murther'd Throp.

Keeper, show me where to fix
On the puppy pair of Dicks:°
By their lantern jaws and leathern,
You might swear they both were brethren:
Dick Fitzbaker, Dick the player,
Old acquaintance, are you there?   150
Dear companions, hug and kiss,

Toast *old Glorious* in your piss;°
Tie them, keeper, in a tether,
Let them stare and stink together;
Both are apt to be unruly,
Lash them daily, lash them duly;
Though 'tis hopeless to reclaim them,
Scorpion rods, perhaps, may tame them.
   Keeper, yon old dotard smoak
Sweetly snoring in his cloak: 160
Who is he? 'Tis humdrum Wynne,
Half encompass'd with his kin.
There observe the tribe of Bingham,
For he never fails to bring 'em;
While he sleeps the whole debate,
They submissive round him wait;
Yet would gladly see the hunks
In his grave, and search his trunks.
See, they gently twitch his coat,
Just to yawn and give his vote,   170
Always firm in his vocation,
For the court against the nation.
   Those are Allens, Jack and Bob,
First in every dirty job,
Son and brother to a queer
Brain-sick brute, they call a peer.
We must give them better quarter,
For their ancestor trod mortar,
And at Howth, to boast his fame,
On a chimney cut his name.   180
   There sit Clements, Dilks, and Carter
Who for Hell would die a martyr:
Such a triplet could you tell
Where to find on this side Hell?
Gallows Carter, Dilks, and Clements,
Souse them in their own ex-crements.
Every mischief's in their hearts;
If they fail, 'tis want of parts.
   Bless us! Morgan, art thou there, man?
Bless mine eyes! art thou the chairman?
Chairman to yon damn'd committee!   190
Yet I look on thee with pity;

Dreadful sight, the learned Morgan
Metamorphos'd to a Gorgon!
For thy horrid looks, I own,
Half convert me into stone.
Hast thou been so long at school
Now to turn a factious fool?
Alma Mater was thy mother,
Every young divine thy brother.   200
O thou disobedient varlet,
Treat thy mother like a harlot!
Thou, ungrateful to thy teachers
Who are all grown rev'rend preachers!
Morgan, would it not surprise one?
Turn thy nourishment to poison!
When you walk among your books,
They reproach you with their looks;
Bind them fast, or from the shelves
They'll come down and right themselves: 210
Homer, Plutarch, Virgil, Flaccus,
All in arms, prepare to back us.
Soon repent, or put to slaughter
Every Greek and Roman author.
Will you, in your factious phrase
Send the clergy all to graze;
And to make your project pass,
Leave them not a blade of grass?
    How I want thee, hum'rous Hogarth!
Thou, I hear, a pleasant rogue art.   220
Were but you and I acquainted,
Ev'ry monster should be painted:
You should try your graving tools
On this odious group of fools;
Draw the beasts as I describe 'em,
Form their features while I gibe 'em;
Draw them like; for I assure you,
You will need no *car'catura*;
Draw them so that we may trace
All the soul in ev'ry face.   230
    Keeper, I must now retire,
You have done what I desire:
But I feel my spirits spent

With the noise, the sight, the scent.
'Pray, be patient; you shall find
Half the best are still behind!
You have hardly seen a score;
I can show two hundred more.'
   Keeper, I have seen enough.
Taking then a pinch of snuff, 240
I concluded, looking round 'em,
May their god, the devil, confound 'em!

A COMPLEAT

COLLECTION

Of genteel and
Ingenious Conversation,

ACCORDING

To the most polite Mode and Method, now used at Court, and in the best Companies of *England*.

In several Dialogues.

By SIMON WAGSTAFF, *Esq;*

AN INTRODUCTION TO THE FOLLOWING TREATISE.

As my life hath been chiefly spent in consulting the honour and welfare of my country for more than forty years past, not without answerable success, if the world and my friends have not flattered me; so, there is no point wherein I have so much laboured, as that of improving and polishing all parts of conversation between persons of quality, whether they meet by accident or invitation, at meals, tea, or visits, mornings, noons, or evenings.

I have passed perhaps more time than any other man of my age and country in visits and assemblies, where the polite persons of both sexes distinguish themselves; and could not without much grief observe how frequently both gentlemen and ladies are at a loss for questions, answers, replies and rejoinders. However, my concern was much abated, when I found that these defects were not occasioned by any want of materials, but because those materials were not in every hand. For instance, one lady can give an answer better than ask a question. One gentleman is happy at a reply; another excels in a rejoinder. One can revive a languishing conversation by a sudden surprising sentence; another is more dexterous in seconding; a third can fill the gap with laughing, or commending what hath been said. Thus fresh hints may be started, and the ball of discourse kept up.

But alas! this is too seldom the case, even in the most select companies.

How often do we see at court, at public visiting-days, at great men's levees, and other places of general meeting, that the conversation falls and drops to nothing, like a fire without supply of fuel. This is what we all ought to lament; and against this dangerous evil I take upon me to affirm, that I have in the following papers provided an infallible remedy.

It was in the year 1695, and the sixth of his late Majesty King William the Third, of ever-glorious and immortal memory, who rescued three kingdoms from popery and slavery, when, being about the age of six-and-thirty, my judgment mature, of good reputation in the world, and well acquainted with the best families in town, I determined to spend five mornings, to dine four times, pass three afternoons, and six evenings every week, in the houses of the most polite families, of which I would confine myself to fifty; only changing as the masters or ladies died, or left the town, or grew out of vogue, or sunk in their fortunes, or (which to me was of the highest moment) became disaffected to the government; which practice I have followed ever since to this very day; except when I happened at any time to be sick, or in the spleen upon cloudy weather; and except when I entertained four of each sex in my own lodgings once a month, by way of retaliation.

I always kept a large table-book in my pocket; and as soon as I left the company, I immediately entered the choicest expressions that passed during the visit; which, returning home, I transcribed in a fair hand, but somewhat enlarged; and had made the greatest part of my collection in twelve years, but not digested into any method; for this I found was a work of infinite labour, and what required the nicest judgment, and consequently could not be brought to any degree of perfection in less than sixteen years more.

Herein I resolved to exceed the advice of Horace, a Roman poet (which I have read in Mr. Creech's admirable translation)° that an author should keep his works nine years in his closet, before he ventured to publish them; and finding that I still received some additional flowers of wit and language, although in a very small number, I determined to defer the publication, to pursue my design, and exhaust, if possible, the whole subject, that I might present a complete system to the world. For, I am convinced by long experience, that the critics will be as severe as their old envy against me can make them: I foresee they will object that I have inserted many answers and replies which are neither witty, humorous, polite, nor authentic; and have omitted others that would have been highly useful, as well as entertaining. But let them come to particulars, and I will boldly engage to confute their malice.

For these last six or seven years I have not been able to add above nine valuable sentences to enrich my collection; from whence I conclude, that what remains will amount only to a trifle. However, if after the publication of this work any lady or gentleman, when they have read it, shall find the least thing of importance omitted, I desire they will please to supply my defects, by communicating to me their discoveries; and their letters may be directed to Simon Wagstaff, Esq. at his lodgings next door to the Gloucester-Head in St. James's Street, (they paying the postage).° In return of which favour, I shall make honourable mention of their names in a short preface to the second edition.

In the mean time, I cannot but with some pride, and much pleasure congratulate with my dear country, which hath outdone all the nations of Europe in advancing the whole art of conversation to the greatest height it is capable of reaching; and therefore being entirely convinced that the collection I now offer to the public is full and complete, I may at the same time boldly affirm, that the whole genius, humour, politeness and eloquence of England are summed up in it. Nor is the treasure small, wherein are to be found at least a thousand shining questions, answers, repartees, replies and rejoinders, fitted to adorn every kind of discourse that an assembly of English ladies and gentlemen, met together for their mutual entertainment, can possibly want, especially when the several flowers shall be set off and improved by the speakers, with every circumstance of preface and circumlocution, in proper terms; and attended with praise, laughter, or admiration.

There is a natural, involuntary distortion of the muscles, which is the anatomical cause of laughter. But there is another cause of laughter which decency requires, and is the undoubted mark of a good taste, as well as of a polite obliging behaviour; neither is this to be acquired without much observation, long practice, and a sound judgment. I did therefore once intend, for the ease of the learner, to set down in all parts of the following dialogues certain marks, asterisks, or *nota-bene's* (in English, *mark-well's*) after most questions, and every reply or answer; directing exactly the moment when one, two, or all the company are to laugh. But having duly considered that the expedient would too much enlarge the bulk of the volume, and consequently the price; and likewise that something ought to be left for ingenious readers to find out, I have determined to leave that whole affair, although of great importance, to their own discretion.

The reader must learn by all means to distinguish between proverbs and those polite speeches which beautify conversation. For, as to the former, I utterly reject them out of all ingenious discourse. I acknowledge indeed, that there may possibly be found in this treatise a few sayings, among so great a number of smart turns of wit and humour, as I have produced, which have a proverbial air. However, I hope it will be considered, that even these were not originally proverbs, but the genuine productions of superior wits, to embellish and support conversation; from whence, with great impropriety, as well as plagiarism (if you will forgive a hard word) they have most injuriously been transferred into proverbial maxims; and therefore ought in justice to be resumed out of vulgar hands, to adorn the drawing-rooms of princes, both male and female, the levees of great ministers, as well as the toilet and tea-table of the ladies.

I can faithfully assure the reader, that there is not one single witty phrase in this whole collection which hath not received the stamp and approbation of at least one hundred years, and how much longer, it is hard to determine; he may therefore be secure to find them all genuine, sterling, and authentic.

But, before this elaborate treatise can become of universal use and ornament to my native country, two points, that will require time and much application, are absolutely necessary. For, *first*, whatever person would aspire to be completely witty, smart, humorous, and polite, must by hard labour be able to retain in his memory every single sentence contained in this work, so as never to be once at a loss in applying the right answers, questions, repartees, and the like, immediately, and without study or hesitation. And, *secondly*, after a lady or gentleman hath so well overcome this difficulty, as to be never at a loss upon any emergency, the true management of every feature, and almost of every limb, is equally necessary; without which an infinite number of absurdities will inevitably ensue. For instance, there is hardly a polite sentence in the following dialogues which doth not absolutely require some peculiar graceful motion in the eyes, or nose, or mouth, or forehead, or chin, or suitable toss of the head, with certain offices assigned to each hand; and in ladies, the whole exercise of the fan,° fitted to the energy of every word they deliver; by no means omitting the various turns and cadences of the voice, the twistings, and movements, and different postures of the body, the several kinds and gradations of laughter, which the ladies must daily practise by the looking-glass, and consult upon them with their waiting-maids.

My readers will soon observe what a great compass of real and useful knowledge this science includes; wherein, although nature, assisted by a genius, may be very instrumental, yet a strong memory and constant application, together with example and precept, will be highly necessary. For these reasons I have often wished, that certain male and female instructors, perfectly versed in this science, would set up schools for the instruction of young ladies and gentlemen therein.

I remember about thirty years ago, there was a Bohemian woman, of that species commonly known by the name of gipsies, who came over hither from France, and generally attended ISAAC the dancing-master° when he was teaching his art to misses of quality; and while the young ladies were thus employed, the Bohemian, standing at some distance, but full in their sight, acted before them all proper airs, and heavings of the head, and motions of the hands, and twistings of the body; whereof you may still observe the good effects in several of our elder ladies. After the same manner, it were much to be desired that some expert gentlewomen gone to decay would set up public schools, wherein young girls of quality, or great fortunes, might first be taught to repeat this following system of conversation, which I have been at so much pains to compile; and then to adapt every feature of their countenances, every turn of their hands, every screwing of their bodies, every exercise of their fans, to the humour of the sentences they hear or deliver in conversation. But above all to instruct them in every species and degree of laughing in the proper seasons at their own wit, or that of the company. And, if the sons of the nobility and gentry, instead of being sent to common schools, or put into the hands of tutors at home, to learn nothing but words, were consigned to able instructors in the same art, I cannot find what use there could be of books, except in the hands of those who are to make learning their trade, which is below the dignity of persons born to titles or estates.

It would be another infinite advantage that, by cultivating this science, we should wholly avoid the vexations and impertinence of pedants, who affect to talk in a language not to be understood, and whenever a polite person offers accidentally to use any of their jargon terms,° have the presumption to laugh at *us* for pronouncing those words in a genteeler manner. Whereas, I do here affirm, that, whenever any fine gentleman or lady condescends to let a hard word pass out of their mouths, every syllable is smoothed and polished in the passage; and it is a true mark of politeness, both in writing and reading, to vary the orthography as well as the sound; because We are infinitely better judges of what will please a distinguishing ear than those who call themselves *scholars*, can possibly be; who, consequently, ought to correct their books, and manner of pronouncing, by the authority of Our example, from whose lips they proceed with infinitely more beauty and significancy.

But, in the mean time, until so great, so useful, and so necessary a design can be put in execution (which, considering the good disposition of our country at present, I shall not despair of living to see) let me recommend the following treatise to be carried about as a pocket companion, by all gentlemen and ladies, when they are going to visit, or dine, or drink tea; or where they happen to pass the evening without cards (as I have sometimes known it to be the case upon disappointments or accidents unforeseen) desiring they would read their several parts in their chairs or coaches, to prepare themselves for every kind of conversation that can possibly happen.

Although I have, in justice to my country, allowed the genius of our people to excel that of any other nation upon earth, and have confirmed this truth by an argument not to be controlled, I mean, by producing so great a number of witty sentences in the ensuing dialogues, all of undoubted authority, as well as of our own production; yet, I must confess at the same time, that we are wholly indebted for them to our ancestors; at least, for as long as my memory reacheth, I do not recollect one new phrase of importance to have been added; which defect in us moderns I take to have been occasioned by the introduction of cant-words° in the reign of King Charles the Second. And those have so often varied, that hardly one of them, of above a year's standing, is now intelligible; nor anywhere to be found, excepting a small number strewed here and there in the comedies and other fantastic writings of that age. The Honourable Colonel James Graham, my old friend and companion, did likewise, towards the end of the same reign, invent a set of words and phrases which continued almost to the time of his death. But, as those terms of art were adapted only to courts and politicians, and extended little further than among his particular acquaintance (of whom I had the honour to be one) they are now almost forgotten.

Nor did the late D. of R——° and E. of E—— succeed much better, although they proceeded no further than single words; whereof, except *bite, bamboozle,* and one or two more, the whole vocabulary is antiquated. The same fate hath already attended those other town-wits, who furnish us with a great variety of new terms, which are annually changed, and those of the last season sunk in oblivion. Of these I was once favoured with a complete list by the Right Honourable the Lord and Lady H——, with which I made a considerable figure one summer in the country; but returning up to town in winter, and venturing to produce them again, I was partly hooted, and partly not understood.

The only invention of late years, which hath any way contributed to advance politeness in discourse, is that of abbreviating or reducing words of many syllables into one, by lopping off the rest. This refinement, having begun about the time of the Revolution,° I had some share in the honour of promoting it, and I observe, to my great satisfaction, that it makes daily advancements, and I hope in time will raise our language to the utmost perfection; although, I must confess, to avoid obscurity I have been very sparing of this ornament in the following dialogues.

But, as for phrases invented to cultivate conversation, I defy all the clubs and coffee-houses in this town to invent a new one equal in wit, humour, smartness, or politeness, to the very worst of my set; which clearly shows, either that we are much degenerated, or that the whole stock of materials hath been already employed. I would willingly hope, as I do confidently believe, the latter; because, having myself, for several months, racked my invention (if possible) to enrich this treasury with some additions of my own (which, however, should have been printed in a different character, that I might not be charged with imposing upon the public) and having shown them to some judicious friends, they dealt very sincerely with me; all unanimously agreeing, that mine were infinitely below the true old helps to discourse, drawn up in my present collection, and confirmed their opinion with reasons, by which I was perfectly convinced, as well as ashamed of my great presumption.

But, I lately met a much stronger argument to confirm me in the same sentiments. For, as the great Bishop Burnet,° of Salisbury, informs us in the preface to his admirable *History of his Own Times*, that he intended to employ himself in polishing it every day of his life (and indeed in its kind it is almost equally polished with this work of mine) so it hath been my constant business, for some years past, to examine, with the utmost strictness, whether I could possibly find the smallest lapse in style or propriety through my whole collection, that, in emulation with the bishop, I might send it abroad as the most finished piece of the age.

It happened one day as I was dining in good company of both sexes, and watching, according to my custom, for new materials wherewith to fill my pocket-book, I succeeded well enough till after dinner, when the ladies retired to their tea, and left us over a bottle of wine. But I found we were not able to furnish any more materials that were worth the pains of transcribing. For, the discourse of the company was all degenerated into smart sayings of their own invention, and not of the true old standard; so that, in absolute despair, I withdrew, and went to attend the ladies at their tea. From whence I did then conclude, and still continue to believe, either that wine doth not inspire politeness, or that our sex is not able to support it without the company of women, who never fail to lead us into the right way, and there to keep us.

It much increaseth the value of these apophthegms that unto them we owe the continuance of our language, for at least an hundred years; neither is this to be wondered at; because indeed, besides the smartness of the wit, and fineness of the raillery, such is the propriety and energy of expression in them all, that they never can be changed, but to disadvantage, except in the circumstance of using abbreviations; which, however, I do not despair, in due time, to see introduced, having already met them at some of the choice companies in town.

Although this work be calculated for all persons of quality and fortune of both sexes; yet the reader may perceive that my particular view was to the OFFICERS of the ARMY, the GENTLEMEN of the INNS of COURT,° and of both the UNIVERSITIES; to all COURTIERS, male and female, but principally to the MAIDS of HONOUR, of whom I have been personally acquainted with two-and-twenty sets, all excelling in this noble endowment; till for some years past, I know not how, they came to degenerate into selling of BARGAINS,° and FREE-THINKING; not that I am against either of these entertainments at proper seasons, in compliance with company who may want a taste for more exalted discourse, whose memories may be short, who are too young to be perfect in their lessons, or (although it be hard to conceive) who have no inclination to read and learn my instructions. Besides, I confess there is a strong temptation for court-ladies to fall into the two amusements above mentioned, that they may avoid the censure of affecting singularity, against the general current and fashion of all about them. But, however, no man will pretend to affirm, that either BARGAINS or BLASPHEMY, which are the principal ornaments of FREE-THINKING, are so good a fund of polite discourse, as what is to be met with in my collection. For, as to BARGAINS, few of them seem to be excellent in their kind, and have not much variety, because they all terminate in one single point; and, to multiply them, would require more invention than people have to spare. And, as to BLASPHEMY or FREE-THINKING, I have known some scrupulous persons of both sexes, who, by a prejudiced education, are afraid of sprights. I must, however, except the MAIDS of HONOUR, who have been fully convinced, by a famous court-chaplain, that there is no such place as hell.

I cannot, indeed, controvert the lawfulness of FREE-THINKING, because it hath been universally allowed, that thought is free. But, however, although it may afford a large field of matter, yet in my poor opinion it seems to contain very little either of wit or humour; because it hath not been ancient enough among us to furnish established authentic expressions, I mean such as must receive a sanction from the polite world, before their authority can be allowed; neither was the art of BLASPHEMY or FREE-THINKING invented by the court, or by persons of great quality, who, properly speaking, were patrons, rather than inventors of it; but first brought in by the fanatic faction, towards the end of their power, and, after the Restoration, carried to Whitehall by the converted *rumpers*,° with very good reason; because they knew that King Charles the Second, from a wrong education, occasioned by the troubles of his father, had time enough to observe that fanatic enthusiasm directly led to atheism,° which agreed with the dissolute inclinations of his youth; and, perhaps, these principles were farther cultivated in him by the French Huguenots, who have been often charged for spreading them among us. However, I cannot see where the necessity lies, of introducing new and foreign topics for conversation, while we have so plentiful a stock of our own growth.

I have likewise, for some reasons of equal weight, been very sparing in DOUBLES ENTENDRES; because they often put ladies upon affected constraints, and affected ignorance. In short, they break, or very much entangle, the thread of discourse; neither am I master of any rules to settle the disconcerted countenances of the females in such a juncture; I can, therefore, only allow *innuendoes* of this kind to be delivered in whispers, and only to young ladies under twenty, who, being in honour obliged to blush, it may produce a new subject for discourse.

Perhaps the critics may accuse me of a defect in my following system of POLITE CONVERSATION; that there is one great ornament of discourse, whereof I have not produced a single example; which, indeed, I purposely omitted for some reasons that I shall immediately offer; and, if those reasons will not satisfy the male part of my gentle readers, the defect may be applied in some manner by an *appendix* to the *second edition*; which *appendix* shall be printed by itself, and sold for *sixpence*, stitched, and with a marble cover, that my readers may have no occasion to complain of being defrauded. The defect I mean is, my not having inserted, into the body of my book, all the OATHS now most in fashion for embellishing discourse; especially since it could give no offence to the *clergy*, who are seldom or never admitted to these polite assemblies. And it must be allowed, that oaths, well chosen, are not only very useful expletives to matter,° but great ornaments of style.

What I shall here offer in my own defence upon this important article, will, I hope, be some extenuation of my fault.

First, I reasoned with myself, that a just collection of oaths, repeated as often as the fashion requires, must have enlarged this volume at least to double the bulk; whereby it would not only double the charge, but likewise make the volume less commodious for pocket carriage.

Secondly, I have been assured by some judicious friends, that themselves have known certain ladies to take offence (whether seriously or no) at too great a profusion of cursing and swearing, even when that kind of ornament was not improperly introduced; which, I confess, did startle me not a little; having never observed the like in the compass of my own several acquaintance, at least for twenty years past. However, I was forced to submit to wiser judgments than my own.

Thirdly, as this most useful treatise is calculated for all future times, I considered, in this maturity of my age, how great a variety of oaths I have heard since I began to study the world, and to know men and manners. And here I found it to be true what I have read in an ancient poet.

> For, now-a-days, men change their oaths,
> As often as they change their clothes.

In short, oaths are the children of fashion; they are in some sense almost annuals, like what I observed before of cant-words; and I myself can remember about forty different sets. The old stock oaths I am confident do not amount to above forty-five, or fifty at most; but the way of mingling and compounding them is almost as various as that of the alphabet.

Sir John Perrot° was the first man of quality whom I find upon record to have sworn by G[od]'s W[ound]s. He lived in the reign of Queen Elizabeth, and was supposed to have been a natural son of Henry the Eighth, who might also have probably been his instructor. This oath indeed still continues, and is a stock oath to this day; so do several others that have kept their natural simplicity. But, infinitely the greater number hath been so frequently changed and dislocated, that if the inventors were now alive, they could hardly understand them.

Upon these considerations I began to apprehend, that if I should insert all the oaths as are now current, my book would be out of vogue with the first change of fashion, and grow as useless as an old dictionary. Whereas, the case is quite otherwise with my collection of polite discourse; which, as I before observed, hath descended by tradition for at least an hundred years, without any change in the phraseology. I, therefore, determined with myself to leave out the whole system of swearing; because, both the male and female oaths are all perfectly well known and distinguished; new ones are easily learnt, and with a moderate share of discretion may be properly applied on every fit occasion. However, I must here, upon this article of swearing, most earnestly recommend to my readers, that they would please a little to study variety. For, it is the opinion of our most refined swearers, that the same oath or curse, cannot, consistent with true politeness, be repeated above nine times in the same company, by the same person, and at one sitting.

I am far from desiring, or expecting, that all the polite and ingenious speeches, contained in this work, should, in the general conversation between ladies and gentlemen, come in so quick and so close as I have here delivered them. By no means: on the contrary, they ought to be husbanded better, and spread much thinner. Nor, do I make the least question, but that, by a discreet thrifty management, they may serve for the entertainment of a whole year to any person who doth not make too long or too frequent visits in the same family. The flowers of wit, fancy, wisdom, humour, and politeness, scattered in this volume, amount to one thousand, seventy and four. Allowing then to every gentleman and lady thirty visiting families (not insisting upon fractions) there will want but a little of an hundred polite questions, answers, replies, rejoinders, repartees, and remarks, to be daily delivered fresh, in every company, for twelve solar months; and even this is a higher pitch of delicacy than the world insists on, or hath reason to expect. But, I am altogether for exalting this science to its utmost perfection.

It may be objected, that the publication of my book may, in a long course of time, prostitute this noble art to mean and vulgar people. But, I answer, that it is not so easily acquired as a few ignorant pretenders may imagine. A footman may swear; but he cannot swear like a lord. He can swear as often: but can he swear with equal delicacy, propriety, and judgment? No, certainly, unless he be a lad of superior parts, of good memory, a diligent observer; one who hath a skilful ear, some knowledge in music, and an exact taste, which hardly falls to the share of one in a thousand among that fraternity, in as high favour as they now stand with their ladies; neither perhaps hath one footman in six so fine a genius as to relish and apply those exalted sentences comprised in this volume, which I offer to the world. It is true, I cannot see that the same ill consequences would follow from the waiting-woman, who, if she hath been bred to read romances, may have some small subaltern, or second-hand politeness; and if she constantly attends the tea, and be a good listener, may, in some years, make a tolerable figure, which will serve, perhaps, to draw in the young chaplain or the old steward. But, alas! after all, how can she acquire those hundreds of graces and motions, and airs, the whole military management of the fan, the contortions of every muscular motion in the face, the risings and fallings, the quickness and slackness of the voice, with the several tones and cadences; the proper junctures of smiling and frowning, how often and how loud to laugh, when to gibe and when to flout, with all the other branches of doctrine and discipline above recited? I am, therefore, not under the least apprehension that this art will be ever in danger of falling into common hands, which requires so much time, study, practice, and genius, before it arrives to perfection;

and, therefore, I must repeat my proposal for erecting public schools, provided with the best and ablest masters and mistresses, at the charge of the nation.

I have drawn this work into the form of a dialogue, after the pattern of other famous writers in history, law, politics, and most other arts and sciences, and I hope it will have the same success. For, who can contest it to be of greater consequence to the happiness of these kingdoms, than all human *knowledge* put together? Dialogue is held the best method of inculcating any part of knowledge; and, as I am confident, that public schools will soon be founded for teaching wit and politeness, after my scheme, to young people of quality and fortune, so I have determined next sessions to deliver a petition to the House of Lords for an Act of Parliament, to establish my book as the standard *grammar* in all the principal cities of both kingdoms where this art is to be taught, by able masters, who are to be approved and recommended by me; which is no more than Lilly obtained° only for teaching words in a language wholly useless. Neither shall I be so far wanting to myself, as not to desire a patent granted of course to all useful projectors; I mean, that I may have the sole profit of giving a licence to every school to read my *grammar* for fourteen years.

The reader cannot but observe what pains I have been at in polishing the style of my book to the greatest exactness; nor have I been less diligent in refining the orthography, by spelling the words in the very same manner that they are pronounced, wherein I follow the chief patterns of politeness, at court, at levees, at assemblies, at playhouses, at the prime visiting-places, by young templars,° and by gentlemen-commoners of both universities, who have lived at least a twelvemonth in town, and kept the best company. Of these spellings the public will meet with many examples in the following book; for instance, *can't*,° *han't*, *sha'nt, didn't, coodn't, woodn't, isn't, e'n't*, with many more; besides several words which scholars pretend are derived from Greek and Latin, but now pared into a polite sound by ladies, officers of the army, courtiers and templars, such as *jommetry* for *geometry*, *verdi* for *verdict*, *lard* for *lord*, *larnen* for *learning*; together with some abbreviations exquisitely refined; as, *pozz* for *positive*; *mobb* for *mobile*; *phizz* for *physiognomy*; *rep* for *reputation*; *plenipo* for *plenipotentiary*; *incog* for *incognito*; *hypps*, or *hippo*, for *hypochondriacs*; *bam* for *bamboozle*; and *bamboozle* for *God knows what*; whereby much time is saved, and the high road to conversation cut short by many a mile.

I have, as it will be apparent, laboured very much, and I hope with felicity enough, to make every character in the dialogue agreeable with itself; to a degree that whenever any judicious person shall read my book aloud, for the entertainment and instruction of a select company, he need not so much as name the particular speakers; because all the persons, throughout the several subjects of conversation, strictly observe a different manner, peculiar to their characters, which are of different kinds. But this I leave entirely to the prudent and impartial reader's discernment.

Perhaps the very manner of introducing the several points of wit and humour may not be less entertaining and instructing than the matter itself. In the latter I can pretend to little merit; because it entirely depends upon memory and the happiness of having kept polite company. But, the art of contriving that those speeches should be introduced naturally, as the most proper sentiments to be delivered upon so great a variety of subjects, I take to be a talent somewhat uncommon, and a labour that few people could hope to succeed in, unless they had a genius particularly turned that way, added to a sincere disinterested love of the public.

Although every curious question, smart answer, and witty reply be little known to many people; yet, there is not one single sentence in the whole collection for which I cannot bring most authentic vouchers whenever I shall be called; and even for some expressions which to a few nicer ears may perhaps appear somewhat gross, I can produce the stamp of authority from courts, chocolate-houses, theatres, assemblies, drawing-rooms, levees, card-meetings, balls, and masquerades, from persons of both sexes, and of the highest titles next to royal. However, to say the truth, I have been very sparing in my quotations of such sentiments that seem to be over free; because, when I began my collection, such kind of converse was almost in its infancy, till it was taken into the protection of my honoured patronesses at court, by whose countenance and sanction it hath become a choice flower in the nosegay of wit and politeness.

Some will perhaps object, that when I bring my company to dinner, I mention too great a variety of dishes, not always consistent with the art of cookery, or proper for the season of the year, and part of the first course mingled with the second, besides a failure in politeness, by introducing a black pudding to a lord's table, and at a great entertainment. But, if I had omitted the black pudding, I desire to know what would have become of that exquisite reason given by Miss Notable for not eating it; the world perhaps might have lost it for ever, and I should have been justly answerable for having left it out of my collection. I therefore cannot but hope, that such hypercritical readers will please to consider, my business was to make so full and complete a body of refined sayings, as compact as I could; only taking care to produce them in the most natural and probable manner, in order to allure my readers into the very substance and marrow of this most admirable and necessary art.

I am heartily sorry, and was much disappointed to find, that so universal and polite an entertainment as cards, hath hitherto contributed very little to the enlargement of my work. I have sat by many hundred times with the utmost vigilance, and my table-book ready, without being able in eight hours to gather matter for one single phrase in my book. But this, I think, may be easily accounted for by the turbulence and jostling of passions upon the various and surprising turns, incidents, revolutions, and events of good and evil fortune, that arrive in the course of a long evening at play; the mind being wholly taken up, and the consequence of non-attention so fatal. Play is supported upon the two great pillars of deliberation and action. The terms of art are few, prescribed by law and custom; no time allowed for digressions or trials of wit. Quadrille in particular bears some resemblance to a state of nature, which, we are told, is a state of war, wherein every woman is against every woman: the unions short, inconstant, and soon broke; the league made this minute without knowing the ally, and dissolved in the next. Thus, at the game of quadrille, female brains are always employed in stratagem, or their hands in action.

Neither can I find that our art hath gained much by the happy revival of masquerading° among us; the whole dialogue in these meetings being summed up in one sprightly (I confess, but) single question, and as sprightly an answer. 'Do you know me?' 'Yes, I do.' And, 'Do you know me?' 'Yes, I do.' For this reason I did not think it proper to give my readers the trouble of introducing a masquerade, merely for the sake of a single question, and a single answer. Especially, when to perform this in a proper manner, I must have brought in a hundred persons together, of both sexes, dressed in fantastic habits for one minute, and dismissed them the next. Neither is it reasonable to conceive, that our science can be much improved by masquerades; where the wit of both sexes is altogether taken up in contriving singular and humoursome disguises; and their thoughts entirely employed in bringing intrigues and assignations of gallantry to a happy conclusion.

The judicious reader will readily discover, that I make Miss Notable my heroine, and Mr. Thomas Neverout my hero. I have laboured both their characters with my utmost ability. It is into their mouths that I have put the liveliest questions, answers, repartees, and rejoinders; because my design was to propose them both as patterns for all young bachelors and single ladies to copy after. By which I hope very soon to see polite conversation flourish between both sexes, in a more consummate degree of perfection than these kingdoms have yet ever known.

I have drawn some lines of Sir John Linger's character, the Derbyshire knight, on purpose to place it in counterview or contrast with that of the other company; wherein I can assure the reader, that I intended not the least reflection upon Derbyshire, the place of my nativity. But, my intention was only to show the misfortune of those persons, who have the disadvantage to be bred out of the circle of politeness; whereof I take the present limits to extend no further than London, and ten miles round; although others are pleased to confine it within the bills of mortality. If you compare the discourses of my gentlemen and ladies with those of Sir John, you will hardly conceive him to have been bred in the same climate, or under the same laws, language, religion, or government. And, accordingly, I have introduced him speaking in his own rude dialect, for no other reason than to teach my scholars how to avoid it.

The curious reader will observe, that where conversation appears in danger to flag, which, in some places, I have artfully contrived, I took care to invent some sudden question, or turn of wit, to revive it; such as these that follow. 'What! I think here's a silent meeting!'° 'Come, madam, a penny for your thought';° with several others of the like sort.

I have rejected all provincial or country turns of wit and fancy, because I am acquainted with a very few; but, indeed, chiefly because I found them so much inferior to those at court, especially among the gentlemen-ushers, the ladies of the bedchamber, and the maids of honour; I must also add, the hither end of our noble metropolis.

When this happy art of polite conversing shall be thoroughly improved, good company will be no longer pestered with dull, dry, tedious story-tellers, or brangling disputers. For, a right scholar, of either sex, in our science, will perpetually interrupt them with some sudden surprising piece of wit, that shall engage all the company in a loud laugh, and, if after a pause, the grave companion resumes his thread in the following manner 'Well, but to go on with my story', new interruptions come from the left and right, till he is forced to give over.

I have likewise made some few essays toward SELLING OF BARGAINS, as well for instructing those who delight in that accomplishment, as in compliance with my female friends at court. However, I have transgressed a little in this point, by doing it in a manner somewhat more reserved than as it is now practised at St. James's.° At the same time, I can hardly allow this accomplishment to pass properly for a branch of that perfect polite conversation, which makes the constituent subject of my treatise; and for this I have already given my reasons. I have likewise, for further caution, left a blank in the critical point of each *bargain*, which the sagacious reader may fill up in his own mind.

As to myself, I am proud to own, that except some smattering in the French, I am what the pedants and scholars call, a man wholly illiterate; that is to say, unlearned. But, as to my own language, I shall not readily yield to many persons: I have read most of the plays, and all the miscellany poems that have been published for twenty years past. I have read Mr. Thomas Brown's° *Works* entire, and had the honour to be his intimate friend, who was universally allowed to be the greatest genius of his age. Upon what foot I stand with the present chief reigning wits, their verses recommendatory, which they have commanded me to prefix before my book, will be more than a thousand witnesses. I am, and have been, likewise, particularly acquainted with Mr. Charles Gildon, Mr. Ward, Mr. Dennis, that admirable critic and poet, and several others. Each of these eminent persons (I mean, those who are still alive) have done me the honour to read this production five times over with the strictest eye of friendly severity, and proposed some, although very few, amendments, which I gratefully accepted, and do here publicly return my acknowledgment for so singular a favour.

And I cannot conceal, without ingratitude, the great assistance I have received from those two illustrious writers, Mr. Ozell and Captain Stevens. These, and some others, of distinguished eminence, in whose company I have passed so many agreeable hours, as they have been the great refiners of our language, so it hath been my chief ambition to imitate them. Let the Popes, the Gays, the Arbuthnots, the Youngs, and the rest of that snarling brood, burst with envy at the praises we receive from the court and kingdom.

But to return from this digression.

The reader will find that the following collection of polite expressions will easily incorporate with all subjects of genteel and fashionable life. Those, which are proper for morning-tea, will be equally useful at the same entertainment in the afternoon, even in the same company, only by shifting the several questions, answers, and replies, into different hands; and such as are adapted to meals will indifferently serve for dinners or suppers, only distinguishing between day-light and candle-light. By this method no diligent person, of a tolerable memory, can ever be at a loss.

It hath been my constant opinion, that every man who is intrusted by nature with any useful talent of the mind, is bound by all the ties of honour and that justice which we all owe our country, to propose to himself some one illustrious action to be performed in his life for the public emolument. And I freely confess that so grand, so important an enterprise as I have undertaken and executed to the best of my power, well deserved a much abler hand, as well as a liberal encouragement from the Crown. However, I am bound so far to acquit myself as to declare, that I have often and most earnestly entreated several of my above-named friends, universally allowed to be of the first rank in wit and politeness, that they would undertake a work so honourable to themselves, and so beneficial to the kingdom; but so great was their modesty that they all thought fit to excuse themselves, and impose the task on me; yet in so obliging a manner, and attended with such compliments on my poor qualifications, that I dare not repeat. And, at last, their entreaties, or rather their commands, added to that inviolable love I bear to the land of my nativity, prevailed upon me to engage in so bold an attempt.

I may venture to affirm, without the least violation of modesty, that there is no man, now alive, who hath, by many degrees, so just pretensions as myself, to the highest encouragement from the CROWN, the PARLIAMENT, and the MINISTRY, towards bringing this work to its due perfection. I have been assured that several great heroes of antiquity were worshipped as gods, upon the merit of having civilized a fierce and barbarous people. It is manifest I could have no other intentions; and I dare appeal to my very enemies, if such a treatise as mine had been published some years ago, and with as much success as I am confident this will meet, I mean, by turning the thoughts of the whole nobility and gentry to the study and practice of polite conversation; whether such mean stupid writers, as the *Craftsman* and his abettors,° could have been able to corrupt the principles of so many hundred thousand subjects, as, to the shame and grief of every whiggish, loyal, true protestant heart, it is too manifest they have done. For, I desire the honest judicious reader to make one remark, that after I have exhausted the whole *in sickly pay-dey** (if I may so call it) of politeness and refinement, and faithfully digested it in the following dialogues, there cannot be found one expression relating to politics; that the MINISTRY is never mentioned, nor the word KING, above twice or thrice, and then only to the honour of Majesty; so very cautious were our wiser ancestors in forming rules for conversation, as never to give offence to crowned heads, nor interfere with party disputes in the state. And indeed, although there seem to be a close resemblance between the two words *politeness* and *politics*, yet no ideas are more inconsistent in their natures. However, to avoid all appearance of

---

* This word is spelt by Latinists, *Encyclopædia*; but the judicious author wisely prefers the polite reading before the pedantic.

disaffection, I have taken care to enforce loyalty by an invincible argument, drawn from the very fountain of this noble science, in the following short terms that ought to be writ in gold, 'MUST is for the King'° which uncontrollable maxim° I took particular care of introducing in the first page of my book; thereby to instil only the best Protestant loyal notions into the minds of my readers. Neither is it merely my own private opinion that politeness is the firmest foundation upon which loyalty can be supported. For, thus happily sings the never-to-be-too-much-admired Lord H——,*° in his truly sublime poem, called *Loyalty Defined*:

> Who's not polite, for the Pretender is;
> A Jacobite, I know him by his phiz.

In the like manner, the divine Mr. Tibbalds, or Theobalds, in one of his birthday poems.

> I an no schollard; but I am polite:
> Therefore be sure I am no Jacobite.

Hear likewise, to the same purpose, that great master of the whole poetic choir, our most illustrious laureat Mr. Colley Cibber.

> Who in his talk can't speak a polite thing,
> Will never loyal be to George our King.

I could produce many more shining passages out of our principal poets, of both sexes, to confirm this momentous truth. From whence, I think, it may be fairly concluded that whoever can most contribute towards propagating the science contained in the following sheets, through the kingdoms of Great Britain and Ireland, may justly demand all the favour that the wisest court, and most judicious senate, are able to confer on the most deserving subject. I leave the application to my readers.

This is the work which I have been so hardy to attempt, and without the least mercenary view. Neither do I doubt of succeeding to my full wish, except among the TORIES and their abettors; who being all *Jacobites*, and, consequently *Papists* in their hearts, from a want of true taste, or by strong affectation, may perhaps resolve not to read my book; choosing rather to deny themselves the pleasure and honour of shining in polite company among the principal geniuses of both sexes throughout the kingdom, than adorn their minds with this noble art; and probably apprehending (as, I confess, nothing is more likely to happen) that a true spirit of loyalty to the Protestant succession should steal in along with it.

* It is erroneously printed in the London Edition, Mr. Stephen Duck.

If my favourable and gentle readers could possibly conceive the perpetual watchings, the numberless toils, the frequent risings in the night, to set down several ingenious sentences, that I suddenly or accidentally recollected; and which, without my utmost vigilance, had been irrecoverably lost for ever; if they would consider with what incredible diligence I daily and nightly attended at those houses, where persons of both sexes, and of the most distinguished merit, used to meet and display their talents; with what attention I listened to all their discourses, the better to retain them in my memory; and then, at proper seasons, withdrew unobserved, to enter them in my table-book, while the company little suspected what a noble work I had then in embryo: I say, if all this were known to the world, I think it would be no great presumption in me to expect, at a proper juncture, the public thanks of both Houses of Parliament, for the service and honour I have done to the whole nation by my single pen.

Although I have never been once charged with the least tincture of vanity, the reader will, I hope, give me leave to put an easy question: What is become of all the King of Sweden's victories? Where are the fruits of them at this day? Or, of what benefit will they be to posterity? Were not many of his greatest actions owing, at least in part, to Fortune? Were not all of them owing to the valour of his troops, as much as to his own conduct? Could he have conquered the Polish King, or the Czar of Muscovy, with his single arm? Far be it from me to envy or lessen the fame he hath acquired; but, at the same time, I will venture to say, without breach of modesty, that I, who have alone with this right hand subdued barbarism, rudeness, and rusticity; who have established and fixed for ever the whole system of all true politeness and refinement in conversation, should think myself most inhumanly treated by my countrymen, and would accordingly resent it as the highest indignity to be put upon the level, in point of fame, in after-ages, with Charles the Twelfth, late King of Sweden.

And yet, so incurable is the love of detraction, perhaps beyond what the charitable reader will easily believe, that I have been assured by more than one credible person, how some of my enemies have industriously whispered about, that one Isaac Newton, an instrument-maker, formerly living near Leicester-Fields, and afterwards a workman in the Mint° at the Tower, might possibly pretend to vie with me for fame in future times. The man it seems was knighted for making sun-dials better than others of his trade, and was thought to be a conjurer, because he knew how to draw lines and circles upon a slate, which nobody could understand. But, adieu to all noble attempts for endless renown, if the ghost of an obscure mechanic shall be raised up to enter into competition with me, only for his skill in making pot-hooks and hangers° with a pencil, which many thousand accomplished gentlemen and ladies can perform as well with a pen and ink upon a piece of paper, and, in a manner, as little intelligible as those of Sir Isaac.

My most ingenious friend already mentioned, Mr. Colley Cibber, who doth so much honour to the laurel crown he deservedly wears (as he hath often done to many imperial diadems placed on his head) was pleased to tell me, that if my treatise were shaped into a comedy, the representation, performed to advantage on our theatre, might very much contribute to the spreading of polite conversation among all persons of distinction through the whole kingdom. I own, the thought was ingenious, and my friend's intention good. But I cannot agree to his proposal: for Mr. Cibber himself allowed, that the subjects handled in my work, being so numerous and extensive, it would be absolutely impossible for one, two, or even six comedies to contain them. From whence it will follow that many admirable and essential rules for polite conversation must be omitted. And here let me do justice to my friend Mr. Tibbalds, who plainly confessed before Mr. Cibber himself, that such a project, as it would be a great diminution to my honour, so it would intolerably mangle my scheme and thereby destroy the principal end at which I aimed, to form a complete body or system of this most useful science in all its parts. And therefore Mr. Tibbalds, whose judgment was never disputed, chose rather to fall in with my proposal mentioned before, of erecting public schools and seminaries all over the kingdom, to instruct the young people of both sexes in this art, according to my rules, and in the method that I have laid down.

I shall conclude this long, but necessary introduction, with a request, or indeed rather, a just and reasonable demand from all lords, ladies, and gentlemen, that while they are entertaining and improving each other with those polite questions, answers, repartees, replies, and rejoinders, which I have with infinite labour, and close application, during the space of thirty six years, been collecting for their service and improvement, they shall, as an instance of gratitude, on every proper occasion, quote my name, after this or the like manner: 'Madam, as our Master Wagstaff says', 'My Lord, as our friend Wagstaff has it'. I do likewise expect that all my pupils shall drink my Health every day at dinner and supper during my life; and that they, or their posterity, shall continue the same ceremony to my *not inglorious memory*, after my decease, for ever.

DIALOGUE II

LORD SMART *and the former company at three o'clock coming to dine.*

[*After salutations.*]

Lord Smart. I'm sorry I was not at home this morning when you all did us the honour to call here. But I went to the levee to-day.

Ld. Sparkish. Oh! my lord, I'm sure the loss was ours.

Lady Smart. Gentlemen and ladies, you are come into a sad dirty house; I am sorry for it, but we have had our hands in mortar.°

Ld. Sparkish. Oh! madam; your ladyship is pleased to say so, but I never saw anything so clean and so fine; I profess, it is a perfect paradise.

Lady Smart. My lord, your lordship is always very obliging.

Ld. Sparkish. Pray, madam, whose picture is that?

Lady Smart. Why, my lord, it was drawn for me.

Ld. Sparkish. I'll swear, the painter did not flatter your ladyship.

Col. My lord, the day is finely cleared up.

Ld. Smart. Ay, Colonel; 'tis a pity that fair weather should ever do any harm.° [*To* NEVEROUT.] Why, Tom, you are high in the mode.

Neverout. My lord, it is better to be out of the world, than out of the fashion.°

Ld. Smart. But, Tom, I hear, you and miss are always quarrelling; I fear, it is your fault; for I can assure you, she is very good humour'd.

Neverout. Ay, my lord; so is the devil when he's pleased.°

Ld. Smart. Miss, what do you think of my friend Tom?

Miss. My lord, I think, he is not the wisest man in the world; and truly, he's sometimes very rude.

Ld. Sparkish. That may be true; but, yet, he that hangs Tom for a fool, may find a knave in the halter.

Miss. Well, however, I wish he were hanged, if it were only to try.

Neverout. Well, miss, if I must be hanged, I won't go far to choose my gallows; it shall be about your fair neck.

Miss. I'll see your nose cheese first, and the dogs eating it.° But, my lord, Mr. Neverout's wit begins to run low, for I vow, he said this before. Pray, Colonel, give him a pinch, and I'll do as much for you.

Ld. Sparkish. My Lady Smart, your ladyship has a very fine scarf.

Lady Smart. Yes, my lord; it will make a flaming figure in a country church.°

[Footman *comes in.*]

Footman. Madam, dinner's upon the table.

Col. Faith, I'm glad of it; my belly began to cry cupboard.°

Neverout. I wish I may never hear worse news.

Miss. What! Mr. Neverout, you are in great haste; I believe, your belly thinks your throat's cut.°

Neverout. No, faith, miss; three meals a day, and a good supper at night, will serve my turn.

Miss. To say the truth, I'm hungry.

Neverout. And I'm angry, so let us both go fight.°

[*They go in to dinner, and after the usual compliments, take their seats.*]

Lady Smart. Ladies and gentlemen, will you eat any oysters before dinner?

Col. With all my heart. [*Takes an oyster.*] He was a bold man, that first eat an oyster.

Lady Smart. They say, oysters are a cruel meat, because we eat them alive. Then they are an uncharitable meat, for we leave nothing to the poor; and they are an ungodly meat, because we never say grace to them.

Neverout. Faith, that's as well said, as if I had said it myself.

Lady Smart. Well, we are well set, if we be but as well served. Come, Colonel, handle your arms; shall I help you to some beef?

Col. If your ladyship pleases; and, pray, don't cut like a mother-in-law, but send me a large slice; for I love to lay a good foundation. I vow, 'tis a noble sir-loin.

Neverout. Ay; here's cut and come again.

Miss. But, pray, why is it call'd a sir-loin?

Ld. Smart. Why, you must know, that our King James the First, who loved good eating, being invited to dinner by one of his nobles, and seeing a large loin of beef at his table, he drew out his sword, and in a frolic knighted it.° Few people know the secret of this.

Ld. Sparkish. Beef is man's meat, my lord.

Ld. Smart. But, my lord, I say beef is the king of meat.

Miss. Pray, what have I done, that I must not have a plate?

Lady Smart. [*To* LADY ANSW.] What will your ladyship please to eat?

Lady Answ. Pray, madam, help yourself.

Col. They say, eating and scratching wants but a beginning. If you will give me leave, I'll help myself to a slice of this shoulder of veal.

Lady Smart. Colonel, you can't do a kinder thing. Well, you are all heartily welcome, as I may say.

Col. They say, there are thirty and two good bits in a shoulder of veal.

Lady Smart. Ay, colonel; thirty bad bits, and two good ones; you see, I understand you; but I hope you have got one of the two good ones.

Neverout. Colonel, I'll be of your mess.

Col. Then, pray, Tom, carve for yourself. They say, two hands in a dish, and one in a purse; Hah, said I well, Tom?

Neverout. Colonel, you spoke like an oracle.

Miss. [*To* LADY ANSW.] Madam, will your ladyship help me to some fish?

Ld. Smart [*To* NEVEROUT.] Tom, they say fish should swim thrice.

Neverout. How is that, my lord?

Ld. Smart. Why, Tom, first it should swim in the sea, (do you mind me?) then it should swim in butter; and at last, sirrah, it should swim in good claret. I think, I have made it out.

Footman. [*To* LD. SMART.] My lord, Sir John Linger is coming up.

Ld. Smart. God so! I invited him to dinner with me today, and forgot it! Well, desire him to walk in.

[SIR JOHN LINGER *comes in.*]

Sir John. What! are you at it? Why, then, I'll be gone.

Lady Smart. Sir John, I beg you will sit down. Come, the more the merrier.

Sir John. Ay; but the fewer the better cheer.

Lady Smart. Well, I am the worst in the world at making apologies; it was my lord's fault. I doubt you must kiss the hare's foot.°

Sir John. I see you are fast by the teeth.

Col. Faith, Sir John, we are killing that, that would kill us.

Ld. Sparkish. You see, Sir John, we are upon a business of life and death. Come, will you do as we do? You are come in pudden-time.°

Sir John. Ay; this you would be doing if I were dead. What! you keep court-hours I see:° I'll be going, and get a bit of meat at my inn.

Lady Smart. Why, we won't eat you, Sir John.

Sir John. It is my own fault; but I was kept by a fellow who bought some Derbyshire oxen from me.

Neverout. You see, Sir John, we stayed for you, as one horse does for another.

Lady Smart. My lord, will you help Sir John to some beef? Lady Answerall, pray, eat, you see your dinner. I am sure if we had known we should have such good company, we should have been better provided;

but you must take the will for the deed. I'm afraid you are invited to your loss.

Col. And, pray, Sir John, how do you like the town? You have been absent a long time.

Sir John. Why, I find, little London stands just where it did when I left it last.

Neverout. What do you think of Hanover Square? Why, Sir John, London is gone out of town° since you saw it.

Lady Smart. Sir John, I can only say, you are heartily welcome; and I wish I had something better for you.

Col. Here's no salt; cuckolds will run away with the meat.

Ld. Smart. Pray, edge a little, to make room for Sir John. Sir John, fall to, you know half an hour is soon lost at dinner.

Sir John. I protest I can't eat a bit, for I took share of a beefsteak and two mugs of ale with my chapman,° besides a tankard of March beer,° as soon as I got out of bed.

Lady Answ. Not fresh and fasting,° I hope?

Sir John. Yes, faith, madam; I always wash my kettle before I put the meat in it.

Lady Smart. Poh! Sir John; you have seen nine houses since you eat last: Come, you have kept a corner of your stomach for a bit of venison-pasty.

Sir John Well, I'll try what I can do, when it comes up.

Lady Answ. Come, Sir John, you may go further, and fare worse.

Miss. [*To* NEVEROUT.] Pray, Mr. Neverout, will you please to send me a piece of tongue?

Neverout. By no means, madam; one tongue's enough for a woman.

Col. Miss, here's a tongue that never told a lie.

Miss. That was, because it could not speak. Why, colonel, I never told a lie in my life.

Neverout. I appeal to all the company, whether that be not the greatest lie that ever was told.

Col. [*To* NEVEROUT.] Pr'ythee, Tom, send me the two legs and rump and liver of that pigeon; for, you must know, I love what nobody else loves.

Neverout. But what if any of the ladies should long?° Well, here take it, and the devil do you good with it.

Lady Answ. Well; this eating and drinking takes away a body's stomach.

Neverout. I am sure I have lost mine.

Miss. What! the bottom of it, I suppose?

Neverout. No, really, miss; I have quite lost it.

Miss. I should be sorry a poor body had found it.

Lady Smart. But, Sir John, we hear you are married since we saw you last. What! you have stolen a wedding it seems.

Sir John. Well; one can't do a foolish thing once in one's life, but one must hear of it a hundred times.

Col. And pray, Sir John, how does your lady unknown?

Sir John. My wife's well, Colonel; and at your service in a civil way.°
Ha, ha.   [*He laughs.*]

Miss. Pray, Sir John, is your lady tall or short?

Sir John. Why, miss, I thank God, she is a little evil.

Ld. Sparkish. Come, give me a glass of claret.

[Footman *fills him a bumper.*]

Ld. Sparkish. Why do you fill so much?

Neverout. My lord, he fills as he loves you.

Lady Smart. Miss, shall I send you some cucumber?

Miss. Madam, I dare not touch it; for they say cucumbers are cold in the third degree.°

Lady Smart. Mr. Neverout, do you love pudden?

Neverout. Madam, I'm like all fools, I love every thing that is good; but the proof of the pudden is in the eating.

Col. Sir John, I hear you are a great walker when you are at home.

Sir John. No, faith, colonel; I always love to walk with a horse in my hand. But I have had devilish bad luck in horse-flesh of late.

Ld. Smart. Why then, Sir John, you must kiss a parson's wife.

Lady Smart. They say, Sir John, that your lady has a great deal of wit.

Sir John. Madam, she can make a pudden; and has just wit enough to know her husband's breeches from another man's.

Ld. Smart. My Lord Sparkish, I have some excellent cider, will you please to taste it?

Ld. Sparkish. My lord, I should like it well enough, if it were not so treacherous.

Ld. Smart. Pray, my lord, how is it treacherous?

Ld. Sparkish. Because it smiles in my face, and cuts my throat.
                                                        [*Here a loud laugh.*]

Miss. Odd-so, madam; your knives are very sharp, for I have cut my finger.

Lady Smart. I'm sorry for it; pray, which finger? (God bless the mark!)

Miss. Why, this finger: no, 'tis this: I vow I can't find which it is.

Neverout. Ay; the fox had a wound, and he could not tell where, &c. Bring some water to throw in her face.

Miss. Pray, Mr. Neverout, did you ever draw a sword in anger? I warrant you would faint at the sight of your own blood.

Lady Smart. Mr. Neverout, shall I send you some veal?

Neverout. No, madam; I don't love it.

Miss. Then pray for them that do. I desire your ladyship will send me a bit.

Ld. Smart. Tom, my service to you.°

Neverout. My lord, this moment I did myself the honour to drink to your lordship.

Ld. Smart. Why then that's Hertfordshire kindness.°

Neverout. Faith, my lord, I pledged myself, for I drank twice together without thinking.

Ld. Sparkish. Why then, Colonel, my humble service to you.

Neverout. Pray, my lord, don't make a bridge of my nose.°

Ld. Sparkish. Well, a glass of this wine is as comfortable as matrimony to an old maid.

Col. Sir John, I design one of these days to come and beat up your quarters in Derbyshire.

Sir John. Faith, colonel, come and welcome; and stay away, and heartily welcome. But you were born within the sound of Bow bell,° and don't care to stir so far from London.

Miss. Pray, colonel, send me some fritters.

[COLONEL *takes them out with his hand.*]

Col. Here, miss; they say fingers were made before forks, and hands before knives.

Lady Smart. Methinks this pudden is too much boil'd.

Lady Answ. Oh, madam, they say a pudden is poison when it's too much boil'd.

Neverout. Miss, shall I help you to a pigeon? Here's a pigeon so finely roasted, it cries, Come eat me.

Miss. No, sir; I thank you.

Neverout. Why, then you may choose.°

Miss. I have chosen already.

Neverout. Well, you may be worse offer'd, before you are twice married.   [*The* COLONEL *fills a large plate of soup.*]

Ld. Smart. Why, Colonel, you don't mean to eat all that soup?

Col. O my lord, this is my sick dish; when I am well, I have a bigger.

Miss. [*To* COL.] Sup, Simon; good broth.

Neverout. This seems to be a good pullet.

Miss. I warrant, Mr. Neverout knows what's good for himself.

Ld. Sparkish. Tom, I shan't take your word for it; help me to a wing.

[NEVEROUT *tries to cut off a wing.*]

Neverout. Egad, I can't hit the joint.

Ld. Sparkish. Why then, think of a cuckold.°

Neverout. Oh! now I have nick'd it.   [*Gives it* LD. SPARKISH.]

Ld. Sparkish. Why, a man may eat this, though his wife lay a-dying.

Col. Pray, friend, give me a glass of small-beer, if it be good.

Ld. Smart. Why, colonel, they say, there is no such thing as good small-beer, good brown bread, or a good old woman.

Lady Smart. [*To* LADY ANSW.] Madam, I beg your ladyship's pardon; I did not see you when I was cutting that bit.

Lady Answ. Oh, madam; after you is good manners.

Lady Smart. Lord! here's a hair in the sauce.

Ld. Sparkish. Then, Madam, set the hounds after it.

Neverout. Pray colonel, help me, however, to some of that same sauce.

Col. Come; I think you are more sauce than pig.

Ld. Smart. Sir John, cheer up; my service to you. Well, what do you think of the world to come?

Sir John. Truly, my lord, I think of it as little as I can.

Lady Smart. [*Putting a skewer on a plate.*] Here, take this skewer, and carry it down to the cook, to dress it for her own dinner.

Neverout. I beg your ladyship's pardon; but this small-beer is dead.

Lady Smart. Why, then, let it be buried.

Col. This is admirable black-pudden. Miss, shall I carve you some? I can just carve pudden, and that's all; I should never make a good chaplain; I am the worst carver in the world.

Miss. No, thank ye, colonel; for they say, those that eat black-pudden will dream of the devil.

Ld. Smart. O, here comes the venison pasty. Here, take the soup away.

Ld. Smart. [*He cuts it up, and tastes the venison.*] 'Sbuds! this venison is musty.°   [NEVEROUT *eats a piece, and burns his mouth.*]

Ld. Smart. What's the matter Tom? You have tears in your eyes, I think. What dost cry for, man?

Neverout. My lord, I was just thinking of my poor grandmother; she died just this very day seven years.

[MISS *takes a bit, and burns her mouth.*]

Neverout. And pray miss, why do you cry too?

Miss. Because you were not hang'd the day your grandmother died.

Ld. Smart. I'd have given forty pounds, miss, to have said that.

Col. Egad, I think the more I eat, the hungrier I am.

Ld. Sparkish. Why, colonel, they say one shoulder of mutton drives down another.

Neverout. Egad, if I were to fast for my life, I would take a good breakfast in the morning, a good dinner at noon, and a good supper at night.

Ld. Sparkish. My lord, this venison is plaguily pepper'd; your cook has a heavy hand.

Ld. Smart. My lord, I hope you are pepper-proof.° Come, here's a health to the founders.°

Lady Smart. Ay; and to the confounders too.

Ld. Smart. Lady Answerall, does not your ladyship love venison?

Lady Answ. No, my lord, I can't endure it in my sight, therefore please to send me a good piece of meat and crust.

Ld. Sparkish. [*Drinks to* NEVEROUT.] Come, Tom; not always to my friends, but once to you.

Neverout. [*Drinks to* LADY SMART.] Come, madam; here's a health to our friends, and hang the rest of our kin.

Lady Smart. [*To* LADY ANSW.] Madam, will your ladyship have any of this hare?

Lady Answ. No, madam; they say, 'tis melancholy meat.

Lady Smart. Then, madam, shall I send you the brains? I beg your ladyship's pardon; for they say, 'tis not good manners to offer brains.

Lady Answ. No, madam; for perhaps it will make me harebrain'd.

Neverout. Miss, I must tell you one thing.

Miss. [*With a glass in her hand.*] Hold your tongue, Mr. Neverout; don't speak in my tip.°

Col. Well, he was an ingenious man, that first found out eating and drinking.

Ld. Sparkish. Of all vittles, drink digests the quickest. Give me a glass of wine.

Neverout. My lord, your wine is too strong.

Ld. Smart. Ay, Tom; as much as you are too good.

Miss. This almond-pudden was pure good; but it is grown quite cold.

Neverout. So much the better, miss; cold pudden will settle your love.

Miss. Pray, Mr. Neverout, are you going to take a voyage?

Neverout. Why do you ask, miss?

Miss. Because you have laid in so much beef.

Sir John. You two have eat up the whole pudden betwixt you.

Miss. Sir John, here's a little bit left; will you please to have it?

Sir John. No, thankee; I don't love to make a fool of my mouth.

Col. [*Calling to the* butler.] John, is your small-beer good?

Butler. An please your honour, my lord and lady like it; I think it is good.

Col. Why then John, d'ye see? if you are sure your small-beer is good, d'ye mark, then, give me a glass of wine.					[*All laugh.*]

Ld. Smart. Sir John, how does your neighbour Gatherall of the Peak? I hear, he has lately made a purchase.°

Sir John. Oh, Dick Gatherall knows how to butter his bread, as well as any man in Derbyshire.

Ld. Smart. Why, he used to go very fine when he was here in town.

Sir John. Ay; and it became him as a saddle becomes a sow.

Col. I know his lady, and I think she's a very good woman.

Sir John. Faith, she has more goodness in her little finger than he has in his whole body.					[COLONEL *tasting the wine.*]

Ld. Smart. Well, colonel, how do you like that wine?

Col. This wine should be eaten; 'tis too good to be drank.

Ld. Smart. I'm very glad you like it; and pray don't spare it.

Col. No, my lord; I'll never starve in a cook's shop.

Ld. Smart. And pray, Sir John, what do you say to my wine?

Sir John. I'll take another glass first; second thoughts are best.

Ld. Sparkish. Pray, Lady Smart, you sit near that ham; will you please to send me a bit?

Lady Smart. With all my heart. [*She sends him a piece.*] Pray, my lord, how do you like it?

Ld. Sparkish. I think it is a limb of Lot's wife.° [*He eats it with mustard.*] Egad, my lord, your mustard is very uncivil.

Ld. Smart. Why uncivil, my lord?

Ld. Sparkish. Because it takes me by the nose, egad.

Lady Smart. Mr. Neverout, I find you are a very good carver.

Col. O madam, that's no wonder; for you must know, Tom Neverout carves o' Sundays.					[NEVEROUT *overturns the saltcellar.*]

Lady Smart. Mr. Neverout, you have overturned the salt, and that's a sign of anger. I'm afraid, miss and you will fall out.

Lady Answ. No, no; throw a little of it into the fire, and all will be well.

Neverout. O madam, the falling out of lovers,° you know.

Miss. Lovers! very fine! fall *out* with him! I wonder when we were *in*.

Sir John. For my part, I believe the young gentlewoman is his sweetheart; there's such fooling and fiddling betwixt them. I am sure they say in our country, that shiddle-come-sh—'s the beginning of love.°

Miss. Nay, I love Mr. Neverout as the devil loves holy water; I love him like pie, I'd rather the devil would have him than I.°

Neverout. Miss, I'll tell you one thing.

Miss. Come, here 's t'ye, to stop your mouth.

Neverout. I'd rather you would stop it with a kiss.

Miss. A kiss! marry come up, my dirty cousin; are you no sicker?° Lord, I wonder what fool it was that first invented kissing!

Neverout. Well, I'm very dry.

Miss. Then you are the better to burn, and the worse to fry.°

Lady Answ. God bless you, Colonel; you have a good stroke with you.

Col. O madam; formerly I could eat all, but now I leave nothing; I eat but one meal a-day.

Miss. What! I suppose, Colonel, that's from morning till night.

Neverout. Faith, miss; and well was his wont.

Ld. Smart. Pray, Lady Answerall, taste this bit of venison.

Lady Answ. I hope your lordship will set me a good example.

Ld. Smart. Here's a glass of cider fill'd. Miss, you must drink it.

Miss. Indeed, my lord, I can't.

Neverout. Come, miss; better belly burst than good liquor be lost.

Miss. Pish! well in life there was never anything so teasing; I had rather shed it in my shoes. I wish it were in your guts, for my share.

Ld. Smart. Mr. Neverout, you han't tasted my cider yet.

Neverout. No, my lord. I have been just eating soup; and they say, if one drinks in one's porridge, one will cough in one's grave.

Ld. Smart. Come, take miss's glass, she wish'd it was in your guts; let her have her wish for once. Ladies can't abide to have their inclinations cross'd.

Lady Smart. [*To* Sir John.] I think, Sir John, you have not tasted the venison yet.

Sir John. I seldom eat it, madam. However, please to send me a little of the crust.

Ld. Sparkish. Why, Sir John, you had as good eat the devil as the broth he's boil'd in.

Col. Well, this eating and drinking takes away a body's stomach, as Lady Answerall says.

Neverout. I have dined as well as my lord mayor.

Miss. I thought I could have eaten this wing of a chicken; but, I find, my eye's bigger than my belly.

Ld. Smart. Indeed, Lady Answerall, you have eaten nothing.

Lady. Answ. Pray, my lord, see all the bones on my plate. They say, a carpenter's known by his chips.

Neverout. Miss, will you reach me that glass of jelly?

Miss. [*Giving it to him.*] You see, 'tis but ask and have.

Neverout. Miss, I would have a bigger glass.

Miss. What! you don't know your own mind; you are neither well, full nor fasting; I think that is enough.

Neverout. Ay, one of the enoughs; I am sure it is little enough.

Miss. Yes; but you know, sweet things are bad for the teeth.

Neverout. [*To* LADY ANSW.] Madam, I don't like this part of the veal you sent me.

Lady Answ. Well, Mr. Neverout, I find you are a true Englishman; you never know when you are well.

Col. Well, I have made my whole dinner of beef.

Lady Answ. Why, Colonel, a bellyful's a bellyful, if it be but of wheat-straw.

Col. Well, after all, kitchen physic is the best physic.

Ld. Smart. And the best doctors in the world are Doctor Diet, Doctor Quiet, and Doctor Merryman.

Ld. Sparkish. What do you think of a little house well fill'd?

Sir John. And a little land well till'd?

Col. Ay, and a little wife well will'd?

Neverout. My Lady Smart, pray help me to some of the breast of that goose.

Ld. Smart. Tom, I have heard that goose upon goose is false heraldry.°

Miss. What! will you never have done stuffing?

Ld. Smart. This goose is quite raw. Well, God sends meat, but the devil sends cooks.

Neverout. Miss, can you tell which is the white goose, or the grey goose the gander?°

Miss. They say, a fool will ask more questions than twenty wise men can answer.

Col. Indeed, miss, Tom Neverout has posed you.

Miss. Why, Colonel, every dog has his day; but, I believe I shall never see a goose again without thinking on Mr. Neverout.

Ld. Smart. Well said, miss; faith, girl, thou has brought thyself off cleverly. Tom, what say you to that?

Col. Faith, Tom is nonpluss'd; he looks plaguily down in the mouth.

Miss. Why, my lord, you see he is the provokingest creature in life; I believe there is not such another in the varsal world.

Lady Answ. Oh, miss, the world's a wide place.

Neverout. Well, miss, I'll give you leave to call me anything, so you don't call me spade.°

Ld. Smart. Well, but, after all, Tom, can you tell me what's Latin for a goose?

Neverout. O my lord, I know that; why brandy is Latin for a goose, and *tace* is Latin for a candle.°

Miss. Is that manners, to show your learning before ladies? Methinks you are grown very brisk of a sudden; I think the man's glad he's alive.

Sir John. The devil take your wit, if this be wit; for it spoils company. Pray, Mr. Butler, bring me a dram after my goose; 'tis very good for the wholesomes.

Ld. Smart. Come, bring me the loaf; I sometimes love to cut my own bread.

Miss. I suppose, my lord, you lay longest abed to-day?°

Ld. Smart. Miss, if I had said so, I should have told a fib; I warrant you lay abed till the cows came home. But, miss, shall I cut you a little crust now my hand is in?

Miss. If you please, my lord, a bit of undercrust.

Neverout. [*Whispering* Miss.] I find, you love to lie under.

Miss. [*Aloud, pushing him from her.*] What does the man mean? Sir, I don't understand you at all.

Neverout. Come, all quarrels laid aside. Here, miss, may you live a thousand years.   [*He drinks to her.*]

Miss. Pray, sir, don't stint me.

Ld. Smart. Sir John, will you taste my October?° I think it is very good; but I believe not equal to yours in Derbyshire.

Sir John. My lord, I beg your pardon; but they say, the devil made askers.

Ld. Smart. [*To the* Butler.] Here, bring up the great tankard full of October for Sir John.

Col. [*Drinking to* Miss.] Miss, your health; may you live all the days of your life.

Lady Answ. Well, miss, you'll certainly be soon married; here's two bachelors drinking to you at once.

Lady Smart. Indeed, miss, I believe you were wrapt in your mother's smock, you are so well beloved.

Miss. Where's my knife? Sure I ha'n't eaten it. Oh, here it is.

Sir John. No, miss; but your maidenhead hangs in your light.

Miss. Pray, Sir John, is that a Derbyshire compliment? Here, Mr. Neverout, will you take this piece of rabbit that you bid me carve for you?

Neverout. I don't know.

Miss. Why, why, take it, or let it alone.

Neverout. I will.

Miss. What will you?

Neverout. Why, take it, or let it alone.

Miss. Well, you're a provoking creature.

Sir John. [*Talking with a glass of wine in his hand.*] I remember a farmer in our country——

Ld. Smart. [*Interrupting him.*] Pray, Sir John, did you ever hear of parson Palmer?

Sir John. No, my lord; what of him?

Ld. Smart. Why, he used to preach over his liquor.

Sir John. I beg your pardon; here's your lordship's health. I'd drink it up, if it were a mile to the bottom.

Lady Smart. Mr. Neverout, have you been at the new play?

Neverout. Yes, madam; I went the first night.

Lady Smart. Well; and how did it take?

Neverout. Why madam, the poet is *damn'd.*°

Sir John. God forgive you! that's very uncharitable: you ought not to judge so rashly of any Christian.

Neverout. [*Whispers* LADY SMART.] Was ever such a dunce? How well he knows the town! See, how he stares like a stuck pig! Well, but, Sir John, are you acquainted with any of our fine ladies yet? Any of our famous toasts?

Sir John. No; damn your fire-ships,° I have a wife of my own.

Lady Smart. Pray, my Lady Answerall, how do you like these preserved oranges?

Lady Answ. Indeed, madam, the only fault I find is, that they are too good.

Lady Smart. O madam; I have heard 'em say, that too good is stark naught. [MISS *drinking part of a glass of wine.*]

Neverout. Pray, let me drink your snuff.°

Miss. No, indeed; you shan't drink after me, for you'll know my thoughts.

Neverout. I know them already; you are thinking of a good husband. Besides, I can tell your meaning by your mumping.°

Lady Smart. Pray, my lord, did not you order the butler to bring up a tankard of our October to Sir John? I believe, they stay to brew it.

[*The* Butler *brings the tankard to* SIR JOHN.]

Sir John. Won't your lordship please to drink first?

Lord Smart. No, Sir John; 'tis in a very good hand; I'll pledge you.

Col. [*To* LD. SMART.] My lord, I love October as well as Sir John; and I hope, you won't make fish of one, and flesh of another.°

Ld. Smart. Colonel, you're heartily welcome. Come, Sir John, take it by word of mouth, and then give it the Colonel.   [SIR JOHN *drinks*.]

Ld. Smart. Well, Sir John, how do you like it?

Sir John. Not as well as my own in Derbyshire; 'tis plaguy small.°

Lady Smart. I never taste malt liquor; but they say, 'tis well hopp'd.°

Sir John. Hopp'd! why, if it had hopp'd a little further, it would have hopp'd into the river. O my lord, my ale is meat, drink, and cloth; it will make a cat speak, and a wise man dumb.

Lady Smart. I was told, ours was very strong.

Sir John. Ay, madam, strong of the water; I believe the brewer forgot the malt, or the river was too near him. Faith, it is mere whip-belly-vengeance; he that drinks most has the worst share.

Col. I believe, Sir John, ale is as plenty as water at your house.

Sir John. Why, faith, at Christmas we have many comers and goers; and they must not be sent away without a cup of good Christmas ale, for fear they should p–ss behind the door.°

Lady Smart. I hear Sir John has the nicest garden in England; they say, 'tis kept so clean that you can't find a place where to spit.

Sir John. O madam; you are pleased to say so.

Lady Smart. But, Sir John, your ale is terrible strong and heady in Derbyshire, and will soon make one drunk and sick; what do you then?

Sir John. Why, indeed, it is apt to fox one; but our way is, to take a hair of the same dog next morning.—I take a new-laid egg for breakfast; and, faith, one should drink as much after an egg° as after an ox.

Ld. Smart. Tom Neverout, will you taste a glass of October?

Neverout. No, faith, my lord; I like your wine, and I won't put a churl upon a gentleman;° your honour's claret is good enough for me.

Lady Smart. What! is this pigeon left for manners? Colonel, shall I send you the legs and rump?

Col. Madam, I could not eat a bit more, if the house was full.

Ld. Smart. [*Carving a partridge.*] Well; one may ride to Rumford upon this knife, it is so blunt.

Lady Answ. My lord, I beg your pardon; but they say, an ill workman never had good tools.

Ld. Smart. Will your lordship have a wing of it?

Ld. Sparkish. No, my lord; I love the wing of an ox a great deal better.

Ld. Smart. I'm always cold after eating.

Col. My lord, they say that's a sign of long life.°

Ld. Smart. Ay; I believe I shall live till all my friends are weary of me.

Col. Pray, does anybody here hate cheese? I would be glad of a bit.

Ld. Smart. An odd kind of fellow dined with me t' other day; and when the cheese came upon the table, he pretended to faint. So somebody said, Pray, take away the cheese. No, said I; pray, take away the fool. Said I well?   [*Here a long and loud laugh.*]

Col. Faith, my lord, you served the coxcomb right enough; and therefore I wish we had a bit of your lordship's Oxfordshire cheese.

Ld. Smart. Come, hang saving; bring us a half-p'orth of cheese.

Lady Answ. They say, cheese digests everything but itself.

[Footman *brings in a great whole cheese.*]

Ld. Sparkish. Ay; this would look handsome, if anybody should come in.

Sir John. Well; I'm weily brosten,° as they say in Lancashire.

Lady Smart. Oh, Sir John; I wou'd I had something to brost you withal.

Ld. Smart. Come; they say, 'tis merry in hall when beards wag all.

Lady Smart. Miss, shall I help you to some cheese? or will you carve for yourself?

Neverout. I'll hold fifty pounds, miss won't cut the cheese.

Miss. Pray, why so, Mr. Neverout?

Neverout. Oh there is a reason, and you know it well enough.

Miss. I can't for my life understand what the gentleman means.

Ld. Smart. Pray, Tom, change the discourse; in troth you are too bad.

Col. [*Whispers* NEVEROUT.] Smoak miss. Faith, you have made her fret like gum-taffety.°

Lady Smart. Well, but miss (hold your tongue, Mr. Neverout) shall I cut you a bit of cheese?

Miss. No, really, madam; I have dined this half hour.

Lady Smart. What! quick at meat quick at work, they say.

[SIR JOHN *nods.*]

Ld. Smart. What! are you sleepy, Sir John? do you sleep after dinner?

Sir John. Yes, faith; I sometimes take a nap after my pipe; for when the belly's full, the bones will be at rest.

Lady Smart. Come, Colonel; help yourself, and your friends will love you the better. [*To* LADY ANSW.] Madam, your ladyship eats nothing.

Lady Answ. Lord, madam, I have fed like a farmer; I shall grow as fat as a porpoise; I swear my jaws are weary with chawing.

Col. I have a mind to eat a piece of that sturgeon; but I fear it will make me sick.

Neverout. A rare soldier indeed! Let it alone, and I warrant it won't hurt you.

Col. Well, but it would vex a dog to see a pudden creep.

[SIR JOHN *rises.*]

Ld. Smart. Sir John, what are you doing?

Sir John. Swolks,° I must be going, by'r Lady; I have earnest business; I must do as the beggars do, go away when I have got enough.

Ld. Smart. Well, but stay till this bottle's out; you know, the man was hang'd that left his liquor behind him. Besides, a cup in the pate is a mile in the gate;° and a spur in the head is worth two in the heel.

Sir John. Come then; one brimmer to all your healths. [*The* footman *gives him a glass half full.*] Pray, friend, what was the rest of this glass made for? An inch at the top, friend, is worth two at the bottom. [*He gets a brimmer, and drinks it off.*] Well, there's no deceit in a brimmer, and there's no false Latin in this; your wine is excellent good, so I thank you for the next, for I am sure of this. Madam, has your ladyship any commands in Derbyshire? I must go fifteen miles tonight.

Lady Smart. None, Sir John, but to take care of yourself; and my most humble service to your lady unknown.

Sir John. Well, madam, I can but love and thank you.

Lady Smart. Here, bring water to wash; though, really, you have eaten so little, that you have no need to wash your mouths——

Ld. Smart. But, prythee, Sir John, stay a while longer.

Sir John. No, my lord; I am to smoke a pipe with a friend before I leave the town.

Col. Why, Sir John, had not you better set out tomorrow?

Sir John. Colonel, you forget tomorrow is Sunday.

Col. Now, I always love to begin a journey on Sundays, because I shall have the prayers of the church to preserve all that travel by land, or by water.

Sir John. Well, Colonel; thou art a mad fellow to make a priest of.

Neverout. Fie, Sir John, do you take tobacco? How can you make a chimney of your mouth?

Sir John. [*To* NEVEROUT.] What! you don't smoke I warrant you, but you smock. (Ladies, I beg your pardon.) Colonel, do you never smoke?

Col. No, Sir John; but I take a pipe sometimes.

Sir John. I'faith, one of your finical London blades dined with me last year in Derbyshire; so, after dinner, I took a pipe; so my gentleman turn'd away his head. So, said I, What, sir, do you never smoke? So, he answered as you do, Colonel: No, but I sometimes take a pipe. So, he took a pipe in his hand, and fiddled with it till he broke it. So, said I, Pray, sir, can you make a pipe? So, he said No; so, said I, Why, then, sir, if you can't make a pipe, you should not break a pipe. So, we all laugh'd.

Ld. Smart. Well; but, Sir John, they say that the corruption of pipes is the generation of stoppers.°

Sir John. Colonel, I hear, you go sometimes to Derbyshire; I wish you would come and foul a plate with me.

Col. I hope you'll give me a soldier's bottle.

Sir John. Come, and try. Mr. Neverout, you are a townwit, can you tell me what kind of herb is tobacco?

Neverout. Why, an Indian herb, Sir John.

Sir John. No, 'tis a pot herb;° and so here 's t'ye in a pot of my lord's October.

Lady Smart. I hear, Sir John, since you are married you have forsworn the town.

Sir John. No, madam; I never forswore anything but building of churches.

Lady Smart. Well; but, Sir John, when may we hope to see you again in London?

Sir John. Why, madam, not till the ducks have eat up the dirt, as the children say.

Neverout. Come, Sir John; I foresee it will rain terribly.

Ld. Smart. Come, Sir John, do nothing rashly; let us drink first.

Ld. Sparkish. Nay, I know Sir John will go, though he was sure it would rain cats and dogs. But pray stay, Sir John; you'll be time enough to go to bed by candle-light.

Ld. Smart. Why, Sir John, if you must needs go; while you stay, make good use of your time. Here's my service to you, a health to our friends in Derbyshire. Come, sit down; let us put off the evil hour as long as we can.

Sir John. Faith, I could not drink a drop more, if the house was full.

Col. Why, Sir John you used to love a glass of good wine in former times.

Sir John. Why, so I do still, colonel; but a man may love his house very well, without riding on the ridge. Besides, I must be with my wife on Tuesday, or there will be the devil and all to pay.

Col. Well, if you go today, I wish you may be wet to the skin.

Sir John. Ay; but they say the prayers of the wicked won't prevail.

[SIR JOHN *takes his leave, and goes away.*]

Ld. Smart. Well, miss, how do you like Sir John?

Miss. Why, I think, he's a little upon the silly, or so. I believe he has not all the wit in the world, but I don't pretend to be a judge.

Neverout. Faith, I believe, he was bred at Hog's Norton, where the pigs play upon the organs.

Ld. Sparkish. Why, Tom, I thought you and he had been hand and glove.

Neverout. Faith, he shall have a clean threshold for me; I never darkened his door in my life, neither in town nor country; but he's a queer old duke° by my conscience; and yet, after all, I take him to be more knave than fool.

Lady Smart. Well, come; a man's a man if he has but a nose on his head.

Col. I was once with him, and some other company, over a bottle; and, egad, he fell asleep, and snored so loud that we thought he was driving his hogs to market.

Neverout. Why, what! you can have no more of a cat than her skin; you can't make a silk purse out of a sow's ear.

Ld. Sparkish. Well, since he's gone, the devil go with him and sixpence; and there's money and company too.

Neverout. Faith, he's a true country put. Pray, miss, let me ask you a question?

Miss. Well; but don't ask questions with a dirty face. I warrant what you have to say will keep cold.

Col. Come, my lord, against you are disposed, here's to all that love and honour you.

Ld. Sparkish. Ay, that was always Dick Nimble's health. I'm sure you know he is dead.

Col. Dead! Well, my lord, you love to be a messenger of ill news. I'm heartily sorry, but, my lord, we must all die.

Neverout. I knew him very well. But, pray, how came he to die?

Miss. There's a question! you talk like a poticary: Why, he died because he could live no longer.

Neverout. Well; rest his soul. We must live by the living, and not by the dead.

Ld. Sparkish. You know, his house was burnt down to the ground.

Col. Yes; it was in the news. Why, fire and water are good servants, but they are very bad masters.

Ld. Smart. Here, take away, and set down a bottle of Burgundy. Ladies, you'll stay, and drink a glass of wine before you go to your tea.

[*All's taken away, and the wine set down.* MISS *gives* NEVEROUT *a smart pinch.*]

Neverout. Lord, miss, what d'ye mean! D'ye think I have no feeling?

Miss. I'm forced to pinch, for the times are hard.

Neverout. [*Giving* MISS *a pinch*.] Take that, miss; what's sauce for a goose is sauce for a gander.

Miss. [*Screaming*.] Well, Mr. Neverout, if I live, that shall neither go to heaven nor hell with you.

Neverout. [*Takes* MISS's *hand*.] Come, miss, let us lay all quarrels aside, and be friends.

Miss. Don't be mauming and gauming a body so!—Can't you keep your filthy hands to yourself?

Neverout. Pray, miss, where did you get that pick-tooth case?

Miss. I came honestly by it.

Neverout. I'm sure it was mine, for I lost just such a one; nay, I don't tell you a lie.

Miss. No; if you lie, it is much.

Neverout. Well; I'm sure 'tis mine.

Miss. What! you think everything is yours, but a little the king has.

Neverout. Colonel, you have seen my fine pick-tooth case; don't you think this is the very same?

Col. Indeed, miss, it is very like it.

Miss. Ay; what he says, you'll swear.

Neverout. Well, but I'll prove it to be mine.

Miss. Ay, do if you can.

Neverout. Why, what's yours is mine, and what's mine is my own.

Miss. Well, run on till you're weary, nobody holds you.

[NEVEROUT *gapes*.]

Col. What, Mr. Neverout, do you gape for preferment?

Neverout. Faith, I may gape long enough, before it falls into my mouth.

Lady Smart. Mr. Neverout, my lord and I intend to beat up your quarters one of these days: I hear you live high.

Neverout. Yes, faith, madam; live high and lodge in a garret.

Col. But, miss, I forgot to tell you, that Mr. Neverout got the devilishest fall in the Park today.

Miss. I hope he did not hurt the ground. But how was it, Mr. Neverout? I wish I had been there to laugh.

Neverout. Why, madam, it was a place where a cuckold had been buried, and one of his horns sticking out, I happened to stumble against it; that was all.

Lady Smart. Ladies, let us leave the gentlemen to themselves; I think it is time to go to our tea.

Lady Answ. & Miss. My lords and gentlemen, your most humble servant.

Ld. Smart. Well, ladies, we'll wait on you an hour hence.

[*The* Gentlemen *alone.*]

Ld. Smart. Come, John, bring us a fresh bottle.

Col. Ay, my lord; and, pray, let him carry off the dead men (as we say in the army).   [*Meaning the empty bottles.*]

Ld. Sparkish. Mr. Neverout, pray, is not that bottle full?

Neverout. Yes, my lord; full of emptiness.

Ld. Smart. And, d'ye hear, John? bring clean glasses.

Col. I'll keep mine; for I think, the wine is the best liquor to wash glasses in.

Hic depositum est Corpus
IONATHAN SWIFT S.T.D.
Hujus Ecclesiæ Cathedralis
Decani,
Ubi sæva Indignatio
Ulterius
Cor lacerare nequit.
Abi Viator
Et imitare, si poteris,
Strenuum pro virili
Libertatis Vindicatorem.

Obiit 19 Die Mensis Octobris
A.D. 1745. Anno Ætatis 78.

[*from*] DR. SWIFT's

WILL.

IN the Name of God, *Amen.* I JONATHAN SWIFT, Doctor in Divinity, and Dean of the Cathedral Church of St. *Patrick, Dublin*, being at this Present of sound Mind, although weak in Body, do here make my last Will and Testament, hereby revoking all my former Wills.

Imprimis, I bequeath my Soul to GOD, (in humble Hopes of his Mercy through JESUS CHRIST) and my Body to the Earth. And, I desire that my Body may be buried in the great Isle of the said Cathedral, on the South Side, under the Pillar next to the Monument of Primate *Narcissus Marsh*, three Days after my Decease, as privately as possible, and at Twelve o'Clock at Night: And, that a Black Marble of   Feet square, and seven Feet from the Ground, fixed to the Wall, may be erected, with the following Inscription in large Letters, deeply cut, and strongly gilded. *HIC* DEPOSITUM EST CORPUS *JONATHAN SWIFT*, S.T.D. HUJUS ECCLESIÆ CATHEDRALIS DECANI, *UBI* SÆVA INDIGNATIO ULTERIUS COR LACERARE NEQUIT. ABI VIATOR, ET IMITARE, SI POTERIS, STRENUUM PRO VIRILI LIBERTATIS VINDICATOREM. OBIIT ANNO   MENSIS   DIE   ÆTATIS ANNO   .

NOTES

ABBREVIATIONS

Correspondence Sir H. Williams (ed.), *The Correspondence of Jonathan Swift*, 5 vols. (Oxford, 1963–5; vols. iv and v rev., 1972).

Guthkelch A. C. Guthkelch and D. Nichol Smith (eds.), *A Tale of a Tub* [etc.] (rev. edn. with corr., Oxford, 1973).

Journal to Stella Sir H. Williams (ed.), *The Journal to Stella*, 2 vols. (Oxford, 1948).

*ODEP*³ *The Oxford Dictionary of English Proverbs*, 3rd ed., rev. by F. P. Wilson (Oxford, 1970).

Poems Sir H. Williams (ed.), *The Poems of Jonathan Swift*, 3 vols. (2nd edn., rev., Oxford, 1958).

Prose H. J. Davis *et al.* (eds.), *The Prose Works of Jonathan Swift*, 14 vols. (Oxford [Blackwell], 1939–68).

SL George Faulkner's *Sale Catalogue* of Swift's Library, 1745; reprinted in Sir H. Williams, *Dean Swift's Library* (Cambridge, 1932).

Works 1735 *The Works of Jonathan Swift, D.D., D.S.P.D.*, 4 vols. (Dublin, 1735), printed by George Faulkner with significant direction from Jonathan Swift.

1 *The Battle of the Books*. This piece springs directly from Swift's life during the 1690s in Sir William Temple's circle at Moor Park near Farnham. Although not published until 1704, in the volume that contained *A Tale of a Tub*, it was written, probably not all at once, at a time when Temple had embroiled himself in the so-called 'Ancients and Moderns Controversy', an exchange of insults in a pamphlet war at the end of the seventeenth century, first in France, then in England. Temple was himself in many respects an important representative of modern self-consciousness. The impulse to publish his own *Memoirs* and *Letters* is in tune with the empirical spirit of the age, though he was no simple-minded believer in progress. The whole-hearted devotion of the 'modern' writers to the self-confident acquisition of information, in the conviction that this alone led to truth, was seen by Temple as the modern form of pride, the primal sin, what he called 'the sufficiency of some of the learned'. In his *Miscellanea. The Second Part* (1690), Temple published 'An Essay upon Ancient and Modern Learning', occasioned partly by a general, literary controversy in France. He deploys a cyclical view of history to attack modern presumption in thinking that a full and clear knowledge of a limited body of extant classical writing would be the key to all knowledge. Looking round for examples of really ancient writing which he might advance as evidence 'in favour of the ancients, that the oldest books we have are still in their kind the best', in a single paragraph out of the sixty-four of which his 'Essay' is comprised, Temple unluckily pitched on the *Fables* of

Aesop and the *Epistles* of Phalaris, 'both living at the same time, which was that of Cyrus and Pythagoras [*c.* sixth century BC]'. Richard Bentley, the greatest classical scholar in England, had little difficulty in demonstrating that the *Epistles* were a late Greek forgery, and that the *Fables* also contained much later material. Temple indeed mentions this judgement of the *Epistles*, but rejects it on subjective grounds of taste, and indicates that he was drawn to the text as the writing of a ruler, because of his own interests as a man of affairs and a letter-writer, rather than for any more technical reason. Temple, who was no rigid enemy of modern writing, was bewildered at attacks on his polite 'Essay'. His lordly tone itself, however, was calculated to enrage professional scholars like Bentley. In 1693, a defensive edition of Phalaris's *Epistles* was undertaken (published 1695) ostensibly by the Hon. Charles Boyle, an adolescent undergraduate at Christ Church, Oxford. This exercise was really carried out by senior members, but according to custom was associated with a well-connected pupil to gain prestige for the foundation. Meanwhile, William Wotton took the opportunity to produce *Reflections upon Ancient and Modern Learning* (1694). Wotton's book is by no means abusive of Temple, but it seeks to demolish his idea of 'the mighty reservoirs and lakes of knowledge' of Egypt and the pre-classical East, and to destroy Temple's cyclical theory of cultural history, which indeed could not be accommodated to orthodox Christian theology. In 1697, the date given in 'The Bookseller to the Reader' as the date of composition of *The Battle of the Books*, Wotton printed a second edition of his *Reflections*, 'with large additions'; the latter included Bentley's essay, *A Dissertation upon the Epistles of Phalaris, Themistocles, Socrates, Euripides and Others; and the Fables of Aesop*. A personal note entered into the second purpose of Bentley's paper, which was to show that the 'Boyle' edition was a shoddy piece of work by incompetent Oxford dons. Temple considered replying to Wotton. The Christ Church party in 1698 issued *Dr. Bentley's Dissertation on the Epistles of Phalaris and the Fables of Aesop, Examined by the Honourable Charles Boyle, Esq.*, which did everything that wit could do to mock Bentley's conclusive argument. In 1697-8 half a dozen other pamphlets were prompted by the controversy, and more in the next year, among the latter Bentley's enlarged and corrected version of his *Dissertation* which answers in slashing style Boyle's *Examination*. In 1701 Swift printed Temple's *Miscellanea. The Third Part*, which contains 'Some Thoughts upon Reviewing the Essay of Ancient and Modern Learning', the answer to Wotton which he had worked on with his late employer. *The Battle of the Books* is Swift's own satirical descant on Temple's original 'Essay' and his later 'Thoughts'.

Bookseller. The publisher; but the sentences were probably written by Swift.

Books in St. James's Library. The royal library, inadequately housed in St James's Palace.

2 *Vide Ephem. de Mary Clarke; opt. edit.* 'Vincent Wing's' sheet almanac (see p. 639) printed by Mary Clark; it contained the annual calendar [ephemerides],

prognostications, and other material. Swift's jocular reference parodies 'modern' pedantic citation and specifies the 'best edition'.

in the Republic of Dogs . . . A satirical version of Hobbes's political philosophy; see note to p. 79 (2).

3 *especially towards the East.* Referring to Temple's notions of traditional and unrecorded wisdom in Egypt, India, and the east.

4 *representatives, for passengers to gaze at.* Books were advertised by pasting up copies of their title-pages in the street.

a certain spirit, which they call brutum hominis. Guthkelch, 222, cites Thomas Vaughan's *Anthroposophia Theomagica* (1650), p. 58, quoting Paracelsus, as Swift's source for this phrase. Vaughan is one of the mystical, alchemical 'dark authors', whose works are satirized in *A Tale of a Tub*.

5 *to bind them to the peace with strong iron chains.* Swift's main joke refers to the books in chained libraries, but he also utilizes the magistrates' sentence of 'binding over to keep the peace'.

the works of Scotus. John Duns Scotus (?1265–1308), the 'Subtle Doctor', contributed to the already dominant Aristotelianism of European theology.

the guardian . . . chiefly renowned for his humanity. Richard Bentley, Keeper of the Royal Library; Boyle in the preface to his edition of Phalaris's *Epistles* complained of Bentley's refusal of sufficient access to a manuscript, 'pro singulari sua humanitate' ('with that courtesy which distinguishes him'); Bentley, in replying, chose to take this as meaning 'out of his singular humanity', i.e. care of readers [in the dangerous building]. *Humanity* could also mean classical literature and civilization.

two of the Ancient chiefs. Phalaris and Aesop.

6 *a strange confusion of place among all the books in the library.* Bentley argued that the royal library was so disorganized when he took it over in 1693, that he could not safely allow public access to it.

the Seven Wise Masters. 'The seven sages' of Greece, was a collective description, also as 'the seven wise men', of any seven of a group of sages of the sixth century BC, including Solon and Thales. 'The Seven Wise Masters', however, or 'The Seven Sages of Rome', is the title of various medieval collections of stories nested in a tale concerning a young prince and his seven teachers.

Withers. George Wither or Withers (1588–1667), poet and writer of Puritan pamphlets in verse, commonly at this time cited as a hack rhymester, as in Dryden's *Essay on Dramatic Poesy* (1668); Swift yokes him with Dryden, and contrasts Dryden with the great poet Virgil, whose *Aeneid* Dryden had translated.

light-horse, heavy-armed foot, and mercenaries. Poets, historians, and translators.

7 *the Moderns were much the more ancient of the two.* The paradox was made by,

among others, Bacon in *The Advancement of Learning*, I. v. l, '. . . These times are the ancient times, when the world is ancient. . . .'

9 *my improvements in the mathematics*. The advances in mathematics during the previous decades, together with improvements in navigation and fortification as well as the work of the Royal Society, all formed the most powerful 'modern' arguments for the superiority of the modern age.

the regent's humanity. Bentley; see note to p. 5 (3).

10 *the borrowed shape of an ass*. In his *Dissertation*, Bentley quoted the Greek proverb, 'Leucon carries one thing, and his ass quite another', in relation to Boyle's mistaken view of the authorship of 'Phalaris's' *Epistles*. Boyle chose to say that Bentley distinguished between the Greek text and the ass who edited it.

a large vein of wrangling and satire. Temple's 'Essay': '. . . the vein of ridiculing all that is serious and good, all honour and virtue, as well as learning and piety . . . is the itch of the age and climate, and has over-run both the court and the stage . . .'

sweetness and light. A phrase taken up by Matthew Arnold in *Culture and Anarchy* (1869).

11 *consults*. '. . . the great consult [of Satan and his followers] began': Milton, *Paradise Lost*, i. 798.

Despréaux. Nicholas Boileau (1636–1711), known as Despréaux, was one of the chief French supporters of the Ancients; here as one of the leading Modern poets, along with Abraham Cowley (see note to p. 17 (1)).

the bowmen . . . Des Cartes, Gassendi, and Hobbes. Philosophers . . . Swift names as their leaders three of the leading Moderns in this field, united in Swift's eyes by 'sufficiency', belief in the uniqueness and novelty of their arguments. Each of them, too, elaborates a mathematico-physical framework for their ideas. Temple in his 'Essay' knows 'of no philosophers that have made entries upon that noble stage for fifteen hundred years past, unless Descartes and Hobbes should pretend to it'.

that [arrow] of Evander. In the *Aeneid*; although attention is drawn to king Evander's 'noble quiver of Lycian arrows' (viii. 166), it was during the archery contest (v. 485–544) that the arrow of *Acestis* 'caught fire, defined its track with flames and vanished into thin air, as shooting stars . . .'.

Paracelsus . . . Harvey, their great aga. Theophrastus Bombast von Hohenheim (1493–1541), Swiss alchemist and physician, took the name Paracelsus [the equal of Celsus, the principal Roman writer on medicine]; he struck out against medical dogma drawn from the traditional study of the writings of Aristotle and Galen . . . William Harvey (1578–1657) demonstrated the circulation of the blood; Temple reasonably enough in his 'Essay' says that this had at that date made no change 'in the practice of physic', but it had far-reaching theoretical implications. Harvey is given the title of a Turkish commander-in-chief.

Guicciardine, Davila, Polydore Virgil, Buchanan, Mariana, Cambden. Francisco

Guicciardini (1483–1540), Florentine author of *Historia d'Italia* (1521; translated into English 1579); Enrico Davila (see note to p. 357 (2)); Polydore Vergil (1470–1555), an Italian who became naturalized and wrote a history of England (1534); George Buchanan (1506–82), Scottish humanist, the author of a *History of Scotland* in Latin (1582); Juan de Mariana (1537–1627), author of *Historia d'España* (1601); William Camden (1551–1623), historian and antiquary, author of the compilation *Britannia* (in Latin, 1586; translated into English from 1610).

engineers . . . Regiomontanus and Wilkins. Mathematicians . . . Johann Muller (1436–76) of Königsberg; John Wilkins (1614–72), one of the founders of the Royal Society, later Bishop of Chester; in his 'Thoughts on Reviewing the Essay', Temple sneers at Wilkins's *The Discovery of a World in the Moon . . . that . . . there may be another habitable World in the Planet* (1638–40) and at his *Essay towards a Real Character and Philosophic [universal] Language* (1668). Swift jokes about the latter ideal in *Gulliver's Travels*, 'Voyage to Laputa', chapter V.

Bellarmine. Cardinal Roberto Bellarmino (1542–1621), Roman Catholic apologist, who is linked with two of the great Schoolmen.

calones . . . led by L'Estrange. Roman grooms or lower servants . . . Sir Roger L'Estrange (1616–1704), translator of, among other things, *The Fables of Aesop and Others* (1692); see p. 606 above.

Vossius. Isaac Vossius (1618–89), Dutch scholar and canon of Windsor; Swift read his work on classical prosody, *De Sibyllinis*, in 1698 and owned a copy of it (*SL* 434).

12 *Momus, the patron of the Moderns . . . Pallas*. Momus, in mythology a son of primeval Night, became the personification of carping criticism; contrasted with Pallas Athena, daughter of Zeus and tutelary goddess of Athens.

second causes. See note to p. 394 (3).

13 *schoolboys judges of philosophy*. 'A boy at fifteen is wiser than his father at forty, the meanest subject than his prince or governors; and the modern scholars because they have, for a hundred years past, learned their lesson pretty well are much more knowing than the ancients their masters' (Temple, 'Essay').

seminaries of Gresham and Covent Garden. In London, the Royal Society met at Gresham College in Broad Street until 1710; Covent Garden, the area of the theatre, of Will's coffee-house, and others, and of the Rose Tavern (see notes to p. 538 (1) and p. 99 (4)), was the 'college' of the wits.

14 *Galen*. Greek physician (*c*.129–99); see note to p. 11 (5).

Hic pauca desunt . . . Swift parodies the formulae by which scholars indicated incomplete manuscripts: 'Here a little is missing', 'Not a little wanting', 'A large hiatus in the manuscript', 'A hiatus greatly to be mourned'.

Bacon. Mentioned by Temple in his 'Essay' as one of the 'great wits among the moderns'; he is significantly not wounded.

Des Cartes . . . his own vortex. See note to p. 11 (3); Descartes' mathematico-physical picture of the universe involved a theory of *vortices*, which attracted hostile theological criticism as materialistic.

15 *Gondibert*. Sir William Davenant (1606–68) projected a heroic poem set in medieval Lombardy; this was published at some length, but unfinished, in 1651. 'Are . . . the flights of Boileau above those of Virgil? If . . . this must be allowed, I will then yield Gondibert to have exceeded Homer, as is pretended . . .' (Temple, 'Essay').

Denham, a stout Modern . . . Sir John Denham (1615–69) was best known for a blank-verse play, *The Sophy* (1642), and for his innovatory topographical poem, *Cooper's Hill* (1642).

Wesley. Samuel Wesley (1662–1736) the elder, rector of Epworth in Lincolnshire and father of John and Charles. His extensive verse writings, especially *The Life of our blessed Lord and Saviour Jesus Christ: an heroic poem* (1693) and *History of the Old and New Testament in Verse* (1701–4), attracted scorn.

Perrault . . . Fontenelle. Charles Perrault (1628–1703), French poet and writer of fairy-tales, reformer of the French Academy, whose poem in praise of the Moderns, *Le Siècle de Louis le Grand* (1687), initiated the controversy in France . . . Bernard Le Bovier, Sieur de Fontenelle (1657–1757), secretary of the French Academy of Sciences and author of several works on the side of the Moderns, principally *Nouveaux Dialogues des Morts* (1683) and *Digression sur les Anciens et les Modernes* (1688).

the lady in a lobster. A small, bony structure in a lobster's stomach.

16 *Dryden, in a long harangue*. Dryden published his translation of *The Works of Virgil* in 1697; a particularly long dedication to the Marquis of Normanby was prefixed to the *Aeneis*, dealing with epic poetry and the translation itself.

Lucan. Marcus Annaeus Lucanus (39–65), author of the unfinished epic poem *Pharsalia: De Bello Civili* [*On the Civil War*] in ten books.

Blackmore. Sir Richard Blackmore. Aesculapius, the god of medicine, takes a charitable view of his practice as a doctor.

Creech. Thomas Creech (1659–1700), translator; his version of *Lucretius* (1682) is quoted in *A Tale of a Tub*, and was followed by his *Horace* (1684).

Ogleby. John Ogleby or Ogilby (1600–76) translated *Aesop* into verse (1650); his *Virgil* (1649) and *Homer* (1660–5) were lavishly printed and illustrated; the plates of the former were re-used in Dryden's volume.

Oldham . . . and Afra the Amazon. Both John Oldham (1653–83), a notable satirist, and Mrs Afra Behn (1640–89), novelist and dramatist, tried their hands (as did Swift himself) at the fashionable, complicated Pindaric odes.

17 *Cowley*. Abraham Cowley (1618–67) had a very high reputation as a poet in his own day; he introduced the fashion for Pindaric odes in English; he published a collection of love poems, *The Mistress* (1647), which gains him here the protection of Venus.

scarce a dozen cavaliers . . . '. . . a giant stone . . . this, scarce twice six chosen

men, of such build as earth now produces, could lift on their shoulders . . .'
(*Aeneid*, xii. 896 ff.), an epic formula, also in Homer; several others are
buried here and there in Swift's text.

a thousand incoherent pieces. Critics scorned Bentley's habit of stitching
together numerous quotations from classical texts, which they claimed he
drew not from wide reading but from dictionaries and lexicons: cf. *A Tale of a
Tub*, p. 131 above.

an Etesian wind. Regular winds [Greek, 'yearly'].

18 *Scaliger.* Joseph Justus Scaliger (1540–1609), a classical scholar whose bad
manners are noticed in Boyle's *Examination*, but defended by Bentley in his
Dissertation.

thy study of humanity. See note to p. 5 (3).

19 *Aldrovandus's tomb.* Ulisse Aldrovandi (1522–1605), a Bolognese naturalist,
who spent his life on his compilations, his *tomb*.

roaring in his bull. See note to p. 429 (3).

20 ————. Francis Atterbury.

21 *new polished and gilded.* Boyle's editing of Phalaris's *Epistles* (1695).

23 *When I come to be old.* This single leaf of paper, endorsed by Swift with the
year, must have been written either just before the death of Sir William
Temple, which took place at 1 a.m. on 27 January 1699, or more likely after
his death, during the few months Swift remained at Moor Park. It has
autobiographical interest, certainly, but more interesting rhetorical implications, a kind of dramatic doodle, in which a young man gives advice to an old
man (himself), reversing the scheme of traditional 'wisdom' literature. May
we not also hear ironic use of the tones of the urbane Temple in the second
last resolution, with its modish French word *opiniâtre*, meaning stubborn or
opinionated? Self-mockery is not absent either.

Et eos qui hereditatem captant, odisse ac vitare. 'To hate and avoid those who
angle for an inheritance.'

24 *Contests and Dissensions.* Looking back on the appearance in October 1701 of
this pamphlet, Swift recollects that the anonymous work 'was greedily
bought, and read . . .', adding that 'the vanity of a young man prevailed with
me, to let myself be known for the author: upon which my Lords Somers and
Halifax . . . desired my acquaintance, with great marks of esteem and
professions of kindness: not to mention the Earl of Sunderland, who had
been of my old acquaintance . . .' (*Prose*, viii. 119 ff.). *Contests and Dissensions*,
however, is less a partisan defence of these Whig statesmen than an
elucidation of certain deeply held ideas given form by Swift's alarm at the
disorderly parliamentary session in 1701. The immediate context of Swift's
Discourse was the frenetic political and journalistic activity in London that
marks the interval between the Peace of Ryswick, signed in September 1697
and concluding the first part of the war against Louis XIV's French
expansionist policy, and the outbreak in 1702 of the second part of the
struggle, the War of the Spanish Succession. Immediately after the

conclusion of the Peace, William's English ministers, the so-called Whig Junto which included Lord Chancellor Somers, Secretary of State Sunderland, Halifax as Chancellor of the Exchequer, and Orford, first Lord of the Admiralty, came under severe attack from the political Opposition. The group lost cohesion, and over the next four years were forced out of office. At the same time, a continuing struggle by the House of Commons to seize more power in the government of the State was directed partly against the King, and partly against the House of Lords. The twin encroachments became a no-holds-barred onslaught on William's ministers, both as peers and as royal favourites. The Tories, led by Harley in the Commons, extended the discussion to foreign policy, hitherto an area of unquestioned royal action. In March 1698, William had negotiated between the Dutch, England and France (one of the claimants to the Spanish inheritance) a secret Partition Treaty, agreeing on a division of the huge Spanish Empire after the death of the ailing king, Carlos II, who had no direct heir. The English ministers advised against this treaty, but allowed the Great Seal to be fixed to it. Another Partition Treaty, more public than the first, was almost immediately made necessary by changes in circumstances, and was signed in February 1700. The immediate denunciation of this second treaty by the Austrian Emperor (another claimant), and its repudiation by Louis XIV on the death of Carlos II in October 1700, so that his second grandson could by the Spanish king's will inherit the whole Spanish Empire as Philip V, precipitated the War of the Spanish Succession. The treaty negotiations formed the basis of articles of impeachment by the Tories against Somers, Halifax, Orford, and the King's Dutch favourite Portland, the 'Lords Partitioners'. These impeachments, prosecutions of peers by the Commons before the rest of the Lords, became a principal concern of William III's fifth Parliament, which met on 10 February 1701. Swift, who had arrived in London in May 1701, is correct in believing that the issues raised fundamental considerations of political power. *Contests and Dissensions* is not a truly controversial pamphlet like Defoe's contributions to the foreign policy debate; it provoked no detailed refutation. In tone and intention, it scorns the popular press, though echoing several contemporary pamphlets. It is aimed at the men of taste to whom he appeals in *An Apology for A Tale of a Tub* (below, p. 71). In fact, it belongs to the end of the spectrum of Swift's writing occupied by that great and difficult satire. *Contests and Dissensions* is a 'historical allegory'. Swift makes free use of the form, appealing to his literate audience's sense of reading as a game, and finds parallels and similarities in ancient history for a bewildering array of details and figures on the contemporary political scene. Considering the brief period available for composition, he probably used abstracts of his wide reading made in Sir William Temple's library. The working out of the pamphlet, however, was not so smooth as its tone suggests. The first four chapters are obviously written to apply to the heat of the power struggle in Parliament. The end of chapter IV is in effect the conclusion of the argument. On 24 June 1701, William cooled the situation by proroguing Parliament, thus effectively quashing the impeachments. Chapter V, dropping the classical allegory, clearly comes *after* 'the late public proceedings'. It contains some of the best generalized political writing in the book, such as the three paragraphs on political parties (pp. 52–3), and in spirit and expression is quite close to some parts of *A Tale of a Tub*, perhaps embodying material associated with that text.

Note A. Some obvious personal references may be tabulated as follows:

Alcibiades, Orford as 33–4; Montague as 33–4

Appius Claudius Sabinus, Lord Haversham as 39

Clodius, Sir Edward Seymour as 53

Coriolanus, Danby as 39

Curio, Charles Davenant as 53

Gracchi, Tories as 42

Miltiades, Orford as 32, 46

Pericles, Montagu as 33, 35

Phocion, Bentinck as 34, 35, 46

Polyperchon, Marlborough as 34

Roman Tribunes, Tory leaders as 38 ff.

Scipio Africanus, Publius, Lord Partitioner as 42

Scipio, Lucius, Lord Partitioner as 42

Servius Tullius, Cromwell as 38

Tarquinius Priscus, Charles I as 37–8

Tarquin the Proud, James II as 38

Themistocles, Orford as 33, 35

Note B. Swift frequently, but not always, cites his classical sources in marginal notes. Though perhaps capable of reading the Greek texts, he seems to have used Latin versions of them, and English versions of both Greek and Latin. He also makes use of Temple's own comments on ancient history, political theory, and citation of classical historians. Swift's principal sources are set out below:

Appian of Alexandria (AD 160), compilation of twenty-four books of histories of the Roman wars to Vespasian; ten survive plus fragments.

Caius Julius Caesar (? 102–44 BC), *Civil War*, unfinished in three books.

Marcus Tullius Cicero (106–43 BC), *Letters to Marcus Brutus; De Re Publica* (*c.*51 BC), three books and fragments.

Diodorus Siculus (*c.*40 BC), Greek compilation of world history centred on Rome, to Caesar's conquest of Gaul.

Dionysius of Halicarnassus (*c.*25 BC), *History of Rome* in Greek, an introduction to Polybius, ten books and fragments surviving (*SL* 234).

Herodotus (*c.*480–425 BC), digressive and anecdotal Greek *History* deals with the war between Asia and Greece, from Croesus to Xerxes (*SL* 92 and 384).

Livius, Titius [Livy] (59 BC–AD17), *History of Rome*, appearing from 26 BC (*SL* 157).

Plutarch (*c.*46–126), *Lives* (*SL* 243).

Polybius (*c.*202–120 BC), Greek *History* of the rise and supremacy of Rome to the destruction of Carthage, forty books, of which the last five, plus fragments, survive.

Thucydides (*c.*460–400 BC), unfinished *History of the Peloponnesian War* (431–404 BC) (*SL* 368), translated by Hobbes.

Xenophon (*c.*430–*c.*355 BC), *History of Greece* and *Memorabilia* [Recollections of Socrates] (*SL* 81).

24 —— *Si tibi vera . . . accingere contra.* 'If it appears to you true, throw in the sponge; and if it is false, prepare yourself to fight': Lucretius, *De Rerum Natura*, ii. 1042–3.

one eminent spirit . . . The modern references are specifically to William III, the Lords, and the Commons.

26 *the truest account of . . . Tyranny.* Swift elaborates a particular, anti-Tory definition of tyranny.

to endeavour to force a lady of great virtue: the very crime. The decemvir Appius Claudius tried to abduct Virginia; earlier, Tarquinius had raped Lucretia.

27 *Regno, Optimatium, et Populi Imperio.* Polybius writes in Greek; the Latin phrases come from the paraphrase in Isaac Casaubon (ed.), *Historiae* (Paris, 1609). [Ellis]

Reges, Seniores, et Populus. 'The [two] kings, the elders, and the people.'

28 *each party.* Each part, constituent.

Inherent Right . . . a dormant power . . . privileges . . . Specific references to the claims advanced on behalf of the Commons by the Tory majority, the impeachers.

29 *Not to consent . . . unless another law* . . . The parliamentary manœuvre of 'tacking' partisan legislation on to bills for supplying the Government with funds.

great changes and alienations of property . . . The estates forfeited by the Catholics in Ireland after the defeat there of James II.

whatever attempt is begun by an assembly ought to be pursued . . . The Whig Lords Partitioners were acquitted in June 1701, but the Tories were reported resolved to pursue the matter further.

the Most Christian King. Louis XIV, who was commonly accused of aiming at the 'universal monarchy' of Europe.

32 *when Athens was at the height of its glory.* Swift is setting out on a specific and extended allegory of the impeached Lords Partitioners (see above, p. 613).

ostracism . . . removed from their presence and councils for ever. For ostracism see note to p. 47 (3) . . . The request of the Tory majority in the Commons to William concerning the impeached Ministers.

34 *to Philippize.* The word was introduced (330 BC) by Demosthenes to describe an Athenian who sided with the enemy, Philip of Macedon; here, it signifies anti-Williamites who had been paid by Louis XIV to support the French claim to the Spanish inheritance for Louis's grandson, Philip of Anjou.

37 *entering on a war . . . only permitted at the King's pleasure.* The main constitutional point at issue; the Crown claimed uncontrolled power in making peace and war, i.e. the direction of foreign policy.

populi impetratâ veniâ. 'After obtaining the good will of the people.'

38 *Servius Tullius . . . King.* Oliver Cromwell was offered the crown in May 1657.

Tribunes of the People. The Tory leaders, protected by parliamentary privilege.

39 *the conquered lands*. The forfeited estates in Ireland.

the Consuls themselves. The King's Ministers, who were peers.

41 *those abuses and corruptions which in time destroy a government* ... A central belief of Swift's, following a preoccupation of Sir William Temple's; the reference should be to Polybius, vi. 10. [Ellis]

42 *the age of the Gracchi*. The political struggle following the Peace of Ryswick, September 1697.

a great private estate left by a king. William granted James II's own large Irish property to his former mistress, Elizabeth Villiers, Countess of Orkney, later a friend of Swift's.

46 *make Demosthenes philippize*. See note to p. 34.

affairs of the last importance. The approach of the War of the Spanish Succession: above, p. 612.

47 *a cloud of witnesses*. Hebrews 12: 1.

made Plato say. *Republic*, vii. 520 d–521 a.

the petalism was erected at Syracuse. The Syracusan voter wrote the name of a citizen he was nominating for banishment on an olive leaf (*petalos*), instead of the Athenian potsherd (*ostrakon*, giving 'ostracism').

50 *a sickness unto death*. John 11: 4.

Quod procul ... persuadeat ipsa. 'May Fortune that directs things steer this fate from us. And may rational thought, rather than the event itself, convince': Lucretius, *De Rerum Natura*, v. 107–8.

some prince in the neighbourhood. In September 1701, on the death in exile of James II, Louis XIV violated the Treaty of Ryswick by publicly recognizing James's son, the Old Pretender, as James III of England.

51 *Tyranny ... of a single person*. Oliver Cromwell.

two weak princes. Charles II and James II.

popularity. Tyranny of the plebs, the people.

a sort of rotation, that the author of the Oceana never dreamed on. James Harrington (1611–77), the Republican author of *The Commonwealth of Oceana* (1656; 1658), a Utopia carefully studied by Swift, was a member of a political club called the *Rota*, that met towards the end of the Commonwealth; one of the ideas canvassed was Harrington's notion of rotation in membership of the Senate.

52 *The raging of the sea, and the madness of the people*. Jude 13, which throughout denounces the ungodly.

Hitherto shalt thou pass, and no farther. Job 38: 8–11.

potter, What dost thou make? Isaiah 45: 9.

53 *Periculosae plenum opus aleæ.* 'A task fraught with perilous chance': Horace, *Odes*, II. i. 6.

imitatores, servum pecus. 'Imitators, that slavish herd': Horace, *Epistles*, I. xix. 19.

what Diodorus tells us. Diodorus Siculus, xii. 17.

54 *during the present lucid interval.* Parliament was prorogued on 24 June 1701.

55 *a House of Commons to lose the universal favour of the numbers they represent.* Refers to the uproar over the imprisonment in May of the five Kentish petitioners who in a carefully orchestrated move advocated support for William against Louis XIV, and the ensuing Whig propaganda victory of Defoe's *Legion's Memorial.*

55–6 *the Act passed some years ago against bribing of elections . . . the late Parliament.* 21 January 1696 . . . William III's fourth Parliament, 6 December 1698 to 19 December 1700, which passed several measures hostile to the King. Swift is defending the legitimacy of the Crown's influence in elections.

56 *tanquam . . . Romuli.* Slightly altered quotation from Cicero's *Letters to Brutus*, no. 21 (II. 1): '[Cato speaks in the Senate] as though he were living in Plato's Republic instead of Romulus' cesspool.' [D. R. Shackleton Bailey]

[*There is . . . the people*]. The final paragraph was omitted by Swift from all editions after the first.

57 *Humble Petition of Frances Harris.* In 1699 Swift was given the modest preferment of domestic chaplain to the Earl of Berkeley and lived with the family in the Castle in Dublin. The Lords Justices formed a commission to carry out the office of the king's representative in Dublin, and the date of this poem is determined as early as 1701 by the impending arrival of one of a new series of Lords Justices, the Earl of Drogheda (see note to p. 58 (3)). Frances Harris was a waiting-woman of Lady Berkeley's.

l. 1. *Lady Betty's chamber.* Lady Elizabeth Berkeley (1680–1769), second daughter of the earl; she married Sir John Germain in 1706, and remained one of Swift's oldest, firmest friends and a steady correspondent.

l. 23. *Mrs. Dukes.* A footman's wife.

l. 24. *Whittle.* The earl's valet.

58 l. 25. *dame Wadgar.* The housekeeper.

l. 27. *Lord Colway's folks are all very sad.* Like the Berkeley household, the Earl of Galway's people regret the impending loss of their importance.

l. 28. *Lord Dromedary.* Earl of Drogheda (?1650–1714).

l. 30. *Cary.* Clerk of the kitchen.

l. 32. *the steward.* 'that beast Ferris . . . scoundrel dog . . .' (*Journal to Stella*, 21 December 1710).

l. 38. *three skips of a louse.* Proverbial since mid-sixteenth century, *ODEP*[3], 817.

l. 41. *service is no inheritance.* Proverbial since 1412, *ODEP*[3], 716.

l. 43. *money can't go without hands*. Cf. 'Nothing is stolen without hands', proverbial since 1616, *ODEP³*, 580.

l. 49. *the Chaplain*. Swift.

l. 55. *Nab*. Diminutive of 'Abigail', a female servant.

59 l. 75. *shall ever pray*. 'for your Lordships' good estate': the concluding formula of a petition, as 'Humbly sheweth' at the start of the poem is the beginning.

60 *Meditation upon a Broom-Stick*. This piece is the occasion of an anecdote from Lady Betty Germain, that during the visits he made to England in the first decade of the eighteenth century, Swift often spent some time with her father, the Earl of Berkeley. The countess was in the habit of asking him to read aloud from Boyle's 'Meditations', but Swift inserted his own *Meditation* in the volume and read it to her great satisfaction. When the hoax was revealed, she took it in good part. Swift indeed visited Berkeley Castle in August 1702. *A Meditation* is not particularly like any of the Hon. Robert Boyle's *Occasional Reflections upon Several Subjects . . .* (1665); Boyle (1627–91), a chemist and natural philospher, was, however, one of the founders of the Royal Society. His religion was strongly Puritan, and his science accommodated a close interest in the hermetic writers satirized in *A Tale of a Tub*. There are several interesting links between *A Meditation* and *A Tale*.

62 *A Tale of a Tub*. Swift's title contains several jokes working simultaneously. It makes use of both an old expression meaning a cock-and-bull story and also the icon, to which he himself refers (p. 79), of the mariners throwing out an empty barrel to distract an inquisitive and threatening 'whale'. In all this he plays with the tone of a jocular formula in handling serious and complex ideas, and introduces the undercurrent of menace and bravado, fear and daring into which he immerses himself in the course of the satire. An imprecise tradition with a respectable pedigree drives back the composition or sketch of part of the work, perhaps the parable or allegory, to Swift's student days at Trinity College, Dublin. Most of the ostensible subject-matter, however, and the bulk of the writing clearly date from his employment by Sir William Temple at Moor Park. The years 1696 and 1697, to which period there are several specific references in the text, probably saw the definitive assembling and elaboration of the text as we now have it; these references give the work its place in the chronological sequence of the present selection. In form, *A Tale* consists of a parable of the development of the Christian religion in Europe, the allegory of the Father, his will, and his three sons with their coats, accompanied by a group of 'Digressions' in which are placed a set of variations on different themes that preoccupied Swift. The whole is embellished with a comic assemblage of the kind of 'preliminaries' that puffed out Grub Street volumes, and a manic 'Conclusion' from the modern and mercantile pen of 'The Author'. Swift's Christian fable develops an argument that Martin [Anglicanism] holds a moderate position between the peremptory institutionalism of Peter

[Catholicism], and the anarchic, egotistical individualism of Jack [radical personal belief]. Swift's brief service in 1695–6 as a Church of Ireland (Anglican) priest in a predominantly presbyterian area at Kilroot, near Belfast, without doubt sharpened his ecclesiastical and political sensibilities. The force of individualistic religion Swift chose to attack as 'zeal' or 'enthusiasm', and to ascribe it to pride, that 'sufficiency' which Temple saw as the root of political dissidence and intellectual arrogance (p. 605). The corruptions of learning flowed from the same sufficiency. These encompassed not only the scornful 'Moderns' like Bentley, who hectored the 'Ancients' he professed to study and attacked those like Temple, who revered the ancient wisdom, but also all the 'edifices in the air', the elaborate intellectual structures that Swift's wide reading in Temple's library had disinterred. Swift makes a sparkling mosaic of fragments from alchemy, hermetic, and occult systems, philosophical, medical, and scientific schemes. The Gnostic teachers of the first two centuries of Christianity, offering secret religious illumination, rub shoulders in the allusive text with Paracelsus, Sendivogius, and Thomas Vaughan offering secret knowledge of nature, Descartes offering a programme for certain reasoning, the charismatic religious leaders like Jack of Leyden, military and political leaders like Alexander the Great and Louis XIV offering themselves at their own valuation to obedient followers. 'The Author' of *A Tale* is himself an instance of such pride and complacency. All are types of sufficiency and fair game for attack, ridicule, and mockery. Joined with this, however, is the freest, liveliest, and most trenchant expression of a deeply satirical temperament that Swift was ever to achieve, completely transcending the aims, interests, quarrels, and preoccupations of the Temple circle, or even of his co-religionists. *A Tale of a Tub* establishes Swift with Juvenal, Rabelais, Sterne, and James Joyce as one of the great European writers in a particular mode. The text of *A Tale*, like the text of *Finnegans Wake*, is dense and capricious, full of unsignalled references and hints. The following table indicates how the piece is put together:

[PRELIMINARIES]

Treatises written by the same Author (1 page)

An Apology for the [Tale of a Tub] (10 pages)

[Printed here in the place traditionally given to it from the fifth edition (1710) onwards: this section was listed by Swift for independent publication, and is really a later commentary on an earlier work and its reception, not a prefatory statement: cf. 'Richard Sympson' to Benjamin Motte (p. 477 above).

Dedication to Somers (3 pages)

The Bookseller [publisher] *to the Reader* (1 page)

The Epistle Dedicatory to Prince Posterity (4 pages)

The Preface (7 pages)

Section I. The Introduction (9 pages)

[DIGRESSIONS]	[PARABLE]
	Section II (10 pages)
	The Father, his will, his three sons, and their coats; sect of tailor-worshippers and the religion of clothing; scholastic interpretation; the eldest son takes over a lord's house, expels his children, and takes in his two brothers.
Section III. A Digression concerning Critics (7 pages)	*Section IV* (9 pages)
	Peter names himself; his projects; the brothers steal a copy of the will, and he kicks them out of doors.
Section V. A Digression in the Modern Kind (5 pages)	*Section VI* (5 pages)
	Martin [Luther] and Jack [Calvin] name themselves; their divergent behaviour in reforming their coats; Jack runs mad and founds the sect of the Aeolists.
Section VII. A Digression in Praise of Digressions (4 pages)	*Section VIII* (5 pages)
	The learned Aeolists and their sect.
Section IX. A Digression on Madness (10 pages)	
Section X. [A Further Digression] (4 pages)	*Section XI* (11 pages)
	Jack's adventures.
[Though indicated in the text as 'A Tale of a Tub' (the heading for the Parable), this is a Digression, suggesting some disturbance in the text, perhaps the loss of a section on Martin: see Guthkelch, 306 ff.]	

The Conclusion (3 pages)

An adequate commentary on *A Tale of a Tub* would far out-run the space available here, but the following notes suggest obviously necessary information. The vast literature on *A Tale* vouches for the power of the text in attracting interpretations.

62 *Diu multumque desideratum.* 'Deeply desired for a long time.'

Basima eacabasa . . . camelanthi. Iren. Lib. *1.* C. *18.* Based on 'certain Hebrew words', mumbo-jumbo used by the Marcosian heretics, 'the more thoroughly to bewilder those who are being initiated' according to the second-century father, Irenaeus, attacking Gnosticism in his work *A Refutation and Overthrowing of Knowledge falsely so called*, commonly entitled *Adversus Haereses*; Swift made an abstract of Irenaeus in 1697 (Guthkelch, p. lvi).

Juvatque novos . . . tempora Musæ. 'It is a delight to gather fresh flowers and to seek a noble garland for my head from a source which the Muses never before used to deck the brow of any man': Lucretius. *De Rerum Natura*, i. 928–31.

Terra Australis incognita. 'The unknown southern land [near Australia].'

treatises written expressly against it. William King, *Some Remarks on the Tale of a Tub* (1704); William Wotton, *Observations upon the Tale of a Tub*; see Guthkelch, 315–28, for the text of the *Observations*.

63 *a late discourse.* [? Francis Gastrell], *The Principles of Deism truly represented and set in a clear Light, in two Dialogues between a Sceptic and a Deist* (1708).

64 *nondum tibi defuit hostis.* 'You have never yet been in want of an enemy': Lucan, *De Bello Civili*, i. 29.

the weightiest men in the weightiest stations. Traditionally taken to refer to Dr John Sharp, Archbishop of York: see p. 376.

another book . . . Letter of Enthusiasm. Anthony Ashley Cooper, 3rd Earl of Shaftesbury, *A Letter concerning Enthusiasm* (1708).

the tritest maxim in the world. The worst is the best corrupted.

65 *L'Estrange.* Sir Roger L'Estrange.

Dryden . . . in one of his prefaces. The lengthy *Discourse concerning the Original and Progress of Satire* (1693); reprinted in G. Watson (ed.), *Dryden's Critical Essays*, ii (1963).

the number Three . . . a dangerous meaning. Some shadow-boxing by Swift, to defend himself from charges of meddling with the doctrine of the Trinity; *four* was the 'perfect number'.

Eachard . . . the Contempt of the Clergy. The Revd John Eachard, (d. 1697), *The Grounds and Occasions of the Contempt of the Clergy and Religion Enquired into* (1670), provoked several violent replies, answered by Eachard the following year.

66 *Marvell's Answer . . . Orrery's Remarks.* Samuel Parker (later Bishop of Oxford), *A Discourse of Ecclesiastical Polity* (1670), strongly attacked toleration; it was part of the occasion of Andrew Marvell's answer to attacks on Nonconformists, *The Rehearsal Transpros'd*, i and ii (1672 and 1673) . . . The 'Remarks' on Bentley's *Dissertation* on Phalaris were by Charles Boyle; see p. 606.

one . . . first . . . as from an unknown hand. Dr William King's *Remarks*.

person of a graver character. The Revd William Wotton.

a certain great man. Sir William Temple.

67 *Porsenna's case, idem trecenti juravimus.* 'Three hundred of us have sworn the same oath': Lucius Annaeus Florus (second century AD), *Epitome* [of the Wars in Roman History to Augustus], i. 10. 6. This is Gaius Mucius Scaevola's answer to the Etruscan Porsenna, whom he had failed to murder and before whom as a captive he thrust his hand in the fire to show his contempt for pain.

another antagonist. Richard Bentley.

a Letter of . . . Buckingham. George Villiers (1628–87), 2nd Duke of Buckingham, 'To Mr. Clifford on his Humane-Reason'.

Peter's banter . . . his Alsatia phrase. Swift assigns the currency of one of his most hated, cant words (see p. 254) to a district between Fleet Street and the Thames, where a legal sanctuary for debtors and criminals was abolished in 1697.

68 *Combat des Livres.* [*Battle of the Books*]. François de Callières, *Histoire Poëtique de la Guerre nouvellement déclarée entre les Anciens et les Modernes* [*Poetical Account of the War newly declared between the Ancients and the Moderns*] (1688).

the answerer and his friend. Wotton and Bentley.

69 *Minnellius or Farnaby.* Jan Minell (*c.* 1625–83), Dutch scholar and editor of Latin school texts; Thomas Farnaby (*c.* 1577–1647), grammarian and schoolmaster.

optat . . . piger. Using an older editorial lack of punctuation, Swift makes the classical commonplace *optat ephippia bos, piger optat arare caballus* read 'The lazy ox longs for the horse's trappings, [the horse yearns to plough]' (Horace, *Epistles*, I. xiv. 43).

that the author is dead. Wotton in his *Observations* hinted at Temple as the author of the *Tale*.

the publishers. The editors; the modern *publisher* was indicated by 'bookseller'.

put it into the bookseller's preface. See note to p. 1 (2).

70 *the bullies in White-Friars.* See note to p. 67 (4).

impedimenta literarum. 'Pieces of literary luggage'.

71 *some explanatory notes.* The first four editions of *A Tale* have a series of marginal notes, all part of the joking and certainly placed there by Swift. A further series of footnotes was added in the fifth edition of 1710 and also separately printed as a set in *An Apology for the Tale of a Tub. With Explanatory Notes by W. W[o]tt[o]n, B.D. and Others* (1711), for the convenience of owners of earlier editions. Swift was also certainly responsible for this second series of notes, which offers a 'commentary' on *A Tale*, and (using material from Wotton's hostile criticism of the book) satirizes the critic as 'the learned commentator' (see p. 95, n. †).

a prostitute bookseller . . . a foolish paper. A Complete Key to the Tale of a Tub: with some Account of the Authors, and the Occasion and Design of writing it, and Mr. Wotton's Remarks examined (1710), published by Edmund Curll; reprinted in Guthkelch, 329–48. *A Complete Key* preserves the remembrance of Swift's cousin, the Revd Thomas Swift, about the early stages of the making of *A Tale of a Tub*. Thomas's copy of the first edition of *A Tale* in the Cornell University Library contains his manuscript notes on the text, which advance claims, not supported by his surviving writing, that he was at least co-author of certain portions of the complex.

The gentleman who gave the copy. 'Ralph Noden, Esq; of the Middle Temple': Curll's manuscript note in a copy of the *Key* in the British Library C. 28. b. 11).

72　*a maxim . . . title to the first.* Perhaps Themistocles after the defeat of Xerxes.

73　*your enemies . . . brought to light.* Somers was impeached in 1701 (see p. 612), but acquitted.

a late reign. King William III died 8 March 1702.

74　*formerly used to tedious harangues.* In the Commons, when he was a Crown law officer; and in the Lords, when he presided as Lord Chancellor.

in his preface. p. 79.

Boccalini . . . Troiano Boccalini (1556–1613), some of whose journalistic pieces, *Ragguaglia di Parnaso*, appeared as *Advertisements from Parnassus . . . Newly done into English, and adapted to the present Times by N.N.*, 3 vols. (1704), part of a spate of free paraphrases and adaptations that occupied Grub Street at this period.

75　*Marcosian Heretics.* From Marcus, second-century Gnostic teacher.

the person. Time, Posterity's 'tutor'.

76　*maitre de palais.* i.e. *maire du palais*: see p. 311 and ibid., n. (2).

Moloch. In the Old Testament, a divinity who required the sacrifice of children by fire (Jeremiah 32: 35).

77　*the laurel.* Renown in poetry, or the royal office of poet laureate.

posted fresh upon all gates and corners of streets. Books were advertised by pasting up their title-pages.

memorial of them . . . to be found. Phrases reminiscent of the Bible: cf. Deuteronomy 22: 26; Psalm 9: 6.

there is a large cloud near the horizon . . . and topography of them. Striking reminiscences of Shakespeare's *Antony and Cleopatra*, IV. xii. 1–10.

78　*Dryden, whose translation of Virgil.* Dryden's folio appeared in July 1697; with its subscriptions, dedications, engravings, it was a publisher's 'event', enough to attract Swift's satire; he also had political and religious animosities to fuel his bad feeling towards the old poet.

B[en]tl[e]y . . . W[o]tt[o]n. Richard Bentley and William Wotton are obvious members of this group, because of their anti-Temple writing in the Ancients v. Moderns controversy (see pp. 605–6): Bentley's 'near a thousand pages' is his enlarged *Dissertation* (1699) on Phalaris; Wotton's 'good sizeable volume' is his *Reflections* (1697).

a friend of your governor. Sir William Temple, who reveres the Ancients.

79 *a Grand Committee.* In Parliament, a committee of the whole House, or one of the four standing committees of the Commons.

Hobbes's Leviathan. Thomas Hobbes, *Leviathan: or, The Matter, Form and Power of a Common-Wealth, Ecclesiastical and Civil*, was first printed in 1651; it expounded a theory of society rooted in materialism, and its anti-traditional doctrine that all laws are framed by man made him one of the most controversial thinkers of the age.

given to rotation. Discussed by James Harrington's Rota club of political debate: see note to p. 51 (4).

the ship in danger . . . its old antitype, the Commonwealth. Cf. Swift's poem *Horace, Book I, Ode xiv . . . paraphrased . . .* above, p. 461. An antitype is what is shadowed forth or represented by a symbol or *type*; the image is from printing, or impressing with a die.

80 *the Spelling School.* Swift was a stickler for what he understood as the propriety of spelling.

insigne . . . alio. 'Something extraordinary, new, [. . .] unspoken by another voice': Horace, *Odes*, III. xxv. 7–8.

81 *fixed this mercury.* An alchemical phrase, to render mercury solid by combination with some other substance; *mercury* is also a sparkling wit.

the very newest . . . refiners. The Moderns; *refiners* has also an alchemical meaning, but is wider; cf. Temple, 'Of Poetry', '. . . reasoners upon government . . . refiners in politics . . . refined luxurists'.

82 *The tax upon paper.* A sales tax of £17.10s. per cent on the value of paper, vellum, and parchment, imposed in 1697.

Leicester-Fields. Now Leicester Square in London.

83 *the first monarch of this island . . . thistles in their stead.* James VI of Scotland by the Union of the Crowns became the first king of 'Great Britain'. He was attacked for appointing Scotsmen to English offices and dignities. The Scottish Order of the Thistle was revived by Queen Anne in 1703.

84 *all pork . . .*Plutarch.* Plutarch, *Life of Titus Quinctius Flamininus*, gives an early version of a common story. A parsimonious host wishes to make an impression; a rich meal is served in which each course has the same base, pork; but however delicately flavoured, the guest finally realizes that it is all 'pork'.

85 *Vide Xenophon.* Xenophon (*c.*428–*c.*354 BC) was formerly credited with a pamphlet, *The Constitution of Athens* (*c.*431).

C[l]eon . . . Hyperbolus. Cleon and Hyperbolus, two Athenian demogogues, referred to by Aristophanes, *Clouds*, 549–51.

all are gone astray . . . not one. Psalm 14: 3.

Astræa. The goddess of Justice who lived on earth in the Golden Age.

splendida bilis. 'Glittering [black] bile': Horace, *Satires,* II. iii. 141; the ancients supposed it to be a cause of madness.

Covent Garden. Theatre and fashionable red-light district in London.

White-Hall. A London royal palace, centre of the Court and Government offices; the buildings were burned down 4 January 1698.

Inns of Court . . . city. In London: one of the lawyers' centres . . . the financial and commercial district.

86 *A Panegyric upon the World . . . A Modest Defence . . .* Two of 'the Author's' treatises: see p. 62.

Evadere . . . labor est. Virgil, *Aeneid,* vi. 128–9: the translation is from Dryden's *Virgil.*

edifices in the air. Intellectual systems.

Socrates . . . in a basket. In Aristophanes, *Clouds.*

87 *the ladder.* The last standing place of those about to be hanged ('turned off'): often used for addressing the crowd of spectators.

senes . . . recedant. 'So that when they are old, they may withdraw into untroubled leisure': Horace, *Satires,* I. i. 31.

88 *sylva Caledonia.* The Caledonian forest: the austere Calvinist Kirk of Scotland, like many of the 'dissenting' groups in England, emphasized preaching.

the only uncovered vessel . . . human ears. Puritans kept their hats on in church as a protest against ritual. Their emphasis on the individuality of Christian witness made prominent use of the text '. . . [Saul of Tarsus] is a chosen vessel unto me . . .' (Acts 9: 15). English religious and political dissidents in the earlier seventeenth century were sometimes punished by mutilating their ears.

publication of these speeches. From 1698 to 1719 Paul Lorraine, the Ordinary [chaplain] of Newgate prison, organized a lucrative flow of 'last dying speeches and confessions', published in folio sheets.

89 *Corpoream quoque . . . impellere sensus.* 'For we must confess that voice and sound also are corporeal since they can affect our senses': Lucretius, *De Rerum Natura,* iv. 526–7; the translation offered in the footnote is Thomas Creech's (1682).

our modern saints. 'Saint' and 'sanctified' in New Testament use are applied to the elect under the New Covenant, i.e. members of the Christian Church: e.g. 1 Corinthians 1: 2; sixteenth- and seventeenth-century 'covenanted' groups applied the term to themselves, and the ironical use that Swift employs became common among their Anglican opponents.

90 *perorare with a song.* Conclude with the psalm customarily sung at the gallows.

Grub-Street. North of London Wall; symbolically the centre of all literary hacks and catch-penny writers. Swift was its great topologist and toponymist.

Gresham. Gresham College in Broad Street, a City foundation, was the meeting place of the Royal Society from 1660 until 1710.

91 *prodigals ... their husks and their harlots.* The Royal Society's empty investigations as 'husks', which formed the diet of the prodigal son after he had wasted his substance on the 'harlots' of riotous living (Luke 15): the latter part of the allusion is relevant at this time in the aftermath of Jeremy Collier's *Short View of the Immorality and Profaneness of the Stage* (1698).

92 *Pythagoras, Æsop, Socrates.* All traditionally ugly men.

History of Reynard the Fox. A group of beast stories which from medieval times were loaded with political and social satire.

92–3 *Tom Thumb ... Dr. Faustus ... Whittington and his Cat ... the Wise Men of Gotham.* All chap-book subjects: *The Hind and Panther*—Dryden's allegorical poem, published 1687, defending the Roman Catholic Church to which he had been converted; *Tommy Potts*—a broadside ballad, *The Lovers' Quarrel*, about fair Rosamund of Scotland, whose love was won by 'the Valour of Tommy Potts'. The critique assigned to each title mocks a different 'corruption' of learning.

The paragraph on *Dr. Faustus* is appropriately one of the places where joking about alchemy surfaces in the book. *Artephius*—the half-legendary author of a hermetic text, *Clavis Majoris Sapientiae* [The Key to the Greater Wisdom], who is supposed to have reached his great age by taking his own elixir; *adeptus*—adept, the alchemical code-word for an initiate in the study; *reincrudation*—chemical reduction, but also given mystical meaning; *via humida*—the humid or watery path, a chemical process involving water or a liquid; *the male* and *female dragon*—symbolic terms in alchemy for sulphur and mercury, using favourite sexual and organic analogies.

The paragraph on *Dick Whittington* calls to mind the traditional rabbinical study of the Talmud ('doctrine'); this collection of texts sets out the Jewish law as it crystallized, after centuries of oral transmission, into the Hebrew Mishnah ('learning'), finally codified at the end of the second century AD by rabbi Juda Ha-Nasi, accompanied by the Aramaic *Gemarah* ('commentary').

The paragraph on *The Wise Men of Gotham* flirts with the Ancients and Moderns controversy (see p. 605).

93 *meal-tubs.* A meal-tub, named in evidence as the hiding-place of treasonable papers, gave its name to one of the factitious 'conspiracies' of 1679, peripheral to the main Popish Plot.

94 *conscience void of offence [towards God and towards Men].* Acts 24: 16.

Dryden ... a multiplicity of godfathers. Dryden in his translation of Virgil dedicated the *Eclogues*, the *Georgics* and the *Aeneid* to three separate noblemen, and the hundred full-page engravings each bore the name and the arms of a top-rate subscriber, including Temple's sister, Martha, Lady Giffard.

95 *Garments of the Israelites.* Deuteronomy 8: 4.

... *Lambin*. Denys Lambin, French scholar (1516–72), ed. Cicero's works (Strasburg, 1581) (*SL* 402) and ed. Plautus (Paris, 1576) (*SL* 593).

the first seven years. i.e. seven centuries of the Christian era.

96 *Locket's*. Adam Locket's fashionable eating-house at Charing Cross.

97 *Jupiter Capitolinus*. In 390 BC the sacred geese in the Roman temple of Jupiter on the Capitol gave the alarm as a party of invading Gauls silently entered the citadel.

Hell. Where the tailor throws his scraps of cloth.

deus minorum gentium. 'A god of the lesser nations' (the *goyim*).

that creature. A louse, 'cracked' as the renovating tailor smoothed a seam.

primum mobile. 'The first moving heaven' (in the medieval cosmography).

98 *ex traduce*. 'Transmitted by propagation'; theologians disputed whether the soul was derived from the parents like the body (traduction), or whether a new soul was created at each birth.

in them we live ... being. Acts 17: 28.

all in all. Corinthians 15: 28.

all in every part. 'Anaxagoras ... asserts that there is in everything a mixture of everything': Lucretius, *De Rerum Natura*, i. 874.

vein and race. Two words used excessively by Sir William Temple; *race* is an adaptation of a French word, which '... applied to wines, in its primitive sense, means the flavour of the soil' (Johnson, 'Life of Thomson', who notes Temple's use of the term in 'An Essay upon the Ancient and Modern Learning').

99 *shoulder-knots*. A French mode which became fashionable in the 1670s.

ruelles. A lady at this time admitted visitors of a morning to the ruelle, or space between her bed and the wall; hence, a levee, or a boudoir generally.

sculler. A boat propelled by one man, thus cheaper and less fashionable than oars, i.e. a boat with two rowers.

the Rose. A tavern at the Drury Lane (theatre) end of Russell Street.

temper. Compromise, adjustment.

100 *jure paterno*. 'By paternal law'; cf. the *jure divino* ('by divine law') by which the exiled James II was still said to be king.

101 *altum silentium*. 'Deep silence': Virgil, *Aeneid*, x, 63.

circumstantial. Unimportant.

aliquo ... adhærere. 'In some manner inhere in the essence.'

Aristotelis ... Interpretatione. There is no specific work by Aristotle called *Dialectica* (Logic); this represents some college collection of pieces translated into Latin: *De Interpretatione* is a straightforward piece, probably by Aristotle, on the relation of thought to language.

conceditur . . . negatur. A formula of scholastic disputation: 'I agree. But, if the same thing be affirmed of the nuncupatory, I deny it.'

102 *a codicil annexed.* The Apocrypha.

written by a dog-keeper. Tobit 5: 16; 11: 4.

105 *Edinburgh streets in a morning.* In the apartments of Edinburgh's multi-storeyed 'lands', after 10 p.m. the filth collected by each householder was by custom emptied from the windows into the street, nominally to be collected at 7 a.m. the next morning by the inadequate force of street cleaners.

Momus . . . Hybris . . . Zoilus . . . Tigellius. For *Momus*, 'the patron of the Moderns', and the descent of criticism, see p. 12 above and ibid., n. (1). *Hybris*, in Greek 'insolence, violence coming from pride in strength', hence pride personified; *Zoilus*, fourth-century BC. Cynic philosopher of Amphipolis, notorious for his bad-tempered attacks on Homer; *Tigellius* was an ungenerous critic of Horace (*Satires*, 1. ii. 3); for *Perrault* see p. 15 and ibid., n. (4).

as Hercules most generously did. Hercules, mortally sick by the poison on the shirt of Nessus which his credulous wife Deianira had given him to regain his love, committed suicide on Mt. Oeta and was elevated to heaven by Jupiter.

106 *the proper employment of a . . . critic.* There follows a parody of the exploits and labours of Hercules: he killed Cacus, a fire-breathing monster living on the Palatine Hill; he killed the Hydra; cleaned out the Augean stables; and exterminated the carnivorous birds of prey that infested the shores of Lake Stymphalis in Arcadia.

107 *noble moderns . . . volumes I turn . . . over . . .* 'For yourselves, turn over the Greek models in your hands night and day': Horace, *Epistle to the Pisos* [*Art of Poetry*], 269.

Pausanias is of opinion. Greek geographer *c.*150 AD; the reference is to his *Description of Greece*, ii. 38.

108 *Herodotus. c.*480–*c.*425 BC: *Histories*, iv. 191.

Ctesias yet refines. A Greek from Coridos (*fl.* late fifth century BC), a doctor at the Persian court; Swift cites a work on India as found in a compilation of extracts from Greek and Latin prose works, the *Bibliotheca* of Photius, ninth-century patriarch of Constantinople, of which work he possessed an edition (Rouen, 1653) in folio, *SL* 104.

our Scythian ancestors. Temple, *Introduction to the History of England*, believed they came from Norway and were the ancestors of the Scots.

Diodorus . . . ventures. Apparently not. Guthkelch, 99 n., suggests that 'Dio (dorus)' is a mistake for 'Dic (aearchus)' (Greek miscellaneous writer, *fl. c.* 300 BC), fr. 60, who mentions a plant on Pelion the shade of which, when it flowered, killed those who slept under it.

Lucretius gives exactly the same relation. 'And on the great peaks of Helicon there is a tree which generally kills men by the foul smell of the blossom': vi. 786–7. The verse translation at n. § is by Creech. Swift probably substituted *retro* ('on the back-side') for Lucretius's *tetro* ('foul') intentionally.

108–9 *Ctesias . . . these remarkable words.* See note to p. 108 (2).

109 *Terence makes . . . mention . . . malevoli.* Prologues to his comedies *Andria, Heautontimorumenos,* and *Adelphi . . .* 'spiteful people'.

like Themistocles and his company. Plutarch. *Themistocles,* 2: 'When, therefore, he was laughed at, long after, in company where free scope was given to raillery . . . he was obliged to answer . . . : " 'Tis true I never learned how to tune a harp, or play upon a lute, but I know how to raise a small and inconsiderable city [Athens] to glory and greatness" ' (trans. J. and W. Langhorne).

110 *composition of a man.* 'Nine tailors make a man': proverbial (*ODEP*³, 567).

sine mercurio. Without mercury: cf. p. 81 and ibid., n. (1).

112 *Terra Australis Incognita.* See p. 62 above and ibid., n. (4).

sovereign remedy for the worms. . . This paragraph (with p. 6) calls to mind contemporary patent medicine advertisements.

repeating poets. Who give readings of their own verse.

112–13 *office of insurance . . . damage by fire.* Indulgences were issued to protect against Hell Fire, just as the recently founded insurance offices (e.g. the Friendly Society itself) issued insurance policies to cover damage by fire.

113 *powder pimperlim-pimp. Poudre de perlimpinpin*; a quack medicine, thence an ironical phrase for the magic ingredient, the universal remedy.

114 *bulls of Colchos.* Before he could carry off the Golden Fleece from Colchis, Jason had to yoke a pair of fire-breathing bulls to sow the dragon's teeth.

the metal of their feet . . . sunk into common lead. A papal bull takes its name from the *bulla* or lead seal, depicting SS Peter and Paul with the Pope's name, attached to the bottom of the document.

Varias inducere plumas . . . Atrum desinit in piscem. 'To insert many coloured feathers' . . . 'turns into a black fish': Horace, *Epistle to the Pisos [Ars Poetica],* 2–4, laughs at the licence of imagination in a painting of a grotesque figure made up of a human head, horse's neck, feathered limbs, and fish's tail. The less formal papal *brief* (letter) was sealed in red wax with the Pope's personal seal depicting St Peter fishing.

appetitus sensibilis. Or *sensitivus*: in Thomas Aquinas's system the natural 'appetite' or inclination towards a particular form of behaviour with which all sensitive life is endued; in addition, man possesses a rational or intellectual 'appetite', the will.

pulveris exigui jactu. '*By the scattering of a little dust* these passionate turmoils, these fierce contests [of bees] are borne down and quieted': Virgil, *Georgics,* iv. 87.

115 *bull-beggars.* The connection of this word for spectres or bug-bears with papal bulls was common.

the north-west. Cf. p. 87.

most humble | *man's man.* The opening formula of a bull named the Pope as *servus servorum dei,* 'servant of the servants of God'.

tax cameræ apostolicæ. The apostolic *Camera* was the papal treasury, and the 'tax' was the fee for engrossing and expediting a papal writing.

verè adepti. 'Truly adepts, initiates'; this phrase introduces more alchemical references: *arcana,* 'the operation', 'sons of [the] art'.

119 *Chinese waggons.* '. . . where Chineses drive | With sails and wind their canie waggons light': Milton, *Paradise Lost,* iii. 438–9.

120 *Quemvis perferre laborem . . . vigilare serenas.* Addressing Gaius Memmius, Lucretius says that '[the delight I hope to draw from our enjoyable friendship] persuades me to endure many labours and makes me keep awake through the nights of stillness': *De Rerum Natura,* i. 141–2.

a very strange, new, and important discovery . . . A satirical mishandling of a maxim of classical critical theory: Horace, *Epistle to the Pisos* [*Ars Poetica*], 343–4: 'He gains every vote who mixes the pleasant and profitable, delighting and instructing the reader at the same time.'

121 *fastidiosity, amorphy, and oscitation.* Fastidiousness, shapelessness, and yawning; the first and second of these pedantic word-forms seem to have been used first by Swift (*OED*).

whether there have been ever any ancients or no. Bentley had 'annihilated' Phalaris as a letter-writer, as well as Aesop: but there is also the paradox that the Moderns are the true Ancients; see note to p. 7.

O. Brazile. Or *Hy-Brazil:* an imaginary island to the west of Ireland.

Painters Wives Island. The earliest mention of this in print seems to be Walter Ralegh, *History of the World* (1614), i, cap. 23, sect. 4: 'while the fellow drew that map, his wife sitting by, desired him to put in one country for her . . .'

balneo Mariæ . . . Q.S. A *bain-marie* or kitchen steamer . . . *quantum sufficit* ('as much as is needed': in cooking or medicine).

sordes . . . caput mortuum. 'Dregs . . . the residue after distillation' (pictographically represented in alchemical texts by a skull).

Catholic. Universally applicable or effective (medical and Rosicrucian).

121-2 *medullas, excerpta quædams, florilegias.* Marrows or piths, certain extracts, anthologies (collections of flowers, garlands), all in Swift's opinion examples of the Moderns' superficial drive to acquire knowledge without labour, thinking, or serious study. The 'reader's digest' was a characteristic of two contemporary developments, a popular audience and a literary market.

122 *Homerus omnes . . .* 'Homer covered all human topics in his poem': Xenophon (*c.*427–*c.*354 BC), *Symposium,* iv. 6.

cabalist. Specifically, a student of the cabbala ('what is received'), the mystical tradition of interpreting the Jewish Scriptures; this has a strong likeness to Gnostic teaching: more generally, one skilled in secret meaning.

opus magnum. The 'great work' in alchemy, the transmutation of base metals into gold.

Sendivogius, Behmen, or Anthroposophia Theomagica. Michael Sędjiẃoj (b. Poland 1566, d. Silesia 1636), alchemist and metallurgist, author of an often-printed alchemical treatise, *De Lapide Philosophorum* [*On the Philosophers' Stone*], 1604, as well as a dialogue on mercury and a tractate on sulphur; his hermetic teaching was influenced by Paracelsus. Jacob Boehme (1575–1625), German theologian, mystic, and prophet; all his writings were made available in English in the mid-seventeenth century. Thomas Vaughan, *AnthroposophiaTheomagica: or, A Discourse of the Nature of Man and his State after Death; grounded on the Creator's Proto-Chymistry, and verified by a practical examination of Principles in the great World . . . Zoroaster in Oracul.* [*The Oracles*, a work attributed to Zarathustra, the sixth-century Iranian magus]. *Audi Ignis Vocem* ['I have heard the voice of the fire'] (1650).

the answer to it writ by the learned Dr. Henry More. Henry More (1614–87), the Cambridge Platonist, published two replies to Vaughan (1650).

sphæra pyroplastica. 'Fire-globe' or 'sphere of fire', a term peculiar to Thomas Vaughan in his recipe for the universal medicine, and related to the mysterious 'third principle' of Boehme.

vix crederem . . . vocem. 'I should find it difficult to believe that this author ever heard of fire': cf. preceding note.

123 *these last three years.* Wotton's *Reflections* first appeared in 1694.

political wagering. See note to p. 217 (2).

124 *proceed critics and wits by reading nothing else.* See p. 132.

127 *zeal . . . the most significant word.* This biblical word was of some standing as a pejorative characterization of religious feeling held to be too unrestrained and probably hypocritical: cf. Ben Jonson's Puritan, Zeal-of-the-Land Busy, in *Bartholomew Fair* (1614).

129 *Exchange-women.* The Royal Exchange on the north of Cornhill and the New Exchange in the Strand both had shops, mostly kept by women.

the fox's arguments. When he had lost his tail, in Aesop's fable.

Dutch Jack. Jack of Leyden (Jan Bockleszoon or Beukelsz) became leader of the Anabaptists who took over Münster; the bishop regained the city in 1535 and Jack was put to death by torture.

the sect of Æolists. See Section VIII, p. 133, and note to p. 133 (2).

130 *—Mellaeo . . . Lepore.* Lucretius, *De Rerum Natura*, i. 934: *Mellaeo* should be *Melleo* (honeyed), which would be a false quantity; Lucretius wrote *Musaeo*: 'touching all with the Muse's charm'.

131 *get a thorough insight into the index.* A common accusation against Bentley: see note to p. 17 (3).

the wise man's rule, of regarding the end. Solon's unwelcome advice to Croesus.

like Hercules's oxen, by tracing them backwards. The monster Cacus stole some of the cattle of Geryon from Hercules (see note to p. 106), dragging them backwards into his cave to avoid detection.

not at this present . . . matter left in nature to furnish . . . a volume. Cf. '. . . in every part of natural and mathematical knowledge . . . the next Age will not find much work of this kind to do' (Wotton, *Reflections upon Ancient and Modern Learning*, quoted in Guthkelch, 146).

132 *Ctesiæ fragm. . . .* A fragment of Ctesias quoted by Photius (see note to p. 108 (2)).

sed quorum . . . pertingentia. 'But whose genitals were gross and reached to their ankles.'

133 *everlasting chains . . . in a library.* See p. 5 and ibid., n. (1).

The learned Æolists. This section operates in very dangerous territory for Swift and his contemporary readers. Wotton in his *Observations* notes: 'His whole *VIII*th section concerning the Æolists [is] a mixture of impiety and immodesty . . .', adding, '. . . So great a delight has this unhappy writer, to play with what some part or other of mankind have always esteemed as sacred!'

Quod procul . . . gubernans. 'May the Fortune that governs things avert this from us': Lucretius, *De Rerum Natura*, v. 107.

134 *anima mundi.* Thomas Vaughan, *Anthroposophia Theomagica* (quoted by Guthkelch, 150 n. 3), dilates on the 'World Soul', identifying it as 'etherial Nature', a middle Spirit, by means of which man is made subject to the influence of the stars, and 'partly disposed of by the *celestial harmony*'; elsewhere he identifies it as the 'universal spirit of Nature'.

forma informans. 'The *form* which imparts form', one of the 'distinctions' of a term in the Aristotelian dualism of form and matter employed by the Schoolmen.

the breath of our nostrils. Genesis 2: 7.

three distinct animas. The traditional scholastic threefold division of the vital principle into vegetative (life), sensitive (feeling), rational (reason).

cabalist Bumbastus . . . the four cardinal points. For *cabalist*, see note to p. 122 (2); for *Paracelsus*, see note to p. 11 (5). Made from the four elements, man the *microcosm* had a correspondence with the four cardinal points of the compass of the *macrocosm*, the face with the east, the posteriors with the west.

135 *learning puffeth men up.* 1 Corinthians 8: 1.

the choicest . . . belches . . . through that vehicle. Swift in common with other contemporary satirists plays on the 'twang of the nose' said to be characteristic of popular preaching: see *The Mechanical Operation of the Spirit*, pp. 174 ff.

latria. 'divine worship' (Greek).

omnium deorum . . . celebrant. 'They worship the North Wind more than all other gods': Pausanias, *Description of Greece*, VIII. xxxvi. 6.

136 Σκοτία. Gr. 'darkness, gloom'; also *Scotia*, 'Scotland'.

Pancirollus. Guido Pancirolli (1523–99), *Rerum Memorabilium jam olim deperditarum libri II* (1599); i, arts and discoveries of the ancients now lost; ii, inventions of the moderns (*SL* 457).

ex adytis and penetralibus. 'From the inner shrines and sanctuaries': Virgil, *Aeneid*, ii. 297.

138 *Laplanders . . . buy their winds . . . from the same merchants . . . retail them . . . to customers much alike*. They 'buy' them from dishonest *shamans* and sell them to merchants (i.e. Puritans and Nonconformists, or perhaps the credulous): 'This, that we have reported concerning the Laplanders, is by Olaus Magnus, and justly, related of the Finlanders, who . . . sell winds to those merchants that traffic with them' (John Scheffer, *History of Lapland* (Oxford, 1674), xi. 58).

Delphos. An erroneous form of *Delphi* used in English by Temple, for which he was rebuked by Bentley. The oracle of Apollo answered through the Pythia, a woman in a state of possession.

139 *A certain great prince*. Henry IV of France (1553–1610), assassinated by a Catholic fanatic.

140 *corpora quaeque*. A Lucretian phrase, 'any bodies'; iv. 1065.

Idque petit . . . gestitque coire. 'And the body seeks that object by which the mind is wounded in love. He tends to that by which he is struck and desires to unite with it': Lucretius, *De Rerum Natura*, iv. 1048 and 1055.

[*Cunnus*] *teterrima belli | Causa* ——. '[A cunt], most dreadful cause of war': Horace, *Satires*, i. iii. 107.

a mighty king. Louis XIV.

dragoon. The dragonnades in the Cevennes against the Protestant *camisards*, a French 'enthusiastic' sect: see note to p. 197.

141 *academy of modern Bedlam*. Bedlam (originally the priory of Bethlehem), a mental hospital for 150 patients, in 1675 moved into a new building in Moorfields near London Wall, not far from where the Royal Society met (see note to p. 13 (2).

Apollonius. Of Tyana, *fl.* at the beginning of the Christian era, a sage who held Pythagorean doctrines and was reputed to have miraculous powers.

clinamina. Lucretius (ii. 292) used *clinamen* ('inclination') to render Epicurus's *parenklisis*, the deviation from the straight path which allowed atoms to collide by chance and create the matter of the world.

Cartesius . . . his romantic system . . . vortex. See p. 11. and ibid., n. (3), and p. 14 and ibid., n. (4).

142 *our hackney-coachmen . . . Est quod gaudeas . . . viderere*. The joke springs from two letters written in May and December 54 BC by Cicero to his young friend C. Trebatius Testa, whom he was recommending to Julius Caesar for employment in the invasion of Britain. (1) '. . . enter a [caveat] for yourself

against the tricks of those charioteers in Britain ...'; (2) 'You have good reason to rejoice in having arrived [in Gaul] where you can appear as a knowledgeable man! Had you gone to Britain as well, I dare say there would have been no greater expert than you in the whole vast island': Cicero, *Letters to Friends*, vii. 6 and 10.

143 *to cut the feather.* To split hairs, to make a fine distinction.

Jack of Leyden. See note to p. 129 (3).

145 *the films and images that fly off ... from the superficies of things.* Lucretius, *De Rerum Natura*, iv. 30–2: '... *What we call "images" of things*, a sort of outer skin perpetually peeling off the surface of objects and flying about this way and that through the air ...'

146 *one man ... leaps into a gulf.* Marcus Curtius to save Rome leaped fully armed, on horseback, into the chasm that had opened in the Forum.

another ... unluckily timing it ... Empedocles. fl. 450 BC, philosopher and mystagogue, said to have perished on entering the crater of Mt. Etna, either to show he was a god, or out of curiosity.

the elder Brutus. Lucius Junius Brutus, traditional founder of the Roman republic; he was said to have feigned stupidity to avoid the vengeance of the Tarquin kings.

ingenium par negotiis. 'A character equal to its duties': Tacitus, *Annals*, vi. 39 and xvi. 18.

Sir E[dwar]d S[eymou]r ... Leading Tory MPs.

Bedlam. see p. 141 and ibid., n. (1); the following passage will remind the reader of the Academy of Lagado in *Gulliver's Travels*, Book III. iv, and also of *The Legion Club* (see pp. 556 ff.).

threepence in his pocket. The traditional share of the (shilling) coach-hire for each of a party of four lawyers from the Inns of Court to Westminster Hall.

147 *ecce cornuta erat ejus facies.* Exodus 34: 29, 30.

the society of Warwick Lane. The Royal College of Physicians stood in Warwick Lane from 1674 to 1825.

148 *the orator of the place.* The guide.

149 *Will's ... Gresham College ... Moorfields ... Scotland Yard ... Westminster Hall ... Guildhall.* Will's coffee-house was the resort of the wits and poets ... The Royal Society met in Gresham College, Broad Street ... Bedlam was in Moorfields ... There was a barracks in Scotland Yard, 'where gentlemen soldiers lie basking in the sun, like so many swine upon a warm dunghill' (Ned Ward, *The London Spy*, ed. A. L. Hayward (1927), p. 172) ... The law courts met in Westminster Hall ... The Lord Mayor and aldermen of the City of London meet in Guildhall, north of Cheapside.

the famous Troglodyte philosopher. Probably one of the series of covert (and ambivalent) references in *A Tale of a Tub* to Francis Bacon, who earns this sobriquet by his image of the *Idols of the Cave* in *The New Organum*, I. liii–lviii:

'The *Idols of the Cave* take their rise in the particular constitution, mental or bodily, of each individual . . .' They include 'certain particular sciences and speculations' to which men become attached, 'either because they fancy themselves the authors and inventors thereof [folly embossed], or because they have bestowed the greatest pains upon them and become habituated to them [folly inlaid] . . .' The whole passage is relevant to Swift's satire.

150 *Dr. Bl[ackmo]re*. Richard Blackmore.

L[estran]ge. Sir Roger L'Estrange.

rectifier of saddles. 'Set the saddle on the right horse': lay the blame on those who deserve it; proverbial from 1607 (*ODEP*³, 690).

furniture of an ass. See note to p. 10 (1).

151 *the Rosicrucians*. The secret society of the Rosicrucians, one of the interests of Thomas Vaughan (see note to p. 122 (5)), is supposed to have been founded by Christian Rosenkreuz in the fifteenth century, to preserve a system of occult wisdom allowing the attainment of knowledge into all the secrets and mysteries of Nature. The brotherhood were required to conceal their membership and their hermetic knowledge.

152 *Bythus and Sigè*. Bythus, Sigè (depth, silence, two of the primary 'aeons' or religious principles), and Acamoth (representing the Hebrew word for wisdom) come from the account of the teaching of Valentinian the Gnostic, in Irenaeus, *Adversus Haereses* (see note to p. 62 (2)), I. iv. 2.

à cujus lacrymis . . . timore mobilis. 'From the tears of the Demiurge proceeds the damp substance, from his laughter the bright, from his sorrow the solid, from his fear the mobile': Irenaeus, see above.

Anima Magica Abscondita. Thomas Vaughan (see note to p. 122 (5)), *Anima Magica Abscondita: Or, A Discourse of the Universal Spirit of Nature, With his strange, abstruse, miraculous Ascent and Descent . . .* (1650).

153 *reduce all thing into types*. See note to p. 79 (4): typological or symbolic reading of the Scriptures, and relating this typology to politics and historical events, are characteristics of some Christian groups, such as seventeenth-century 'Puritans' or the modern Jehovah's Witnesses.

154 *a passage near the bottom*. Guthkelch, 191, suggests Revelations 22: 11: 'he which is filthy, let him be filthy still', omitted in some manuscripts.

155 *It was ordained*. A passage mocking the Calvinistic emphasis on predestination.

156 *Vide Don Quixote*. Part I, chap. xviii; silver was used in nasal prosthesis.

an ancient temple of Gothic structure. Stonehenge, 'Gothic' because it was judged rude and barbarous, supposedly built by the Druids.

157 *a strange kind of speech*. See note to p. 135 (2) above.

the Spanish accomplishment of braying. Don Quixote, Part II, chapters xxv and xxvii; the adventure of the alderman braying to recover a lost ass.

the stinging of the tarantula. Those bitten by the tarantula spider were believed to be afflicted with hysterical dancing (tarantism), which could be calmed by music.

feared no colours. 'Feared no enemy', from 'colours' meaning 'flags'; 'colours' may also mean embellishments of style, rhetorical ornaments.

leap . . . into the water. Total immersion in adult baptism.

pilgrim's salve. An ointment made from pork fat and isinglass.

a-groaning, like the famous board. Elm boards made to groan in this way, by virtue of their fibrous structure, were exhibited as prodigies.

159 *Effugiet . . . Proteus.* 'But Proteus, the rascal, will still escape from these bonds': Horace, *Satires*, II. 71.

artes perditae. 'Lost arts': see note to p. 136 (2).

slitting of one ear *in a stag* . . . A remark of Aristotle's in *Historia Animalium*, vi. 29 (578ᵇ).

160 *improve the growth of ears.* The cropped hair of male Puritans (Roundheads) gave prominence to the ears.

161 *six senses . . . *Including Scaliger's.* J. C. Scaliger, *De Subtilitate* (1537), p. 358; cf. Robert Burton, *The Anatomy of Melancholy* (1628), Pt. I. sect. 1, memb. 1, subsect. 6: '. . . to which you may add Scaliger's sixth sense of titillation, if you please'.

oscitancy. See note to p. 121 (1).

162 *that noble Jesuit.* Father Pierre-Joseph d'Orleans (*fl.* 1688–1734) SJ, *Histoire de M. Constance* (1690), 'Avertissement'.

163 *to write upon nothing.* Cf. Rochester's poem 'Upon Nothing' (*c.* 1680) and, later, Henry Fielding, 'Essay on Nothing' (1743).

ut plenus vitæ conviva. 'Like a dinner guest full of life': Lucretius, *De Rerum Natura*, iii. 938.

a very polite nation in Greece. The people of Troezen; Pausanias, ii. 31. 5.

165 *The Mechanical Operation of the Spirit.* The third and last piece that made up the miscellany volume, *A Tale of a Tub* (1704), furnished like the others with its own title-page, is cast in the popular form of a 'Letter to a Friend'. It attacks another modern intellectual fashion, the communication of abstruse scientific information to a society of *virtuosi*, eager to hear, and be known to hear, the latest advances in human knowledge. Descartes's metaphysics, by divorcing mind from matter, had turned *spirit* or the divine force into a kind of 'mechanical spirit' brought in to keep the argument from becoming totally atheistic. *The Mechanical Operation of the Spirit* also takes up Swift's attack on one of the abuses of religion, the cultivation of 'enthusiasm' (Greek, 'possession by the god'). Swift associates this false inspiration in *A Tale of a Tub* with Jack. *The Mechanical Operation of the Spirit* is clearly part of the complex of *A Tale of a Tub*, and particularly related to Section XI of *A Tale* itself. The exact relationship is complex and obscure.

T. H. Esquire. Possibly Thomas Hobbes, a theorist of 'motion' (see note to p. 11 (3)).

New Holland. Australia: by the mid-seventeenth century, Dutch seamen voyaging from the Dutch East Indies had sailed down the west coast of the as yet unexplored continent.

166 *Iroquois Virtuosi . . . Gresham . . . the Literati of Tobinambou.* In 1687, Charles Perrault read his modern poem lauding *Le Siècle de Louis le Grand* to the French Academy, provoking several epigrams by Boileau; Sir William Temple reprinted one of them in his 'Thoughts upon Reviewing the Essay of Ancient and Modern Learning'; it concludes: 'Where can anyone have said such a shameful thing? Among the Huron Indians? Among the Topinambous?' 'No! In Paris.' 'In the mad-house then?' 'No! In the Louvre, at a full meeting of the French Academy.' The Topinambous were a tribe of Brazilian Indians. The Royal Society was meeting at this time in Gresham College, Broad Street.

168 *The Planetary Worlds.* The plurality of inhabited worlds was an old speculation given new life by sixteenth- and seventeenth-century discoveries in optics and astronomy: see note to p. 11 (7), and cf. Fontenelle, *Entretiens sur la pluralité des mondes habités* (1686).

The Squaring of the Circle. An impossible problem solved, as he believed, by Thomas Hobbes.

Hippocrates tells us. De Aere, Aquis, et Locis, 35, 36, but in his mention of the [long-heads] he says nothing of the Scythians (see note to p. 108 (3)).

169 *Roundheads.* See note to p. 160.

the following fundamental. The Aristotelian antithesis of 'corruption' and 'generation' was a scholastic commonplace and the source of many jokes: see p. 599.

170 *modern saints.* See note to p. 89 (2).

the second chapter of the Acts. i.e. Acts of the Apostles, dealing with the day of Pentecost, when the Holy Spirit appeared to the Apostles as cloven tongues of fire, and they spoke with 'other tongues'.

while their hats were on. See note to p. 88 (2).

Jauguis. Yogis: Yoga is union with the supreme spirit.

Guagnini . . . Alexander Guagninus, *Sarmatiae* [Poland and south-east Russia] *Descriptio* (1578), 'Moschoviae Descriptio' *sub* 'Mulierum conditio' ['the condition of women'].

172 *Dum fas . . . avidi—.* 'When furious with passion they distinguish right and wrong by the narrow line their desire marks out': Horace, *Odes,* I. viii. 10, 11.

173 *the picture of Hobbes's Leviathan.* At the top of the engraved title-page of the first edition of Hobbes, *Leviathan* (1651), a crowned figure holding a sword and a crozier rises behind a view of hills and a city; the torso and arms are made up of diminutive figures.

174 *the choice and cadence of the syllables*. An important critical principle for Swift: cf. p. 372.

enigmatically meant by Plutarch. Convivium VII Sapientium, 5.

Sir H[u]mphrey Edw[i]n. A presbyterian Lord Mayor, 1697–8; see p. 162.

Thy word . . . paths. Psalm 119: 105.

Canting. See p. 62.

175 *a Banbury saint.* Banbury, Oxfordshire, was famous for the zeal of its Puritans, who in 1602 demolished the famous cross there.

176 *Rippon spurs.* Ripon in the West Riding of Yorkshire was the centre of a celebrated equestrian accessories industry, including saddlery and the proverbial 'right Ripon spurs'.

lecture. An exposition of a scripture passage, often held in mid-week, not part of the Sunday services.

the Rod of Hermes. The winged *caduceus*, herald's staff (or magic wand) of Mercury, messenger of the gods: see note to p. 394 (7).

the snuffle of a bag-pipe. 'Bagpipe' glimmers throughout this passage to represent the Scottish Kirk; see also note to p. 88 (1).

as Darius did . . . the day before. Darius conspires with six other Persian noblemen to kill Smerdis, the usurper; when they have done so, the assassins agree that he should be king whose horse neighs first after sunrise. Darius' groom arranges the previous night for his master's stallion to cover a mare, and the next morning, on encountering the mare, Darius' horse neighs.

177–8 *The most early traces we meet with of fanatics in ancient story . . .* i.e. history. The references in this dense paragraph on ancient ecstatic religion, amusing as many of them are individually, may be so congested as to have driven the whole piece out of *A Tale* proper. The following are a few suggestions for elucidating it: *Orgia*—secret rites, e.g. the Eleusinian Mysteries; *Panegyres*—an assembly of a whole nation; *Dionysia*—festival (orgia) of Dionysus, a Thracian god of an ecstatic religion; *Orpheus*—to whom is attributed in Greek mythology the foundation of the mystic religion of Orphism, involving Demeter and Dionysus; *Melampus*—a Greek prophet who used the voices of birds and reptiles, which he (like Orpheus) understood, for divination; *Diod. Sic. L.1.*—Diodorus Siculus, [*World History*], i (Egypt), 97, 286;—*scouting through the index*—see note to p. 131 (1); *Herod. L.2.*—Herodotus, *Histories*, ii. 77, 'they drink a wine made from barley'; *the Scarlet Whore*—Revelations 17, identified by the sectaries with the Pope and mitred bishops.

178 *Dionysia Brauronia.* Brauron, on the east coast of Attica, was the centre of a quinquennial festival of Dionysus.

Vide Photium . . . Photius, *Bibliotheca*, iii, preserves fifty stories from Greek mythology by Conon, *fl.* 90 BC.

Simon Magus . . . Eutyches. Simon the Magician (or the Revealer) was a name to which many stories in early Christian legend were attracted; Irenaeus,

Adversus Haereses, I. xxiii, identifies him with the Simon of Acts 8: 9–24 and further names him as the original Gnostic teacher. . . . Eutyches was a fifth-century heresiarch, archimandrite of Constantinople, who taught that Christ possessed only a divine essence; this in turn implied the deification of human nature.

179 *John of Leyden, David George, Adam Neuster*. For the Dutch-born Anabaptist, Jan Bockleszoon, see note to p. 129 (3); David George or Joris (1501–56), another Dutch Anabaptist, founded the 'Familists' or Family of Love; Adam Neuster (d. 1576) was a German Socinian theologian, i.e. he denied the divinity of Christ (see note to p. 225 (1)).

Family of Love, Sweet Singers of Israel. By using these generic names, Swift introduces into his catalogue of 'enthusiasts' the Anabaptist or 're-baptized' groups that proliferated in England in the middle decades of the seventeenth century. He gives an undeserved prominence to these extreme groups, provocatively associating them with quietists like the Quakers.

furor [*Uterinus*]. 'Mania of the uterus': nymphomania.

180 *that philosopher . . . into a ditch*. An ancient jest sometimes attributed to Thales.

181–6 *Apothegms and Maxims*. All his life, Swift practised the art of writing terse, significant pieces, to which we have given this title. Some (numbered by the editors) appear in collections, reminiscent of La Rochefoucauld's celebrated *Réflexions ou Sentences et Maximes Morales* (1665), a text which Swift admired; others occur as dense nuggets placed in the texture of other modes of writing. The diverting side of Swift's interest in 'thoughts' is represented, in the present selection, by some passages from the *Journal to Stella*, chosen from over thirty quasi-proverbs.

187 *Baucis and Philemon*. 'Written, 1706', the poem was printed in *Miscellanies in Prose and Verse* (1711). This version embodies the normalizing and smoothing revisions recommended by Swift's friend Joseph Addison. The present text is taken in part from Swift's earlier autograph, so far as it goes, now in the Pierpoint Morgan Library, New York. Swift's original conception is more racy, direct, and idiosyncratic. The story is from Ovid, *Metamorphoses* viii. 611–724.

189 l. 118. *English Mall*. The exploits of Mary Ambree, the legendary English female captain in the Flanders wars of Queen Elizabeth's time, were celebrated in ballads. Swift metamorphoses these, together with illustrated broadsides carrying popular tales of other worthies, into memorial tablets to male and female ancestors and their progeny.

192 l. 210. *believe me jealous*. i.e., a cuckold, with horns.

193 *from* THE BICKERSTAFF PAPERS

This cluster of satirical papers is arranged around two April Fool's Day jokes. Swift's satire is not primarily aimed at the 'science' of astrology. William Lilly, who had died discredited in 1681, was the last astrologer in London widely consulted by an impressive official clientele including the

Privy Council. It remained true, however, that men like the great Isaac Newton himself strayed into strange speculations, and in humbler company kept old habits of thinking and belief. The widely circulated yearly almanacs written by the astrologers, their crass tone, and the extremely large profits made by their publication are the real target of Swift's irony and attack. These publications were the most valuable literary properties of the day; monopoly in the several titles of the half a million or so almanacs printed each autumn was held, under royal charter, by members of the Stationers' Company. An almanac, often published under the registered 'authorship' of some long-dead but well-known astrologer, like Lilly himself, not only contained a calendar with astronomical information, astrological prognostications, and weather forecasts. A wide range of other materials, which varied from almanac to almanac, drew to each of some thirty titles its particular public. Gardening hints, interest tables, patent medicine advertisements, as well as innumerable other topics, are covered, and amidst all this, of course, politics are not absent. John Partridge, the butt of Swift's satire, may or may not have been a reliable prognosticator; his was the leading almanac title, *Merlinus Liberatus*, with an annual circulation of over 20,000 copies. It was a further provocation that the speciality of Partridge's almanac was vituperative, Low-Church, anti-Tory *verse*, and in particular, strong opposition to the religio-political Sacramental Test (see p. 641). Almanacs were distributed to the booksellers in October. Swift arrived in London soon after 6 December 1707. At the end of February, he published *Predictions for the Year 1708*, in which he nests an announcement of the approaching death of John Partridge. Swift also wrote at this time *An Answer to Bickerstaff*, the joke within the joke, which opens up all the levels of the hoax for those quick enough to see them; he did not, however, print this, perhaps drawing back from its direct autobiographical confession. It was first made public through Deane Swift in *Works* 1765. On the evening of 29 March 1708, the date foretold for Partridge's death, a verse broadside was being cried in the streets, with the title, *An Elegy on Mr. Partridge, the Almanac-Maker*. On 31 March, in time for April Fool's Day, appeared *The Accomplishment of the First of Mr. Bickerstaff's Predictions*. The joke was too good to drop, especially since Partridge was angrily replying. The next year, Swift opened fire again in February with *A Famous Prediction of Merlin* (not printed here), and issued perhaps as his second April Fool's Day piece, *A Vindication of Isaac Bickerstaff*, advertised 7 April.

193 *Bickerstaff*. Swift took the name from a locksmith's in Long Acre (note in *Works*, 1735); Steele adopted the mask for his *Tatler*.

194–5 *the miscarriage at Toulon...Admiral Shovel*. Marlborough planned for 1707 a combined operations attack on the French base at Toulon. Returning from the unsuccessful attempt, on 22 October Sir Cloudesley Shovell's flagship, the *Association*, and two other vessels, unsure of their position in the fog, ran on the Bishop Rock off the Scillies with the loss of the Admiral and 2,000 men.

195 *battle at Almanza*. The defeat on 25 August (NS) 1707 of the Earl of Galway

by a Franco-Spanish army destroyed the last hope of making the allied candidate, the Archduke Charles, accepted as King of Spain.

the Old Style. England did not adopt until 1752 the sixteenth-century reform of the calendar decreed by Pope Gregory XIII; in Swift's day, the difference in dates was 11 days.

196 *Aries ... Libra.* The sun entered the zodiac sign of Aries (the Ram) on 10 March (OS) and the sign of Libra (the Balance) on 12 September (OS).

197 *the Prophets.* Groups of French refugees from Louis XIV's ferocious persecution of the Calvinist *camisards* in the Cevennes (Dauphiné) brought to London a set of extreme, visionary beliefs, which included prophesying; English adherents were attracted to the sect, numbering among them several well-to-do men and women, to whom the name 'French Prophets' was also applied.

199 *Alter erit jam Tethys ... | Dilectos heroas.* 'Another Tethys shall at last arise, and a second Argo to carry chosen heroes'; Virgil, *Eclogue* iv. 34–5. Virgil's own text specifies Tiphys, the pilot of the *Argo*. Could Swift mean the female sea deity *Tethys* to refer to good Queen Anne in a renewed naval attack on Toulon?

200 *Captain H[alley].* Edmund Halley, FRS, later Astronomer Royal, had made several voyages to prepare a southern star map and investigate magnetic variations.

202 *An Answer to Bickerstaff. sic cecidit Phaeton.* 'So Phaeton tumbled.'

203 *the French prophets.* See note to p. 197.

204 *The General History of Ears.* One of the list of 'Treatises' facing the title-page of *A Tale of a Tub* (see p. 62); a rash explicit avowal of the authorship of that work.

205 *An Elegy on Mr. Partridge.* l. 15. *Aries.* This sign of the zodiac, the Ram, marks the start of the year when the sun enters it at the spring equinox, 12 March; it also covers 1 April, April Fool's Day.

l. 31. *Boötes.* The Waggoner, a bright star in the constellation known as the Wain (or Arcturus in the Great Bear).

206 l. 61. *Mercury.* Contemporary treatments for venereal diseases used compounds of mercury.

l. 63. *in Lucian read.* In Lucian's *Menippus*, the Cynic philosopher on his visit to Hades sees Philip of Macedon, father of Alexander the Great, sitting in a corner, trying to earn a living as a cobbler.

207 l. 77. *Argo.* The ship in which Jason sailed to find the Golden Fleece.

l. 85. *Virgo.* The constellation of the Virgin.

l. 86 n. *Tibi brachia ... Scorpius.* 'For you, huge [blazing] Scorpio draws in his arms and has left for you more than a fair share of the heavens': Virgil, *Georgics,* i. 34–5 (*ingens* for *ardens*).

l. 95 n. *Sed nec ... legeris Orbe,* &c. 'But do not choose your seat [Caesar,] in the Northern sky ...'; Lucan, *De Bello Civili,* i. 53.

ll. 96–100. *St. James's . . . Moor Fields.* The fashionable, or court, end of London lay to the west, near St James's palace . . . Bedlam was in Moorfields, north of the city limits.

l. 102n. *Neve tuam . . . Romam.* 'Nor look down aslant, [Caesar,] at your city of Rome': ibid. 55 (*Neve* for *Unde*).

212 *A Vindication of Isaac Bickerstaff. the Inquisition in P[ortugal]* . . . 'This is fact, as the Author was assured by Sir Paul Methuen, then ambassador to that crown' [Swift's note in *Works* 1735].

213 *Illustrissimo Bickerstaffio . . . vir doctissimus.* 'The quotations here inserted, are in imitation of Dr. Bentley; in some part of the famous controversy between him and Charles Boyle Esq., afterwards Earl of Orrery' [Swift's note]. 'To the most illustrious Bickerstaff founder of astrology' . . . 'Thus most recently [has written] Bickerstaff, that great star of England' . . . 'Bickerstaff the great Englishman, easily first among astrologers of the present age' . . . 'I should say, in spite of the great man' . . . 'perhaps rather the printer's error, since otherwise Bickerstaff, that most learned man' . . .

217 *An Argument against Abolishing Christianity.* The powerful irony of this piece, written in 1708, which has kept it alive despite the intricacy of its ostensible subject-matter, centres in certain paradoxes of the so-called Test Act of 1673 and the ambiguous attitude towards it held by Swift in company with other committed churchmen. Charles II's strongly Tory, High-Church Parliament in that year forced the enactment of a law requiring all office-holders, military or civil, under the central or the local Government, to take the Sacrament of the Lord's Supper according to the use of the Church of England and to swear oaths of supremacy (of the King over the Church). The purpose was to exclude Roman Catholics and Dissenters from power and office, and control the King's use of his prerogative to buy support from these groups by rewarding them. In 1704, as a clause in an anti-Popery Act, the Test was extended to Ireland. All his life, Swift staunchly supported the Test against many attempts by the Whigs to repeal it, first in Ireland and by that example in England, and the whole basis of this legislation caused him deep problems. By the Act, Parliament had used its power in matters of transcendent, theological importance. Further, it had been made clear to Swift that the ruling Whig Junto were willing to advise the Queen to grant the Church of Ireland the relief from the Crown's right to certain payments, a favour that Swift, commissioned by the Irish bishops, was soliciting in London, but only on condition that the abolition of the Test Act in Ireland was not opposed. Thus, the phrase in the complex title of the piece, 'as things now stand', represents a grimly immediate rub for Swift himself. He forthrightly believed in the State's right to require specific religious observances. He recognizes, however, as in Maxims [R4], [R5], and [R6] above (p. 185), that coercive power cannot touch belief itself. At the same time, Swift always maintains the validity and necessity of 'primitive Christianity', which he identifies as the necessary basis of civilized life in England. Thus, the speaker in *An Argument* is crazy to use a word like

'abolishing' in connection with Gospel truth, and doubly so to sneer at 'the system of the Gospel, after the lapse of other systems', implying that Christianity is only one of a series of alternatives. Yet it may be thought that Swift's irony undercuts his own avowed position of support for the Test Act, since Christianity cannot be 'enacted' either.

217 *lay wagers against the [Union].* In 1708 an Act was passed penalizing laying bets on the outcome of events relating to the war with France: see p. 303, *n* (2). The Treaty and Act of Union, a subject of extreme discontent to Swift with his strong Anglican and Anglo-Irish feelings, incorporated England and Scotland under a British Parliament, and took effect on 1 May 1707.

218 *the proposal of Horace. Epode* xvi, a lament over tyranny and civil strife.

nominal Christianity. Specifically, 'occasional conformity', i.e. token observance of the communion requirements of the Test and Corporation Acts, in order to hold office.

219 *Deorum offensa diis curæ.* 'Insults to the gods are the gods' concern': Tacitus, *Annals,* I. 73.

the allies. The alliance against France in the War of the Spanish Succession (see p. 612).

free-thinkers . . . Asgil . . . and forty more. The deists, regularly opposed by Swift, rejected in varying degrees the visionary or supernatural elements of Christian doctrine, and often drew on contemporary scientific thinking to offer a religion of nature and reason. See the relevant entries in the Biographical Index below.

220 *an old dormant statute or two.* Neglected laws enforcing religious conformity on office-holders, such as the Corporation Act (1661) and the Test Act itself.

Empson and Dudley. Sir Richard Empson and Edmund Dudley, two of Henry VII's Civil Servants accused of penal reactivation of obsolete statutes; Henry VIII courted popularity by arresting them the day after he acceded and executing them in 1510.

the wise regulations of Henry the Eighth. See p. xxvi.

221 *the chocolate-house.* Gaming was associated with these raffish establishments where liquid refreshment was not limited to chocolate.

222 *the Monument.* Sir Christopher Wren's great Doric column stands in Fish Street Hill, near London Bridge, commemorating the Great Fire of London of 1666. The statement attributing the calamity to the 'Popish faction' was removed from the inscription in 1831.

the Trimmers. Compromisers; appropriately, Valentini was a castrato, or male soprano.

Prasini and Veniti. Two of the four rival teams in the Roman (and Byzantine) chariot races, the greens and the blues, and hence warring factions of supporters so distinguished. Blue and green are respectively the colours of the knightly Orders of the Garter [English] and the Thistle [Scottish].

prohibited silks . . . wine. Imports from France, officially forbidden on account of the war, were supplied by a thriving smuggling trade.

223 *a scheme for comprehension.* Swift sought to refute the argument that the abolition of the Test Act would lead to a beneficial union of the Protestant interests in England and Ireland, since to accept this would destroy his position that the Church of England uniquely represented the pure, unsectarian Christian faith.

224 *choqued.* Shocked; Swift keeps the French form of this newly introduced word.

225 *Socinians.* Specifically, followers of two sixteenth-century Italian 'free-thinkers', but at this time used in a general sense of Christians who held the doctrine of the Trinity to be unscriptural and who offered human reason as the test of the truth of theological teaching.

jus divinum of Episcopacy. Divine right, presumably descended from the Apostles.

'The Rights of the Christian Church'. By Matthew Tindal; the book is the target of Swift's incomplete *Remarks*, 'Written in the year 1708 . . .' (*Prose*, ii. 65–107).

226 *sorites.* In logic, a series of more than two linked propositions leading to a conclusion.

228 [*Answer to Verses from May Fair*]. l. 2. *May Fair.* The fair held in May, in Brookfields, then a country district between what is now Brook Street and Shepherd Market, has given its name to this fashionable district of London. Its rowdiness attracted hostility and it was later discontinued. 'Society' left London in the spring to spend summer and autumn on country estates.

ll. 19 ff. *fair Ardelia . . . Worsley's . . . Harry.* The exact references in the last two stanzas, which turn this gay set of verses into an occasional poem, are unclear; but *Ardelia* is Mrs Anne Finch, later Countess of Winchilsea; in 1710 Miss Frances Worsley married Lord Carteret and later still became important in Swift's life.

229 *A Description of the Morning.* This ironic pastoral, a 'town eclogue', was first printed as part of the section of Steele's *Tatler*, No. 9, 28–30 April 1709, date-lined from 'Will's Coffee-house'.

ll. 9–10. *The youth . . . where wheels had worn the place.* 'To find old nails' [note in *Works* 1735].

l. 11. *cadence deep.* In Addison's *Spectator*, No. 251, 18 December 1711, on the street cries of London, Will. Wimble calls them '*the ramage de la ville* [city bird song or town chorus]'. Marcellus Laroon's *The Cryes of London Drawn after the Life*, engraved by René Tempest, was first published in 1709, the year of Swift's verses.

brickdust Moll. Was selling powdered brick for scouring, also mentioned by Addison.

to steal for fees. Gaolers depended for their living on exacting payments from their prisoners in return for subsistence and privileges.

230 *Swift to Esther Johnson and Rebecca Dingley.* Between his arrival in London in September 1710 and his departure from England in June 1713 to be installed Dean of St Patrick's, Swift wrote a series of sixty-five letters to Esther Johnson and her companion Rebecca Dingley in Dublin, though the former of course is the real correspondent. These letters form practically the only surviving remnant of his lifelong correspondence with Esther Johnson, and clearly this series was preserved, while the rest was destroyed, because of its depiction of his career in political, social, and literary London. The series has a complicated publication history, which includes the invention in 1779 of the distracting title, *Journal to Stella*, and its adoption by later editors. Twenty-five of the letters survive in Swift's original manuscript. Swift tried to write a daily entry of informal comment and information, often as he went to bed, in bed, or before he rose. He addresses Esther Johnson, somewhat less often Rebecca Dingley, and frequently both ladies, in tender personal messages for which he employs a private code, *ourrichar gangridge* ('our little language') (11 March 1712), based on abbreviations and the childish pronunciation of newly learned words. 'When I am writing in our language, I make up my mouth just as if I was speaking it' (7 March 1711). The chief abbreviations are 'MD', 'Md' for *My dear* or *My dears*; 'Ppt' for *poppet* or perhaps *poor pretty thing*; 'Dd' for *Dingley*; 'Pdfr' (pronounced 'Podefar') for *poor dear foolish rogue* or perhaps *poor dear foolish fellow*; 'FW' for *foolish wenches*. He wrote quickly and impulsively in a very small hand which poses many problems. The series is not uniform; it was interrupted by illness in the spring and early summer of 1712, and never perfectly resumed. Though made up of intimate writing, Swift's series of letters is not unguarded; and although he became an intimate of the Ministers, his insights and views are sometimes hasty and not completely informed. The significant figures mentioned in the two letters included in the present selection, nos. VI and XXX (pp. 230 and 272), are given entries in the Biographical Index.

230 *my memorial.* The Church of Ireland's request for remission by the Crown of the First Fruits (see p. 641).

the Archbishop. William King: 10 October 1710; *Correspondence*, i. 183.

my poetical Description of a Shower. See p. 256.

Patrick, the extravagant whelp. Swift's Irish servant, given to drink.

231 *Mr. Addison's election.* He was MP for Malmesbury from 1709 until his death.

one Captain Lavallin. Charles Lavallée.

Doctors' Commons. The College of Advocates, near St Paul's, whose members had the monopoly of pleading in the ecclesiastical and admiralty courts; abolished in 1857.

my Tatler. Possibly the hint and heads for ['The History of a Shilling'], *Tatler*, No. 249, 11 November 1710, claimed as his by Swift (*Journal*, 30 November).

Presto. Swift.

232 *your 6th 'Miscellanea'.* Tonson's *Poetical Miscellanies: The Sixth Part* (1709), 629.

Lord Halifax . . . his country house. He was ranger of Bushy Park, across the road from Hampton Court.

233 *a lady just come to town.* Perhaps Mrs Vanhomrigh, mother of Esther Vanhomrigh.

till I turn over. To the next page.

Dawson's office at the Castle. Joshua Dawson, under-secretary to the Lord-Lieutenant.

poor Lady Berkeley. See p. 617; the Earl had died on 24 September.

Stellakins. Deane Swift omitted most passages in Swift's 'little language', but retains something representing one here; Swift did not use the name 'Stella' until some years later; perhaps it should be 'Sluttakin' (Williams).

234 *My lampoon.* Swift's poem, sent to the printer 4 October, *The Virtues of Sid Hamet the Magician's Rod*, satirizing the newly dismissed Lord Treasurer, Sidney Godolphin, one of whose ensigns of office was the white staff.

my Tatler about shortening of words. Tatler, No. 230; see p. 252.

bobbed. Ducked or bowed to.

Lord President of Scotland. Sir Hew Dalrymple, Lord President of the Court of Session in Edinburgh.

the Smyrna. A coffee-house in Pall Mall, opposite Marlborough House, noted for political and literary gossip.

235 *Brazil tobacco.* To be rasped for snuff.

Mr Sterne. Enoch Stearne, clerk to the Irish House of Lords, cousin of Dean Stearne.

Irish wine. Claret, which was good in Ireland.

my Miscellany. Miscellanies in Prose and Verse, published at the end of February 1711, not with Benjamin Tooke's imprint but John Morphew's.

the letter to the Bishop of Killaloe. Perhaps an editorial or printing error for 'Killala' (Williams). Swift's *List of Subjects for a Volume* (1708), setting out the proposed contents for the 1711 *Miscellanies*, includes a 'Letter to the Bishop of K————' (Ehrenpreis, *Swift* . . . ii. 768). This piece is not known.

237 *A Short Character of . . . Thomas Earl of Wharton.* Published at the beginning of December 1710, this pamphlet is one of several detached pieces associated with Swift's series of *Examiner* essays (p. 648). Perhaps *A Short Character* contains material assembled earlier, which in turn would explain the apparently disparate nature of the contents framing the four paragraphs of invective against Wharton. The public reasons behind Swift's contempt for 'Honest Tom', the leading Whig borough-monger, are obvious; as he wrote later, 'His brethren [in the Junto] were forced out of mere justice to leave Ireland at his mercy; where he had only time to set himself right.' There were personal reasons, too, for Swift's hatred. In the débâcle of the dismissal of the Whig Ministry, Wharton resigned his Lieutenancy on 30

August 1710, the date Swift chooses to place on *A Short Character*, so that he may appear to attack the governor in office.

238 *grand climacteric.* The sixty-third year was supposed to be physiologically of special significance.

239 *one kingdom . . . another.* England . . . Ireland.

242 *a moderate deanery.* Connor.

244 *Mrs. L[loy]d . . . box-money.* Wharton's 'cast wench' mentioned earlier (p. 241) . . . The money given at each throw to the owner of the dice-box, and so perhaps money given by the gamblers to repay service and attendance.

the expedition to Cadiz. A combined operations attack on Cadiz was planned by Marlborough and William III before his death. It was carried out in 1702 under the Duke of Ormonde and Admiral Sir George Rooke, but incompetent direction and indiscipline led to its failure.

245 *Chapelizod gate.* One of the gates into the great royal enclosure of Phoenix Park to the west of Dublin was at Chapelizod, where the Lord-Lieutenant had a country house.

248 *the affair of Trim.* 25 miles from Dublin, Trim lay near Laracor, to which vicarage Swift had been appointed in 1700 and used as a retreat; the 'affair' was the disputed election of the mayor.

Dr. L[a]mb[e]rt. Ralph Lambert, Swift's successful rival for the position of chaplain to Wharton which he used as a stepping-stone to the Deanery of Down (1709); in 1727, he became Swift's diocesan as Bishop of Meath.

249 *Mr. Whitshed.* Later Lord Chief Justice Whitshed.

251 *Mrs. Fl[oy]d.* Mrs Lloyd (see p. 244).

252 *[The continual Corruption of our English Tongue]*. The letter which makes up this entire *Tatler* is undoubtedly by Swift; 'To-day I dined with Mr. Stratford at Mr. Addison's retirement near Chelsea; then came to town; got home early, and began a letter to the *Tatler* about the corruption of style and writing &c.' (*Journal to Stella*, 18 September 1710). It was included in *Works* 1735.

253 *Tom . . . the plenipo's.* Thomas Harley, cousin of Robert Harley and MP for Radnorshire. Appointed one of the Secretaries of the Treasury, he did not, however, go with the plenipotentiaries when the peace conference got under way, though he took instructions to them in 1712.

The Jacks . . . hipps . . . rep. The Jacobites . . . hypochondria . . . reputation.

255 *simplex munditiis.* 'Natural elegance': Horace, *Odes*, I. v. 5.

Hooker. Richard Hooker (*c.*1554–1600), author of a massive argument in defence of the Anglican Church, *Of the Laws of Ecclesiastical Polity*, in eight books (printed 1593–1661), a monument of English prose.

Parsons the Jesuit. Robert Parsons (1546–1610), SJ, controversialist and educationist. His chief work was a book of devotional instruction, *A Christian Directorie* (1581), which also appeared in a Protestant version.

Sir H. Wotton, Sir Robert Naunton, Osborn, Daniel the historian. Sir Henry

Wotton (1586–1639), poet, diplomat, and Provost of Eton, whose writings appeared in a posthumous collection, *Reliquiae Wottonianae* (1651); Sir Robert Naunton (1563–1635), Secretary of State 1617–18, whose *Fragmenta Regalia: Observations on the late Queen Elizabeth, her Times and Favourites* was several times reprinted from 1641 to 1663 and in later collections; Francis Osbourne (1593–1659), sceptical controversialist and historian, best known for his popular and witty *Advice to a Son* (Oxford, 1656–8); Samuel Daniel (1563–1619), dramatist, historian, and Poet Laureate; his historical writing is partly in verse, *The Civil War between the Houses of Lancaster and York* (1595–1609), and partly in prose, *The Collection of the Historie of England to the death of Edward III* (1612–18).

256 *A Description of a City Shower.* This set of verses made up *Tatler*, No. 238, 14–17 October 1710: 'And now I am going in charity to send Steele a *Tatler*, who is very low of late' (*Journal to Stella*, 7 October). Swift thought this piece twice as good as *A Description of the Morning* (ibid., 30 November).

l. 10. *a-ches.* Pronounced 'aitches'.

257 l. 38. *her oil'd umbrella's sides.* Umbrellas (of oiled silk) were at this time for women only.

l. 41. *Triumphant Tories, and desponding Whigs.* Godolphin was dismissed as Lord Treasurer on 5 August 1710; Swift arrived in London on 7 September. At the beginning of October the general election returned a Commons with a large Tory majority.

l. 51. *Laoco'n struck the outside.* Virgil, *Aeneid*, ii. 50–3.

l. 58. *From Smithfield, or St. 'Pulchre's.* The drainage from the butchers' shops and cattle and sheep pens in West Smithfield ran down Cow Lane to meet, at Holborn Conduit, the drainage from the St Sepulchre's Church area running down Snow Hill; the joint flow ran west until it fell into the Fleet River, or Ditch, then open and navigable, at Holborn Bridge.

ll. 61–3. *Sweepings from butchers' stalls . . . down the flood.* 'These three last lines were intended against the licentious manner of modern poets, in making three rhymes together, which they call *triplets*; and the last of the three was two or sometimes more syllables longer, called an *Alexandrian*. These triplets or alexandrians were brought in by Dryden, and other poets of the reign of Charles II. They were the mere effect of haste, idleness and want of money, and have been wholly avoided by the best poets, since these verses were written' [note in *Works* 1735, probably by Swift].

258 *from THE EXAMINER*

Harley induced Swift to join his new team at the beginning of October 1710. On 2 November appeared Swift's first *Examiner* essay, No. 14, the start of his series of thirty-three weekly ministerial 'leaders', which ran during the crucial opening session of the new Tory Parliament and the new administration. *The Examiner* had first been published on Thursday, 9 August, the week after Lord Treasurer Godolphin was dismissed. It was a weekly folio half-sheet, comprising a single essay with no news, one of the very earliest political essay journals. Swift's regular contributions ceased with No. 45 of 7 June 1711, the conclusion of this essay forming the opening of No. 46. Each *Examiner* essay is about 2,000 words long, and not only presents some central theme, but associates with it several of the preoccupations of the Harley administration. Swift's *Examiner* was meant to mould opinion, to create a favourable climate for financial reform at home and peace abroad. Swift abandoned the contemporary form of political controversy, the 'examining' passage by passage of Opposition writing, in favour of expressing lofty, amusing disdain for 'those little antagonists, who may want a topic for criticism'.

[*Marlborough*]. Swift wrote severe things about the Duke and Duchess of Marlborough, but a remark in the *Journal to Stella* ought also to be noted: '. . . the Duke pretended to think me his greatest enemy, and got people to tell me so, and very mildly to let me know how gladly he would have me softened towards him. I bid a lady of his acquaintance and mine let him know, that I had hindered many a bitter thing against him, not for his own sake, but because I thought it looked base, and desired every thing should be left to him except power' (6 January 1713).

Qui sunt? . . . 'Who are the good citizens? Who are they that serve their country well in peace and war; who else but those who keep in mind all that their country has done for them?': Cicero, *Pro Gnaeo Plancio*, 80.

259 *two persons allied by marriage to the general.* The Earl of Godolphin, Lord Treasurer, whose eldest son married Henrietta; and the Earl of Sunderland, who married Anne; two of Marlborough's daughters, ladies of the bedchamber to Queen Anne.

260 *The lands of Woodstock.* The Queen's grant to Marlborough of the royal manor of Woodstock, near Oxford, was confirmed by an Act of Parliament at the beginning of 1705; the following year royal and parliamentary money was voted to build Blenheim Palace.

The grant at the Pall Mall, the rangership. In 1702, the Queen granted the Duchess of Marlborough 'the office of Ranger of the great and little Parks at Windsor', with the lodge and 'the grounds in St. James's Park upon which [Marlborough House] stands'.

262 *a saying of Seneca. De Beneficiis,* I. i. 4.

263 [*The Rage of Party*].——*Garrit . . . fabellas.* '[Cervius] chatters on with nursery stories to the point': Horace, *Satires* II. vi. 77–8.

a passage out of Plato. Symposium, 189–92.

264 *Mr.*——. Matthew Prior.

265 *the undertakers for the late m[inistr]y.* Party managers.

the Nonjurors. Clergy of the Church of England, including the Archbishop of Canterbury, who in conscience could not take the oaths to William and Mary, having sworn loyalty to James II; in consequence they lost their preferments.

267 [*The Criminals in the late Ministry*]. *Indignum est ... legibus.* 'In a commonwealth that is preserved by law, all departure from law is a disgrace': adapted from Cicero, *Pro Cluentio*, 146.

quam prope ... possint accedere. 'How near they can come to sin, without actually sinning.'

268 *the other sex, of which ... I could produce an instance.* Perhaps the Duchess of Marlborough.

the ambassador of a great prince. At the beginning of 1709, Czar Peter the Great's departing ambassador, A. A. Matveof, was arrested at the instance of his creditors and manhandled from his coach. An Act of Parliament, still in force, was immediately introduced and passed, declaring the diplomatic immunity of envoys.

A commissioner of the stamped paper. Richard Dyot, tried at the Old Bailey on 13 January 1711, but acquitted of felony since his crime was a breach of trust.

the notorious cheat of the brewers at Portsmouth. In January and February 1711, the Commons were exercised with a naval victualling scandal.

269 *the Act of Indemnity.* 7 Ann. c. 22, 1708; despite Swift's invective, such an Act to protect Ministers from future prosecution was fairly common Government practice.

the address made to the Qu[een] about three years ago. From both Houses of Parliament, 23 December 1707: '... no peace can be honourable or safe, for your Majesty, or your allies, if Spain, the West Indies, or any part of the Spanish monarchy be suffered to remain under the power of the House of Bourbon'.

271 *their conduct in the City about a fortnight ago.* In the election for the governor and court of directors of the Bank of England on 22 and 23 April, all the Whig candidates were returned. They had been trying to sabotage Harley's financial management.

272 *Swift to Esther Johnson and Rebecca Dingley.* For the *Journal to Stella*, see p. 644.

Lord Treasurer. Robert Harley, Earl of Oxford.

Mr Masham. Husband of Abigail Masham.

my brother ... and some others of our Society. 'The Society' or (Brothers') Club was set up in June 1711 with twelve members, rising to twenty-three; it was composed of men of 'wit and learning' or 'power and influence'. Swift's notion was that the latter should help the former, and that the Society should be a Tory counterpart to the famous Whig Kit-cat Club.

Lord Keeper, Mr Secretary. Simon Harcourt, and Henry St John.

Noble fruit, and I dare not eat a bit. Swift believed that his lifelong disability, 'Menière's syndrome' of vertigo, deafness, and nausea, was caused by eating fruit. Could it have been an allergy, as his symptoms suggest?

something I am doing. The first reference to writing *The Conduct of the Allies* (see p. 651).

Lady Giffard and Mrs Fenton. Martha, Lady Giffard, the widowed sister of Sir William Temple, with whom Swift was on bad terms . . . Mrs Jane Fenton, Swift's sister, married to a currier and living in poor circumstances, whom both Swift and Lady Giffard aided.

273 *an account of Prior's Journey. A New Journey to Paris: Together with some secret Transactions between the Fr——h K——g, and an Eng—— Gentleman. By the Sieur de Baudrier. Translated from the French*; written to laugh away the Government's embarrassment at the detection of Prior's secret mission to France to initiate the unilateral peace negotiations.

Bouchain being taken. Marlborough's last, and in some ways most remarkable, victory was the forcing on 4–5 March (NS) of Marshal Villars's famous *Ne plus ultra* defensive lines, running through Arras to Valenciennes; Bouchain itself fell on 12 September (NS).

the Archbishop of Dublin's. William King.

trembled for my shillings. A shilling was the standard hackney-coach hire.

274 *the two Secretaries.* Henry St John and the Earl of Dartmouth.

Bernage. Lt. Moses Bernage, a former student at Trinity College, and protégé of Swift's.

Mrs Van. Mrs Vanhomrigh, mother of Esther Vanhomrigh.

275 *some business. The Conduct of the Allies* (see p. 280).

Lord Harley and Lord Dupplin. Harley's (Oxford's) son and son-in-law.

Mrs Hill . . . one of the dressers. Alice Hill . . . one of the Queen's ladies of the bedchamber, sister of Abigail Masham.

276 *Cranburn.* Cranbourne, three miles south of Windsor, seat of the 3rd Earl of Ranelagh.

the Green Cloth. The Board of Green Cloth was the executive committee that ran the royal household; it kept a daily table at court for the entertainment of distinguished visitors.

the Duchess of Somerset is thought to gain ground daily. Harley owed his private access to the Queen to Mrs Masham, and used it to oust Godolphin and the Whig Junto. The Duchess (see note to p. 377 (6) succeeded Mrs Masham as the Queen's favourite.

sent you over all your bills. For the method of 'approving' Irish legislation, see note to p. 458 (1).

the affair of the mayoralty. Of Dublin; a continuing Irish dispute since 1709; the Dublin corporation was Whig in complexion; the Government was trying to have a Tory elected mayor.

I must write larger . . . able to read this. 'Written enormously large' [editorial note by Deane Swift].

278 *Billy Swift.* Swift's cousin, who had died in 1711; he was a solicitor, son of Swift's uncle William.

Sterne. See p. 421 and ibid., n. (1).

279 *poor Jenny*. Swift's sister.

those that threw the merit on the Duke of Ormond. For obtaining the remission by the Crown to the Church of Ireland of the First Fruits; instead of recognizing Swift's efforts and credit with Harley.

280 *The Conduct of the Allies.* Published on 27 November 1711, this was Swift's second major contribution to the Harley administration. By secret diplomacy, Harley followed a deep personal conviction and committed himself to negotiating peace with France. He clearly accepted the consequence that this would probably involve a breach of treaty obligations to the allies. The war in Europe had reached a stalemate. Marlborough had undoubtedly won brilliant victories, but there was at that time no European conception of 'unconditional surrender' to match Marlborough's strategy, and no national or allied political or technical capacity to wage the total war Marlborough hankered after. Harley and St John cut the knot. They made a separate deal with France, offering substantial advantages to Britain. In return, the allies were to be pressured into abandoning the Habsburg claim to the crown of Spain and the Empire of the Spanish Indies, as well as giving up other particular aims. Allied agreement thus obtained, the British Ministers calculated that the fury of the Whig Opposition would be disarmed by the fulfilment of the popular desire for peace. The allies resisted the pressure put on them longer than was thought possible, however, and the administration was faced with a very ugly situation as the new parliamentary session approached. *The Conduct* is not an impartial examination of general arguments in favour of peace, though it contains such arguments. Its publication was a political act; and the meeting of parliament was delayed until it was ready. The piece is tendentious, even misleading. Swift seized the advantage of attack, and thereafter most Whig arguments became answers to *The Conduct.* Swift's pamphlet also offered a scenario for the Tories in the bitter parliamentary debates. The layout of the piece is worth some attention, and may be summarized as follows:

First comes a *Preface* of four paragraphs stating, 'freely and impartially', several general maxims, closely and constructively connected, however, with the precise arguments that are about to be offered to justify the Ministers' peace policy. The body of the pamphlet thereafter falls into five sections, indicated by the square-bracketed letters supplied by the editors in the margin of the text:

[A] A general theoretical and historical framework of ten paragraphs.
[B] A section of ten paragraphs on the immediate historical origins of the War of the Spanish Succession. Here Swift employs a tactic which lends *The Conduct* some of its particular force, namely a comparison and analysis of actual State papers supplied by the administration, in this case the Declarations of War against France made by the Dutch and the Queen in 1702.
[C] Forty-eight paragraphs containing the substance of Swift's case, developed under three heads. The third subsection marshals the

Ministry's case for concluding a unilateral agreement with France preparatory to forcing a general peace.

[D] After a hinge paragraph of summary, Swift's argument turns to a ten-paragraph attack on the previous administration, the second thrust of the entire piece which is indicated in its full title. The last three paragraphs offer interpretation of the change of ministry in 1710. This section may have begun life as a separate piece.

[E] The concluding section is a discussion, in five subsections, of the Whig war aim of 'No Peace without Spain', i.e. that the French king's grandson must be removed from the Spanish throne. This section shows signs of strain; perhaps it too had an independent origin. Swift again prints an actual text, the eighth Article of the Grand Alliance, setting out the 'Demands to be insisted on by the Allies . . .', but in a carefully slanted translation. The success of Swift's piece as writing is amply attested by its publication history. Its political effectiveness, however, is to be measured by the survival of Oxford's ministry.

——*Partem tibi . . . vincente perit*——. 'Gaul snatched some of us from you; Spain took others in cruel battles; some lie in Italy. All over the world your troops die while you are victorious. What good is it to have spilt blood on the lands of the North, conquering the Rhone and the Rhine?': Lucan, *De Bellum Civili*, v. 264–7.

Odimus . . . armis. 'We hate the hawk, for all his life is spent in war': Ovid, *Ars Amatoria*, ii. 147.

—— *Victrix Provincia plorat.* 'The victorious province weeps': Juvenal, *Satire* 1. 50 (altered).

281 *the treaty of Gertruydenburg.* After Marlborough's victory at Ramillies in May 1706, French morale slipped badly, in a period of increasing military and economic crisis, even civil disorder. Louis opened a diplomatic offensive to detach first Savoy, then the Dutch, from the alliance against him. A peace conference ('treaty') was held at Geertruidenberg in North Brabant, from September 1709 to March 1710. The British Ministers were forced to keep the Dutch in the alliance by negotiating a bilateral agreement extremely favourable to the States-General, the so-called Barrier Treaty. The conference failed in the last resort because, though Louis seemed to be willing to concede most of the allied demands, he stuck at the impossible British requirement that he should assist with a French army in dispossessing his grandson, Philip of Anjou, of the Spanish throne.

the confederates. The Dutch and the British (the Maritime Powers), the Habsburg Empire, 'Spain' under the Habsburg Pretender, Portugal, Savoy, and some smaller European principalities.

282 *pro aris et focis.* 'For altars and homes.' [Sallust, *Cataline Conspiracy*, 59.5]

284 *author of so detestable a project.* Gilbert Burnet.

the late king. William III.

the terms of a peace. The Peace of Ryswick, September 1697, offered England only Louis XIV's recognition of William III as King of England (see p. 611).

285 *the famous treaty of partition.* Of Spain and the Spanish Empire, negotiated by William III (see p. 612); the prelude to the War of the Spanish Succession.

the late King of Spain. Carlos II (d. 1700).

a certain great person . . . then in the church interest. Sidney Godolphin.

one whose advantage . . . he was engaged to promote. John Churchill, later Duke of Marlborough.

286 *K. Charles.* The Archduke Charles of Austria (1685–1740), Habsburg Pretender to the Spanish throne as 'Charles (or Carlos) III'.

289 *allowed to Augustus by his enemy of Sweden . . . Stanislaus.* Charles XII of Sweden deposed Augustus, Elector of Saxony.

292 *our general.* Marlborough.

the States. The seven United Provinces of the Netherlands acted together through the States-General.

293 *the only general . . . at last called home in discontent.* The Earl of Peterborough, the Tory hero, recalled after his successful campaign of 1705.

294 *what was performed by some private men at Bristol.* A Bristol syndicate in 1708 sent Captain Woodes Rogers with two ships on a privateering expedition against the Spaniards in the Pacific. He captured the Acapulco galleon with a rich cargo.

Mr. Hill's expedition. John Hill, brother of Abigail Masham, was in 1711 put in military command of the combined operation against Quebec promoted by St John. The expedition was a notorious failure.

295 *two alliances with Portugal.* The offensive treaty signed May 1703 brought Portugal into the war, and the better-known 'Methuen' treaty, signed in December and still in force, is a defensive and trade agreement: both were negotiated by Paul Methuen, the British ambassador, and his father.

297 *the barrier treaty.* See note to p. 281 (1).

298 *the French refugees.* The Protestant Huguenots who fled from Louis XIV's persecution, following the revocation of the Edict of Nantes in 1685.

299 *only signed by one of our plenipotentiaries.* Lord Townshend; Marlborough, the other, refused to sign, describing the terms as 'prejudicial to England'.

300 *the battles of Hochstet and Ramillies.* i.e. Blenheim, 13 August 1704; Ramillies, 12 May 1706.

Bouchain. See note to p. 273 (2).

302 *neither of the two last emperors.* Leopold I (1658–1705) and Joseph I (1705–11).

to make large presents to one single person. Marlborough, who was made Prince of Mindelheim in the Empire, and offered the lucrative office of Governor-General of the Spanish Netherlands; Swift also implies grants of money.

303 *the business of Toulon.* See note to p. 194.

the creature of a certain great man . . . the base mercenary end of getting money by wagers. Arthur Maynwaring, like the Duchess of Marlborough herself, placed bets on the outcome of the Toulon expedition. Maynwaring was a protégé of Lord Treasurer Godolphin, a devotee of the card-table and the turf, referred to elsewhere by Swift as 'a sharper' (*Examiner*, No. 19, 7 December 1710): for wagers on the war, see note to p. 217.

the Maréchal de Tessé's troops. René de Froulai (1651–1725), comte de Tessé and Marshal of France, was the commander in Provence, defending Toulon.

305 *a million of patacoons.* A little less than £250,000; the Spanish *patacon*, Portuguese *patacão*, was a piece of eight, a dollar.

by the noble conduct of that general being forced to retire into Valencia. By the end of the summer of 1706, it had become clear that Galway's risky occupation of Madrid could not be made secure.

Palatines. Protestant refugees who fled from the persecution of the Catholic Elector of the Rhenish Palatinate.

306 *the battle of Almanza.* See note to p. 195 (1). There was a long and acrimonious inquisition in Parliament into Galway's defeat.

308 *by which the whole power at home and abroad . . . upon that family.* See note to p. 259. Henrietta became Duchess of Marlborough in her own right after the death of her father in 1722.

309 *lest their* tables should be overthrown. Matthew 21: 12.

310 *offers of a peace after the battle of Ramillies.* See note p. 281 (1).

the Prince of Denmark's death. The death in October 1708 of Queen Anne's husband, Lord High Admiral, was used to produce an important political shift, in which the Whig Junto gained power and Somers and Wharton entered the Cabinet against the Queen's will.

as they waxed the fatter did but kick the more. Deuteronomy 32: 15.

memorials and messages. The Dutch war leaders made every effort to save Godolphin from dismissal in 1710 and in June, following a fall in the funds, four directors of the Bank of England waited on the Queen to advise her against a change of Ministers.

her story. Her history.

311 *the advice of Solomon . . .* 'It is better to dwell in a corner of the housetop, than with a brawling woman in a wide house': Proverbs 21: 9.

the old masters of the palace in France. In the Frankish kingdom, the chief royal office of 'mayor of the palace' was usurped by various rebellious magnates, turning the Merovingian kings into puppets. Finally, in the eighth century, Charles Martel seized power, and founded the Carolingian royal dynasty.

a g[enera]l during pleasure . . . into a king. Swift several times makes this allegation against Marlborough: e.g. *Memoirs relating to that Change which happened in the Queen's Ministry*, 'written in October 1714'; *Prose*, viii. 114.

312 *the Duke of Anjou.* The Dauphin's second son, to whom the Spanish crown was bequeathed by Carlos II.

313 *the partition treaty.* See p. 612.

till malt and land were mortgaged . . . a general excise . . . the dixième denier. The Government's chief source of income, increasingly devoted to servicing debt, was the land tax. Of the excises, or duties on domestic consumption, the most profitable was that on malt, i.e. barley prepared for brewing . . . It was a common bogey that the Government was contemplating a 'general excise' or duty on all domestic consumption. Though this was obviously attractive to the tax gatherers, contemporary administration could scarcely have collected it . . . The 'tenth penny' represents a feudal or arbitrary exaction, perhaps a reference to the abortive scheme floated in the 1690s for a capitation tax; the French phrase no doubt hints at ruinous taxation of the kind Louis XIV was alleged to impose.

a discourse by itself. Some Remarks on the Barrier Treaty, between Her Majesty and the States-General, 'By the Author of the Conduct of the Allies', published 22 February 1712.

314 *the treaty of Gertruydenberg.* See note to p. 281 (1).

the secretary of the embassy. Horatio Walpole (1678–1757), Robert Walpole's younger brother.

315 *the emperor's death.* Joseph I died in March 1711, and was succeeded by his brother, the Archduke Charles, Austrian Pretender to the Spanish throne.

316 *the augustissima casa.* 'The most august house' [of Habsburg].

321 *the present King of France has but few years to live.* Louis XIV was then 73; he died in 1715.

322 *who lay heavy burthens upon others . . . one of their fingers.* Matthew 23: 4.

after the battle of Ramillies. 12 May 1706.

324 *the treaty of Travendal.* The agreement at Traventhal, near Lübeck, 18 August 1700, between Denmark and Sweden, detached Denmark from the coalition against Sweden and was guaranteed by the Maritime Powers.

Monsieur Lilienroot. Nils Eosander, comte de Lillieroot (1636–1705), was the Swedish mediator at the Treaty of Ryswick, 1695 (see p. 611); an Anglo-Swedish treaty was finally signed in 1700.

the treaty of Alt Rastadt. For the terms of the treaty of Altranstadt, 1707, see *Stanislaus Leczinski*, p. 716.

325 *If the King of Sweden returns.* Charles XII.

326 *this edition.* To the fourth edition (December 1711) and to all later printings there was added the *Postscript*. The nervousness of Swift, or the Ministers, about the issue of the succession to the Crown was prophetic, since after the peace was concluded it was the successful smear of 'Jacobite sympathies' that finally destroyed the political power and credibility of the Tories on the

accession of George I. Swift's pamphlet, quickly translated into French and Spanish, attracted a host of replies (*Teerink*, pp. 285–9). The chief answer was by Marlborough's chaplain, Dr Francis Hare, later Bishop of Chichester, *The Allies and the Late Ministry defended against France, and the present Friends of France*, in four parts (1711–12). Swift never referred to any of the replies again in the text of *The Conduct*.

327 *Dunkirk to be Let . . . A Hue-and-Cry after Dismal.* This is a 'penny paper', a voluminous class of (often anonymous) cheap, publications printed as a folio half-sheet, with a title at the top, place and date of imprint at the bottom, but often without a printer's name. It is one of 'at least seven' that Swift says he wrote (*Journal to Stella*, 7 August 1712) to beat the censorship introduced on 1 August by the Stamp Act (see note to p. 331 (3)). Swift uses the technical challenge of this small-scale, popular format to attack the Earl of Nottingham, popularly known as 'Dismal', an opponent of the Ministry in the Lords. On 6 June, the Queen, in outlining the general terms of the peace agreed with the French, mentioned that Louis XIV had agreed to a cautionary British occupation of Dunkirk and the demolition of its port installations, long formidable protection for enterprising privateers. The release of this information was an attempt to head off some of the ferocious opposition to the peace. The Whigs stayed with the Dunkirk question, however, and nagged at the delay in effecting the occupation, despite entry of a British force under General Jack Hill on 8 July. They raged even more bitterly at Louis's attempts to avoid sacrificing his huge investment in the port. In this context Swift's mockery of Nottingham takes on its political force as well as its humour. This short text has been left unmodernized, as an example of Swift's prose in its contemporary dress.

Squash. A traditional contemptuous name; it also refers to *Quashie* or *Quashee*, the personal name (from Fanti) taken by a West Indian slave born on Sunday, and hence a name given unspecifically in English households to a black slave or servant.

330 *[Part of] The Seventh Epistle of the First Book of Horace Imitated.* Swift wrote this poem following his return to London on 9 September 1713 after being installed Dean of St Patrick's in Dublin. By pretending that his reward of the Deanery of St Patrick's was a practical joke on Oxford's part, Swift offers his patron the kind of jesting compliment the latter relished. His 'imitation' of Horace is freely related to an urbane ninety-eight-line epistle in which the Roman poet addresses his patron, Maecenas, on the subject of the necessity of maintaining his own independence. Swift embellished his poem with nineteen footnotes setting out in short passages of a line or two the parallels in Horace's satire, omitted from modern printings. His poem, however, does not depend like Pope's imitations on carefully worked-out allusive references, but on bold and lucky identifications.

331 l. 37. *the Faction.* The Whigs.

l. 38. *the Junto.* A form of the Spanish *junta*, commonly used for the united directing group of Whig grandees, Halifax, Orford, Somers, Sunderland, Wharton.

l. 43. *the paper-stamp.* A clause was introduced in the Supply Bill, effective 1 August 1712, which (known as the Stamp Act) attempted to censor political writing by placing a tax on all printed newspapers and pamphlets, a halfpenny on a folio half-sheet or less and a penny on a whole sheet and not more. A red stamp indicated payment made.

332 l. 94. *borrow'd money.* Swift convinced himself that Oxford promised him £1,000 to clear his expenses; but the Treasurer was dismissed before anything was done about this, supposing the promise genuine.

l. 99. *silver verge.* The wand of office carried by a verger.

l. 104. *'Cheats.* i.e. 'escheats', claims on the new incumbent by former holders; also a suggestion of 'cheats'.

333 l. 120. *Old Read.* Oxford's 'famous lying porter . . . an old Scotch fanatick' (*Journal to Stella*, 17 August 1711).

334 *Cadenus and Vanessa.* Esther, or Hester, Vanhomrigh (Vanessa) was twenty-one years younger than Swift. Her mother brought her to London at the end of 1707. Swift became intimate with the family and took the daughter under his wing as a kind of pupil, in a relationship that has a parallel in that between himself and Esther Johnson. The relationship with 'Misshessy' developed into something deep, which became for Swift an impossible, but for the passionate girl an irreversible, situation. To try to cool the affair, some time in 1713 Swift wrote this poem, not intended for publication. Manuscript copies got into circulation after Vanessa's unhappy death in 1723, with an obvious hint of scandal. Unauthorized editions of it were published in London in 1726, and Faulkner included it in *Works* 1735.

l. 2. *the Cyprian queen.* Venus, goddess of love and beauty; as Aphrodite she was said to have risen from the sea-foam near Paphos in Cyprus. She is here presiding over a Court of Love.

l. 9. *His altar now no longer smokes.* Worshippers no longer seek his aid by sacrifices.

ll. 17–19. *Against our sov'reign lady's peace . . . crown.* These are the technical phrases of an English legal charge ('against our sovereign Lady the Queen, her Crown and Dignity') and are used to support the poem's 'Court-of-Love' structure.

335 l. 46. *equipage and park parades.* The turn-out of coach, horses and servants that enabled a fine lady to take a creditable part in driving round the Ring (see below, l. 389 and note). The fashionable walk was The Mall in St James's Park.

336 l. 93. *their king's.* The *Muses* were represented as young, beautiful, and modest virgins, the daughters of Jupiter (Zeus), but led by Apollo.

l. 96. *the Graces.* (Usually three) maidens, attendants of Venus, representing beauty and charm.

l. 107. *Fletas, Bractons, Cokes.* Three English lawbooks. *Fleta* is the title of *Commentarius Juris Anglicani* [*Commentary on English law*], *c.*1290, traditionally because the anonymous writer was in London's Fleet prison; Henry de Bracton (d. 1268), *De Legibus et Consuetudinibus Angliae* [*Concerning the Laws and Customs of England*], the earliest systematic discussion; Chief Justice Sir Edward Coke (1552–1634), whose four *Institutes* (1628–44) with his *Law Reports* formed at this time the basis of English legal study.

l. 109. *Ovid, Book the Second.* Publius Ovidius Naso (43 BC–AD 17) among his works wrote three books of love poems (*Amores*) and *The Art of Love* (*Ars Amatoria*) also in three books, I–II for men, III for women.

l. 111. *Dido's case.* The story of Dido and Aeneas in Virgil's *Aeneid*, IV.

l. 112. *Tibullus's Reports.* The works of the poets of love are the *Law Reports* proper for Venus' court; Albius Tibullus (*c.* 50–19 BC) wrote on his love for Delia and other mistresses, as well as for a boy, Marathus.

l. 114. *Cowley's briefs, and pleas of Waller.* The lyric poetry of Abraham Cowley (1618–61) includes *The Mistress* (1647), a poem about love addressed to the reader's intellect. The occasional verse of Edmund Waller (1606–87) was at this time passing out of favour.

337 l. 122. *Demur, imparlance . . . essoign.* All pleas for delay in legal proceedings: *demurrer*, admitting the opponent's statement but denying that legal redress is available and asking for this to be decided first; *imparlance*, asking for an extension of time to answer a case, theoretically allowing a possible amicable settlement; *essoign* or *essoin*, offering an excuse for non-appearance in court at the appointed time.

l. 126. *Clio.* The Muse of history.

l. 136. *Lucina's aid.* A Roman deity who brought babies to see the light of day.

338 l. 187. *Pallas.* Among Pallas Athena's attributes was the personification of wisdom; she was also a war goddess, portrayed with a helmet, fully armed (see l. 250 below).

341 l. 308. *Atalanta's star.* Atalanta was a maiden averse to marriage, who killed her unsuccessful suitors.

l. 324. *a new Italian.* Opera singer.

343 l. 367. *none will burn her for a witch!* Proverbial, cf. *ODEP*[3], 93.

l. 369. *the purlieus of St. James.* The fashionable quarter of west-end London, near St James's Palace.

l. 389. *the Ring.* A circular track in Hyde Park round which the fashionable world drove in their equipages (see above, l. 46), to see and be seen.

l. 397. *Tunbridge.* The spa at Tunbridge Wells was a fashionable holiday resort.

344 l. 426. *to patch her face.* Ladies placed small pieces of black silk or other material on their faces and exposed flesh, to throw the complexion into contrast or hide blemishes.

345 l. 466. *Cadenus'.* i.e. *Decanus*, the Dean (Swift).

l. 487. *Plutarch's Morals*. Mestrius Plutarchus (*c.*50–*c.*120) wrote a number of short moral essays which were popular school texts.

353 l. 782. *Constr'ing*. Construing (= translating and interpreting), a continuation of the reversed pupil–teacher motif.

354 l. 854. *project*. A word of bad connotation for Swift. A projector was an unreliable enthusiast, exemplified by the irresponsible Venus, who could escape the consequences of her dangerous meddling with human life because she is a goddess (cf. l. 906).

l. 857. *Coram Regina, prox. die Martis*. 'Before the Queen [in the Court of the Queen's Bench] next Tuesday.'

356 l. 903. *O yes!* Oyez! The thrice-repeated call by the public crier or court officer (Old French, 'Hear ye!'), to gain silence.

l. 906. *at six and sev'n*. Proverbial from the eighteenth century, *at sixes and sevens*; ODEP[3], 739.

357 *Swift to Miss Esther Vanhomrigh. if the thing you know of had been published. The History of the Four Last Years of the Queen* (see note to p. 411 (5)).

How does Davila go on? Enrico Davila, *Historia delle Guerre Civili di Francia* (1630); Swift possessed and annotated a copy of the English translation (1647–8); *SL* 594.

358 *The Importance of the Guardian Considered*. Richard Steele's periodical, *The Guardian*, was not a political paper, but politics intruded into its columns. In particular, Steele entered the violent controversy over the French delay in demolishing Dunkirk (p. 656). Having been elected to Parliament on 25 August, as one of the members for the rotten borough of Stockbridge in Hampshire, Steele sought to be a leading Opposition writer. On 22 September 1713 he published a sixty-three-page shilling pamphlet, *The Importance of Dunkirk Considered*. Though diffuse, it went into three editions in a month. The compilation takes the form of a letter to John Snow, the bailiff or chief magistrate of Stockbridge; it reprints the Memorial against the demolition presented to the Queen by M. Tugghe, a representative of the burghers of Dunkirk. Steele offers a point-by-point rebuttal of the Memorial, a personal vindication of 'a true, grateful and loyal heart', a discussion of the argument that criticism of the administration is an infringement of the royal prerogative, and other material. When he returned from Ireland in September 1713, Swift could find no way of adequately exercising his talents as a political writer. The feud between Bolingbroke and Oxford paralysed any coherent propaganda campaign. His friendship with his old schoolfellow Steele, like his intimacy with Addison, was a casualty of the increasingly divisive party-war that characterized the closing years of the Queen's reign. Swift's answer to Steele's pamphlet, one of only four pieces he wrote and published for the Oxford administration during its last embattled year, came out at the end of October 1713. He takes the offensive in *The Importance of the Guardian* by choosing the style and tone of Steele's writing as his main topic. Steele's rhetoric is bombastic and sentimental. Swift's may be described as the rhetoric of wit. The quarrel

between Swift and Steele is not a misunderstanding, and only begins with personalities; it represents a deep and fundamental antagonism. To a modern reader, Steele is correct in arguing that private men have a right to criticize the Government and comment on public affairs. Swift's denial of this right, for argument's sake, puts him in a false position; at his most characteristic, of course, he himself breaches this denial.

359 *Mr. Steele is author of two tolerable plays.* The Funeral, or Grief à la Mode (1701–2) and *The Tender Husband, or The Accomplished Fools* (1705).

Gazetteer. The official Government news-sheet was *The London Gazette*; in the spring of 1707 Steele was appointed to run it, at an enhanced yearly salary of £300. He resigned in October 1710, with the fall of his patron, the Whig Secretary of State Sunderland.

360 *Sacheverell's trial.* Henry Sacheverell, a popular High-Church preacher, delivered an anti-Government sermon before the Lord Mayor in St Paul's Cathedral on 5 November 1709. Godolphin sought to make an example of him. He was impeached for seditious libel. His trial before the Lords was a *cause célèbre*, and though he was found guilty on 23 March 1710, the small majority of seventeen and the light sentence awarded represented a defeat for the Government; Sacheverell became a popular hero.

his subject . . . Mr. Harley. Steele could not leave the political crisis alone. The sketch of Polypragmon in *Tatler*, No. 191, 28–9 June 1710, is taken to satirize Harley; as is the letter about a 'deep intriguer' who had taken over the 'theatre', *Tatler*, No. 193, 2–4 July 1710.

the style . . . of Englishman. *The Guardian*, written daily by 'Nestor Ironside Esq.', ceased publication with No. 175 on 1 October 1713. On 6 October appeared the first number of the thrice-weekly *The Englishman, being the sequel of the Guardian.*

361 *to provoke . . . another pamphleteer.* The anonymous author of *The Honour and Prerogative of the Queen's Majesty Vindicated and Defended against the unexampled Insolence of the Guardian, in a Letter from a Country Whig to Mr. Steele.* Perhaps Defoe.

I could instance Abel Roper. Abel Roper, the Tory journalist, heads a list of regular advertisers in the newspapers.

364 *if you had not relieved him . . . St. Stephen's chapel.* The Commons met in St Stephen's chapel in the Palace of Westminster, and Steele's membership conferred on him the privileges of Parliament, one of which was immunity from arrest for debt during the session.

strip off the very garments . . . flesh. Jude 23.

his colleague. Thomas Broderick.

365 *Socinians.* See note to p. 225.

367 *publishing.* Steele's portentous style of political writing not only made use of italics and capitalization, but ran to a good deal of black letter.

alchemist. Steele's money troubles in the period 1697 to 1702 drove him to join a syndicate employing an alchemist to find the 'philosopher's stone', which would transmute base metals into gold.

371 *de contemptu mundi, et fuga seculi.* About scorn of the world and fleeing from the times.

he somewhere else calls 'the sins of his youth'. Swift's apparently casual reference is to Steele's signed letter in *Guardian*, No. 53, of 12 May 1713, which he took as an unforgivable insult. Steele wrote: '[I] am now heartily sorry I called him [Swift] a Miscreant [in *Guardian*, No. 41, of 28 April] that word I think signifies an unbeliever, Mescroyant I take it is the old French word. I will give myself no manner of liberty to make guesses at him, if I may say him; for tho' sometimes I have been told by familiar friends, that they saw me talking to the *Examiner* [Swift]; others who have rallied me upon the sins of my youth, tell me it is credibly reported that I have formerly lain with the *Examiner* [Mrs Mary de la Rivière Manley, who wrote papers in that periodical]. I have carried my point and have rescued innocence from calumny, and it is nothing to me, whether the *Examiner* writes against me in the character of an estranged friend or an exasperated mistress.'

372 *the bill of commerce being rejected.* Britain signed a Treaty of Peace and a Treaty of Commerce with France at the Peace of Utrecht, March 1713. The Treaty of Commerce was Bolingbroke's brain-child and the Bill to make it effective was defeated in the Commons on 18 June, largely by the votes of eighty rebel Tories.

some horrible expectations. The Queen being in poor health, Defoe was not the only one who offered *An Answer to a Question Nobody thinks of, viz. But what if the Queen should Die?* (1713).

his predecessor Ridpath. George Ridpath.

374 *choqued.* See note to p. 224.

376 *The Author upon Himself.* Giving up all hope of reconciling Oxford and Bolingbroke, Swift left London on 31 May 1714 to live in seclusion with his friend the Revd John Geree, rector of Letcombe Bassett in the Berkshire Downs, near Wantage. There he remained until mid-August, and during these ten weeks he wrote this set of thirty-seven couplets.

374 ll. 1–2. *hag . . . prelate . . . prude.* The notes are from Faulkner's printing in *Works* 1735, presumably prompted by Swift.

377 l. 41. *Walpole and Aislaby.* Robert Walpole and John Aislabie; the latter, (nominally Tory) MP for Ripon, who in 1713–14 was co-operating with the Whig Opposition.

l. 46. *Perkin.* The Pretender, from *Perkin Warbeck*, pretended son of Edward IV.

l. 47. *from Lambeth sent.* Lambeth Palace is the London residence of the Archbishop of Canterbury, the 'headquarters' of the Anglican Church.

l. 48. *A dang'rous treatise. A Tale of a Tub.*

l. 52. *He sues for pardon. Journal to Stella,* 23 and 26 April 1713. The message, however, from Swift's 'mortall enemy' was 'by a third hand'.

l. 53. *Madam Coningsmark.* Another slur on the character of the Duchess of Somerset. Swift refers to the story that in 1682, after the Duchess's flight to Lady Temple's from her second husband Thomas Thynne, her lover Count von Königsmark procured Thynne's murder. Swift's suicidal verse broadside attack on the Duchess, *The Windsor Prophecy* (December 1711), politically valueless, made the Queen implacably hostile to his claims for preferment.

377–8 ll. 58–62. *the vengeful Scot . . . sleight.* Swift's second attack on Steele, *The Public Spirit of the Whigs set forth in their Generous Support of the Author of the Crisis,* was published in February 1714. It contained a slighting reference to beggarly Scots peers, later removed, but not before in March Wharton, at the instigation of the Duke of Argyll and other Scottish lords, complained of the pamphlet in the upper House. Oxford had to agree to a proclamation being issued offering a reward for the discovery of the author of the 'seditious' libel (whom everyone knew). Proceedings were stopped a few days later on a technicality.

379 *Swift to Joseph Addison. upon being Secretary.* On 12 April 1717, following a crisis involving the resignation of Walpole and other Whig Ministers, Sunderland became the dominant political figure and Addison reached the climax of the public career he had assiduously followed, being appointed Secretary of State for the Southern Department.

380 *The Testimony of Conscience.* Although Swift was in holy orders for half a century, and after 1714 for many years he preached his turn in St Patrick's every fifth Sunday barring absence from Dublin, only twelve sermons ascribed to him are known. This suggests that he did not consider his sermons part of his *œuvre*, an impression that is strengthened by several slighting references to them in his correspondence, as well as by his ironical maxim [72] that preaching affects only the virtuous (see p. 182). On the other hand, he took the art of preaching seriously, as he did every duty of his profession and station. He attracted hearers to St Patrick's, and expounded his views on preaching and sermons in *A Letter to a Young Gentleman, lately entered into Holy Orders,* first printed in 1720, as well as in a sermon on sermons, now known as *Sleeping in Church.* The sermon selected for this anthology appeared with two others in a little volume published in London a year before Swift's death. In its plainness, it is typical of what is known of his preaching.

381 *the heathen Emperor who said.* Tiberius: apparently one of Swift's favourite quotations (see note to p. 219 (1)).

385 *the advice of Jethro to . . . Moses.* Exodus 19: 21.

387 *Stella's Birthday* written AD 1718 [i.e. 1719]. This poem appears to mark the start of Swift's yearly custom of addressing a set of verses to Esther Johnson [Stella] on her birthday, 13 March. She transcribed this poem, with others for 1721 and 1722, into her manuscript book now in the possession of the Duke of Bedford at Woburn Abbey.

l. 1. *thirty-four.* Actually, thirty-eight.

388 *Swift to Bishop Evans. refused to accept my proxy*. John Evans, Bishop of Meath, was holding his diocesan visitation, at which Swift as vicar of Laracor was bound to attend or send a proxy. Evans had complained of 'the insolent rudeness of Dr. Swift' at his visitation the previous year, when 'he endeavoured to arraign me before my clergy for unkind usage towards 3 of them . . .' (Evans to Wake, Archbishop of Canterbury, 10 June 1718).

your first coming over. Evans was translated from the See of Bangor to Meath in 1716.

389 *Phyllis, or, The Progress of Love*. This poem is transcribed by Esther Johnson and assigned to 1719 in her manuscript book now in the possession of the Duke of Bedford at Woburn Abbey.

390 l. 56. *marriages are made in Heaven*. Proverbial from 1567, cf. *ODEP³*, 514.

392–5 *The Progress of Beauty*. This poem is transcribed by Esther Johnson and dated 1719 in her manuscript book now in the possession of the Duke of Bedford at Woburn Abbey.

393 ll. 51–2. *adore | The workmanship . . . hands*. Cf. Jeremiah 1: 16, Acts 7: 41.

l. 60. *White lead . . . Lusitanian*. A paste compounded of lead salts was used as a cosmetic. Its use is cumulatively poisonous . . . Fine Portuguese tin-glazed ware with attractive chinoiserie decoration was imported at this time.

394 l. 73. *the Pell-Mell*. Pall Mall, the fashionable street south of, and parallel with, Piccadilly, between the Haymarket and St James's Palace.

l. 74. *the glasses of your chair*. The windows of your sedan-chair.

ll. 89–90. *Partridge . . . cause Efficient*. John Partridge, the astrologer . . . In Aristotle's metaphysics, there was a fourfold account of causality. Swift mentions the first three terms in the poem: *material cause*, the stuff out of which a thing is made; *formal cause*, the essence of that thing; *efficient cause*, the impetus or effect by which a thing is produced: *final cause* is the aim or idea of the change.

ll. 91–2. *Cancer . . . milky way*. Cancer (the Crab) is one of the signs of the zodiac, but Swift also refers to a cancer of the breast, part of the poem's network of conceits on wasting or venereal diseases, visible tokens that break apart illusions, reveal secret misbehaviour, and command human obedience.

l. 93. *Gadbury*. John Gadbury, an astrologer.

l. 95. *swain Endymion*. The youth whose beauty excited the love of the frigid Selene (the Moon).

l. 96. *Mercury's her foe*. In astrology, Mercury is the planet nearest the sun; compounds of mercury were used in Swift's day in the treatment of venereal diseases, but their unpleasant and poisonous side-effects imposed seclusion on the patient, and the treatment was almost as bad as the disease.

395 l. 99. *Flamsteed*. John Flamsteed, the astronomer.

396 *To Stella, who collected and transcribed his Poems*. First printed in the

Pope–Swift *Miscellanies. The Last Volume* (1727). Dated 1720 in *Works* 1735, a later date (1723) is more apt; see H. Davis, *Stella*, 1942, p. 63.

l. 4. *Inigo Jones.* 1573–1652; the first great English classical architect, designer of the Banqueting House in Whitehall.

397   l. 44. *tippling under ground.* In a cellar drinking-den.

ll. 45–6. *Sylvia beating flax . . . tracks.* Imprisonment with hard labour in Bridewell (see note to p. 534, l. 41) . . . punishment by the lash.

l. 50. *Curll's collections.* Edmund Curll.

l. 63. *What stoics call without our power.* Stoic doctrine taught that the passions arose when a man mistakenly judged 'indifferent' things (i.e. outside our power) to be good or bad.

l. 71. *Mævius.* See note to p. 543, ll. 301–2.

l. 72. *suburb.* Outlying slum district.

l. 74. *crambo.* Rhyme, derived from the word-game: see note to p. 592 (2).

398   l. 78. *lost her nose.* By syphilis.

399   l. 121. *Thus Ajax.* One of the Greek chiefs at the siege of Troy, a man of obstinate bravery; he and Odysseus contended for the arms and armour of Achilles on the latter's death. Ajax lost, and in demented rage slaughtered a flock of sheep, thinking them to be Greeks. Bitter shame at this act led to his suicide.

400   *A Proposal for the Universal Use of Irish Manufacture.* This is the first in the long series of pieces in prose and verse that Swift wrote in Ireland, defying English oppression, which as Swift perceived the situation, was both political and economic. In *A Proposal*, he concentrates on the mercantilist anti-Irish economic legislation of the English (British) Parliament, but his efforts to raise the consciousness of the Anglo-Irish was a political act. The Dublin establishment therefore took political action against the provocative publication. Lord Chief Justice Whitshed sought and obtained the presentment of the pamphlet as seditious by the Dublin grand jury and, against the trial jury's dogged resistance, the conviction of the printer. Swift used his influence in London and the proceedings were stopped before sentence. The whole legal affair is touched on in *An Excellent New Song*, which follows *A Proposal* in the present collection (p. 406). Swift also gives his interpretation of it in his letter to Alexander Pope, 10 January 1721 (see pp. 411–17).

penal clauses absolutely prohibiting their tenants from ploughing. Swift is drawing attention to a change in Irish land-use, though the conclusions he draws need qualification. After the Woollens Act of 1699 (see next note), pasturage for sheep actually contracted. But as the export trade in beef and butter grew, a long-term result of the English Act of 1667 forbidding the importation of Irish cattle on the hoof, the area of pasturage expanded again to meet the success of this trade, favouring the enterprise of large landowners. Although a sign of economic expansion, the change was of course bad news for other agricultural interests and for country-folk in general, who made up the majority of the Irish population.

to make our wool a drug to us. The English woollen industry lobby secured the passage in 1699 of the Irish Woollens Act, which forbade the export of Irish wool anywhere but to England, levying a duty on its importation there, as well as barring the exportation of Irish woollen cloth. There was a vigorous clandestine trade in wool with France.

in case Barnstaple should be overstocked. This small seaport in Devon was the chief mart for imported Irish wool.

401 *the late Archbishop of Tuam.* The Revd John Vesey (1638–1716), for whom Swift had some friendship.

Non tanti mitra . . . ostrum. 'A mitre is not worth so much; the robes of a judge are not of so much importance.'

402 *the present Archbishop of Dublin.* The Revd William King.

the fable in Ovid of Arachne and Pallas. Ovid, *Metamorphoses*, vi. Fable 1.

oppression makes a wise man mad. Ecclesiastes 7: 7.

403 *Mostyn and Whitehaven.* Ports in Flintshire and Cumberland.

Sanderson and Suarez . . . civilians. Robert Sanderson (1587–1663), Bishop of Lincoln, a leading Anglican casuist whose works would have been studied by Swift for his ordination: Francisco Suárez (1548–1617), SJ, Spanish theologian, casuist, and political philosopher . . . writers on the Civil Law.

a person who by his style and literature. A note in *Works* 1735 identifies the translation as 'supposed to be Caesar's *Commentaries* dedicated to the Duke of Marlborough', implying Martin Bladen (1680–1746), a soldier and client of the Duke's.

404 *Little Britain.* A London street running from Aldersgate Street westwards to St Bartholomew's Hospital, Smithfield; together with an offshoot, Duck Lane, it was an area of printers, journalists, second-hand book shops, and old clothes stalls.

the author of a play. Viscount Grimston.

a dispensing power in the Queen. The power claimed by the Crown as part of the royal prerogative, of overriding statutes in special circumstances.

405 *canting their own lands.* Setting parcels of land at lease.

a thing they call a Bank. In 1720, a proposal was made for the foundation of a National Bank of Ireland with a capital of £500,000; the project received royal approval in 1721, but was killed by the Irish Parliament. Swift joined in the attack on it, arguing that it was another 'job' of the moneyed men.

406 *An Excellent New Song on a Seditious Pamphlet. To the tune of Packington's Pound.* These verses were clearly written during the uproar over *A Proposal for the Universal Use of Irish Manufacture*, to keep the provocation open. *Packington's Pound* was a sixteenth-century dance-tune; throughout the

seventeenth and early eighteenth centuries it was the second most popular tune for political and other ballads, imposing its form with a refrain on such pieces. Gay used it in *The Beggar's Opera* (1728), III. ii. Air 43.

l. 9. *Journeyman Waters*. Edward Waters, printer of Swift's piece, *A Proposal for the Universal Use of Irish Manufacture*.

l. 10. *In England the dead in woollen are clad*. An Act of 1667 sought to encourage the woollen industry by requiring that corpses be buried in woollen shrouds; it was not repealed until 1815.

l. 13. *a living dog better is than a dead lion*. Ecclesiastes 9: 4; then proverbial from 1566; cf. *ODEP*[3], 476.

l. 16. *our horns pull in*. Like snails; i.e. curtail our activities; proverbial from 1374; cf. *ODEP*[3], 201.

407 l. 29. *coram nobis*. 'Before us'; i.e. the Court of King's Bench.

408 *The Run upon the Bankers*. Esther Johnson copied the poem, 'Written in A:D: 1720', into her manuscript volume, now at Woburn Abbey. The set of witty variations on the theme of the bankers' misuse of credit, playing with biblical allusions, mythology, and business terms, is clearly prompted by the collapse in 1720 of the South Sea Bubble. Swift wrote a more elaborate and specific poem on this financial and political crisis, *The Bubble* (*Poems*, 248–59).

ll. 5–6. *The multitude's . . . seas*. Isaiah 17: 12.

ll. 14–16. *Quakers . . . have levees . . . of duns*. Quakers refused to pay tithes to the incumbents of the established Church; they were frequently prosecuted for payment, when 'duns' or debt-collectors would gather as clients did at a great man's levee.

l. 21. *the wisest monarch sings*. Solomon: Proverbs 23: 5.

l. 27. *the wish of Nero*. 'If asked to sign the usual execution order for a felon, [Nero] would sigh: "Ah how I wish that I never learned to write"' (G. Suetonius Tranquillus, trans. Robert Graves, *The Twelve Caesars*).

409 l. 32. *images of wax*. A conceit identifying the wax seals attached to legal instruments with the wax images in witchcraft; as the latter waste away or are damaged, those they represent are sympathetically harmed.

l. 42. *the god of gold and hell*. Plutus was god of gold, Pluto of hell; they were often confused.

ll. 45–8. *conj'rer . . . the bloody bond*. So necromancers signed their pacts with the devil.

l. 49. *baited*. 'Harassed', 'under attack', as in *bear-baiting*; but perhaps also 'deficient', 'lacking': see *OED*, s.vv. *bait* and *bate*.

l. 52. *the writing on the wall*. At Belshazzar's feast, Daniel 5: 30.

l. 57. *universal call*. The summons to the Day of Judgement; but a *call* is also a demand to a subscriber or stockholder for payment of capital.

410 l. 64. *Weigh'd in the balance . . .* Daniel 5: 27.

411 *Swift to Alexander Pope*. Clearly drafted as a pamphlet or personal statement, in 1722 and after (see Ehrenpreis, *Swift*, iii. 136, 445, nn.).

gentlemen of the long robe to those in furs. Lawyers (pleaders) to judges.

a discourse. *Some Free Thoughts upon the Present State of Affairs*, not printed
until 1741 and also included in that year in the Faulkner volume containing
this letter: *Prose*, viii. 75 ff. and 205 ff.

a certain great Minister. Bolingbroke.

some Memorials of the four last years of the Queen's reign . . . disdained to accept it.
The piece now known as *The History of the Four Last Years of the Queen*, in
length one of Swift's principal works, was drafted as a pamphlet intended to
serve as a scenario for the ministerialists in the session of Parliament that
opened on 9 April 1713. The quarrel between Oxford and Bolingbroke,
however, prevented publication, and gradually Swift began to think of it as a
history of the Oxford administration and its peace negotiation. Swift
unsuccessfully sought the office of Historiographer Royal which fell vacant
in December 1713, on the death of Thomas Rymer. The Duke of
Shrewsbury, Lord Chamberlain, appointed the scholar Thomas Madox.

412 *a discourse*. *A Proposal for the Universal Use of Irish Manufacture* (see above,
p. 400).

a person in great office here. Lord Middleton, Lord Chancellor of Ireland.

the Duke of Grafton . . . was pleased to grant a noli prosequi. Swift solicited this
action of discontinuing the prosecution from his friend Grafton.

413 *a treatise*. *A Dedication to a Great Man, concerning Dedications*, usually
attributed to the Whig pamphleteer and journalist Thomas Gordon (d.
1750).

414 *Non obtusa adeo . . . jungit ab urbe*. 'Our Punic hearts are not so
undiscriminating, nor does the sun harness his horses so far from this city of
Tyre': Virgil, *Aeneid*, i. 567–8.

tanquam in equo Trojano. 'As if in the Trojan horse': Cicero, *Phillipics*, ii.
13.

415 *Mr. Addison, when he first came over hither Secretary*. On 21 April 1709.

416 *the necessity of suspending any law . . . to see it repeated*. The Habeas Corpus Act
was suspended in 1715 for six months in the panic at the Jacobite Rebellion.

417 *I have often known an innocent man seized and imprisoned*. Oxford was arrested
in June 1715, and held in the Tower until his release in July 1717, when no
impeachment prosecution was forthcoming.

418 *A Satirical Elegy on the Death of a late Famous General*. The Duke of
Marlborough died on 16 June 1722, aged 72. The poem was never published
by Swift, and first appeared in the *Gentleman's Magazine*, 34 (May 1764).

l. 6. *The last loud trump*. 1 Corinthians 16: 52.

l. 17. *his funeral appears*. Marlborough was accorded a very elaborate State
funeral in Westminster Abbey on 9 August.

419 *Upon the Horrid Plot discovered by Harlequin, the Bishop of Rochester's French Dog.* The financial disaster of 1720–1, known as the South Sea Bubble, became a grave political crisis. Naturally, the Jacobites wished to exploit the serious difficulties of the Hanoverian regime in London, and they evolved an unrealistic plan, which provided for the Duke of Ormonde to sail into the Thames with substantial finance and supplies of arms, together with a nucleus of Irish officers to raise an army; risings were to be organized at the same time in the West Country and in the north. Francis Atterbury, Bishop of Rochester, at first allowed himself against his better judgement to become one of the organizers of these preparations. It was apparent by the beginning of 1722 that the Jacobite apparatus lacked the capacity to succeed. Atterbury withdrew. The Jacobite agents in England, however, criminally neglected the security of their communications. Further, in Paris the Earl of Mar was buying his rehabilitation from the Hanoverian Government by betraying his colleagues, including Atterbury. In the aftermath of the financial débâcle Walpole was brought back into the administration. Despite the fact that the Jacobite threat had collapsed, Walpole decided to consolidate his position with the King and in the country at large by exaggerating the Jacobite menace and in particular by destroying Atterbury, one of his most formidable opponents in Parliament. He produced a narrative of a complex Jacobite conspiracy, which was based on the collation of the original plan, the muddle that followed, and the lunatic projects of an irresponsible Norwich attorney, Christopher Layer, who had no official Jacobite support. Atterbury was arrested on 24 August 1722 and held for nine months in the Tower, in conditions of extreme severity. Habeas Corpus was suspended. Layer was tried and hanged, drawn, and quartered. The evidence against the subtle and circumspect bishop was insufficient for a treason trial in a court of law, but Walpole struck at him through a parliamentary Bill of Pains and Penalties, virtually a finding of guilt and sentence by legislative vote. The Bill was passed on 16 May 1723, and from 18 June Atterbury was deprived, banished for ever from the kingdom, and condemned to suffer as a convicted felon if he returned. One of the chief links in Walpole's chain of evidence was the little spotted dog, Harlequin, sent by Mar to Atterbury's dying wife, which was mentioned in letters. Atterbury's treatment shocked Swift, and Walpole's use of reported, decoded messages is referred to in the famous passage in *Gulliver's Travels*, Part III, chapter vi, towards the end, about the project for discovering 'Plots and Conspiracies'. This poem was first published in *Works* 1735.

l. 10. *Porter, and Prendergast, and Oates.* George Porter and Thomas Prendergast (*c.* 1660–1709) were concerned in the Jacobite plot to assassinate William III on 15 February 1696 at Turnham Green; Porter turned king's evidence. Titus Oates (1649–1705), the perjured informer in the so-called Popish Plot of 1678–9.

l. 12 *this dog was lame.* Harlequin broke his leg on the way from France, hence the 'mysterious meaning' in *Gulliver's Travels*, 'a lame dog an invader'.

l. 15. *help your lame dog o'er the stile.* Proverbial since 1546; *ODEP³*, 369: the first of several 'dog' proverbs.

l. 20. *cur Plunkett, or whelp Skean.* James Plunket, a down-at-heel Irish adventurer, associate of Christopher Layer and writer of incriminating letters, sentenced in the same Bill as Atterbury to life imprisonment in the Tower, where he died in 1738. Skean, or Skene, was the source of hearsay evidence implicating Atterbury, which, however, he denied on oath.

l. 22. *t'other puppy that was drown'd.* The Revd Philip Neyno, a starving graduate of Trinity College, Dublin, foolishly employed as a copyist of secret letters. Neyno tried to sell Walpole inconsiderable information but was trapped. On 24 September 1722, in a desperate attempt to escape from confinement, he was drowned in the Thames.

l. 23. *Mason, that abandon'd bitch.* Layer's lodging-house keeper, Elizabeth Mason, in whose possession two fatal bundles of the former's papers were found. At Layer's trial, she was harried over her sexual habits.

l. 28. *dogs-heads in a porridge-pot.* Proverbial since *c.*1579 (*ODEP³*, 376).

l. 30. *every dog must have his day.* Proverbial since 1561 (*ODEP³*, 195).

l. 32. *a hog or dog on't.* Proverbial (*ODEP³*, 500).

420 l. 40. *teach dead dogs to bite.* Cf. (*a*) 'You cannot teach an old dog new tricks', proverbial from 1523 (*ODEP³*, 805); and (*b*) 'Dead dogs do not bite', proverbial from 1571 (*ODEP³*, 171).

l. 52. *decipher'd, and translated.* Walpole's case depended on the versions of a number of letters produced in his efficient decoding office.

l. 54. *the secret wise Committee.* The Select Committee of the Commons, packed with Walpole's supporters, set up on 15 January 1723 to examine the evidence for the plot.

l. 56. *set his mark.* As an illiterate 'signs' by a cross; *mark* is also, in hunting parlance, an animal's footprint.

l. 58. *a dog in a doublet.* Proverbial since *c.*1549 (*ODEP³*, 195).

l. 60. *dog-tricks.* Proverbial since 1540 (*ODEP³*, 197).

l. 70. *the bishop's foot was in it.* Proverbial from 1528, referring to burnt food, because bishops could burn heretics (*ODEP³*, 61); Swift again uses this formula in *Polite Conversation,* i (*Prose,* iv. 134).

421 *Swift to Bishop Stearne. the old club.* Consisting of Archdeacon and Mrs Walls, Esther Johnson, and Rebecca Dingley.

422 *from* THE DRAPIER'S LETTERS CONTROVERSY

Some time in 1720, the British administration had to find a modest financial provision for George I's mistress, Gräfin Melusine von der Schulenburg, who had become a naturalized British subject and, in 1719, Duchess of Munster in the Irish peerage. It no doubt seemed convenient, using the Irish establishment to maintain absentee pensioners, that a royal patent should be issued for minting Irish copper halfpence and farthings and disposed of for the benefit of the Duchess. A taker was found for the bargain in William Wood, a Wolverhampton entrepreneur; perhaps he had suggested the scheme. His price was £10,000, and the patent for the minting (over fourteen years) of coins to the face value of £100,800 was issued under the King's signature on 12 July 1722. In August 1722, a month after the issue of the patent, the Commissioners of the Irish Revenue in Dublin complained to the Lord-Lieutenant, the Duke of Grafton, then in England. This conflict touched on an ancient source of dispute in Ireland, the coinage. Since Tudor times, the English executive had consistently refused to allow the Irish Government control over a mint, one of the most open signs of the subjugation of Ireland and the subordination of its Anglo-Irish rulers. The circulation of money in Ireland was as a result full of difficulties. A similar situation, though less severe, existed in Scotland, and a worse one in the American plantations. Receiving no reply to their first remonstrance, the Irish Revenue Commissioners in September complained to the Treasury in London. This suggests that something had gone wrong with the management of the Irish establishment, and in this respect it is relevant to note that the Ministers in London were in the midst of a bitter power struggle. The apparently parochial argument over copper coins in Ireland had therefore much wider implications for both sides. For the Ministry in London and their representatives in Dublin, it was a test of strength in a situation made uncomfortable and uncertain by intrigue. After temporizing, and trying administrative and technical review which offered concessions on the amount of copper coin to be minted, the London Government, and in this matter principally Walpole, was forced to concede defeat. Wood's patent was withdrawn and the patentee compensated. In the great flurry of pamphlets on the affair, seven of Swift's prose pieces are cast in the form of the Drapier's Letters; associated with the Letters are several small prose pieces by Swift as well as verse epigrams and poems. Swift's main titles are set out below: the three pieces offered in the present selection are distinguished by an asterisk:

*I. *A Letter to the Shop-keepers, Tradesmen, Farmers, and Common-People in General, of the Kingdom of Ireland ... (Very Proper to be kept in every Family)*, March 1724.

II. *A Letter to Mr. Harding the Printer. Upon Occasion of a Paragraph in his News-Paper of August 1st.*, 4 August 1724. Swift's response to the Government leak of Wood's agreement to limit his issue of coins to the amount of £40,000.

III. *Some Observations upon a Paper, Called, The Report of the Committee of ... the Privy Council in England*, 5 September 1724; addressed 'To the Nobility and Gentry of the Kingdom of Ireland', the Anglo-Irish political nation. The Report had been carefully drawn for publication and flatly set out the case based on precedents for the dependency of the Government of Ireland.

A Serious Poem upon William Wood, Brazier, Tinker. Hard-Ware-Man, Coiner, Counterfeiter, Founder and Esquire, anonymous half-sheet, September 1724.

*IV. *A Letter to the Whole People of Ireland*, 13 October 1724. Printed in time to be on the streets of Dublin the day Carteret lands in Ireland, 22 October.

Seasonable Advice to the Grand Jury, 11 November 1724. Swift urges the Dublin grand jury called to present Harding, the printer of Letter IV who had been arrested on 4 November, to refuse to do so. They follow his advice, and also refuse a call to present *Seasonable Advice* itself.

*[fifth]. *A Letter to the Lord Chancellor Middleton*, dated 26 October 1724, though referring to Carteret's proclamation against Letter IV issued on 27 October. Unpublished at the time, it is not strictly a Drapier's Letter, but it is Swift's justification for trenching on the wider Anglo-Irish controversy in Letter IV, and is therefore included in the sequence; it was first printed in *Works* 1735, where it is called VI in order of publication.

[sixth]. *A Letter to Viscount Molesworth*, 14 December 1724. Keeps the controversy going by justifying Swift's attitudes and arguments in opposition to the condemnation in the proclamation issued against Letter IV. Called V in order of publication.

VII. *An Humble Address to both Houses of Parliament*, written in the summer of 1725 to be ready for the opening of the Irish Parliament. This was originally called for 6 August but prorogued until the announcement that Wood had surrendered his patent could be made by Carteret; the turn of affairs made the pamphlet unnecessary; it was first printed in *Works* 1735.

To the Shop-keepers, Tradesmen, Farmers, and Common-People in General, of the Kingdom of Ireland. The significance, if any, of the initials 'M.B.' (Marcus Brutus has been suggested) does not seem to have been indicated anywhere by Swift; nor the reason for his adoption of the curious form 'Drapier' for 'Draper'. Swift's Dublin 'Liberty' of St Patrick's, an exempt district which he ruled as Dean, had a concentration of fiercely Protestant (including some Huguenot) weavers and linen and woollen drapers.

the printer to sell it at the lowest rate. The printer was John Harding, arrested in November for publishing Letter IV: see above. Letter 1 was offered at the rate of 36 for 2s., Swift claiming in advertisements that the author had 'undertaken to pay the printer the charge of publishing them'.

a little book . . . found him guilty. A Proposal for the Universal Use of Irish Manufacture, May 1720 . . . see above, p. 400, and ibid., n. (1).

423 *four score and ten thousand pounds.* Actually £100,800 = 360 tons of copper.

425 *'Squire C——y.* William Connolly.

the brass money in K. James's time. During his months in Ireland in 1689–90, James II was forced to strike a base coinage to pay his troops; in several proclamations he threatened penalties against those who refused to accept his coins and promised to redeem them at face value for silver and gold in due course.

426 *run all into sheep.* A point reiterated by Swift in his Irish writing, but see note to p. 400 (2).

427 *'The Mirror of Justice'* ... *as my Lord Coke says.* Andrew Horne (d. 1328), *The Mirror of Justices,* an antiquarian compilation rather than a lawyer's case-book.... Sir Edward Coke (1552–1634), judge and opponent of the use of the royal prerogative by James I and Charles I: Swift's quotations are from *The Second Book of the Institutes of the Laws of England* (1642), 576–7.

Henry the 4th. chap. 4. Should be 4 Hen. IV, c. 10.

428 *another Act in this King's reign ... and by an Act made in the eleventh year of his reign.* A small tangle in the legal mumbo-jumbo which Swift has perhaps obtained from a lawyer: 9 Edward III, c. 4 ... this should be 11 Henry IV, c. 5; a galley halfpenny was a foreign silver coin introduced into England perhaps by Genoese Sailors (*OED*).

Davis's Reports. Sir John Davies (1569–1626), Attorney-General for Ireland: *Le Primer Report des Cases et Matters en Ley resolves et adjuges en les Courts del Roy en Ireland* (Dublin, 1615); Swift's reference is to p. 18, 'Le Case de Mixt Monyes'.

429 *His Majesty ... obliges nobody to take these halfpence.* Wood's patent states that his coin was 'to pass and be received as current money by such as shall be willing to receive the same'.

the accursed thing. Joshua 6: 18.

a bull of brass. Perillus invented the brazen bull for Phalaris, the tyrant of Acragas in Sicily, in the early sixth century BC, and was himself the first victim of the device.

431 *Swift to Lord Carteret. two small tracts.* i.e. his own Drapier's Letter 1 and probably the eight-page piece also printed by Harding, *The True State of the Case Between the Kingdom of Ireland of the one Part, and of Mr. William Wood of the other Part. By a Protestant of Ireland,* which is attributed to Lord Abercorn.

432 *Swift to Lord Carteret. a great Minister.* Lord Treasurer Oxford.

434 *A Letter to the Whole People of Ireland.* This is the most provocative of the Drapier's Letters printed during the controversy, not only in the timing of its publication on 22 October, the day the new Lord-Lieutenant landed at Ringsend, but also in its broadening of the scope of the argument into the basis of the governance of Ireland itself. Five days after Carteret's arrival, he held a Privy Council, and all the members present, except Archbishop King, signed an order for prosecuting Harding the printer by due process of law and all but King and two others signed a proclamation against the 'wicked and malicious pamphlet'. Carteret could not obtain outright condemnation of the whole Letter, but forced mention of 'several seditious and scandalous paragraphs ...' The proclamation went on to offer £300, which was never claimed, for the discovery of the author. Carteret's secretary mentions a 'quotation out of scripture got by rote, by men, women and children ... And the people said unto Saul, Shall Jonathan die, who hath wrought this great

salvation in Israel? God forbid: as the Lord liveth, there shall not be one hair of his head fall to the ground, for he hath wrought with God this day. So the people rescued Jonathan, that he died not [1 Samuel 14: 45]' (PRO SP 63, vol. 384).

Esau . . . a mess of pottage. Genesis, 25: 29–34.

435 *sending base money hither.* See Letter I, p. 428 above.

the opinion of the great Lord Bacon. The sentence seems to be an allusion to an idea that Bacon expresses more than once, but not in these words, namely the parallel between 'rules of nature, and the rule of policy'. Bacon was a supporter of the kingly power and nowhere denies the Crown's power to alter the valuation at will.

436 *which those of English birth . . . Wood's halfpence.* This was one of the paragraphs against which the proclamation of 27 October was directed.

a Report altogether in favour of Wood . . . former letter. The Report of the Committee of the . . . Privy Council, Whitehall, 24 July 1724, printed in *The London Journal* and separately . . . Swift commented on it in Letter III, see above p. 671.

I have shown it at large. Letter III. This was another 'treasonable' paragraph which attracted Carteret's censure.

437 *the Parliament . . . is . . . to assemble.* Carteret did not finally summon Parliament until 21 September 1725, when he could announce that Wood had surrendered his patent.

438 *All considerable offices for life here are possessed by . . . followers of the chief governors.* The monopolizing of offices by English aspirants, at the expense of the Anglo-Irish born in the country, is a sore point with Swift: see p. 474f., Swift to Peterborough, 28 April 1726.

the reversion of several employments during pleasure. The right, exercised by leave of the Crown, of succeeding to an office or place.

a favourite secretary. Edward Hopkins (d. 1726), appointed by the Duke of Grafton, 1722.

439 *closeting.* Intimidating or influencing by private conferences; ironically, a favourite tactic of the Catholic James II.

440 *lately made primate.* Hugh Boulter.

441 *Ireland is a 'depending kingdom'.* This passage sets out the nub of the Anglo-Irish argument against the administration, and it is marked as legally exceptionable in Carteret's copy. Swift follows closely the case put forward by William Molyneux in his famous book, *The Case of Ireland's being bound by Acts of Parliament in England, Stated* (1698). The British 'Declaratory Act' (1720) makes the strongest statement of the contrary view.

a statute made here in the 33d year of Henry 8th. In June 1541, Henry VIII had a Parliament in Dublin substitute for his inherited title 'Lord of Ireland', the new title 'King of his land of Ireland as united, annexed, and knit for ever to the imperial crown of the realm of England'.

at Preston. On 14 November 1715, the Jacobite rebels in arms in England surrendered to General Carpenter, who commanded a loyalist force including troops from Ireland.

the Parliaments of England ... the famous Mr. Molineux. The English Parliament in the reigns of Charles II and William III enacted protectionist legislation restricting Irish trade; attack on these pretensions formed a central part of Swift's Anglo-Irish defiance (see note to p. 400 (3)) ... In 1698, the Commons in London voted Molyneux's *The Case of Ireland* to be a book 'of dangerous consequence to the crown and people of England ...'. Molyneux's book was reprinted in Dublin in 1725.

442 *somebody in England*. Walpole.

a pamphlet ... of near 50 pages. Some farther Account of the Original Disputes in Ireland, about Farthings and Half-pence. In a Discourse with a Quaker of Dublin (1724).

444 *a Dutch reckoning*. A bill that gives only the total owed, without particulars.

445 *a short paper printed at Bristol. A Short Defence of the People of Ireland, Occasioned by the View of a Letter from Mr. Wood to one of the Managers of his Copper Halfpence in Bristol* (1724; reprinted in Dublin).

the true English people of Ireland. See p. 471.

another newsletter but of yesterday. [Dublin], *The Flying Post*, 12 October 1724.

446 *fifty thousand operators*. 'Ireland is represented as in a state of slavery, and treated as slaves by England; nay, when [Swift] mentions 50,000 operators as a necessary number to distribute his fire-balls, I doubt he means something which he dared not name [i.e. the army], and insinuates as if we are to be borne down by main force' (Lord Middleton to Thomas Broderick, in W. Coxe, *Memoirs of ... Walpole* (1798), ii. 397).

as remote from thunder as ... from Jupiter. An ancient saying found in Greek and Latin forms; cited by Erasmus, *Adagia*, 'Procul a Jove atque fulmine'.

447 *A Letter to the Lord Chancellor Middleton*. This piece was intended to be even more provocative than Letter IV, since by signing it 'J.S.' and dating it from 'Deanery House', Swift declares that he is the Drapier. Carteret in a letter to the Duke of Newcastle, Secretary of State, 31 October 1724, says '... no man in the kingdom how great and considerable soever he might think himself was of weight enough to stand a matter of this nature ...', adding that following legal advice, he considered Letter IV treasonable (H. J. Davis (ed.), *The Drapier's Letters* (1935), pp. xlvi–xlvii). Not surprisingly, Swift did not publish the *Letter to Middleton* until it appeared in *Works* 1735 with the *Advertisement to the Reader*.

after many years' intermission. In 1720 there was a coolness between Swift and Middleton, since the Dean believed the Chancellor had pressed for the prosecution of Edward Waters, printer of *A Proposal for the Universal Use of Irish Manufacture* (see Swift to Pope, p. 412).

448 *an affair of state . . . not now a preaching.* A matter attracting a prosecution for seditious libel (or even treason). Carteret believed the Drapier's Letter IV 'contained such seditious and in my opinion treasonable matter as called upon a Chief Governor here to exert his utmost power in bringing the author of it to justice . . . I am fully determined to summon him before the Council . . . I shall think it my duty to order his being taken into custody, and to detain him if I can by law . . .' . . . Several statutes providing for the prosecution of treasonable acts specify 'preaching, teaching and advised speaking'.

Whitshed . . . the device upon his coach. Swift says he noted the motto on Whitshed's coach, *Libertas et natale solum* ('Liberty and my native country'), while the judge was trying Harding for printing Letter IV. He wrote a bitter lampoon against Whitshed with the lines, '. . . Could nothing but thy chief Reproach, | Serve for a Motto on thy Coach . . .' (*Poems*, 347-9).

449 *the Duke of Grafton, and Mr. Walpole.* Both hostile to Middleton.

450 *to make a speech directly against me.* 'I heard at court, that Walpole (a great Whig member) said, that I and my whimsical club writ [*An Excellent New Song, Being the Intended Speech of a famous Orator against Peace*, a Grub Street lampoon on Nottingham] at one of our meetings, and that I should pay for it' (*Journal to Stella*, 18 December 1711).

451 *Pepper-harrow.* Peper Harrow, Middleton's seat in Surrey, near Moor Park, between Godalming and Milford.

452 *bellum atque virum.* 'A contest and a man.'

453 *in one of his former pamphlets.* Letter I; see p. 427.

nummorum famulus. 'The slave of money'; tokens for doing the dirty work.

454 *that destructive project for a bank in Ireland.* See note to p. 405 (2).

455 *Sir Edward Coke.* See note to p. 427 (1).

Lord Somers, the greatest man I ever knew of your robe. Swift had mixed opinions about Somers: he attacked him as a Junto member in *Examiner*, No. 27, 1 February 1711, but had dedicated *A Tale of a Tub* to him (see p. 71).

a printer prosecuted . . . Edward Waters; see p. 400 and ibid., n. 1.

I did very lately . . . preach. Doing Good: a Sermon on the Occasion of Wood's Project (*Prose*, ix. 232 ff.).

456 *Sir George Rook.* Rooke lived at St Laurence, near Canterbury.

controlled. Overruled, therefore not allowed to operate as a maxim; see p. xii.

a passage of Signor Leti. Gregorio Leti or Lati (1630-1701), a voluminous historian and traveller; the story is told in Anthony Hamilton's account of the court of Charles II in his *Mémoires du Comte de Grammont* (trans. Abel Boyer, 1714).

garlands. Miscellanies or collections of popular songs and ballads, from the common title, *A Garland of . . .*

458 *Poining's act.* This was basically the legal instrument that defined the legislative arrangements for Ireland until 1783. Henry VII sent Sir Edward

Poynings to Ireland as Lord Deputy. Poynings called a carefully selected Parliament at Drogheda on 1 December 1494. Various measures were passed, intended to make the central Government of the Crown supreme; amongst these, what became known as Poyning's Law (or Act) was interpreted in Swift's day as requiring that all Irish bills be approved by the Privy Council in London before the Irish Parliament voted on them. The Irish Parliament, and the Irish Privy Council, could draft the 'heads of bills' to be offered for approval, amendment, or rejection by the Council in London. When (and if) these were sent back to Dublin (with or without amendments), the Irish Parliament could accept or reject the proposed legislation, but not themselves amend it.

all your purchases . . . a hundred years' purchase. All your acquisitions of landed property for money (as distinct from acquisition by inheritance) . . . paying for the property 100 times the annual return on the land.

459 *more papers have been written . . . the maker of ballads.* H. J. Davis (ed.), *The Drapier's Letters* (1935), Appendix II, lists forty-five 'Other Pamphlets and Broadsides in Prose concerning Wood's Coinage' . . . Swift himself wrote eleven known pieces of verse concerning the controversy (*Poems*, 331 ff.).

the madman in Don Quixote. The story is in the 'Prologue' to the second part of Cervantes's book.

460 *I will go and whisper among the reeds.* Ovid, *Metamorphoses*, xi. 174 ff., the Fable of Midas, whose barber found that the king had asses' ears hidden under his purple turban. Not daring to reveal the shameful secret, the barber dug a hole in the ground into which he whispered what he had seen, and threw the earth back in again. A thick bank of reeds began to appear there, however, and when they were fully grown, stirred by the south wind, they revealed the truth.

461–2 *Horace, Book I, Ode xiv, paraphrased and inscribed to Ireland.* Horace's *Ode* consists of five stanzas, each of four short lines, and is an elaboration of the figure of the ship of state; Swift further amplifies the figure in his prefatory 'Inscription'. His version and expansion of Horace's lines is probably to be dated to the Wood's halfpence controversy; a contemporary manuscript, now in the Cambridge University Library, carries the date 17 November 1724. The poem, with eleven accompanying citations from the Latin text, was first printed in Dublin in 1730, and reprinted in *Works* 1735.

Inscription. Dedication.

l. 3. *moving Delos.* The floating island eventually anchored by Poseidon.

462 l. 41. *Ierne's claim.* Hibernia's claim that the Catholic Irish (descended from the ancestors of the royal Stuarts) are forced to fight for France, who formerly fought for the true England (possibly in support of Charles I).

l. 44. *French records for twenty long campaigns.* Recórds: the French kings made considerable use of Irish mercenaries.

463–4 *On Dreams. An Imitation of Petronius.* The starting-point of Swift's poem is a set of sixteen hexameters assigned to Titus Petronius Arbiter, d. AD 65,

'Somnia quae mentes ludunt volitantibus umbris, | non delubra deum nec ab aethere numina mittunt, | sed sibi quisque facit . . .': 'Neither the sanctuaries of the gods nor the spirits of the air send the dreams which delude our minds with flitting shadows; each of us makes dreams for himself . . .' Swift's examples differ from these of Petronius.

464 l. 30. *dead men's shoes.* Proverbial from 1530; cf. *ODEP*³, 171.

465 *Swift to Charles Ford.* The text of this letter and the next has been left unmodernized to give an indication of the spelling and punctuation in Swift's holograph.

somebody for whose Advantage. The Duchess of Kendal, mistress of George I.

our Friend with the weak Stomack. Esther Johnson (Stella).

466 *Swift to Charles Ford. Quilca.* Dr Thomas Sheridan's small country house in Co. Cavan, where Swift was staying from April to October 1725, and which he visited at other times.

Lᵈ Oxford. Edward Harley, 2nd Earl.

Mʳ Lewis. Erasmus Lewis.

467 *I have some Reasons not to be in Dublin.* He was still intending that the Drapier's *Letter* [VII] *to both Houses of Parliament*, which he was writing at this time, should be published just as the session opened (see p. 671).

my Travells. Gulliver's Travels.

468–9 *Swift to the Rev. Thomas Sheridan. a discarded courtier.* Carteret appointed Sheridan as one of his chaplains, and at Swift's request presented him to the living of Rincurran in Co. Cork. On Sunday, 1 August 1725, the anniversary of George I's accession, Sheridan was asked as a visitor to preach in Cork; he chose to talk on the text 'sufficient unto the day is the evil thereof' (Matthew 6: 34). In the circumstances, Carteret was obliged to strike him off the list of the Lord-Lieutenant's chaplains and exclude him from the Castle.

as Don Quixote said to Sancho. Cervantes, *Don Quixote*, Part I, Book III, chapter xi.

the apostle's expression. Philippians 4: 11.

470 *Swift to Alexander Pope. Mr. Stopford's management.* The Revd James Stopford, a young protégé of Swift's, had delivered a letter to Pope but not made personal contact.

those dominions where I govern. 'The Liberties' (of St Patrick's Cathedral).

my Travels . . . a printer shall be found brave enough. Gulliver's Travels . . . Waters and Harding had already been imprisoned and threatened for printing works by Swift.

done with translations. Pope's lucrative translation of Homer: the *Iliad* (1715–20); the *Odyssey* (1725–6).

not in Timon's manner. Lucian's dialogue *Timon* makes the fifth-century Athenian misanthrope rail directly against mankind and his treacherous friends.

a blunder. Pope's villa at Twickenham was on one side of the high road, his five-acre garden on the other; they were linked by the famous underground grotto.

471 *The lady . . . at court*. Mrs Howard.

a passage in Bede. *A History of the English Church and People* (*c.*731), iii. 3; the Roman dating of Easter officially replaced the Celtic use of the Greek dating in England by a decision of the Synod of Whitby in 664.

473 *Swift to the Earl of Peterborough*. Following his arrival in London in mid-March 1726, Swift and some of his friends were invited by Walpole to dine with him at Chelsea. Swift then requested a second interview to discuss the grievances of the Anglo-Irish, and interpreted the outcome as having 'entirely broke with the Court ministers'.

474 *a University in Ireland*. Trinity College, Dublin, was and is the only college of the University of Dublin.

477–8 *'Richard Sympson' to Benjamin Motte*. Amid all the Drapier's dangerous writing, Swift was completing the work for which he is most widely known. When he arrived in London for his visit in 1726, he carried with him a manuscript of *Gulliver's Travels*. A few days before he left, with the help of Pope, arrangements were made for its publication. This Letter, which survives in the Pierpoint Morgan Library, was obviously drafted by Swift, but was written out by Gay. It was sent to a reputable London publisher, accompanied by part of the manuscript of the *Travels*. Motte replied accepting the offer, but postponing payment of the considerable advance, because it was 'in vacation time (the most dead season of the year)'. The book was published by him on 28 October 1726, after Swift's departure for Ireland.

479 *Stella's Birthday, 1727*. This is the last of the poems (see p. 387) which Swift gave to Esther Johnson (Stella) each year to mark her birthday on 13 March. Swift left Dublin for his final visit to England in the second week of April 1727. The ladies stayed in the Deanery while he was away, and he heard in London of the onset of what proved to be Stella's last sickness; he returned to Dublin, ill and agitated, at the end of September.

l. 26. *virtue, styled its own reward*. Proverbial from 1596; cf. *ODEP³*, 861.

484 *On the Death of Mrs. Johnson [Stella]*. First printed by Deane Swift in *Works* [4to], viii (1765), pt. 1, pp. 255–64.

another lady. Rebecca Dingley.

going to visit my friends in England . . . the death of a person. Temple; see pp. xxix, xxx.

485 *her sayings . . . bon mots*. *Bon Mots de Stella* was first printed, probably from Swift's manuscript, in *Miscellanies* (1745), x; *Prose*, v. 237–8.

490 *Dr. Stephens's Hospital*. Richard Steevens (*c.*1654–1710), MD, left his estate to found this Dublin Hospital; standing to the east of the Guinness Brewery, it was built by his sister and opened 1733; Swift became a trustee in 1721.

492 *A Modest Proposal.* The best-known single piece of Swift's Anglo-Irish writing, *A Modest Proposal* was written during the late summer of 1729, and printed by Mrs Harding in October. It is the satirical obverse of Swift's straightforward economic and social comment on the ills of Ireland. It had surely become clear to Swift that there were to be no political solutions to the twisted and immovable animosities in that unhappy country. He can take no side without qualification. A scornful attack on most of the Anglo-Irish political nation, only sympathetic with the native Irish on the grounds of common humanity, natural feeling, and hatred of tyranny, the piece deals the shrewdest blow to the English reader, and indeed the hypocritical reader of any age or culture, whose slow, complacent, and dishonest responses are savaged by the cannibal joke.

this great town. Dublin.

strolling. Begging from door to door; one of Swift's last pamphlets offered a project for dealing with the severe problem of begging in Dublin, *A Proposal for giving Badges to the Beggars in all the Parishes of Dublin* (1737).

fight for the Pretender in Spain. The Pretender gained economic and political importance by his ability to attract the Catholic Irish to fight for his European backers, France and Spain.

493 *the number of souls . . . of these I calculate . . .* Sir William Petty, 'A Treatise on Ireland' (1687), estimated the population of Ireland at 1,300,000. Swift owned a copy of Petty's *Essays in Political Arithmetick* (1699), *SL* 412 . . . In this passage and elsewhere, Swift makes his projector adopt the computing tone in which Sir William and other political arithmeticians talk of many alarming schemes such as 'the transplantation of a million people' (Petty advocating the depopulation of Ireland), or 'that a teeming woman, at a medium, bears a child every two years and a half' (ibid.).

nor cultivate land. See note to p. 400 (1).

494 *upon a medium.* On an average.

a grave author. François Rabelais (?1494–?1553), *Pantagruel,* v. xix.

495 *the famous Psalmanazar.* George Psalmanazar published a spurious *History of Formosa* (1704); in the second edition (1705) he recounts the story given by Swift from memory.

497 *other expedients.* All recommended by Swift at different times, cf. *A Proposal for the Universal Use of Irish Manufactures* (1720) (p. 400 above).

Topinamboo. See note to p. 166.

497–8 *like the Jews . . . the very moment their city was taken.* During the last desperate siege of Jerusalem by the emperor Titus in AD 70, the defenders were split by a bitter civil war between three factions.

498 *not to sell our country . . . for nothing.* '[Ireland] this land of slaves | Where all are fools, and all are knaves | Where every knave and fool is bought | Yet kindly sells himself for nought . . .': Swift's then unpublished *Holyhead Journal* (1727); *Poems,* 421.

500 *The Grand Question Debated.* In 1728, 1729, and 1730, Swift spent a considerable period of time with Sir Arthur and Lady Acheson near Armagh. Swift's visits produced a number of sets of verses arising from domestic jokes, generally known as the Market Hill poems (*Poems*, 847–908). *The Grand Question Debated* dates from 1729. In 1609, one Hamilton, who had been granted land at Mullabrack in James I's Ulster plantations, built a stone bawn (from the Irish *bábhun*) to serve a settlement there.

501 l. 21. *poundage and drawbacks.* Taxes on payments by the Government, usually in excise.

l. 49. *my dream's out.* My dream is fulfilled.

502 l. 76. *her picture by Jervis.* Charles Jervas.

l. 84. *a cup in thy pate.* Taken a drink; proverbial from 1656; see p. 598.

503 l. 116. *curchies.* Obsolete form of *curtsies*.

l. 117. *Kit.* Lady Acheson's footman.

504 l. 148. *cast a sheep's eye.* To look amorously; proverbial since 1529 (*OEDP³*, 722).

l. 152. *Jinny.* Dr Henry Jenny (d. 1742), ten years older than Swift, Archdeacon of Dromore.

l. 158. *cry Bo to a goose.* Proverbial since 1572 (*ODEP³*, 701).

505 l. 178. *hips.* Usually, *hyp* or *hyps*: hypochondria, depression.

506 *Swift to Lord Carteret.* Carteret relinquished his Lord-Lieutenancy of Ireland when he sailed for England on 20 April 1730.

his ancestor, the Earl of Cork. Richard Boyle (1566–1643), 1st Earl of Cork and Lord Treasurer of Ireland, erected the largest monument in St Patrick's Cathedral, chiefly to the memory of his second wife but also housing numerous other effigies, including one of himself.

the great Duke of Schomberg. A tablet was erected at the expense of the Dean and Chapter, carrying a phrase implying the neglect of the family, which brought Swift into more disrepute with the court in London.

507 *your successor.* The Duke of Dorset.

I let him pass unpreferred. Probably the Revd Stafford Lightburne, Swift's curate at Laracor, 1722–33, married to a relative of Swift's.

508 *Death and Daphne.* This is another Market Hill poem (see p. 680). Daphne is Lady Acheson, whose slight build served Swift for a number of jokes.

l. 2. *Pluto's hall.* Pluto was the god of the underworld.

l. 5. *the weekly bills.* 'Of mortality'; publication of these returns of deaths, with their causes, for the 109 parishes of the city of London began at the end of the sixteenth century.

l. 7. *since the Peace.* Of Utrecht, 1713.

l. 21. *Megaera.* One of the Greek avenging Furies.

l. 24. *toupees*. Wigs fashionable at this time, in which the front hair was combed back over a pad ... the black adder formed a queue or pigtail.

509 l. 37. *new-flux'd*. Just recovered from the mercury salivation treatment for venereal disease.

l. 42. *aconite*. A piece of the root of aconite (or monk's hood) was chewed to numb toothache; the poison aconitin (an alkaloid) is the active agent.

ll. 46–7. *Warwick Lane ... The faculty*. The College of Physicians (the Faculty), whose official dress was a scarlet gown, stood in Warwick Lane to the north-west of St Paul's cathedral in London.

l. 58. *Adonis*. In Greek mythology, a beautiful youth beloved of Aphrodite.

510 l. 79. *rooks*. Card-sharpers.

l. 80. *cards ... are Pluto's books*. Cf. 'Cards are the devil's books', proverbial since 1676 (*ODEP³*, 102).

l. 84. *Proserpine*. Wife of Pluto, and Queen of the underworld.

l. 85. *Elysian shades*. In later mythology, the part (fields) of Hades inhabited by the shades of the blessed.

l. 87. *Styx*. One of the principal rivers of the underworld, over which the shades of the dead must pass into Hades.

l. 100. *in the suds*. In the 'dumps' or sulks.

511 *An Excellent New Ballad*. 'There is a fellow here from England, one Sawbridge, he was last term indited for a rape. The plea he intended was his being drunk when he forced the woman; but he bought her off. He is a Dean and I name him to your lordship, because I am confident you will hear of his being a Bishop ...' (Swift to the Earl of Oxford, 28 August 1730; *Correspondence*, iii. 405). Sawbridge was indicted in Dublin for ravishing Susanna Runkard, tried on 12 June 1730, and acquitted on his evidence that he was in Co. Wexford at the time of the alleged offence.

512 l. 39. *without a commendam*. A second benefice was sometimes held *in commendam* ['commended by the Crown'] by a dignitary ill-provided for by his nominally higher office.

l. 44. *great Smedley's successor*. Jonathan Smedley.

l. 47. *in Atherton's shape*. John Atherton, Bishop of Waterford and Lismore, was in 1640 degraded, unfrocked, and hanged in Dublin.

l. 49. *Colonel Chartres*. Francis Charteris.

l. 58. *to pay the devil and all*. 'The devil and all to pay', proverbial from 1400, (*ODEP³*, 184).

514 *Verses on the Death of Dr. Swift*. One of Swift's most famous poems, this set of 484 verses is linked with another set of 202 verses, *The Life and Character of Dean Swift*, printed perhaps as an April Fool's joke in 1731, which starts from the same maxim, also uses dialogue, and overlaps in some topics. A text of *Verses*, which was widely known in Dublin from Swift's manuscript, was first printed in 1739 by Pope, who omitted almost a third of the poem as well

as the accompanying notes, on the grounds of literary tact, because there were inaccuracies of fact in the text, and to prevent Swift from giving further offence to the Queen and the Ministers, and appearing too vain.

a Maxim in Rochefoucault. François, duc de la Rochefoucauld, *Réflexions . . .* (1665), no. xcix; see p. 638.

l. 11. *your patience move.* Upsets your patience.

516 l. 61. *drove me out of date.* By writing *The Craftsman,* the leading anti-Walpole journal (see below).

517 l. 117. *they talk in tropes.* Rhetorical figures, using a word or a phrase in a sense other than that proper to it.

l. 123. *daily Howd'y's come of course.* Daily messages (generally delivered by a servant) of enquiry about the Dean's health begin, as custom decrees.

519 l. 186. *I only was the Princess then.* George I died in June 1727; the Prince of Wales became George II and his wife, Caroline, Queen.

520 l. 191. *died without his shoes.* Cf. 'To die in his shoes' (to be hanged), proverbial since 1666 (*ODEP³*, 186).

521 l. 227. *doleful dumps.* Cf. 'To be in the dumps', proverbial since 1529 (*ODEP³*, 208).

ll. 230, 238. *vole . . . quadrille.* Quadrille, a four-hand card game then fashionable, in which the *vole* is a grand slam, the play which wins or loses all the tricks.

l. 240. *dearest friends . . . must part.* Cf. 'Best of friends . . .', proverbial since 1380 (*ODEP³*, 290).

l. 241. *ran his race.* A commonplace; cf. Hebrews 12: 1.

522 l. 258. *Duck-lane.* See note to p. 404 (1).

l. 260. *to the pastry-cook's.* Waste paper was used by pastry-cooks for cases and wrapping.

l. 274. *Against the Craftsman and his friend.* See note to p. 579.

523 l. 278. *Mr. Henly's.* 'Orator' Henley.

l. 293. *as sure as God's in Glo'ster.* Proverbial since 1655 (*ODEP³*, 789).

l. 300. *at the Rose.* The Rose Tavern (see note to p. 99 (4)); it was a haunt of men-about-town.

524 ll. 317–18. *To steal a hint . . . all his own.* Cf. 'To him no author was unknown, | But what he writ was all his own' (Sir John Denham, *On Mr. Abraham Cowley* (1677), 29–30).

l. 323. *Stars and Garters.* Walpole received the Order of the Garter in 1726, and ostentatiously wore the star.

l. 326. *Nor persons had in admiration.* Jude 16.

l. 342. *In princes never put his trust.* Psalm 146: 3.

525 ll. 351–2. *Two kingdoms . . . set a price upon his head.* See note to p. 377–8 and p. 673 n.

526 l. 370. *He left the court in mere despair.* See p. 378; *mere*, 'complete'.

l. 381. *By solemn League and Cov'nant bound.* The Solemn League and Covenant, drafted in Edinburgh in 1643, was accepted by the English Parliament. In return for agreement to presbyterianise the Church in England and Ireland, a Scottish army was sent south to be used against the Royalist forces. Swift insinuates that the 'Good old Cause' of the Whigs is the lineal descendant of the regicide, anti-Anglican, arbitrary Government of the Protectorate.

l. 388. *Story.* History.

527 ll. 403–6. *ev'n his own familiar friends . . . against him lifting up their heels.* John 13: 18.

l. 420. *modern Scroggs, or old Tressilian.* Sir William Scroggs (?1623–85), Lord Chief Justice 1678, terrorized those arraigned before him in the 'Popish Plot'. In 1680, he was impeached and removed from office for, among other alleged misconduct, illegally discharging the Middlesex Grand Jury. This charge prompts Swift to bracket him with Whitshed (see p. 664). Sir Robert Tressilian, Chief Justice of the King's Bench, presided with severity at trials following the Peasants' Revolt in 1381; he was impeached for treason in 1381 and hanged.

528 l. 422. *Nor fear'd he God, nor man regarded.* Luke 18: 2.

l. 428. *topics.* Abstruse points of law for strained arguments.

l. 440 n. *one single Act.* By the Declaratory Act (1720), the British Parliament denied appellate jurisdiction to the Irish House of Lords.

529 ll. 449–50. *Go snacks . . . keep the peace.* Divide the profits, go shares with . . . act as Justices of the Peace.

530 l. 480. *a house for fools and mad.* St Patrick's Hospital was opened in 1757, the first in Ireland for the care of the mentally disabled.

531 *The Place of the Damned.* The poem first appeared as an anonymous Dublin broadside in 1731. It was collected as Swift's in *Works* 1735.

532 *The Day of Judgement.* The poem is mentioned by the Earl of Chesterfield, who in a letter to Voltaire, 27 August 1752, says he possesses the manuscript of it in Swift's hand. It was first printed in *The St. James's Chronicle, or British Evening Post*, No. 2,052, 9–12 April 1774.

533 *A Beautiful Young Nymph going to Bed. Works* 1735 assigns this poem to 1731.

Pars minima est ipse Puella sui. 'A mistress is the least part of herself' (i.e. lacking cosmetics and aids to beauty): Ovid, *Antidotes against Love*, i. 334.

l. 1. *Drury Lane.* The red-light district of London, extending to Covent Garden.

534 l. 41. *Bridewell and the Compter. Bridewell* (from 'St Bride's Well'), a house between Fleet Street and the Thames; after the Great Fire used as a prison

for whores and vagrants. *Compter* (from 'counter', a mayor's or magistrate's court-room), the prison attached to a municipal court; there were two in the City of London.

l. 46 n. —— *Et longam . . . viam.* 'She seems to be left lonely, to make her endless way': Virgil, *Aeneid*, iv. 467–8.

l. 47. *Fleet-ditch's oozy brinks.* See note to p. 257 (4).

ll. 54–6. *religious clubs . . . pays 'em all in kind.* Local societies for the reformation of manners became active towards the end of the seventeenth century. Swift considered the societies by 1709 had 'dwindled into factious clubs' (*Prose*, ii. 57), Whiggish and sectarian. He insinuates that such zealots left Corinna alone in return for favours received.

l. 63. *issue-peas.* Pellets placed in a running sore to keep it open.

535 *On Poetry. A Rhapsody.* This satire first appeared in London on 31 December 1733. The publication was followed by a flurry of police activity caused by the appearance in November of two other poems by Swift, *An Epistle to a Lady* with *On Reading Dr. Young's Satires, called the Universal Passion.* Wilford, the printer of these, was taken into custody, as well as the bookseller who had purchased the copyright, Lawton Gilliver. Swift's printer, Motte, was also arrested though his name did not appear on the offending publication, as was Matthew Pilkington, who sold the copyright, and another protégé of Swift's, Mrs Barber, who had brought the manuscripts over from Ireland. The Government decided against a prosecution for seditious libel.
    See Note on the Text, p. xxxv.

l. 3. *Young's universal passion*, pride. Edward Young's popular series of seven satires, *The Universal Passion* (1725–8), was published as *Love of Fame* in 1728.

l. 36. *Bridewell.* See note to p. 534, l. 41.

536 l. 50. *The wealthy have you in derision.* Psalm 119: 51.

ll. 54–8. *one annual hundred pound . . . on Grub Street line.* In 1730, Colley Cibber succeeded Laurence Eusden as Poet Laureate. Swift's lines say that Cibber has introduced a stain of dishonour in the 'line' of Poets Laureate; the succession is now, for ever, fixed by divine right in Grub Street writers, either by Cibber as 'King of the Dunces' as Pope later made him in the 1743 *Dunciad*, or because George II, patron of Dunces, has so decreed.

l. 72. *spirits to discern.* Cf. 1 Corinthians 12: 10.

538 l. 117. *Will's.* A coffee-house, called after its proprietor, on the north side of Russell Street, Covent Garden. Its heyday was towards the end of the seventeenth century, when Dryden presided over his circle in the first-floor 'Wits' Room'.

l. 122. *swallow down your spittle.* Job 7: 19.

539 l. 162. *a South Sea jobber.* A financier who made money in the crooked share deals in South Sea Company stock, which led to the South Sea Bubble (swindle that burst) of 1720–1; perhaps Walpole.

preceding l. 187. *D'Anvers*. The fictitious 'Caleb D'Anvers' conducted the Tory periodical *The Craftsman* (see note to p. 579 (1)).

l. 187. *Sir Bob's defence*. Sir Robert Walpole.

540 l. 194. *baubles in the Tower*. The crown jewels, kept in the Tower of London.

ll. 209–13. *scenes of endless woe . . . Charon's boat . . . a sop*. Charon's boat carried the dead, stripped of their earthly possessions, across the River Styx to Hades; the dead were given a cake to offer as a 'sop' to Cerberus, Pluto's three-headed dog that guarded the nether regions.

l. 215. *the iv'ry gate of dreams*. Delusive visions, in classical mythology, came through the ivory gate, true visions through the gate of horn.

l. 216. *excise*. Walpole staked his power and influence in 1732–3 on his Excise Bill; this sought to reduce smuggling and reform the frauds in the Customs by instituting the taxation of internal distribution of commodities from bonded warehouses. The public outcry forced him to withdraw the measure, the first check to his political success.

541 l. 236. *puny judge*. i.e. feeble, but also the legal term *puisne*, junior.

ll. 249–50. *Judicious Rymer . . . Wise Dennis . . . profound Bossu*. Swift links modern critical authorities with the ancients: Thomas Rymer . . . John Dennis (see above, p. 78) . . . René le Bossu (1631–80), French critic.

ll. 256–62. *peri hupsous . . . quotation on quotation. On the Sublime* was attributed to Longinus (*c.* 213–73); it became very influential in eighteenth-century criticism of the arts. Nicholas Boileau (1636–1711) rendered it into French (1674); it was translated into English 'from Boileau's French version' by John Pulteney in 1680; Leonard Welsted published his translation in 1712.

542 l. 264. *Battus*. Dryden was the presiding critical spirit at Will's forty years before this poem was written: see note to p. 538, l. 117.

l. 280. *Augusta Trinobantum*. Roman London, the city of the Trinobantes.

543 l.300. *Smithfield drolls*. Smithfield was the site of Bartholomew Fair, held at the end of August and the scene of booths offering farces and drolleries. Swift introduces a condensed geography of the dunces' London, extending from Wapping in the south-east on the Thames to Kentish Town in the north.

ll. 301–2. *Bavius . . . Mævius*. Two poetasters: 'Let him who does not hate Bavius, admire your songs, Maevius': Virgil, *Eclogues*, iii. 90.

ll. 303–4. *Tigellius . . . from Ludgate . . . to Temple Bar*. Tigellius was an accomplished but disagreeable mimic, jester, and musician, patronized by Julius Caesar and Augustus: Horace, *Satires*, i. ii. 3 ff. and iii. 4 ff. . . . Ludgate is at the east end of Fleet Street, Temple Bar at the west.

ll. 319–20. *Hobbes clearly proves . . . state of war by nature*. See p. 2 and ibid., n. (2).

544 l. 369. *Flecknoe . . . Howard*. Richard Flecknoe (*c.*1600–78), poet and playwright, attacked by Dryden as the father of Dulness in *Mac Flecknoe*

(1682); Pope in *The Dunciad* (1728), l. 200, mentions 'high-born Howard' (Edward Howard (1624–c. 1700), poet and playwright) as one of the 'Dull of ancient days'.

545 l. 399. *Jemmy Moore.* James Moore Smythe.

546 l. [35]. *Neb-cadnezers.* Nebuchadnezzar, King of Babylon, punished by being made to 'eat grass as oxen'; Daniel 4: 31 ff.

l. 411. *thy monarch.* George II.

547 l. 424. *Short by the knees.* On bended knee; the reference is to Horace, *Epistles*, I. xii. 28.

l. 425. *The* consort. Queen Caroline.

l. 429. *divine Iülus.* Or Ascanius, the son of Aeneas: Frederick Louis (1707–51), the Prince of Wales, father of George III.

ll. 439–40. *Bright goddesses . . . Duke William.* Anne, Amelia, Caroline Elizabeth, Mary, Louise, the five daughters of King George and Queen Caroline; William Augustus, Duke of Cumberland, later the butcher of Culloden.

l. 441. *the* minister of state. Portly Sir Robert Walpole, whose marital misfortunes attracted satire.

l. 446. *prudent Fabius . . . *Unus homo . . . restituis rem.* Quintus Maximus Cunctator [Delayer], voted dictator of Rome after the defeat at Lakę Trasimene, 217 BC; he wore down Hannibal's invading army by refusing battle . . . [You,] 'the single man who by delaying restores the state': from Virgil, *Aeneid*, vi. 846.

547–8 ll. 461–4. *St. George . . . string cerulean.* Walpole, as a Knight of the Garter, wore across his great bulk the star of St George and the blue sash.

548 ll. 473–6. *on Lewis . . . rascals lied.* Louis XIV of France, humbled (to Swift's mind) by the allies in the War of the Spanish Succession.

l. 486 n. *Divisum imperium cum Jove Caesar habet.* 'Caesar has divided supremacy with Jove': Virgil (attrib.) in some manuscripts of Aelius Donatus, *Life of Virgil*, from Suetonius' *Life* (p. 66 in Reifferscheid's edn. of Suetonius (Leipzig, 1860)).

l. 494. *Woolston.* Thomas Wolston.

l. 494f. *Caetera desiderantur.* 'The rest is wanting.'

549–55 *Directions to Servants.* This piece was posthumously and simultaneously published in Dublin and London in November 1745. The first section, 'Rules that concern all servants in general', printed here, seems to have been reasonably complete, as well as the articles on the Butler, the Cook, the Footman; thereafter the pieces on the Coachman, Groom, House-Steward and Land-Steward, Porter, Dairy-Maid, Chamber-Maid, Nurse, Laundress, House-Keeper, Tutoress or Governess are more or less 'heads' only. Swift perhaps started jottings at the same period as *Mrs. Harris's Petition* (1701) (p. 57 above). The milieu of the 'author' of *Directions to Servants* is clearly London, from which, for example, a 'brother servant . . . was running away to Ireland'. He may have fiddled with the work until 1739. From ancient times in Western literature, in comedy and fiction, the bond between master and servant has been a type of the human lot. The mockery not only plays on the men and women in the servants' hall. The quality above stairs are thoughtless, tyrannical, greedy, and foolishly negligent. Dr Johnson charged: 'To his domestics, [Swift] was naturally rough; and a man of rigorous temper . . .' But Swift also suffered Patrick's misdemeanours for some reason, interest or humanity, and placed a tablet in his cathedral to the memory of another servant, Alexander McGee.

556 *The Legion Club*. This invective is one of Swift's last pieces. It was not printed by him, though it appeared in 1736 in a London volume, *Swift contra Omnes. An Irish Miscellany*. It also circulated in manuscript, finally being published among Swift's *Works* in the London *Miscellanies . . . the fifth volume* (1745); Faulkner first included the poem in *Works* (1762). The verses represent an important aspect of his Anglo-Irish writing, the contempt and hatred he felt for the Dublin Parliament. In addition, there is a reinforcing, particular impulse to attack, arising from the Irish Parliament's refusal in 1736 to award the Church of Ireland its undoubted legal right to a tithe of the produce of grazing land, the so-called 'tithe of agistment'. With the expansion of the Irish trade in exported beef, this was becoming very valuable indeed. Swift contributed several prose pieces to this controversy. The title refers to the Scriptures (Mark 5): Jesus asks the 'unclean spirit' possessing the man 'out of the tombs', 'What is thy name?' The answer is, 'My name is Legion: for we are many.' Thereafter, in freeing the man from his possession, Christ allows 'the devils' to enter the bodies of the great herd of Gadarene swine feeding nearby. The members of the Irish Parliament are therefore a legion of unclean spirits, a herd of feeding swine, a procession of the damned, and, sitting in their stately new building, a 'club' of the inmates of a madhouse. The members named have entries in the Biographical Index.

l. 2. *a building large and lofty*. The noble Irish Parliament house, now the Bank of Ireland, was begun on College Green opposite Trinity College in 1729. Far larger and more splendid than the then accommodation of Parliament in London, it was in use by 1732, though not completed until seven years later.

l. 6. *against the church* . . . St Andrew's, the 'round church', built after the Restoration, stood across College Street from the Parliament building.

l. 7. *my grandam's jest*. '(The) near(er) the church, (the) far(ther) from God', proverbial from *c.*1303 *ODEP*[3], 557.

l. 18. *Jackpudden*. A buffoon or merry andrew at a fair, often drumming up an audience for a quack doctor.

l. 20. *a far less villain's nose*. In the pillory.

l. 28. *den of thieves*. Matthew 21: 13.

l. 35. *should Swift endow*. See p. 530. and ibid., n.

557 l. 52. *dabble in their dung*. See pp. 146 f.

l. 54. *How to plague and starve the city*. Parliament is pursuing the narrow interests of the landowners at the expense of the mercantile, professional, and working classes in Dublin.

l. 60. *heads of bills*. See note to p. 458 (1).

l. 62. *their Votes*. Printed lists were circulated of how MPs voted on certain measures.

ll. 63–4. *Sir Tom . . . flax and grass*. Sir Thomas Prendergast . . . In 1733, to encourage the growth of flax and hemp, it was proposed to reduce the tithe on these crops by two-thirds of the legal rate, and to settle payment by a long-term composition, known as a *modus*; both suggestions were against the interests of the clergy. Swift joined in the controversy with *Some Reasons against the Bill for settling the Tithe of Hemp, Flax, etc. by a Modus*. *Grass* refers to the dispute over the tithe of agistment.

l. 67. *At the parsons, Tom*. A hunting cry.

558 l. 83 n. *Di quibus . . . audita loqui, &c*. 'You gods who rule the shades, you silent shadows, you Chaos and you Phlegethon, you wide, silent spaces of night, let me tell what I heard . . .': Virgil, *Aeneid*, vi. 264 ff.

l. 87 n. *Vestibulum . . . ultrices, &c*. 'Before the doorway itself, and within the very jaws of hell, Grief and the avenging [Cares have made their lairs]': ibid. 273–4.

l. 91 n. *Discordia . . . innexa cruentis*. 'Mad Strife, her snaky locks entwined with a bloody headband': ibid. 280–1.

l. 93 n. *Corripit . . . venientibus offert*. 'Suddenly, at this moment, Aeneas shaking with fear grasps his sword and turns the naked blade against them as they come forward': ibid. 290–1.

l. 97 n. *Et ni docta . . . vitas*. 'Had not his wise companion [warned him] that they were shadowy beings without body': ibid. 292.

l. 103 n. *Et centumgeminus Briareus*. 'And the hundred-fold Briareus' (one of the hundred-handed giants): ibid. 287.

559 l. 113. *three hundred brutes*. There were three hundred members in the Irish Commons.

l. 125. *Lake Avernus*. Near Cumae and Naples, in the crater of an extinct volcano. Its deep waters give off poisonous fumes; the cave where Aeneas entered the underworld is close by.

l. 146. *pair of Dicks*. Richard Tighe and Richard Bettesworth.

l. 152. *old Glorious*. William III, victor of the Boyne.

563 *A Compleat Collection of Genteel and Ingenious Conversation*. This represents the last substantial achieved piece which engaged Swift's creative energies. Motte and Bathurst brought it out in London, in March 1738, and Faulkner simultaneously in Dublin under Swift's own supervision. The beginning of the piece lay far back in the past, in 1704 or earlier. The work falls into two

parts. Three dialogues take part in the house of Lord and Lady Smart, near St James's Park in London. The date is not specified, but the tone is reminiscent of Swift's society milieu in the last years of Queen Anne's reign. There is noticeably no Irish element in the conversations. The dialogues are prefaced by an ironical essay from the pen of their compiler, Simon Wagstaff, obviously a relative of Swift's early creation, Isaac Bickerstaff (see p. 193 and n.). The Introduction, in outline at least an early piece, mocks handbooks on behaviour and conversation, reliance on translations, and complacent group judgement, in the spirit of *A Tale of a Tub*. In the present selection, the Introduction to Swift's work is followed by Dialogue II. Swift's theme is a serious one, the importance for civilization of the supreme social art of conversation; it occupied him all his life. Instead of engaging in an easy, open, and improving exchange, the speakers in *Polite Conversation* perform stiff, closed, and mechanical motions. They are each equipped with a store of counters, which they present in turn like unintelligent children, flashing old proverbs, proverbial phrases, stylized social jokes, stale toasts, and flat sentiments, the small change of social life. But here, on closer consideration, a certain powerful and entirely Swiftian ambiguity may be discerned in the text. The often ancient proverbs and phrases have a life of their own. By the late seventeenth century, the proverb had descended from the position of valued receptacle of traditional wisdom given to it by Bacon and earlier writers. It was becoming low and old-fashioned. Yet Swift, in his own writing (see p. 183 above), relished the un-Augustan qualities in the best proverbs, unexpectedness, gnarled wisdom, and pithy undercutting humour. *Polite Conversation* is frequently cited as a source in dictionaries and lists of proverbs. The dialogues preserve real linguistic observation and real feeling for speech. It is quite possible that Swift remembered and noted down conversations he had heard; it is equally probable, indeed it would be characteristic, that perhaps predominantly he used collections and lists of proverbs and phrases. Two collections in particular seem likely sources: John Ray, *A Collection of English Proverbs* (1670; 2nd edn. enlarged, 1678) and James Kelly, *A Complete Collection of Scottish Proverbs explained and made intelligible to the English Reader* (1721). Space does not permit the listing of all the more than 200 proverbs, proverbial phrases, or catch phrases which Swift stitches together in Dialogue II. To show the nature of the material, thirty examples are set out in the notes with entries as appropriate in the *Oxford Dictionary of English Proverbs*, 1970 (*ODEP³*), Ray 1670 or 1678, and Kelly 1721, as well as the earliest date of usage recorded.

564 *the advice of Horace . . . translation.* Horace, *Epistle to the Pisos* [*Ars Poetica*], 386–9: 'If you ever write anything . . . put your manuscript in a drawer and suppress it for nine years . . .' For Thomas Creech's translation (1684), see p. 16, n. (4).

565 *paying the postage.* The recipient of a letter normally paid the postage.

566 *the whole exercise of the fan.* A popular topic of satire; Addison's *Spectator*, No. 102, 27 June 1711, gives an account of an academy for 'the exercise of the fan' with words of command.

567 *Isaac the dancing master.* Mr Isaac (d. 1742), French dancing-master, mentioned by Steele in *Tatler*, No. 34, 28 June 1709.

jargon terms. Unintelligible terms in the discourse of scholars, philosophers, or scientists (cf. p. 252).

568 *cant-words.* Terms peculiar to the discourse of a group (e.g. criminals); modish vocabulary of smart society. See note to p. 253 (2).

the late D. of R—— . . . Charles Lennox, 1st Duke of Richmond.

the Revolution. Of 1688; the withdrawal of James II and accession of William and Mary.

569 *Bishop Burnet . . . every day of his life.* In the 'Preface' to *History of My own Time*, i (1724), Gilbert Burnet writes: 'I look on the perfecting of this work, and the carrying it on through the remaining part of my life, as the greatest service I can do to God, and to the world . . . over and over again retouched and polished by me . . .' Swift commented in his copy: 'Rarely polished; I never read so ill a style' (*Prose*, v. 266).

570 *gentlemen of the inns of court.* See note to p. 85 (8).

selling of bargains. Hoaxing or 'catching' in conversation, specifically by luring the victim to ask a question to which an obscene answer might be given; also with the implication of court bribery and corruption like Wood's 'purchase' of his patent.

570–1 *the fanatic faction . . . the converted rumpers.* The Puritans . . . the remnant of the Long Parliament (the Rump), dissolved by Cromwell in 1653, recalled by Monck in 1659–60, and 'converted' to monarchy as the restoration of Charles II unfolded.

571 *fanatic enthusiasm . . . atheism.* For enthusiasm see p. 635 and p. 179, n. (2).

expletives to matter. Useless words, to pad out a sentence or cadence.

572 *Sir John Perrot . . . G[od]'s W[ound]s.* Queen Elizabeth's aggressive Lord Deputy in Ireland (1584–8); on his return to England he was tried for treason on the basis of 'undutiful words' about his mistress; he died in the Tower. Anecdotes about his uncourtly diction are preserved by Sir Robert Naunton (see above, p. 255 and ibid., n. (4)) . . . God's [Christ's] Wounds, often as *swounds* or *zounds*, a common oath.

574 *no more than Lilly obtained.* A collaborative Latin grammar, dating from the reign of Henry VIII, passing under the authorship of William Lilly (?1468–1522), was the standard school-book until the mid-eighteenth century.

young templars . . . gentlemen-commoners . . . in town. Gentlemen ostensibly studying law in the Inns of Court (e.g. the Inner and Middle Temple) . . . undergraduates of good birth given the disciplinary and domestic privileges of fellows (senior members) of Oxford and Cambridge colleges and thus staying out of college in London.

for instance, can't . . . bam. One of Swift's long-standing linguistic concerns: see pp. 253 ff.

576 *masquerading.* At a public masked ball, with the participants in fancy dress, affording relaxation of strict social etiquette.

577 *here's a silent meeting!* A Quaker Meeting.

a penny for your thought. ODEP³, 619 (1522; after Swift's time, '. . . thoughts').

at St. James's. At court, St James's palace.

578 *Mr. Thomas Brown's* . . . Notes on contemporary writers mentioned in the *Introduction* will be found in the Biographical Index.

579 *the Craftsman and his abettors.* The *Craftsman* (later *The Country Journal: or,* . . .), 'by Caleb D'Anvers' (No. 1, Sept. 1725, to No. 1111, Oct. 1747 . . .), the leading journal of the Opposition to Walpole, was edited by Nicholas Amherst and backed by Bolingbroke, William Wyndham, the Earl of Chesterfield, Arbuthnot, and others.

580 *Must is for the King. ODEP³*, 552 (1603).

uncontrollable maxim. Incontrovertible principle.

Lord H——. Probably Lord Hervey of Ickworth.

581 *Isaac Newton* . . . *afterwards a workman in the Mint.* Sir Isaac Newton as Warden of the Mint gave his certificate to the trial of the pyx which declared Wood's Irish coin to be good and sufficient: see p. 670.

582 *pot-hooks and hangers.* A common phrase for the elementary strokes in learning to write; cf. p. 199; here, astronomical or astrological symbols.

583 *we have had our hands in mortar.* '. . . fingers . . .', *ODEP³*, 259 (1665); we have building going on.

'tis a pity that fair weather should ever do any harm. ODEP³ 240 (1616).

better to be out of the world, than out of the fashion. ODEP³, 602: 'As good to be out of the world as out of the fashion' (1639).

very good humour'd . . . so is the devil when he's pleased. ODEP³, 182: 'The Devil is good when he is pleased' (1581; Kelly 1721, 333).

I'll see your nose cheese first, and the dogs eating it. ODEP³, 709: 'I will see your nose cheese first' (Kelly 1721, 224: 'I would sooner see your nose cheese, and myself the first bite').

it will make a flaming figure in a country church. ODEP³: 'It will make a fair figure in a country church' (Ray 1670, 192; Kelly 1721, 207); cf. *Journal to Stella*, 9 February 1711: 'Will she pass in a crowd? Will she make a figure in a country church?'

584 *my belly began to cry cupboard. ODEP³*, 44: 'My belly cries cupboard' (1671; Ray 1678, 237).

your belly thinks your throat's cut. ODEP³, 45: 'The belly thinks the throat is cut' (1540; Kelly 1721, 379).

To say the truth, I'm hungry . . . And I'm angry, so let us both go fight. ODEP³, 393: 'If thou be hungry, I am angry: let us go fight' (Ray 1678, 65).

our king James the First . . . in a frolic knighted it. Sirloin is the *surloigne* or choice upper loin of beef; the hoary knighting story is also told of Henry VIII and Charles II.

585 *kiss the hare's foot.* i.e. to starve, or be late: *ODEP³*, 430 (1598).

in pudden-time. A lucky or favourable time: *ODEP³*, 653 (1546).

you keep court-hours I see. The traditional dinner hour in the country was noon. In town it was at this time 3 p.m. and becoming later as the century wore on.

586 *Hanover Square... London is gone out of town.* The Hanover Square complex was laid out at the north of Mayfair *c.*1715.

my chapman. The man who had bought Sir John's cattle.

March beer. A strong ale or beer made in March.

fresh and fasting. A medicinal direction found in patent medicine advertisements: cf. p. 112.

if any of the ladies should long. Another of Neverout's leers? Have a food craving related to pregnancy.

587 *my wife's... at your service in a civil way.* Cf. *Journal to Stella*, 8 January 1712: 'I am sorry in a civil way, that's all...'

cucumbers are cold in the third degree. Cf. 'As cool as a cucumber'; *degree*, applied in the natural philosophy of the Middle Ages to (four) successive stages of intensity of the elementary qualities of bodies (heat, cold, moisture, dryness) (*OED*).

588 *my service to you.* I drink to you.

Hertfordshire kindness. i.e. drinking back to one who drinks to you: *ODEP³*, 371 (1662).

don't make a bridge of my nose. 'To make a bridge of your nose' (i.e. to pass you over in drinking with or serving): *ODEP³*, 85; (Ray 1678, 281).

born within the sound of Bow bell. i.e. a Cockney: *ODEP³*, 76 (1571).

you may choose... before you are twice married. Perhaps a flirtatious speech by Neverout, offering himself as a 'pigeon' or befooled lover to Miss Notable.

589 *I can't hit the joint... think of a cuckold...* i.e., imagine two horns (the traditional badge of a cuckold) and cut between them.

S'buds! this venison is musty. God's Body... mouldy, gone bad.

590 *pepper-proof.* Cf. Ray 1678, s.v. 'One that hath the French Pox': he is not pepper-proof.

here's a health to the founders. i.e. to the founders of the feast (the host and hostess); Lord Smart does not know what he is saying.

don't speak in my tip. Perhaps 'in my tipple' (*OED*).

591 *lately made a purchase.* Bought some real estate.

a limb of Lot's wife. Very salty: Lot's wife turned into a pillar of salt (Genesis 19: 26).

the falling out of lovers . . . '. . . is the renewing of love', *ODEP*[3], 242 (1578).

592   *shiddle-come-sh—'s the beginning of love.* 'Shitten-come-shites is the beginning of love' (Howel, *English Proverbs*, 6, in *Lexicon Tetraglotton*, 1659).

as the devil loves holy water; I love him like pie . . . have him than I. (*a*) 'The Devil loves no holy water', *ODEP*[3], 182 (1500); (*b*) *ODEP*[3], 492 ('I love thee like pudding, if thou wert pye I'd eat thee', Ray 1678, 349) . . . (*c*) Miss ends with a rhyming clause to make a 'crambo'.

marry come up, my dirty cousin; are you no sicker? [Neverout snatches a kiss]; 'Marry come up', *ODEP*[3], 515 (*c*.1595, Shakespeare, *Romeo and Juliet.*, II. v. 64) . . . 'my dirty cousin', *ODEP*[3], 515 (1674).

very dry . . . the worse to fry. Another crambo, in which Miss completes Neverout's sentence with a rhyming sequel.

593   *goose upon goose is false heraldry.* Cf. 'Metal upon metal is false heraldry', *ODEP*[3], 529 (1643).

which is the white goose . . . gander. A trick question.

594   *don't call me spade.* Eunuch; from *spayed*.

brandy is Latin for a goose, and tace is Latin for a candle. (*a*) An apology for dram-drinking at table (*Marprelate Tracts*, 1588); (*b*) *tace* (Lat.), 'be silent': *ODEP*[3], 797 (1676).

October. (Strong) ale brewed in October.

595   *the poet is damn'd.* The dramatist is hissed.

fire-ships. (Diseased) prostitutes.

drink your snuff. 'To take (in) snuff' (to take offence at something): *ODEP*[3], 749 (1560).

tell your meaning by your mumping. (*Mumping*, grimacing); *ODEP*[3], 436 ('. . . gaping', 1659).

596   *make fish of one, and flesh of another.* (To make an invidious distinction): *ODEP*[3], 264 (1639; Ray 1670, 9).

plaguy small. Horribly like (weak) small-beer.

well hopp'd. Hops give the ale taste, not strength.

for fear they should p—ss behind the door. 'A rustic gesture of contempt for the niggardly' (Eric Partridge).

to fox one . . . take a hair of the same dog . . . drink as much after an egg. To intoxicate or stupify with drink . . . 'a hair of the dog that bit you': *ODEP*[3], 343 (1546) . . . 'One should drink as much after an egg as after an ox'; *ODEP*[3], 203 (Ray 1670, 36).

put a churl upon a gentleman. (Implying that beer is the drink of the lower classes): *ODEP*[3], 655 (1586; Kelly 1721, 187) cf, 'Aleto claret adit basis', Swift's Latino-Anglicus version (1734–5) of this saying, printed by Mayhew in his *Rage and Raillery* (1967), 147.

596–7 *cold after eating . . . sign of a long life.* Eric Partridge cites (without ascription), 'If you eat till you're cold, you'll live to be old'.

597 *weily brosten.* Well-nigh burst.

fret like gum-taffety. To fret like gummed taffeta (velvet) (the material, stiffened with gum, quickly frayed): *ODEP*[3], 287 (1604).

598 *Swolks.* A form of *Swounds* ('God's wounds').

a cup in the pate is a mile in the gate. (i.e. 'road'): *ODEP*[3], 160 (1694).

599 *the corruption of pipes is the generation of stoppers.* See p. 169 and ibid., n. (2); pieces of broken clay pipes were used to tamp down burning tobacco.

'tis a pot-herb. i.e. not a kitchen herb, but for use while drinking.

600 *queer old duke.* '*Queere* duke, c. a poor decayed gentleman', *A New Dictionary of the Canting Crew* (1699): there is evidence that Swift used this compilation of criminal argot.

603–4 *Swift's Epitaph.* 'Here is laid the body of Jonathan Swift, Doctor of Sacrosanct Theology, Dean of this cathedral church, where savage indignation can no longer tear his heart. Depart, wayfarer, and imitate if you can a man who to his utmost strenuously championed liberty.

'He died on the 19th day of October in the year of our Lord 1745, in the 78th year of his age.'

Swift had a long experience in drafting such lapidary inscriptions; satirical modulations of the epitaph form may be found in his poems on John Partridge, the astrologer (pp. 205 ff.), and on the death of the Duke of Marlborough (pp. 418 ff.). The opening of the second sentence, *Abi Viator*, employs a commonplace of epitaphs in addressing the living. The phrase has its origin in classical appeals to the passer-by on the tombs that bordered roads near towns, particularly those of great families on the outskirts of Rome. Swift evokes Juvenal, *Satire* I. 79, in the previous sentence. He contrasts the formulaic peace of death with a most unconventional *saeva Indignatio*; his famous phrase echoes the line in which the great Roman poet sardonically characterizes his own satire: 'si natura negat, facit indignatio versum' ('though natural endowment forbids, indignation makes the poem'). There may be a further Roman and Juvenalian strand at the close of the command to the reader. The final word, *Vindicatorem*, is not classical. Polished Latinity, and Swift was practised, demands *vindex* for 'vindicator' or 'defender'. *Vindicator* is found only in late, ecclesiastical Latin, meaning 'avenger', a sense not required here. It has been plausibly suggested that Swift, in deliberately using the out-of-the-way word, may be seeking to render, or recalling, a recognizable and significant English phrase. This occurs in Dryden's very well-known essay on satire of 1693: '[Juvenal's] indignation against vice is more vehement; his spirit has more of the commonwealth genius; he treats tyranny, and all the vices attending it, as they deserve, with the utmost rigour: and consequently, a noble soul is better pleased with *a zealous vindicator of Roman liberty* than with a temporizing poet [i.e. Horace], a well-mannered Court slave . . .'

FURTHER READING

BIBLIOGRAPHIES

L. A. Landa and J. E. Tobin, *Jonathan Swift. A List of Critical Studies published from 1895 to 1945* (New York, 1945).

R. H. Rodino, *Swift Studies 1965–1980. An Annotated Bibliography* (New York, 1984).

J. J. Stathis, *A Bibliography of Swift Studies, 1945–1965* (Nashville, 1965).

H. Teerink, *A Bibliography of the Writings of Jonathan Swift* (1937); 2nd edn., rev. A. H. Scouten (Philadelphia, 1963).

D. M. Vieth, *Swift's Poetry 1900–1980. An Annotated Bibliography* (New York, 1982).

SWIFT'S WORKS

(a) Collected Editions

The following four sets make up the standard text:

H. J. Davis *et al.* (eds.), *The Prose Works of Jonathan Swift*, 14 vols. (Oxford [Blackwell], 1939–68); vols. xv and xvi have been added, containing *The Journal to Stella*, ed. H. Williams (1948).

Sir H. Williams (ed.), *The Poems of Jonathan Swift*, 3 vols. (Oxford, 1937; 2nd edn., rev., 1958).

—— (ed.), *The Journal to Stella*, 2 vols. (Oxford, 1948); fully annotated.

—— (ed.), *The Correspondence of Jonathan Swift*, 5 vols. (Oxford, 1963–5); vols. i–iii await revision; vols. iv and v partially rev. David Woolley (1972); annotated.

(b) Principal Editions of Individual Works

A Discourse of the Contests and Dissensions Between the Nobles and Commons in Athens and Rome, ed. F. H. Ellis (Oxford, 1967).

A Tale of a Tub, to which is added *The Battle of the Books* and *The Mechanical Operation of the Spirit*, eds. A. C. Guthkelch and D. Nichol Smith (Oxford, 1920; 2nd edn., rev., 1958; with corrections, 1973).

The Drapier's Letters to the People of Ireland, ed. H. J. Davis (Oxford, 1935; rev. bibliography, 1965); full Introduction and notes; needs some revision in the light of modern Irish historical scholarship.

Gulliver's Travels. There are many editions of this work: a selection is given in chronological order of those with notable features:

H. Williams (ed.), *Gulliver's Travels: the Text of the First Edition* (1926); Introduction, valuable textual material, notes, and bibliography.

R. A. Greenberg (ed.) (Norton Critical Edition, New York, 1961; enlarged, 1970); with fifteen reprinted essays and extracts.

A. E. Case (ed.), 1938.

P. Turner (ed.) (Oxford, 1971); notes suggest classical references.

A. Ross (ed.) (Longman, 1972, 1976); text based on first edn.; Introduction, notes, glossary, and five essays on aspects of the satire, including a discussion of the 'foreign languages'.

COMMENTARY

(a) Biography

I. Ehrenpreis, *Swift: the Man, his Works and the Age*, vol. i. *Mr. Swift and his contemporaries* [1667–99] (1962; 1964); vol. ii. *Dr. Swift* [1700–14] (1967); vol. iii. *Dean Swift* [1714–45] (1983); a monumental work based on an impressive grasp of the documents and works; the most substantial modern biography of Swift.
—— *The Personality of Jonathan Swift* (1958).
P. Greenacre, *Swift and [Lewis] Carroll: a Psychoanalytic Study of Two Lives* (New York, 1955); straightforward Freudian reading.
L. Landa, *Swift and the Church of Ireland* (Oxford, 1954).

(b) General Works

J. M. Bullitt, *Jonathan Swift and the Anatomy of Satire: a Study of Satiric Technique* (Cambridge, Mass., 1953).
H. J. Davis, *Jonathan Swift: Essays on his Satire and other Studies* (Oxford, 1964).
D. Donoghue, *Jonathan Swift: a critical Introduction* (Cambridge, 1969); not for the beginner.
J. A. Downie, *Jonathan Swift, Political Writer* (1984).
A. C. Elias, Jr., *Swift at Moor Park* (1982).
M. Price, *Swift's Rhetorical Art: a Study in Structure and Meaning* (New Haven, 1953).
R. Quintana, *Swift: an Introduction* (1955); an excellent starting-point.
—— *The Mind and Art of Jonathan Swift* (1936; 2nd edn., 1953).
E. Rosenheim, Jr., *Swift and the Satirist's Art* (Chicago, 1963).
P. Steele, *Jonathan Swift, Preacher and Jester* (Oxford, 1978).

Much interesting writing on Swift's works is to be found in essays and articles, often scattered through issues of periodicals and journals, for example:

A. N. Jeffares (ed.), *Swift, Modern Judgements* (1968).
—— *Fair Liberty was all his Cry: a Tercentenary Tribute to Jonathan Swift, 1667–1745* (1967).
R. McHugh and P. Edwards (eds.), *Jonathan Swift, 1667–1967: a Dublin Tercentenary Tribute* (Dublin, 1967).
C. Probyn (ed.), *The Art of Jonathan Swift* (Vision Critical Study, 1978); contains nine new essays, including notably W. B. Carnochan's 'The Consolations of Satire'.
C. Rawson (ed.), *The Character of Swift's Satire: A revised Focus* (1983).
J. Traugott (ed.), *Discussions of Jonathan Swift* (Boston, 1972); contains N. O. Brown's Freudian interpretation of Swift from his *Life against Death* (1959) (see below).
E. Tuveson (ed.), *Swift, A Collection of Critical Essays* (Englewood Cliffs, NJ, 1964); contains ten useful reprinted studies.
B. Vickers (ed.), *The World of Jonathan Swift* (Oxford, 1968).

K. Williams (ed.), *Swift: the critical Heritage* (1970); reprints pieces and extracts up to the early nineteenth century.

(c) Studies of Specific Texts

A Tale of a Tub

J. R. Clark, *Form and Frenzy in* A Tale of a Tub (Cornell UP, 1970).

P. Harth, *Swift and Anglican Rationalism: the religious Background of* A Tale of a Tub (1961).

R. Paulson, *Theme and Structure in Swift's* Tale of a Tub (New Haven, 1960).

F. N. Smith, *Language and Reality in Swift's* A Tale of a Tub (Columbus, Ohio, 1979).

M. K. Starkman, *Swift's Satire on Learning in* A Tale of a Tub (Princeton, 1950).

Gulliver's Travels

F. Brady (ed.), *Twentieth Century Interpretations of* Gulliver's Travels (Englewood Cliffs, NJ, 1968).

F. Brady, 'Vexations and Divisions: Three Problems in *Gulliver's Travels*', *Modern Philology*, 75 (1978); discusses the uncertainty of 'interpreting' details.

A. E. Case, *Four Essays on* Gulliver's Travels (Princeton, 1945; repr., Gloucester, Mass., 1958); on the text; the geography and chronology; personal and political satire; the significance of the book.

R. S. Crane, 'The Houyhnhnms, the Yahoos and the History of Ideas', in J. A. Mazzeo (ed.), *Reason and Imagination, Studies in the History of Ideas* (1962).

M. P. Foster (ed.), *A Casebook on Gulliver among the Houyhnhnms* (New York, 1961; repr., 1963); text of Part IV and a substantial collection of pieces written between 1752 and 1960.

P. Harth, 'The Problem of Political Allegory in *Gulliver's Travels*', in *Modern Philology*, 73 (1976).

A. Ross, *Swift:* Gulliver's Travels (Edward Arnold, 1968).

Poems

In the last decade there has been a growth of serious interest in Swift as a poet. The published work is stronger in good readings of particular poems than in any persuasive general evaluation.

A. B. England, *Energy and Order in the Poetry of Swift* (Bucknell UP, Lewisburg, Pa., 1980).

J. I. Fischer, *On Swift's Poetry* (Gainesville, Fla., 1978).

M. Shinagel, *A Concordance of the Poetry of Swift* (Ithaca, New York, 1972).

BACKGROUND READING

J. C. Beckett, *The Anglo-Irish Tradition* (1976); with bibliography.

N. O. Brown, *Life against Death: the psychoanalytical Meaning of History* (1959).

A. Carpenter, *Place, Personality and the Irish Writer.* (Irish Literary Studies, 1; Dublin, 1977).

R. C. Elliott, *The Power of Satire: Magic, Literature, Art* (Princeton, 1960); contains a valuable discussion of *Gulliver's Travels*.

O. Ferguson, *Swift and Ireland* (Urbana, Ill., 1962).

R. Foster, *Modern Ireland: 1600–1972* (1988).

P. Fussell, *The Rhetorical World of Augustan Humanism: Ethics and Imagery from Swift to Burke* (Oxford, 1965).

G. Holmes, *British Politics in the Age of Anne* (1967).

F. G. James, *Ireland in the Empire, 1688–1770* (Cambridge, Mass., 1973); useful bibliography; generally informative, and suggestive on economic history; stresses parallels with American history.

E. M. Johnson, *Ireland in the Eighteenth Century* (The Gill History of Ireland, 8; Dublin, 1974); sections 1–5; bibliography.

J. R. Jones, *Country and Court: England 1688–1714* (Edward Arnold, 1977).

R. F. Jones, *Ancients and Moderns: a Study of the scientific Movement in Seventeenth-century England* (Berkeley, 1965).

M. MacCurtain, *Tudor and Stuart Ireland* (The Gill History of Ireland, 7; Dublin, 1972), sections 8, 9, and 10; bibliography.

V. Mercier, *The Irish Comic Tradition* (Oxford, 1962).

F. O'Connor, *The Backward Look: a Survey of Irish Literature* (1967).

C. Probyn (ed.), *Jonathan Swift: the contemporary Background* (Manchester, 1978); twenty-three short selections from writers from 1656 to 1732.

P. Rogers, *Grub Street: Studies in a Sub-Culture* (1972).

W. A. Speck, *Stability and Strife: England 1714–1760* (Edward Arnold, 1977).

Some Recent Titles

C. Fabricant, *Swift's Landscape* (Baltimore, 1982); a materialist discussion.

J. I. Fischer, H. J. Real, J. Woolley (eds.), *Swift and His Contexts* (NY, 1989); a recent miscellany.

F. P. Lock, *Swift's Tory Politics* (1983); a brisk account.

E. Pollak, *The Poetics of Sexual Myth* (Chicago, 1985); on Swift, Pope and gender.

P. Reilly, *Jonathan Swift: The Brave Desponder* (Manchester, 1982).

J. A. W. Rembert, *Swift and the Dialectical Tradition* (1988); an important introduction to a central Swiftian concern.

D. B. Wyrick, *Jonathan Swift and the Vested Word* (Chapel Hill, NC, 1988); takes up some modern criticism: good bibliography.

E. Zimmerman, *Swift's narrative Strategies: Author and Authority* (Ithaca, NY, 1983); Swift and narratology.

GLOSSARY

abroach, streaming, running.

adust, burned up with heat (also a medical term).

afflatus (literally) breathing upon; inspiration.

alamode, in the fashion.

album, a blank book for autographs, notes, etc.

all to naught, completely vicious, immoral.

amarant (*Amaranth; anaranthine*) unfading (flower).

ambages, circuitous, roundabout ways.

an, if (an archaic word surviving only in dialect and proverb: 'ifs and ans').

anatomy, skeleton.

anima, air exhaled and inhaled, the breath of life.

animal rationale, rational animal.

animus (literally) wind; the rational and feeling soul, as opposed to *anima*, physical life.

antitype, the impression corresponding to the die; in typological interpretation, what is shadowed forth or indicated by the 'type' or symbol.

approves, shows, affirms.

arcanum, a mystery or hermetic secret.

argent, silver.

arrect, pricked up.

ars poetica, poetic art (as *The Art of Poetry*, the common title of a poem by Horace).

atramentous, black as ink.

bagnio (literally) baths or a bathing establishment; notoriously, a brothel.

bait, to stop for rest and refreshment.

basso relievo (bas-relief); low-relief carving, in which the figures are raised only a little from the background.

beaver, a hat made from beaver's fur.

bedlam, a bedlamite, inmate of the St Mary of Bethlehem Hospital for the insane in London (see note to p. 141 (1)), or any mad person.

beeves, oxen, cattle; *pl.* of 'beef'.

bere, barley

bills of mortality, regular published returns of deaths (and births) in certain districts; first published in 1592 for 109 London parishes; hence the area covered by such official statistics; London.

birth-day night, celebration for a royal birthday, royal reception.

bite (a modish word) *vb.* to hoax, also *n.*; *bit*, hoaxed, caught.

black money, copper coins; contrasted with *white money*, silver.

bolus, a large pill.

boutade, a sudden motion, like a kick from a horse's hind legs.

break, go bankrupt; or, decay.

briefs, abridgements, summaries.

briguing, intriguing, conspiring, from F *briguer.*

brocado's, brocades (from Sp. and Port. *broccado*; It. *broccato*, embossed); 'flowered' fabrics woven with a pattern of raised figures.

broke, cashiered, deprived of an army commission.

bubble, swindle, *vb.* and *n.*

bulks, frameworks projecting from the fronts of buildings in a street, stalls; used for sleeping rough.

bullion, melting-house (mint) or place of exchange.

bully, pimp.

butter weight, good measure, 18 or more ounces to the pound.

cabal *vb.* & *n.*, to intrigue; the intrigue itself; a small clique of intriguers.

cant, jargon.

case (physical) condition; *in case,* in good condition.

cast a nativity, frame a horoscope for prediction.

cells, small, humble dwellings, cabins.

chair, sedan-chair, a common mode of transport in London.

chancres, see *shankers.*

chapman, purchaser.

character (printing) type; cf. *On Poetry,* ll. 95–104 (p. 537).

cheapen, bargain to reduce the price.

christiana religio absoluta et simplex, the Christian religion, complete, all of a piece.

clap, venereal disease, usually gonorrhoea.

classis, kind, division; it was also a Puritan word for the ministers of a district.

clipping, to defraud by paring the rim of a silver or gold coin; hence generally to curtail or diminish with ill intent.

clyster-pipes, enemas.

cockle, the weed corn cockle (*Agrostemma githago*), whose seeds had to be sifted out of the seed corn; the task gave rise to several proverbs.

coelum empyreum, the highest heaven.

coif, close-fitting cap.

coil, uproar, fuss.

colberteen, plain, open, network lace.

come to, come round to agreement or reconciliation.

commons, daily fare.

complaisance, courtesy.

complexion, character, temperament.

congee, bow, originally at taking leave (*congé*).

conjurer, a person with occult powers; a fortune-teller.

control, to overrule.

conversed, an old form of *conversant.*

copia vera, true copy.

copperas, green vitriol or ferrous sulphate, used in making ink.

copy-hold, an English tenure of land, bound by the custom of the manor, less absolute than 'freehold'.

cottiers, peasants renting small parcels of land on an annual (or very short) tenure.

cotton, to agree or 'get on' with.

cully, a simpleton, gull.

cum appendice, with an appendix.

cum grano salis, with a grain of salt, sceptically.

cunning man, a fortune-teller with occult power, consulted to find missing property.

custodium (*custodiam*) in Irish law, a three-year grant of Crown lands.

deshabille, informal or leisure dress.

desiderata, things that are desired (to fill up blanks).

desunt nonnulla, not a few words are missing.

devoted, consecrated, doomed.

dispensible, subject to dispensation, able to be allowed; a royal 'dispensing power' was claimed by Charles II and James II, to set aside laws in special cases.

distress, seizure of goods for the payment of a debt.

division, the disposition of material in a discourse, preliminary classification (in rhetoric and scholastic logic).

dizened, decked out; now only in *bedizened.*

drawing room (royal) reception.

duo sunt genera, there are two kinds.

elogy (elogies), characterization(s); since these were usually favourable, the word became confused with *eulogy* and lost its separate existence.

ends, shoemakers' threads pointed with bristles.

exantlation, drawing or pumping out, as water from a well (L *exantlare*).

ex cathedra, from the bishop's chair, infallibly.

exploded, clapped or hissed off the stage (L *explaudere*).

ex post facto (a law) made to punish a crime after it has been committed; retrospective.

expostulate the case, argue through, discuss, enlarge on.

fact, crime (in legal parlance).

fade, wan, commonplace.

fee-simple, absolute heritable possession.

flammed, deceived, tricked.

flight-shot, long-distance shot in archery.

fluctuate, to be tossed up and down (as on waves), unstable, unsettled.

fob, small pocket in a waistcoat or the waist of breeches, for a watch or valuables.

fonde, foundation, (financial) support.

free-thinkers, unbelievers, atheists.

fresh and fasting, medicinal direction found in patent medicine advertisements.

fugitive, volatile (in chemistry).

garnish, money extorted by a gaoler in return for better treatment, particularly allowing light manacles, or freedom of movement within the prison.

gasconnade, vainglorious boasting or fiction, from the reputed character of the inhabitants of Gascony in south-west France.

gawses (*gauzes*) thin transparent fabrics of silk, linen, or cotton.

goody, goodwife; i.e. mistress or Mrs.

goose, tailor's smoothing-iron, with a goose-neck handle.

gossips, the women friends invited to be present at a birth.

grand monde, the great world.

Grands Titres, Noble Titles.

grimace, pretence, sham.

groaning chair, the bed-side chair at (or after) the lying in, or 'groaning'.

groat, fourpence; i.e. a small sum, in proverbial use.

grogram, a stiff silk fabric, sometimes containing a mixture of mohair and wool.

hamated, hooked (L *hamatus*).

hermitage, a renowned red wine from a hill so-called on the bank of the Rhone twelve miles north of Valence.

heydukes (*heyducks*, from a Turkish word for brigands) picked Hungarian footsoldiers given noble rank.

hic multa desiderantur, a great deal is missing here.

hobb, in some fireplaces, the flat area of brick or more usually metal, at one or both sides of the grate, level with the top, used for heating pans and kettles.

hobby-horses, obsessions.

horsed for discipline, placed piggyback to be flogged on the posteriors by a schoolmaster.

hung by geometry (usually of clothes) hanging at an angle.

impar, unequal to the task.

in capite, in chief, holding land directly from the Crown.

inclusivè, inclusively, comprehensively (L *adv.* used in scholastic disputation).

Index expurgatorius, the list of books which Roman Catholics are forbidden to read, reviewed annually by the cardinals of the Congregation of the Index.

in foro conscientiae, in the court of conscience.

innuendo, an explanation in parenthesis (legal and scholastic use).

in petto, secretly (It., literally 'in the breast').

instinct, animated, impelled.

interessed, concerned (archaic even in Swift's day).

in terminis, in the exact words.

interstitia, intervals.

jack, a contrivance for turning a spit to roast meat in front of the fire, often worked by weights like a clock.

jakes, a privy.

job, a trust or public action turned to private advantage; also thieves' slang, a robbery or crime.

jordan, chamber-pot.

jure ecclesiae, by the law of the Church.

kennel, the open drain or gutter in a street, usually in the middle.

kilderkin, a cask for liquid.

King's Bench, the highest court of common law in England (and similarly in Ireland).

lantern, a case for carrying a light, with transparent side(s) sometimes made of oiled paper.

last, a model of the foot on which a shoemaker or cobbler places the footwear on which he works.

levee, a (royal) morning reception, literally at the rising of the patron.

list, a strip of cloth, a head- or sweat-band.

lover, affectionate friend, well-wisher.

lurry, hubbub, uproar.

mamelukes, the military group (and

their descendants) who in 1254 seized and held Egypt; originally Caucasian slaves, they ruled until 1811.

mangé votre bled en herbe (having) eaten your corn in the blade; i.e. lived on your capital.

marish, obsolete form of 'marsh'.

medium, average.

meum et tuum, mine and thine.

mobile, *mobile vulgus* ('the volatile crowd'), the mob.

mopus, a stupid or moping person.

morsure, biting.

multa absurda sequerentur, many absurdities would follow.

mutatis mutandis, the necessary changes being made.

needle, not only the tailor's needle, but also the magnetic needle of the compass.

nemine contradicente, no one speaking against; unanimously.

nog, a strong beer brewed in East Anglia, Sir Robert Walpole's country.

noli prosequi, see next entry.

nolle prosequi (literally) 'to be unwilling to pursue'; a certificate made when the pursuer abandons the case; the writ issued by the Attorney-General to stop a Crown prosecution. (Also *pl.*)

nuncupatory, oral.

olios, stews, cf. *olla podrida.*

ombre (pronounced *omber*) a three-handed card game of Spanish origin for which the eights, nines, and tens of the pack are discarded. The play is described in J. Butt (ed.), *Poems of Alexander Pope,* ii (1954 etc.), Appendix C. The game was succeeded in popularity by *quadrille* (q.v.).

opus magnum, great work; in alchemy, changing base metal to gold.

ordinaries, public eating-houses where a meal was regularly offered at a fixed price, as a *five-penny ordinary.*

os sacrum, 'the sacred bone'; a triangular structure at the base of the vertebrae, of which it is a continuation. A Jewish tradition explains its 'sacredness' as, resistant to decay, it will be the growth-point at the resurrection of the 'new body'.

pale, an area within certain bounds, subject to a specific jurisdiction; cf. the effective English jurisdiction round Dublin established in 1547.

pandect, originally, Justinian's compendium of Roman law; hence any body of laws and, more generally, a complete digest of any subject.

partie carrée, a foursome (two men and two women).

parts, talents.

party, part, constituent.

passing-bell, death-bell.

patshaws, Swift's version of *padishah* or *padshah,* a Persian title ('Great King'), applied in Europe to the Sultan of Turkey.

'peach, give evidence against, incriminate.

pennyworth, bargain.

pericranies, brains (from L *pericrania*).

philologer, lover of letters or learning.

philomath, a lover of learning, especially a student of mathematics or natural philosophy; frequently ar astrologer.

physic, medicine.

picquet, a two-handed card game for which the low cards, twos to sixes, are discarded.

pinner, coif (q.v.) with two long hanging strips pinned on each side, worn by ladies of rank.

pistole, used for certain foreign gold coins, particularly a Spanish coin worth about 17 shillings or the French Louis d'Or worth about £1.

plate, precious metal, usually silver.

plebscita, ordinances or regulations passed by the *plebs* (people).

plight (good) condition.

pocket, a small bag or pouch, commonly not attached to the dress.

points, laces for fastening together parts of the dress.

porringer, a small basin or bowl.

port-reeve, mayor or chief magistrate.

postulatum (postulata) thing(s) demanded or taken for granted before an argument starts.

prerogative, the royal pre-eminent right, theoretically subject to no restriction, particularly the claim to be able to be outside the common law, also to make peace and war etc.

pretend, claim. *Pretender,* Claimant.

primordium, first principle.

professors, professionals (of any science, art, or activity).

projector, promoter; for Swift always in a bad sense, a cheat, a speculator.

propriety (proprieties), property; an older form favoured by Swift.

pure bite, completely successful hoax.

puris naturalibus, in a state of nature; naked.

put (country) bumpkin, 'buffer'.

quadrille, a four-handed card game in which the eights, nines, and tens are discarded; it succeeded *ombre* (q.v.) as the popular game in the 1720s and was in turn displaced in the 1740s by whist.

quartum principium, fourth principle, or element.

quean, trollop, hussy.

quinta essentia, the 'fifth essence' drawn from the four elements (earth, air, fire, water); in ancient and medieval philosophy it was the substance of the heavenly bodies.

quit, requite, repay.

quoad magis et minus, as far as, more or less.

racking, raising rent above a normal or reasonable level.

rally, to banter, to treat with good-humoured ridicule.

rationis capax, capable of reason.

rattle, scold.

receipt, recipe, prescription.

relievo, a work of art in relief, i.e. parts of it raised from a plane surface.

resent, feel deeply, take badly. *Resentments*, feelings of indignation.

returning, investing for a 'return'.

rubs, disagreeable experiences.

sack-posset, a drink made of hot curdled milk, white wine (cf. F *sec*), and perhaps spices.

salivation, the contemporary treatment by mercury of venereal disease; it stimulated the flow of saliva.

sans consequence, without repercussions; unimportant.

save-all, a holder that allows the candle to be burned to the last.

scandalum magnatum, libelling magnates (peers).

scantling, a sample or specimen.

schools, universities, from the places of disputation which formed a main part of the academic programme in Swift's day.

screwing, extorting money from (a tenant or dependant).

scrub, mean, contemptible.

senatusconsulta, decrees of the [Roman] senate.

serve the king, enlist as a soldier.

shankers, chancres (cancers), venereal ulcers.

shaver, 'a smart fellow', *Dictionary of the Canting Crew* (1699).

shed, pour out.

sheet, broadside, or folded to a four-page pamphlet.

si mihi credis, if you will believe me.

sink, cesspool or sewer.

smatter, talk ignorantly, prate.

smock, fornicate.

smoke (smoak), 'get', 'rumble'.

snap-dragon, a Christmas game in which raisins are snatched from a bowl of burning brandy and eaten as they flame.

sophisters, at Trinity College, Dublin, third- or fourth-year students.

spargefaction, sprinkling.

sparkish, smart or elegant, likely to please a *spark* or dandy.

special verdict, when the jury find on the facts only, leaving matters of law to the judge.

specie, kind, sort.

spleen, melancholy, ill humour, peevishness, depression; all thought to come from a disorder in that organ.

sponging-house, a bailiff's house, in which he held debtors before their committal to prison.

stand out, refuse to place a bet or take part in gambling.

stews, brothels, or in general the red-light district.

story, history.

stroll, to wander as a vagabond.

stuffs, fabrics made from wool.

sub dio, in the open air.

summity, summit (an obsolete form).

summum bonum, the supreme good.

surtout, an overcoat.

tabbies, glossy materials containing silk (taffetas), sometimes striped.

table-book, a pocket- or memorandum-book.

taking off, distracting or diverting; also, putting to death.

Teague, from the Irish name *Tadhg,* a nickname for a (stage) Irishman.

tell, count.

Templar (in London) a young man-about-town, nominally enrolled to study law at one of the Inns of Court such as the Middle or Inner Temple.

tentiginous humour, an inclination to lust (from L *tentigo,* an erection).

terms of art, technical expressions.

tertio modo, in the third way.

toilets, the morning ceremony of dressing.

toils, nets.

totidem syllabis, in so many syllables.

totidem verbis, in so many words.

totis viribus, with all [our] strength.

trait, a touch or stroke.

troll it, roll along (see note to p. 335); cf. *tooling along.*

truckling, subservient, obsequious.

turned head, opposite of *turned tail.*

turnpikes, spiked barriers across a road.

twelve-penny gallery, the cheapest (and uppermost) range of theatre seats, traditionally occupied by footmen.

uncontrollable, unalterable, independent.

undertaker, promoter of a speculative [for Swift, usually fraudulent] business enterprise; contractor.

use, interest, hence *usury.*

vales (*vails*) tips to servants, especially when a guest left the house.

vamped, refurbished, patched.

vapours, hysterics.

villeinage, the feudal state of being a *villein* or bond-servant; serfdom.

virga genitalis, phallus.

virtuoso (usually) antiquary, scientific dilettante [from It., 'one specially skilled']; *pl. virtuoso*[*es*]; or *virtuosi*; also *adj.*

vizard, visor (of a helmet); also, mask.

vox populi (**vox Dei**), the voice of the people (is the voice of God).

water tabby, wavy or water-silk.

yard, a straight piece of wood, a stick; (nautical) the spar at right angles to the mast which extends the sail; a tailor's measure; the erect penis.

z[oun]ds, God's wounds!

BIOGRAPHICAL INDEX OF
CONTEMPORARIES

ABERCORN, James Hamilton (1656–1734), 6th Earl of; friend of Swift and leading opponent in Ireland of Wood's coinage patent.

ADDISON, Joseph (1672–1719), writer, moralist, and politician; close and admired friend of Swift to whom in 1705 he presented a copy of his *Remarks on Several Parts of Italy*, inscribed 'The most agreeable companion | The truest friend | And the greatest genius of his age'; party differences estranged them after 1710; one of the principal contributors to Steel's *Tatler* (1709–11) and co-editor with him of the *Spectator* (1711–12); Under-Secretary of State, 1705–8; MP; Secretary (i.e chief executive of the Irish Government) to Wharton, Lord-Lieutenant 1708–10; Secretary to the Lords Justices in London (regents), 1714–15; Secretary of State, 1717–18.

ALLEN, John, son of Joshua, 2nd Viscount Allen (see next entry); MP for Carysfort, Co. Wicklow.

ALLEN, Robert, brother of Joshua, 2nd Viscount Allen, who in 1730 attacked Swift as a Jacobite libeller; Robert was MP for Co. Wicklow; Joshua's great-grandfather was a builder.

ANNE Stuart (1665–1714), second legitimate daughter of James II; married Prince George of Denmark, 1683; succeeded her sister's husband, William III, as Queen of England, Ireland, and Scotland, 1702: Swift's attitude to her was ambivalent; she denied him preferment.

ARBUTHNOT, Dr John (1667–1735), wit, satirist, miscellaneous writer; born Kincardinshire, Scotland; physician to Queen Anne from 1705; the central figure in the Scriblerus Club (see below, POPE); author of *The History of John Bull* (five pro-peace pamphlets, 1712); correspondent of Swift and a friend valued for his amiable honesty and nobility of character.

ASGILL, John (1659–1738), deist; he had an extensive law practice in Ireland and was an MP: an eccentric pamphlet on death brought him under attack and he fled to England, 1705: Swift names him several times.

ASHE, Dillon or Dilly (c.1666–1718), younger brother of St George Ashe; a contemporary of Swift at Trinity College, Dublin; vicar of Finglas near the city; Archdeacon of Clogher, 1704; Chancellor of Armagh, 1706; a punning friend of Swift.

ASHE, St George (c. 1658–1718), Swift's tutor at Trinity College, Dublin, and later esteemed friend; Provost of the College, 1692; Bishop of Cloyne, 1695; of Clogher, 1697; of Derry, 1717.

AUGUSTUS II ('the Strong'), Friedrich August (1670–1733), hereditary Elector of Saxony, 1694; bought election as King of Poland, 1697; resigned after defeat in Nordic War by Charles XII of Sweden, 1706; regained crown after Charles's defeat, 1709.

BENTLEY, Richard (1662–1742), classical scholar, critic, and theologian; Keeper of the Royal Library, 1694; Master of Trinity College, Cambridge, 1700; Bentley united to his formidable learning a turn for sarcasm and personalities which embroiled him in foolish controversy with the Christ Church wits; Swift hated his 'pert style'.

BERKELEY, Charles Berkeley (1649–1710), 2nd Earl of; in 1699 one of the Lords Justices of Ireland and took Swift with him as chaplain; returned, 1701. Swift maintained a friendship with him, and especially his daughter Lady Betty (Germain). He married Elizabeth, daughter of Lord Campden.

BERKELEY OF STRATTON, William Berkeley (?–1741), 4th Baron; descended from a Lord-Lieutenant of Ireland; married to a Temple; he was Chancellor of the Duchy of Lancaster in Harley's ministry, 1710–14.

BETTESWORTH, Richard (c. 1689–1741), serjeant-at-law and Irish MP. In 1733, provoked at one of the lampoons in which he was a frequent butt, he threatened to cut Swift's ears off with a penknife, and confronted him though without hurt.

BLACKMORE, Sir Richard (1654–1729), poet, Whig political writer, and physician to William III and Queen Anne; knighted, 1697; the author of several long, dull poems, e.g. *Prince Arthur* (1697) and later *The Creation: a philosophical poem* (1712).

BOLINGBROKE, Henry St John (1678–1751), 1st Viscount, 1712: Tory MP 1701; Secretary at War in Godolphin's ministry, 1704–8; Secretary of State, 1710–14, in which office he showed dash and hard work; undermined Oxford but was not made Lord Treasurer on the latter's fall; dismissed by George I and fled to France in 1715, taking service with the Pretender; for this attainted; bribed his way back to England, 1723, pardoned but barred from the House of Lords; one of the leaders of the Opposition to Walpole and a Tory theorist in his contributions to *The Craftsman*; retired to France in 1735. Swift knew him well, corresponded with him, admired his conversation and abilities.

BOLTON, the Revd John (c. 1656–1724); ordained in Ireland, 1677; prebendary of St Patrick's, 1691; Dean of Derry, 1701; Swift, who thought he ought to have received this deanery himself, was given Bolton's prebends.

BOULTER, Hugh (1672–1742), Archbishop of Armagh; chaplain to Tenison, Archbishop of Canterbury; chaplain to George I; Bishop of Bristol, 1719; succeeded Lindsay as Archbishop and Primate of All Ireland, 1724. Following the Wood coinage patent controversy, Boulter became the aggressive leader of the 'English interest' in Ireland and Walpole's instrument in tightening English control of the Irish Government.

BOYLE, the Hon. Charles (1674–1731); as an aristocratic pupil at Christ Church, Oxford, his name was put to an edition of *The Epistles of Phalaris* (1695); given the credit of writing the riposte of the Christ Church wits, *Dr. Bentley's Dissertation ... Examined ...* (1698); succeeded as 4th Earl of Orrery, 1703; major-general, 1709; he was a supporter of Swift's 'Society' (see note to p. 272 (4)); committed to the Tower in Walpole's Jacobite scare of 1722 (see p. 668n.).

BRODRICK, Thomas (c. 1654–1730), elder brother of Lord Middleton; MP for Stockbridge and later Guildford, Surrey, where his estate lay.

BROWN or BROWNE, Peter (d. 1735); Provost of Trinity College, Dublin, 1679; Bishop of Cork and Ross, 1710; Swift did not like him, but mentions him as a friend of Esther Johnson's.

Human Souls (1702) was attacked as materialistic and prosecuted by Parliament; Swift several times lists him with deist writers.

CURL or CURLL, Edmund (1675–1747), bookseller and publisher; specialized in scandal, pornography, and unauthorized printing.

DENNIS, John (1657–1734), dramatist and critic; his later cantankerous judgements gained him the contempt of the important writers of the time; he is very much underrated as a critical theorist.

DILKES, Michael O'Brien; MP for the borough of Castlemartyr, Co. Cork.

DINGLEY, Rebecca (*c.*1665–1743); lifelong, older companion of Esther Johnson; daughter of a cousin of Sir William Temple.

DODINGTON, George Bubb (1691–1762), took the name Dodington on inheriting the Irish and other estates of his uncle George (d. 1720), who had been Secretary to the Earl of Pembroke, Lord-Lieutenant 1707–9; a supporter of Walpole, and later one of the Lords of the Treasury.

DORSET, Lionel Cranfield Sackville (1688–1765), 7th Earl of; Duke of, 1720; Lord-Lieutenant of Ireland, 1730–7.

DUBLIN, Archbishop of; see KING, William.

DUCK, Stephen (1705–56), the 'thresher poet'; a self-educated agricultural labourer from Wiltshire, whose verses gained him the patronage of Queen Caroline; *Poems on Several Subjects* (1730), to which Pope and Swift both subscribed; he was ordained, beneficed, and later committed suicide.

D'URFEY, Thomas (1653–1723), dramatist and song-writer; a butt for satirists from the time of Dryden; many of his songs were extremely popular and his topical plays succeeded.

ÉPINE, Francesca Margherita de l' (d. 1746); a celebrated Italian singer performing in London in the second decade of the eighteenth century.

EVANS, John (d. 1724), translated from the See of Bangor to that of Meath in Ireland, 1716, and thus diocesan of Swift's vicarage of Laracor; one of the most zealous Whig ecclesiastics in Ireland, a watch-dog for the 'English interest', writing regular reports to the Archbishop of Canterbury which often denounce Swift.

FENTON, Mrs Jane (1666–1738), only other child of Swift's parents; married Joseph Fenton, a currier, whom Swift disliked.

FLAMSTEED, the Revd John (1646–1719), first Astronomer Royal, 1675.

FORD, Charles (1682–1741); born in Dublin and one of Swift's closest friends; Swift helped him to become Gazetteer, 1712; important correspondent of Swift (see D. Nichol Smith (ed.), *Letters of Swift to Ford* (1935).

FOUNTAINE, Sir Andrew (1676–1753); art collector and virtuoso; knighted, 1699; official at Dublin Castle; Warden of the Mint, 1727.

GADBURY, John (1627–1704), almanac-maker and astrologer; crypto-Catholic, Jacobite.

GALWAY, Henry de Massue (1648–1720), Marquis de Ruvigny; Viscount, 1692; and Earl of, 1697; Huguenot refugee in the service of William III; fought in Ireland; a brave and experienced general, he held command of the allied armies in Spain and Portugal but was decisively beaten at Almanza, April 1707; his conduct became the focus of Tory attacks on the war.

1711; on his return, his salary in arrear, he died penniless 14 February 1713 as Swift brought him aid.

HENLEY, Anthony (d. 1711), wit and MP; a friend of Swift, he helped with Harrison's *Tatler*.

HENLEY, John (1692–1756), 'Orator'; ordained in the Church of England, he abandoned the establishment and set himself up as an eccentric subscription speaker and preacher; he taught elocution and worked as a journalist for Walpole.

HERVEY, Lord John (1696–1743), son of the Earl of Bristol; a supporter of Walpole; Vice-Chamberlain, 1730; Baron Hervey of Ickworth, 1733; he took part with Lady Mary Wortley Montagu in the literary skirmishing against Pope.

HILL, John (d. 1735), colonel and later major-general; younger brother of Abigail Masham; he commanded a brigade at Almanza and in 1711 was the army commander in the unsuccessful expedition against Quebec promoted by Bolingbroke; he commanded the Dunkirk garrison, 1713.

HOLT, Sir John (1642–1710); Lord Chief Justice of the King's Bench in England, 1689.

HOPKINS, Edward (d. 1726), Secretary to the Duke of Grafton, Lord-Lieutenant of Ireland; his appointment as Master of the Revels, 1722, with a salary to be raised from the theatre in Dublin prompted a satirical poem by Swift (*Poems*, 306).

HOWARD, Mrs Henrietta; see SUFFOLK, Henrietta Hobart.

JERVAS, Charles (*c.* 1675–1739), born in Ireland; a fashionable portrait-painter practising in London and Dublin; translator of *Don Quixote*; a friend of Swift, he painted several portraits of him (e.g. those in the Bodleian Library, Oxford, and in the National Portrait Gallery), and at least one of Esther Johnson (possibly that in the National Gallery of Ireland).

JOHNSON, Esther or Hester (1681–1728), 'Stella'; beloved friend of Swift; her father had some connection with Sir William Temple's household and her mother was in Lady Giffard's service. Sir William left her a small legacy, on which after 1702 she lived in Ireland with her older companion Rebecca Dingley. Swift had some part in her education at Moor Park and came to be a dominant influence on her life. A lively and intelligent woman, she moved in good Dublin society, but did not always enjoy good health.

KING, William (1650–1729); Bishop of Derry, 1691; Archbishop of Dublin, 1703; of strong Revolution Whig principles, also a staunch supporter of the Anglo-Irish interest and so was refused the senior Archbishopric of Armagh; an untiring worker for the good of the Church of Ireland. The two men had an eventful relationship, especially in 1710–14 when Swift became a supporter of Harley's Tory administration; in later controversy with the 'English' interest, Swift returned to admiration for the doughty old fighter.

LECZINSKI, Stanislaus; see STANISLAUS LECZINSKI.

L'ESTRANGE, Sir Roger (1616–1704), Tory journalist, pamphleteer, press censor, and translator.

LEWIS, Erasmus (1670–1754), diplomat and Civil Servant; secretary to the English ambassador in Paris, 1701; secretary to Harley; secretary to the embassy at Brussels, 1708; Under-Secretary of State, 1710–14; a friend of Swift, Prior, Pope, Arbuthnot, Gay.

LILLIEROOT, Nils Eosander (1636–1705), comte de; Swedish diplomat.

LINDSAY, Thomas (?–1724); Bishop of Killaloe, 1696; of Raphoe, 1713; and since he was regardful of the 'English' interest, promoted Archbishop of Armagh and Primate, 1714; Swift viewed him ambivalently, but supported his promotion.

LINTOT(T), (Barnaby) Bernard (1675–1736), bookseller, whose shop was a meeting-place for writers; he published poems by Dryden, and works by Gay, Farquhar, Parnell, and Pope (with whom he had uneasy relations).

MARGARITA; see ÉPINE.

MARLBOROUGH, John Churchill (1650–1722), 1st Duke of, 1702; Prince of Mindelheim in the Empire, 1704; Captain General and Master of the Ordnance, 1702; Commander-in-Chief of the allied armies in Flanders and English ambassador extraordinary and plenipotentiary to the allied powers. A brilliant general and organizer, he was the military half of the duumvirate (with Godolphin), that led the British part of the war against Louis XIV. His financial dealings became a major target of the Tory opposition to the war. After the defeat by Harley in 1710 of the Whigs who had forced themselves into Godolphin's administration, and who were strongly supported by the Duchess of Marlborough, the Duke resigned the Duchess's offices on her behalf in January 1711 and was himself dismissed from all his offices in December. In 1713 they went into exile. The Duke was reinstated on the accession of George I. After 1710, Swift took a leading part in attacking Marlborough (but see note to p. 258 (2)).

MARLBOROUGH, Sarah Churchill (*née* Jennings) (1660–1744), Duchess of; married John Churchill, 1678; she became the domineering friend of the Princess Anne, daughter of James II. When Anne became Queen in 1702, she made Sarah Mistress of the Robes, Groom of the Stole, and Keeper of the Privy Purse. Sarah's partisan Whiggism gradually alienated her mistress. Swift wrote many hard things about the Duchess, who in turn dealt him a few shrewd blows in her *Memoirs*.

MASHAM, Abigail Hill (d. 1734), wife of Samuel (later Lord) Masham; a young cousin of the Duchess of Marlborough, she was introduced by the latter into the Queen's service, and by her quietness gradually supplanted the Duchess as the royal confidante. She was also a cousin of Robert Harley, who used her as a private channel to the Queen in his manœuvres to oust Lord Treasurer Godolphin.

MAYNWARING, Arthur (1668–1712), Whig politician and publicist; secretary and political adviser to the Duchess of Marlborough; MP; Godolphin made him a Commissioner of the Customs and Auditor of the Imprests; a member of the Whig political and literary group, the Kit-cat Club, he was one of the few controversialists who could approach Swift in effective writing.

MIDDLETON, Alan Brodrick (1660–1728), Baron, 1715; 1st Viscount, 1717; Irish politician (and also an English MP); Solicitor-General for Ireland, 1695; Lord Chief Justice of the Queen's Bench in Ireland, 1709–11; Lord Chancellor of Ireland, 1714. In spite of his Whig and 'English' background (e.g. he was strongly opposed to the Irish Test Act), he gained Swift's approbation by his resistance to Wood's coinage patent.

MOLYNEUX, William (1656–98), mathematician, philosopher, and Irish patriot; educated at Trinity College, Dublin; Irish MP representing the college; correspondent of Locke; his book, *The Case of Ireland's being bound by Acts of Parliament in England, Stated* (1698), is the classic early Anglo-Irish declaration of independence.

MOORE, i.e. James Moore SMYTHE (1702–34), the son of Arthur Moore, a Commissioner of Trade. James wrote a comedy, *The Rival Modes* (1727), incorporating some lines by Pope; he appears in *The Dunciad* and in various squibs.

MORGAN, Marcus Antonius; MP for the borough of Athy, Co. Kildare, and chairman of the Irish Commons committee to consider the petition of graziers for relief from the tithe on grazing lands, 1736: the committee duly provided this relief, angering Swift and the churchmen.

NOTTINGHAM, Daniel Finch (1647–1730), 2nd Earl of; a Tory High Churchman, appointed senior Secretary of State, 1702–4; at the end of 1711 he agreed to support the Whigs against the Peace, in return for their (cynical) support of his bill against Occasional Conformity; his nickname 'Dismal' came from his swarthy complexion. Swift several times attacked him.

ORFORD, Edward Russell (1652–1727), naval commander and member of the Whig Junto; admiral, 1689; 1st Lord of the Admiralty, 1694–9, 1709–10, 1714–17; he had been impeached with Somers, 1700–1.

ORMOND(E), James Butler (1665–1745), 2nd Duke of; soldier, courtier, and leading Irish peer; Lord-Lieutenant of Ireland, 1703–7 and 1710–13; Commander-in-Chief on Marlborough's dismissal, 1712, with 'restraining' orders not to fight the French; impeached for high treason, 1715; fled to serve the Pretender; he was to have led the abortive Jacobite descent on England in 1722; died in exile. He was a friend of Swift, and presented him, but not without prompting, to the Deanery of St Patrick's.

OXFORD, Robert Harley (1661–1724), 1st Earl of; he came of a Puritan family; politician and statesman; Speaker of the House of Commons, 1701–5; Secretary of State, 1704–8, and fell after an unsuccessful bid to oust Godolphin; Chancellor of the Exchequer when he succeeded, 1710; his main policy was the end of the War of the Spanish Succession. After the assassination attempt on him in 1711 by Guiscard, he became Lord Treasurer and a peer. Oxford and Bolingbroke quarrelled, as Bolingbroke led the Tories and Oxford sought to continue as the Queen's 'manager'; he was dismissed in August 1714 just before the Queen's death. Swift became an intimate of Oxford's circle and a valued conversationalist. On the accession of George I, Oxford was warded in the Tower for two years but released and acquitted by the Lords of all charges of treason. Swift's relations with him and judgement of him are complex.

OZELL, John (d. 1743); an industrious verse translator; mentioned in *The Dunciad.*

PALMERSTO(W)N, Henry Temple (c. 1673–1757), Baron; a nephew of Sir William Temple, and sinecurist Chief Remembrancer of Ireland.

PARTRIDGE, John (1644–1715); said to have been a shoemaker, he became a leading almanac-maker and astrologer; his annual *Merlinus Liberatus* (from 1680) specialized in anti-High Church verse. Swift built his Bickerstaff joke round the prediction of Partridge's death.

PARVISOL, Isaiah (d. 1718), from 1708 Swift's steward and tithe-collector; of French extraction (possibly a Huguenot); sometimes querulously mentioned in the *Correspondence*.

PATRICK, Swift's best-known servant; drunken and feckless, he was yet taken on a second time on 9 February 1710 (*Journal to Stella*), but finally dismissed in April 1712.

PEMBROKE, Thomas Herbert (*c.*1653–1733), 8th Earl of; Lord-Lieutenant of Ireland, 1707–8; Swift was a member of his domestic circle at Dublin Castle, where he encouraged punning in 'the Castilian language'.

PETERBOROUGH, Charles Mordaunt (*c.*1658–1735), 1st Earl of Monmouth, 1690; 3rd Earl of, 1697; courageous soldier and erratic diplomat, joint commander in Spain with Admiral Sir Cloudesley Shovell, 1705–7; the Tories' answer to Marlborough; a valued friend and correspondent of Swift after 1701, and also of Pope, Gay, Arbuthnot, and other men of letters.

PHILIPS, Ambrose (1674–1749), poet, dramatist and Irish office-holder; his *Pastorals* (in the same volume with Pope's, 1709) gave him his nickname; his verses addressed to infantine aristocratic children gave rise to the word 'Namby-Pamby'; secretary to Archbishop Boulter, 1724.

POPE, Alexander (1688–1744), poet and correspondent of Swift; he was a member of the Scriblerus Club (also Arbuthnot, Gay, Oxford, Parnell), which met to satirize pedantry. Pope invokes Swift at the opening of *The Dunciad*. The two men produced joint *Miscellanies*, but there are differences between them in their attacks on dullness, Walpole, irreligion, and wickedness. Swift willed a miniature of Oxford to his 'dearest friend' Alexander Pope.

PORTLAND, Hans Willem Bentinck (1649–1709), 1st Earl of; courtier and diplomat; favourite of William III; impeached with Somers over the Partition treaties, 1701.

PRENDERGAST, Sir Thomas (d. 1760), 2nd Baronet; MP for Chichester in England, and Clonmel in Co. Tipperary; Postmaster-General for Ireland, 1733; a Protestant convert, hated by Swift for enmity to the Church of Ireland clergy over tithing; his father, a Jacobite, betrayed a plot to kill William III in 1696 and was given the baronetcy.

PRETENDER, the (i.e. claimant), James Francis Edward Stuart (1688–1766), son of James II and titular Prince of Wales, also known as the Chevalier de St George, and 'the Old Pretender'; became titular James III in 1701. Charles James Stuart (1720–88), son of the above, was 'the Young Pretender' (Bonnie Prince Charlie).

PSALMANAZAR, George (*c.* 1679–1763), French literary impostor who lived in London; his bogus *Description of Formosa* appeared in 1704.

PULLEYN (PULLEIN), Tobias (1648–1713); Bishop of Cloyne, 1694; of Dromore, 1695.

PULTENEY, William (1684–1764), MP, 1705; supporter of Walpole, Secretary at War, 1714; after 1725 joined Bolingbroke in Opposition and ran the chief anti-Walpole journal *The Craftsman*; removed from the Privy Council, 1731; on Walpole's fall, he refused office and became Earl of Bath.

RICHMOND, Charles Lennox (1672–1732), 1st Duke of; illegitimate son of Charles II; Swift had some acquaintance with him.

RIDPATH, George (?–1726), a Scotsman, leading Whig journalist and editor of the *Flying Post*, all incurring Swift's disfavour; Ridpath was committed to Newgate for seditious libel, 1712; tried, found guilty, but fled, 1713.

RIVERS, Richard Savage (*c.*1654–1712), 4th Earl; Lieutenant-General and Constable of the Tower of London, 1709; sent as envoy to Hanover, 1710.

ROLT, Patty; a favourite 'cousin' of Swift; deserted by her first husband; she married again but was given financial help by Swift as late as 1735.

ROOK(E), Sir George (1650–1709), admiral; a Tory, unsuccessfully set up as a 'blue water' naval hero against Marlborough, the land-based military strategist.

ROPER, Abel (1665–1726), journalist, who started the leading Tory newspaper, the thrice-weekly *Post-Boy*, in 1695, to which Swift contributed paragraphs 1710–14.

RYMER, Thomas (1641–1713), literary critic and theorist, Historiographer Royal, and important editor of historical documents: see e.g. his *The Tragedies of the Last Age Considered . . .* (1678) and *Foedera* [*Treaties*] (1704 etc.); Swift sought his office when he died.

ST JOHN, Henry; see BOLINGBROKE, Henry St John.

SAWBRIDGE, Thomas (? 1690–1733), son of a Leicestershire parson and himself beneficed there until he was deprived in 1713; 'late chaplain to the East India Company at Bombay' when appointed by the Crown Dean of Fearns, 1728; indicted for rape, 1730, but acquitted.

SCHOMBERG, Frederick Herman von Schönberg (1615–90), created by William III 1st Duke of; general; killed at the Battle of the Boyne.

SHARP(E), John (1645–1714), Archbishop of York, 1691; Queen Anne's chief adviser in ecclesiastical matters, who Swift rightly thought had dissuaded her from giving him (as author of *A Tale of a Tub*) preferment in England.

SHERIDAN, Dr Thomas (1687–1738), priest and schoolmaster; grandfather of Richard Brinsley Sheridan, the dramatist; in 1737 Swift ended the twenty-year friendship between them, during which they had exchanged countless riddles, puns, and domestic verses.

SHREWSBURY, Charles Talbot (1660–1718), 12th Earl of; 1st Duke of, 1694; statesman and courtier; Lord Chamberlain, 1710; ambassador to France, 1712; Lord-Lieutenant of Ireland, 1713–15; appointed Lord Treasurer at Queen Anne's death-bed to forestall Bolingbroke's accession to power; a member of the Society (see p. 272 n. 4) and a friend of Swift.

SMEDLEY, Jonathan (b. 1671), educated at Trinity College, Dublin; army chaplain and Whig supporter; Lord-Lieutenant Townshend made him Dean of Killala, 1718; exchanged for the richer Deanery of Clogher, 1724. His enmity to Swift brought him into popular disfavour and his attacks on Pope placed him in *The Dunciad*; in 1727 he resigned his office and in 1729 he sailed for Madras (see Swift's *Dean Smedley Gone to seek his Fortune* (1729) in *Poems*, 454–6).

defeated and captured by Marlborough at the Battle of Blenheim; released from captivity in England, 1712, and made a Duke.

TATE, Nahum (1652–1715), poetaster and dramatist; educated at Trinity College, Dublin; Poet Laureate, 1692.

TEMPLE, Sir William (1628–99), Baronet; diplomat, statesman, and author; ambassador at The Hague, he helped draft the Triple Alliance, and arranged the marriage of Princess Mary and William of Orange; in 1681, having refused the Secretaryship of State, he retired from public life, though he continued to advise William III. His 'Essay upon the Ancient and Modern Learning' in *Miscellanea. The Second Part* (1690) embroiled him in the Ancients and Moderns controversy. Swift worked for him and lived with him at Moor Park, near Farnham in Surrey, for most of the decade 1689–99.

THEOBALD, Lewis (1688–1744), dramatist, journalist, translator, and editor of Shakespeare (1734); he worked for Curll; after criticizing Pope's edition of Shakespeare, he appeared as the 'hero' of the first version of *The Dunciad* (1728).

THROP (d. 1736), the Revd Roger, rector of Kilcorman, Co. Limerick; persecuted by his patron, John Waller, he was popularly said to have succumbed to the attacks.

TICKELL, Thomas (1686–1740), poet; a protégé of Addison, who made him his Under-Secretary in Ireland and later Secretary to the Lords Justices there; edited Addison's *Works* (1721) with a famous elegy on his patron; Secretary to Lord-Lieutenant Carteret, 1724.

TIGHE, Richard; Irish privy councillor and MP for Belturbet, Co. Cavan; Swift called him 'Fitz-Baker' on account of his descent from one of Cromwell's army-contractors.

TINDAL, Matthew (1657–1733), lawyer and anti-Christian deist; he turned Roman Catholic under James II, reconverting after 1688; one of the *bêtes noires* of Swift, who began *Remarks* in answer to Tindal's anti-clerical *The Rights of the Christian Church Asserted*; published *Christianity as Old as the Creation* (1730).

TOFTS, Catherine (c. 1680–1756), singer in London.

TOLAND, John (1670–1722), born in Ireland, political agent, deist, and sceptic, author of *Christianity not Mysterious* (1696), a correspondent of Oxford.

TOWNSHEND, Charles Townshend (1674–1738), 2nd Viscount; Whig peer; one of the British plenipotentiaries at Utrecht; relative and ally of Robert Walpole.

VALENTINI; an Italian male contralto, in London 1707–15.

VANHOMRIGH, Esther or Hester (1688–1723), called by Swift 'Vanessa'; daughter of Bartholomew Vanhomrigh, Lord Mayor of Dublin (d. 1703); from 1708 Swift allowed a friendship to develop between him and the young girl in London; she fell violently in love with him. He wrote *Cadenus and Vanessa* (1713), perhaps in an unsuccessful attempt to cool the affair. In 1714, Vanessa followed him to Dublin in a vain effort to make him return her passion. She died in Ireland.

WALLER, John, of Castletown, Co. Limerick; MP for Doneraile, Co. Cork; grandson of Sir Hardress Waller, one of the regicides.

WALLS, Thomas (*c.* 1672–1750), Archdeacon of Achonry and master of the St Patrick's Cathedral school; he and his wife, Dorothy Newman, were friends of Esther Johnson, who lived with them for a time in the years 1714–17.

WALPOLE, Sir Robert (1676–1745); MP for King's Lynn in Norfolk from 1701; leader of the Commons Opposition to Harley's administration; his financial ability made him Chancellor of the Exchequer, 1721, in the crisis of confidence following the South Sea Bubble. Walpole's parliamentary skill, unscrupulous intelligence, and ruthlessness made him the dominant politician and virtual Prime Minister, until his resignation was forced by a foreign policy crisis, 1742. In common with Pope, Gay, and many of the leading writers, Swift devoted considerable energy to attacking Walpole's corruption and monopoly of power; his contempt for Ireland and Irish problems also fanned Swift's enmity.

WARD, Edward (1667–1731), voluminous miscellaneous and comic writer; author of the racy monthly, *The London Spy* (1698–1700).

WATERS, Edward (*fl.* 1708–36), Dublin printer; tried for printing Swift's *Proposal for the Universal Use of Irish Manufacture* (1720).

WELSTED, Leonard (1688–1747), minor Civil Servant and poet; he published a translation of Longinus' *Peri Hupsous* [*On the Sublime*], 1712; having attacked Pope, he appears twice in *The Dunciad.*

WHARTON, Thomas Wharton (1648–1715), 2nd Baron; 1st Earl of, 1706; Whig politician and parliamentary manager; Lord-Lieutenant of Ireland, 1708–10; became an object of hatred to Swift (e.g. as Verres, the corrupt proconsul, in *Examiner*, No. 19).

WHITSHED, William (*c.* 1656–1727); Lord Chief Justice of the Queen's Bench in Ireland; Chief Justice of the Common Pleas, 1726.

WILLIAMSON, Sir Joseph (1633–1701), career diplomat; Secretary of State, 1674.

WOLSTON (WOOLSTON), Thomas (1670–1733); became a free-thinker and was deprived of his Cambridge fellowship and his holy orders; author of *The Old Apology for the Truth of the Christian Religion* (1705), and other tracts denying the historical truth of the Scriptures.

WOOD, William (1671–1730), Wolverhampton iron-master; contractor for the supply of copper coinage to Ireland and American colonies.

WOTTON, the Revd William (1666–1726), scholar and cleric; a Cambridge graduate, and rector of Middleton Keynes from 1693; his *Reflections upon Ancient and Modern Learning* (1694) attacked Temple's 'Essay upon Ancient and Modern Learning'; the second edition of the *Reflections* (1697) also contains the first version of Bentley's *Dissertation upon the Epistles of Phalaris . . . and the Fables of Aesop* showing that the work attributed to these writers, praised by Temple, was spurious; the third edition of Wotton's *Reflections* (1705) adds *A Defence of the Reflections . . . with Observations upon a Tale of a Tub* (also printed separately).

WYNDHAM, Sir William (1687–1740), Baronet; Tory MP for Somerset; a supporter of Bolingbroke, he became Secretary at War, 1712; a leading English Jacobite.

WYNN (WYNNE), John; MP for Castlebar, Co. Mayo; Owen Wynne was MP for Co. Sligo; Owen Wynne (? son) was MP for the borough of Sligo.

INDEX OF SHORT TITLES

Italics indicate a poem

INDEX OF FIRST LINES

INDEX OF ADDRESSEES

OF SWIFT'S LETTERS